New Geography in Action

Junior Cycle Geography

Norma Lenihan & Jason O'Brien

educate.ie

PUBLISHED BY:

Educate.ie

Walsh Educational Books Ltd

Castleisland, Co. Kerry, Ireland

www.educate.ie

PRINTED AND BOUND BY:

Walsh Colour Print,

Castleisland, Co. Kerry, Ireland

ISBN: 978-1-912239-41-2

Contents

Please note that you do not have to follow the order below. Chapters have been written so they can be taught in any order.

Introduction .... **vi**

SECTION 1: FIRST YEAR

Chapter 1 **Geographical Skills for First Years: Ordnance Survey and graph skills** **1**
Introduction to Geography 1
Ordnance Survey map skills 1 3
Charts and graphs 14

Chapter 2 **The Earth's Surface: Shaping the crust** **20**
The structure of the Earth 20
Plates 21
Volcanic activity 23
Earthquakes 28
Fold mountains 32

Chapter 3 **Rocks: How they are formed and used** **38**
Types of rock 38
Igneous rocks 40
Sedimentary rocks 42
Metamorphic rocks 43
Uses of rock 44

Chapter 4 **Primary Economic Activities: How we use the world's natural resources** **51**
Economic activities and natural resources 51
Water: a renewable resource 54
Fishing in Ireland: over-exploitation of a renewable resource 59
Farming in Ireland 61
Forestry in Ireland – a growing renewable natural resource 64

Chapter 5 **Energy and the Environment: How fuelling our needs impacts on the world we live in** **71**
Energy resources 71
Non-renewable energy resources 72
Renewable energy resources 77
Ireland and renewable energy 80
Environmental consequences of energy production 82

Chapter 6 **Weathering and Mass Movement: The changing face of the Earth** **89**
Weathering and erosion 89
Carbonation and karst landscapes 92
Mass movement 97

SECTION 2: SECOND YEAR

Chapter 7 **Geographical Skills for Second Years: Ordnance Survey and aerial photograph skills** **106**
Ordnance Survey maps 2 106
Introduction to aerial photographs 114
Distance, ratio, range and mean 120

Chapter 8 **Secondary Economic Activities: Industry in Ireland** **122**
Secondary economic activities 122
Factors that influence the location of a factory 123
Types of manufacturing industry 126
Industry and conflict 132

Chapter 9 **Rivers: Shaping our landscape** **136**
Rivers 136
The work of rivers 139
River landforms 140
People and rivers 147
Drainage features (rivers) on Ordnance Survey maps 151

Chapter 10 **The Sea: How it shapes our coastline** **158**
Waves 158
Landforms of coastal erosion 160
Coastal transportation and deposition 164
People and the sea 168

Chapter 11 **Glaciation: The work of ice** **178**
Glaciation 178
Landforms of glacial erosion 180
Glacial transportation and deposition 184
People and glaciation 187

Chapter 12 **Settlement and Urbanisation: Where we live and why** **196**
Introduction to settlement 197
History of settlement in Ireland 202
Urban settlement in Ireland today 204
Rural settlement in Ireland today 208
Introduction to urbanisation 210
Solutions to urbanisation problems 213
Focus on urban areas 217

Chapter 13 **Weather: How it impacts on our lives** **226**
The atmosphere 226
The sun 227
Wind 229
Ocean currents 231
Air masses and fronts 232
Clouds 236
Precipitation 237
Weather 239

Chapter 14 **Climates: Classifying climate types and Ireland's climate** **252**
Climate 252
Global climates 256
Factors influencing Ireland's climate 260
Climate change 262

SECTION 3: THIRD YEAR

Chapter 15 **Geographical Skills for Third Years: Ordnance Survey, aerial photograph and satellite imagery skills** **272**
Comparing Ordnance Survey maps and aerial photographs 273
Aerial photograph sketch maps 275
Satellite imagery 280

Chapter 16 **Soil: A vital natural resource** **284**
Soil 284
Soil formation 288
Irish soil types 290
Natural vegetation and soil 293
Human interference with soil 295

Chapter 17 **Tertiary Economic Activities: Transport and tourism** **304**
Tertiary economic activities 304
Tourism 305
The physical world and tourism in Ireland 307
Transport 311
Tourism and transport on Ordnance Survey maps 315

Chapter 18 **Population: How population changes over time** **322**
World population growth 322
Factors that influence the rate of population change 325
The demographic transition model 329
Population pyramids 330
Population change 333

Chapter 19 **Migration: People on the move** **342**
Migration 342
Organised migration 348

Chapter 20 **Economic Inequality: A world divided** **352**
Levels of economic development 352
The North–South divide 357
Development assistance/aid 361
Life chances in the developed and developing worlds 365

Chapter 21 **Globalisation: Living in an interconnected world** **374**
Introduction to globalisation 374
Impact of globalisation 376
Globalisation and the world we live in today 379

Key Words 385
Index 404
Maps 410
Acknowledgements 418

Introduction

Welcome to *New Geography in Action*! We hope you enjoy your Junior Cycle Geography course.

Here are some features to look out for:

In this chapter, you will learn tells you what you will learn about in the chapter.

There is an **Ice-breaker Activity** at the start of every chapter. This will get you thinking about the topics you will cover.

Chapters are broken into topics. Every topic has **Learning Intentions**, **Key Words**, **Questions** and a **Self-Assessment Checklist**.

Each section has **bronze**, **silver** and **gold** questions to test students' learning at different levels.

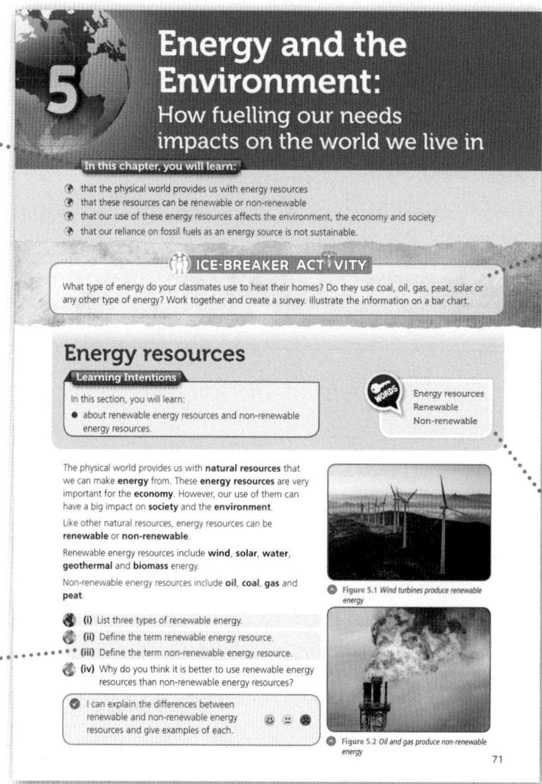

5

Energy and the Environment:
How fuelling our needs impacts on the world we live in

In this chapter, you will learn:

- that the physical world provides us with energy resources
- that these resources can be renewable or non-renewable
- that our use of these energy resources affects the environment, the economy and society
- that our reliance on fossil fuels as an energy source is not sustainable.

ICE-BREAKER ACTIVITY

What type of energy do your classmates use to heat their homes? Do they use coal, oil, gas, peat, solar or any other type of energy? Work together and create a survey. Illustrate the information on a bar chart.

Energy resources

Learning Intentions

In this section, you will learn:

- about renewable energy resources and non-renewable energy resources.

KEY WORDS
Energy resources
Renewable
Non-renewable

The physical world provides us with **natural resources** that we can make **energy** from. These **energy resources** are very important for the **economy**. However, our use of them can have a big impact on **society** and the **environment**.

Like other natural resources, energy resources can be **renewable** or **non-renewable**.

Renewable energy resources include **wind**, **solar**, **water**, **geothermal** and **biomass** energy.

Non-renewable energy resources include **oil**, **coal**, **gas** and **peat**.

(i) List three types of renewable energy.
(ii) Define the term renewable energy resource.
(iii) Define the term non-renewable energy resource.
(iv) Why do you think it is better to use renewable energy resources than non-renewable energy resources?

I can explain the differences between renewable and non-renewable energy resources and give examples of each.

Figure 5.1 *Wind turbines produce renewable energy*

Figure 5.2 *Oil and gas produce non-renewable energy*

71

There are lots of Activities (including Numeracy and Portfolio Activities), Video Lessons and Case Studies throughout!

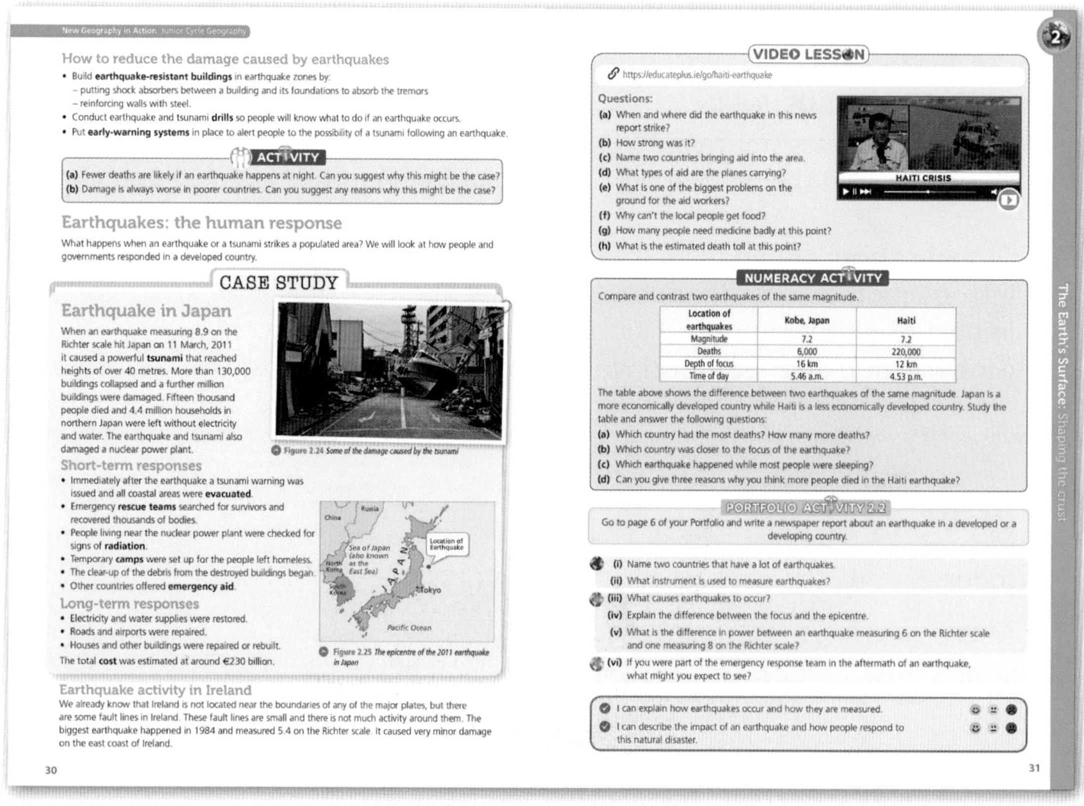

New Geography in Action Junior Cycle Geography

How to reduce the damage caused by earthquakes

- Build **earthquake-resistant buildings** in earthquake zones by:
  - putting shock absorbers between a building and its foundations to absorb the tremors
  - reinforcing walls with steel.
- Conduct earthquake and tsunami **drills** so people will know what to do if an earthquake occurs.
- Put **early-warning systems** in place to alert people to the possibility of a tsunami following an earthquake.

ACTIVITY

(a) Fewer deaths are likely if an earthquake happens at night. Can you suggest why this might be the case?
(b) Damage is always worse in poorer countries. Can you suggest any reasons why this might be the case?

Earthquakes: the human response

What happens when an earthquake or a tsunami strikes a populated area? We will look at how people and governments responded in a developed country.

CASE STUDY

Earthquake in Japan

When an earthquake measuring 8.9 on the Richter scale hit Japan on 11 March, 2011 it caused a powerful **tsunami** that reached heights of over 40 metres. More than 130,000 buildings collapsed and a further million buildings were damaged. Fifteen thousand people died and 4.4 million households in northern Japan were left without electricity and water. The earthquake and tsunami also damaged a nuclear power plant.

Figure 2.24 *Some of the damage caused by the tsunami*

Short-term responses

- Immediately after the earthquake a tsunami warning was issued and all coastal areas were **evacuated**.
- Emergency **rescue teams** searched for survivors and recovered thousands of bodies.
- People living near the nuclear power plant were checked for signs of **radiation**.
- Temporary **camps** were set up for the people left homeless.
- The clear-up of the debris from the destroyed buildings began.
- Other countries offered **emergency aid**.

Long-term responses

- Electricity and water supplies were restored.
- Roads and airports were repaired.
- Houses and other buildings were repaired or rebuilt.

The total **cost** was estimated at around €230 billion.

Figure 2.25 *The epicentre of the 2011 earthquake in Japan*

Earthquake activity in Ireland

We already know that Ireland is not located near the boundaries of any of the major plates, but there are some fault lines in Ireland. These fault lines are small and there is not much activity around them. The biggest earthquake happened in 1984 and measured 5.4 on the Richter scale. It caused very minor damage on the east coast of Ireland.

30

VIDEO LESSON

https://educateplus.ie/go/haiti-earthquake

Questions:

(a) When and where did the earthquake in this news report strike?
(b) How strong was it?
(c) Name two countries bringing aid into the area.
(d) What types of aid are the planes carrying?
(e) What is one of the biggest problems on the ground for the aid workers?
(f) Why can't the local people get food?
(g) How many people need medicine badly at this point?
(h) What is the estimated death toll at this point?

NUMERACY ACTIVITY

Compare and contrast two earthquakes of the same magnitude.

Location of earthquakes	Kobe, Japan	Haiti
Magnitude	7.2	7.2
Deaths	6,000	220,000
Depth of focus	16 km	12 km
Time of day	5.46 a.m.	4.53 p.m.

The table above shows the difference between two earthquakes of the same magnitude. Japan is a more economically developed country while Haiti is a less economically developed country. Study the table and answer the following questions:

(a) Which country had the most deaths? How many more deaths?
(b) Which country was closer to the focus of the earthquake?
(c) Which earthquake happened while most people were sleeping?
(d) Can you give three reasons why you think more people died in the Haiti earthquake?

PORTFOLIO ACTIVITY 2.2

Go to page 6 of your Portfolio and write a newspaper report about an earthquake in a developed or a developing country.

(i) Name two countries that have a lot of earthquakes.
(ii) What instrument is used to measure earthquakes?
(iii) What causes earthquakes to occur?
(iv) Explain the difference between the focus and the epicentre.
(v) What is the difference in power between an earthquake measuring 6 on the Richter scale and one measuring 8 on the Richter scale?
(vi) If you were part of the emergency response team in the aftermath of an earthquake, what might you expect to see?

I can explain how earthquakes occur and how they are measured.

I can describe the impact of an earthquake and how people respond to this natural disaster.

The Earth's Surface: Shaping the crust

2

31

There are questions at the end of every chapter to help you revise what you have learned.

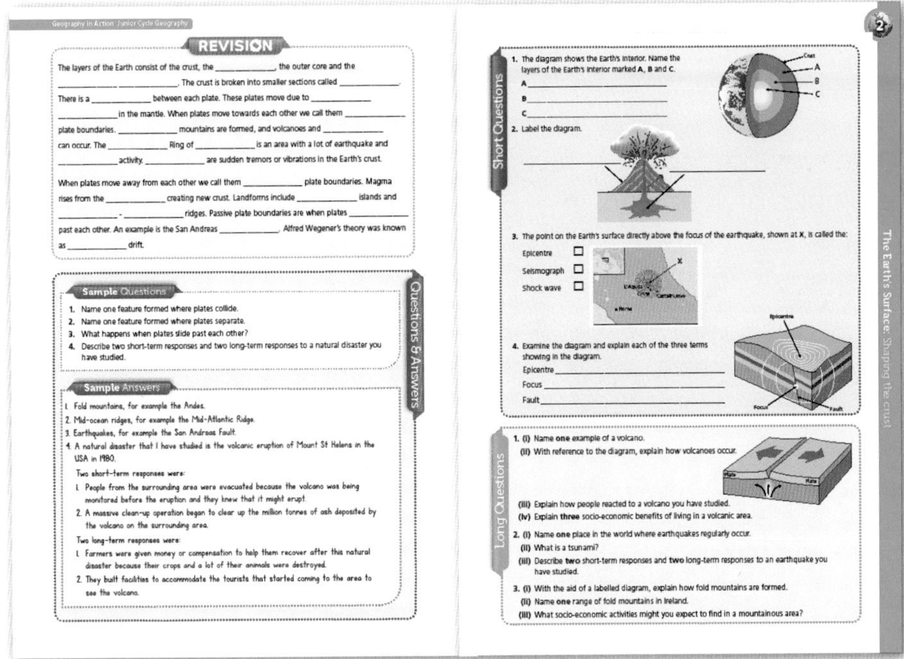

REVISION

The layers of the Earth consist of the crust, the ____________, the outer core and the ____________ ____________. The crust is broken into smaller sections called ____________. There is a ____________ between each plate. These plates move due to ____________ ____________ in the mantle. When plates move towards each other we call them ____________ plate boundaries. ____________ mountains are formed, and volcanoes and ____________ can occur. The ____________ Ring of ____________ is an area with a lot of earthquake and ____________ activity. ____________ are sudden tremors or vibrations in the Earth's crust.

When plates move away from each other we call them ____________ plate boundaries. Magma rises from the ____________ creating new crust. Landforms include ____________ islands and ____________ - ____________ ridges. Passive plate boundaries are when plates ____________ past each other. An example is the San Andreas ____________. Alfred Wegener's theory was known as ____________ drift.

Questions & Answers

Sample Questions

1. Name one feature formed where plates collide.
2. Name one feature formed where plates separate.
3. What happens when plates slide past each other?
4. Describe two short-term responses and two long-term responses to a natural disaster you have studied.

Sample Answers

1. Fold mountains, for example the Andes.
2. Mid-ocean ridges, for example the Mid-Atlantic Ridge.
3. Earthquakes, for example the San Andreas Fault.
4. A natural disaster that I have studied is the volcanic eruption of Mount St Helens in the USA in 1980.

   Two short-term responses were:
   1. People from the surrounding area were evacuated because the volcano was being monitored before the eruption and they knew that it might erupt.
   2. A massive clean-up operation began to clear up the million tonnes of ash deposited by the volcano on the surrounding area.

   Two long-term responses were:
   1. Farmers were given money or compensation to help them recover after this natural disaster because their crops and a lot of their animals were destroyed.
   2. They built facilities to accommodate the tourists that started coming to the area to see the volcano.

Short Questions

1. The diagram shows the Earth's interior. Name the layers of the Earth's interior marked **A**, **B** and **C**.
   A ____________
   B ____________
   C ____________
2. Label the diagram.
3. The point on the Earth's surface directly above the focus of the earthquake, shown at **X**, is called the:
   Epicentre ☐
   Seismograph ☐
   Shock wave ☐
4. Examine the diagram and explain each of the three terms showing in the diagram.
   Epicentre ____________
   Focus ____________
   Fault ____________

Long Questions

1. (i) Name **one** example of a volcano.
   (ii) With reference to the diagram, explain how volcanoes occur.
   (iii) Explain how people reacted to a volcano you have studied.
   (iv) Explain **three** socio-economic benefits of living in a volcanic area.
2. (i) Name **one** place in the world where earthquakes regularly occur.
   (ii) What is a tsunami?
   (iii) Describe **two** short-term responses and **two** long-term responses to an earthquake you have studied.
3. (i) With the aid of a labelled diagram, explain how fold mountains are formed.
   (ii) Name **one** range of fold mountains in Ireland.
   (iii) What socio-economic activities might you expect to find in a mountainous area?

Features Key

	Activities that you will carry out as part of a group.		Tells you where to go in the book to find out more.
	Activities that you will carry out with a partner.		Tells you that there is an animation of the illustration available on www.educateplus.ie.
	Tells you what a word means.		

Key Skills

All of the Activity boxes are colour-coded according to the relevant Key Skill.

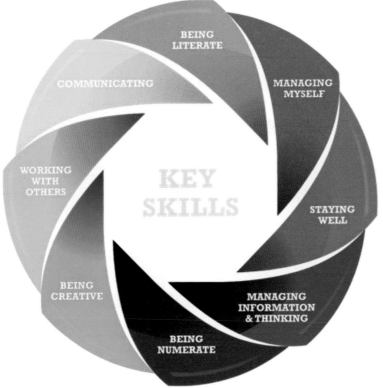

KEY SKILLS

BEING LITERATE
MANAGING MYSELF
STAYING WELL
MANAGING INFORMATION & THINKING
BEING NUMERATE
BEING CREATIVE
WORKING WITH OTHERS
COMMUNICATING

Explore More *New Geography in Action* Student Resources

Portfolio

Keep fantastic examples of your work in your Portfolio book.

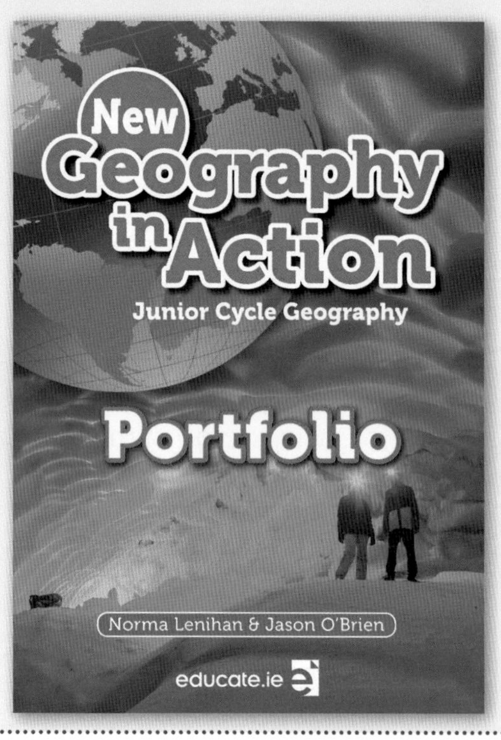

Activity Book

The Activity Book contains a lot of extra questions based on the chapters in your textbook.

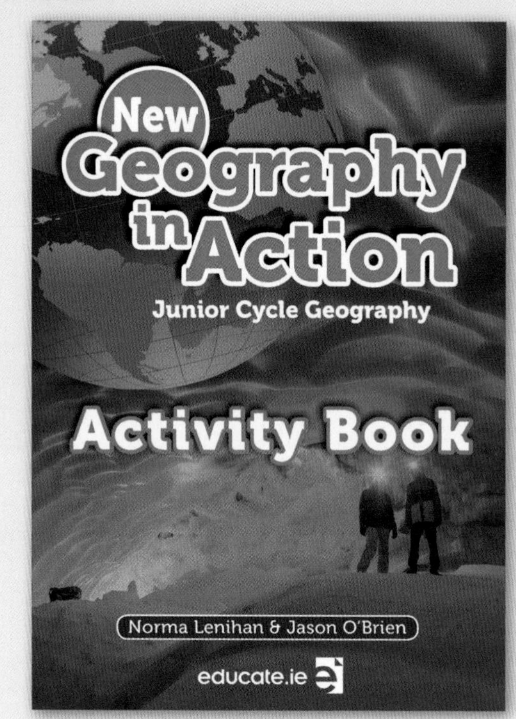

Digital Resources for Students

You'll find chapter quizzes, animations and videos on

www.educateplus.ie/resources/new-geography-action

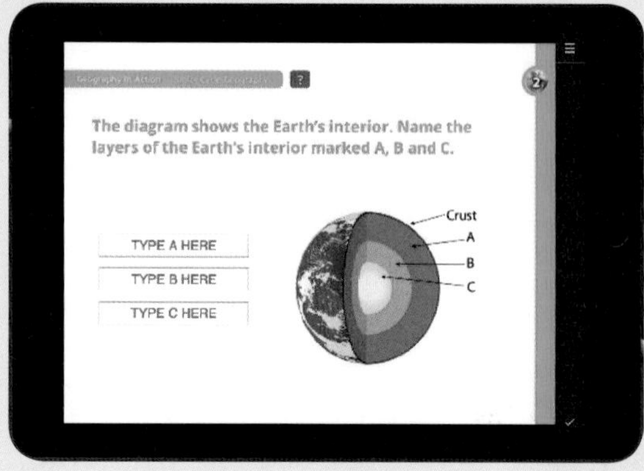

Information for Teachers

The invaluable *New Geography in Action* Teacher's Resource Book provides the ultimate support for planning, teaching and assessing Junior Cycle Geography. We've included the Learning Outcomes by Chapter here as a handy reference guide but don't forget to check out the Teacher's Resource Book for additional information.

Learning Outcomes by Chapter

There are three strands in the Junior Cycle Geography specification:

- **Strand One: Exploring the physical world** (Strand One Learning Outcomes are in green below)
- **Strand Two: Exploring how we interact with the physical world** (Strand Two Learning Outcomes are in blue below)
- **Strand Three: Exploring people, place and change** (Strand Three Learning Outcomes are in purple below)

Chapter 1: Geographical Skills for First Years

Element: Geographical Skills

Chapter 2: The Earth's Surface

1.1 describe the formation and global distribution of volcanoes, earthquakes, and fold mountains in the context of plate tectonics and structure of the Earth

1.10 investigate a range of physical processes active in a chosen location and the connections between them

2.1 describe the economic and social impacts of how we interact with the occurrence of volcanoes, earthquakes, and fold mountains

2.3 identify how the physical landscape influences the development of primary activities

2.8 investigate how people respond to a natural disaster

2.9 assess the interrelationships between the physical world, tourism and transport

Chapter 3: Rocks

1.2 distinguish between different categories of rock type, referring to composition and formation

1.10 investigate a range of physical processes active in a chosen location and the connections between them

2.2 evaluate the environmental, economic, and social consequences of rock exploitation and energy resources

2.7 investigate examples of how people interact with and manage surface processes

Chapter 4: Primary Economic Activities

2.3 identify how the physical landscape influences the development of primary activities

2.4 assess the exploitation of water, fish stocks, forestry, and soil as natural resources

Chapter 5: Energy and the Environment

1.9 differentiate between the types of energy resources produced by the physical world
2.2 evaluate the environmental, economic, and social consequences of rock exploitation and energy resources
2.6 examine the causes and implications of climate change
2.7 investigate examples of how people interact with and manage surface processes

Chapter 6: Weathering and Mass Movement

1.3 analyse the processes and effects of weathering and mass movement on our landscape
1.10 investigate a range of physical processes active in a chosen location and the connections between them
2.7 investigate examples of how people interact with and manage surface processes
2.8 investigate how people respond to a natural disaster
2.9 assess the interrelationships between the physical world, tourism and transport

Chapter 7: Geographical Skills for Second Years

Element: Geographical Skills

Chapter 8: Secondary Economic Activities

2.5 describe a local secondary activity in relation to its function and the factors that influence its location

Chapter 9: Rivers

1.5 explain how the processes of erosion, deposition and transportation shape our fluvial, marine, and glacial landscapes
1.10 investigate a range of physical processes active in a chosen location and the connections between them
2.7 investigate examples of how people interact with and manage surface processes
2.8 investigate how people respond to a natural disaster
2.9 assess the interrelationships between the physical world, tourism and transport

Chapter 10: The Sea

1.5 explain how the processes of erosion, deposition and transportation shape our fluvial, marine, and glacial landscapes
1.10 investigate a range of physical processes active in a chosen location and the connections between them
2.7 investigate examples of how people interact with and manage surface processes
2.8 investigate how people respond to a natural disaster
2.9 assess the interrelationships between the physical world, tourism and transport

Chapter 11: Glaciation

1.5 explain how the processes of erosion, deposition and transportation shape our fluvial, marine, and glacial landscapes

1.10 investigate a range of physical processes active in a chosen location and the connections between them

2.3 identify how the physical landscape influences the development of primary activities

2.7 investigate examples of how people interact with and manage surface processes

2.9 assess the interrelationships between the physical world, tourism and transport

Chapter 12: Settlement and Urbanisation

3.4 consider the factors affecting the location and origin of rural and urban settlement in Ireland

3.5 examine the causes and effects of urban change in an Irish town or city

Chapter 13: Weather

1.7 investigate the formation and behaviour of a significant weather event

1.8 gather, record and interpret weather data

2.8 investigate how people respond to a natural disaster

Chapter 14: Climates

1.6 classify global climates, and analyse the factors that influence the climate in Ireland

2.6 examine the causes and implications of climate change

Chapter 15: Geographical Skills for Third Years

Element: Geographical Skills

Chapter 16: Soil

1.4 assess a soil type in a local area in relation to composition and vegetation

1.10 investigate a range of physical processes active in a chosen location and the connections between them

2.3 identify how the physical landscape influences the development of primary activities

2.4 assess the exploitation of water, fish stocks, forestry, and soil as natural resources

2.7 investigate examples of how people interact with and manage surface processes

Chapter 17: Tertiary Economic Activities

2.7 investigate examples of how people interact with and manage surface processes

2.9 assess the interrelationships between the physical world, tourism and transport

Chapter 18: Population

3.1 use the demographic transition model to explain populations' characteristics and how populations change

3.3 examine population change in Ireland and in a developing country

Chapter 19: Migration

3.2 investigate the causes and consequences of migration

3.3 examine population change in Ireland and in a developing country

Chapter 20: Economic Inequality

3.6 identify global patterns of economic development

3.7 compare life chances for a young person in relation to gender equality, health care, employment and education opportunities in a developed and a developing country

3.8 evaluate the role of development assistance in human development

Chapter 21: Globalisation

3.9 synthesise their learning of population, settlement and human development within the process of globalisation.

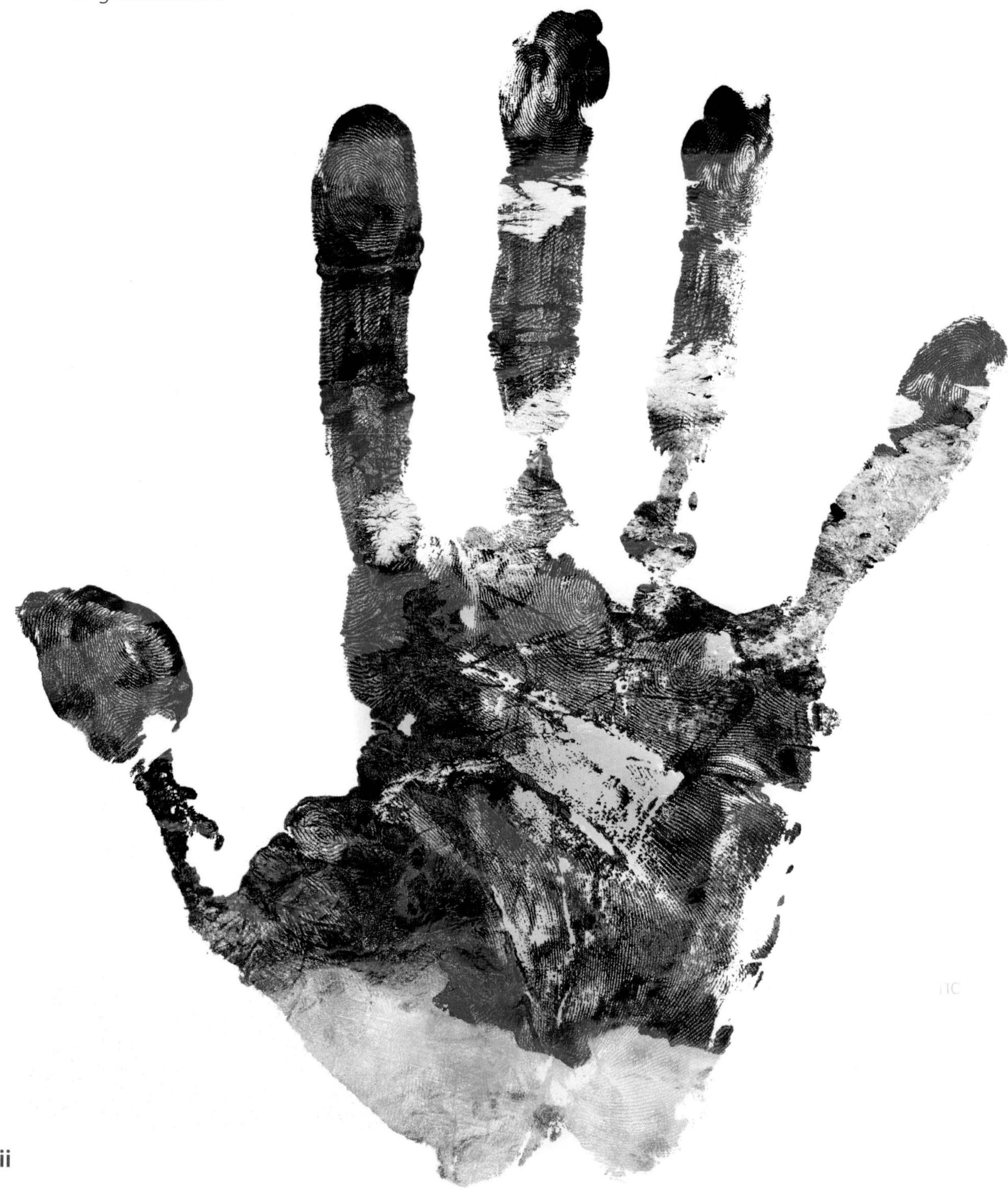

1 Geographical Skills for First Years: Ordnance Survey and graph skills

In this chapter, you will learn:

- what Geography is
- how you can use the skills you learn in Geography class in everyday life
- skills to help you interpret Ordnance Survey maps
- how to understand data and show it on graphs
- about common units of measurement.

ICE-BREAKER ACTIVITY

Before you start your Junior Cycle Geography course, answer the following questions in groups of four:

1. List four things that you already know about Geography.
2. Why do you think it is important to study Geography in school?
3. How do you think you will use what you learn in Geography class when you leave school?

Introduction to Geography

What is Geography?

Geography is the study of **the world around you**. It helps you to explore where you live. It will make you think more about your village/town/city, your country and the whole world!

It also helps you to understand the way the world is **physically** (what it looks like), **socially** (the people that live in it and why they live where they do) and **economically** (the flow of money and goods around the world).

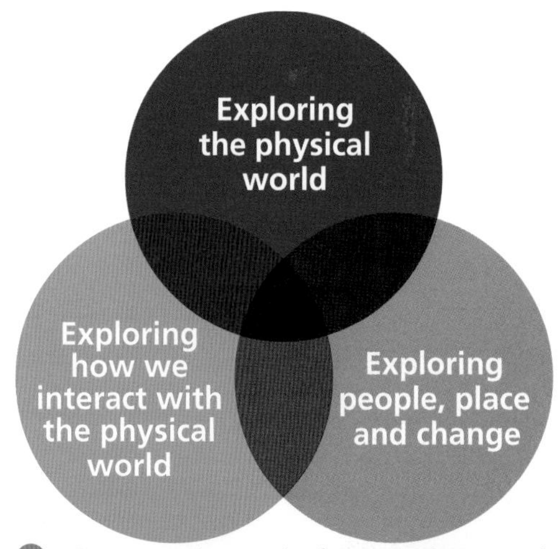

Figure 1.1 *The strands of Junior Cycle Geography*

Geography strands

There are **three strands** in Junior Cycle Geography. They are:

1. **Exploring the physical world**: looking at the physical world around us and how and why the world is shaped the way it is.

   For example, we will look at the **formation of soil** in Chapter 16.

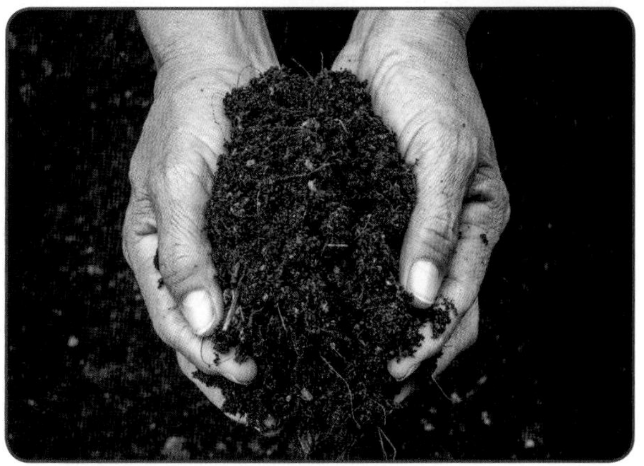

Figure 1.2 *Soil: the physical substance*

2. **Exploring how we interact with the physical world**: looking at how we interact with the world we live in, how we use the planet Earth to our advantage and the impact this can have.

   For example, we will look at **how people use soil** to grow crops in Chapter 4.

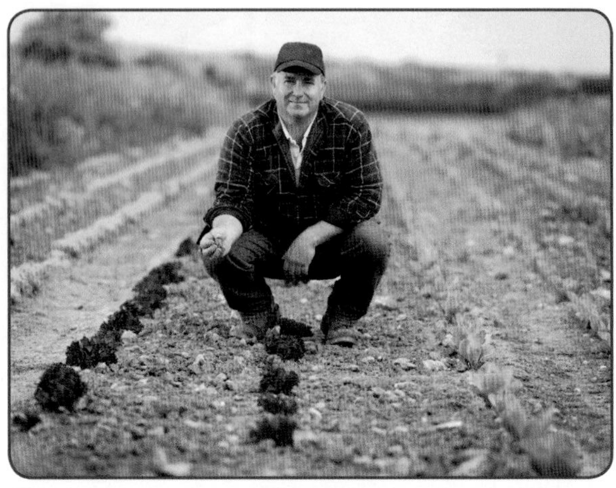

Figure 1.3 *Soil and people: growing crops*

3. **Exploring people, place and change**: looking at the people in the world, the places where they live and the conditions in which they live and why.

   For example, we look at how the **overexploitation of soil** leads to desertification (grassland changing into desert) in Chapter 16.

Figure 1.4 *Soil, people, place and change: desertification*

You can see from the examples on soil above that the three strands **overlap**.

What can you do with Geography?

The **skills** you learn in Geography class will allow you to understand what's going on in the world. You will also learn to think about how to solve the different problems you come across.

Take a look at the video lesson below to find out some exciting ways people use Geography in their daily lives.

Follow this link to watch a video about Geography:

https://educateplus.ie/go/geo-video

(a) Which job did you think was the most interesting?

(b) Google Earth is mentioned in the video. Go to Google Earth (https://earth.google.com/web/) and find:

- **(i)** your school
- **(ii)** your house
- **(iii)** a place you would like to visit.

(c) Eric Larsen says, 'Being an explorer is basically being a geographer'. Discuss this in groups of four.

Geography skills

In order to be a good geographer you will learn and practise many **skills**. This chapter will teach you some of the skills that you will need in your first year of Geography. Your class can dip in and out of this chapter throughout the year.

The skills you will need in First Year are broken into two groups:

1. **Ordnance Survey map skills**
2. **Graph skills.**

We will also look at **units of measurement** at the end of the chapter.

Ordnance Survey map skills 1

Learning Intentions

In this section, you will learn:

- the scale and national grid used for OS maps
- how to locate places on an OS map using grid references
- how to read the legend of an OS map
- the way height is identified on an OS map
- how to give directions on an OS map
- how to draw a sketch map from an OS map.

Cartographer
Scale
Ratio
National grid
Subzone
Easting
Northing
Grid reference
Legend
Contour
Triangulation pillar
Spot height
Summit
Cardinal points
Compass

Maps are representations of the world that have been created by people called **cartographers**. Maps help people to **navigate** (find their way around) the world.

There are many **different types** of map. Look at pages 12, 61, 128, 233 and 258 of this book to see some of the different types. You will also find maps of Ireland, Europe and the world on pages 410–417.

ACTIVITY

Many people use Google Maps to help them find and explore places. Go to Google Maps (www.google.ie/maps) and find some of the following places, which you will learn more about in your First-Year Geography course:

- Iceland
- Mount St Helens
- Haiti
- Dubai
- The Burren
- Nevado del Ruiz

ACTIVITY

Can you identify where in the world you are by looking at your surroundings on Google Street View? Go to https://geoguessr.com/ to have a go!

Draw a map of your school and its grounds (yard, pitches, car park, etc.). Use an A4 page and remember to label and colour your map.

Ordnance Survey maps

Ireland's national mapping agency is called **Ordnance Survey Ireland** or **OSI**. OSI produce printed and digital maps of Ireland. You will find lots of examples of **Discovery Series** maps (a series of maps produced by the OSI) throughout this book.

Go to https://maps.scoilnet.ie. (Your Geography teacher will need to create an account to log in.) Find your local area on the OSI map.

We are now going to look at the skills you will need to interpret Ordnance Survey maps in First Year.

Scale

The scale of a map is the **ratio** of the distance on the map to the corresponding distance on the ground.

The scale on the Ordnance Survey Discovery Series maps is **1:50,000**. This means that every centimetre on the map is equal to 50,000 centimetres (500 m) on the ground.

50,000 cm = 500 m or 0.5 km

Therefore, every **2 cm on an Ordnance Survey map is equal to 1 km on the ground**.

A-Z

Ratio:
how much of one thing there is compared to another thing. To work out a ratio, the trick is to multiply or divide the numbers by the same value.

SCALE 1:50 000 SCÁLA 1:50 000 **WWW.OSI.IE**

1 KILOMETRES 0 1 2 3 4 5 6 7 KILOMETRES 8

1 STATUTE MILES 0 1 2 3 4 STATUTE MILES 5

2 ceintiméadar sa chiliméadar (taobh chearnóg eangaí) 2 centimetres to 1 Kilometre (grid square side)

Figure 1.5 *Map scale 2 cm = 1 km*

NUMERACY ACTIVITY

If there are four teachers in a school and 100 students, calculate the teacher-to-pupil ratio.

National grid

The **national grid** is used to locate places or regions on Ordnance Survey maps. Each square on the grid measures **100 km by 100 km** and is represented by a **letter** of the alphabet. In total there are 25 squares. The only letter that is not used is the letter 'I'. These boxes, called **subzones**, can be divided into smaller squares measuring 1 km by 1 km.

These squares have vertical and horizontal lines called **eastings** and **northings**.

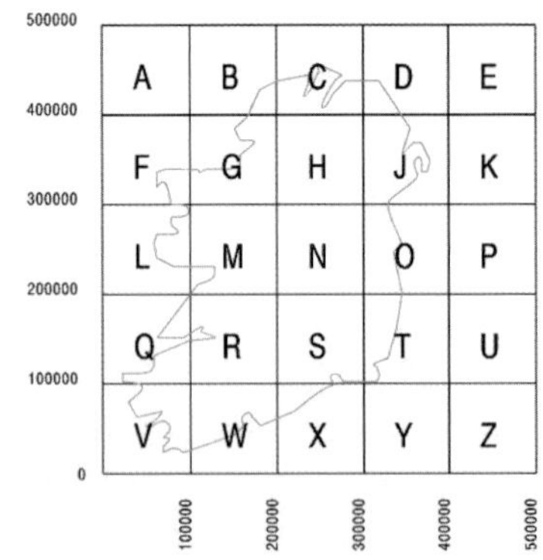

Figure 1.6 *Irish national grid*

Eastings

These are **vertical lines** on Ordnance Survey maps, giving coordinates. The numbers get higher as you go further east.

Northings

These are the **horizontal lines** on Ordnance Survey maps, also giving coordinates. The numbers get higher as you go further north.

Grid references

Grid references are used to locate an area or an exact **location** on an Ordnance Survey map.

The term **LEN** will help you remember what you have to do when you are using a grid reference:

L – letter of subzone | **E – the easting** | **N – the northing**

Four-figure grid reference

This kind of grid reference is used to locate an area or a **single grid square**.

We always give the **eastings before the northings**. A simple way to remember this is, 'go in the door before you go upstairs'. This will give the location of any single square on the map. The area of any square on the map is **1 km²**.

Example: You can work out the four-figure grid reference for the square with the ★ as follows:

1. Write down the subzone letter – on this map it is **V**.
2. Go in along the easting lines and write down the two-digit number the grid box is **beyond** – on this map **44**.
3. Go up along the northing lines and write down the two-digit number the grid box is **above** – on this map **99**.
4. The four-figure grid reference is **V 44 99**.

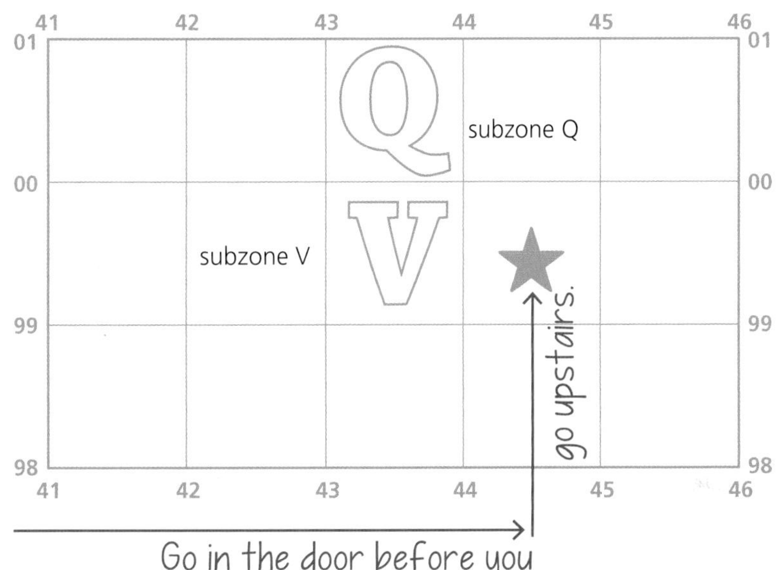

Figure 1.7 *Finding a four-figure grid reference*

See Video 1: Location: Four-figure grid reference

Six-figure grid reference

This kind of grid reference will pinpoint the **exact location** of something on the map, for example a post office or church.

Example: You can work out the six-figure grid reference for the location indicated by a ★ as follows:

1. Write down the subzone letter – on this map it is **V**.
2. Go in along the easting lines and write down the two-digit number the location is beyond. Now, imagine that the grid square is further broken up like graph paper. Add a number to your two digits to show how far into the grid box the location is – on this map it is **447**.
3. Go up along the northing lines and write down the two-digit number the location is above. Again, add a number to your two-digit northing to show how far up the grid box the location is – on this map it is **996**.
4. The six-figure grid reference is **V 447 996**.

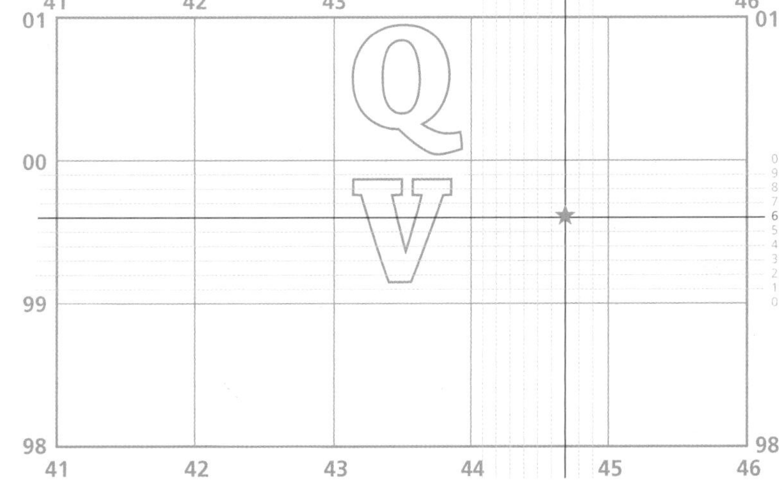

Figure 1.8 *Finding a six-figure grid reference*

See Video 2: Location: Six-figure grid reference

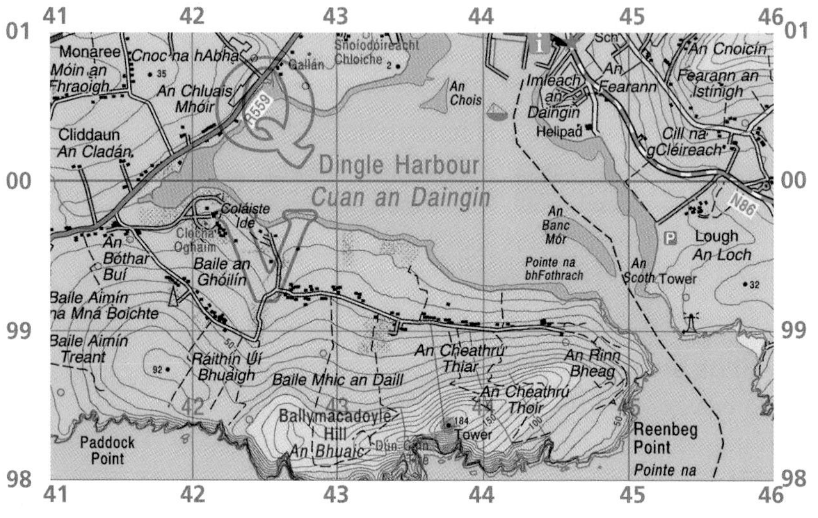

Figure 1.9 *Ordnance Survey map showing subzone letter, eastings and northings*

ACTIVITY

Look at Figure 1.9. There is a car park located in the grid square V 45 99. The car park's exact location is V 453 997.

Take another look at the map and answer the following questions:

(a) Which grid square is the ogham stone (Clocha Oghaim) located in?

(b) Give the six-figure grid reference for the ogham stone.

Symbols

Ordnance Survey maps come with a **legend**. A legend helps us identify what the symbols on the map stand for. It is important that we know what the symbols represent.

Look at the legend of OS symbols opposite.

(a) Every person in the class must draw ten symbols from the legend on a piece of paper.

(b) Swap it with a partner in your class.

(c) Write down the name of the symbols on the piece of paper.

(d) Swap it back and get your partner to correct it.

Figure 1.10 *Legend key*

Ordnance Survey Ireland
Suirbhéireacht Ordanáis Éireann

DISCOVERY SERIES SRAITH EOLAIS

egend Eochair

Mótarbhealach
Motorway (Junction number)

Bóthar príomha náisiúnta
National Primary Road

Bóthar tánaisteach náisiúnta
National Secondary Road

Carrbhealach dúbailte
Dual Carriageway

Bóthar príomha /tánaisteach náisiúnta beartaithe
Proposed Nat. Primary / Secondary Road

Bóthar Réigiúnach
Regional Road

4 metres min
4 metres max
Bóthar den tríú grád
Third Class Road

Boithre de chineál eile
Other Roads

Bealach
Track

Líne tarchurtha leictreachais
Electricity Transmission Line

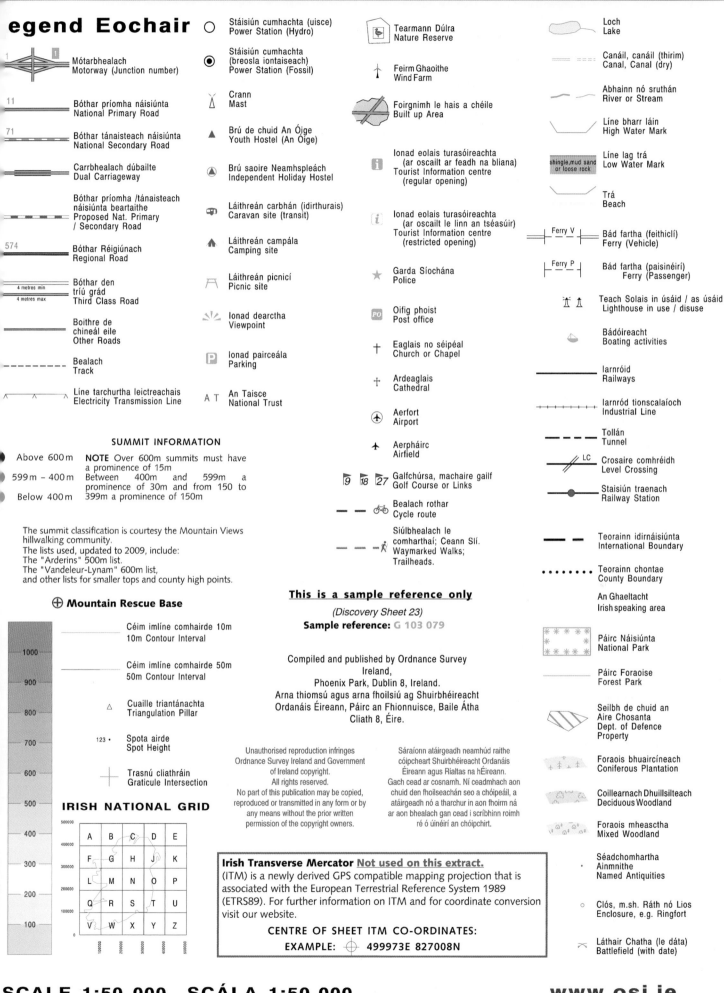

Stáisiún cumhachta (uisce)
Power Station (Hydro)

Stáisiún cumhachta (breosla iontaiseach)
Power Station (Fossil)

Crann
Mast

Brú de chuid An Óige
Youth Hostel (An Óige)

Brú saoire Neamhspleách
Independent Holiday Hostel

Láithreán carbhán (idirthurais)
Caravan site (transit)

Láithreán campála
Camping site

Láithreán picnicí
Picnic site

Ionad dearctha
Viewpoint

Ionad pairceála
Parking

A T An Taisce
National Trust

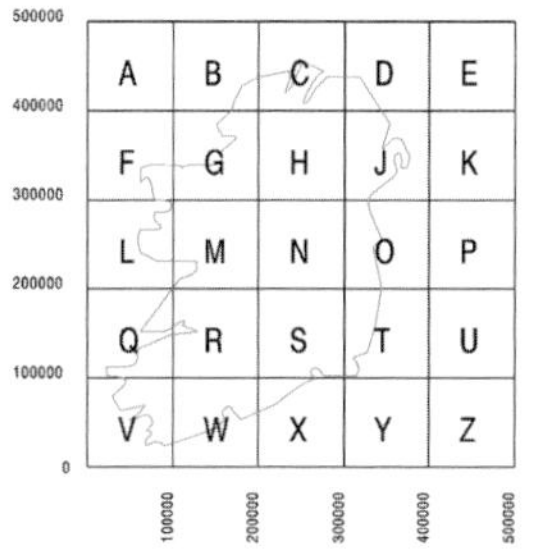

Tearmann Dúlra
Nature Reserve

Feirm Ghaoithe
Wind Farm

Foirgnimh le hais a chéile
Built up Area

Ionad eolais turasóireachta (ar oscailt ar feadh na bliana)
Tourist Information centre (regular opening)

Ionad eolais turasóireachta (ar oscailt le linn an tséasúir)
Tourist Information centre (restricted opening)

Garda Síochána
Police

Oifig phoist
Post office

Eaglais no séipéal
Church or Chapel

Ardeaglais
Cathedral

Aerfort
Airport

Aerpháirc
Airfield

9 18 27 Galfchúrsa, machaire gailf
Golf Course or Links

Bealach rothar
Cycle route

Siúlbhealach le comharthaí; Ceann Slí.
Waymarked Walks; Trailheads.

Loch
Lake

Canáil, canáil (thirim)
Canal, Canal (dry)

Abhainn nó sruthán
River or Stream

Líne bharr láin
High Water Mark

shingle,mud sand or loose rock
Líne lag trá
Low Water Mark

Trá
Beach

Ferry V
Bád fartha (feithiclí)
Ferry (Vehicle)

Ferry P
Bád fartha (paisinéirí)
Ferry (Passenger)

Teach Solais in úsáid / as úsáid
Lighthouse in use / disuse

Bádóireacht
Boating activities

Iarnróid
Railways

Iarnród tionscalaíoch
Industrial Line

Tollán
Tunnel

LC
Crosaire comhréidh
Level Crossing

Staisiún traenach
Railway Station

Teorainn idirnáisiúnta
International Boundary

Teorainn chontae
County Boundary

An Ghaeltacht
Irish speaking area

Páirc Náisiúnta
National Park

Páirc Foraoise
Forest Park

Seilbh de chuid an Aire Chosanta
Dept. of Defence Property

Foraois bhuaircíneach
Coniferous Plantation

Coillearnach Dhuillsilteach
Deciduous Woodland

Foraois mheasctha
Mixed Woodland

Séadchomhartha Ainmnithe
Named Antiquities

Clós, m.sh. Ráth nó Lios
Enclosure, e.g. Ringfort

Láthair Chatha (le dáta)
Battlefield (with date)

SUMMIT INFORMATION

Above 600m — **NOTE** Over 600m summits must have a prominence of 15m

599m - 400m — Between 400m and 599m a prominence of 30m and from 150 to

Below 400m — 399m a prominence of 150m

The summit classification is courtesy the Mountain Views hillwalking community.
The lists used, updated to 2009, include:
The "Arderins" 500m list.
The "Vandeleur-Lynam" 600m list,
and other lists for smaller tops and county high points.

⊕ Mountain Rescue Base

1000
900
800
700
600
500
400
300
200
100

Céim imlíne comhairde 10m
10m Contour Interval

Céim imlíne comhairde 50m
50m Contour Interval

Cuaille triantánachta
Triangulation Pillar

123 • Spota airde
Spot Height

Trasnú cliathráin
Graticule Intersection

IRISH NATIONAL GRID

A	B	C	D	E
F	G	H	J	K
L	M	N	O	P
Q	R	S	T	U
V	W	X	Y	Z

500000 400000 300000 200000 100000 0
100000 200000 300000 400000 500000

This is a sample reference only

(Discovery Sheet 23)

Sample reference: G 103 079

Compiled and published by Ordnance Survey Ireland,
Phoenix Park, Dublin 8, Ireland.
Arna thiomsú agus arna fhoilsiú ag Shuirbhéireacht Ordanáis Éireann, Páirc an Fhionnuisce, Baile Átha Cliath 8, Éire.

Irish Transverse Mercator **Not used on this extract.**
(ITM) is a newly derived GPS compatible mapping projection that is associated with the European Terrestrial Reference System 1989 (ETRS89). For further information on ITM and for coordinate conversion visit our website.

CENTRE OF SHEET ITM CO-ORDINATES:
EXAMPLE: ⌖ 499973E 827008N

SCALE 1:50 000 SCÁLA 1:50 000

www.osi.ie

1 KILOMETRES 0 1 2 3 4 5 6 7 KILOMETRES 8
1 STATUTE MILES 0 1 2 3 4 STATUTE MILES 5

2 ceintiméadar sa chiliméadar (taobh chearnóg eangaí) 2 centimetres to 1 Kilometre (grid square side)

Height

Height is identified in five ways on an Ordnance Survey map: **colour**, **contours**, **triangulation pillars**, **spot heights** and **summit heights**.

1. Colour

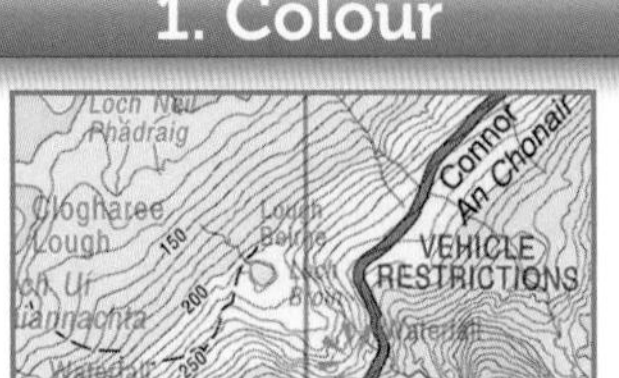

The colour **green** represents **lowland** areas. These are areas up to a height of 200 m. As the height increases, the colour changes from green to **light cream** to **light brown** to **dark brown**, which indicates an **upland** area.

2. Contours

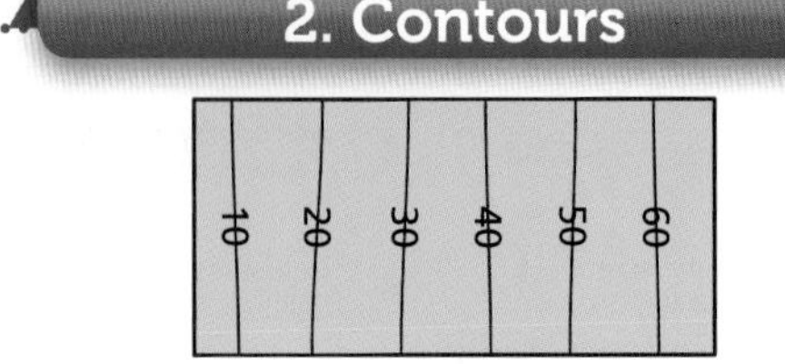

These are **lines** on the map showing areas of **equal height**. The height in metres is written on them. They are placed **10 metres** apart. The closer the lines are together the steeper the slope.

3. Triangulation pillars

△ 136

These **triangle** shapes show where there is a concrete pillar used by map-makers. They are usually found on mountain **peaks** or hilltops. The height of the mountain is given in metres beside the triangle.

4. Spot heights

• 310

These can be found anywhere on the map showing height in metres of a particular place. They are represented by a small, **black spot** with a number beside it.

5. Summit heights

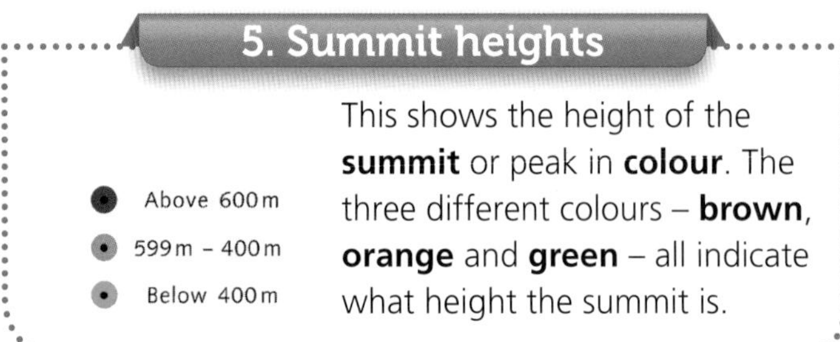

This shows the height of the **summit** or peak in **colour**. The three different colours – **brown**, **orange** and **green** – all indicate what height the summit is.

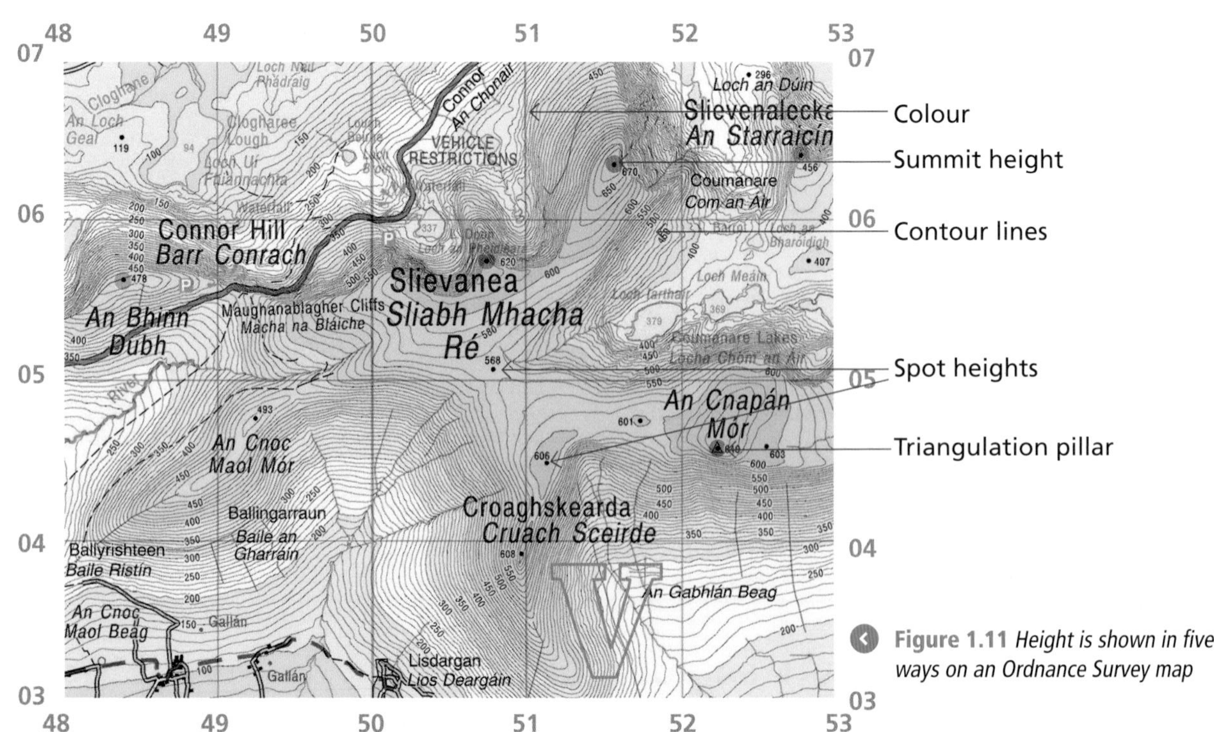

Figure 1.11 *Height is shown in five ways on an Ordnance Survey map*

Direction

Directions are usually given using the compass **cardinal points** of the **compass**: north, south, east and west. In between the cardinal points are other compass points. Look at the compass in Figure 1.12 to familiarise yourself with the directions on it. **North** is always shown on Ordnance Survey maps, see Figure 1.13.

When referring to direction, remember to note whether you are travelling towards an area or coming from that area.

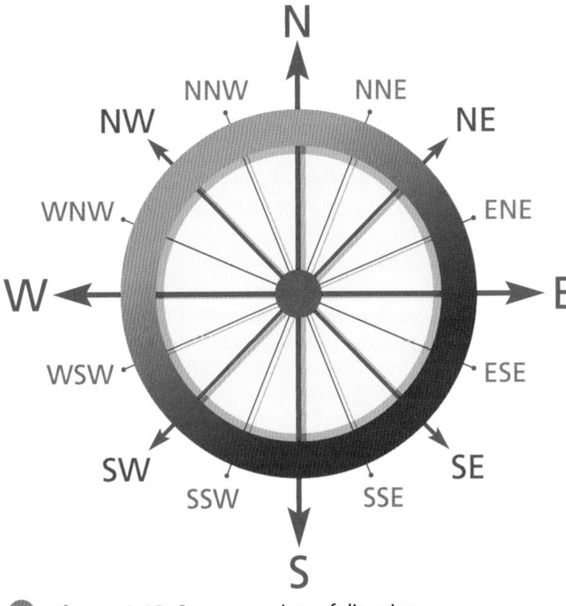

Figure 1.12 *Compass points of direction*

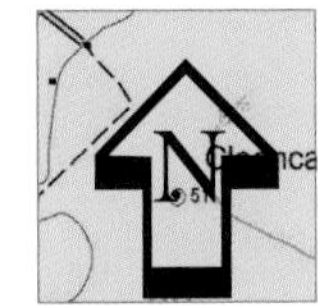

Figure 1.13 *The symbol for north on an Ordnance Survey map*

In groups of four, discuss ways in which you can work out direction without using technology. Think about these possibilities: sun, stars, trees, buildings, well-known landmarks.

Share your thoughts with the class.

In pairs, see if you can answer these questions:

(a) What direction does the front door of your school face?

(b) What direction do you travel on the way to school from your home?

(c) If you were to travel to Dublin city centre from your home, what direction would you be going?

(d) If you were to fly directly on a plane to the following cities from Dublin Airport, what direction would you be travelling?

(i) London **(ii)** Madrid **(iii)** New York

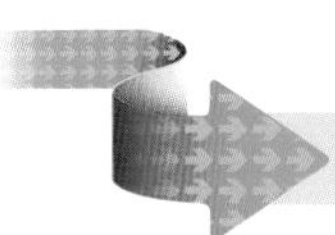

Go to Chapter 7 to learn more about Ordnance Survey maps.

Sketch map

A sketch map is a hand-drawn copy of a part of an Ordnance Survey map.

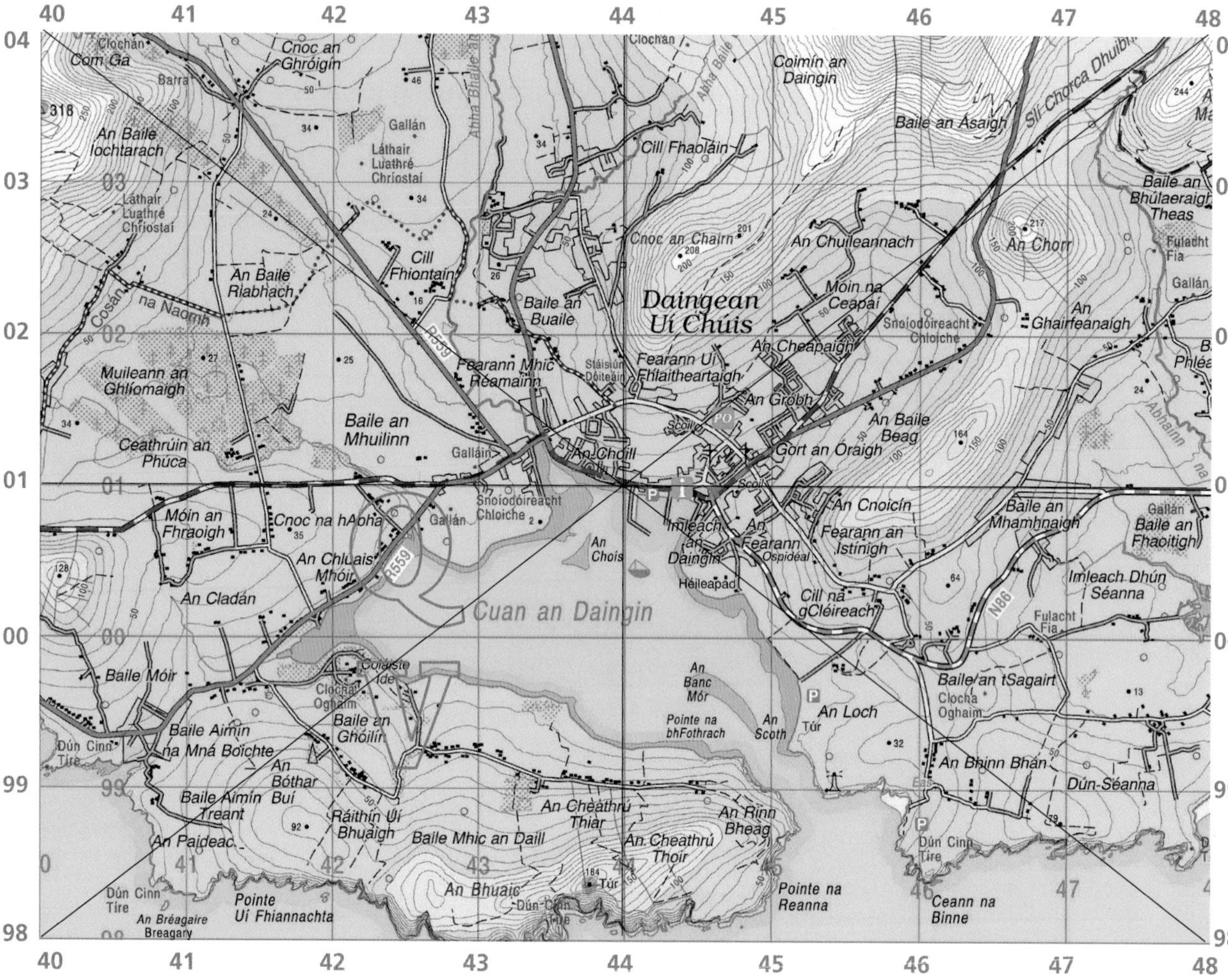

Figure 1.14 *OS map of Dingle harbour, Co. Kerry*

How to draw a sketch map:

When drawing a sketch map, follow the guidelines below:

1. Always use a **pencil**.
2. Draw a **frame** for your sketch map. First measure the width of the OS map in centimetres and divide by two. Then measure the height of the OS map and again divide by two. This will be the size of your sketch map frame in centimetres.
3. Put a **title** across the top of the map. Titles should read: 'Sketch map of ___________ OS map'.
4. Using a ruler, divide the OS map into eight **sections** as shown in Figure 1.14.
5. Using a pencil and ruler, divide the sketch map into **sections** in the same way. This will help you draw the sketch. See Figure 1.15.

Sketch map of Dingle OS map

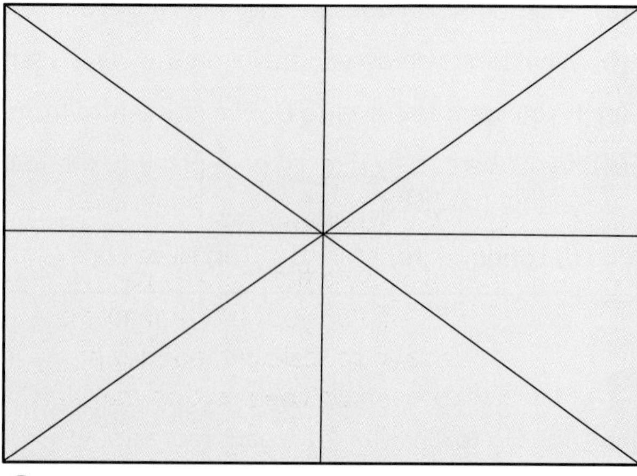

Figure 1.15 *The frame is divided into sections*

6. If there is a major **physical feature** such as an upland area, coastline, river or large lake, draw it to help with location. See Figure 1.16.
7. Then draw on the sketch the **features** you have been asked to show. Only put in what is asked in the question.
8. Draw a **key/legend** at the side or bottom, using different symbols and colours for each feature you include on your sketch.
9. Draw the **north** sign and the **subzone** letter on your sketch.
10. Finally, **rub out** the section lines that you drew in step 5, and add colour.

Sketch map of Dingle OS map

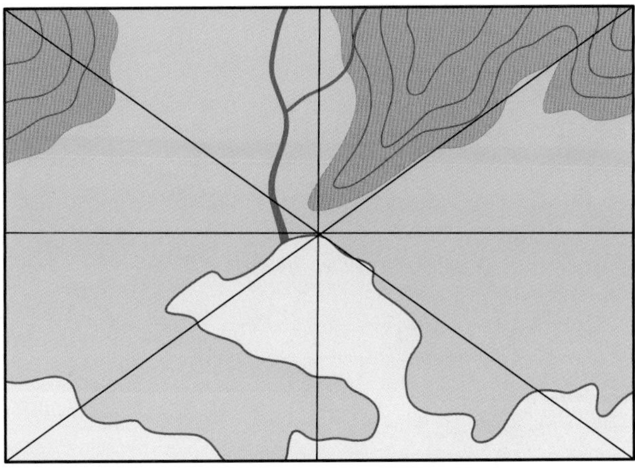

Figure 1.16 *Major physical features are added*

Sketch map of Dingle OS map

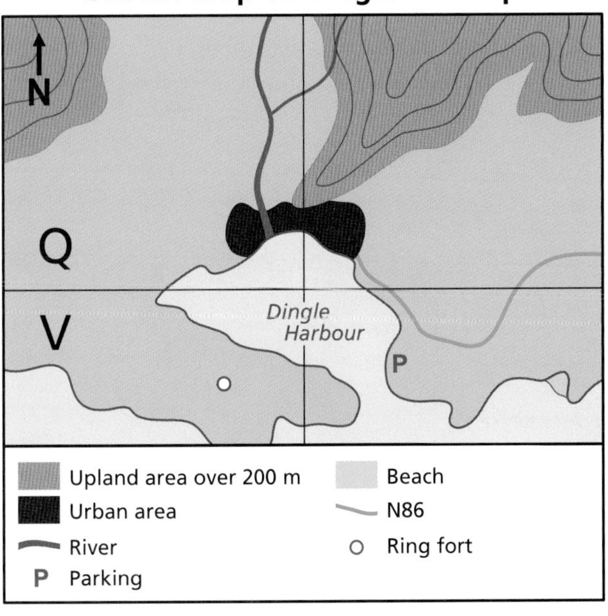

Figure 1.17 *The completed sketch map of Dingle harbour*

Top Tip

Make sure the features you include on your sketch map are drawn to scale and not out of proportion compared to the OS map.

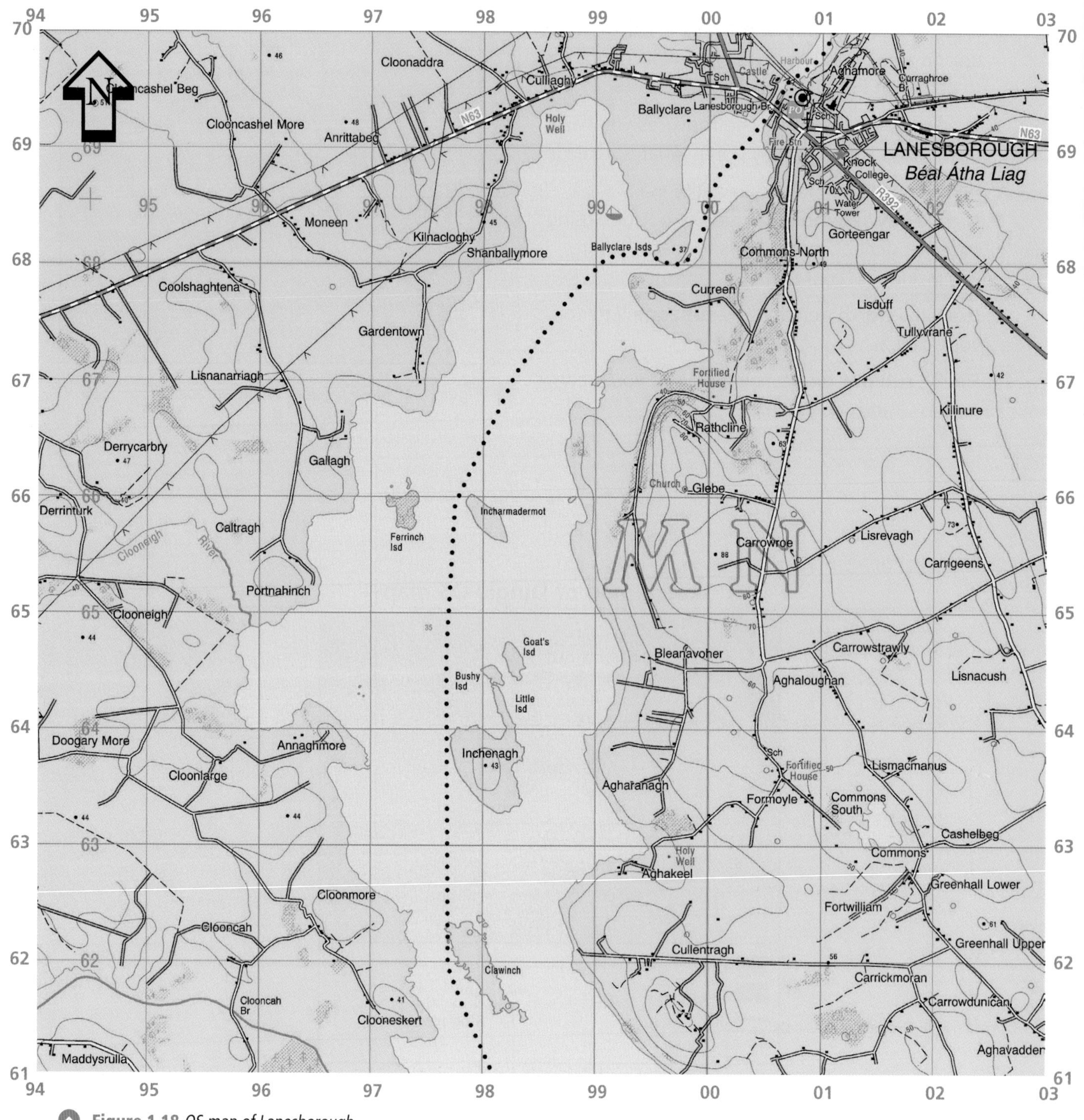

Figure 1.18 *OS map of Lanesborough*

Examine the Ordnance Survey map of Lanesborough above and answer these questions.

1. **(a)** Name the townland area at M 95 63.
   (b) Name the townland area at N 00 65.
   (c) Name the island at M 97 65.
   (d) Name the island at M 99 68.

2. Give the four-figure grid reference for the following:
   - **(a)** A deciduous woodland area
   - **(b)** A coniferous plantation
   - **(c)** Goat's Island
3. What antiquities are located at the following six-figure grid references?
   - **(a)** M 985 694
   - **(b)** N 007 637
4. What is the spot height at the six-figure grid reference M 967 693?
5. What service is located at N 012 689?
6. Give the six-figure references for the following:
   - **(a)** Boating activities
   - **(b)** A post office
   - **(c)** An old church
   - **(d)** A ring fort
7. What direction would you be travelling in the following situations?
   - **(a)** You leave Goat's Island and go towards Lanesborough.
   - **(b)** You leave Lanesborough and go towards the boating activities.
   - **(c)** You are travelling along the N63 from where it enters the map at 940 675 to Lanesborough.
8. Draw a sketch map of the Lanesborough Ordnance Survey map and include the following on your sketch:
   - **(a)** Lanesborough urban area
   - **(b)** The lake
   - **(c)** The N63
   - **(d)** The county boundary
   - **(e)** A fortified house
   - **(f)** A mixed woodland area

Practise the Ordnance Survey skills you have learned as you progress through your First-Year course. You will learn more OS skills in Chapters 7 and 15.

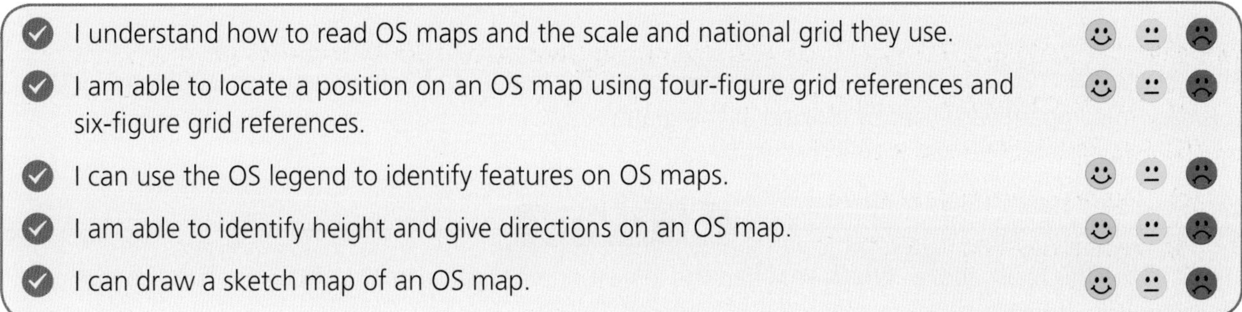

I understand how to read OS maps and the scale and national grid they use.
I am able to locate a position on an OS map using four-figure grid references and six-figure grid references.
I can use the OS legend to identify features on OS maps.
I am able to identify height and give directions on an OS map.
I can draw a sketch map of an OS map.

Charts and graphs

Learning Intentions

In this section, you will learn:

- that data can be shown on charts and graphs
- that different charts and graphs can be used to illustrate different types of information
- how to draw bar charts, pie charts and trend graphs.

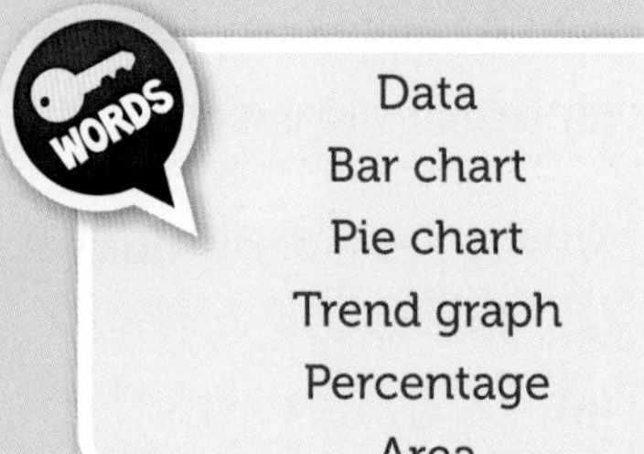

Data
Bar chart
Pie chart
Trend graph
Percentage
Area

Data

Data is a collection of **facts**. You'll see data presented visually in **charts** and **graphs** throughout this book. This section will help you to interpret these charts and graphs. You will also learn how to create your own!

We will look at:

- **Bar charts**
- **Pie charts**
- **Trend graphs**

Bar charts

Bar charts show data in a very simple form. They can help us to make comparisons between two or more pieces of information.

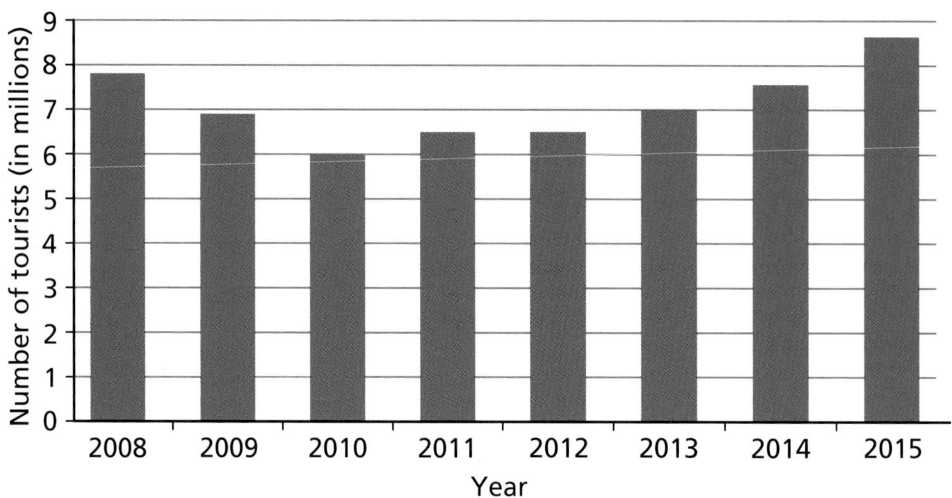

Figure 1.19 *Tourist visitors to Ireland 2008–2015*

Look at the bar chart above. It shows the number of tourist that visited Ireland between 2008 and 2015. It is easy to compare each year by looking at the graph.

Look at the bar chart above. Which year had the lowest number of visitors? Which year had the highest number of visitors?

How to draw a bar chart:

- Write a title for the chart. This should be an explanation of the information you are showing. For example, the title for the bar chart above is 'Tourist visitors to Ireland 2008–2015'.
- Draw an x-axis and a y-axis.
- Start with the x-axis. Work out how many groups you have to show on the x-axis. For example, there are eight bars in the chart above because we wanted to show eight years.
- Write a title for the x-axis. For example, the title for the x-axis for the bar chart above is 'Year'.
- Then move on to the y-axis. The y-axis always starts at 0. Work out the units of measurement you will use (for example, in the bar chart on the previous page the units are millions.) Then, decide what intervals to put on the chart (for example, the intervals on the bar chart above are 0, 2, 4, 6, etc.).
- Write a title for the y-axis. For example, the title for the y-axis for the bar chart above is 'Number of tourists'.

Top Tip

Remember **SALT** when you are drawing a graph:

S – Draw a **S**cale on the axes.

A – Check the intervals are even on the **A**xes.

L – Check the axes are **L**abelled.

T – Give your graph a **T**itle.

Top Tip

When drawing the bars on the chart, be sure to make the bars the **same width**. You should also use the **same space** between the bars.

NUMERACY ACTIVITY

Thirty students in a class were asked to select their favourite subject. See their answers below and illustrate this information using a bar chart.

Subject	No. of students
History	5
Geography	15
Science	7
Business	3

Pie charts

A pie chart is a circular graph. The data is shown in slices or sectors. The size of the slice shows how important that slice is.

Pie charts usually show data in percentages.

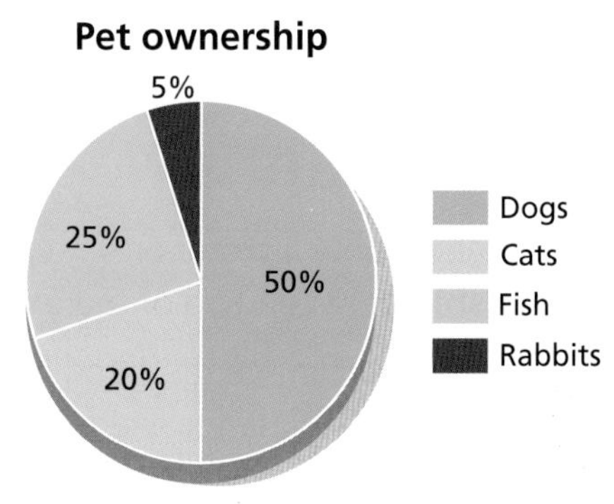

Figure 1.20 *Pie chart showing pet ownership*

ACTIVITY

Look at the pie chart above. What percentage of people own rabbits? Do more people own fish or dogs?

How to draw a pie chart:

You will need a calculator, a compass and a protractor.

- There are 360 degrees in a circle. Therefore the total of the data you want to display is equal to 360 degrees or 100 per cent.
- The first step is to work out what the total is. You do this by adding each sector. For example, the total number of pets in the pie chart above is 20.
- We now have to work out what percentage and degrees each of the sectors is:
  - To get the percentage, divide each value by the total and multiply by 100.
  - To get the degrees, divide each value by the total and multiply by 360.

	Dogs	Cats	Fish	Rabbits	Total
	10	4	5	1	20
Percentage	$\frac{10 \times 100}{20} = 50\%$	$\frac{4 \times 100}{20} = 20\%$	$\frac{5 \times 100}{20} = 25\%$	$\frac{1 \times 100}{20} = 5\%$	100%
Degrees	$\frac{10 \times 360^\circ}{20} = 180^\circ$	$\frac{4 \times 360^\circ}{20} = 72^\circ$	$\frac{5 \times 360^\circ}{20} = 90^\circ$	$\frac{1 \times 360^\circ}{20} = 18^\circ$	360°

- Once this is done, draw a circle on your page with a compass.
- Draw a line from the centre of the circle to the edge.
- Measure out the angle for each sector using a protractor.

NUMERACY ACTIVITY

This table shows the different ways 20 students travel to school. Look at the information below and draw a pie chart.

How students travel to school	No. of students
Walk	6
Car	8
Bus	4
Cycle	2

Trend graphs

Trend graphs show a **trend** or pattern for data **over a period of time**. They can also show the **relationship** between two or more sets of data.

For example, we can see the trend for energy supply and demand in the world in the trend graph on the next page. The demand for energy is going up, so the red line is increasing.

We can also see from the graph that renewable energy and fossil fuels trends are linked. The demand for renewable energy is increasing as the supply of fossil fuels is decreasing.

How to draw a trend graph:

- Write a title for the graph.
- Draw an x-axis and a y-axis.
- Start with the x-axis. Work out how many groups you have to show on the x-axis. For example, on this trend graph the time is measured in decades from 2000 to 2050.

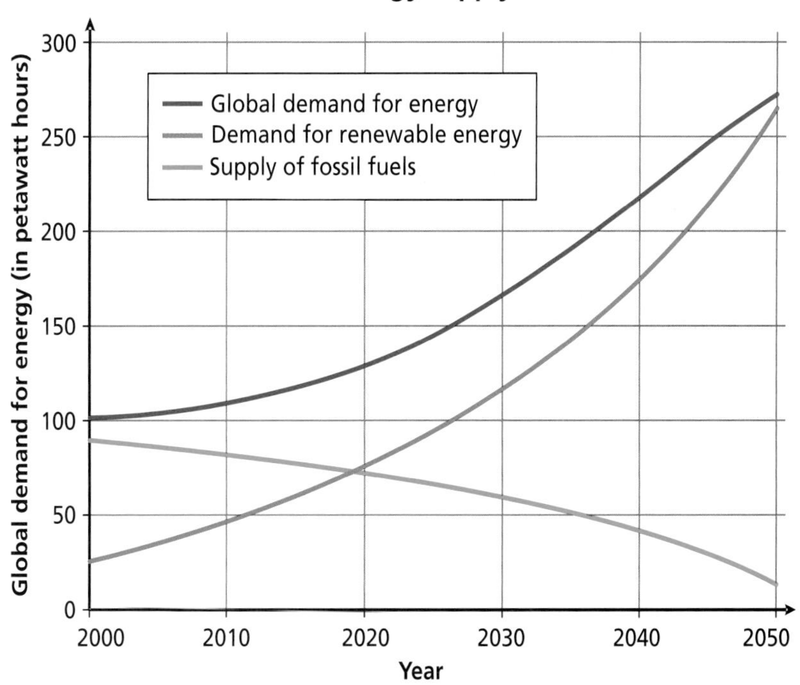

Figure 1.21 *Trend graph showing past and future energy supply and demand*

- Write a title for the x-axis. For example, the title for the x-axis for the trend graph above is 'Year'.
- Then move on to the y-axis. The y-axis always starts at 0. Work out the unit of measurement you will use. For example, the unit of measurement for the trend graph above is petawatt hours. Then, decide what intervals to put on the chart. For example, the intervals on the trend graph above are 0, 50, 100, 150, etc.
- Write a title for the y-axis. For example, the title for the y-axis for the trend graph above is 'Global demand for energy (in petawatt hours)'.
- Plot the data on the graph for each group.
- When all the data has been plotted, join the points together to show the data in a trend line.

NUMERACY ACTIVITY

This table shows the hours of sunshine in Dublin and the Costa del Sol in June, July and August. Look at the information below and draw a trend graph.

Month	June	July	August
Dublin	6.5 hours	5 hours	5 hours
Costa del Sol	9 hours	10 hours	9 hours

- I can read and interpret data from bar charts, pie charts and trend graphs.
- I can draw bar charts, pie charts and trend graphs.

First-Year skills

Learning more about units of measurement will also help you throughout the year. Here is more information on:

- Percentages
- Area
- Height

Percentages

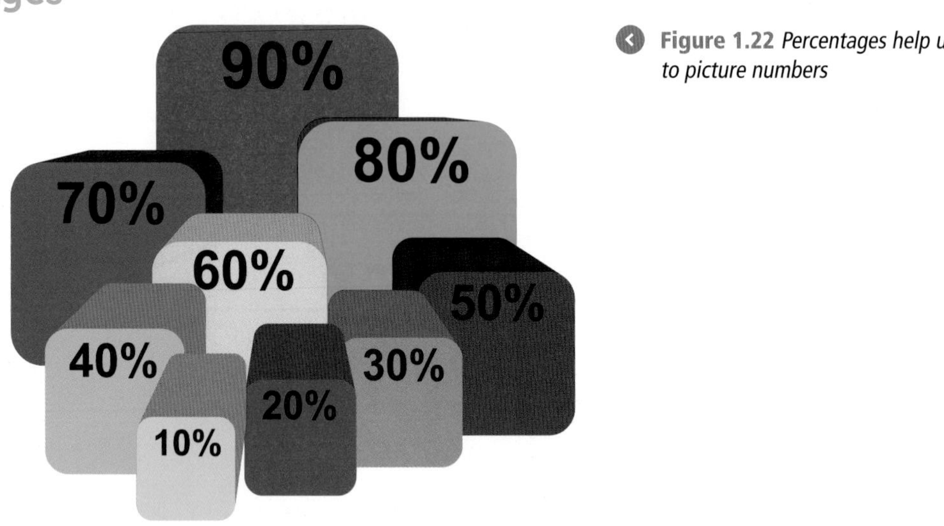

Figure 1.22 *Percentages help us to picture numbers*

You will be dealing with percentages in First Year. Percentages can help us to picture numbers more easily.

To get a percentage, divide the number by the total and multiply by 100.

For example $\frac{18}{30}$ x 100 is 60 per cent.

NUMERACY ACTIVITY

(a) If 17 out of 30 students in a class are girls, calculate the percentage of the class who are girls.

(b) If 20 per cent of a class of 30 have iPhones, how many students have iPhones?

Area

You will also be using area in First Year.

We calculate area using various units of measurement, from square millimetres to square kilometres. We also deal in units of acres and hectares when it comes to farming and forestry. An acre is just over 4,000 m². A hectare is 10,000 m².

To calculate area, we multiply length by width.

For example, an OS map that is 8 grid squares across and 10 grid squares down has an area of 80 km².

NUMERACY ACTIVITY

The minimum length of a GAA pitch is 130 m. The minimum width is 80 m. Calculate the minimum area of a GAA pitch.

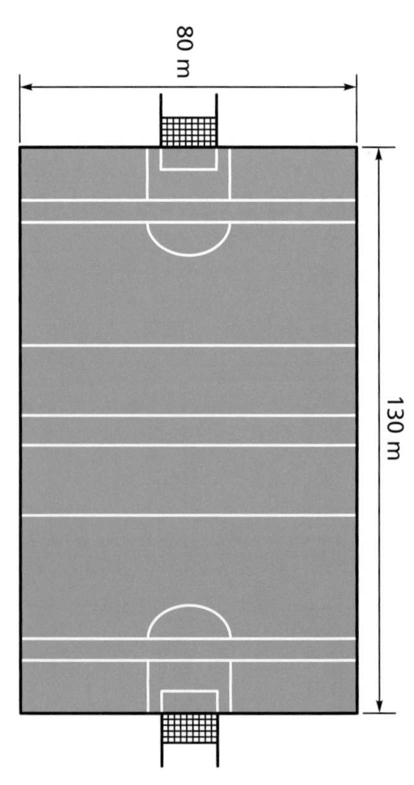

Figure 1.23 *The dimensions of a GAA pitch*

Height

In Geography we discuss height of land above sea level. We also discuss the heights of buildings. Height is usually measured in metres.

Figure 1.24 *Height is not always easy to judge. The height of the Eiffel Tower is 324 m. A standard double-decker bus is 4.4 m. Can you work out how many buses you would have to stack on top of each other to reach the top of the Eiffel Tower?*

NUMERACY ACTIVITY

Mount Everest is 8,848 m. Carrauntoohil is 1,038 m. What is the difference in height?

ACTIVITY

For the following questions, estimate your answer first and then find the exact answer afterwards:

(a) What height are you?

(b) What height is the ceiling in your classroom?

(c) What height is the spire in O'Connell Street in Dublin City?

(d) What height is the Eiffel Tower in Paris, France?

(e) What is the height of the Cliffs of Moher in Co. Clare?

2 The Earth's Surface: Shaping the crust

In this chapter, you will learn:

- that the Earth is made up of layers
- what plates are and how they move
- what happens when plates meet or separate
- how to describe volcanoes, earthquakes and fold mountains and the effects they have on people
- how people respond to natural disasters like volcanoes and earthquakes.

ICE-BREAKER ACTIVITY

The map of the world on the right shows the largest 'plates' that make up the Earth's crust and the locations of earthquakes, volcanoes and fold mountains. In pairs, look at the map and discuss these questions:

1. What do you notice about the distribution of fold mountains?
2. What do you notice about the distribution of earthquakes and volcanoes?
3. Do you see any patterns?

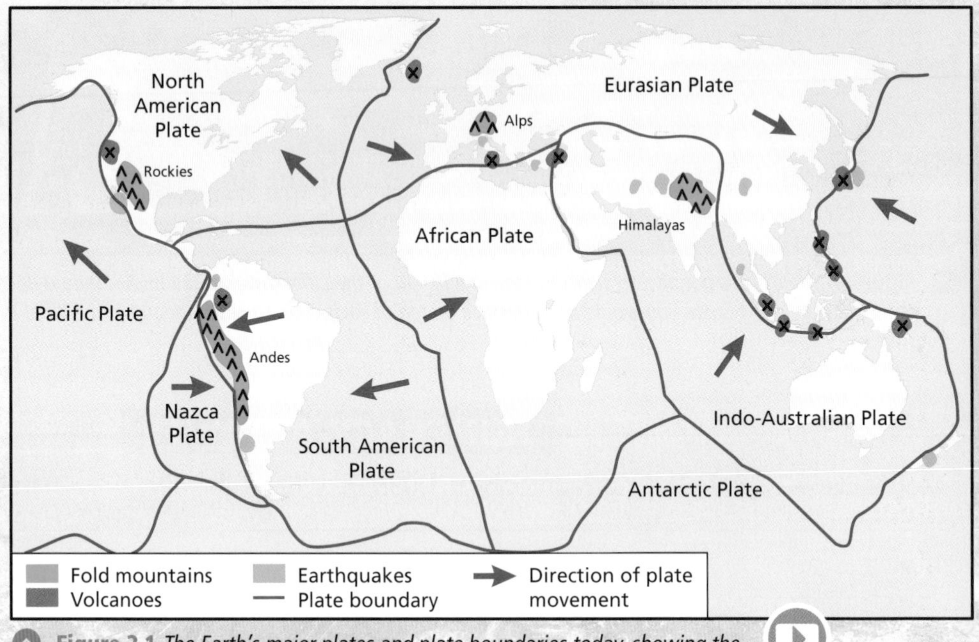

Figure 2.1 *The Earth's major plates and plate boundaries today, showing the location of major earthquakes, volcanoes and fold mountains*

The structure of the Earth

Learning Intentions

In this section, you will learn:

- that the Earth is made up of layers.

Crust
Mantle
Core
Magma

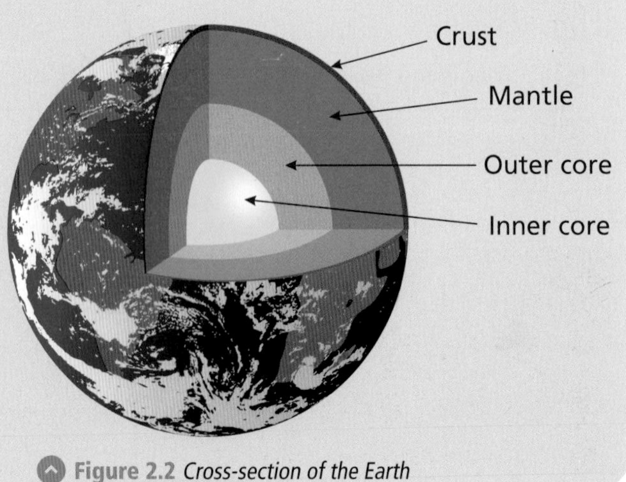

Figure 2.2 *Cross-section of the Earth*

The Earth is made up of three different layers – the **crust**, the **mantle** and the **core**:

The Crust

The crust is the outside layer. It is made of solid rock. The oceans and continents lie on top of the crust.

The Mantle

The mantle lies under the crust. It is made of molten (melted) or semi-molten rock called **magma**. The magma is moved around by currents, like bubbles in a pot of boiling water.

The Core

The core is the centre of the Earth. It is made of iron and nickel. It is the hottest part of the Earth at 6,000 °C. The core can be divided into the inner core and outer core.

 **(i)** What are the three layers of the Earth called?

 **(ii)** On which layer of the Earth are the oceans and continents found?

 I can name and describe the layers of the Earth.   

Plates

Learning Intentions

In this section, you will learn:

- what plates are and how they move.

Plate	Destructive
Plate boundary	Subduction
Convection currents	Constructive
Plate tectonics	Sea-floor spreading
Pangaea	Passive
Continental drift	Fault line

The Earth's crust is broken into pieces called **plates**. It is like the cracked shell of a hard-boiled egg.

The plates with land on top are called **continental plates** and the plates with oceans on top are called **oceanic plates**. The line where two plates meet is called a **plate boundary**.

The plates sit on top of the mantle. The magma in the mantle is moved around in a circular motion by **convection currents**. This causes the plates to move. Sometimes the plates collide (crash against each other), separate from each other or slide past each other at the plate boundaries.

Convection currents explained

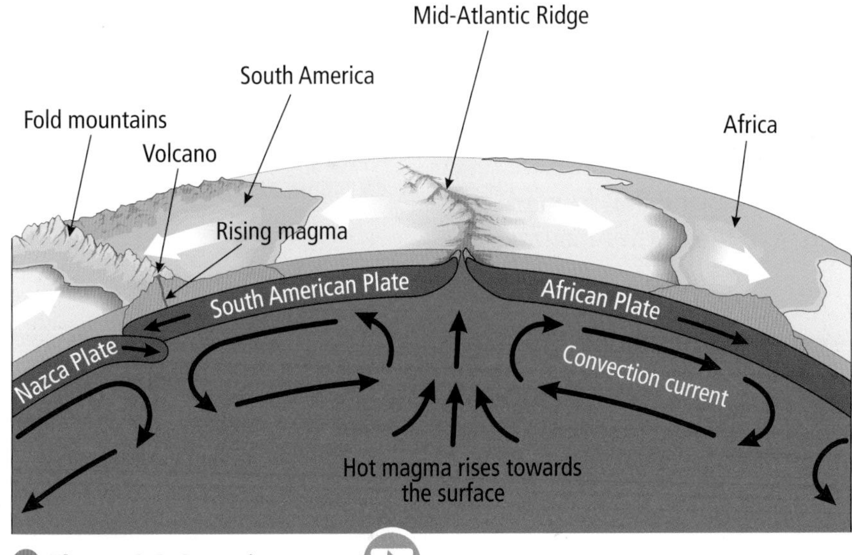

Figure 2.3 *Convection currents*

1. When magma is heated in the mantle, it rises towards the crust.
2. As it rises it cools and moves sideways. This causes friction between the magma and the crust and pulls the plates.
3. The magma cools and sinks back down into the mantle.
4. This process is constantly repeated.

Plate tectonics

The study of plates and their movements is called **plate tectonics**. We didn't always know about plate tectonics. The first person to come up with the idea was a German called Alfred Wegener. When he looked at the shapes of the continents he thought they looked like pieces of a jigsaw puzzle, and his theory was that they were once all joined together. He called this huge land mass **Pangaea**, meaning 'all land'.

Pangaea then broke up and the continents moved to the positions they are in today. Wegener called this **continental drift**.

Few people believed Wegener until the 1950s when scientists discovered the **Mid-Atlantic Ridge**. This is the boundary where the American Plate is separating from the Eurasian Plate.

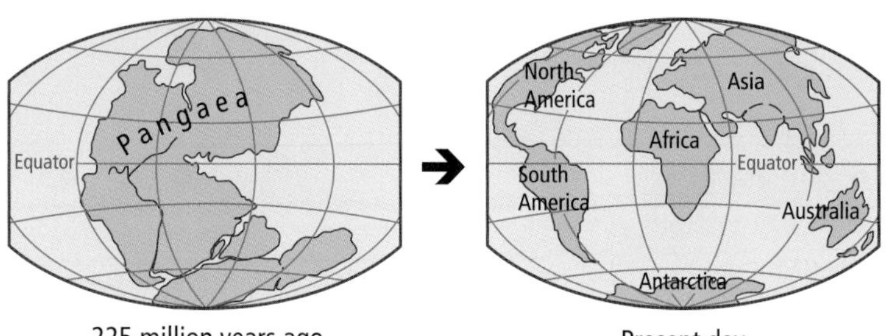

Figure 2.4 *From Pangaea to our world*

ACTIVITY

Work in pairs. Can you see how the shape of South America fits into the shape of Africa in Figure 2.4? Can you see how other land masses look like jigsaw pieces?

What happens at each of the boundaries?

Plates collide

Plates that collide with each other have **destructive (or convergent) boundaries**. Here, the crust is destroyed.

Huge pressure is built up and the heavier plate is pushed under the lighter plate. This is called **subduction**. The heavier plate melts back into the mantle. The lighter plate is lifted up, forming **fold mountains**. Plates that collide also cause **earthquakes** and **volcanoes**.

Example: The **Andes** are fold mountains that formed where the Nazca Plate is colliding with the South American Plate.

Figure 2.5 *Plates collide*

Plates separate

Plates that separate from each other have **constructive boundaries**. Here, new crust is created.

Plates move apart from each other and a gap is formed between the two plates. Magma rises out of the mantle to fill the gap. The magma then cools and hardens to form new crust. When this happens under the sea it is called **sea-floor spreading**.

Plates that separate form **volcanic mountains**, **volcanic islands** and **mid-ocean ridges**.

Example: Iceland is an example of a volcanic island that formed because the Eurasian Plate is separating from the North American Plate.

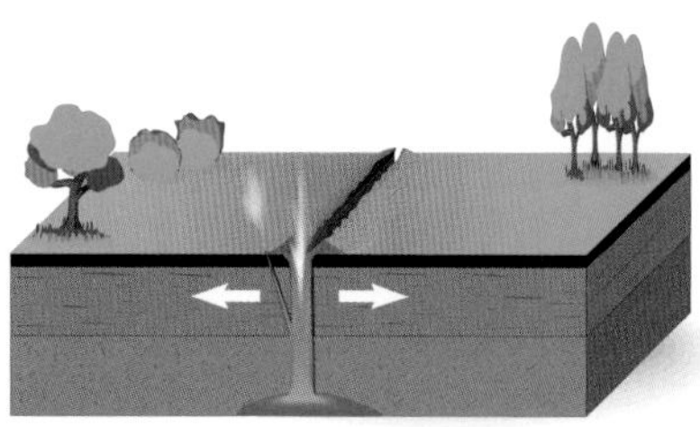

Figure 2.6 *Plates separate*

Sliding plates

Plates that slide past each other have **passive boundaries**. Crust is neither created nor destroyed.

These plates are locked together and then release a huge amount of energy when they slide past each other. Sliding plates cause **earthquakes** and **fault lines**.

Example: The **San Andreas Fault** in California is a fault line formed where the Pacific Plate is sliding past the North American Plate.

Figure 2.7 *Sliding plates*

ACTIVITY

Choose a term from this Wordle and describe it. Your partner has to guess what it is without you using the word!

Mantle Continental Drift Boundary Core Pangaea Crust Convection Current Oceanic Plate Magma

 **(i)** Name the two different types of plates.

 **(ii)** What happens where plates collide?

(iii) What happens where plates separate?

(iv) What happens where plates slide past each other?

(v) Explain how plates move.

- I can explain what plates are and how they move.
- I can give evidence to prove the theory of plate tectonics.
- I can explain what happens at each type of plate boundary.

Volcanic activity

Learning Intentions

In this section, you will learn:

- where volcanic activity takes place
- about the features formed when volcanoes erupt
- about the different parts of a volcano
- about the different types of volcano
- about the positive and negative impacts of volcanic eruptions
- how people respond to natural disasters such as volcanoes.

KEY WORDS

Mid-ocean ridge, Magma chamber, Vent, Lava, Cone, Crater, Active, Dormant, Extinct, Socio-economic, Geyser, Lahar, Geothermal energy, Sustainability

Now that we understand that volcanic activity can occur at boundaries where plates separate or collide, we will look at **volcanic activity** in more detail.

Most volcanic activity happens around the edge of the Pacific Plate, which is why this area is known as **the Pacific Ring of Fire**.

Volcanic activity creates **mid-ocean ridges**, **volcanic islands** and **volcanic mountains**.

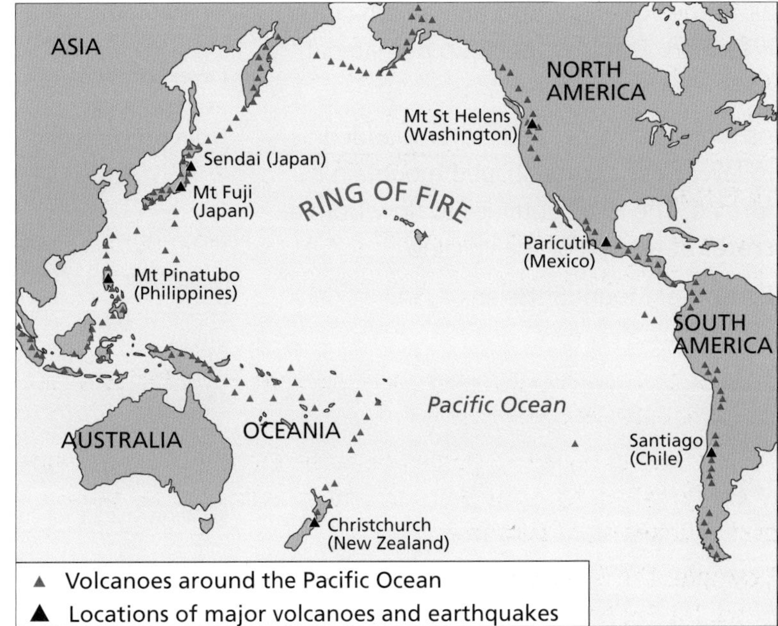

Figure 2.8 *The Pacific Ring of Fire*

Mid-ocean ridges

Hot molten rock, known as **magma**, rises up from the mantle through the cracks in the crust. The magma then cools, hardens and builds up, forming a ridge of rock.

Example: In the middle of the Atlantic Ocean, the American plates are separating from the Eurasian and African plates and the magma that rises up through the cracks or **fissures** there is creating a chain of mountains on the seabed known as the **Mid-Atlantic Ridge**.

Figure 2.9 *The Mid-Atlantic Ridge*

Volcanic islands

Mountains on the seabed, formed when magma wells up through the cracks in the crust, sometimes rise above the surface of the ocean. These mountains are called **volcanic islands**.

Example: Iceland.

DID YOU KNOW? The word volcano comes from the Latin name Vulcan – the Roman god of fire.

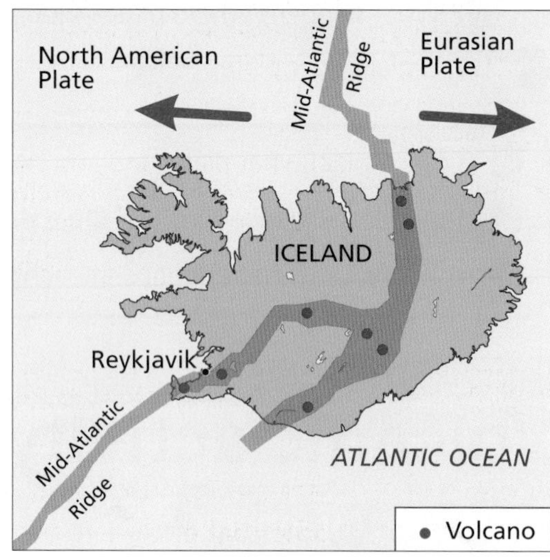

Figure 2.10 *The Mid-Atlantic Ridge through Iceland*

Volcanic mountains

Magma can also rise up from a **magma chamber** in the Earth's crust through a **vent**. A vent is a narrow tube in the crust. When the magma reaches the surface, we call it **lava**.

Lava, hot ash and rocks are thrown into the air as the volcano erupts and an ash cloud is formed. There is a build-up of material around the vent.

As more eruptions occur, layer is added to layer until a **cone**-shaped mountain is formed. The lava continues to flow from a **crater** at the top of the volcano.

Example: Mount St Helens, USA.

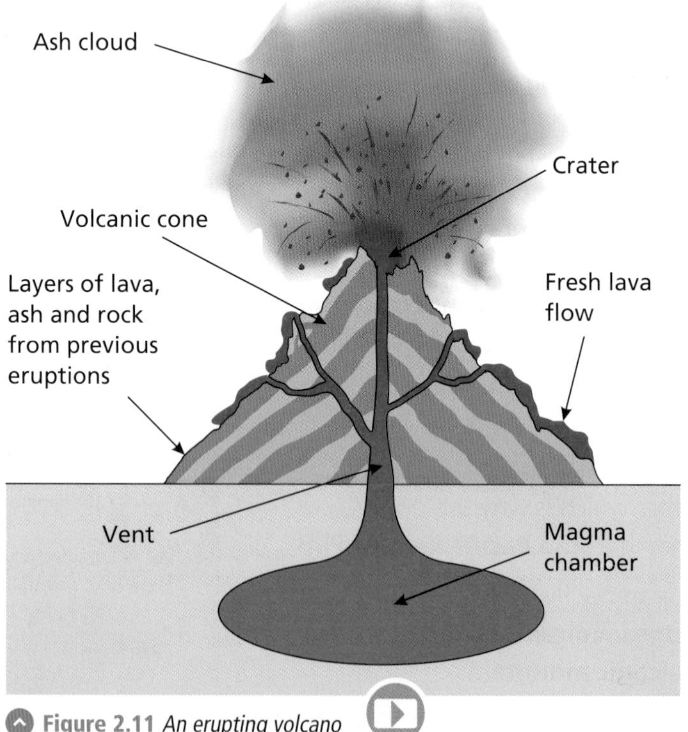

Figure 2.11 *An erupting volcano*

Types of volcano

There are three types of volcano – **active**, **dormant** and **extinct**:

Active

Active volcanoes erupt regularly, e.g. Mount Etna in Sicily and Mount St Helens in the USA.

Dormant

Dormant volcanoes have not erupted for a long time, but might erupt again, e.g. Mount Vesuvius in Italy.

Extinct

Extinct volcanoes will not erupt again, e.g. Croghan Hill in Co. Offaly.

Socio-economic effects of volcanoes

Socio-economic:
to do with both social factors (i.e. people) and economic factors (i.e. money) and how they relate to each other.

Positive effects

- The soils made from lava are rich in **minerals** and so are very suitable for agriculture. People who live in volcanic areas can grow crops to sell. For example, Campania in Italy is a **fertile** region because of Mount Vesuvius.
- **Tourists** visit the sites of some famous volcanoes, such as Mount Etna in Sicily, Italy. Hot springs, called **geysers**, are also tourist attractions.
- Water heated underground by volcanic activity can be used to generate **geothermal energy** to heat people's homes.

Figure 2.12 *Tea plantation beside a volcano in Kerinci, Indonesia*

Negative effects

- Gases produced by volcanoes, such as **sulfur dioxide**, can poison people who live nearby and cause **acid rain**. This can affect economic activities such as agriculture, fishing and forestry.
- A lava flow burns everything in its path. There can be huge **loss of human life** when a volcano erupts.
- When volcanic material mixes with water from rivers or rain or melting snow and ice, a river of mud called a **lahar** can be created. Lahars can destroy towns and villages in their path. This happened in Colombia in 1985.

Figure 2.13 *House buried by lava from Mount Etna, Sicily*

Go to Chapter 6, pages 98–99, to learn more about lahars.

ACTIVITY

Watch this video about volcanoes: https://educateplus.ie/go/volcanoes-video. Then answer the following questions:

(a) How many eruptions happen each year?

(b) What percentage occur in the Pacific Ring of Fire?

(c) What is a volcano's 'pyroclastic flow'?

CASE STUDY

Volcanic activity: Iceland

There is a lot of volcanic activity in Iceland because it is on the **Mid-Atlantic Ridge**. The physical landscape has influenced the economic and social activities of the people who live there.

Geothermal energy

Geothermal energy is energy produced from the **heat of the Earth**. This type of energy production is a major positive effect of volcanic activity in Iceland.

- The **steam** from the hot water is used to create electricity, which provides power for factories, offices and houses.
- Water heated by geothermal energy is piped into offices, schools and people's homes and used to heat them.
- It is one of the cheapest and most **sustainable** forms of energy.

Figure 2.14 *A geothermal power plant in Iceland*

A-Z **Geothermal energy:** heat energy produced by and stored in the Earth.

A-Z **Sustainability:** using the Earth's resources in a responsible way so that they are still available for future generations.

Go to Chapter 5, p. 78, to learn more about **geothermal energy**.

Agriculture

Agriculture is a very important **socio-economic** activity in Iceland. Although much of the island is mountainous and unsuitable for agriculture, about 20 per cent of the land area is fertile because it is rich in volcanic **minerals**.

- Iceland is completely **self-sufficient** in the production of meat, dairy products and eggs. This means that they don't have to import any of these food sources.
- Crops such as tomatoes, cucumbers and peppers, as well as flowers, are grown in **greenhouses** that are heated using geothermal energy.
- The water used for the geothermal heating systems is reused to water the plants. This is an example of a **sustainable** use of water.
- Because Iceland is so far north, there are few hours of sunlight during winter. Cheap **geothermal energy** allows people in Iceland to create **artificial light**, which the plants need to grow.

Figure 2.15 *Greenhouses heated by geothermal energy*

Tourism

Tourism in Iceland has grown a lot over recent years. More than **two million** people visit the country each year. That is six times the population of the country. Attractions include black-sand **beaches, geysers** and **geothermal spas** like the Blue Lagoon. These, as well as the 32 active volcanoes, are all the result of volcanic activity.

Tourism has positive and negative **socio-economic effects**:

- Tourism provides many **job opportunities**. For example, locals work as tour guides and lifeguards.
- Tourism can lead to **soil erosion** and increasing property prices.

Figure 2.16 *The Blue Lagoon is a top tourist attraction*

The government of Iceland works to promote sustainable tourism. You can find out more about it here: https://educateplus.ie/go/iceland

Read the article and answer these questions:

(a) According to Iceland Naturally, what is Iceland's brand?

(b) Visitors to Iceland can support sustainable tourism. Explain two ways they can do this.

Volcanoes: the human response

We have learned why natural disasters such as volcanic eruptions occur and about the economic benefits to people who live in areas affected by volcanic activity. What happens to these people when a volcano erupts? We will look at one example of human response to a natural disaster like this.

CASE STUDY

Natural disaster: Mount St Helens

Mount St Helens in the USA erupted in 1980, causing massive destruction over an area of 600 km^2. About 7,000 large animals and hundreds of thousands of smaller ones were killed. All surrounding forests were flattened. A river of mud caused by melting snow destroyed about two hundred homes. The height of the mountain was reduced by 400 metres.

Figure 2.17 *The eruption of Mount St Helens*

Short-term responses

- The volcano was monitored before the eruption. This meant that authorities were able to **evacuate** the areas surrounding Mount St Helens. The death toll of 61 would have been much higher if the area had not been evacuated.
- A million tonnes of **ash** took ten weeks and millions of dollars to remove. It also provided jobs for 200,000 people.
- Electricity was restored.

Long-term responses

- Millions of trees were **replanted**. These trees will not be fully grown until 2050.
- Farmers were given money as **compensation** for their losses.
- The government gave money to **rebuild** damaged buildings and transport routes.
- **Tourist facilities** were built to accommodate the people who came to visit the area.

Figure 2.18 *Forests were flattened for kilometres by the force of the eruption*

PORTFOLIO ACTIVITY 2.1

Go to page 4 of your Portfolio to create a tourism leaflet about an active volcano.

ACTIVITY

Check out this link: https://educateplus.ie/go/mount-etna. This website constantly monitors the active volcano Mount Etna in Sicily, Italy. When was the most recent activity?

Volcanic activity and Ireland

There have been no active volcanoes in Ireland for many millions of years because we are no longer beside a plate boundary, but there is **evidence** of volcanic activity in the past. For example, Lambay Island off the coast of Co. Dublin is an extinct volcano that was active over 450 million years ago. The Giant's Causeway in Co. Antrim also formed as a result of volcanic activity.

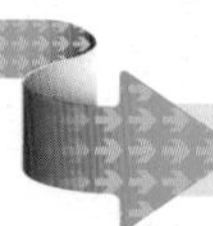

Go to Chapter 3, page 40, to learn more about the Giant's Causeway.

(i) Name a volcano you have studied.

(ii) Name an area with lots of volcanic activity.

(iii) Draw a labelled diagram of a volcano.

(iv) List three things that happened as a result of a volcano you have studied.

(v) Can you explain why people might want to live in an area prone to volcanic activity?

- I can name and describe three features of volcanic activity.
- I can list the three different types of volcano.
- I can explain the socio-economic impacts of volcanoes for a region that I have studied.
- I can describe the impact of a volcano and how people respond to this natural disaster.

Earthquakes

Learning Intentions

In this section, you will learn:

- how earthquakes occur and where they occur in the world
- how people measure and record earthquakes
- about the damage that can be caused by earthquakes
- how people can reduce the damage done by earthquake activity.

Tremor
Focus
Epicentre
Aftershock
Seismologist
Seismograph
Richter scale
Tsunami

Earthquakes are sudden **tremors** or **vibrations** in the Earth's crust.

When plates are pressing against (colliding with) or sliding past each other, there can be **a build-up of pressure** along the fault line. When the plates move, the sudden **release of pressure** results in an **earthquake**.

The point beneath the surface where the earthquake happens is called the **focus**.

The point on the surface directly above the focus is called the **epicentre**. The tremors or vibrations are strongest here and they reduce in strength the farther away you move from the epicentre. Therefore, the greatest damage occurs close to the epicentre.

The smaller tremors that follow an earthquake are called **aftershocks**.

Example: There have been many earthquakes along the San Andreas Fault in the United States.

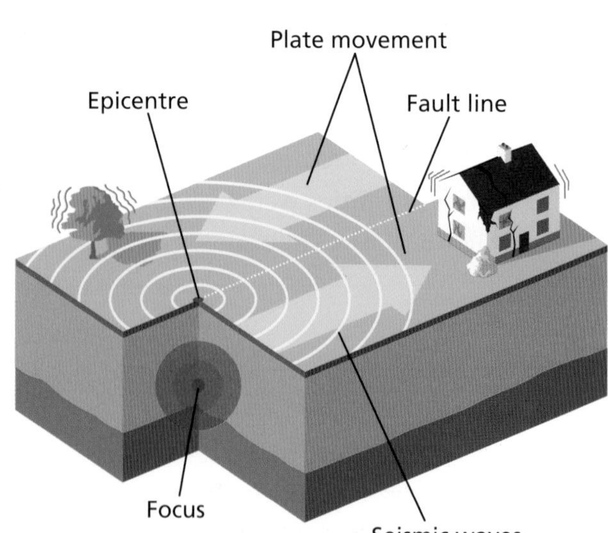

Figure 2.19 *The structure of an earthquake*

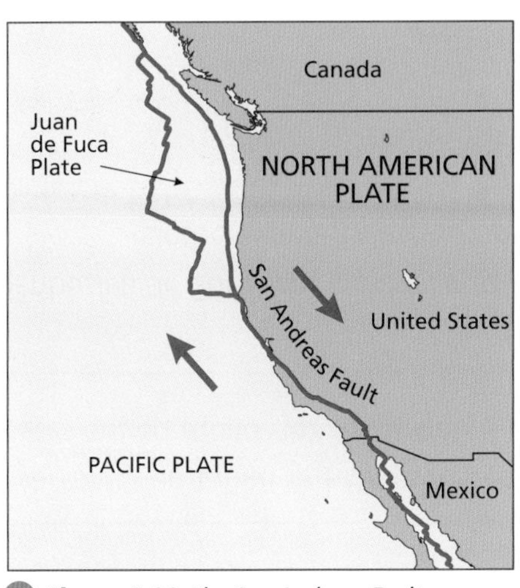

Figure 2.20 *The San Andreas Fault. Earthquakes occur here because the Pacific Plate and the North American Plate are sliding past each other*

Figure 2.21 *Satellite view of the San Andreas Fault*

Measuring earthquakes

A person who studies earthquake activity is called a **seismologist**. A seismologist uses instruments called **seismographs** to measure tremors in the Earth's crust.

The **Richter scale**, and more recently the **Moment Magnitude Scale** (*Mw*) are used to show the strength of an earthquake. The Richter scale ranges between 1 and 10. Each unit is ten times stronger than the one before. For example, an earthquake measuring 6 on the Richter scale is ten times stronger than one that measures 5.

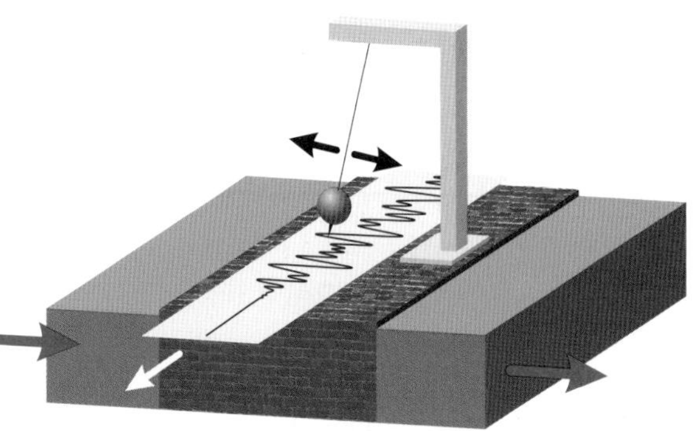

Figure 2.22 *Seismographs measure tremors in the Earth's crust*

Damage caused by earthquakes

- There is **loss of life**.
- Buildings are damaged or collapse.
- Damage to electricity lines or gas pipelines may cause **fires**.
- Damage to sewers and water supplies may cause the spread of **disease**.
- Bridges, roads and railway lines are damaged, often making it difficult to get help into the area.
- Landslides and avalanches can be triggered, causing more death and destruction.
- When an earthquake occurs under the sea, water can be displaced, making a huge wave called a **tsunami**. This may eventually crash onto the coastline, causing devastation.

Figure 2.23 *Buildings ruined during an earthquake in Turkey in 2011*

Research the impact of a tsunami, such as the one in South-East Asia in 2004. Work in groups and answer the following questions:

(a) What countries were affected?
(b) What was the death toll?
(c) How many people were left homeless?
(d) What was life like for people living in these areas afterwards?

How to reduce the damage caused by earthquakes

- Build **earthquake-resistant buildings** in earthquake zones by:
  - putting shock absorbers between a building and its foundations to absorb the tremors
  - reinforcing walls with steel.
- Conduct earthquake and tsunami **drills** so people will know what to do if an earthquake occurs.
- Put **early-warning systems** in place to alert people to the possibility of a tsunami following an earthquake.

(a) Fewer deaths are likely if an earthquake happens at night. Can you suggest why this might be the case?
(b) Damage is always worse in poorer countries. Can you suggest any reasons why this might be the case?

Earthquakes: the human response

What happens when an earthquake or a tsunami strikes a populated area? We will look at how people and governments responded in a developed country.

CASE STUDY

Earthquake in Japan

When an earthquake measuring 8.9 on the Richter scale hit Japan on 11 March, 2011 it caused a powerful **tsunami** that reached heights of over 40 metres. More than 130,000 buildings collapsed and a further million buildings were damaged. Fifteen thousand people died and 4.4 million households in northern Japan were left without electricity and water. The earthquake and tsunami also damaged a nuclear power plant.

Figure 2.24 *Some of the damage caused by the tsunami*

Short-term responses

- Immediately after the earthquake a tsunami warning was issued and all coastal areas were **evacuated**.
- Emergency **rescue teams** searched for survivors and recovered thousands of bodies.
- People living near the nuclear power plant were checked for signs of **radiation**.
- Temporary **camps** were set up for the people left homeless.
- The clear-up of the debris from the destroyed buildings began.
- Other countries offered **emergency aid**.

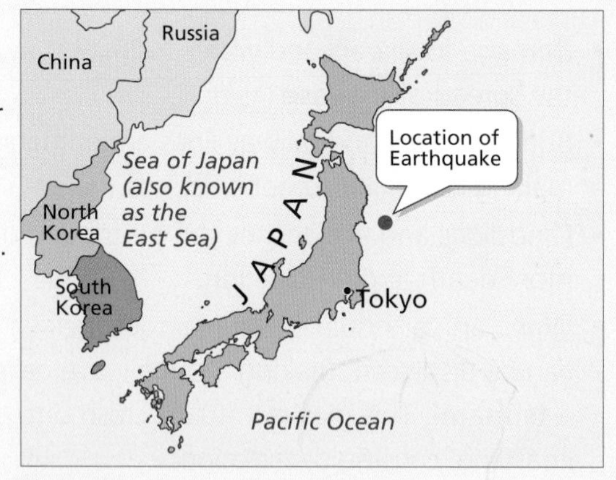

Figure 2.25 *The epicentre of the 2011 earthquake in Japan*

Long-term responses

- Electricity and water supplies were restored.
- Roads and airports were repaired.
- Houses and other buildings were repaired or rebuilt.

The total **cost** was estimated at around €230 billion.

Earthquake activity in Ireland

We already know that Ireland is not located near the boundaries of any of the major plates, but there are some fault lines in Ireland. These fault lines are small and there is not much activity around them. The biggest earthquake happened in 1984 and measured 5.4 on the Richter scale. It caused very minor damage on the east coast of Ireland.

VIDEO LESSON

https://educateplus.ie/go/haiti-earthquake

Watch the video in the link above and answer these questions:

(a) When and where did the earthquake in this news report strike?
(b) How strong was it?
(c) Name two countries bringing aid into the area.
(d) What types of aid are the planes carrying?
(e) What is one of the biggest problems on the ground for the aid workers?
(f) Why can't the local people get food?
(g) How many people need medicine badly at this point?
(h) What is the estimated death toll at this point?

NUMERACY ACTIVITY

Compare and contrast two earthquakes of the same magnitude.

Location of earthquakes	Kobe, Japan	Haiti
Magnitude	7.2	7.2
Deaths	6,000	220,000
Depth of focus	16 km	12 km
Time of day	5.46 a.m.	4.53 p.m.

The table above shows the difference between two earthquakes of the same magnitude. Japan is a more economically developed country while Haiti is a less economically developed country. Study the table and answer the following questions:

(a) Which country had the most deaths? How many more deaths?
(b) Which country was closer to the focus of the earthquake?
(c) Which earthquake happened while most people were sleeping?
(d) Can you give three reasons why you think more people died in the Haiti earthquake?

PORTFOLIO ACTIVITY 2.2

Go to page 6 of your Portfolio and write a newspaper report about an earthquake in a developed or a developing country.

(i) Name two countries that have a lot of earthquakes.
(ii) What instrument is used to measure earthquakes?

(iii) What causes earthquakes to occur?
(iv) Explain the difference between the focus and the epicentre.
(v) What is the difference in power between an earthquake measuring 6 on the Richter scale and one measuring 8 on the Richter scale?
(vi) If you were part of the emergency response team in the aftermath of an earthquake, what might you expect to see?

- I can explain how earthquakes occur and how they are measured.
- I can describe the impact of an earthquake and how people respond to this natural disaster.

Fold mountains

Learning Intentions

In this section, you will learn:
- how fold mountains form and where they form on the Earth's surface
- about the different periods of folding
- how people have interacted with fold mountains.

Anticline
Syncline
Alpine
Armorican
Caledonian

Fold mountains form when **two plates collide** with each other. Here is how it happens:
- When a heavier plate and a lighter plate are pushed together and collide, the heavier plate sinks underneath the lighter plate and into the mantle.
- The lighter plate then buckles upwards because it has nowhere else to go, causing **fold mountains** to form.
- The **magma** (formed from the heavier plate melting into the mantle) can move to the surface, forming volcanoes.

Example: The **Andes** mountains were formed by the heavier Nazca Plate colliding with the lighter South American Plate.

If **two lighter plates** collide, both buckle upwards.

Example: The **Himalayas**, where the Indo-Australian Plate is colliding with the Eurasian Plate.

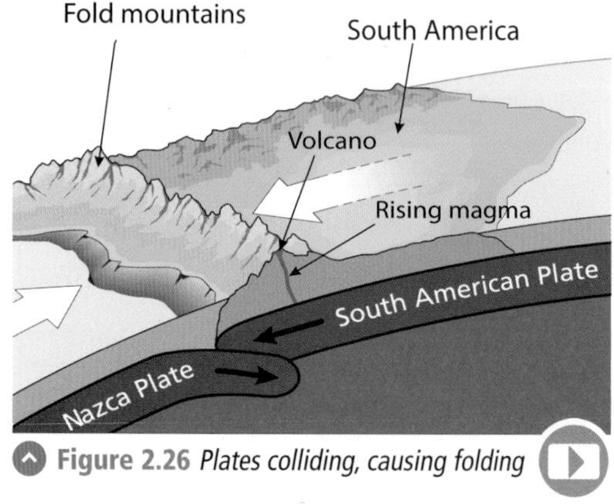

Figure 2.26 *Plates colliding, causing folding*

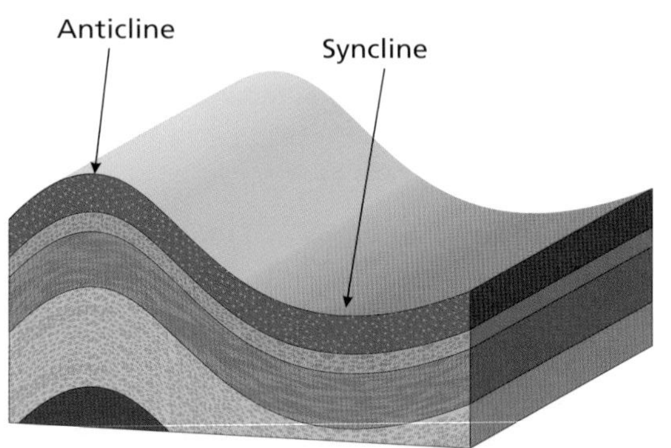

Figure 2.27 *Fold mountains: an **anticline** is an up-fold, a **syncline** is a down-fold*

Periods of folding

Alpine

The highest mountains in the world were formed about 30 to 35 million years ago during the Alpine folding period.

Examples: The **Alps** in Europe, the **Andes** in South America, the **Rockies** in North America and the **Himalayas** in Asia.

Armorican

This period of folding occurred when the Eurasian and African plates collided about 250 million years ago.

Examples: MacGillycuddy's Reeks, the **Galtee**, **Comeragh** and **Knockmealdown** mountains in Ireland and the mountains of the Black Forest in Germany.

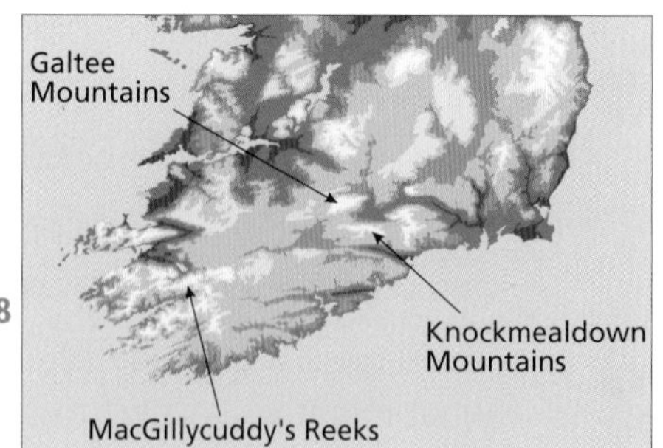

Figure 2.28 *The fold mountains of Munster*

Caledonian

This period of folding occurred about 400 million years ago when the Eurasian Plate and the American Plate collided.

Examples: The **Dublin** and **Wicklow** mountains in Ireland, the **Appalachian** mountains in North America and the mountains of Norway, Sweden and Scotland.

Mountains and people

While living in mountainous areas can be very challenging, there are also lots of benefits for the local people. The following points can be applied to mountainous regions in Ireland such as the Wicklow Mountains and the mountains around Killarney in Kerry. It can also be applied to mountainous regions in Europe such as the Alps.

Tourism

- People are attracted to the **beautiful scenery** in mountainous areas and the opportunity to take part in a variety of **activities**, including mountaineering, hillwalking, skiing, river rafting and rock climbing.
- Tourism provides **employment** for local people. There are many jobs for people who work directly with tourists, such as tour guides, bus drivers and waiters. Tourism also provides jobs indirectly – to people who supply food to the restaurants, for example.
- Tourism in mountainous areas can also have a negative impact on the **environment** and the local people. Buses and traffic cause **pollution**. **Litter** can also be an issue. **Avalanches** can occur on ski slopes because skiers dislodge the snow.

Figure 2.29 *A ski resort in the Austrian Alps*

Farming

While farming is challenging in mountainous areas, it is still an important economic activity for the people who live there.

- The main type of farming in mountainous areas is **cattle** and **sheep** rearing.
- Crops are not usually grown in mountainous areas because it is difficult to use machinery on the slopes and the weather conditions are not favourable.
- In some mountainous areas, such as the Alps, cattle are brought up to summer pastures when the snow melts and fruit and vines are planted where **terraces** have been cut into the steep slopes.

Forestry

The physical landscape in mountainous areas means that forestry is sometimes the only suitable economic activity. However, when the trees are cut down it can lead to **soil erosion**, landslides and flooding.

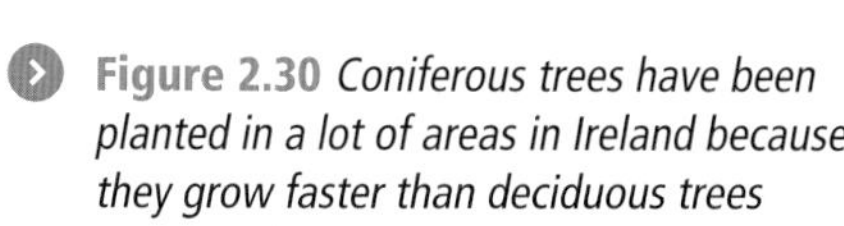

Figure 2.30 *Coniferous trees have been planted in a lot of areas in Ireland because they grow faster than deciduous trees*

NUMERACY ACTIVITY

The highest mountain in Ireland is Carrauntoohil at 1,038 m. Mont Blanc is the highest mountain in the Alps at 4,810 m. Calculate the difference in height.

Fold mountains and maps

Study the map and answer the following questions:

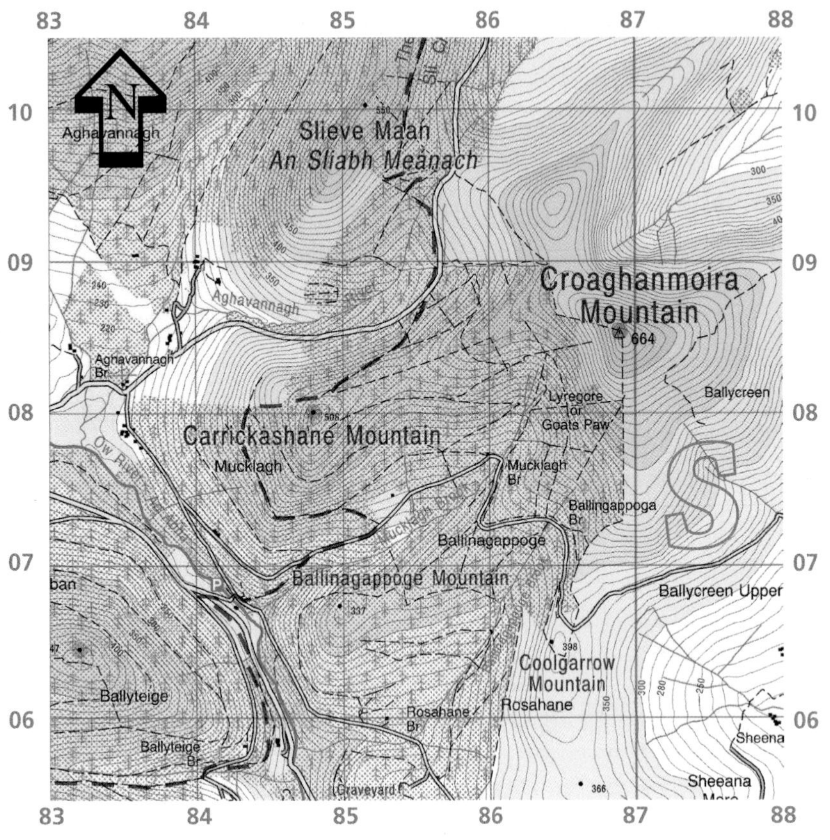

Figure 2.31 *OS map of part of the Wicklow Mountains*

(a) What is the height and grid reference of the highest point you can see on this map?

(b) Give two pieces of evidence that show that tourists visit this area.

(c) Draw a sketch of this map and show:

- Car park
- Land over 400 m
- The distance of the trail shown on the map.

(d) Identify three ways in which height is shown on this map.

(e) Name two land uses shown on this map.

(i) Name two fold mountain ranges in Ireland.

(ii) Name a fold mountain range in South America.

(iii) Name a fold mountain range in Asia.

(iv) What happens when a lighter plate and a heavier plate collide?

(v) What happens when two lighter plates collide?

(vi) Can you explain why the Himalayas are still getting bigger but the mountains in Ireland are not?

- I can explain how fold mountains are formed.
- I can say when fold mountains were formed.
- I can describe how people make a living in mountainous areas.

REVISION

The layers of the Earth consist of the crust, the ______________, the outer core and the ______________ ______________. The crust is broken into smaller sections called ______________. There is a ______________ between each plate. These plates move due to ______________ ______________ in the mantle. Alfred Wegener's theory was known as ______________ drift.

When plates move towards each other we call them ______________ plate boundaries. ______________ mountains are formed, and volcanoes and ______________ can occur. The ______________ Ring of ______________ is an area with a lot of earthquake and ______________ activity. ______________ are sudden tremors or vibrations in the Earth's crust.

When plates move away from each other we call them ______________ plate boundaries. Magma rises from the ______________ creating new crust. Landforms include ______________ islands and ______________ - ______________ ridges. Passive plate boundaries are when plates ______________ past each other. An example is the San Andreas ______________.

Questions & Answers

Sample Questions

1. Name one feature formed where plates collide.
2. Name one feature formed where plates separate.
3. What happens when plates slide past each other?
4. Describe two short-term responses and two long-term responses to a natural disaster you have studied.

Sample Answers

1. Fold mountains, for example the Andes.
2. Mid-ocean ridges, for example the Mid-Atlantic Ridge.
3. Earthquakes, for example the San Andreas Fault.
4. A natural disaster that I have studied is the volcanic eruption of Mount St Helens in the USA in 1980.

   Two short-term responses were:

   1. People from the surrounding area were evacuated because the volcano was being monitored before the eruption and they knew that it might erupt.
   2. A massive clean-up operation was begun to clear up the million tonnes of ash deposited by the volcano on the surrounding area.

   Two long-term responses were:

   1. Farmers were given money or compensation to help them recover after this natural disaster because their crops and a lot of their animals were destroyed.
   2. They built facilities to accommodate the tourists that started coming to the area to see the volcano.

Short Questions

1. The diagram shows the Earth's interior. Name the layers of the Earth's interior marked **A**, **B** and **C**.

   A ______________________

   B ______________________

   C ______________________

2. Label the diagram.

3. The point on the Earth's surface directly above the focus of the earthquake, shown at **X**, is called the:

   Epicentre ☐

   Seismograph ☐

   Shock wave ☐

   [tick (✓) the correct box]

4. Examine the diagram and explain each of the three terms shown in the diagram.

   Epicentre ______________________

   Focus ______________________

   Fault ______________________

Long Questions

1. **(i)** Name **one** example of a volcano.

   (ii) With reference to the diagram, explain how volcanoes occur.

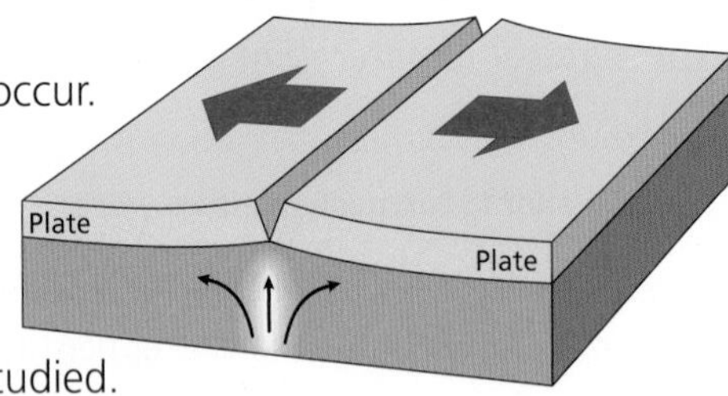

   (iii) Explain how people responded to a volcano you have studied.

   (iv) Explain **three** socio-economic benefits of living in a volcanic area.

2. **(i)** Name **one** place in the world where earthquakes regularly occur.

   (ii) What is a tsunami?

   (iii) Describe **two** short-term responses and **two** long-term responses to an earthquake you have studied.

3. **(i)** With the aid of a labelled diagram, explain how fold mountains are formed.

   (ii) Name **one** range of fold mountains in Ireland.

   (iii) What socio-economic activities might you expect to find in a mountainous area?

Visual Summary

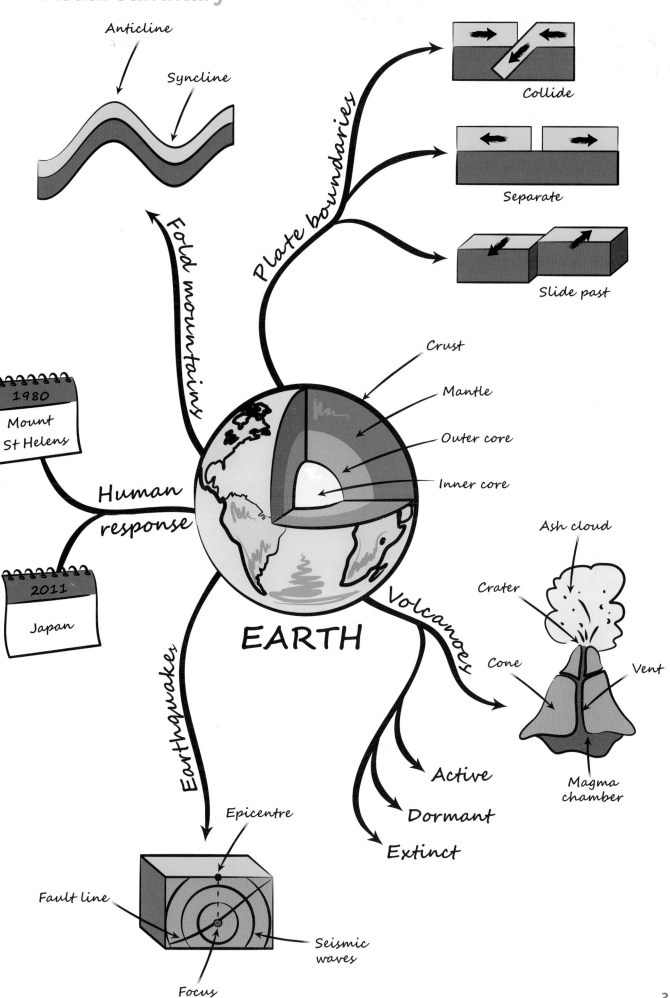

Anticline
Syncline
Fold mountains

Plate boundaries
Collide
Separate
Slide past

Crust
Mantle
Outer core
Inner core

1980
Mount St Helens
Human response
2011
Japan

EARTH

Volcanoes
Ash cloud
Crater
Cone
Vent
Magma chamber
Active
Dormant
Extinct

Earthquakes
Epicentre
Fault line
Seismic waves
Focus

3 Rocks:
How they are formed and used

In this chapter, you will learn:

- that rocks can be divided into three different groups, depending on how they are formed
- about the physical landscapes different rocks produce, and where they are located
- how people use rocks for their benefit and the impact that this can have on the environment.

ICE-BREAKER ACTIVITY

Examine different rock samples. Compare and contrast each rock, making notes on colour, texture (what it feels like), size, weight, strength, hardness and what you think each rock might be used for.

Types of rock

Learning Intentions

In this section, you will learn:

- how to divide rocks into three different groups
- how rocks are formed.

KEY WORDS

Mineral
Igneous
Sedimentary
Metamorphic

As we saw in the previous chapter, the Earth's crust is made up of rock. Rocks are composed of different **minerals**. These minerals are held together by a **natural cement**. They differ from one another in the following ways:

- Hardness
- Texture (how they feel)
- Colour
- Mineral content

ACTIVITY

As a group, write a list of names of all the rocks that you know. What are the similarities and differences between these rocks?

There are many different types of rock. However, all rocks can be divided into **three groups** depending on how they were formed. The three groups are:

1. **Igneous rocks**
2. **Sedimentary rocks**
3. **Metamorphic rocks**

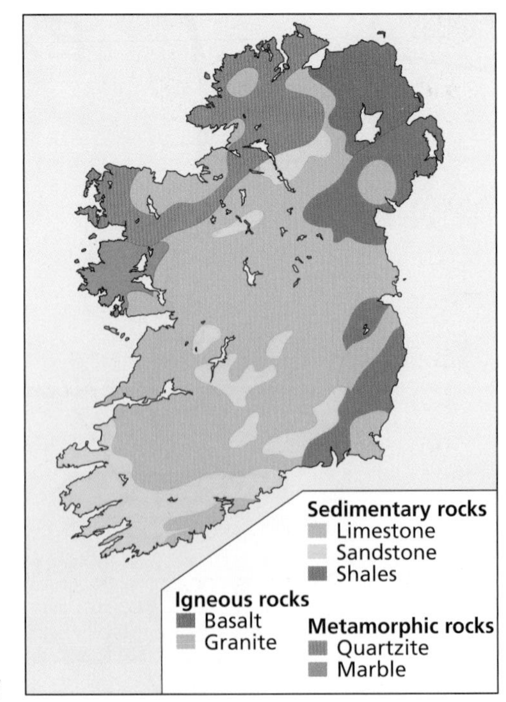

Figure 3.1 *The locations of the main rock types in Ireland*

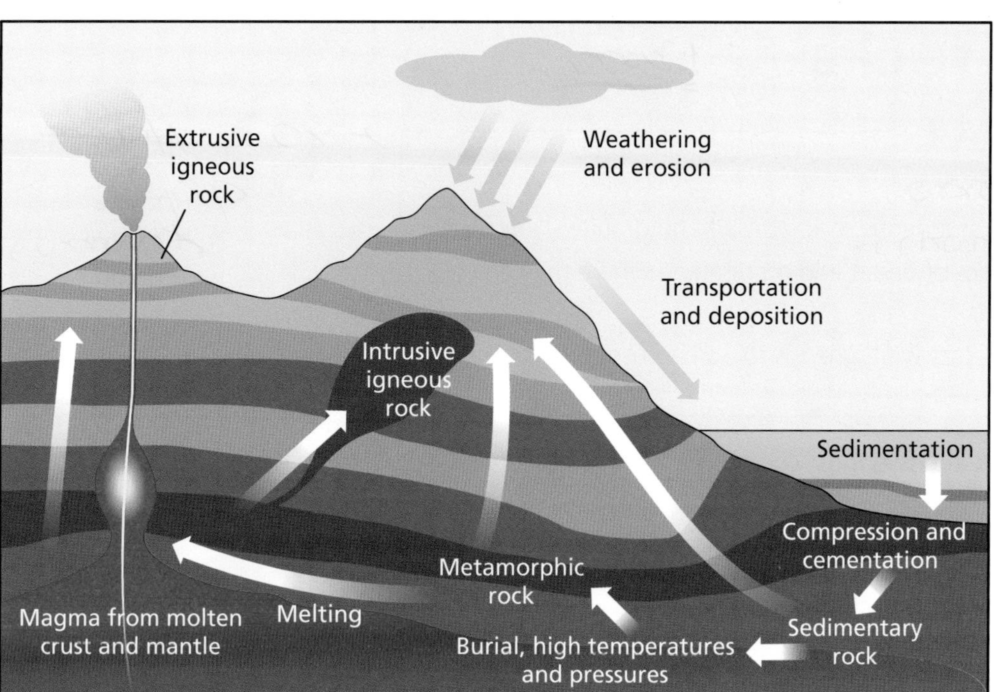

Figure 3.2 *The rock cycle: how rocks are formed*

Igneous rocks

Igneous rocks are formed as a result of **volcanic activity**. When hot molten **magma** escapes from the mantle it cools and hardens. If it reaches the **surface** as lava, it cools and **solidifies quickly**, whereas the magma **inside the crust** cools more **slowly**.

Sedimentary rocks

Sedimentary rocks are formed from **particles** of other rocks, as well as dead plants and animals. These **sediments** are **deposited** on sea and lake beds as well as on land. Layers of this material build up over time and are **compressed** and **cemented**, creating solid rock.

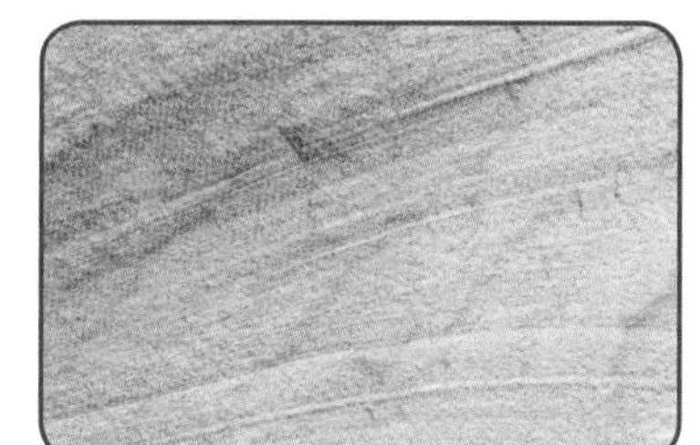

Metamorphic rocks

Metamorphic rocks are formed from rocks that already exist. They form when igneous or sedimentary rocks are **changed** into new, harder rocks by great **heat** or **pressure** or sometimes both.

 **(i)** List two ways in which rocks differ from one another.

(ii) List three different categories of rocks.

(iii) Which rock type has different layers?

(iv) Briefly describe how igneous rocks form.

(v) Briefly describe how sedimentary rocks form.

(vi) Briefly describe how metamorphic rocks form.

- I can list the ways in which rocks differ from each other.
- I know the three rock groups and I can explain how they are formed.

Igneous rocks

Learning Intentions

In this section, you will learn:

- how two types of igneous rock – basalt and granite – are formed
- the characteristics of basalt and granite and where they are found in Ireland
- how people interact with igneous rocks and use them to their advantage.

Basalt
Granite
Extrusive
Crystal
Hexagonal
Intrusive

Basalt and **granite** are the two most common **igneous** rocks in Ireland. As we have already learned, igneous rocks are formed from volcanic activity.

Basalt

Colour: Grey/black

Texture: Medium grained

Formation: Basalt is an **extrusive** rock. It is formed when **lava** spreads out **over the surface** of the Earth's crust due to **volcanic activity**. It then cools and hardens. Basalt has **tiny crystals** which cannot be seen without the use of a microscope. This is because the lava cooled and hardened very quickly in the open air when it reached the surface.

Use: Basalt is used for **road chippings** due to its hardness. The landscape created by basalt can also be a tourist attraction.

Example: Basalt is found in the **Antrim–Derry Plateau** in the north-east of Ireland. The **Giant's Causeway** is part of this plateau. As the lava there was so thick, when it cooled it contracted to form the **hexagonal** (six-sided) shapes that can be seen today.

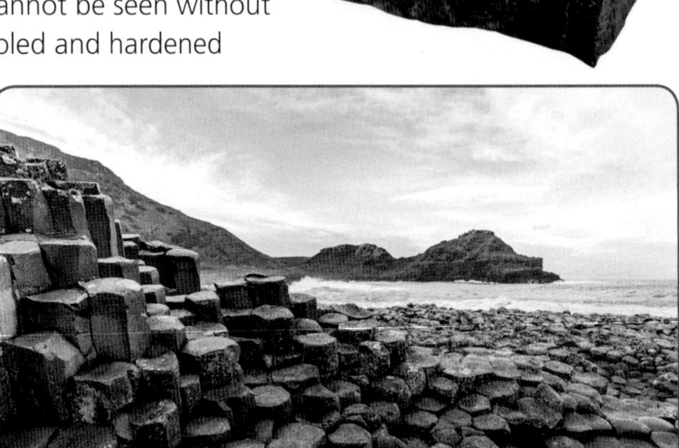

Figure 3.3 *Giant's Causeway, Co. Antrim*

Extrusive rock is formed **above** the surface of the Earth.

PORTFOLIO ACTIVITY 3.1

Go to page 10 of your Portfolio to create an article about tourism and the Giant's Causeway.

Granite

Colour: Range of colours, including black, grey, pink and cream

Texture: Coarse grained

Formation: Granite is an **intrusive** rock. It is formed when molten **magma** pushes its way into the crust and cools and hardens there, **under the surface**. Granite has **large crystals**. This is because the molten magma cooled very slowly over millions of years. Some of these crystals include the minerals **quartz**, **feldspar** and **mica**. Granite is eventually exposed at the surface when rock lying over it is worn away.

Use: Granite is used in a variety of everyday products such as **counter tops** in kitchens because of its hardness and durability.

Example: Granite is found in the **Mourne Mountains** in the east of Ireland.

Intrusive rock is formed **below** the surface of the Earth.

Figure 3.4 *The Mourne Mountains*

In groups of four, imagine you own a quarry and are setting up a new company that sells granite products. You want to promote and sell your products to potential clients (i.e. classmates). Outline the following:

- Name of company
- How granite is quarried and the location of your quarry in Ireland
- The products created from granite, and their uses
- Why granite is such a suitable rock for these products.

Present your sales pitch to the class.

Figure 3.5 *More than two million tourists visit Mount Rushmore each year to see the sculptures of four former US presidents carved into the granite rock*

ACTIVITY

You can find out more about Mount Rushmore at https://educateplus.ie/go/mount-rushmore

(i) List three characteristics of basalt rock.

(ii) List three characteristics of granite rock.

(iii) Explain the differences in formation between basalt and granite.

(iv) Explain why granite forms much more slowly than basalt.

- I can name two types of igneous rock.  
- I know how igneous rocks are formed and can give examples of where they are found in Ireland.  

Sedimentary rocks

Learning Intentions

In this section, you will learn:

- how two types of sedimentary rock – limestone and sandstone – are formed
- the characteristics of limestone and sandstone and where they are found in Ireland
- how people interact with sedimentary rocks and use them to their advantage.

Limestone
Sandstone
Sediment
Compress
Cement
Strata
Permeable
Soluble
Deposit

Limestone and **sandstone** are the most common **sedimentary** rocks in Ireland.

Limestone

Colour: Grey

Texture: Coarse grained

Formation: The limestone in Ireland was formed about 350 million years ago when Ireland was located close to the equator. Limestone is made from particles of **shells** and the remains of **skeletons of sea creatures**. When these particles sink to the seabed they are called **sediment**. The sediment piled up at the bottom of a **warm, shallow sea** over millions of years. The weight of the upper layers of sediment **compressed** and **cemented** the lower layers of sediment into **strata** (layers) of solid rock.

Limestone is **permeable**. This means that water can pass through it. It is also **soluble**, which means that it dissolves in water.

Use: Limestone is often used to make **monuments**. It is used in the construction of buildings, and to make **cement**. It is also ground down into **lime** and added to soil to improve soil fertility.

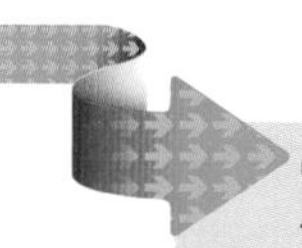

Go to Chapter 16 to learn more about the connection between soil and rocks.

Figure 3.6 *Limestone in the Burren, Co. Clare*

Example: Limestone is the most common type of rock in Ireland. We will learn more about the limestone landscape in the **Burren**, one of the biggest tourists attractions in the west of Ireland, in Chapter 6.

Sandstone

Colour: Reddish/brown

Texture: Coarse grained

Formation: Sandstone is formed from sand that has been worn away from the Earth's surface. This sand is carried by the wind and rivers and then **deposited** as sediment in seas, lakes and deserts, where the layers build up over time. The layers are **compressed** and **cemented** together to form sandstone.

Use: Sandstone is used in **patios** and as a **building material** in the construction industry.

Examples: Sandstone is found in **MacGillycuddy's Reeks** in Co. Kerry and the **Galtee Mountains** in the south of Ireland.

Figure 3.7 *Uluru, or Ayers Rock, is one of the best-known sandstone areas in the world. About half a million people visit this site every year*

(i) What is the most common rock found in Ireland?

(ii) Where in Ireland do we find sandstone rock?

(iii) Limestone is a permeable and soluble rock. What does this mean?

(iv) Using information from the previous chapter, can you explain how Ireland moved from its position at the equator to where it is today?

- I can name two types of sedimentary rock.
- I know how sedimentary rock is formed and can give examples of where it is found in Ireland.

Metamorphic rocks

Learning Intentions

In this section, you will learn:

- how two types of metamorphic rock – marble and quartzite – are formed
- the characteristics of marble and quartzite and where they are found in Ireland
- how people interact with metamorphic rocks and use them to their advantage.

KEY WORDS

Marble
Quartzite
Heat
Pressure

Two examples of **metamorphic** rocks found in Ireland are **marble** and **quartzite**.

Marble

Colour: White/red/green/black

Texture: Smooth

Formation: Marble is formed when **limestone** is put under great **heat** or **pressure** due to plate movement or when **molten magma** comes in contact with limestone. It is a **very hard** rock that can vary in colour.

Use: Marble can be cut to whatever size is required and **polished** to make its appearance more appealing, so it is used to make **monuments**, **floor tiles**, **fireplaces** and **ornaments**.

Examples: Marble is found in Co. Antrim (white), Co. Cork (red), Connemara, Co. Galway (green) and Co. Kilkenny (black).

Quartzite

Colour: White/grey

Texture: Granular (grainy)

Formation: Quartzite is formed when **sandstone** is put under great **heat** or **pressure** due to plate movement or when **molten magma** comes in contact with sandstone. Quartzite is an **extremely hard** rock and it is found on the top of many of Ireland's mountains. This is because it is not easily broken down.

Use: Quartzite is used in objects such as **counter tops** and **road chippings**, and to make **glass**.

Examples: Croagh Patrick in Co. Mayo and the Great Sugarloaf in Co. Wicklow.

(i) List the two forces that can change rocks into metamorphic rocks.

(ii) What is the benefit of being able to cut and polish marble?

(iii) What is quartzite used for? List two things.

(iv) Why is quartzite commonly found on the peaks of Ireland's mountains?

- I can name two types of metamorphic rock.
- I know how metamorphic rock is formed and can give examples of where it is found in Ireland.

PORTFOLIO ACTIVITY 3.2

Go to page 12 of your Portfolio and complete the rock fact files.

Uses of rock

Learning Intentions

In this section, you will learn:

- that rocks are a natural resource that can be used in a variety of ways
- that we get different energy sources such as coal, oil and gas from mining rocks
- that we quarry rocks for building purposes
- that mining and quarrying can have both positive and negative socio-economic impacts.

KEY WORDS

Natural resource
Exploit
Energy
Building materials
Mining
Quarrying
Ore
Galvanise

Rocks are a **natural resource** that can be used, or **exploited**, in many different ways. We will now look at how rocks can be used as **sources of energy** and as **building materials**. The production of energy and building materials are of great socio-economic importance.

Natural resource: something in the natural world that people can use to their advantage.

Energy

Some rocks can be used to create energy because they contain what are called **fossil fuels**. We will learn more about fossil fuels in Chapter 5. There are **three** fossil fuels, and they are extracted from the crust in different ways.

Coal

Coal is mined in **open pits** if it is close to the surface, or from underground **mines** if it is deeper in the Earth's crust. The process of extracting coal from within the Earth's crust is called **shaft mining**. Vertical wells are drilled and a **shaft** is constructed. **Corridors** are mined out on various levels to take out the coal. **Castlecomer**, Co. Kilkenny, is an example of an Irish town where coal mining used to take place.

Figure 3.8 *Coal mining in an open pit*

(a) Imagine there is a coal mine in your local area. List the positive and negative impacts on the area. Work in pairs.

(b) Do you think coal mining is a sustainable activity? Give three reasons to justify your answer.

Oil and gas

Oil and gas are extracted from rock by **drilling** and **pumping**. The process involves drilling deep into the Earth's crust and pumping the oil and gas to the surface. This can also be done offshore from a rig in the sea. The oil or gas is then piped ashore.

Figure 3.9 *An offshore oil drilling platform*

Building materials

We extract rock from the Earth's surface for **building** purposes every day. This is done through the process of **quarrying**. Large machinery is used to cut rock out of the crust, or **explosives** are used to break rock away from the crust. Rocks that are used as building materials include **limestone**, **sandstone** and **marble**.

Figure 3.10 *A marble quarry*

ACTIVITY

Take a look at https://educateplus.ie/go/gsi and find a quarry near you. Record the following information:

(a) the name of the quarry

(b) the type of rock that is extracted

(c) how the rock is extracted

(d) what the rock is used for

(e) any additional information that you find interesting.

CASE STUDY

Quarry: McMonagle Stone, Mountcharles, Co. Donegal

McMonagle Stone is a company that owns five quarries and employs more than 70 people. It extracts **quartzite**, **sandstone** and **granite** in various locations throughout Co. Donegal. The main quarry at **Glencolmcille** extracts gold quartzite, also known as brown quartzite. The head office and display centre is located at Mountcharles. The company sells more than 2,000 different types of stone product, both nationally and internationally. Most of the products are used in **building** and **garden paving**.

Figure 3.11 *McMonagle Stone quarry*

Check out www.mcmonaglestone.ie to find out more about this quarry.

Figure 3.12 *The stone is used in buildings and gardens*

Impacts of mining and quarrying

Mining and quarrying have **social**, **environmental and economic impacts**, and sometimes they can be in conflict with each other. This can make mining or quarrying a controversial activity. Below is a list of some of the positive and negative impacts of mining and quarrying.

Positive impacts:

- They provide **employment**, which supports the local economy.
- They support other **economic activities** by providing material used in areas such as construction and energy production.
- They also provide the **raw materials** to make copper, steel, iron and glass.

Negative impacts:

- They can cause noise, water and air **pollution**.
- They can be an **eyesore** (i.e. they look bad) because the bare rock is exposed. Many people don't want to live near a mine or quarry.
- The material extracted from a mine or quarry needs to be transported, which can lead to **traffic congestion**. Heavy traffic damages the environment.

Figure 3.13 *A quarry can make a big mark on the landscape*

Can you think of any other impacts of mining, either positive or negative? Discuss in small groups and make a list of your suggestions. Then share your results with the class.

CASE STUDY

Mining in Ireland: Boliden Tara mine

The Tara mine is located in Navan, Co. Meath. It produces **lead** and **zinc ore**. The mine opened in 1977, and is now owned by the Swedish-based Boliden company. It is **Europe's largest zinc mine**.

Figure 3.14 *Boliden Tara mine*

Since 1977 the mine has produced over **85 million tonnes** of ore. In 2016 it produced 2.6 million tonnes. The ore is mined at a depth of between **150 and 1,000 metres underground** and blasting techniques are used to mine the rock.

The mine employs 580 people directly and has also created a lot of employment in the local area as a result of the number working in the mine. The mine is therefore very important to the local **community**.

Ore:
rock from which valuable metals or minerals can be extracted.

Using the metals

The rock that is blasted below the surface is brought above ground, where it is crushed. It is then transported to Boliden processing plants in other countries to **extract** the metals. These are sent on to factories to use in manufacturing products.

- **Lead** is used in making **car batteries**, keels for yachts, and ammunition.
- **Zinc** is used to **galvanise** other metals to prevent rusting, and in the manufacture of paint and ink.

Figure 3.15 *Most of the lead Boliden produce is used in making car batteries like this one*

Mining and the environment

Boliden, the company that owns the Tara mine, is very aware of the importance of the **environment** and **sustainability**. When a mine or parts of a mine are no longer in use, the company carries out projects to restore the landscape to what it was like before mining started. This is called **reclamation**.

Figure 3.16 *A car body is galvanised by dipping it in molten zinc*

ACTIVITY

Investigate www.boliden.com to learn about its reclamation program. Click on the link **Sustainability** and look at the **Reclamation and restoration** section to see what the company is doing to help restore the landscape to its previous state.

 **(i)** Name three fossil fuels.

 **(ii)** What are the two ways we extract rock from the crust?

 **(iii)** Explain one positive and one negative effect of mining and quarrying.

- I know how rocks can be used.  
- I can explain the positive and negative socio-economic and environmental impacts of mining and quarrying. 

REVISION

There are three groups of rocks: ____________, ____________ and ____________. Igneous rocks form when ____________ cools down and ____________. Examples of these types of rock are ____________ and ____________. A tourist attraction in Ireland is an area of basalt rock known as the ____________ ____________.

Sedimentary rocks form when particles of ____________ or dead ____________ and plants build up and are ____________ under pressure to form rocks. Two examples of sedimentary rock are ____________ and ____________. ____________ is the most common type of rock in Ireland and can be found in the ____________, Co. Clare.

Metamorphic rocks form as the result of either great ____________ or great ____________ on igneous or sedimentary rock. For example, limestone changes to ____________ and sandstone changes to ____________. Marble has many uses and can be cut and ____________ and comes in many different ____________.

Rocks can be used in a wide variety of ways, including as building materials and sources of ____________. This means that they are of great ____________ importance.

Questions & Answers

Sample Questions

1. Name **two** rock groups that you have studied.
2. Explain how **one** of these types of rock forms.
3. Explain **one** positive and **one** negative socio-economic impact of mining/quarrying.

Sample Answers

1. Igneous and sedimentary.
2. Igneous: Igneous rocks are formed due to volcanic activity. Hot molten magma escapes from the mantle. It cools and solidifies quickly into rock on the Earth's surface or slowly deep inside the crust. Two types of igneous rock are formed – basalt on the surface and granite in the crust.
3. Mining can have both positive and negative socio-economic impacts. A positive socio-economic impact would be the creation of employment for people living in the local area. This would be great for the local economy and the services nearby.

   A negative socio-economic impact would be the traffic congestion that would result from the heavy machinery and the need for heavy good vehicles to transport the rock that is extracted. The heavy traffic can also have a negative impact on the environment in the local area.

Short Questions

1. The rock in photograph **A** is sometimes used to make kitchen worktops, as shown in photograph **B**.

   The rock is called:

   Limestone ☐

   Basalt ☐

   Granite ☐ [tick (✓) the correct box]

2. The rock shown in this photograph is a piece of marble.

   It is:

   An igneous rock ☐

   A sedimentary rock ☐

   A metamorphic rock ☐ [tick (✓) the correct box]

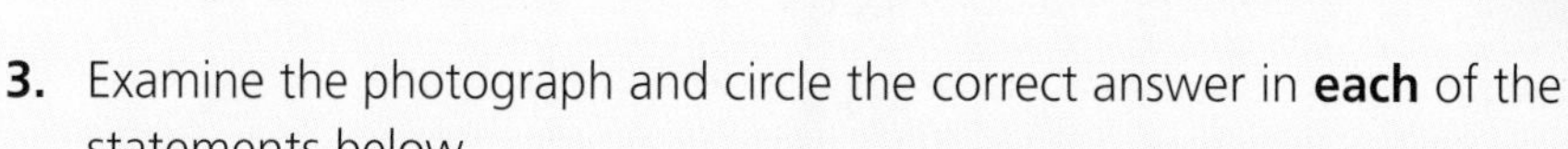

3. Examine the photograph and circle the correct answer in **each** of the statements below.

   (i) The name of the rock is **granite / basalt**.

   (ii) The rock is **an igneous / a sedimentary** rock.

   (iii) An example of this rock is found in **the Burren / Wicklow**.

A rock with large crystals that formed inside the Earth's crust

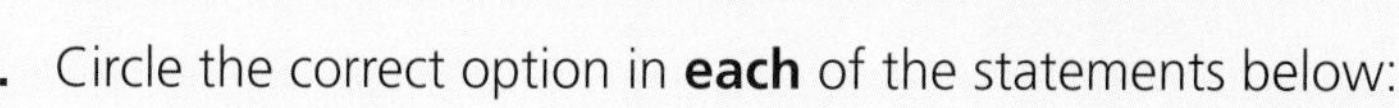

4. Circle the correct option in **each** of the statements below:

   (i) Limestone is a permeable rock. **True / False**

   (ii) Basalt is a white rock. **True / False**

   (iii) Marble is a sedimentary rock. **True / False**

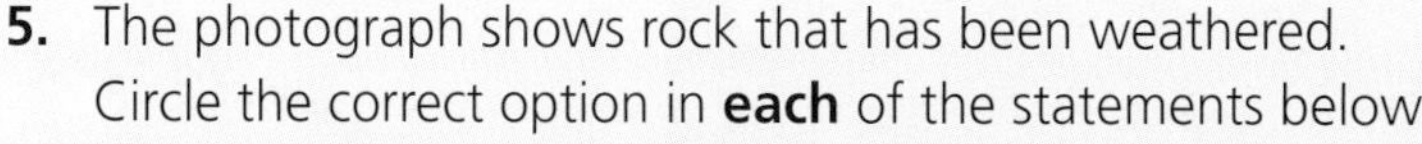

5. The photograph shows rock that has been weathered. Circle the correct option in **each** of the statements below.

   (i) The rock is **sandstone / limestone**.

   (ii) An example of this rock can be found in **the Giant's Causeway / the Burren**.

Long Questions

1. **(i)** 'Volcanoes result in the formation of igneous rocks.'
   Select **one** igneous rock and explain how it was formed.

   (ii) 'Rocks are useful for economic activities.'
   Name and explain **two** ways rocks may be used in economic activities.

2. **(i)** Name the category of rock to which limestone belongs.

   (ii) Name a location where limestone is found.

3. **(i)** Name any **two** rocks.

   (ii) People use rocks in many different ways.
   Describe **one** use of each rock you named.

4. **(i)** Name **one** rock you have studied and state if it is igneous, sedimentary or metamorphic.

   (ii) Describe how the rock you have chosen in part (i) above was formed.

   (iii) Give **two** reasons why people might object to a quarry being opened near their home.

Visual Summary

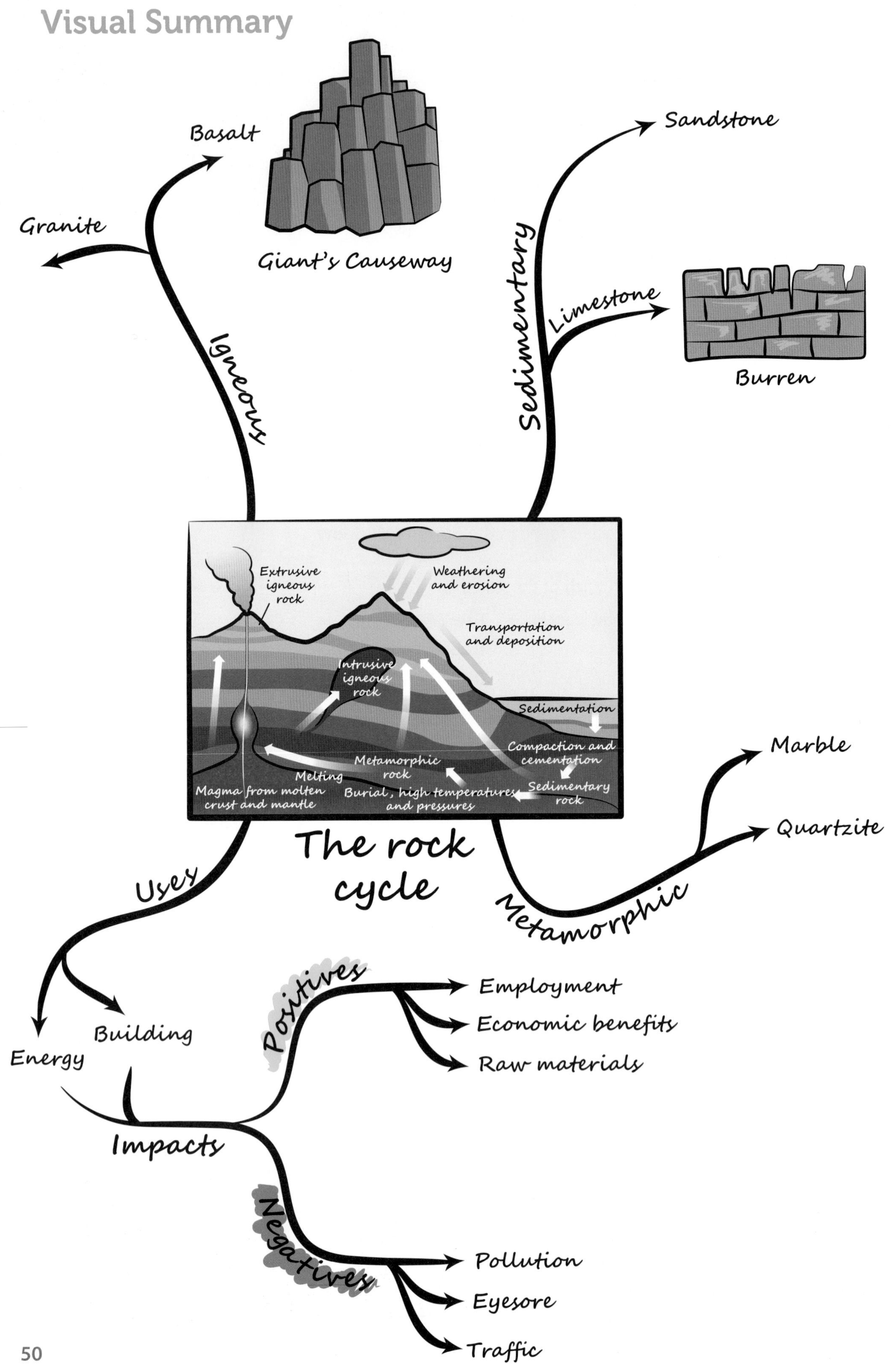

Basalt
Granite
Giant's Causeway
Igneous
Sandstone
Sedimentary
Limestone
Burren
Extrusive igneous rock
Weathering and erosion
Transportation and deposition
Intrusive igneous rock
Sedimentation
Compaction and cementation
Metamorphic rock
Melting
Magma from molten crust and mantle
Burial, high temperatures and pressures
Sedimentary rock
The rock cycle
Marble
Quartzite
Metamorphic
Uses
Energy
Building
Impacts
Positives
Employment
Economic benefits
Raw materials
Negatives
Pollution
Eyesore
Traffic

4 Primary Economic Activities:

How we use the world's natural resources

In this chapter, you will learn:

- what economic activities and natural resources are
- that water is a renewable resource
- about primary economic activities (fishing, farming and forestry)
- that natural resources can be exploited in a sustainable way.

ICE-BREAKER ACTIVITY

Nature provides us with many things that we can use. Can you and your classmates make a list of these things? How do we use them?

Economic activities and natural resources

Learning Intentions

In this section, you will learn:

- that there are three types of economic activity
- that natural resources can be both renewable and non-renewable.

KEY WORDS

Primary	Renewable
Secondary	Non-renewable
Tertiary	Infinite
Natural resources	Finite

Economic activities

Economic activities are what people do to earn a living. They can be put into three groups – **primary** economic activities, **secondary** economic activities and **tertiary** economic activities.

ACTIVITY

Divide into groups of three and write down 12 economic activities. Make a list of (i) what is similar about these economic activities, and (ii) what is different about these economic activities.

Primary activities are jobs which involve working **directly** with the Earth's rocks, soils and waters.	**Secondary activities** are jobs which involve making or **manufacturing** something.	**Tertiary activities** involve providing a **service** that is useful to people.
Jobs: Farmer, Fisher, Forestry worker, Miner	**Jobs:** Carpenter, Factory worker, Baker, Builder	**Jobs:** Teacher, Garda, Solicitor, Shopkeeper
Figure 4.1a *Forestry*	**Figure 4.1b** *Factory work*	**Figure 4.1c** *Teaching*

In Ireland, less than 10 per cent of the working population is employed in the primary sector. In less economically developed countries it can be up to 90 per cent. Discuss this with your group. Why do you think this might be the case?

Natural resources

Natural resources are things in the **natural world** which are useful to people such as **land**, **rivers** and **seas**. People have been using these natural resources for their own benefit for thousands of years.

There are two types of natural resources – **renewable** resources and **non-renewable** resources.

Renewable resources

- Renewable resources can be used over and over again.
- If you look after them and use them in a **sustainable** way, they will not run out.
- Renewable resources are also called **infinite** resources.
- **Water** is an example of a renewable resource.

Non-renewable resources

- Non-renewable resources are resources that can only be used **once**. Each time a non-renewable resource is used, less of that resource is left for the future.
- Non-renewable resources will eventually **run out** because they cannot be replaced quickly enough.
- Non-renewable resources are also called **finite** resources.
- **Oil** is an example of a non-renewable resource.

When we use natural resources it is called **exploitation**. If we **over-exploit** natural resources they might not be available for future generations. This sort of exploitation is **unsustainable**.

ACTIVITY

(a) Work in pairs. Match each of the pictures A–H to the resources in the box below.

Iron ore	Water	Fish	Gas
Peat	Oil	Wood	Wind

(b) Are these resources renewable or non-renewable? Discuss with your partner.

(i) Name the three types of economic activity.

(ii) Name one primary economic activity.

(iii) Explain the term infinite resource.

(iv) Explain the term finite resource.

(v) Choose any non-renewable resource and suggest how it might be exploited in a more sustainable way.

- I can list the three types of economic activity. 
- I can explain the difference between renewable and non-renewable resources and give examples of each. 

Water: a renewable resource

Learning Intentions

In this section, you will learn:

- that water is an important natural resource that we need in order to survive
- how the water cycle works
- how a local water supply works in Ireland
- how water can be used in a sustainable way
- how an irrigation scheme waters the land.

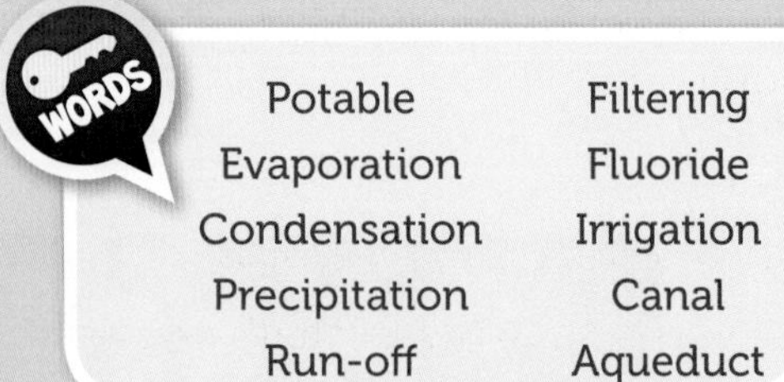

Water is a **renewable natural resource**. That means it can be used over and over again. Water is very important because people and animals need **potable** water to survive and plants need water to grow.

A-Z
Potable water:
water that is safe for people and animals to drink.

The water cycle

The Earth has a limited amount of water. This water is continuously **recycled** to provide a steady water supply. This recycling of water is called the **water cycle**. There are four main stages of the water cycle:

1. Evaporation
2. Condensation
3. Precipitation
4. Run-off

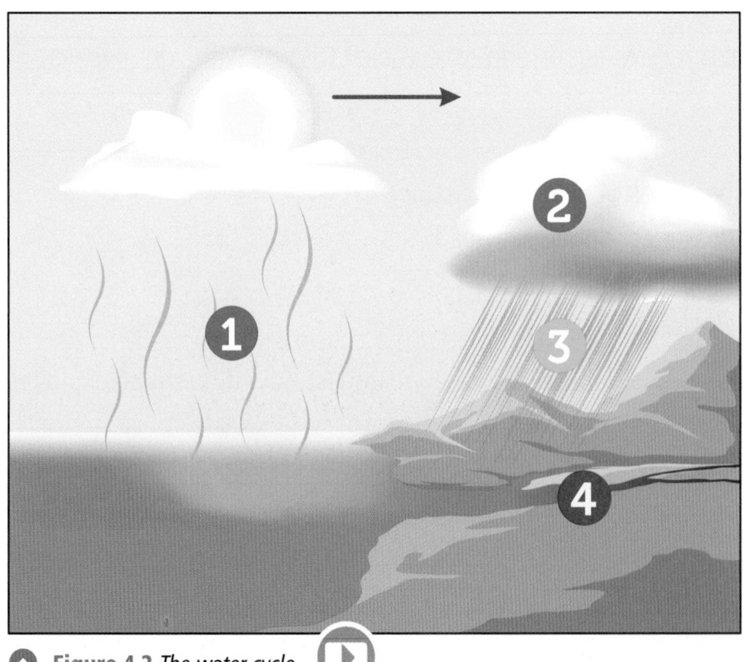

Figure 4.2 *The water cycle*

1. Evaporation

Evaporation occurs when the sun heats up water in rivers, lakes, oceans, trees and plants and turns it into **water vapour**.

2. Condensation

The water vapour **rises** into the air. As the air rises, it **cools**. The water vapour **condenses** into tiny droplets which come together to form a **cloud**. The wind blows these clouds towards the land.

3. Precipitation

Precipitation occurs when so much water has condensed that the air cannot hold it any more. The clouds get heavy and water falls back to the Earth in the form of **rain**, **hail**, **dew**, **sleet** or **snow**.

4. Run-off

When the water falls back to Earth as precipitation, it may fall back into the oceans, lakes or rivers or it may end up on land. When it ends up on land, it will either soak into the soil and become part of the **groundwater** that plants and animals use to drink or it may **run off** the soil into oceans, lakes or rivers where the cycle starts all over again.

Water in Ireland

Divide up into groups of four and answer the following questions:

(a) How does water end up in our taps?

(b) Where does the waste water from our homes go?

Irish Water is responsible for the public water supply in Ireland. It is also responsible for looking after Ireland's waste water.

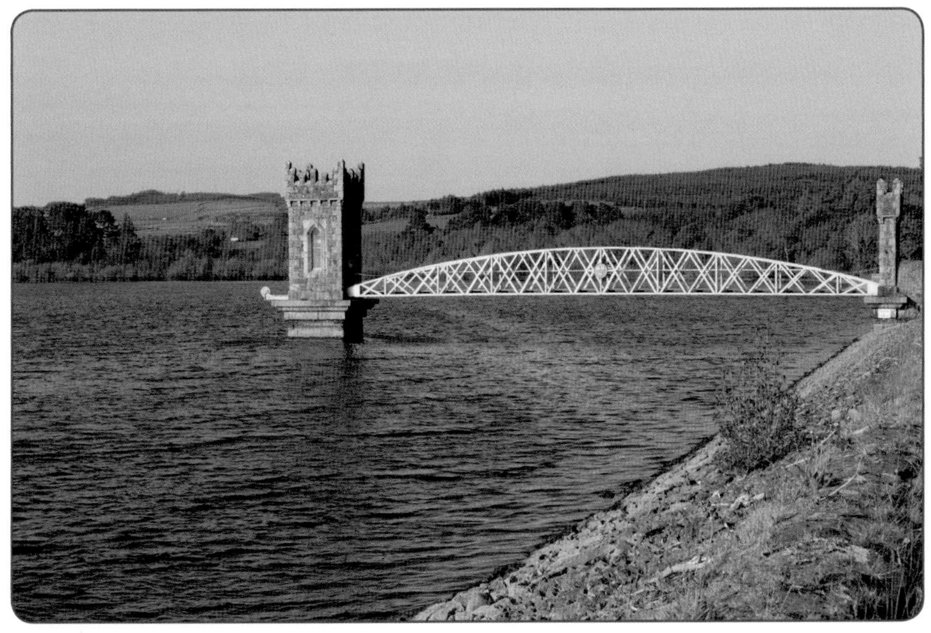

Figure 4.3 Vartry reservoir, near Roundwood, Co. Wicklow

CASE STUDY

Local water supply: Limerick City

The water in the taps all around Limerick City comes from the **River Shannon**, but before it gets to people's homes it has to be **treated** so it is safe to drink.

Limerick City and County Council produces 60 million litres of potable water each day in its **water treatment plant**. This water is taken from the river at Clareville and Clonlara.

Figure 4.4 *Water treatment plant in Limerick*

Filtering

The water goes through **filters** to take out any bacteria and viruses.

Adding chemicals

A number of **chemicals** are then added to the water. **Chlorine** is added to make sure the water is clean. **Fluoride** is added to help stop tooth decay.

Storage

The water is then pumped to **storage reservoirs** in Castletroy which store up to 75 million litres at any one time. From there it flows through **mains** (the largest pipes) to Limerick City and into **distribution pipes** supplying homes, businesses and other users.

In 2017, Irish Water invested €6.6 million in a project to improve this water distribution network by replacing and fixing old water mains around Limerick City.

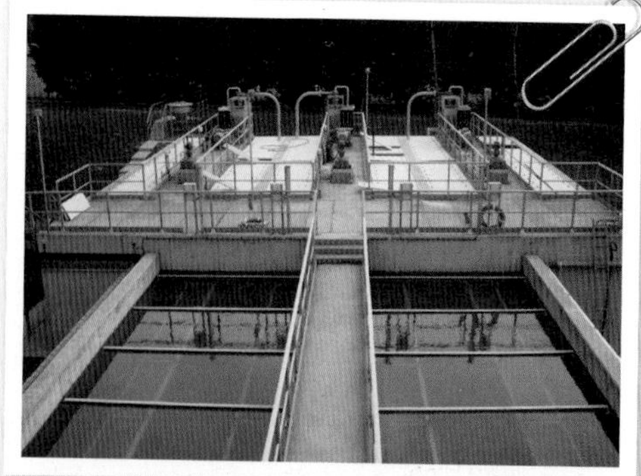

Figure 4.5 *Filtering system at the water treatment plant*

Waste water

Waste water is treated at the **Castletroy** Waste Water Treatment Plant to make it safe to drink again.

Sustainable water exploitation in Ireland

Water is our most precious **natural resource** and it is vital that we manage it in a way that meets our needs and the needs of future generations. Water is something that we take for granted and we need a more **sustainable** approach to how we use water in order to protect our supply.

ACTIVITY

(a) Make a list of small changes we can make in our daily lives to reduce our consumption of water. Work in pairs.

(b) Do you think Irish people should pay for the water they use? Discuss everyone's views in class and conduct a class vote.

Water and the sustainable development goals

In 2015, world leaders agreed that we all need to **work together** to make sure that people around the world can live better lives without damaging the planet. States will work towards achieving the **Global Goals for Sustainable Development** between 2015 and 2030.

PORTFOLIO ACTIVITY 4.1

Go to page 16 of your Portfolio to learn about Goal 6 (Clean Water and Sanitation) of the United Nations' Global Goals for Sustainable Development, and write a letter to your TD about it.

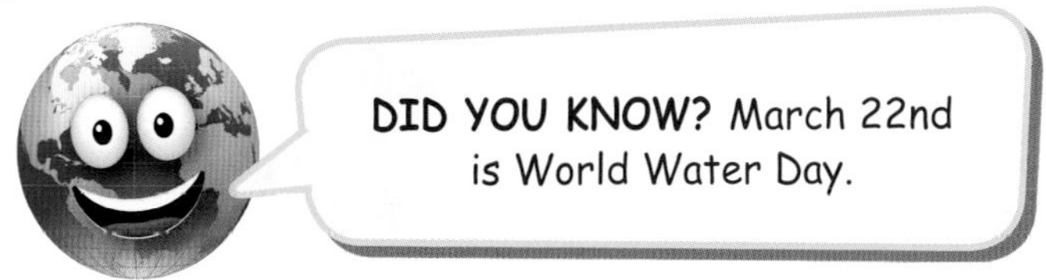

DID YOU KNOW? March 22nd is World Water Day.

Irrigation

In Ireland there is no shortage of rainfall. However, some parts of the world can go through long periods of **drought** when there is a **shortage of rainfall**.

Irrigation is the **artificial watering** of the land. It is done to help crops grow in areas where there is a shortage of rainfall. There are many examples of **irrigation schemes** throughout the world.

Figure 4.6 *Irrigation can enable people to grow crops that need a lot of water, even in dry climates*

CASE STUDY

Irrigation scheme: Central Valley Project, California

Why does the valley need irrigation?

The area has a very **warm climate** with mild winters. There are very **hot summers** from June to August each year. The region often suffers from **drought** (a lack of rainfall). This used to mean that it was difficult to grow crops on the farmlands of the San Joaquin Valley in the south. However, the **Sacramento River** in the northern region of California has been used to irrigate the valley and provide water for drinking.

Figure 4.7 *Map of San Joaquin Valley and Sacramento River*

About the Central Valley Project

- **Dams** were built on the river to create large **reservoirs** where water can build up.
- **Canals** and **aqueducts** (human-made channels) were then used to pipe the water from the north of the valley to the south.
- The valley is now a region that produces a variety of **crops** such as vegetables and fruit.

Advantages of the scheme

- The valley is irrigated in times of drought.
- The towns and cities in the area have a water supply.

Disadvantages of the scheme

- It was very **expensive** to build the dams, and the cost of pumping the water is high, so it increases the cost of the produce.
- A lot of water **evaporates** from the reservoirs. This leaves a high salt content and can lead to poisoning of the land.

Figure 4.8 *An aqueduct running through farmland in Central Valley*

 **(i)** What are the four main stages of the water cycle?

 **(ii)** Name a chemical that is added to water. What does it do?

 **(iii)** Why are there no irrigation schemes in Ireland?

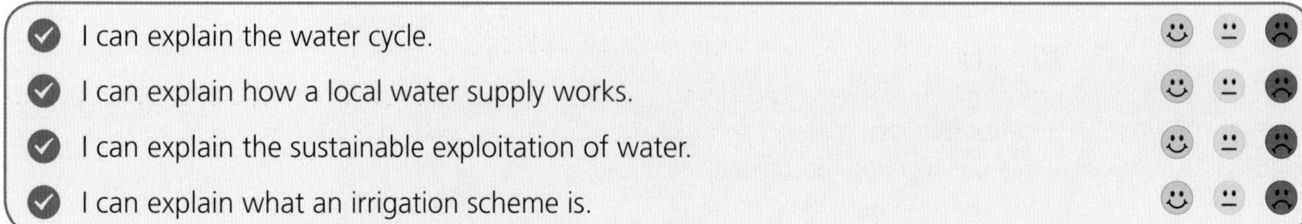

I can explain the water cycle.
I can explain how a local water supply works.
I can explain the sustainable exploitation of water.
I can explain what an irrigation scheme is.

Fishing in Ireland: over-exploitation of a renewable resource

Learning Intentions

In this section, you will learn:

- that fishing is a primary economic activity
- why overfishing occurs
- about the sustainable exploitation of fish.

Over-exploitation	Photosynthesis
Continental shelf	Overfishing
Plankton	Conservation zone

Ireland's fishing history

Ireland has many **fishing ports**. This is mainly because we are located beside the Atlantic Ocean. The shallow waters of the **continental shelf** create ideal conditions for fish to live and grow. There is also a lot of **plankton**, the small and microscopic organisms that fish and whales feed on.

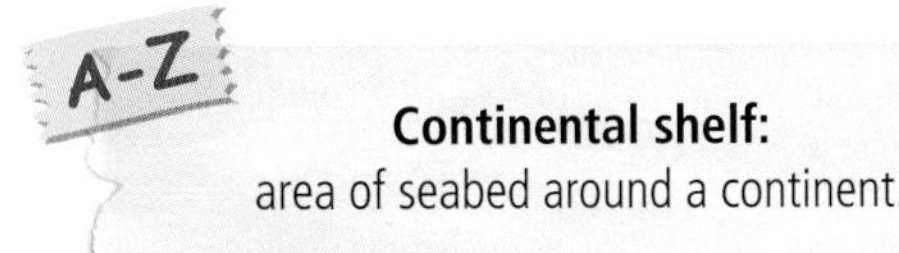

Continental shelf:
area of seabed around a continent.

In recent years, Ireland has become more heavily involved in the **fishing industry** and fishing plays a very important part in many people's lives. It is extremely important to a number of villages and towns as a source of **income** and **employment**.

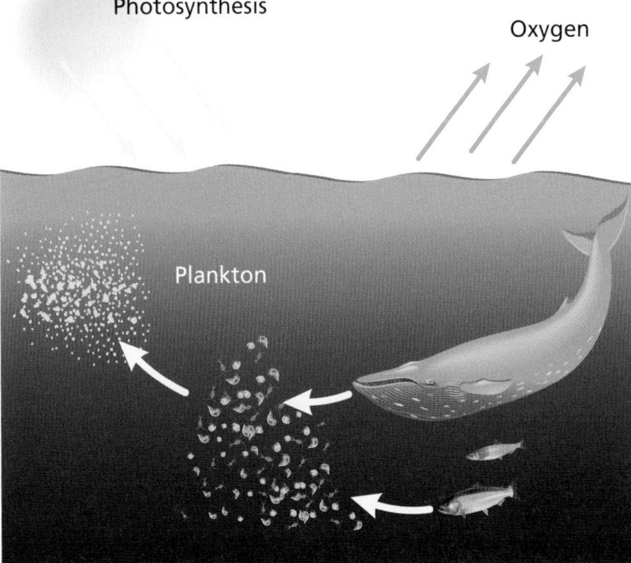

Figure 4.9 *Plankton*

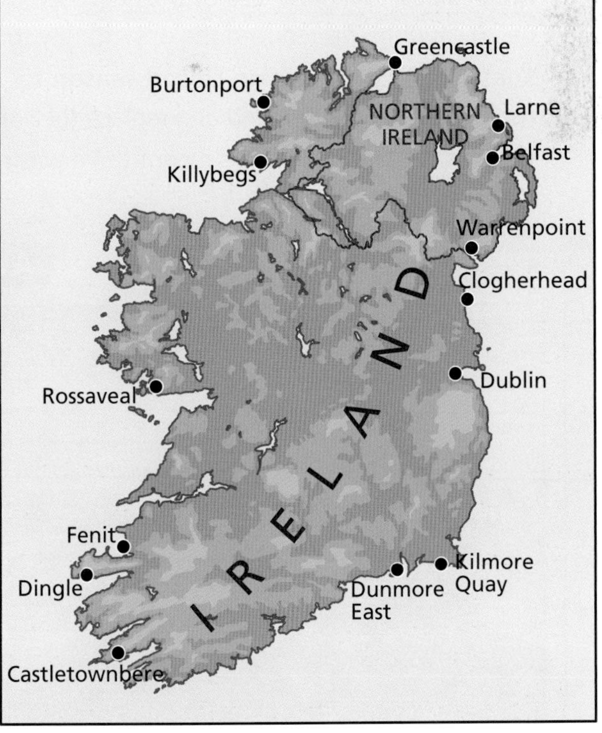

Figure 4.10 *Ireland's fishing ports*

DID YOU KNOW? Like plants, some types of plankton convert the sun's energy into food energy through a process called **photosynthesis**.

Overfishing

Fish are a renewable natural resource, but they can be over-exploited by **overfishing**. This is when fish are taken from the water faster than they can reproduce. This is a major problem in Ireland and elsewhere, causing many people to lose their jobs.

Reasons for overfishing

Overfishing has occurred for the following reasons:

- **Membership of the EEC (EU)**: When Ireland joined the **EEC** in 1973, we gave up **control** of our waters and how we fish. We then had to share our fish with other member countries. This meant that **foreign trawlers** could now fish in Irish fishing areas. This led to more and more fish being caught.
- **Modern technology**: The improvement in **sonar** technology and **radar** equipment means fish are easier to locate and catch. The increase in the **size** of trawlers means they can stay out at sea for longer and therefore catch more. Trawlers are also now accompanied by **factory ships** which are able to process the fish at sea and keep them **refrigerated**, allowing trawlers to stay at sea for even longer.
- **Mesh sizes**: The mesh size of the nets used to be too small and it led to young, underdeveloped fish being caught. This reduced the opportunity for the fish to breed and **replace their stocks**.
- **Seasons**: As there was **no closed season** for fishing, all fish could be caught all year round. This meant fish were not able to breed and replace their stocks.
- **Quotas**: The lack of quotas meant there was **no limit** to the amount of fish a trawler could catch.

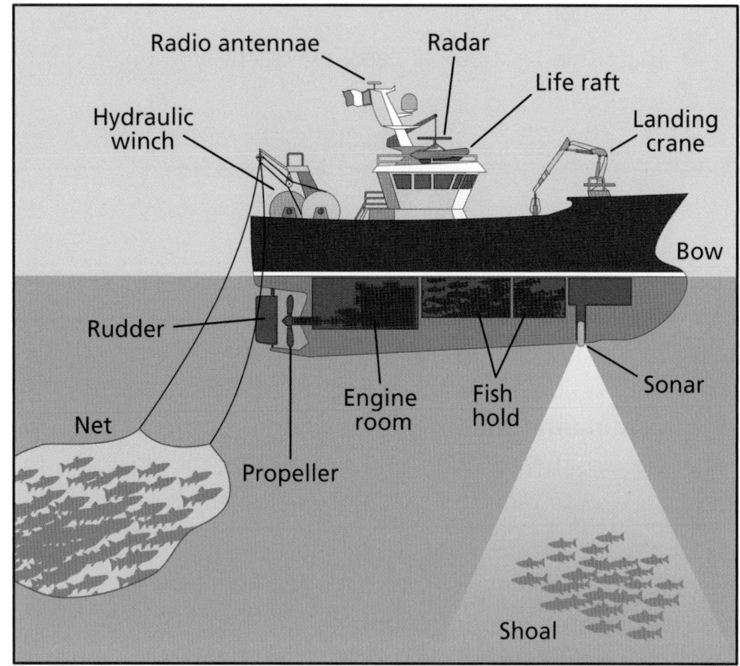

Figure 4.11 *Modern trawlers use technology in everything they do*

ACTIVITY

Figure 4.12 *A trawler from thirty years ago*

Figure 4.13 *A modern 'supertrawler'*

Compare these two photographs. How has fishing changed? Why do you think we need to be worried about the size of supertrawlers?

Sustainable exploitation of fish

Many types of fish are now **endangered** because of overfishing. In Irish waters, species such as **cod**, **herring** and **haddock** are under threat. This has led the Irish government and the EU to try to **limit** the amount of fish being caught.

The following steps have been taken:

- The creation of **conservation zones** around Ireland
- The introduction of yearly **quotas** for fish catches
- A **ban** on the fishing of some **endangered** species
- The **shortening** of the fishing **season** for some types of fish
- An **increase** in net **mesh** sizes.

The Irish Conservation Box

In 2003, a **Conservation Box** was created. Fishing in this area is restricted and strict **quotas** have been set in this zone to help **fish stocks** to recover. It covers an area of **100,000 km²** off the coast of Ireland.

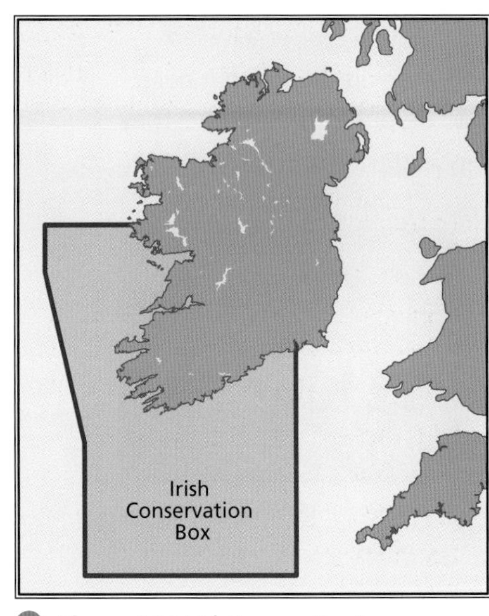

Figure 4.14 *Irish Conservation Box*

 **(i)** Name one thing fish feed on.

 **(ii)** List and explain two reasons for overfishing in Ireland.

(iii) List and explain ways that the Irish government and the European Union have tried to reduce the over-exploitation of fish.

 **(iv)** Why is it important to preventing overfishing?

- I understand how overfishing has occurred in Ireland.  
- I understand the steps that have been taken to exploit fish sustainably in Ireland. 

Farming in Ireland

Learning Intentions

In this section, you will learn:

- that farming is a primary economic activity
- that farming is a system made up of inputs, processes and outputs.
- that there are many different types of farm
- about the impacts that farming has on the environment
- how we can continue to farm in a sustainable way.

Agriculture
Inputs
Processes
Outputs
Dairy
Arable
Tillage
Horticulture
Pastoral
Livestock

Farming is an example of a **primary economic activity**. Farming is a very important economic activity. It provides people with **employment** and a **food supply**.

In Ireland **5.7 per cent** of people are employed in **agriculture**, and **12.3 per cent** of Ireland's total exports are **agri-food products** (food produced from agriculture).

Farms are run as a system of **inputs**, **processes** and **outputs**.

Inputs

These are things that need to be put into the farm. They include cattle and machinery, such as tractors.

Figure 4.15a *Input: cattle*

Processes

These are tasks or jobs done by the farmer throughout the year on his or her farm, such as milking, ploughing and cutting silage.

Figure 4.15b *Process: milking*

Outputs

These are the products of the farm and what the farmer sells, including milk, vegetables and livestock.

Figure 4.15c *Output: milk*

ACTIVITY

Can you make a list of other inputs, processes and outputs on a farm? Try and link the three together to create a system.

Types of farm

There are many different types of farming which produce different types of produce.

Examples include:

- **Dairy** farming (cows for milk, butter, cheese, etc.)
- **Arable** farming or **tillage** (maize, wheat, barley, etc.)
- **Horticulture** or market gardening (vegetables, flowers, fruits, salad, etc.)
- **Pastoral** farming (grazing sheep or cattle)
- **Livestock** (cattle, sheep, pigs, horses)
- **Mixed** farming (livestock, crops, vegetables)

Figure 4.16 *Different types of farming*

A *Arable*

B *Dairy*

C *Horticulture*

D *Pastoral*

E *Livestock*

C

D

E

The type of agriculture in an area depends on the type of **soil** in the area. We will learn more about soil types in Chapter 16.

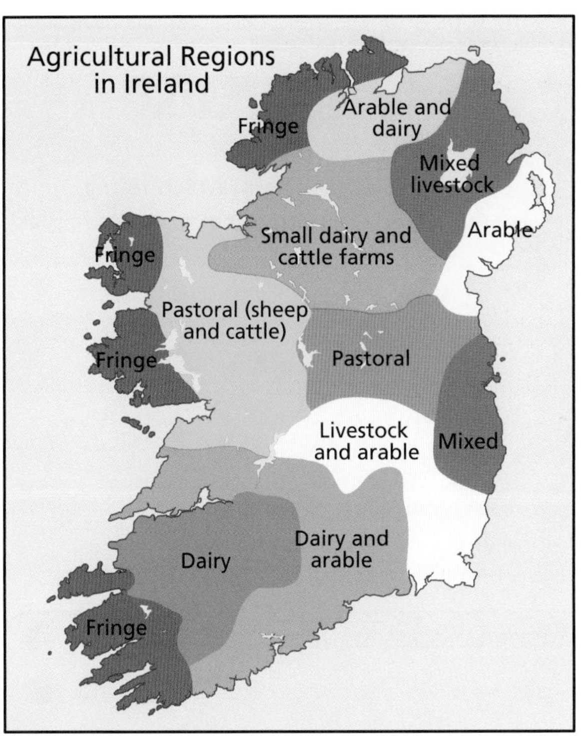

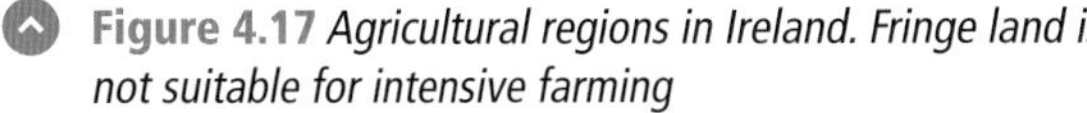

Figure 4.17 *Agricultural regions in Ireland. Fringe land is not suitable for intensive farming*

ACTIVITY

Some farmers grow crops on their land while other focus on the production of meat. Suggest some reasons for this. Discuss in groups of four. Outline your opinions to the class.

ACTIVITY

Take a look at the map on the left, which shows the types of agriculture in Ireland. What is the main type of agriculture in your region?

Impact on the environment

While farming is essential, it can result in damage to the **environment**.

- Insect **sprays** used on crops can be harmful and can end up in our food.
- **Fertilisers** used on the land to increase the fertility of the soil can run off into streams and rivers. This **pollutes** our water supply.
- The **illegal dumping** of silage, slurry, and sometimes milk, can lead to rivers becoming polluted. This can result in the killing of fish. Strict laws can help to prevent illegal dumping.

Figure 4.18 *Slurry being spread; slurry is a mixture of manure and water used to fertilise fields*

Sustainable agriculture

As a member of the European Union, agriculture in Ireland is strongly influenced by the EU's **Common Agricultural Policy (CAP)**. The main aims of the CAP are:

1. To provide **income support** to farmers
2. To ensure **guaranteed market prices** for farmers in the EU
3. To support **rural development** programmes
4. To provide Europe with a good **supply** of quality food.

The CAP has invested billions of euros in agriculture and rural development in Ireland. In 2013 the CAP decided to focus on '**Greening**'. Now farmers are rewarded for using more **sustainable** agricultural practices. These include:

1. **Diversifying** crops – farmers should grow different types of crops and the main crop cannot cover more than 75 per cent of the land.
2. Farmers must keep **permanent grassland**. This helps to protect a variety of plants and animals.
3. Farmers must protect **water sources** on their land.

These measures are to ensure the **sustainability** of agriculture and reduce its negative impact on the environment.

ACTIVITY

Visit www.origingreen.ie to research the various ways in which farming in Ireland is becoming more sustainable.

(i) List an input to a farm.
(ii) List an output from a farm.

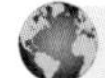
(iii) Explain any process that occurs on a farm.
(iv) Name any type of farm. What does it produce?

(v) Explain two ways in which farmers can farm sustainably.

- I understand that farming is a system of inputs, outputs and processes.
- I can explain the different types of farm.
- I am aware that farming can have a negative impact on the environment and of the importance of sustainable farming.

Forestry in Ireland – a growing renewable natural resource

Learning Intentions

In this section, you will learn:

- that forestry is a primary economic activity
- that wood is a natural resource that is exploited by people
- about the impact of deforestation on the global climate
- how people are being encouraged to increase reforestation.

KEY WORDS

Deciduous
Coniferous
Deforestation
Reforestation
Semi-state body
Coillte
Teagasc

The **forestry** industry in Ireland employs 12,000 people. This makes it a very important **primary economic activity**.

Wood is a natural resource that has been **exploited** by people for a very long time. It is a **renewable** resource if it is managed in a sustainable way.

Types of forest in Ireland

The natural vegetation of Ireland is **deciduous** forest. Deciduous trees lose their leaves in winter. **Beech**, **birch**, **oak** and **ash** are examples of deciduous trees.

Figure 4.19 *Deciduous woodland: birch trees in Co. Kildare*

The first settlers who came to Ireland **cleared** a lot of the natural woodlands for **agriculture** and **settlement**. Wood was used for **tools**, as a **building** material and as **fuel**.

During the plantations, English landowners introduced **coniferous** trees. These are trees such as spruce and pine that are **evergreen**. They don't lose their leaves in winter. Coniferous trees grow faster than deciduous trees.

Ireland has the **lowest forest cover** of all European countries (10.7 per cent in 2016). However, the amount of **forest area** in Ireland has been **increasing** significantly in the past few decades.

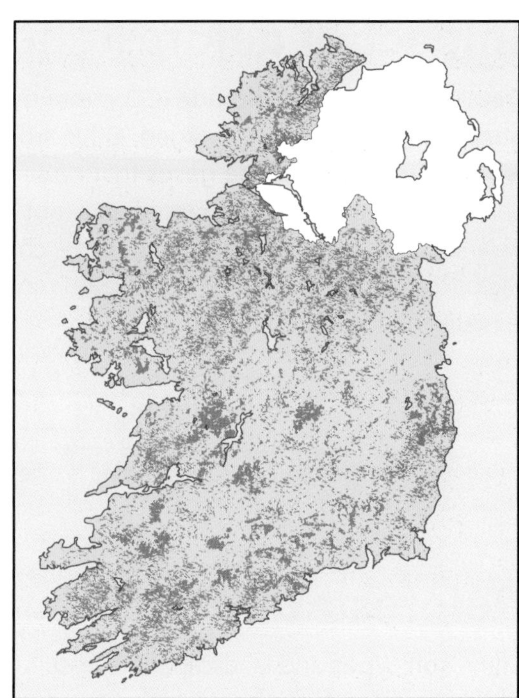

Figure 4.20 *Map of Ireland's forests*

Figure 4.21 *Coniferous woodland in the Mourne Mountains, Co. Down*

The table below shows the forest area in Ireland since 1656.

Year	Area (hectares)	% of Total Land Area
1656	170,000	2.5
1841	140,000	2.0
1908	125,200	1.8
1918	100,717	1.4
1928	89,000	1.2
1949	144,000	2.1
1965	254,350	3.7
1973	323,654	4.6
1985	411,529	5.9
2006	697,730	10.1
2012	731,650	10.5
2016	757,090	10.7

NUMERACY ACTIVITY

(a) In which year was the percentage of total land aea at its lowest?

(b) Calculate the increase in percentage of total land area between 1985 and 2016.

(c) Draw a trend graph to display the increase in the percentage of total land area in this table.

Impact of deforestation on the global climate

Trees **absorb carbon dioxide** (CO_2) from the atmosphere and **release oxygen** (O_2). Carbon dioxide is one of the **greenhouse gases** that cause climate change. The reduction of forested area, not just in Ireland but all over the world, has been a contributing factor to **climate change**. We will learn more about climate change in Chapter 14.

Figure 4.22 *Deforestation in the Amazon rainforest, Brazil*

Deforestation:
the clearing of all trees from an area by burning or cutting. The cleared land is then used in other ways.

Reforestation in Ireland

Some **soil types** and landscapes are unsuitable for large-scale agriculture. In such areas, **forestry** is the best option for land use and many acres of coniferous forest have been planted in marginal areas such as the Wicklow Mountains and the **gley soils** of west Limerick and north Kerry.

Reforestation:
the planting of trees on areas of land that were once covered by forest but were affected by deforestation.

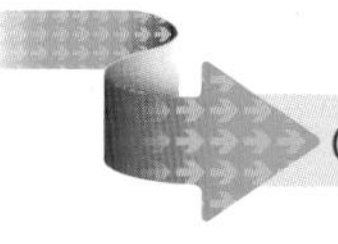

Go to Chapter 16 to learn more about soil types and gley soils.

The **Forest Service** of the Department of Agriculture, Food and the Marine is responsible for the development of forestry in Ireland. The **semi-state body Coillte** owns more than half of the forests in Ireland. Farmers and landowners can apply for **grants**, funded by the government and the EU, from the Department of Agriculture, Food and the Marine. There are numerous private companies and the semi-state body **Teagasc** offers advice and assistance in this area.

Semi-state body:
an organisation partly owned and run by the government. The minister of the relevant department is responsible for the semi-state body.

 **(i)** What percentage of Irish land area is covered by woodland?

 **(ii)** Name and explain two factors that have led to the increase in forestry development in Ireland.

 **(iii)** Suggest and explain ways in which you and your family could reduce the exploitation of wood.

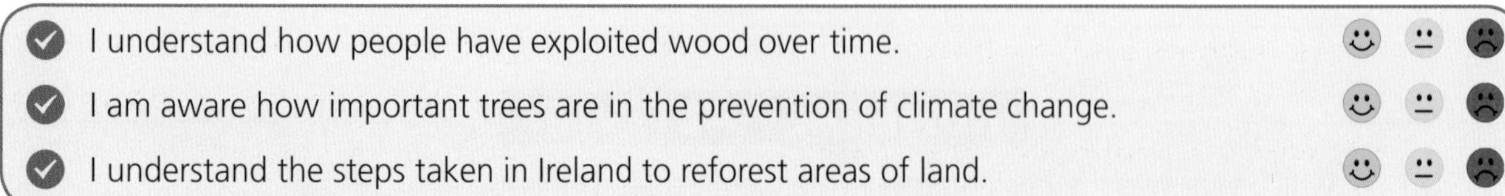

- I understand how people have exploited wood over time.
- I am aware how important trees are in the prevention of climate change.
- I understand the steps taken in Ireland to reforest areas of land.

REVISION

Economic activities can be put into three categories: ________________, ________________ and ________________. ________________ resources can be used again and again, while ________________ resources cannot be used again. ________________ exploitation is when resources are managed so that future generations will also be able to use them.

________________ is the most vital natural resource. ____________ ____________ is responsible for the public water ________________ in Ireland. Before it gets to our taps, water is ________________ to remove bacteria, and ________________ and ________________ are added.

The artificial watering of land is called ________________.

Fish are a ________________ resource. ________________ has led to a decrease in fish stocks. Improved technology, such as ________________ and better ________________, has added to this problem. Fishing is ________________ in the ________________ Box around Ireland.

Farming is a ________________ with inputs, ________________ and outputs.

________________ used to increase soil fertility can cause pollution of rivers. The EU's ____________ ____________ ____________ supports farmers.

The natural vegetation of Ireland is ________________ forest. ________ per cent of land area in Ireland is forested. Trees absorb ____________ ____________.

Questions & Answers

Sample Questions

1. Name **two** Irish fishing ports.
2. Explain **two** reasons for overfishing.
3. Describe **two** measures that can be used to prevent overfishing.

Sample Answers

1. Killybegs, Co. Donegal and Rossaveal, Co. Galway
2. a. The first reason for overfishing is improvements in technology. With developments in sonar technology and radar equipment the fish are easier to locate and catch.
   b. The second reason is Ireland joining the European Union in 1973. This allowed trawlers from other countries to fish in Irish waters, which meant that more and more fish were caught and they did not get a chance to reproduce.
3. a. One measure has been to introduce the quota. Fishers are only allowed to catch a certain amount of fish, which allows for the conservation of fish stocks. This also protects certain species of fish which might be in danger.
   b. Another measure has been to increase the mesh size of fishing nets. This allows younger fish to escape and ensures that the species will not become endangered.

Short Questions

1. The box below contains inputs, processes and outputs on a farm. Circle **three** processes on a farm.

calves	milking	tractors
cutting silage	ploughing	milk
fertilisers	crops	maize

2. Name **three** renewable resources.

(i) ______________________________

(ii) ______________________________

(iii) ______________________________

3. Which of the photographs shows an example of a primary economic activity?

Factory ☐

Gas rig ☐

Garda ☐ [tick (✓) the correct box]

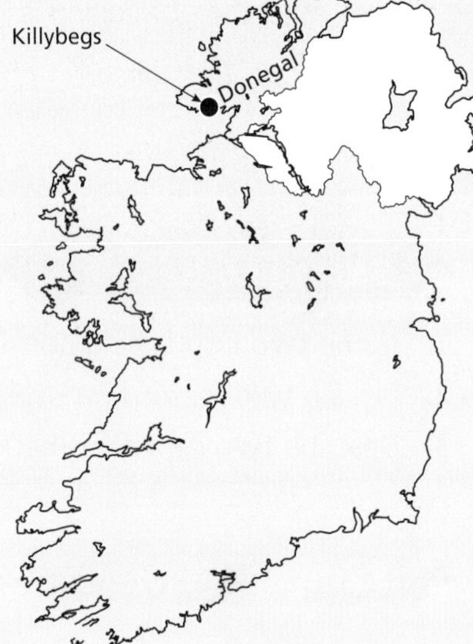

4. Killybegs is best known as the location for:

A tourist resort ☐

A fishing port ☐ 

A large chemical factory ☐ 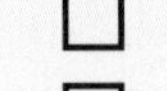

A peat-burning power station ☐ 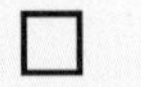

[tick (✓) the correct box]

5. The natural resources shown in the photographs are:

Non-renewable ☐

Renewable ☐ [tick (✓) the correct box]

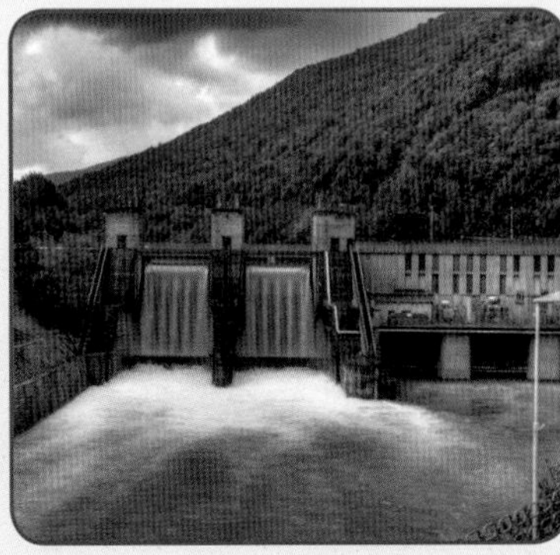

Long Questions

1. With the aid of a labelled diagram, explain the water cycle. Make sure to explain the following terms – evaporation, condensation, precipitation and run-off.

2. The Global Goals for Sustainable Development are about protecting life on the planet. What do you think are the messages behind these two posters?

IMAGINE IF TREES GAVE OFF WIFI SIGNALS, WE WOULD BE PLANTING SO MANY TREES AND WE'D PROBABLY SAVE THE PLANET TOO.

TOO BAD THEY ONLY PRODUCE THE OXYGEN WE BREATHE.

3. **(i)** What is the term given to the artificial watering of crops?
   (ii) Name **one** such scheme that you have studied.
   (iii) Explain **one** advantage and **one** disadvantage of this scheme.

4. Ireland's fish catch, 1997–2000 (tonnes)

Fish Type	1997	1998	1999	2000
Cod	5,706	5,294	3,860	2,928
Herring	57,155	58,248	45,334	42,114

   (i) Describe the trend shown by the figures in the table.
   (ii) Draw a line graph using the figures in the table above.
   (iii) Explain **two** reasons why overfishing occurred in Irish waters.
   (iv) 'The Irish Box is a method of conserving fish stocks.'
      (a) Name **one** country other than Ireland and the UK whose vessels fish in the Celtic Sea.
      (b) Name and describe **one** other method which might be used to conserve fish stocks.

5. Farming is a system with inputs, processes and outputs. Explain these **three** terms and give an example of each.

6. **(i)** Name **two** semi-state organisations that work in forestry in Ireland.
   (ii) Explain **two** reasons why there has been an increase in forestry in Ireland in recent years.

Visual Summary

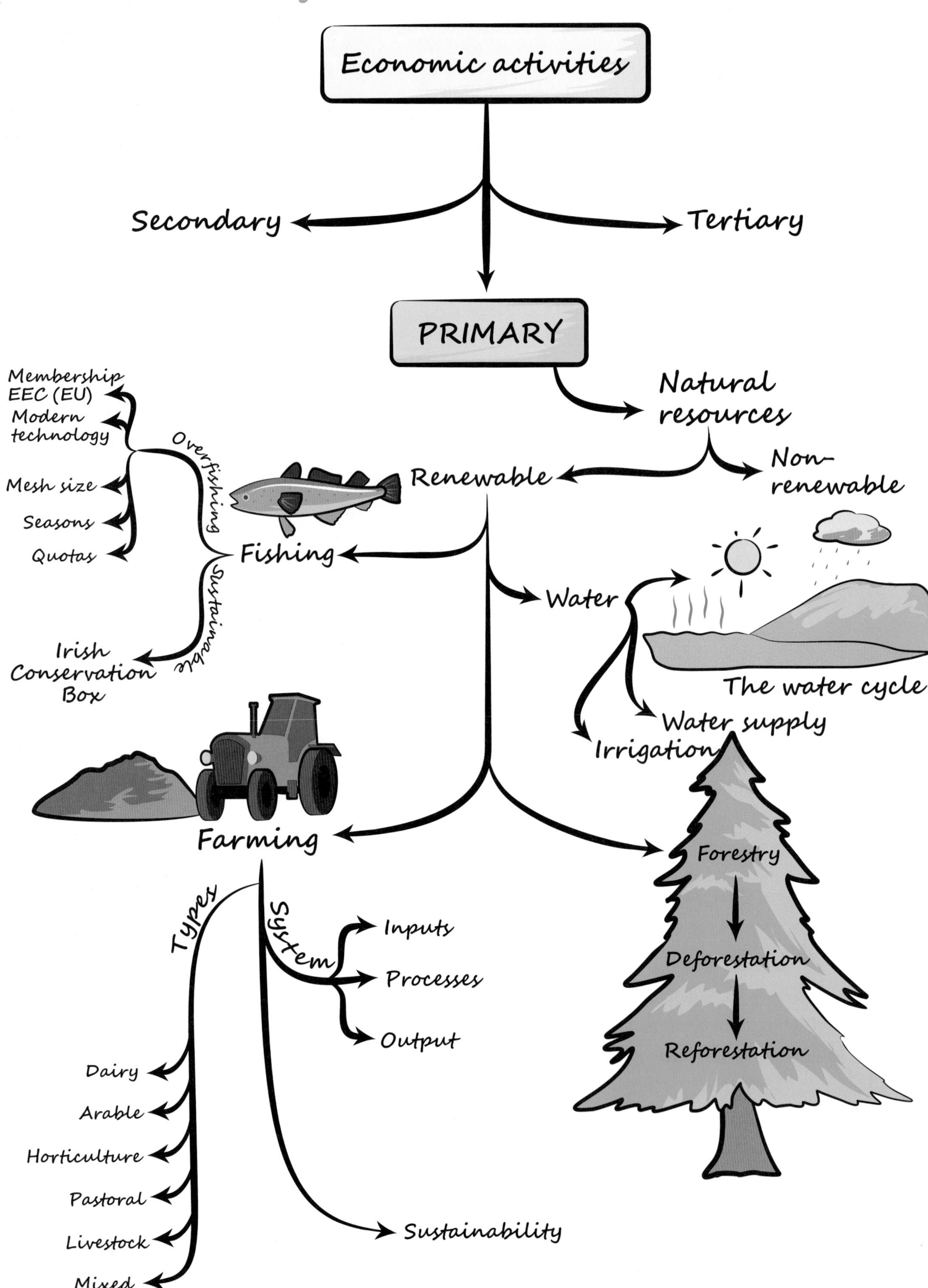

Energy and the Environment: How fuelling our needs impacts on the world we live in

In this chapter, you will learn:

- that the physical world provides us with energy resources
- that these resources can be renewable or non-renewable
- that our use of these energy resources affects the environment, the economy and society
- that our reliance on fossil fuels as an energy source is not sustainable.

ICE-BREAKER ACTIVITY

What type of energy do your classmates use to heat their homes? Do they use coal, oil, gas, peat, solar or any other type of energy? Work together and create a survey. Illustrate the information on a bar chart.

Energy resources

Learning Intentions

In this section, you will learn:

- about renewable energy resources and non-renewable energy resources.

KEY WORDS

Energy resources
Renewable
Non-renewable

The physical world provides us with **natural resources** that we can make **energy** from. These **energy resources** are very important for the **economy**. However, our use of them can have a big impact on **society** and the **environment**.

Like other natural resources, energy resources can be **renewable** or **non-renewable**.

Renewable energy resources include **wind**, **solar**, **water**, **geothermal** and **biomass** energy.

Non-renewable energy resources include **oil**, **coal**, **gas** and **peat**.

Figure 5.1 *Wind turbines produce renewable energy*

(i) List three types of renewable energy.

(ii) Define the term renewable energy resource.

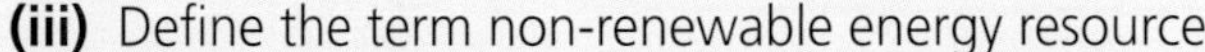

(iii) Define the term non-renewable energy resource.

(iv) Why do you think it is better to use renewable energy resources than non-renewable energy resources?

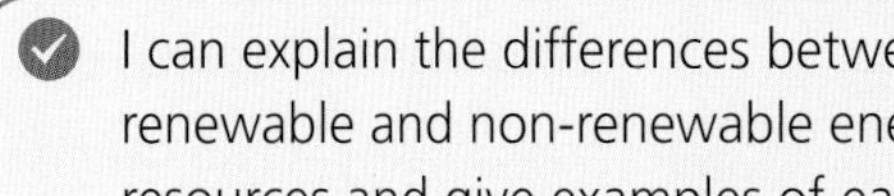

I can explain the differences between renewable and non-renewable energy resources and give examples of each.

Figure 5.2 *Oil and gas produce non-renewable energy*

Non-renewable energy resources

Learning Intentions

In this section, you will learn:

- about the different types of non-renewable energy resources
- where these non-renewable energy resources are located.

Fossil fuel, Dependent, Oil, OPEC, Gas, Coal, Peat

Non-renewable energy comes from sources that will eventually run out. **Fossil fuels** such as oil, coal, gas and peat are all examples of non-renewable energy resources.

Fossil fuels were formed from **decomposing** plants and organisms. They are the world's largest energy source – over **80 per cent** of the world's energy comes from fossil fuels. In Ireland, 91 per cent of our energy comes from fossil fuels.

Unfortunately, these fossil fuels cause great harm to our environment, and people are too **dependent** on fossil fuels. That means that they **rely** on them too much.

NUMERACY ACTIVITY

Ireland does not produce all the energy the country needs. The pie chart on the right shows Ireland's energy imports.

(a) What percentage of Ireland's energy imports are from coal?

(b) What percentage of Ireland's energy imports are from fossil fuels?

(c) Calculate the percentage difference between the amount of natural gas imported and the amount of coal imported.

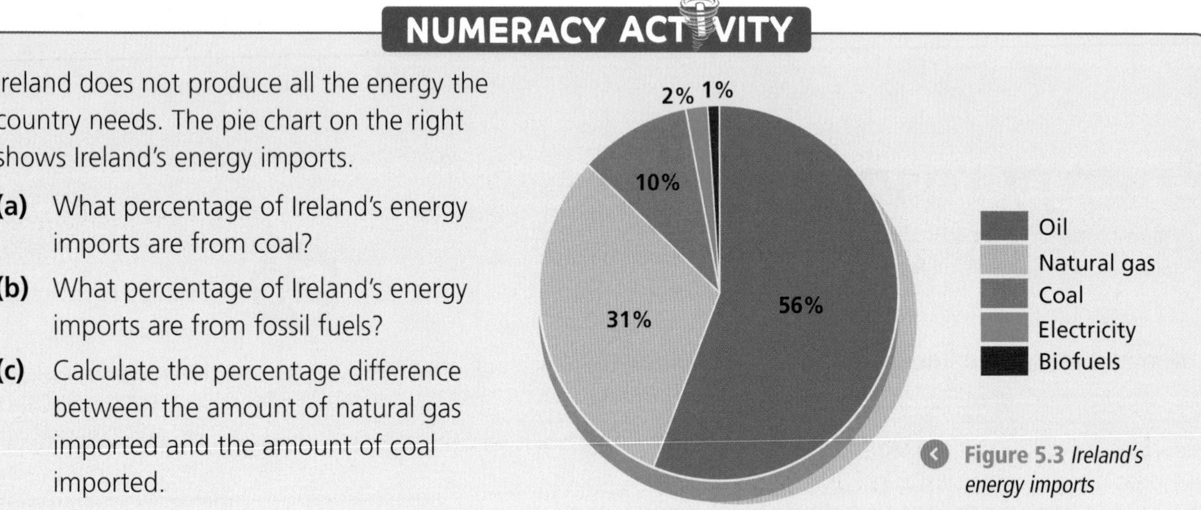

Figure 5.3 *Ireland's energy imports*

Oil

Oil is a very important source of **energy** in our world today. It is a **non-renewable** energy resource. Therefore, it is vital that we try to **conserve** the oil we have. Look at the photographs below to see how we use oil on a daily basis:

Figure 5.4 *How we use oil*

A *Run our cars on petrol*

B *Maintain our cars with oil*

C *Heat our homes with oil*

D *Fly aircraft with aviation fuel*

ACTIVITY

Can you list ways in which you and your family might use oil at home? Go online to research the products we use every day that are made using oil.

There are advantages and disadvantages of using oil:

Advantages of Oil

- It gives off hardly any smoke.
- It produces great heat.
- It is very efficient.
- It is easily transported.

Disadvantages of Oil

- It is expensive.
- We have to import it.
- It must be transported by sea in tankers.
- Oil leaks can cause serious pollution.

Figure 5.5 *Clear-up operation under way after an explosion on the offshore rig Deepwater Horizon in the Gulf of Mexico caused a huge oil spillage in 2010*

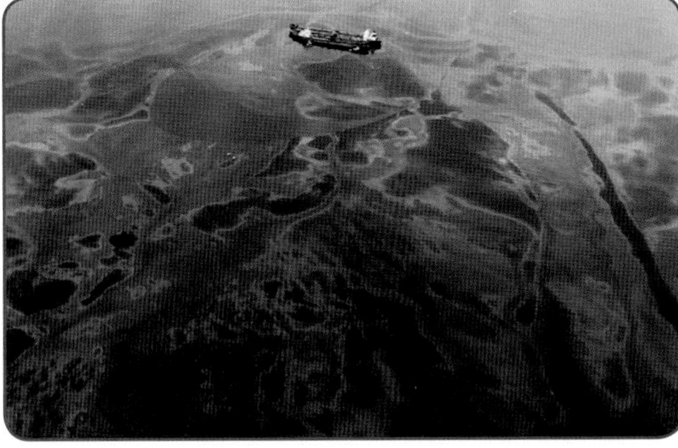

Figure 5.6 *In 1989 the tanker* Exxon Valdez *ran aground in Alaska and spilt more than 40 million litres of oil*

ACTIVITY

Look at the photographs of oil spillages above. Can you describe one economic and one environmental impact of an oil spillage?

Location of oil

Many countries, including the USA and Norway, have **oil reserves**. However, the vast majority of reserves are located around the Persian Gulf in the **Middle East**. Countries in the region include **Saudi Arabia**, **Kuwait**, **Iran**, **Iraq** and the **United Arab Emirates (UAE)**.

Oil prices are set by **OPEC** (Organisation of the Petroleum Exporting Countries), which causes the price to **fluctuate** (rise and fall). For example, prices **fall** if there is a lot of oil available and prices **rise** if it is difficult to access oil because of conflicts in oil-producing countries.

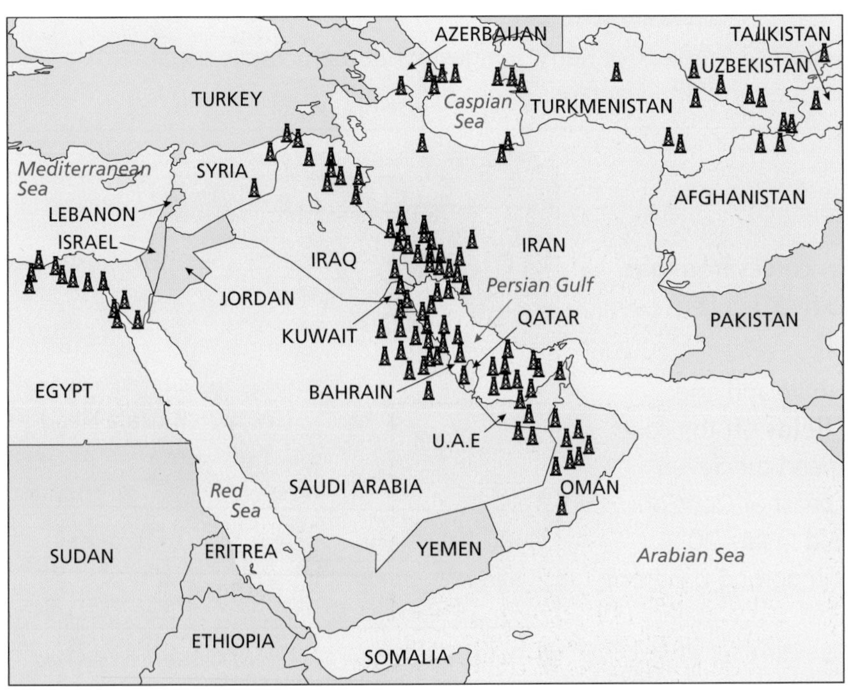

Figure 5.7 *Oil wells in the oil-producing countries of the Middle East*

With your class, find out the cost of oil today. Check the price every few days and see if the price is increasing or decreasing. Suggest reasons for your findings.

Study the picture on the left. What impact has oil had on the economy in Dubai? Discuss in pairs.

Figure 5.8 *The oil-rich city of Dubai in the United Arab Emirates*

Oil in Ireland

In Ireland, **48 per cent** of our energy comes from **oil**. Ireland has not yet **exploited** its oil reserves for a number of reasons. Two of the main reasons are:

1. The **location** of Irish oil reserves makes it very difficult to drill for oil. Improvements in technology may make these oil reserves easier to drill in the future.
2. The oil may not be of a high **quality**.

Therefore, we are completely **dependent** on oil imports in Ireland at the moment.

However, there is a lot of **exploration** work occurring around our coastline. Currently under investigation is the **Barryroe oil field** off the coast of west Cork (see Figure 5.9). After initial research it is thought to contain over 1.6 billion barrels of oil.

ACTIVITY

Imagine oil was discovered off the coast of Dingle, Co. Kerry. Suggest what the possible social, environmental and economic advantages and disadvantages might be.

Gas

In Ireland, **27 per cent** of our energy comes from **gas**. Our use of natural gas has increased by 8 per cent over the past decade.

Ireland's natural gas comes from both Ireland and abroad. There are a number of **gas fields** off the coast of Ireland. Kinsale Head, Ballycotton and the Seven Heads gas fields are located off the coast of Co. Cork. We started using the **Corrib gas field** in late 2015. This will reduce our dependency on importing gas from abroad.

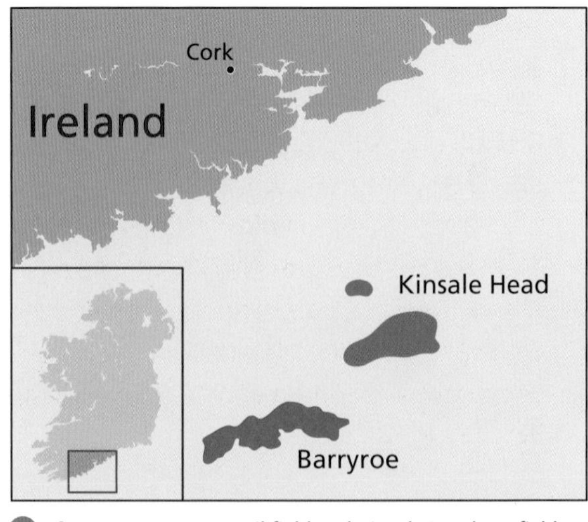

Figure 5.9 *Barryroe oil field and Kinsale Head gas field*

Non-renewable energy: Corrib gas field

The Corrib gas field is located off the **north-west coast** of Ireland, near Co. Mayo. The exploitation of the gas field created a great deal of **controversy**. There was a lot of concern about the location of the **onshore processing plant** and the **route of the pipeline** that was to lead to the plant.

Gas was first brought ashore in **2015** through a pipeline more than 90 km long. It runs along the seabed and then in a tunnel under **Sruwaddacon Bay** and then underground to the **Bellanaboy** terminal near Belmullet in Co. Mayo.

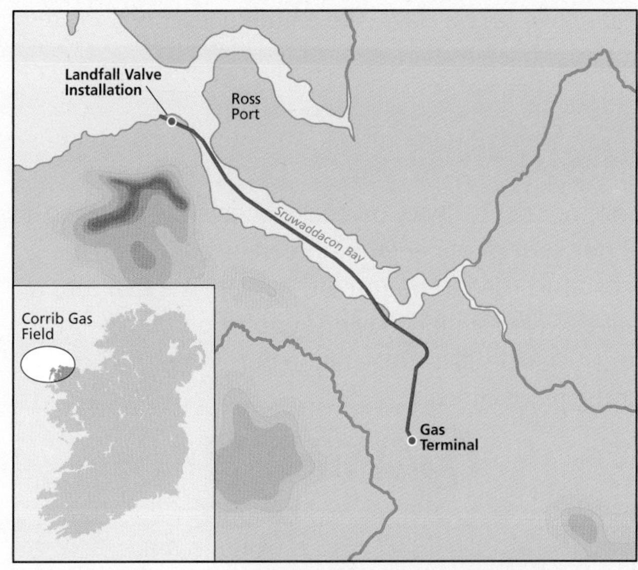

Figure 5.10 *The Corrib gas field and the route of the pipeline*

Positive socio-economic impacts:

- The gas field will be worth **€4.4 billion** to the Irish economy.
- It will provide **60 per cent** of Ireland's gas.
- It created over **1,200 jobs** in the rural area of west Mayo while it was being built. This prevented some local people from migrating in search of employment. It now employs about **175** people.
- The **local communities** have benefitted. For example, the Belmullet GAA club received a contribution of €450,000 towards the development of their training grounds.
- Two **scholarships** are offered to students at local secondary schools to help with their college or university education.

Figure 5.11 *There were many protests against the building of the gas pipeline*

Negative socio-economic impacts:

- There are concerns about the **safety** of the project. For example, some fear an explosion along the route of the onshore pipe and the impact that it would have on the local residents.
- **Environmental issues**, such as harm to local water supply, were of concern during the construction of the site. **Carrowmore Lake**, which is the local source of drinking water, is near the Bellanaboy refinery.
- Some waste material from the terminal is released into **Broadhaven Bay**. The bay is an important site for dolphins, otters, grey seals and whales. There are fears that it will have a major impact on the **wildlife** there.
- There are **fears** that the release of carbon, nitrogen and sulfur into the atmosphere in a rural area with a very clean environment will also have negative impacts.
- Some people complain about the **visual impact** of the Bellanaboy terminal.

Figure 5.12 *Laying the pipeline*

Figure 5.13 *The terminal at Bellanaboy*

With your classmates, research the Corrib gas field online. Write down **three positive** and **three negative** effects that the building of the plant has had on the community. Present your findings to the class, then take a class vote on the question: Should the plant have been built? Record the results of the vote using a pie chart.

Coal

While our dependency on coal is constantly declining, **10 per cent** of our energy still comes from **coal**. It is a solid fuel used to **heat** many homes. The **ESB** runs a coal-powered station in **Moneypoint** on the Shannon Estuary in Co. Clare. The station burns imported coal for the production of electricity.

Watch the video at https://educateplus.ie/go/china-coal to see how China is trying to reduce its reliance on coal. Write down two interesting facts you learned while watching this video. Share them with your partner.

Figure 5.14 *A coal-fired power station*

Peat

Peat is a fuel made of **decayed plants** and other organic matter found in **bogs**. Peat has been an important source of **heating** and **energy** in Ireland for hundreds of years. While the commercial exploitation of peat is being phased out, it is still an important energy source in the raised bogs of the west coast of Ireland. In Ireland, **5.5 per cent** of our energy comes from **peat**.

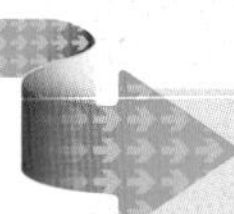

Go to Chapter 16, pages 298–299, to learn more about the sustainable exploitation of peat in Ireland.

Ordnance Survey maps and non-renewable energy resources

We can identify power stations using non-renewable energy resources on Ordnance Survey maps by the symbol on the right:

Stáisiún cumhachta (breosla iontaiseach) Power Station (Fossil)

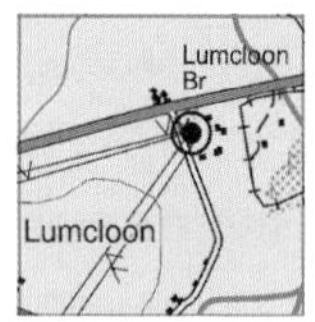

Figure 5.15 *Power station on an OS map*

 **(i)** List three non-renewable energy resources.

 **(ii)** What fossil fuels do we have naturally in Ireland?

 **(iii)** What is the disadvantage of not having natural resources such as oil located in Ireland?

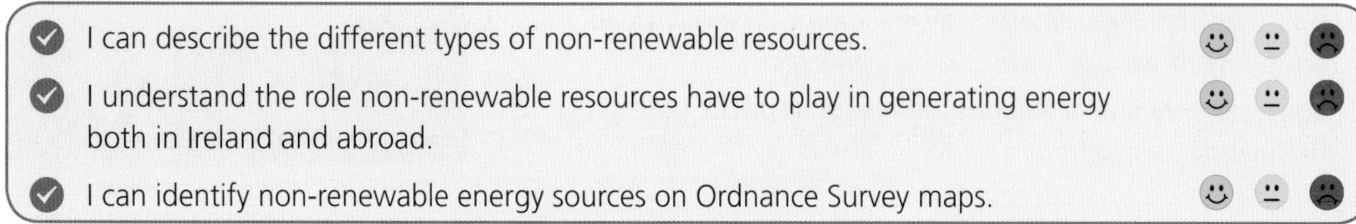

- I can describe the different types of non-renewable resources.
- I understand the role non-renewable resources have to play in generating energy both in Ireland and abroad.
- I can identify non-renewable energy sources on Ordnance Survey maps.

Renewable energy resources

Learning Intentions

In this section, you will learn:

- about the different types of renewable energy resources.

Hydroelectric	Solar panel
Turbine	Geothermal
Wind farm	Biomass
Solar cell	Biofuel

The **energy resources** we rely on now are mostly non-renewable or **finite**, meaning that they will eventually **run out**. They also cost a lot of money. We need to develop our production and use of **renewable energy**. There are many different **types** of renewable energy sources.

- Hydroelectric power (HEP)
- Wind energy
- Solar energy
- Geothermal energy
- Biomass

Hydroelectric power (HEP)

Hydroelectric power is the creation of electricity by using the force of **falling water**.

A **dam** is built across a river to **trap** the water. (A dam is a concrete wall that controls the flow of the water.) When part of the dam is opened water rushes through. The water is used to turn a **turbine**, which generates **electricity**.

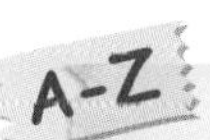

Turbine:
a machine where liquid (water) or gas (wind) flows through and turns a wheel with blades in order to produce power.

Figure 5.16 *A hydroelectric power station*

HEP is the **largest** source of renewable energy. In 2015 it generated over 16 per cent of the world's electricity.

Examples of HEP stations are **Inniscarra** dam in Co. Cork, **Ardnacrusha** dam in Co. Clare and the **Three Gorges** dam in China.

HEP stations need the following:

1. **Water supply**: HEP stations need a constant supply of water. They are built on fast-flowing, high-volume rivers.
2. **Slope**: A HEP station needs to be built where there is a **drop** in the course of the river. This drop causes the water to flow **quickly**.
3. **Bedrock**: The reservoir behind the dam of a HEP station must be built on **impermeable** bedrock. This is so the water in the reservoir does not seep away and remains as a constant water supply.
4. **Climate**: HEP stations need to be situated in areas with high levels of **rainfall**.

Go to the Case Study on page 80 of this chapter to learn more about hydroelectric power .

Wind energy

The **force of the wind** can be used to turn **turbines** and create electricity. The blades on **wind turbines** can deal with winds blowing at up to 320 kph (km per hour). Modern wind turbines are very large in size and are generally grouped together in what is known as a **wind farm**.

Wind energy is becoming a very important source of **renewable** energy. It is a **clean** source of energy and one that is used by more than 80 countries worldwide.

The main **disadvantage** of wind energy is that a **constant supply** of wind is needed. Therefore the **locations** of wind farms have to be chosen carefully.

Figure 5.17 *A wind farm on Prince Edward Island, Canada*

DID YOU KNOW? The largest wind farm in the world is located in the province of Gansu in China.

Solar energy

Solar energy is created using heat and light from the **sun**. It is the biggest renewable energy source in the world.

Solar cells on **solar panels** capture the heat and light and convert this into electricity. In Ireland you can see solar panels on the roofs of homes across the country.

Figure 5.18 *Solar panels on a house*

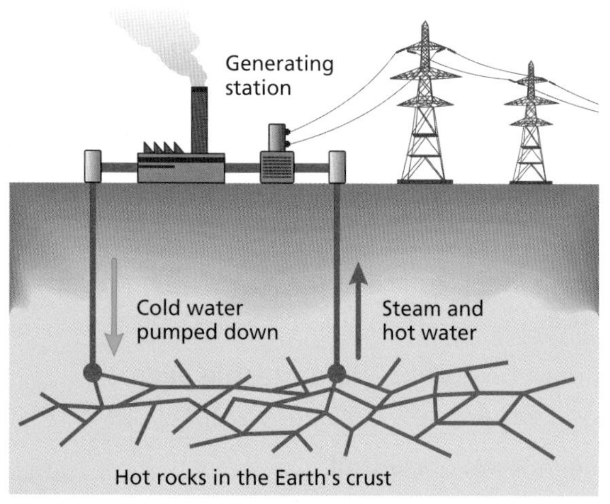

Figure 5.19 *Geothermal energy*

Geothermal energy

Geothermal energy is created by using the **heat** from the **Earth's crust**. Water is **pumped** deep into the Earth's crust and **heated** by the rocks. The heated water is then pumped back to the surface where it can be used to heat homes. The hot water can also be converted to **steam** which is used to turn **turbines** and generate electricity.

Geothermal energy can be exploited in areas where there is **volcanic activity**. **Iceland** and **New Zealand** are two countries that produce huge amounts of geothermal energy.

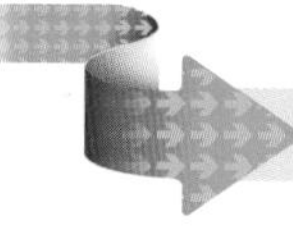

Go to Chapter 2, page 26, to learn more about Iceland and geothermal energy.

Biomass

Biomass energy comes from **organic material**. Examples of the organic materials used include **wood** logs, chips and pellets; **manure**; **sewage** and also certain crops like **rape seed oil**.

Biomass materials are used to produce **biofuels**. These biofuels include **biodiesel**, which is used to power engines, such as those used in **agricultural machinery**. This cuts down on the use of non-renewable fuels like petrol and diesel.

Figure 5.20 *Recycled wood pellets can be used in heaters*

Ordnance Survey maps and renewable energy resources

We can identify renewable energy resources on Ordnance Survey maps with the following symbols:

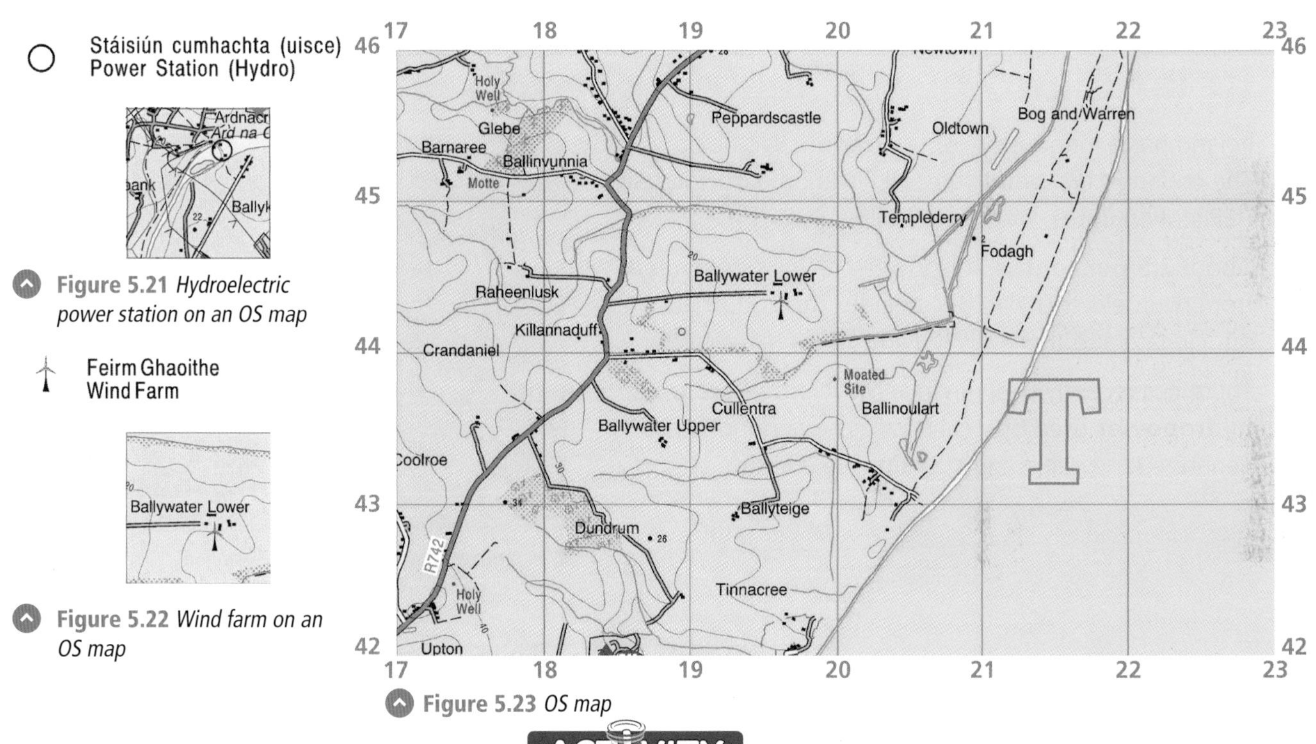

Figure 5.21 *Hydroelectric power station on an OS map*

Figure 5.22 *Wind farm on an OS map*

Figure 5.23 *OS map*

ACTIVITY

Look at the Ordnance Survey map of the Ballywater wind farm in Co. Wexford above. Answer the following questions in your copybook:

1. Give a four-figure grid reference for the location of the wind farm on the map.
2. Explain two reasons why the wind farm was located at its current site.

(i) What percentage of the world's electricity does hydroelectric power generate?

(ii) Name a country that uses geothermal energy. Why is this country suitable for the production of geothermal energy?

(iii) Why should we encourage the use of renewable energy resources over non-renewable energy resources? Give three reasons for your answer.

- I can describe the different types of renewable energy resources.
- I can identify renewable energy resources on Ordnance Survey maps.

Ireland and renewable energy

Learning Intentions

In this section, you will learn:

- about Ireland's production of hydroelectric power
- about Ireland's production of wind energy.

Hydropower
Reservoir
Megawatt

In Ireland, we have excellent **resources** for the production of renewable energy. The government, as well as private individuals and organisations, is working towards producing more energy from **sustainable** renewable sources.

ACTIVITY

Look at www.seai.ie to find out more about Ireland's commitment to cleaner energy.

Ireland and hydroelectric power

Ireland has a long history of using hydroelectric power. The country's first and largest HEP station, **Ardnacrusha** HEP station in Co. Clare, was built in 1927.

About **2.5 per cent** of Ireland's electricity is generated from hydroelectricity. HEP is ideal for this country due to our climate and the levels of **rainfall** we receive annually.

There has recently been an increase in **small-scale hydropower** used by local businesses and industries to generate renewable and **sustainable** energy.

Figure 5.24 *Ardnacrusha HEP station*

CASE STUDY

Hydroelectric power in Ireland: Inniscarra Dam

Inniscarra Dam was constructed in the 1950s as part of the **Lee Hydroelectric Scheme**. The dam is located west of **Ballincollig** in Co. Cork. The dam stands at a height of 44 metres.

The Inniscarra reservoir (also known as Inniscarra lake) was created in 1956. The reservoir was made by flooding parts of the Lee valley west of Cork City.

The reservoir occupies an area of **530 hectares** or 5 km^2. There are approximately 40 km of bank area that can be fished. In recent years there has been a lot of investment in the development of **angling** facilities here.

The HEP station generates **27 megawatts of electricity** for the area. A megawatt (MW) is the unit we use to measure electricity.

Figure 5.25 *Inniscarra Dam, Co. Cork*

Advantages of HEP

- HEP stations and turbines can generate cheap, clean and **renewable** electricity.
- The water that builds up behind the dam wall is known as a **reservoir**. This can be used as a **water supply** for the local area.
- The reservoir can also act as a **leisure facility** for activities such as fishing, rowing and other water-based activities.
- The building of the dam can also help to **prevent flooding.**

Disadvantages of HEP

- The creation of a reservoir behind the dam may mean the **loss** of good **farmland**.
- Families may have to be **relocated** (moved away) as a result of the creation of a reservoir. This can be costly and also a major upheaval for families.
- **New roads and bridges** have to be built around the reservoir and HEP station.
- The dam can stop fish from swimming upstream. This reduces **fish stocks**.

Watch the building of the Three Gorges dam in China here: https://educateplus.ie/go/three-gorges-dam

It is the world's largest HEP station. It has both positive and negative socio-economic impacts for the people of China.

Divide into pairs. One person should take notes on the positive impacts. The other person should take notes on the negative impacts. Share your points with each other after you have watched the video.

Debate the points as a class and then vote on whether or not the building of the Three Gorges dam was a good or a bad decision by the Chinese government.

Ireland and wind energy

There are many **wind farms** in Ireland. Ireland is in an **ideal location** for the production of wind energy because it is located on the edge of Europe. The **strong winds** that come from the **Atlantic Ocean** make the west coast of Ireland one of the best places for a wind farm.

The majority of wind farms are located in **upland** areas , especially near the **west coast**, to take advantage of the windy conditions. Most of the wind farms are also situated in **isolated areas** to prevent visual pollution of the landscape. Many of our wind farms are located on what is known as **cut-away bogs**. These are bogs that are no longer used to produce peat.

Ireland's largest wind farm is **Galway Wind Park** near Oughterard with 58 wind turbines producing energy to power more than 140,000 homes. It was opened by Coillte and Airtricity in October 2017.

Currently **over 20 per cent** of our electricity is produced by wind, saving us in the region of €200m annually. Wind energy is now **employing** more than 3,400 people nationally.

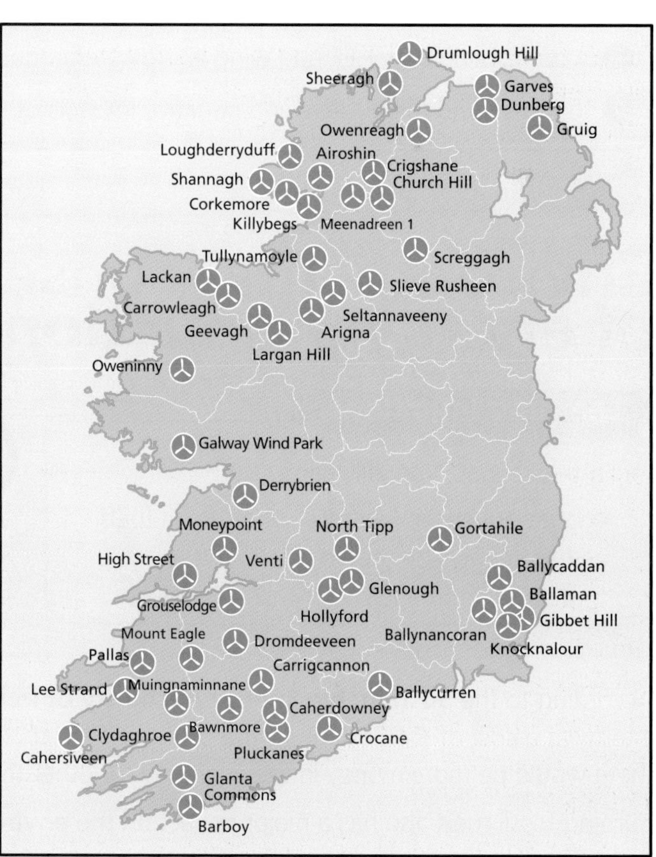

Figure 5.26 *Some of Ireland's wind farms*

Go to Chapter 16, page 299, to learn more about cut-away bogs.

Advantages of wind energy

- **Clean** energy source that is sustainable.
- Cuts **cost** of energy as it reduces our need to import energy sources.
- Creates **employment** in rural areas both in construction and maintenance of the wind farms.

Disadvantages of wind energy

- Wind is **unreliable** from day to day.
- Wind farms are very **expensive** to build.
- Noise and **visual pollution** can impact local residents and lead to planning objections.
- Wind farms can be hazardous for local **wildlife** (e.g. birds).
- Building wind farms in cut-away bogs and increased human activity can lead to **mass movement**. For example, the building of a wind farm contributed to the bog burst that occurred in Derrybrien, Co. Galway, in 2003.

PORTFOLIO ACTIVITY 5.1

Go to page 20 of your Portfolio to write a report on a wind farm.

(i) Name Ireland's first HEP station.

(ii) What percentage of Ireland's electricity comes from the production of wind energy?

(iii) List and explain two positives of the production of HEP.

(iv) List and explain two negatives of the production of wind energy.

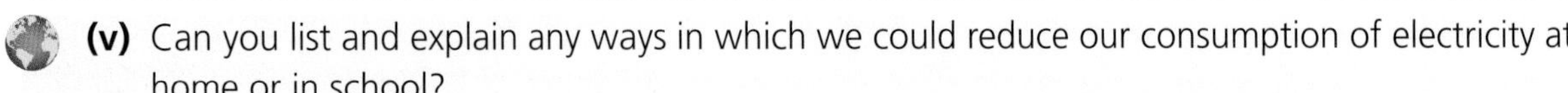

(v) Can you list and explain any ways in which we could reduce our consumption of electricity at home or in school?

- I can explain how HEP and wind energy are produced in Ireland.
- I understand the positive and negative impacts of HEP and wind energy.

Environmental consequences of energy production

Learning Intentions

In this section, you will learn:

- that our continued reliance on fossil fuels has impacts on the economy, the environment and society as a whole.

Global warming
Greenhouse gases
Acid rain
Sulfur dioxide
Nitrogen oxide
pH value
Smog

According to the **Sustainable Energy Authority of Ireland**, in 2015 we **imported** 88 per cent of our energy at a cost of €4.6 billion to the country. If we could reduce our **dependency** on imported energy, there would be more money in the economy for other things.

Burning fossil fuels also has a major impact on the **environment**, both on a local level and on a global scale. The three main impacts of fossil fuel use are:

1. Global warming
2. Acid rain
3. Smog

Global warming

The Earth's **temperature** is gradually rising every year. Since 2000 we have experienced one record-breaking hottest year after another. Although global warming has been happening for hundreds of years, scientists believe that it has got faster since the **Industrial Revolution** in the 1700s. This is because we have been burning more and more **fossil fuels** to produce the energy needed in industry and for the way we live today.

Burning fossil fuels causes an increase in **greenhouse gases**. These gases **trap** the sun's heat in the atmosphere, causing temperatures to rise. The resulting **climate change** is the biggest environmental issue of our time. You will learn more about this in Chapter 14.

Acid rain

Acid rain is formed when **sulfur dioxide** and **nitrogen oxide** are released into the atmosphere. This happens when **fossil fuels** are burned in cars, power stations and factories. The gases produced combine with the **water vapour** in the atmosphere and fall as **acid rain**.

Normal **rain** has a **pH value** of around **5.6** because it mixes with gases in the atmosphere. **Acid rain**, however, can have a **pH value** of around **4**, which means that it is **acidic**.

A-Z

pH value:
a scale of measurement of how acid or alkaline a substance is. Pure water has a pH value of 7 and is neutral. The lower the pH value, the more acidic the substance is.

Problems caused by acid rain

- Acid rain can wash **nutrients** from the soil, which stops crops from growing. This means farmers have to use more **fertilisers**.
- Acid rain can wipe out **fish stocks** in lakes, because fish cannot reproduce if the water in the lake is too acidic.
- **Forests** become vulnerable to **disease** and many trees can die because of the damage done to the soil by acid rain. The Black Forest in Germany is one area where large stretches of forest have been affected by acid rain.
- **Cities** can be damaged as the chemicals in acid rain attack old buildings and **weather** (wear away) the stone.

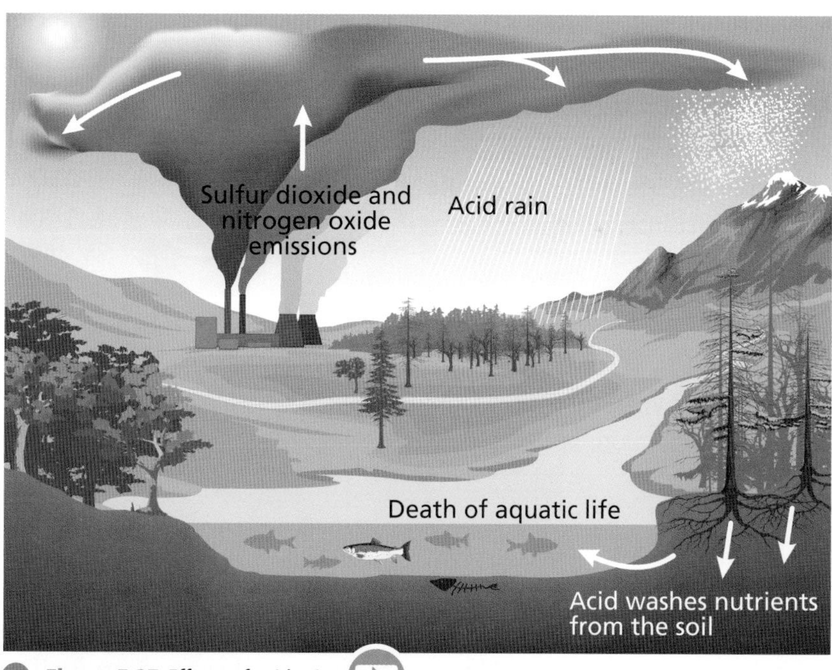

Figure 5.27 *Effects of acid rain*

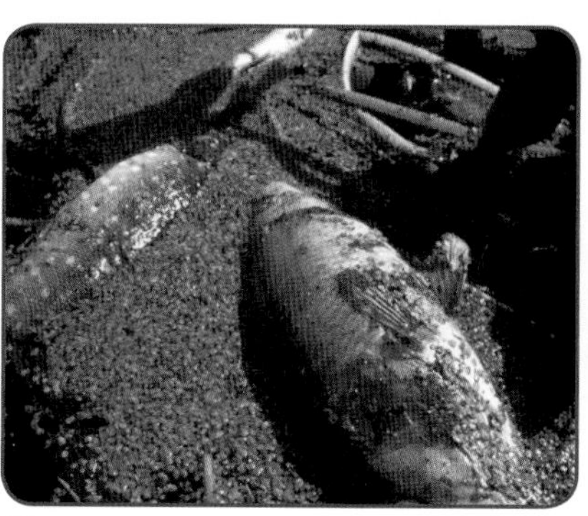

Figure 5.28 *Acid rain can kill fish stocks*

Figure 5.29 *The effects of acid rain on trees in Germany*

Figure 5.30 *Acid weathers stone*

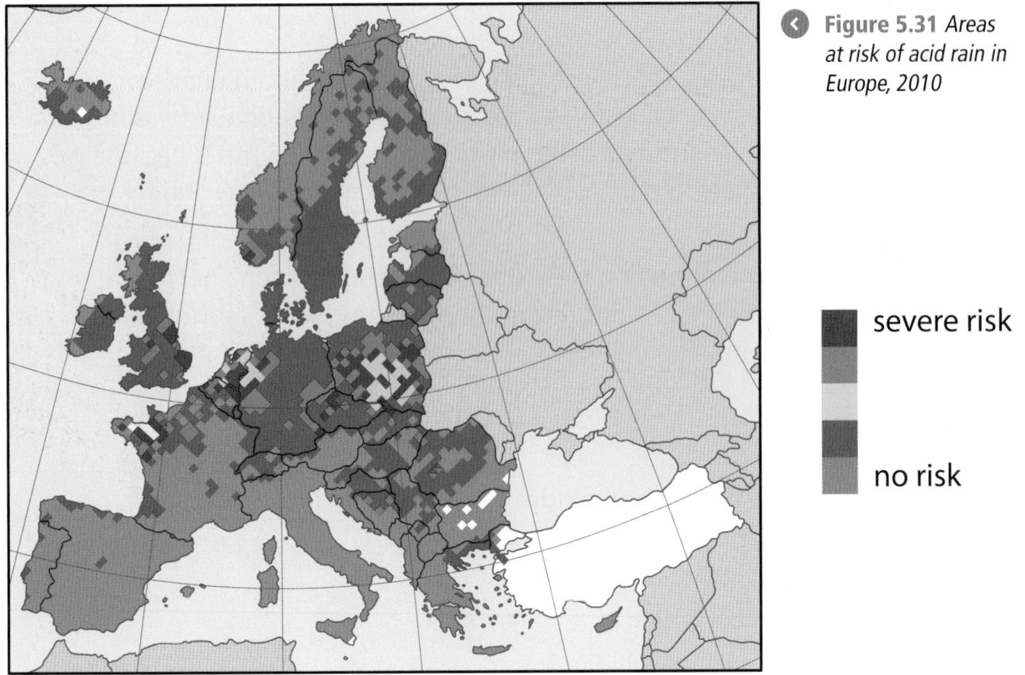

Figure 5.31 *Areas at risk of acid rain in Europe, 2010*

Solutions to acid rain

If we want to **reduce** the amount of harmful chemicals going into the atmosphere, we need to do the following:

- Use more renewable and **clean energy** sources such as **solar** and **wind** power.
- Use **natural gas** instead of coal in power stations because it is a **cleaner** fuel.
- Use **filters** on coal and oil power stations to **reduce** sulfur dioxide **emissions**.
- **Tax cars** with high emissions or develop cleaner technology for cars.
- Encourage people to use **public transport** instead of their cars.

DID YOU KNOW? There are over two million cars in Ireland. All new cars must be electric or hybrid by 2030.

Discuss what you and your classmates could do to encourage people to change their behaviour and reduce air pollution, both locally and nationally.

Fighting acid rain

These measures work. Acid rain was once a big problem in **Europe** and **North America** but in the 1980s and 1990s measures were brought in to replace coal with **natural gas** in power stations, and to **reduce emissions** of sulfur dioxide. Since then, there has been a big **reduction** in the production of acid rain. It is no longer a major problem in these areas.

However, in **Asia**, and especially **China**, where over half of the world's coal is burned each year, acid rain has become a **major environmental problem**.

Smog

Smoke from burning fossil fuels causes **air pollution**. When these gases mix with sunlight and its heat, **smog** is formed. Because it looks like **fog** and is caused by **smoke**, it is called **smog**.

Smog was common during the last century in **industrial areas** because the main form of energy came from burning coal. In 1952 the smog was so bad in **London** that roads, railway lines and airports were closed. It caused 4,000 **deaths**.

It remains a familiar sight in **cities** today, especially in the densely populated and economically booming cities of **China** and **India**.

Figure 5.32 *Smog in Beijing, China*

ACTIVITY

Watch this video: https://educateplus.ie/go/beijing-smog. It shows smog descending on the city of Beijing. How could this affect the people who live and work there?

PORTFOLIO ACTIVITY 5.2

Go to page 21 of your Portfolio to create an Energy Saving Tips poster for your school.

 **(i)** List two impacts of burning fossil fuels.

 **(ii)** List and explain two ways to reduce the amount of harmful chemicals that go into the atmosphere.

 **(iii)** Describe two impacts of acid rain and two ways in which it can be prevented.

- I understand how our reliance on fossil fuels impacts the economy, environment and society.
- I can explain global warming, acid rain and smog.

REVISION

____________________ ____________________ are things provided by nature which are useful to people. ____________________ energy resources can be used repeatedly.

_______-____________________ energy resources are resources that can only be used once. Fossil fuels such as ____________________, ____________________, ____________________ and ____________________ are all examples of non-renewable energy resources. There are many different types of renewable energy sources such as ____________________, ____________________, ____________________, ____________________ and ____________________. Hydroelectric power is the creation of electricity by using the ____________________ of falling water. The force of the wind can be used to turn turbines that produce electricity. Solar energy is created using ____________________ and ____________________ from the sun's rays. It is the ____________________ renewable energy source in the world. Geothermal energy can be exploited in areas where there is ____________________ activity.

Burning fossil fuels also has a major impact on the ____________________. The three main impacts of fossil fuel use are global warming, ____________________ ____________________ and ____________________.

Questions & Answers

Sample Question

Why should Ireland and its government invest in renewable energy?

Sample Answer

Ireland should firstly invest in renewable energy because it is good for the environment. As this energy source is clean and does not release CO_2 into the atmosphere this is a huge positive for the environment and helps in the reduction of smog, acid rain and the greenhouse gases that cause global warming.

Secondly, Ireland should invest in renewable energy because it will reduce the cost of buying imported sources of energy such as coal, gas and especially oil. Renewable energy is a much cheaper type of energy as it is in constant supply and it doesn't have to be imported.

Also we should invest in renewable energy because it is sustainable for future generations. This means that future generations will also be able to benefit from these energy sources as they will not run out.

Short Questions

1. Examine the pie chart showing home energy usage in Ireland in 2013.

   Indicate which three statements below are correct by ticking the correct box.

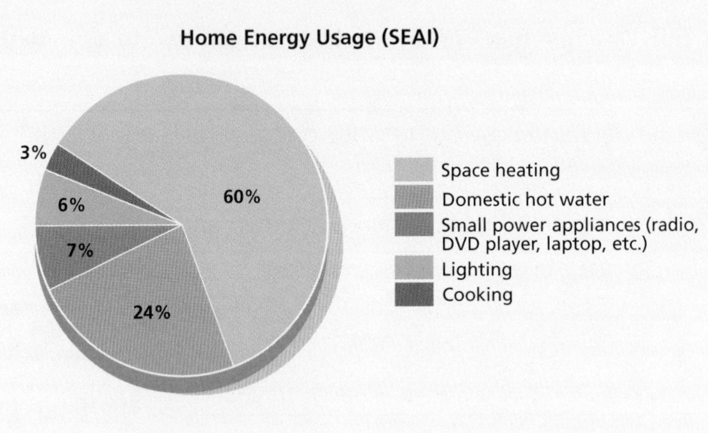

   A Small power appliances accounted for 31% of home energy usage.

   B Lighting and cooking combined accounted for 9% of home energy usage.

   C The percentage usage for small power appliances was greater than the percentage usage for domestic hot water.

   D Space heating accounted for the greatest percentage of home energy use.

   E Domestic hot water accounted for nearly a quarter of home energy use.

   A, B, C ☐ A, C, E ☐ B, C, D ☐ B, D, E ☐

2. The photograph shows a wind farm in Spain.

   Name three other types of renewable energy.

   (i) ______________________

   (ii) ______________________

   (iii) ______________________

3. Examine the map on the right showing areas at risk of acid rain and circle the correct option for each of the following statements.
   (i) The United Kingdom is an area at high risk of acid rain.
   True / False
   (ii) There is no risk of acid rain in Poland.
   True / False
   (iii) Sulfur dioxide is one of the causes of acid rain.
   True / False

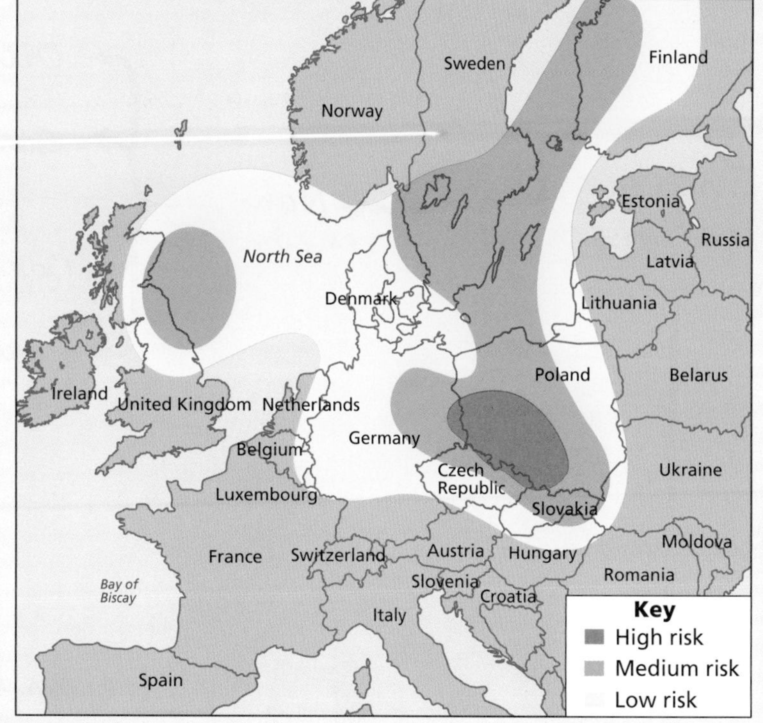

4. Examine the pie chart below showing what sources are used to generate electricity in Ireland.
   (i) What percentage of electricity was generated from coal?
   (ii) What percentage of electricity was generated from natural gas?
   (iii) What percentages of electricity was generated from renewables?
   (iv) What was the percentage difference between electricity being generated by peat and that by coal?
   (v) What was the total percentage of electricity generated by fossil fuels?

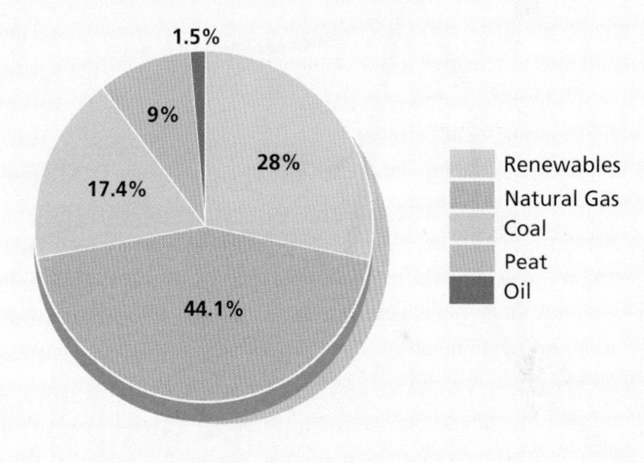

Long Questions

1. What is the benefit of sustainable exploitation for people?
2. Name and describe **one** advantage and **one** disadvantage of oil as an important natural resource?
3. In relation to a case study you have looked at on non-renewable energy sources, explain **two** positive and two negative socio-economic impacts of that project on the local environment and community.
4. **(i)** Name **one** example of renewable energy.
   (ii) Name any **two** physical (natural) factors that are required for the generation of energy using the renewable energy source named in (i) above.
   (iii) Explain **one** advantage of renewable energy.
5. In relation to a renewable energy source in Ireland, describe **two** positives and **two** negatives of that production on the local area.
6. **(i)** Explain **two** effects of acid rain.
   (ii) Describe **two** ways of reducing acid rain.

Visual Summary

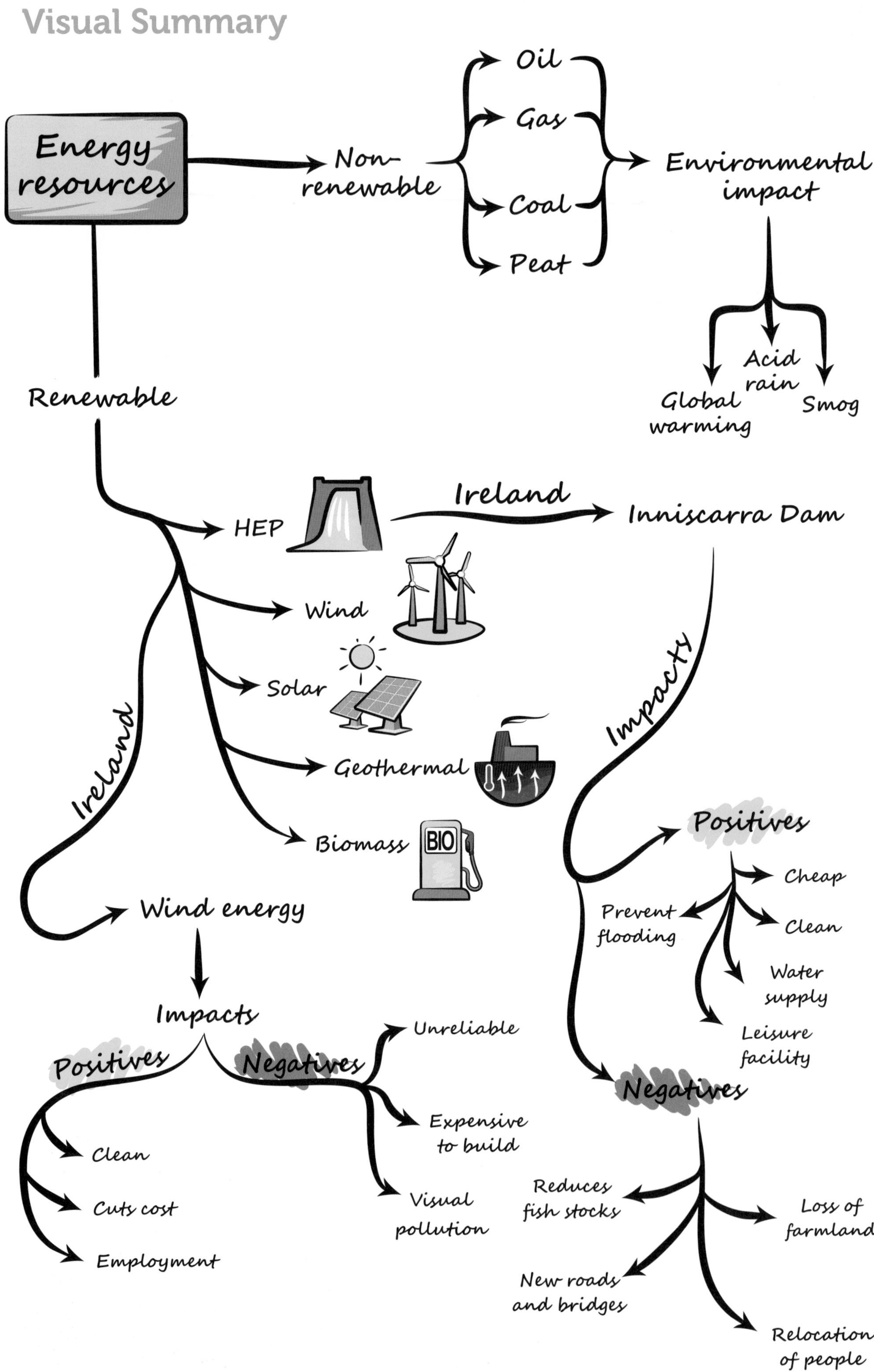

6 Weathering and Mass Movement: The changing face of the Earth

In this chapter, you will learn:

- how to define weathering and erosion
- how the landscape is shaped by different processes of weathering
- how broken-down rocks are moved down slopes by gravity
- how human activity can influence mass movement.

ICE-BREAKER ACTIVITY

Discuss the following questions with your classmates:

1. Can you think of different ways the weather might break down rocks?
2. Can you think of different ways humans and animals might break down rocks?
3. From what you learned about rocks in Chapter 3, can you name an area in Ireland where weathering occurs?

Weathering and erosion

Learning Intentions

In this section, you will learn:

- the difference between weathering and erosion
- about mechanical weathering and chemical weathering.

Denudation	Fluctuating
Weathering	Scree
Mechanical	Carbonation
Chemical	Carbonic acid
Erosion	Calcium carbonate
Freeze-thaw action	

The rocks and soil of the Earth's crust are constantly being worn down by processes known as **denudation**. The two main processes of denudation are **weathering** and **erosion**.

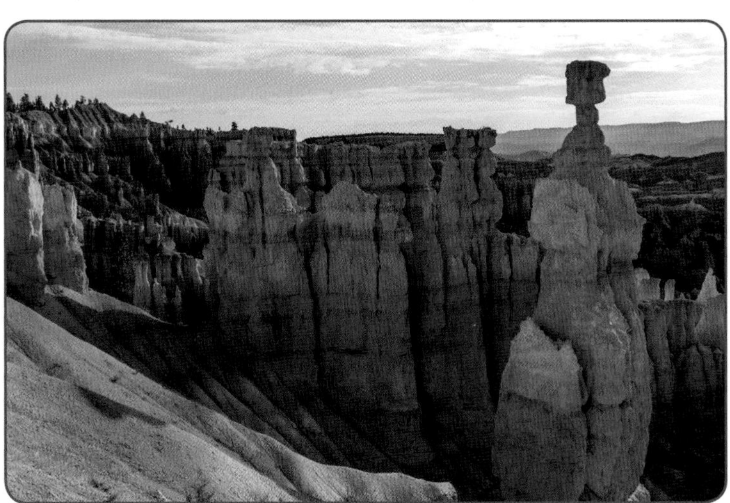

Figure 6.1 *Weathered rock formations in Utah, USA*

Weathering

Weathering is the **breaking down** of rocks and soil that are exposed to the **weather**. The broken-down material does not move from the place where the weathering occurred. There are two types of weathering:

- **Mechanical** weathering
- **Chemical** weathering

Erosion

Erosion is the **breaking down** of rocks and soil and the **transportation** of the eroded material. Erosion is caused by:

- Moving **water** (rivers/seas): see Chapters 9 and 10
- Moving **ice** (glaciers): see Chapter 11
- Moving **air** (wind): see Chapter 13

Mechanical weathering

Mechanical weathering breaks up rocks into smaller pieces by putting **pressure** on the rock. **Freeze-thaw action** is an example of mechanical weathering.

Freeze-thaw action

Freeze-thaw action occurs high up in mountainous areas where there is a lot of **precipitation** (rain, sleet or snow) and the temperatures regularly rise above and fall below **freezing point** (0 °C). Temperatures that repeatedly rise and fall are called **fluctuating temperatures**.

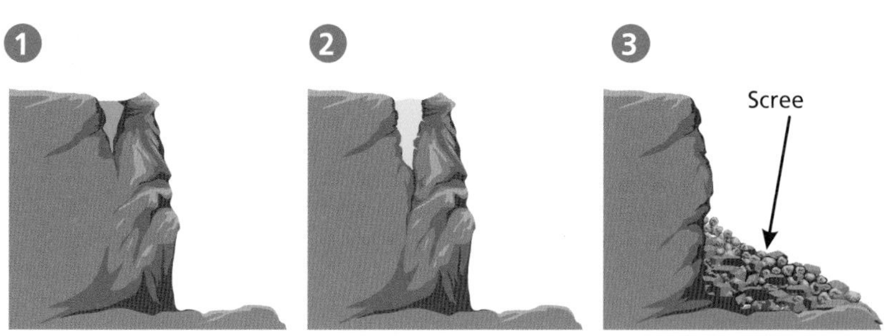

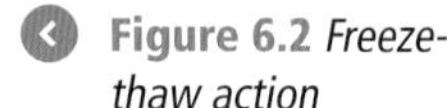
Figure 6.2 *Freeze-thaw action*

1. During the day, **water** seeps into cracks in the rock.
2. At night, **temperatures fall** below freezing point. The water in the cracks **freezes** and **expands** by 9 per cent, putting **pressure** on the rock.
3. This process continues over time, widening the cracks and joints in the rock, causing it to **weaken**, and eventually pieces break off. The broken-down rock is known as **scree**. Scree often builds up at the base of a slope.

Example: Freeze-thaw action occurs in upland areas like **Croagh Patrick** in Co. Mayo. Temperatures here frequently rise above and fall below freezing point.

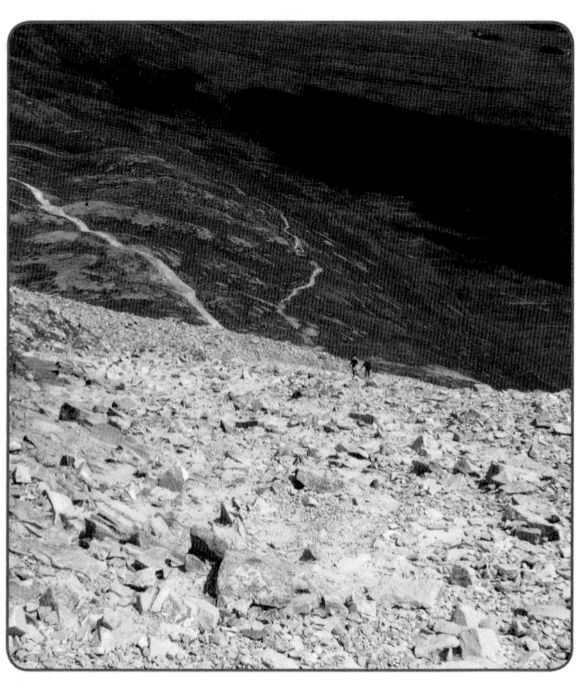

Figure 6.3 *Scree on Croagh Patrick*

Chemical weathering

Chemical weathering is when rocks are **dissolved** because of a **chemical reaction**. **Carbonation** is an example of chemical weathering.

Carbonation

- The atmosphere contains a gas called **carbon dioxide** (CO_2).
- **Rainwater** (H_2O) mixes with the carbon dioxide (CO_2) to form a weak **carbonic acid** (H_2CO_3).
- This weak carbonic acid has a huge effect on **limestone** rock. This is because limestone contains 80 per cent **calcium carbonate**.
- The weak carbonic acid reacts with the calcium carbonate in the limestone and **dissolves** it.
- Limestone is a **permeable** rock, so rainwater can pass right down through the rock.

In the next section we will look at how **carbonation** has created a unique landscape in the **Burren**, a limestone region in Co. Clare.

Figure 6.4 *The effects of weathering on a gravestone*

ACTIVITY

How is weathering affecting the rock in Figures 6.4 and 6.5? Discuss in pairs, then compare your ideas with the rest of the class.

Figure 6.5 *The Burren*

(i) Name two common causes of erosion.

(ii) Name two types of weathering.

(iii) Where does freeze-thaw action commonly occur?

(iv) How does the temperature influence freeze-thaw action?

(v) Where in Ireland is there evidence of freeze-thaw action?

(vi) Explain how carbonation occurs?

(vii) Why does freeze-thaw action not usually occur in hot climates?

- I can explain the difference between weathering and erosion.  
- I can explain processes of mechanical weathering and chemical weathering.  

Carbonation and karst landscapes

Learning Intentions

In this section, you will learn:

- where carbonation occurs in Ireland and how it has created a unique landscape
- how surface and underground features form in a karst landscape
- the positive and negative impacts of tourism in a karst landscape.

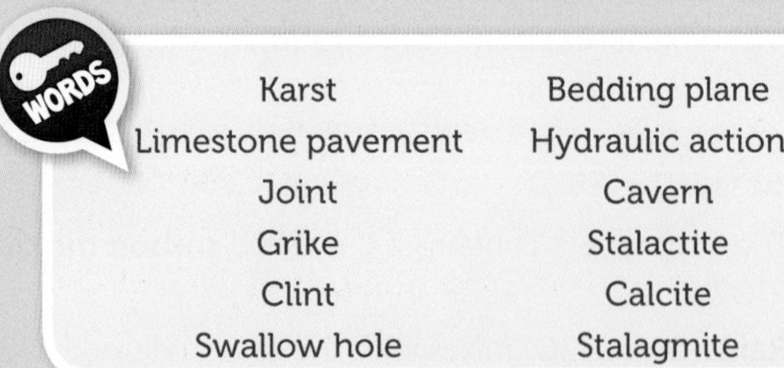

KEY WORDS
Karst
Limestone pavement
Joint
Grike
Clint
Swallow hole
Bedding plane
Hydraulic action
Cavern
Stalactite
Calcite
Stalagmite

Carbonation occurs in areas where bare limestone rock is **exposed** to the weather. These areas are known as **karst landscapes**.

An example of a karst landscape in Ireland is the **Burren in Co. Clare**. The soil was removed from the Burren by **ice-sheets** during the last ice age. This left the bare limestone rock exposed. **Carbonation** has created a unique landscape in the region. We will now look at the **features** that have formed both on the **surface** and **underground** because of carbonation.

Figure 6.6 *A view of the Burren, Co. Clare*

DID YOU KNOW? Karst landscapes are named after a limestone region called Karst in Slovenia.

Surface features

Limestone pavement

The surface of a karst landscape is called a **limestone pavement**. This is how a limestone pavement is formed:

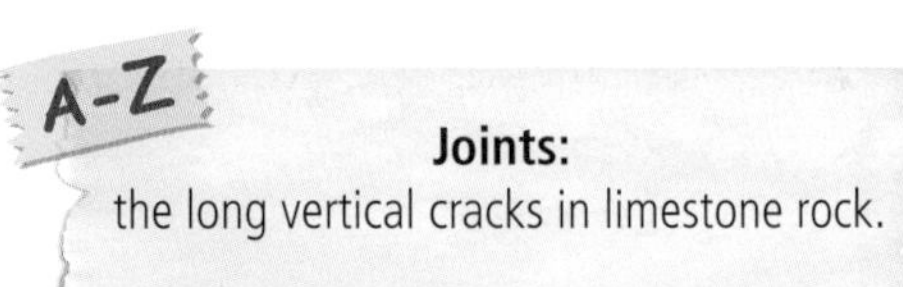

A-Z
Joints:
the long vertical cracks in limestone rock.

- **Rainwater** falls onto the exposed limestone and passes through **vertical joints** or cracks in the limestone.
- **Carbonation** makes the joints wider by dissolving the calcium carbonate in the limestone until they then look like grooves or gaps in the limestone. These grooves or gaps are called **grikes**.
- The blocks left in between the grikes are called **clints**.

Figure 6.7 *Limestone pavement in the Burren, Co. Clare*

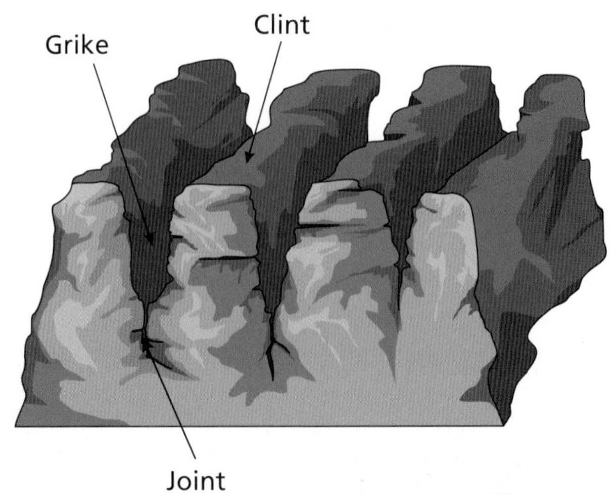

Figure 6.8 *Features of a limestone pavement* 

Swallow hole

Rivers that flow over a limestone surface can disappear underground through a **swallow hole**. This is how a swallow hole is formed:

- As the river flows over limestone, the water widens the **joints** in the rock through **carbonation**.
- Eventually the river disappears from the surface and begins to flow **underground** along the **bedding planes**.
- Carbonation and the physical force of the moving water, called **hydraulic action**, enlarge the joints and bedding planes.
- The place where the river disappears underground is called a **swallow hole**.
- The river continues to flow underground, helping to form underground karst features such as **passages** and **caves**.

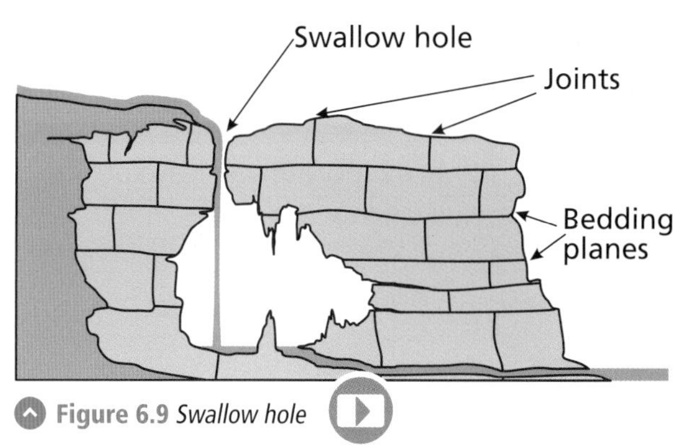

Figure 6.9 *Swallow hole*

A-Z

Bedding planes: the horizontal spaces between the layers or strata in limestone rock.

Swallow holes vary in size depending how large or small the river is. **Pollnagollum** swallow hole in the Burren is over six metres wide and 16 metres deep.

Underground features

Caves and caverns

As rivers flow underground through swallow holes they **enlarge** the passages through which they flow.

DID YOU KNOW? A cavern is an underground cave. If the hollow or the opening is on the surface it's a cave, if it's underground it's a cavern. So, a cavern is a cave, but a cave isn't always a cavern!

- This occurs by the processes of **carbonation** and **hydraulic action**, the physical force of the moving water.
- These processes can widen the spaces underground to create **caves** and **caverns**, such as the **Aillwee Caves** in the Burren, Co. Clare.

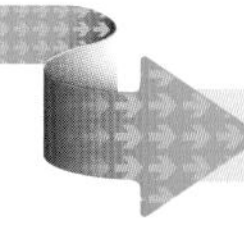

You will learn more about **hydraulic action** in Chapter 9.

Figure 6.10 *Crag Cave in Castleisland, Co. Kerry has many examples of stalactites, stalgmites and pillars*

Stalactites

As the water seeps through the rock, it carries **dissolved limestone** with it. Some of this water eventually reaches the **roof** of a cave or a cavern below ground.

- The drops slowly **evaporate** and leave behind small **deposits** of pure limestone called **calcite**.
- Gradually the calcite builds up to form icicle-like shapes called **stalactites**, which hang from the roof.

Stalagmites

Drops of water may also seep through the rock and fall on the **ground**.

- This water evaporates and leaves **deposits of calcite** on the floor of the cave directly **below** the stalactites.
- The calcite builds up, forming upside-down icicle-like shapes called **stalagmites**.

Pillars

After thousands of years a stalactite and a stalagmite can meet and join, resulting in the formation of a **pillar** or **column**.

Top Tip

Here's a little trick to help you remember which is which. The 'g' in stalagmite stands for ground and the 'c' in stalactite stands for ceiling.

Exam Toolkit

Apply this formula to help you answer long questions on physical geography in your exam.

D – E – P – E –D

Description – **E**xample – **P**rocesses – **E**xplanation – **D**iagram

Try to remember this by using a sentence that contains each first letter, for example:

Do **E**at **P**orridge **E**ach **D**ay.

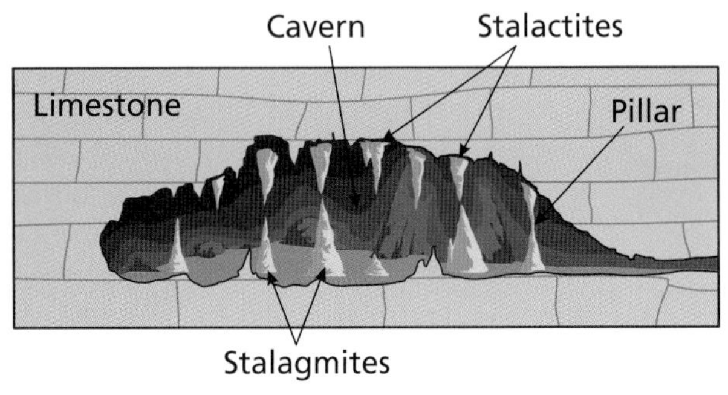

Figure 6.11 *Underground features* 

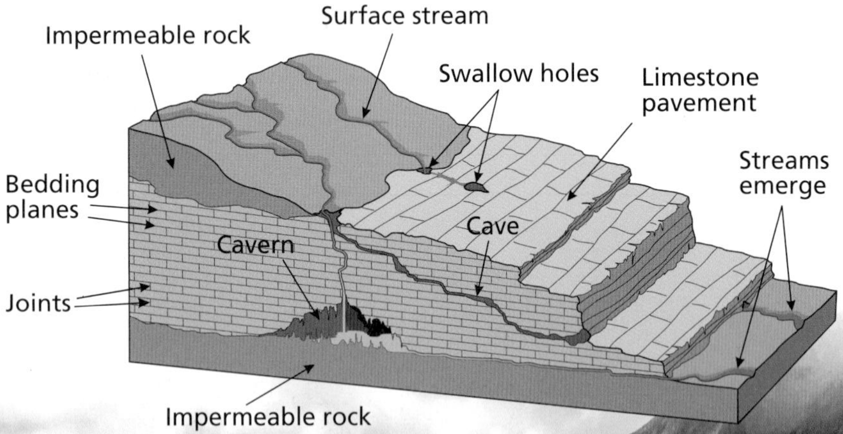

Figure 6.12 *Features of a karst landscape*

Figure 6.13 *Karst landscape in New Zealand*

CASE STUDY

A karst landscape: the Burren, Co. Clare

The limestone of the **Burren** was formed **300 million** years ago under the sea. The Burren is now a region of **exposed** limestone. As we have already seen, **chemical weathering** in the Burren has resulted in a **unique landscape** in Ireland.

The Burren is a major **tourist attraction** for many people with different interests. This provides **employment** for many people in the **tertiary sector**. We will now look at the **advantages** and **disadvantages** of tourism in the Burren:

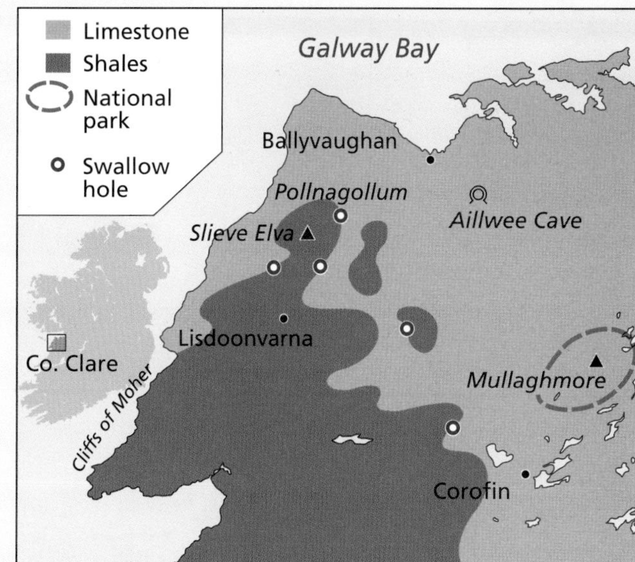

Figure 6.14 *Location of the Burren*

Advantages of tourism

- Provides employment in the area for local people
- Reduces migration from the area
- Brings income to the region and therefore improves services and infrastructure
- Creates spin-off businesses which benefit each other, e.g. restaurants and shops

Disadvantages of tourism

- Increased pollution can cause damage to the limestone
- New buildings and increased services can destroy the scenic beauty of the region
- In the Burren there was conflict over plans to build a visitor centre
- Walkers can cause damage to the rare flora (plants) and fauna (animals) of the region

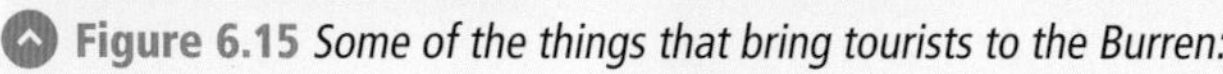

Figure 6.15 *Some of the things that bring tourists to the Burren:*

A *Wildflowers*
B *Potholing*
C *Hiking*
D *Ancient monuments*

PORTFOLIO ACTIVITY 6.1

Go to page 24 of your Portfolio and write a letter to your Principal outlining the reasons both for and against a school visit to the Burren.

The Burren on Ordnance Survey maps

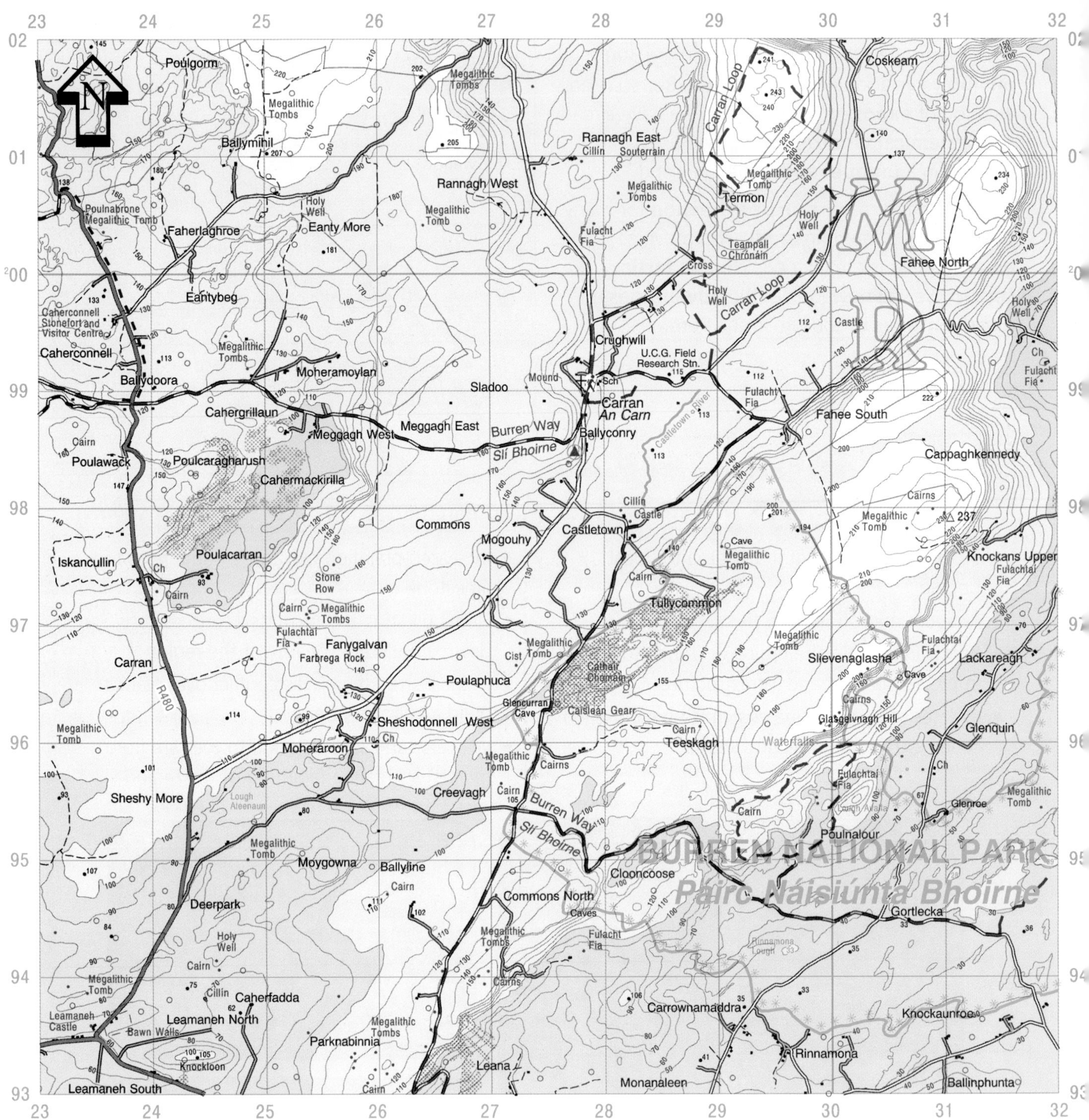

Figure 6.16 *Ordnance Survey map of the Burren*

Study the map and answer the following questions:

(a) Give the four-figure grid reference for Caherconnell Stonefort and Visitor Centre.

(b) Give the six-figure grid reference for three swallow holes. Explain why you think they are located there.

(c) Explain, with reference to the map, why you think this area is an attractive place for tourists to visit.

(d) Can you see any negative impacts that tourism may have on the Burren? Look at the map and describe one disadvantage of tourism in the area.

(i) Name two surface features in karst areas.
(ii) Name two underground features in karst areas.
(iii) Draw a labelled diagram of one surface feature in a karst area and explain how it was formed.
(iv) Draw a labelled diagram of one underground feature in a karst area and explain how it was formed.
(v) Explain two positive and two negative impacts of tourism in the Burren, Co. Clare.
(vi) If limestone was formed under the sea 300 million years ago, can you explain how the Burren is now above the level of the sea?

- I can name and explain the formation of two surface features in a karst area
- I can name and explain the formation of two underground features in a karst area.
- I can explain the link between this physical landscape and tourism.
- I can identify the links between tourism and the physical landscape on OS maps.

Mass movement

Learning Intentions

In this section, you will learn:

- about the factors that affect mass movement
- about the various types of mass movement
- about the impact of mass movement on people.

Regolith
Gradient
Soil creep
Terracette
Bog burst
Saturated
Mudflow
Lahar
Avalanche

Weathering and erosion produce loose material called **regolith**. **Mass movement** is when regolith moves down a slope due to gravity.

Factors that affect mass movement

Gradient

Gradient refers to the **steepness** of the slope. The steeper the slope, the faster the movement of the regolith.

Water content

Water makes regolith **heavier**. Heavier regolith moves downslope faster. Water can also act as a **lubricant**. This makes the movement of the regolith easier. Heavy rain, therefore, can speed up mass movement.

Human activity

People sometimes **dig** into slopes in upland areas during **construction** (of wind turbines and roads, for example) and when **quarrying** or **mining**. Digging into the slope makes the slope **steeper** and more **unstable**. Regolith moves down steep slopes quickly.

Vegetation

Grass and **shrubs** protect the soil from weathering and erosion. The **roots** of plants and trees bind the soil together. They keep it stable and help to **prevent** mass movement.

Animals

Burrowing animals can loosen the soil, making it **unstable**. **Overgrazing** by cattle and sheep removes the vegetation cover **exposing** the soil. This too can make the slope unstable and lead to mass movement.

Types of mass movement

Mass movement is classified by the **speed** at which it occurs. There are **slow** (soil creep) and **fast** (bog bursts, mudflows, landslides and avalanches) mass movements.

Soil creep

Soil creep is the **movement of soil down a slope under the influence of gravity**. It is the **slowest** form of mass movement. It becomes evident only when you examine the landscape closely:

Trees grow **at an angle**, with the base of the tree turned downslope.

As the soil moves downslope, a series of steps called **terracettes** can form, giving the surface a wrinkled appearance.

Fences **bend** and telegraph poles **tilt** downhill.

Walls **crack** and break when soil piles up behind them.

Figure 6.17 *Evidence of soil creep*

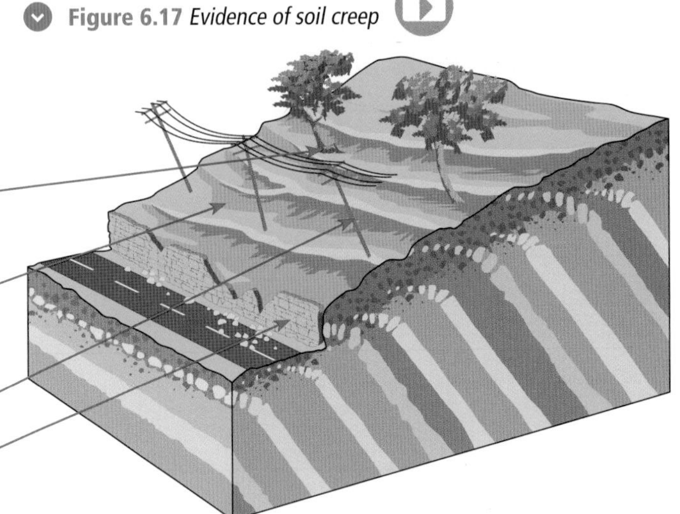

Bog bursts

A bog burst, or bog slide, occurs when a **mass of bog or peat moves down a slope** after a period of **heavy rainfall**. The peat becomes so **saturated** that water can no longer soak downwards. That makes it unstable, so the peat moves downslope and can block roads, knock down trees, damage roads and buildings, and pollute lakes and rivers.

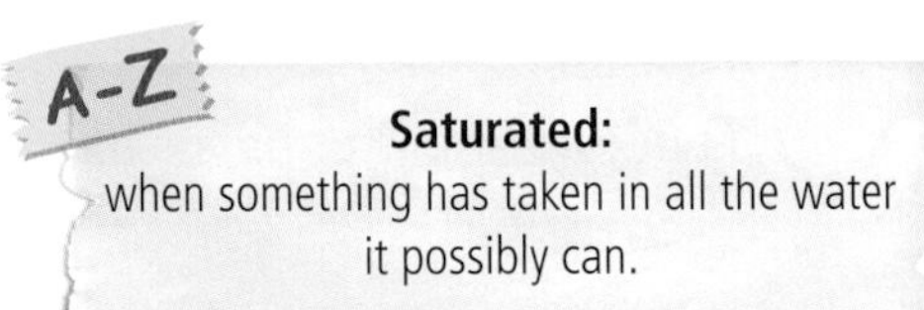

A-Z

Saturated: when something has taken in all the water it possibly can.

ACTIVITY

Watch the video clip 'The Politics of Peat' on YouTube. Write a report on what happened in Derrybrien, Co. Galway in 2003.

Figure 6.18 *A bog burst*

Mudflows

Mudflows occur when **soil and regolith become saturated** with water after periods of **heavy rainfall** and move downslope like a **river of mud**. They are one of the **fastest** forms of mass movement and can reach speeds of over **100 kph**.

Mudflows can also occur in the **aftermath of a volcano**. In snowy regions, a volcanic eruption will cause snow and ice to melt quickly. This **meltwater** mixes with ash, soil and rock fragments to create a particularly dangerous kind of mudflow known as a **lahar**.

CASE STUDY

Lahar: Nevado del Ruiz in Colombia

On the night of 13 November 1985, the volcano of **Nevado del Ruiz** in the **Andes** mountains erupted. The volcano had been **dormant** for 140 years. The hot ash and rock that **erupted** from the volcano melted the snow and ice on the mountain, creating **lahars**. These lahars rushed down the mountainside, picking up rock, soil and ash along the way. The lahars were up to **40 m deep** and travelled at speeds of up to 50 kph.

The town of **Armero**, located 74 km from the crater and at the foot of the mountain, lay directly in the path of a lahar. It took just two and a half hours to reach the town, and the people were not warned in time. Over 23,000 people were killed, and 85 per cent of the town was washed away, making this one of the worst volcanic disasters in history.

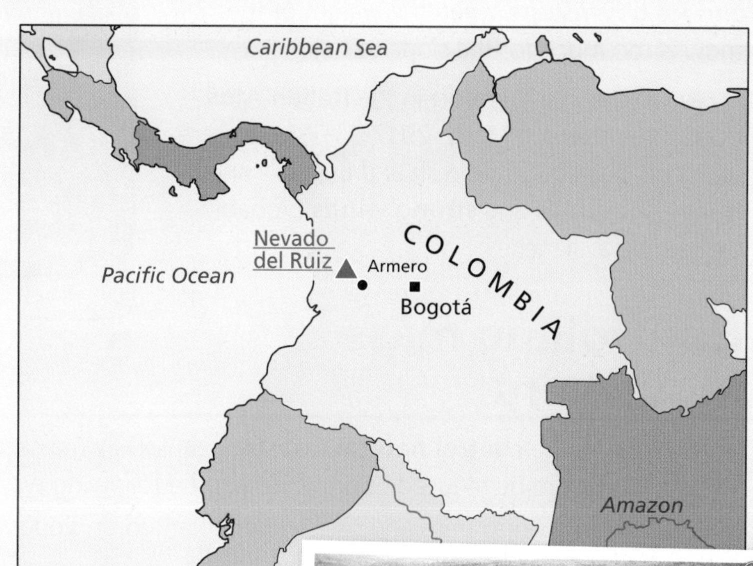

Figure 6.19 *Nevado del Ruiz, Colombia*

Figure 6.20 *The aftermath of the lahar*

Landslides

A landslide is the **rapid movement of regolith down a steep slope** that has become unstable. Causes of landslides include coastal erosion, deforestation, heavy rainfall, earthquakes and **undercutting** by road building or quarrying.

A landslide caused by **heavy rainfall** in south-west China in June 2017 buried 62 homes and more than a hundred people. Thousands of rescue workers with sniffer dogs and life-detection equipment searched in the rubble for the missing people. They also worked on unblocking the local river and roads that had been filled with material from the landslide.

The **lack of vegetation** on the hillside made the disaster much worse than it might have been.

Figure 6.21 *Some of the destruction caused by the China landslide*

DID YOU KNOW? The biggest landslide in recorded history was triggered by the eruption of Mount St Helens in 1980. Nearly 3 km^3 of rock moved downslope.

Avalanches

An avalanche is the **rapid movement of snow and ice downslope** when the weight of the snow is too much for the slope to hold.

An avalanche in a ski resort in the **Italian Alps** killed three skiers in March 2017. The skiers were skiing off-piste through fresh and unstable snow. **Heavy snowfalls** and **strong winds** probably caused the avalanche.

Figure 6.22 *The destructive power of an avalanche*

Controlling mass movement

Humans can try to **control natural disasters** caused by mass movement. These hazards can be reduced or prevented in the following ways.

- **Vegetation** such as trees and vines can be planted on slopes to stabilise them.
- **Steps** can be built into a mountainside to trap moving material.
- **Restricting overgrazing** keeps vegetation cover and stops soil creep.
- **Controlled explosions** in mountainous areas can be used to trigger small avalanches, making large, life-threatening avalanches less likely.

Figure 6.23 *Throwing explosives to control avalanches in Squaw Valley, California*

Figure 6.24 *Old tyres being used to prevent a landslide in Brazil*

PORTFOLIO ACTIVITY 6.2

Choose one type of mass movement listed above and research an example. Go to page 26 of your Portfolio and create your own Case Study.

(i) List five factors that influence mass movement.

(ii) Name two types of mass movement.

(iii) What evidence might prove that soil creep is occurring?

(iv) Give an example of a mudflow that you have studied and explain why it happened.

(v) Explain three things humans can do to try to stop mass movement from occurring.

(vi) Explain two ways that humans cause mass movement with reference to examples you have studied.

- I can list and explain the factors that affect mass movement.
- I can name and explain examples of slow and fast mass movement.
- I understand the impact of mass movement on people.
- I understand the methods used to control mass movement.

REVISION

____________________ is the breakdown of rocks and soil that are exposed on the Earth's surface. The two main types of weathering are ____________________ and ____________________. Erosion is the breakdown of rocks and the ____________________ of this material. ____________________-thaw action is a type of mechanical weathering. This happens mainly in ____________________ areas. Water gets into cracks in the rock, and freezes and ____________________ during the night, putting ____________________ on the rock. The pieces of rock then fall to the base and are known as ____________________.

____________________ is a type of chemical weathering. It occurs when rainwater mixes with ____________________ ____________________ in the atmosphere. It has a huge effect on one type of rock, known as ____________________. Surface features that are formed include limestone ____________________ and swallow ____________________. Underground features that are formed from carbonation include stalactites and ____________________.

Mass movement is the movement of loose, weathered material downhill due to ____________________. The loose material is known as ____________________. Mass movement can be either fast or ____________________. This depends on a number of factors, including gradient, water ____________________, ____________________ activity and ____________________.

Soil ____________________ is the slowest type of mass movement. Evidence of soil creep can be seen when a series of steps called ____________________ form. Bog ____________________ occur when an upland bog becomes ____________________ with water, which helps the bog to move. Mudflows occur when saturated ____________________ flows rapidly downhill. They can also result from ____________________ activity when the slopes are covered with snow. This type of mudflow is also known as a ____________________. Landslides can occur when the land is very eroded, or when new ____________________ are built. An avalanche is a type of mass movement where ____________________ moves rapidly downhill.

Questions & Answers

Sample Questions

1. **Name** the type of rock which occurs in the area shown.
2. **Describe** fully the type of weathering that takes place in the area shown.

Sample Answers

1. Limestone
2. Rainwater (H_2O) passes through the atmosphere and mixes with carbon dioxide (CO_2). It then forms a weak carbonic acid. This falls as rain and sometimes falls onto exposed limestone. This carbonic acid then dissolves the limestone because limestone is permeable and soluble and contains 80 per cent calcium carbonate. It passes through vertical joints in the rock, forming grikes and clints which create a limestone pavement. It continues on through the bedding planes and joints further down to create caves, caverns, stalactites and stalagmites.

Short Questions

1. The broken-down rock found on this upland area, Croagh Patrick, has resulted from:

Solution ☐
Mechanical weathering ☐
Carbonation ☐
[tick (✓) the correct box]

2. The photograph shows the effects of weathering on a public monument.
This is the result of:

Physical weathering ☐
Biological weathering ☐
Sunny weather ☐
Chemical weathering ☐
[tick (✓) the correct box]

3. How has the large rock shown in this photograph been cracked?

Mechanical weathering ☐
Deposition ☐
Chemical weathering ☐
Plants and animals ☐
[tick (✓) the correct box]

4. The diagram shows underground features in a karst region.
Name the **three** limestone features labelled A, B and C on the diagram.

A______________________________

B______________________________

C______________________________

Limestone features

5. The photograph shows limestone that has been weathered.

Circle the correct option in each of the statements below:

(i) This weathered limestone is called **limestone footpath / limestone pavement**.

(ii) This feature is formed by **chemical weathering / mechanical weathering**.

(iii) An example of this feature can be found in the **Burren, Co. Clare / Giant's Causeway, Co. Antrim**.

6. Circle the correct option in each of the statements below.

(i) Mudflows are one of the fastest forms of mass movement. **True / False**

(ii) Mudflows occur in dry areas. **True / False**

(iii) Gradient is very important for mass movement. **True / False**

7. The diagrams show a type of mass movement.
[tick (✓) the correct box in each of the statements below.]

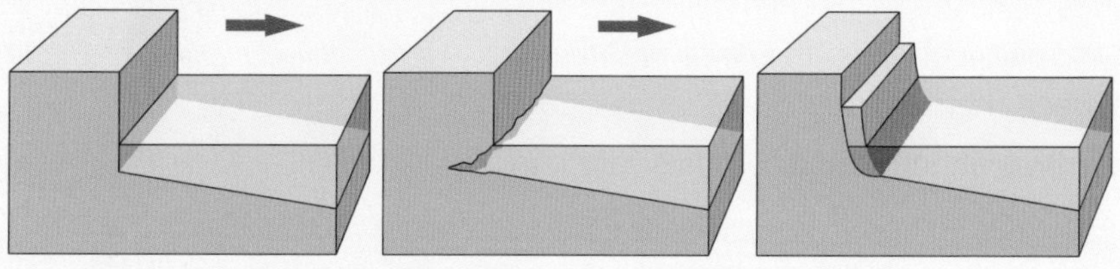

(i) The process shown is: soil creep ☐ a landslide ☐

(ii) The type of mass movement shown is: rapid ☐ slow ☐

(iii) The type of mass movement shown is most likely to occur:
at the side of a calm lake ☐ on a stormy coast ☐

8. The type of mass movement illustrated in the diagrams is:

Soil creep ☐

A mudflow ☐

A landslide ☐

A bog burst ☐ [tick (✓) the correct box]

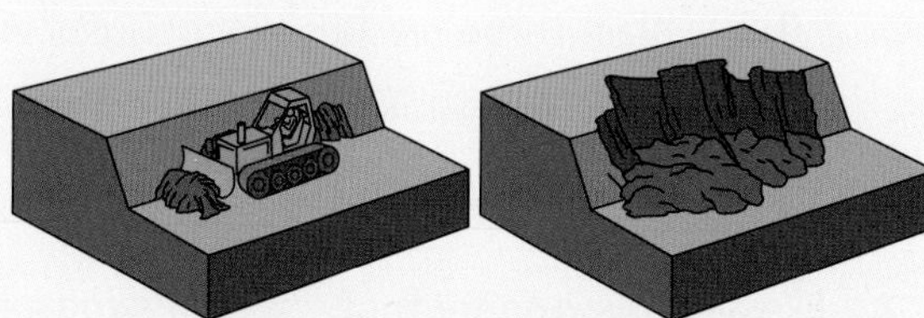

9. Examine the diagram.

Which type of mass movement does it show?

Avalanche ☐

Soil creep ☐

Bog burst ☐

Landslide ☐ [tick (✓) the correct box]

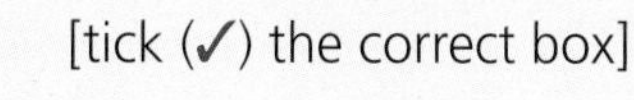

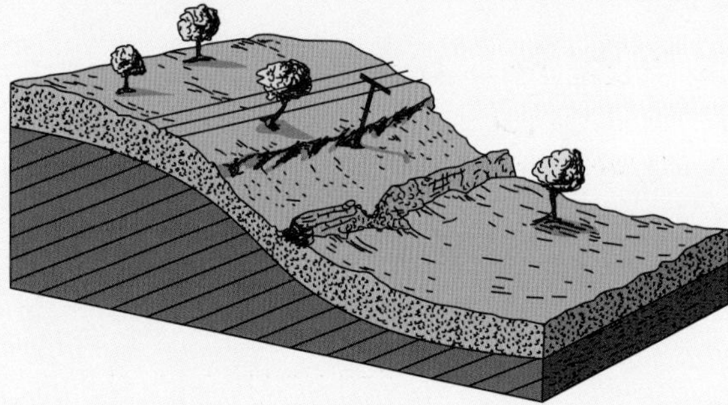

Long Questions

1. The diagrams show one type of weathering.

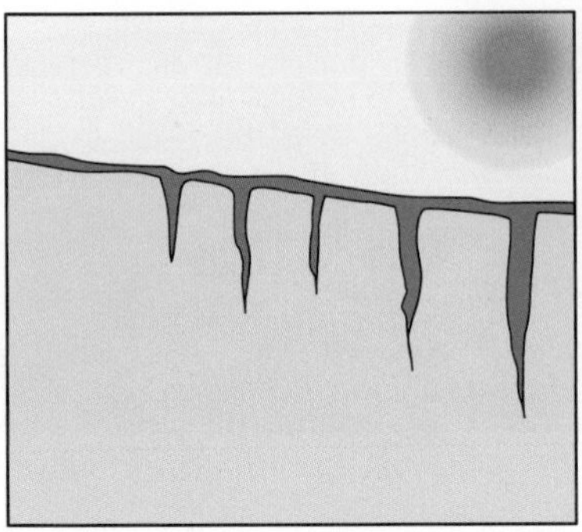
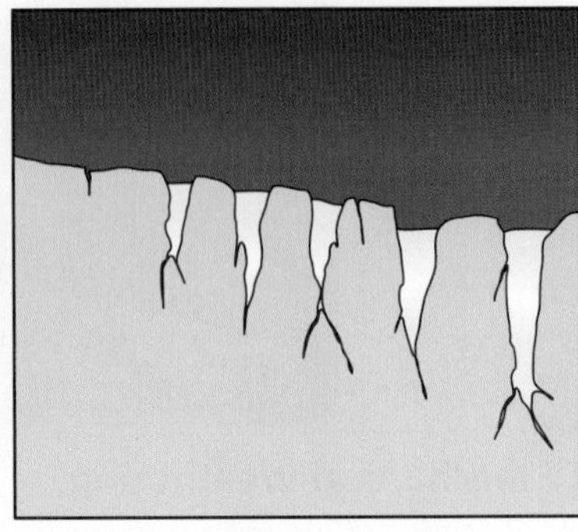
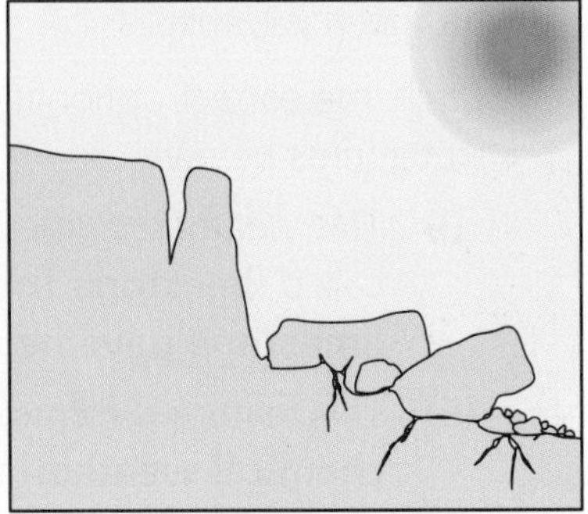

   (i) Name the type of weathering shown in the diagrams.
   (ii) Explain how this type of weathering occurs.

2. Explain why freeze-thaw action is more likely to occur on mountains rather than on lowland.

3. Explain, with the aid of a diagram, how any two karst surface features are formed.

4. **(i)** What type of rock is limestone?
   (ii) This picture shows limestone pavement.
   What is the name given to the slabs of limestone at **X**?
   What is the name given to the deep weathered gaps between them at **Y**?
   (iii) Name any **two** underground features found in the Burren.

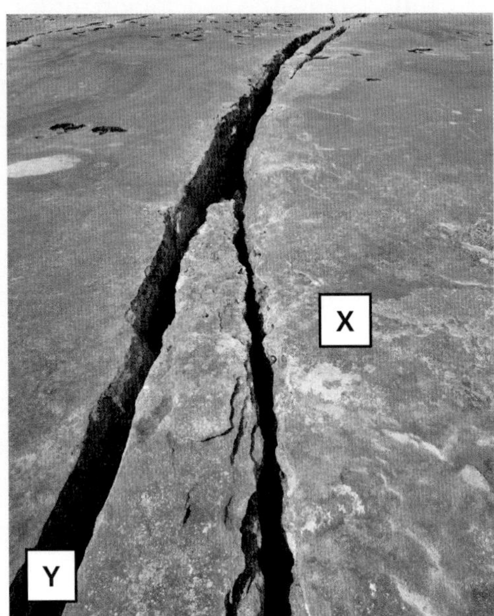

5. **(i)** Explain **three** reasons why tourists might like to visit the Burren in Co. Clare.
   (ii) Describe **one** advantage and **one** disadvantage of tourism in the area.

6. Explain how **three** factors play a role in mass movement.

7. Explain how **one** form of slow mass movement and **one** form of fast mass movement occur.

8. Give an account of a mass movement episode you have studied. Describe its causes and effects.

Visual Summary

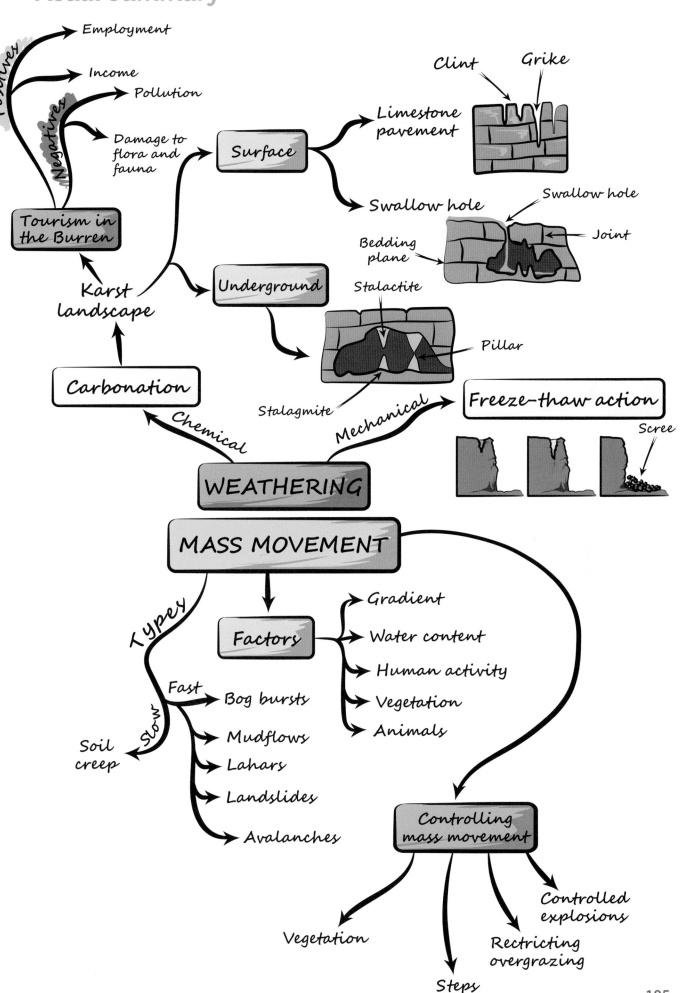

- WEATHERING
  - Chemical → Carbonation → Karst landscape
    - Surface
      - Limestone pavement (Clint, Grike)
      - Swallow hole (Swallow hole, Joint, Bedding plane)
    - Underground (Stalactite, Pillar, Stalagmite)
    - Tourism in the Burren
      - Positives: Employment, Income
      - Negatives: Pollution, Damage to flora and fauna
  - Mechanical → Freeze-thaw action (Scree)
- MASS MOVEMENT
  - Types
    - Slow: Soil creep
    - Fast: Bog bursts, Mudflows, Lahars, Landslides, Avalanches
  - Factors: Gradient, Water content, Human activity, Vegetation, Animals
  - Controlling mass movement: Vegetation, Steps, Rectricting overgrazing, Controlled explosions

Geographical Skills for Second Years:
Ordnance Survey and aerial photograph skills

In this chapter, you will learn:

- the Ordnance Survey skills you will need for Second Year
- the aerial photograph skills you will need for Second Year
- useful numeracy skills.

ICE-BREAKER ACTIVITY

Look at the map of your area on maps.scoilnet.ie, and compare it with the aerial photograph on the same site. Work in groups of four and answer the following questions:

(a) What are the advantages of Ordnance Survey maps?

(b) What are the advantages of aerial photographs?

(c) What are the disadvantages of Ordnance Survey maps?

(d) What are the disadvantages of aerial photographs?

This chapter will teach you some of the skills that you will need in your second year of Geography. Your class can dip in and out of this chapter throughout the year.

The skills you will need in Second Year are broken into two groups:

1. **Ordnance Survey map skills**
2. **Aerial photograph skills**

We will also look at numeracy skills at the end of the chapter.

Ordnance Survey maps 2

Learning Intentions

In this section, you will learn:

- how to calculate distance and area on an Ordnance Survey map
- how to identify different slope types on an Ordnance Survey map
- how to draw a cross-section of an Ordnance Survey map
- how to identify land uses on an Ordnance Survey map.

Regular area, Irregular area, Slope, Concave, Convex, Compound, Cross-section, Land use, Site, Infrastructure, Settlement

You were introduced to Ordnance Survey map skills in Chapter 1. We looked at **scale**, **grid references**, **legends**, **height**, **directions** and **sketch maps**. Go back to Chapter 1 if you want to recap on any these skills.

We are now going to look at new skills you will need to interpret Ordnance Survey maps in Second Year.

Measuring distance

We can be asked to find **distance** on an Ordnance Survey map in two different ways. We need to be able to measure the distance of a **curved line** like a road, and a **straight-line** distance between two locations. Remember that **2 cm** on the map **equals 1 km** on the ground. Whatever the distance is in **centimetres**, you must **divide by two** to get the answer in **kilometres**.

NUMERACY ACTIVITY

If a road measures 13 cm on the map, how many kilometres is that on the ground?

Straight-line method

This is when you measure a distance between two points 'as the crow flies'.

- Place a straight edge piece of paper on the map, making sure it is touching both locations. Mark each location on the paper.
- Using a ruler, measure the distance between the two points.
- Using your **scale**, convert the distance to kilometres.

Curved-line method

This may be used to measure a river.

- Place the edge of a strip of paper at the start point and along the line of the river (or road, etc.) on the map and mark it A.
- Follow the paper along the line until there is a bend in the river. Mark this point and then turn the paper to follow the river, using your pencil to keep the paper in place.
- Repeat the process until you have measured the curved line distance. Mark the end point B.
- Using a ruler, measure the distance between the two points.
- Using your **scale**, convert the distance to kilometres

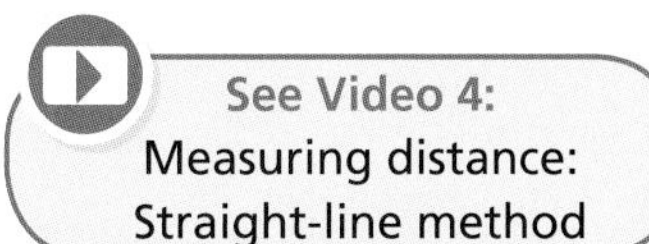

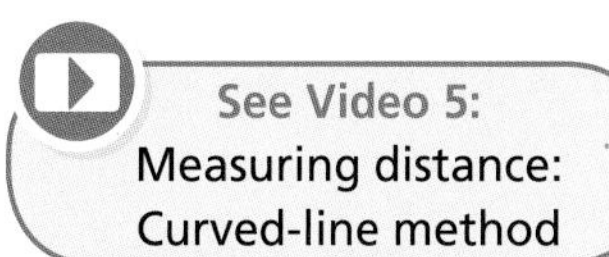

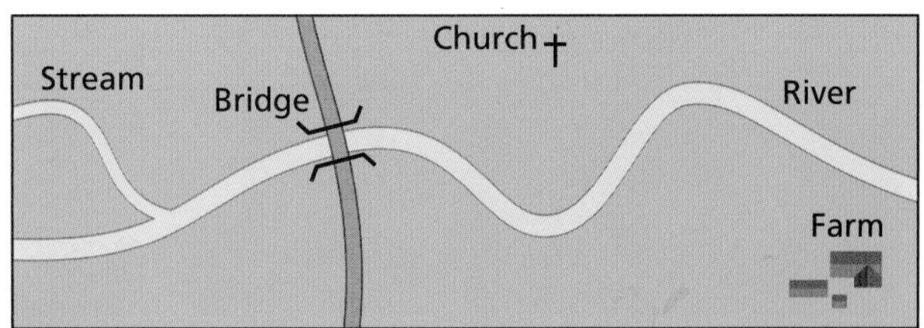

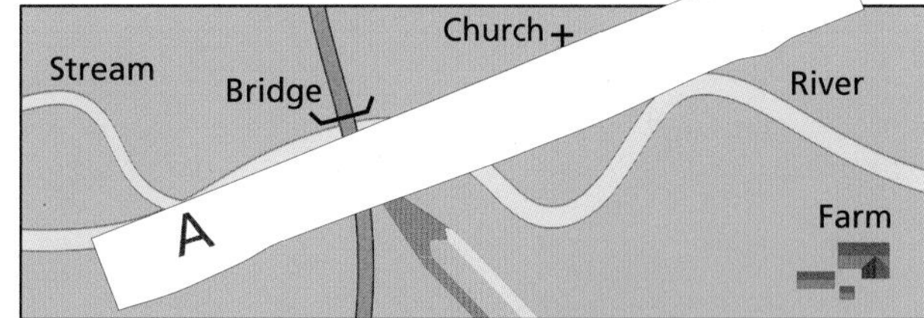

Figure 7.1 *A: We want to measure the length of the river from where the stream comes in, to as far as the farm; B: This can be done using a pencil and a piece of paper.*

ACTIVITY

Look at Figure 7.1 above. The scale is 2 cm = 1 km.

(i) Measure the distance from the bridge to where the river exits the right-hand side of the map using the straight-line method.

(ii) Measure the length of the river from the bridge to where the river exits the right-hand side of the map using the curved-line method.

Calculating area

Finding the **area** of a region or feature on a map can be done in two different ways. This depends on the **shape** of the area in question.

Top Tip

We learned in Chapter 1 that the scale on Ordnance Survey maps is 2 cm to 1 km. Every box on the grid is 1 km by 1 km. This makes **each grid box 1 km²** in area.

Regular area

This can be in the shape of a rectangle or square area on the map. We calculate the area by counting the total number of grid boxes. You can also **multiply** the number of squares across by the number of squares down. Your answer must then be converted to **km²**.

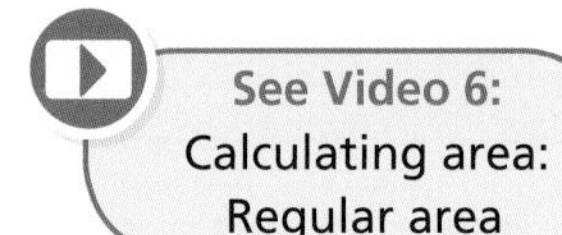

Irregular area

This is the shape of a **non-rectangle** or square area, for example a harbour or a lake. To get the area we must first count the **full boxes** that are taken up by the harbour or lake. We then count any boxes that are **half or more** covered by the harbour or lake. To finish, we **add** the two together and give the answer in **km² approx**.

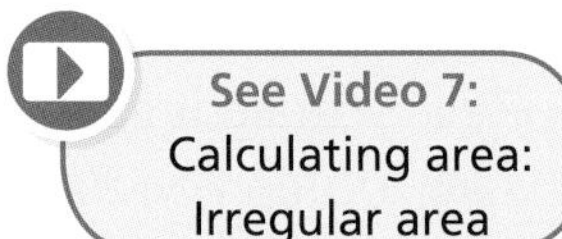

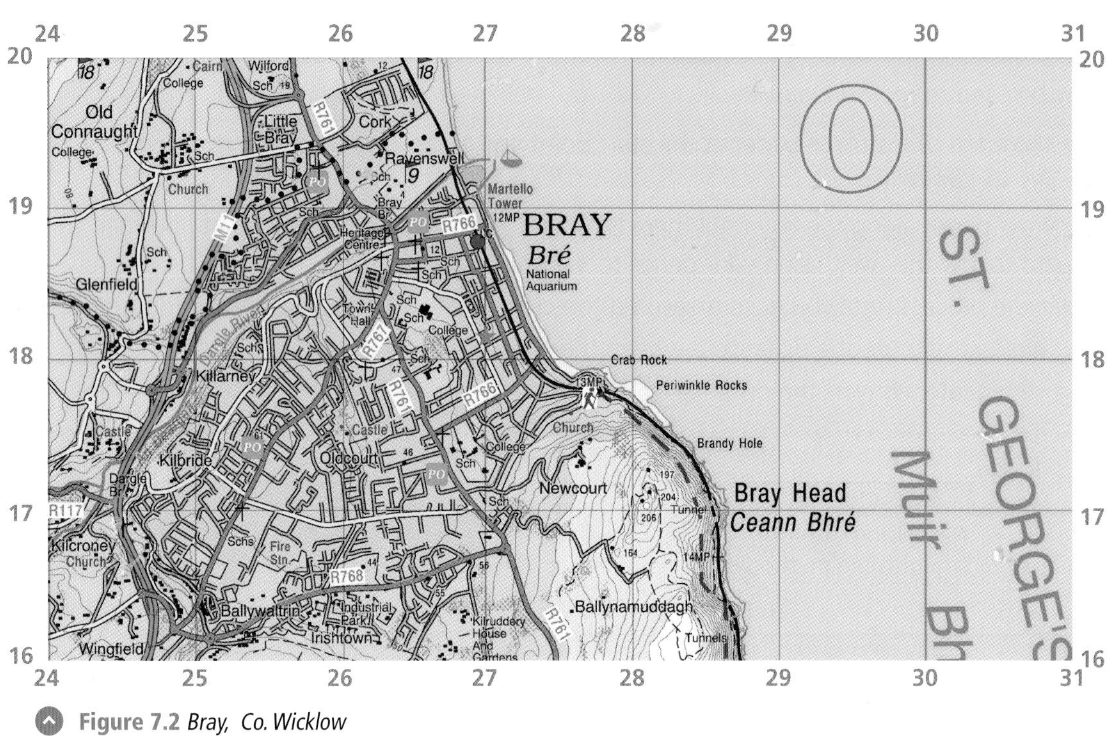

Figure 7.2 *Bray, Co. Wicklow*

NUMERACY ACTIVITY

Look at the OS map of Bray above.

(i) Can you calculate the area of the map in km²?

(ii) Calculate the area of water on the map in km².

Slope

Slopes are identified using the **contour lines** on Ordnance Survey maps. Remember that the contour lines are spaced **10 metres** apart, so the **closer** the contour lines are to each other, the **steeper** the slope. There are four types of slope: even, concave, convex and compound.

Even slope

This slope is even and the contour lines are **evenly** spaced out.

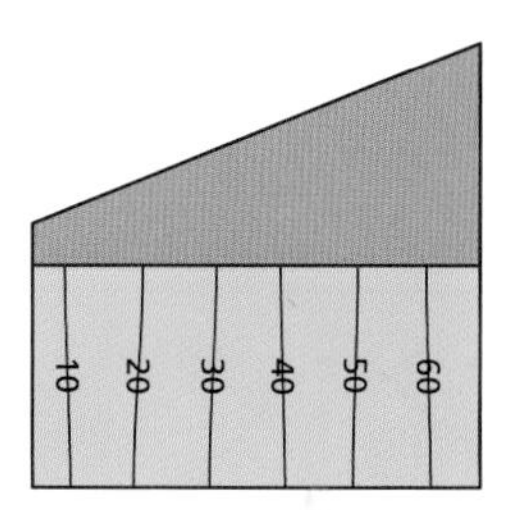

A

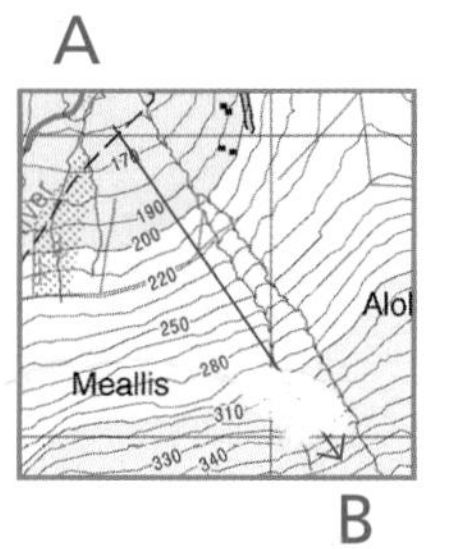

B

Concave slope

This shape of slope is shown using contour lines that are spaced out at the base and getting **closer together as they near the peak**. The slope is gentle at first and then gets steep.

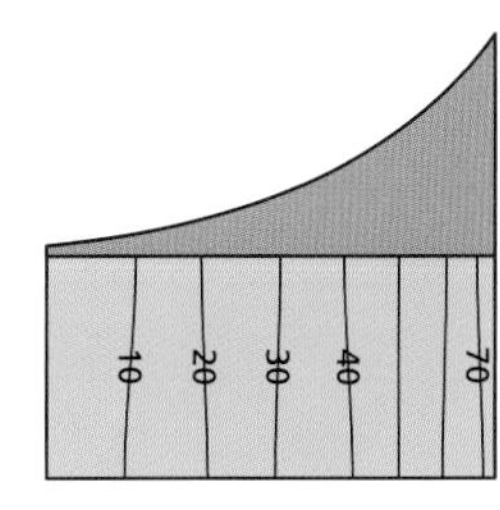

C

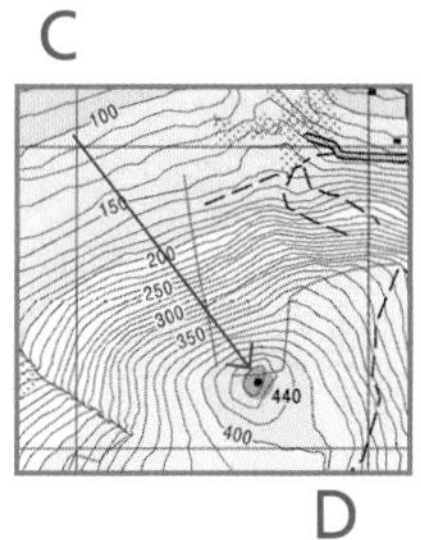

D

Convex slope

This shape of slope is shown using contour lines that are **closer together at the base** and become more spread out as they near the peak. The slope is steep at first and then gets gentle near the top.

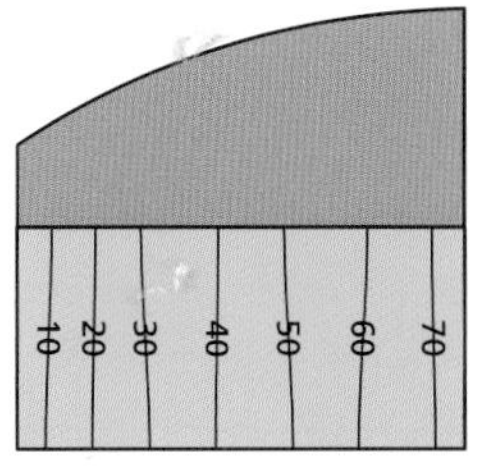

F

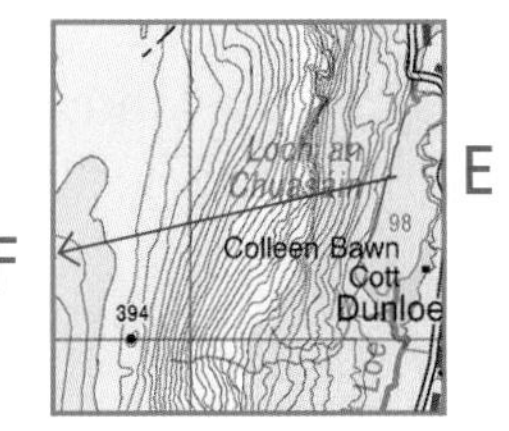

E

Compound slope

The contour lines for this slope are sometimes spaced out and sometimes close together, showing that the slope is steep in places and not steep in other areas. It is also called a **stepped slope**.

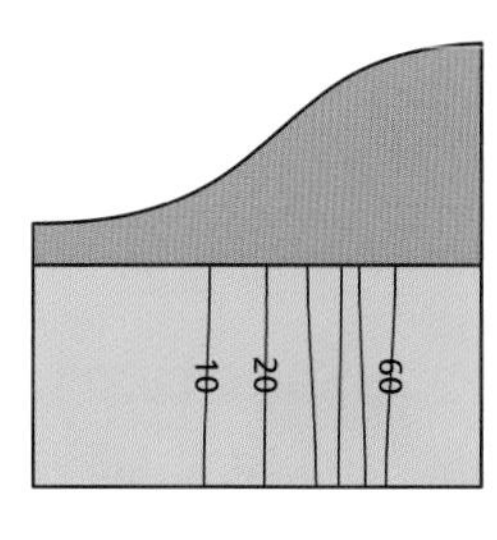

G

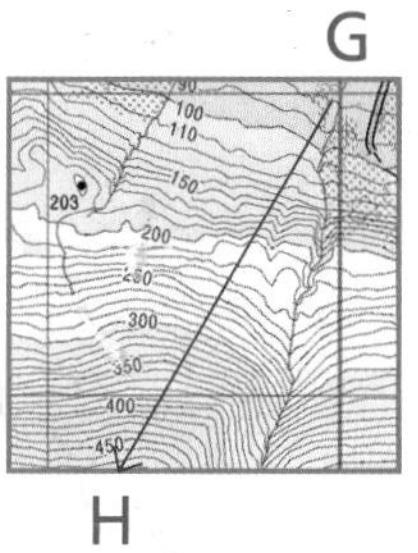

H

ACTIVITY

Read these descriptions of walking up a hill or mountain, and decide what sort of slope each of them describes. It may help you to make drawings.

(a) It was a tough walk. It was quite steep from the beginning and stayed like that all the way to the top.

(b) It wasn't too hard most of the time, but there were several tough, steep sections where we had to use our hands.

(c) It was easy going at first, but the walking got harder and harder as we got closer to the summit.

Cross-section

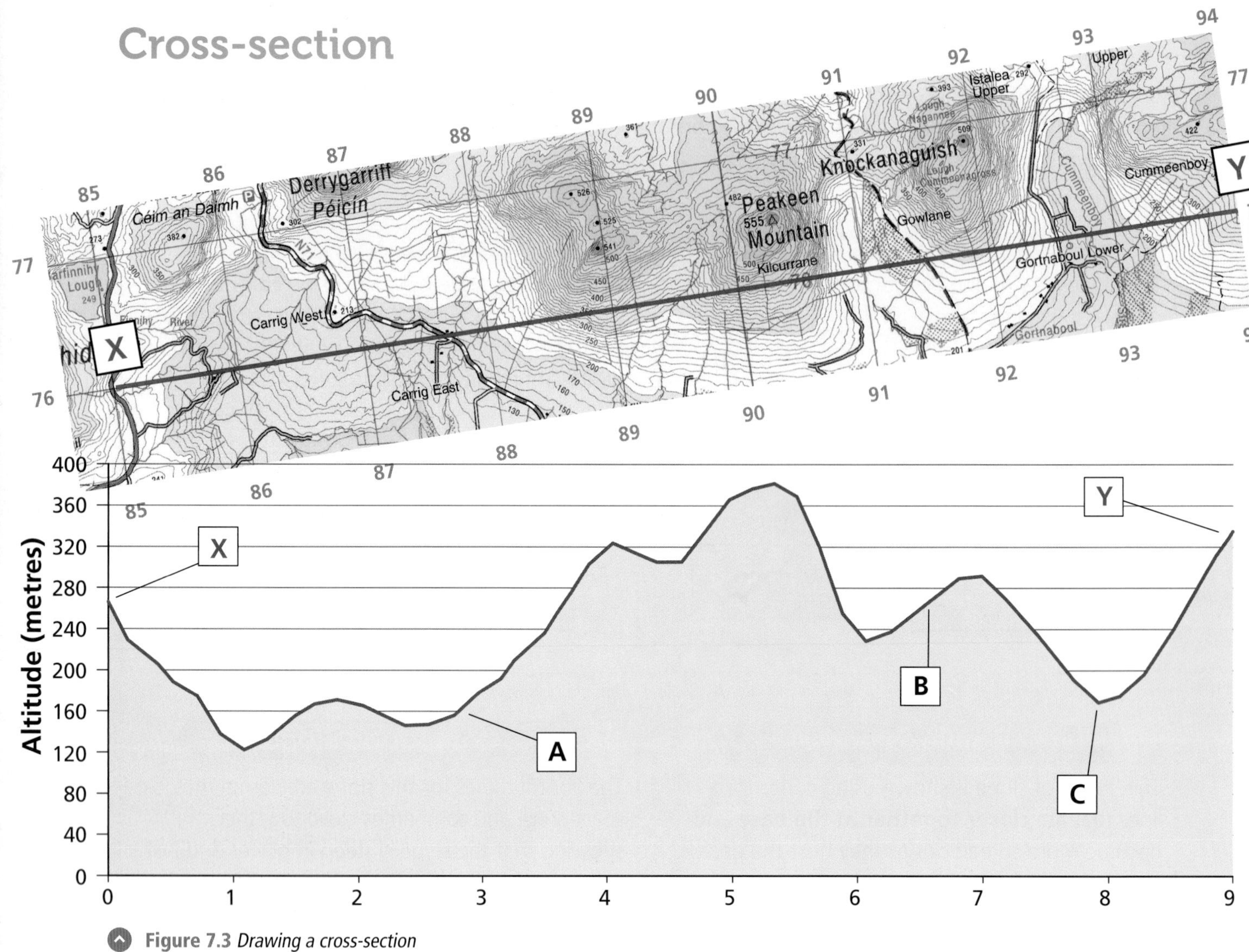

Figure 7.3 *Drawing a cross-section*

A cross-section is a **slice** through a particular feature, in this case the **landscape**. It shows us the slopes and relief features. Hill walkers and mountain climbers often use cross-sections to examine routes.

How to draw a cross-section:

1. Put the straight edge of a piece of paper on the map so that it is touching both points of the map section being calculated. Mark the beginning and end of the cross-section, and write down the grid references and heights of each point.
2. Go along the cross-section line, making a mark every time a contour line touches the paper. Add any height numbers you see. Also mark the position of any main features, e.g. rivers or roads.
3. On graph paper, draw an x-axis and a y-axis to create a graph of what you have on the paper. The length along the bottom (x-axis) should be the same as your cross-section line on your paper. The scale on the side (y-axis) should be in 10 m intervals up to the maximum height in your cross-section.
4. Put your piece of paper along the x-axis and mark a dot on the graph for each contour line that is on the paper. The distance along the bottom should be the same as on the paper, and the distance up the side of the frame should correspond to the height of the contour line. If you don't have a number for a particular line, count up or down from one you do have. Look out for places where the same contour line crosses the paper more than once. **Remember:** there is a gap of 10 m between contour lines, 100 m and 50 m lines are shown in bold and height numbers are towards the top of the slope.
5. Join the dots with a smooth line and check back to the map to make sure your cross-section looks sensible.

Land uses on Ordnance Survey maps

County councils, developers and other organisations use Ordnance Survey maps when they are deciding where to build something. For example, they might use OS maps when they are trying to find the best **location** for a **residential area** (housing estate), a **shopping centre** or a **factory**.

We are going to look at the types of **site**, **infrastructure** and **settlement** that are necessary for each of these.

	Residential area	Shopping centre	Factory
Site	Needs a large, level site that can cater for the development of facilities for residents.	Needs a large, level site that can cater for car parking facilities and be easily extended.	Needs a large, level site that can cater for car parking facilities and be easily extended.
Infrastructure	Needs good access to the main road network for residents. Also needs to be close to public transport facilities.	Needs close and good access to the main road network for customers.	Needs good access to the main road network for transporting goods and for the workers. Also needs to be close to other transport links such as air, sea and rail for the importing and exporting of goods.
Settlement	Larger developments would be on the outskirts of the town as land prices are usually lower than in the town centre.	Often situated on the outskirts, but near a town, with good access for local people.	Important not to situate a factory in the middle of a town. It needs to be near to a workforce and have good access to transport.

Log in to maps.scoilnet.ie with your teacher and class and find your local area.

Identify and highlight any **schools**, **shopping centres**, **factories** and **residential areas** on the OS map. Divide in to groups of four and select one of the above land uses.

(a) Examine the location of the land use in question and, in your group, list the reasons why you think it was located where it is. Make sure to list any disadvantages of its location also.

(b) It is the council's opinion that a new community centre/leisure centre should be built in your local area. With your group, select the most appropriate site and give reasons for your answer. Each group must report their findings to the class. A vote must then be taken to decide upon the most suitable location.

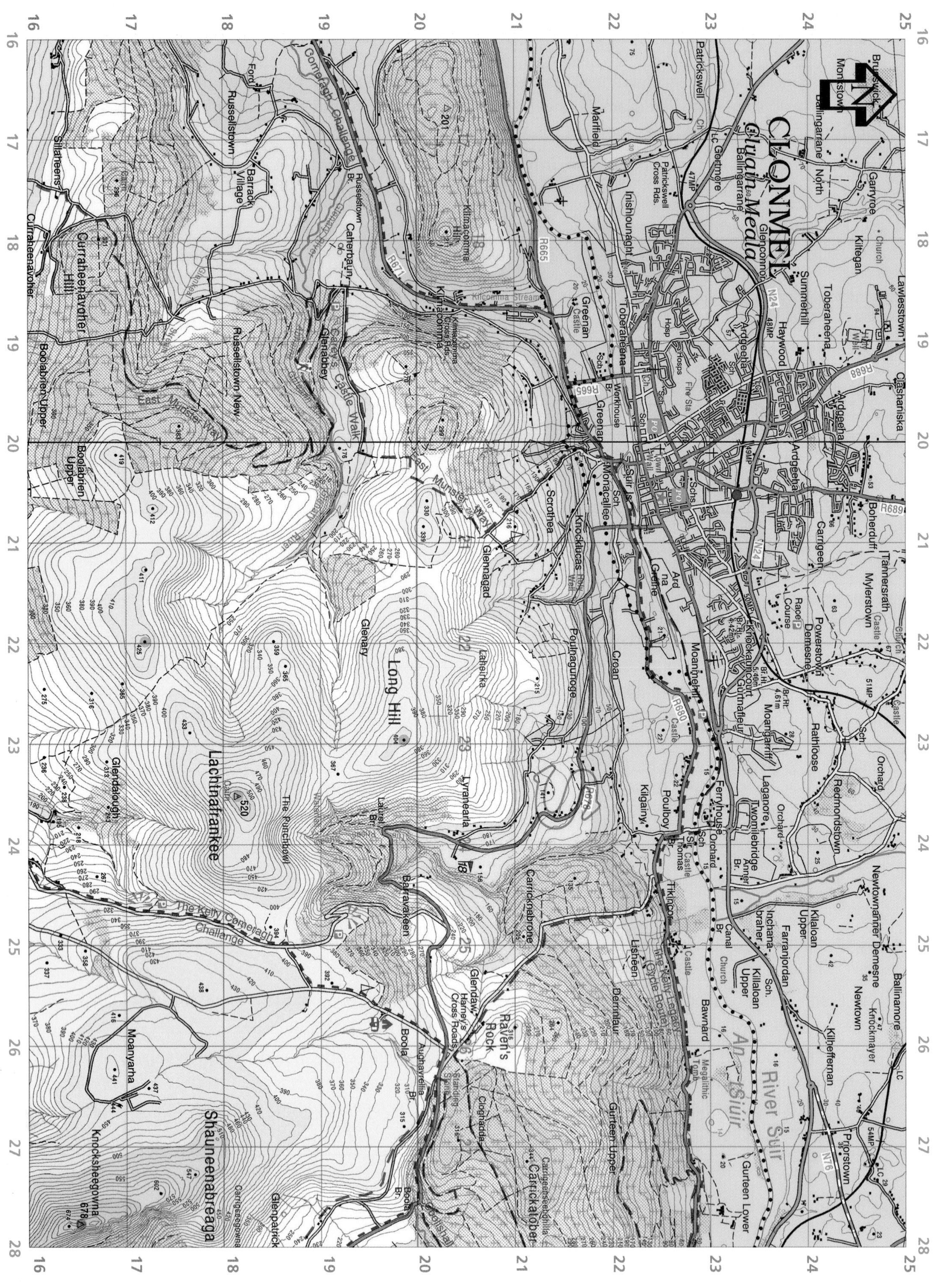

Figure 7.4 *OS map of Clonmel, Co. Tipperary*

Examine the Ordnance Survey map of Clonmel on the opposite page and answer these questions.

1. Measure the following:
   - **(a)** The straight-line distance from the spot height at Long Hill to the triangulation pillar at Lachtnafrankee.
   - **(b)** The straight-line distance from the parking site at S 18 19 to the parking site at S 24 19.
   - **(c)** The distance covered by the N24 from where it enters the map at S 160 239 to where it leaves the map at S 280 237.
   - **(d)** The distance covered by the railway line from where it enters the map at S 160 231 to where it leaves the map at S 230 250.
   - **(e)** The distance of the Kelly Legacy cycle route from where it enters the map at S 160 189 to where it leaves the map at S 280 228.
2. Find the area of the following:
   - **(a)** The total map extract
   - **(b)** The land north of the River Suir
   - **(c)** The land south of the River Suir
   - **(d)** The land under coniferous plantation on the map.
3. What type of slope is at each of the following points?
   - **(a)** S 26 19
   - **(b)** S 23 19
4. Draw a cross-section of the map extract. Draw your cross-section from Kilmacomma Hill S 179 203 to the spot height at S 197 204.
5. Can you suggest a suitable location for a factory in the area shown on the map? Give **two** reasons for your answer.

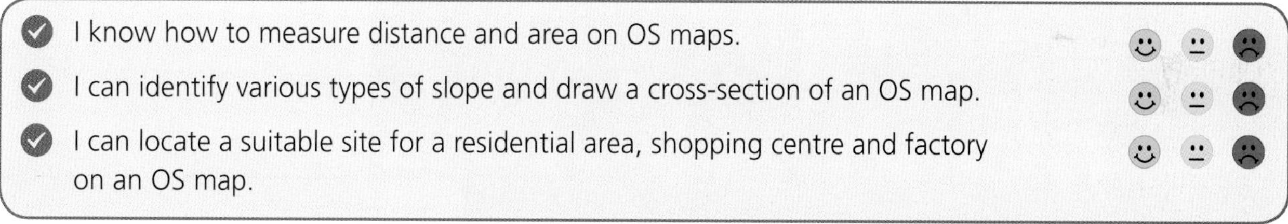

I know how to measure distance and area on OS maps.
I can identify various types of slope and draw a cross-section of an OS map.
I can locate a suitable site for a residential area, shopping centre and factory on an OS map.

Introduction to aerial photographs

Learning Intentions

In this section, you will learn:

- that there are different types of aerial photograph
- to identify the time of year on aerial photographs
- to identify land uses and functions in urban and rural areas on aerial photographs
- to identify transport issues on aerial photographs.

Angle
Vertical
Oblique
Foreground
Background
Horizon
Function

Aerial photographs can be used to show **features** on the landscape. They are taken from the air and give us a **bird's-eye view** of a landscape. We can learn a lot from studying aerial photographs, just as we do when we study OS maps.

We are now going to look at the skills you will need to interpret aerial photographs in Second Year.

Types of aerial photograph

Aerial photographs can be taken from different **angles** in the sky. As a result of this we get two distinct types of aerial photograph. These are referred to as **vertical** and **oblique** aerial photographs.

Vertical photographs

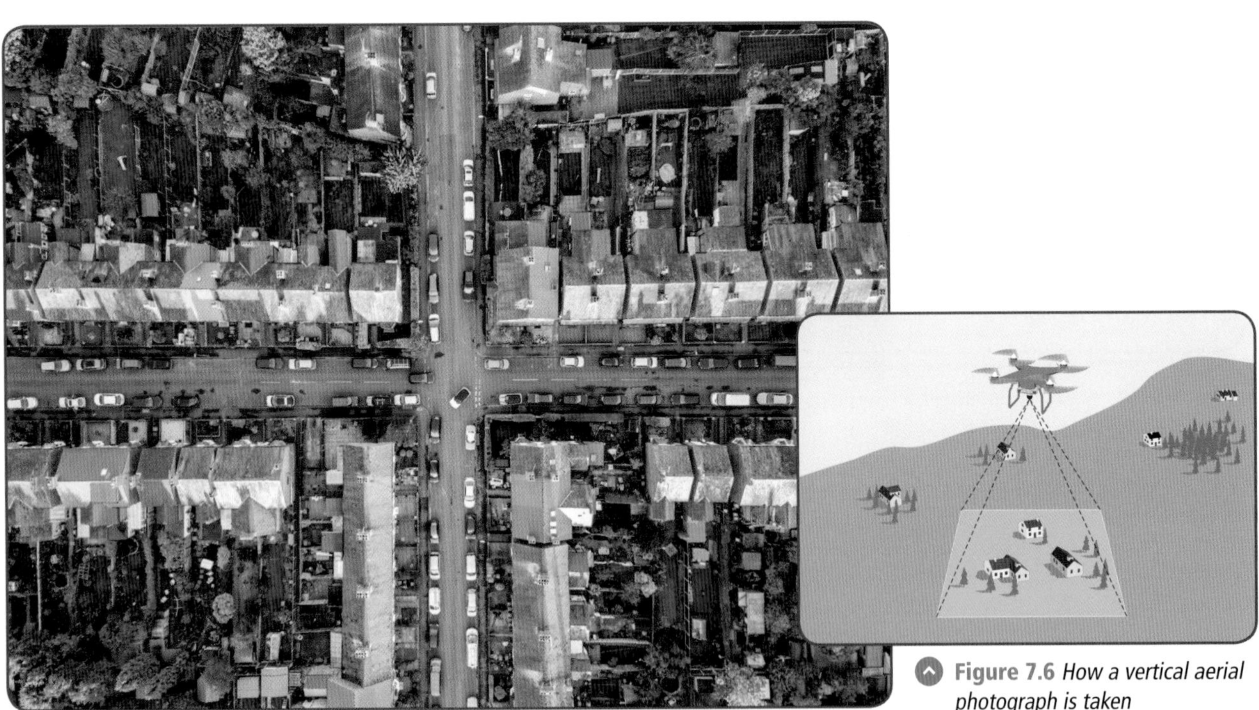

Figure 7.5 *A vertical aerial photograph*

Figure 7.6 *How a vertical aerial photograph is taken*

A **vertical** photograph is taken when the camera is facing **directly downwards**, as in the photograph above. Only the **rooftops** of buildings can be seen and all the features are **scaled down equally**. You **cannot see the horizon** on vertical photographs.

Oblique photographs

Figure 7.8 *How an oblique aerial photograph is taken*

Figure 7.7 *An oblique aerial photograph*

Oblique photographs are taken **at an angle**. Features nearer to the **bottom** of the shot appear **larger** than those at the top. The bottom of the picture is called the **foreground** and the top is called the **background**. Some parts of buildings may be hidden, and on high oblique pictures you can see the **horizon**, as in the photograph above.

Naming locations on an aerial photograph

When giving location on an Ordnance Survey map, we give **grid references**. On aerial photographs, we divide the photograph into **nine sections**. The name we give each section depends on the type of photograph.

Location on vertical photographs

North-west	North	North-east
West	Centre	East
South-west	South	South-east

Location on oblique photographs

Left background	Centre background	Right background
Left middleground	Centre middleground	Right middleground
Left foreground	Centre foreground	Right foreground

Identifying the season

Figure 7.9 *An aerial view of Killala, Co. Mayo*

When examining aerial photographs, we can identify the time of year at which the photograph was taken. The photograph above was taken during the **summer**.

- The trees are in full **foliage**.
- The **grass** has been cut.
- There are **few shadows** because the **sun is high** in the sky.

Other things you may see in a photograph taken in summer:

- **Cattle** grazing in fields
- Bales of **hay/silage** in fields.

Photographs taken in **winter** may show:

- Trees that have **lost their foliage**
- **Ploughed fields**
- **Longer shadows** as the sun is low in the sky
- An **absence of animals** in fields

Look at Figure 7.9. Answer the following questions in pairs:

(a) Is the photo vertical or oblique? Explain how you made your decision.

(b) If a similar photo were taken in winter, describe and give the location of the differences you might expect to see.

Identifying functions on aerial photographs

Identifying urban functions and land uses

The **functions** of a town are related to the **services it provides**. You should ask yourself why people come into this town and what they use it for. Aerial photographs give us a lot of **evidence** about what the functions of a town might be.

Sometimes, you have to **interpret** what the functions are. For example, if you see a building that looks like a school and there are playing pitches and courts around it, then you can **suggest** that the town has an educational function. Many of the following features are seen on aerial photographs and they tell us what the functions might be.

Function	Features	Function	Features
Educational	School, college or university	**Commercial**	Office block
Port	Dock, boats and ships. Fishing if you can see trawlers	**Tourism**	Beach, park, castle in good repair
Ecclesiastical	Church, abbey or graveyard	**Legal**	Courthouse
Recreational	Playing pitches and courts, golf courses	**Residential**	Housing estates
Industry	Industrial estate	**Health**	Hospital
Market	Square	**Retail**	Shops and shopping centres
Transport	Railway line, train station, roads		

Figure 7.10 *An oblique aerial view of Cork City*

ACTIVITY

Look at Figure 7.10. Locate and name as many land uses as possible. Work in pairs.

Identifying rural functions and land uses

Many aerial photographs will show **rural areas** as well as urban areas, with the rural area often appearing in the **background** of the photograph. From such photographs we can sometimes identify **rural patterns of settlement**: **linear**, **clustered** and **dispersed**.

Rural land uses, such as **agriculture** and **forestry**, can also be seen on aerial photographs. You may see cattle grazing in a field, bales of hay or silage, ploughed fields, fields that have recently been harvested, grain silos and areas covered in forest.

Go to Chapter 12, pages 208–209, to learn more about rural patterns of settlement.

Figure 7.11 *An oblique aerial view of Charleville, Co. Cork – A: Clustered; B Dispersed; C: Linear*

Figure 7.12 *An oblique aerial view of Ballina, Co. Tipperary and Killaloe, Co. Clare*

Look at Figure 7.12 above. Can you identify any rural patterns of settlement?

Transport on aerial photographs

It is very easy to identify the various **transport routes** on aerial photographs. We can see types of **roads**, **railway lines**, **stations**, **airports** and **ports**. Photographs of urban areas are often used by those who **manage** transport routes and networks in order to ensure there is no traffic congestion. Indeed, many **traffic calming** and **traffic management** strategies can easily be seen on an aerial photograph.

Yellow boxes	Allow traffic to flow into a main street and keep areas such as in front of fire stations free from traffic.
Roundabouts	Reduce traffic where main road networks meet.
Traffic lights	Direct traffic and give an opportunity for traffic to flow.
Filter lanes	Allow traffic to turn right and therefore avoid cars backing up behind.
One-way streets	Organise and keep traffic flowing in one direction if the street is narrow.
Ring roads	Mean that cars don't have to have to go into town centres. Journey times are shorter and towns are not as congested.
Car parks	Provide an alternative to parking at the side of the road.
Double lines	Prevent people from parking at the side of the road where it is not suitable to do so.
Pedestrianised streets	With no cars allowed, these streets make shopping a more pleasant and easy experience for shoppers.

Figure 7.13 *An oblique aerial view of Mitchelstown, Co. Cork*

ACTIVITY

Look at the photograph above and say what measures have been put in place to help traffic.

- I can identify the difference between vertical and oblique photographs.
- I can identify the time of year on an aerial photograph.
- I can identify the urban and rural functions on an aerial photograph.
- I can identify transport on an aerial photograph.

Distance, ratio, range and mean

Learning the following skills will also help you throughout Second Year. Here is more information on:

- Distance
- Ratio
- Range
- Mean

Distance

Distance is the length of space between two points.

Top Tip

Convert kilometres to miles by multiplying the kilometres by 0.62137.

NUMERACY ACTIVITY

(a) Draw these measurements:
- 1 mm
- 1 cm
- 1 inch
- 30 cm

(b) Does your teacher have a metre stick? If so, measure your height in metres. You might need to get help from a classmate.

(c) How many kilometres is it from your house to your school? Use Google Maps to find out.

(d) Convert the distance from your house to your school from kilometres to miles.

Ratio

A ratio says how much of one thing there is compared to another thing. To work out a ratio, the trick is to always multiply or divide the numbers by the same value.

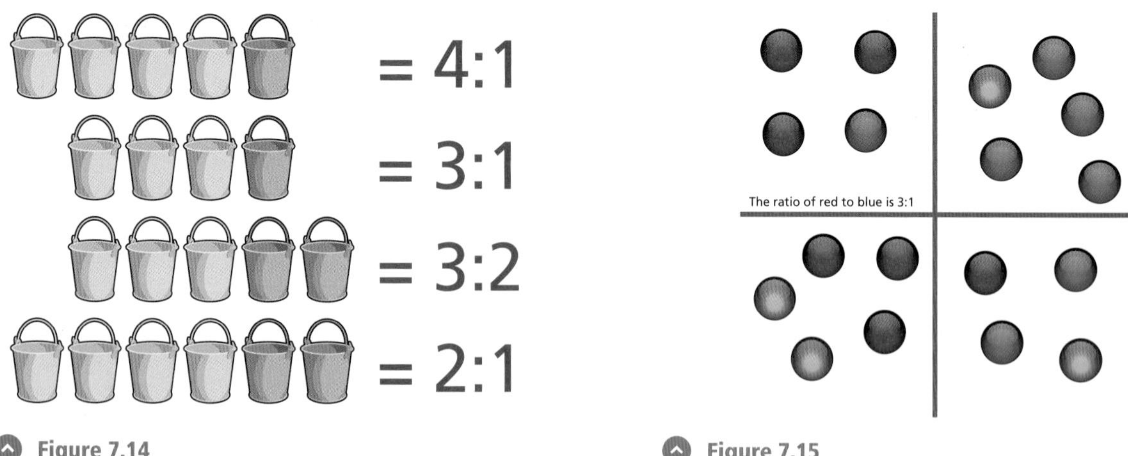

Figure 7.14

Figure 7.15

NUMERACY ACTIVITY

Can you work out the ratios in Figure 7.15 above? The first one is done for you.

Range

Range is the difference between the highest and lowest of a set of numbers. When you have these values you take the lowest from the highest.

For example, if you were asked what is the range of the average temperature in Ireland if the coldest month was 6 °C and the hottest month was 16 °C, the range for the year's temperature would be 10 °C.

NUMERACY ACTIVITY

Look at rainfall for Shannon Airport, 2016. What was the range for the year?

Rainfall at Shannon Airport for 2016												
	Jan	**Feb**	**Mar**	**Apr**	**May**	**Jun**	**Jul**	**Aug**	**Sep**	**Oct**	**Nov**	**Dec**
Rainfall (mm)	107	144	64	42	45	68	66	107	88	35	69	74

Mean

The mean is the **average** of a set of numbers.

For example, if you were asked to find the mean of 24, 27, 19 and 18, you would add up the four numbers and then divide the answer by 4.

$$24 + 27 + 19 + 18 = 88$$

$$\frac{88}{4} = 22$$

The mean of 24, 27, 19 and 18 is 22.

NUMERACY ACTIVITY

Look at the monthly temperatures for Ireland in 2016. What was the mean temperature for Ireland in 2016?

Monthly temperatures in Ireland in 2016												
	Jan	**Feb**	**Mar**	**Apr**	**May**	**Jun**	**Jul**	**Aug**	**Sep**	**Oct**	**Nov**	**Dec**
Temperature (°C)	6	5	7	8	12	15	16	16	14	11	6	6

8 Secondary Economic Activities: Industry in Ireland

In this chapter, you will learn:

- about secondary economic activities
- about the factors that influence the location of a factory
- about the different types of manufacturing industries
- that conflict can arise between industry and the environment.

Name a factory in your area. What happens in this factory? Why do you think the factory is located where it is?

Secondary economic activities

Learning Intentions

In this section, you will learn:

- about secondary economic activities
- that secondary economic activity is a system of inputs, processes and outputs
- about manufacturing in Ireland.

Manufacturing
System
Inputs
Processes
Outputs
Semi-finished product
Finished product

Secondary economic activities involve making or **manufacturing** something.

Secondary economic activities work as a **system** of **inputs**, **processes** and **outputs**.

Processes involve **doing** something. These words often end in **–ing**.

Inputs

These are the things that we need to put in at the start. Examples:

- workers
- money/capital
- raw materials

Processes

These are the things we do to the inputs to turn them into semi-finished or finished products. Examples:

- carving
- assembling

Outputs

These are the things we have at the end. They can be **semi-finished** products which go on to form inputs again, such as a plank of wood.

They can also be **finished products** which are ready for the market. Example:

- furniture

Divide into pairs. One person should write down a list of raw materials required for any industry you choose. The other person should write down a list of outputs that can be made from these raw materials.

Work together to figure out what processes could be used to change the raw materials into outputs.

The following table shows how the system works in The Wood Factory, a furniture manufacturing company in Co. Dublin:

Inputs	Processes	Outputs
• Raw materials (wood, steel)	• Measuring	• Tables
• Electricity	• Cutting	• Beams
• Machinery	• Welding	• Shelves
• Workers	• Carving	• Waste (wood chippings)

ACTIVITY

Make a list of inputs, processes and outputs for factories that make the following:

1 Footballs **2** Bicycles **3** Breakfast cereal

Manufacturing in Ireland

There are over **4,000 manufacturing companies** employing more than 200,000 people **directly** in the manufacturing sector in Ireland. A further 400,000 people are employed **indirectly** (e.g. solicitors, accountants, IT consultants). **Exports** from the manufacturing sector in Ireland in 2016 were worth €117 billion.

- I understand what secondary economic activities are.
- I understand that secondary economic activities are a system of inputs, processes and outputs.

Factors that influence the location of a factory

Learning Intentions

In this section, you will learn:

- about the factors that influence the location of a factory.

Raw materials, Labour force, Markets, Services, Transport, Policy

When **locating** and building a **factory** there are a number of factors that have to be taken into consideration:

- Raw materials
- Markets
- Transport facilities
- Labour force
- Services
- Government policy
- Personal preferences

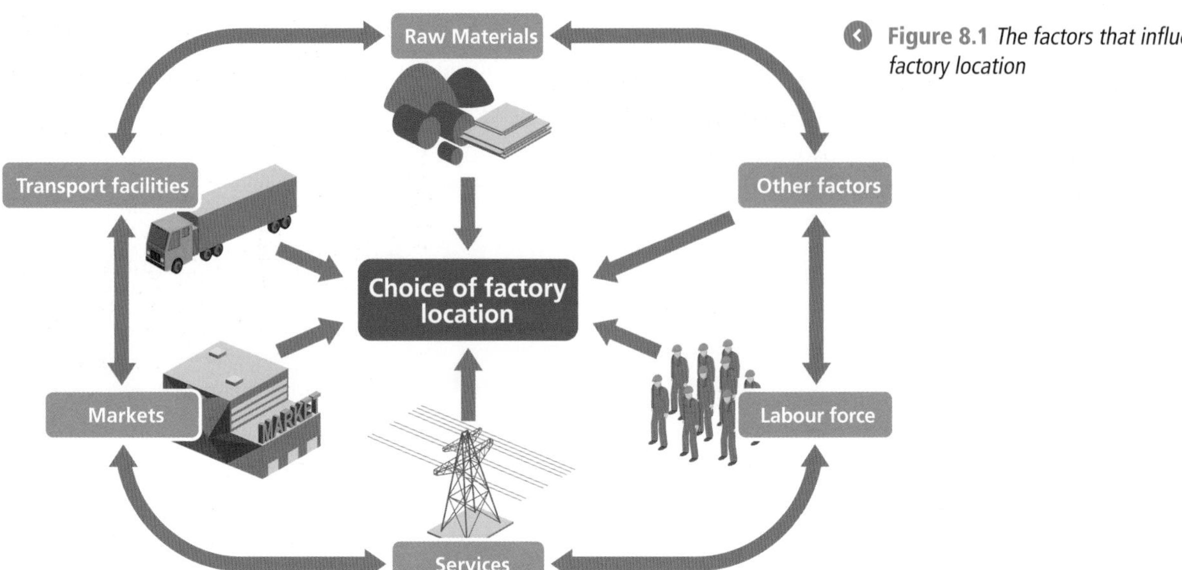

Figure 8.1 *The factors that influence factory location*

Raw materials

If the **raw materials** needed by a factory are big and **heavy** (e.g. steel), the factory may need to be located **close to them** to make the **transportation** of the raw materials easier and less expensive. If raw materials are small and light, transportation is not as difficult or expensive.

Figure 8.2 *Copper is an important raw material in the electronics and construction industries*

Figure 8.3 *The countries of the European Union are a market for Ireland's beef and dairy products*

Markets

Markets are where factories **sell** their products. Factories located **close** to their markets can transport their products quickly and they have **lower transportation costs**. For example in Ireland, many companies locate near Dublin because of the large market.

Transport facilities

All factories need to **transport** their finished products to the **market**. If the products are to be sold in the same country as they are made, then good **road** or **rail** transport is required. If the company is **exporting** products it may also need to be close to an **airport** or a **port**. This reduces transportation costs and makes the movement of goods faster.

Figure 8.4 *Train carrying cargo in containers that have arrived at a port by ship*

Figure 8.5 *Workers in a clothing factory*

Labour force

A factory's labour force are the people who **work** in the factory. Factories must be built where there are enough **workers**, usually near towns and cities. Some factories may locate next to universities or colleges if they need **highly skilled graduates**. **Boston Scientific** is located in Galway for this reason.

Services

Factories need access to **services** like electricity, water, sewage treatment, waste disposal, telephone, broadband and Wi-Fi. This is why **industrial estates** are attractive to companies and why it is more difficult to get companies to locate in rural areas.

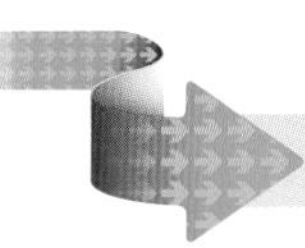

Go to page 129 to learn about industrial estates.

Figure 8.6 *Services such as banks are necessary for industry*

Government policy

Governments do many things to **encourage** companies to set up in their country. The Irish government gives **grants** to help companies to set up here. The **Industrial Development Authority (IDA)** works to attract industry to locate here. Ireland also has a **low corporation tax** rate, which attracts companies.

Corporation tax:
a tax that companies must pay on their profits. The corporation tax in Ireland is 12.5 per cent, which is less than in most countries. In the USA, for example, it is 40 per cent.

ACTIVITY

Look up https://educateplus.ie/go/ida-ireland and make a list identifying the different ways the IDA offers incentives to companies to locate here. Work in pairs.

Figure 8.7 *Government grants and tax relief attract industry*

Personal preferences

Some people may set up a factory in an area where they come from or an area they like. **Ford** in Ireland was located in Cork because the father of the company's founder, Henry Ford, was born there.

ACTIVITY

Local people are often happy when companies set up in their area because it provides jobs. Suggest reasons why people might be unhappy when companies set up near them? Work in groups of three.

PORTFOLIO ACTIVITY 8.1

Go to page 32 of your Portfolio to fill in the template on an industry in your area.

 **(i)** List three factors that influence the location of a factory.

 **(ii)** Explain two factors in detail that influence the location of a factory.

 **(iii)** Explain two things that the government does to attract industry to Ireland.

 I understand the factors that influence the location of a factory.   

Types of manufacturing industry

Learning Intentions

In this section, you will learn:
- that there are different types of manufacturing industry.

Heavy
Light
Footloose
Industrial estate
Industrial inertia
Multinational company (MNC)
Globalisation
Foreign direct investment (FDI)

The **function** (purpose) of a manufacturing industry is to change **raw materials** into a **product** that the customer wants. What a factory does depends on what exactly it aims to produce. We will now examine different **types** of manufacturing industries.

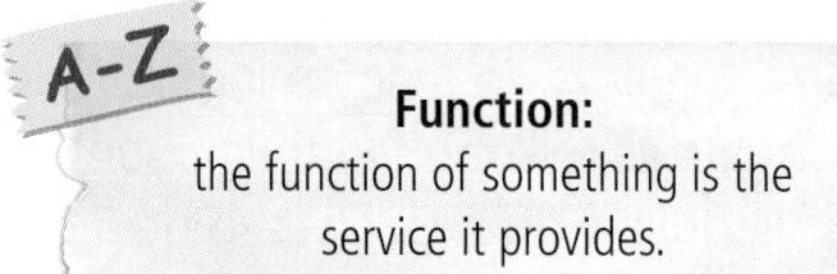

A-Z

Function: the function of something is the service it provides.

Heavy industry

Both the raw materials and the products being made in a **heavy industry** are big and heavy. **Iron** and **steel** making are examples of heavy industry.

Figure 8.8 *When raw materials are heavy, they are more expensive to transport*

Light industry

Products being made in a light industry are **small** and **light**. **Electronic** products and **healthcare** products are examples of products made in light industries.

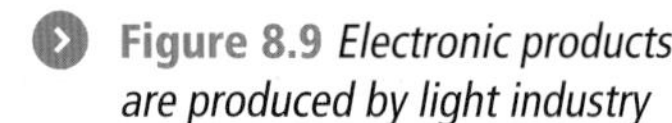

Figure 8.9 *Electronic products are produced by light industry*

CASE STUDY

Heavy industry: RUSAL Aughinish Alumina

An example in Ireland of a **heavy industry** is the RUSAL Aughinish Alumina factory on Aughinish Island in the Shannon Estuary, close to Limerick City. It is part of **RUSAL**, the world's largest aluminium producer.

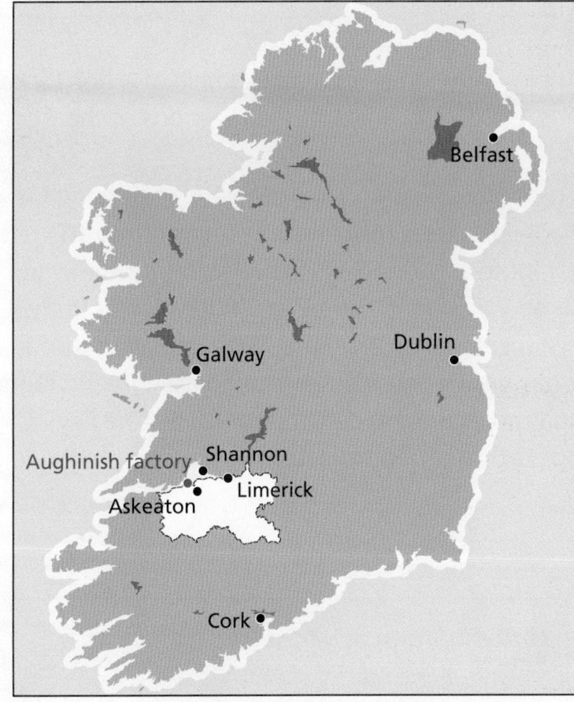

Figure 8.10 *Aughinish Alumina is based on the Shannon Estuary*

RUSAL Aughinish Alumina

The **function** of RUSAL Aughinish Alumina is to produce **alumina** out of the raw material **bauxite**. Alumina is a **semi-finished product**. It is a white powder used to make **aluminium**. The alumina is exported by ship to **aluminium smelters** in the UK and Scandinavia. The RUSAL Aughinish Alumina plant is the largest of its kind in Europe. Production started in 1983 and it now produces over 1.9 million tons of alumina per year.

Reasons for its location:

- **Raw material**: **Bauxite** is the main material used in making alumina. It is a bulky, heavy material that comes from the **Republic of Guinea** in Africa. It is shipped to the Shannon Estuary where there is a **deep-water port** at Aughinish. This port is suitable for the ships bearing the large containers to load and unload.
- **Market**: Ireland is a member of the **EU** and is close to **European markets**. Alumina can be easily exported to smelters in Scandinavia and other European countries.
- **Transport**: The **deep-water port** at Aughinish allows for heavy cargo ships to dock and transport bauxite to the factory and alumina to the smelters around Europe. The **N69** national secondary road connects the factory with Limerick City and nearby Shannon Airport.
- **Labour force**: There are more than 450 people employed at the factory. These workers mostly come from the **nearby towns** and villages, such as Foynes, Askeaton, Kildimo, Rathkeale and Newcastlewest.
- **Aughinish Island** on the Shannon Estuary can **store** large quantities of the bauxite. Therefore, a constant supply of it can remain close to the factory.

Figure 8.11 *The Aughinish processing plant*

Figure 8.12 *The deep-water port at Aughinish*

Inputs	Processes	Outputs
• Bauxite • Caustic soda • Electricity	• Bauxite is crushed and mixed with caustic soda and then heated	• Alumina powder • Waste

ACTIVITY

Check out https://educateplus.ie/go/rusal to find out more about this heavy industry. What other countries are RUSAL located in? Are they committed to sustainable development?

CASE STUDY

Light industry: Apple

Apple Computers Ltd is an example of a **light industry**. It is located in Hollyhill, Cork City. Manufacturing Apple products is one of the functions of the Cork headquarters.

Apple

Apple produces **information technology (IT)** products such as computers, iPads, iPods and iPhones for the world market. The company currently employs 6,000 workers in the Cork City area. It first located in Cork in the 1980s and over the last number of years it has grown considerably due to its high-end range of products and the increasing demand for them. The Cork City plant is the **operational headquarters** for Europe, the Middle East and Asia.

Figure 8.13 *A smartphone manufactured by Apple in Cork*

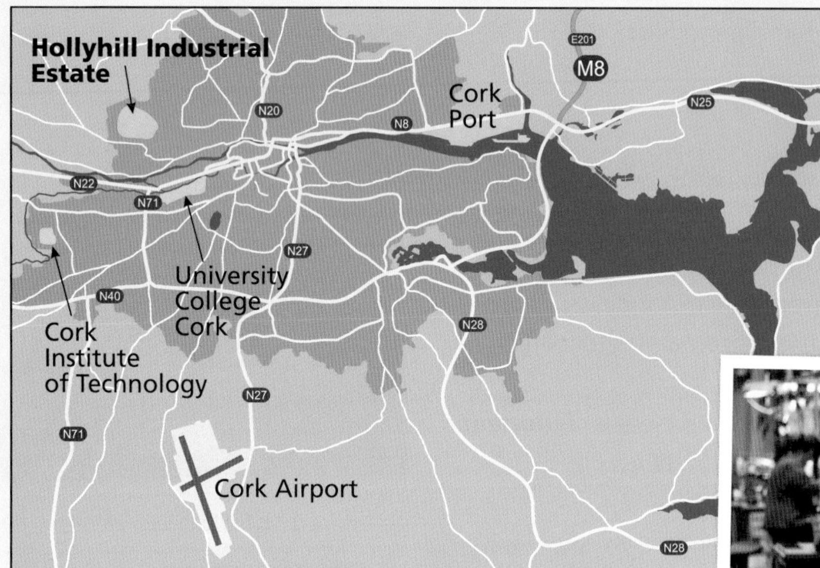

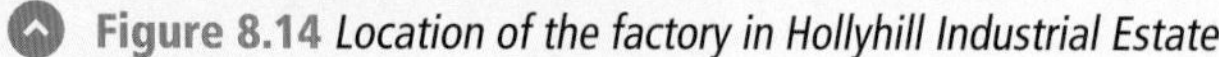
Figure 8.14 *Location of the factory in Hollyhill Industrial Estate*

Figure 8.15 *Inside the Apple factory*

Reasons for its location

- **Corporation tax**: Ireland's low corporation tax encouraged Apple to locate here, and that continued low corporation tax has kept the company in place. The fact that Ireland is a member of the **EU** means Apple can locate its European headquarters here and make use of the free movement of goods.
- **Transport**: Its proximity to the **Port of Cork** and **Cork Airport** means goods can be shipped worldwide and at a lower cost.
- **Labour force**: Being close to University College Cork and the Cork Institute of Technology means there is a steady supply of **skilled graduates** available.

There has been a lot of talk about Ireland's low corporation tax in the news in recent years. Divide up into groups of three. Research the problems that can arise from low corporation tax rates in Ireland. Each group should outline their main findings to the class.

Footloose industry

In the past, manufacturing industries had to set up near **coal fields** as this was the only source of energy. Now that there are new sources of energy, this is no longer the case.

These days, many manufacturing industries can set up in a variety of locations. They are not tied to one place and so they are called **footloose industries**.

Footloose industries are usually **light industries** and they often locate in **industrial estates** or **business parks** close to large cities.

Figure 8.16 *Industrial estates are areas on the edges of cities and towns where footloose industries are encouraged to locate*

Industrial estates

Industrial estates are sites at the **edge** of urban areas that are set aside to be used by industries. Here land is cheaper than in the middle of towns and cities, so there is **space** to build on and expand. Industrial estates also provide a high level of **services** such as water, waste and high-speed broadband connection. Industrial estates are located within easy **access** of routeways such as motorways, providing quick transport to airports, ports and markets.

Manufacturers are often beside other industries that can provide semi-finished products for them.

Examples of industrial estates are **Citywest** Business Park in Dublin, **Raheen** Industrial Estate in Limerick and **Ballybrit** Business Park in Galway.

In groups of four, suggest reasons why light industries would want to locate in industrial estates in your local town or city. Present your reasons to the class.

Industrial inertia

When an industry does not relocate, even though it might make economic sense to do so, it is called **industrial inertia**. This generally occurs when the industry has strong historical links to a particular area.

Industrial inertia: when an Industry stays at its original location even though the reasons for locating there no longer apply.

An example of this is **Sheffield** in England. The area has a long-standing **reputation** for steel production, so even though the coal mines have closed, the steel factories have remained there. In order to survive, they have changed their approach. They now use **new energy sources** and they also producing **new products**, such as surgical instruments.

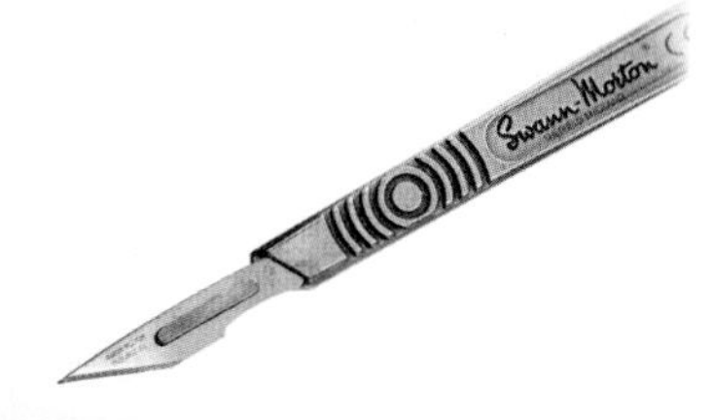

Figure 8.17 *A scalpel manufactured by a Sheffield steel company*

Multinational corporations (MNCs)

Figure 8.18 *Examples of multinational corporations (MNCs) with bases in Ireland*

Multinational corporations make their products in many different countries. Their **headquarters** are located in one country and then they have **branches** in other countries throughout the world. Because of **globalisation**, it is a lot easier for big companies to move to different countries. It makes it easier to buy and sell across all areas of the world.

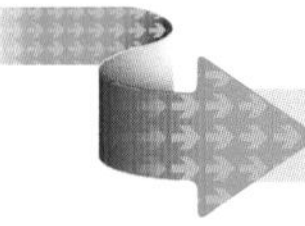

Go to Chapter 21 to learn more about globalisation.

CASE STUDY

MNCs in Ireland: Google

Over recent years Ireland has become a focus point for many of the world's MNCs, especially **technology** companies. Google first came to Ireland in 2003, and provided 100 jobs. It now employs **2,500** people.

Figure 8.19 *Google office, Dublin*

There are several **reasons** why MNCs have chosen to locate in Ireland:

- Ireland is a **member of the EU**. This means that it is easy for the MNC to access **markets** and **labour force**. Google employs 65 different nationalities in Dublin.
- There is a **highly educated** workforce.
- **English** is the language of business and the main language in Ireland.
- **Corporation tax** is low (12.5 per cent).

One in five people in Ireland is now employed by an MNC.

When MNCs locate a base in Ireland, it is known as **foreign direct investment (FDI)**. It is great for the country as it creates **employment**. The major **downside** of this is that the MNCs can leave at any stage they want, leading to devastating job losses. This creates uncertainty in the economy.

DID YOU KNOW? In 2009, Dell announced that it was cutting 1,900 jobs in Limerick because it was moving its production plants to Poland in order to cut costs.

ACTIVITY

When Donald Trump was elected President in 2016, one of his promises was to attract American MNCs back to the USA. Choose one of the MNCs from the map on the right. Assess the socio-economic effects on the local area if this MNC were to leave Ireland.

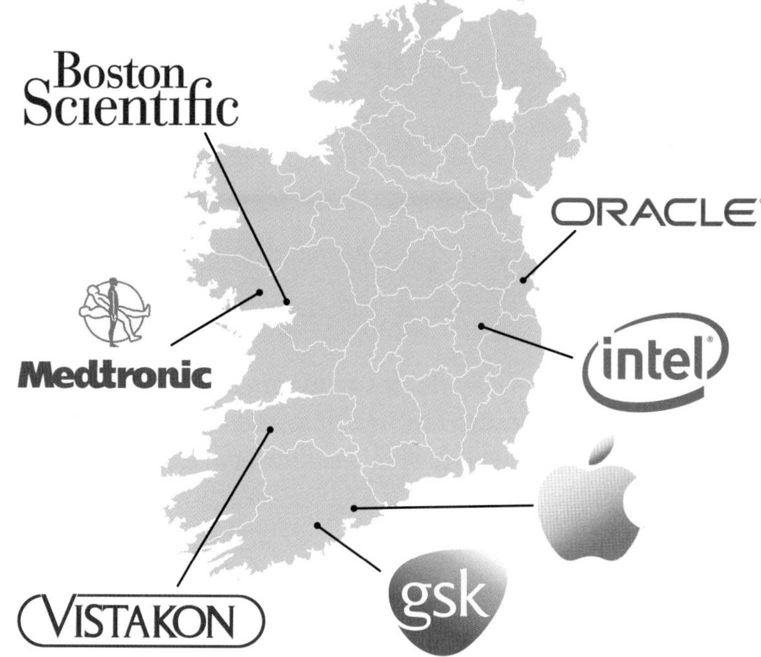

Figure 8.20 *Map of Ireland showing the location of some of the MNC bases in Ireland*

Industries on Ordnance Survey maps

1. Give the four-figure grid reference for an industrial estate on the map extract below.
2. Give two reasons why an industry might locate in this industrial estate.
3. State two reasons why the industrial estate has developed at its current location.

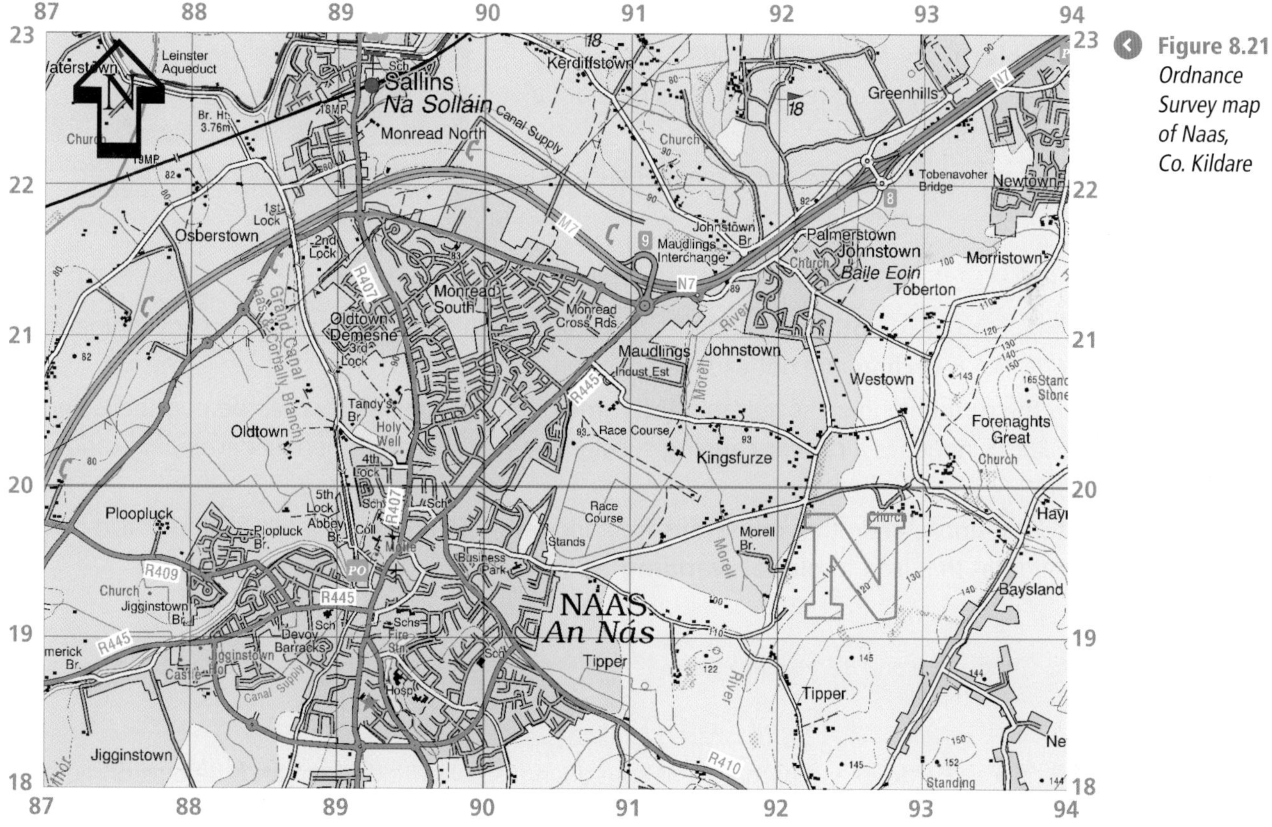

Figure 8.21 *Ordnance Survey map of Naas, Co. Kildare*

(i) List three different types of manufacturing industry.

(ii) Explain two types of manufacturing industry in detail. Give examples.

(iii) Can you describe any positive socio-economic impacts of an MNC locating in a local town/city/region?

- I understand the different types of manufacturing industries. 
- I can use Ordnance Survey maps to understand the location of industrial estates. 

Industry and conflict

Learning Intentions

In this section, you will learn:

- that conflicts may arise between industrial development and sustainability.

Incinerator
Carcinogenic
Waste managementic

Conflict may arise between **factory owners** and the **inhabitants** of the surrounding area. People may fear that gas and smoke **emissions** from factories could damage their health and the environment. An example of this in Ireland would be the huge controversy surrounding the location of **incinerators**, such as the one built by Covanta in **Poolbeg**, Co. Dublin. You can find out more about this at www.dublinwastetoenergy.ie.

Incinerators

Incinerators are factories that **burn waste**. Everywhere they are built, local people protest against them.

Figure 8.22 *Poolbeg incinerator*

Positives of incinerators:

- **Landfill** sites are filling up and there is little room left to dump waste. Incinerators are seen as a sustainable solution to **waste management**. Many countries in the EU use incinerators as a way of getting rid of waste and rubbish.
- They can provide **electricity** for the surrounding area while also attracting other industries to the region. This provides a **sustainable** energy source.
- **Jobs** can be created from the building and maintenance of an incinerator.

Negatives of incinerators:

- They can be seen as an **easy option** for getting rid of rubbish. This can mean that more environmentally friendly solutions, like **recycling**, are not explored enough.
- People living in the surrounding areas fear that the **fumes** from the incinerators can be poisonous and **carcinogenic**. A carcinogen is a **cancer-causing** substance that can lead to people developing various types of cancer.
- Like other factories, smoke and other **emissions** from incinerators could contribute to smog, acid rain and the greenhouse gases that lead to **global warming**.

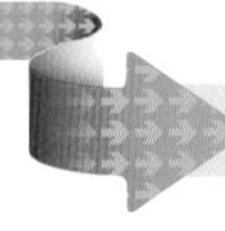

Go to Chapters 5 and 14 to learn more about smog, acid rain and global warming.

PORTFOLIO ACTIVITY 8.2

Go to page 33 of your Portfolio and prepare a debate on industrial development and the environment.

 **(i)** Name one example of the conflict between industrial development and the environment.

 **(ii)** Give one argument in favour of incinerators.

(iii) Give one argument against incinerators.

 **(iv)** Suggest an alternative solution to dealing with waste.

 I understand why there is often conflict between industrial development and environmental issues.   

REVISION

Secondary activities are those which take __________ materials and process them or they take semi-____________________ materials and process them further. They may be seen as a ____________________. The system consists of ____________________, ____________________, and ____________________. A number of ____________________ are involved when choosing the ____________________ of an industry. These include raw materials, ____________________, transport facilities, ____________________ force, ____________________, and government ____________________. An example of a heavy industry in Ireland is ____________________ ____________________ and of a light industry is ____________________. When an industry has no ties to any one location it is known as ____________________. Industry may ____________________ if the location factors change. If an industry does not relocate, even though it may be economically sound to do so, it is called ____________________ ____________________. Factories that burn waste are called ____________________. There is often ____________________ surrounding such factories because people worry they will damage the ____________________.

Questions & Answers

Sample Questions

1. Name a secondary economic activity that you have studied.
2. What are its functions?
3. Explain **three** reasons for the factory choosing this location.

Sample Answers

1. The secondary economic activity I have studied is Rusal's Aughinish Alumina.
2. The function of Aughinish Alumina is to extract alumina from the raw material bauxite in its refinery. Alumina is a semi-finished product. It is a white powder that is used to make aluminium. The alumina is exported by ship to aluminium smelters in the UK and Scandinavia.
3. Rusal's Aughinish Alumina factory is located on Aughinish Island in the Shannon Estuary close to Limerick City. There are many reasons why the factory was located there:
   - (a) Raw materials: The raw material used in making alumina is called bauxite. This is a bulky, heavy material that comes from the Republic of Guinea in Africa. The deep-water port at Aughinish on the Shannon Estuary is suitable for the large container ships transporting this raw material and for exporting the semi-finished product at the end of the process.
   - (b) Markets: Ireland is a member of the European Union and so has access to European markets. The alumina can be exported to RUSAL's smelters in Scandinavia and other European countries.
   - (c) Labour force: Aughinish Alumina employs 450 at its factory. Nearby towns such as Foynes, Askeaton, Kildimo, Rathkeale and Newcastlewest supply the workers for the factory.

Short Questions

1. Factories operate as systems.
   Which of the following is an **output** from a factory system?

   Labour ☐ Buildings ☐
   Transport ☐ Manufactured goods ☐ [tick (✓) the correct box]

2. Indicate which three statements below are correct by ticking the correct box.
   1. Modern industries still need to locate near raw materials.
   2. Modern industries are footloose industries.
   3. Mining is an example of secondary economic activity.
   4. The IDA encourages investment from MNCs into Ireland.
   5. Factories must be built where there are enough workers.

   1, 2, 3 ☐ 2, 3, 4 ☐ 1, 3, 5 ☐ 2, 4, 5 ☐

3. The diagram shows that a factory is a system with inputs, processes and outputs.

   Inputs → Processes → Outputs

   In the box below, circle **three** items, which may be factory inputs.

Labour	Waste material	Transport
Semi-finished products	Capital	Manufactured products

4. Which of the following is an example of a footloose industry?

   Computer manufacture ☐ Cement factory ☐
   Iron and steel ☐ Shipbuilding ☐ [tick (✓) the correct box]

5. Which of the following groups are all examples of people involved in secondary economic activity?

   Dentist, farmer, Garda, taxi driver ☐
   Teacher, insurance official, nurse, journalist ☐
   Bank official, miner, shopkeeper, plumber ☐
   Baker, factory worker, cabinet maker, brewer ☐ [tick (✓) the correct box]

Long Questions

1. **(i)** Name **one** manufacturing industry you have studied.
   (ii) Describe this industry, referring to its inputs, processes and outputs.
2. Explain **two** factors which influence the location of industry.
3. Look at this diagram, showing a factory as a system, with inputs, processes and outputs.

   (i) Name a factory that you have studied.
   (ii) Name **two** inputs, **two** processes and **two** outputs of your chosen factory.
   (iii) Describe and explain **two** reasons why the factory you have named developed at its present location.
4. Explain **three** reasons why conflict often arises when a factory is planned to be built in an area. Give an example that you have studied.

Visual Summary

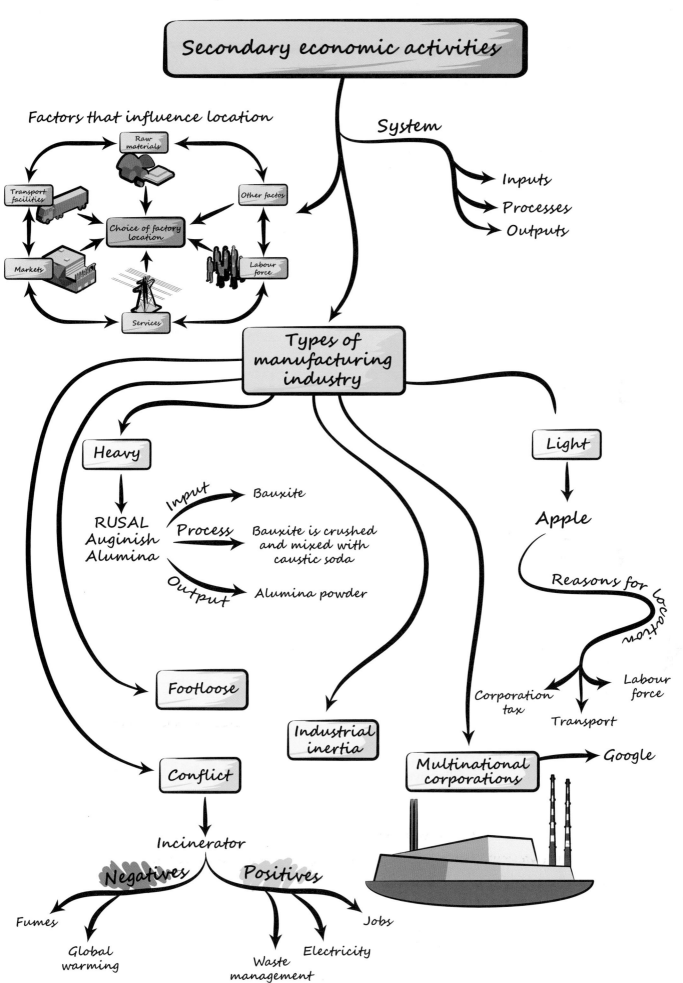

Secondary economic activities

Factors that influence location

Raw materials

Transport facilities

Other factos

Choice of factory location

Markets

Labour force

Services

System

Inputs

Processes

Outputs

Types of manufacturing industry

Heavy

RUSAL Auginish Alumina

Input → Bauxite

Process → Bauxite is crushed and mixed with caustic soda

Output → Alumina powder

Light

Apple

Reasons for location

Corporation tax

Transport

Labour force

Footloose

Industrial inertia

Multinational corporations → Google

Conflict

Incinerator

Negatives

Fumes

Global warming

Positives

Waste management

Electricity

Jobs

Rivers: Shaping our landscape

In this chapter, you will learn:

- how to name and describe the main landforms of a river
- how rivers erode, transport and deposit material
- how people interact with and try to manage rivers
- how human interaction impacts on river processes
- how to recognise drainage features on OS maps.

What words come to mind when you think of a river? Write down as many words as you can in 30 seconds. Work in pairs. Share your list with the rest of the class.

Rivers

Learning Intentions

In this section, you will learn:

- about features that are commonly found along the route of a river
- about the three stages of a river
- about the different characteristics and landforms of the three stages of a river.

Source
Course
Confluence
Tributary
Mouth
Drainage basin
Watershed
Estuary

Rivers are very important as they **drain** the land of rainwater and carry it out to sea.

Source	The **beginning** or start of a river
Course	The **route** a river takes to the sea
Confluence	The point at which two rivers or streams **join** together
Tributary	A stream or **smaller river** that flows into a larger stream or river
Mouth	The point where a river comes to the **end**, usually when entering the sea
Drainage basin	The area of land **drained** by a river
Watershed	The area of **high ground** which **separates** two drainage basins
Estuary	The part of a river mouth that is **tidal**

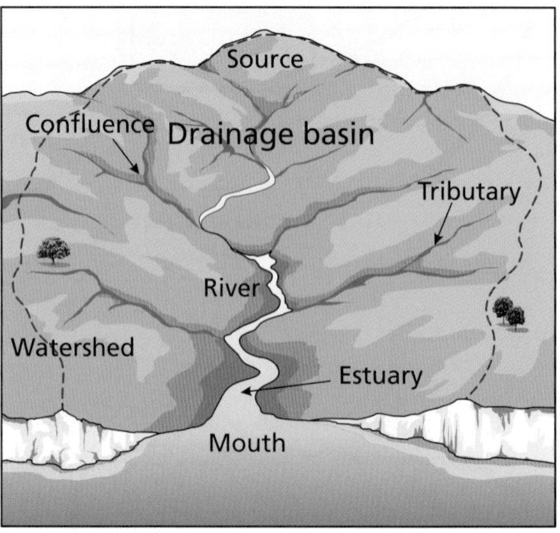

Figure 9.1 *Common features of a river*

Stages of a river

A number of **surface processes** take place on rivers. These surface processes create many **features** along the route of the river.

> A-Z
> **Surface processes:** the ways in which weathering and erosion create different features on the Earth's surface, and so shape the landscape.

The river course can be divided into **three** stages that reflect the change in **gradient** (slope) from the river's **source** high up in the mountains to its **mouth** at sea level. The three stages are:

- Youthful stage (Upper)
- Mature stage (Middle)
- Old stage (Lower)

The **characteristics** and **landforms** of each stage are set out in the table below. The landforms will be explained throughout the chapter.

	Youthful stage (Upper)	Mature stage (Middle)	Old stage (Lower)
Gradient	Steep	Gently sloping	Levelling off
Speed	Fast-flowing	River starts to slow down	Slow-moving
Water quantity	Low volume of water	Higher volume of water	Largest volume of water
Erosion/Deposition	Erosion	Erosion and deposition	Deposition
Profile of river	Steep, V-shaped valley Narrow, shallow channel High level of material on river bed (larger rocks)	Open, gently sloping valley with flood plain Wider, deeper channel Suspended sediment	Flat and wide flood plain Very wide and very deep channel High levels of suspended sediment
Landforms	V-shaped valleys Interlocking spurs Waterfalls	Meanders Oxbow lakes	Flood plains Levees

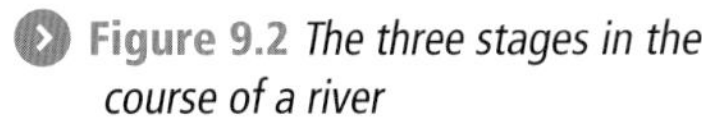

Figure 9.2 *The three stages in the course of a river*

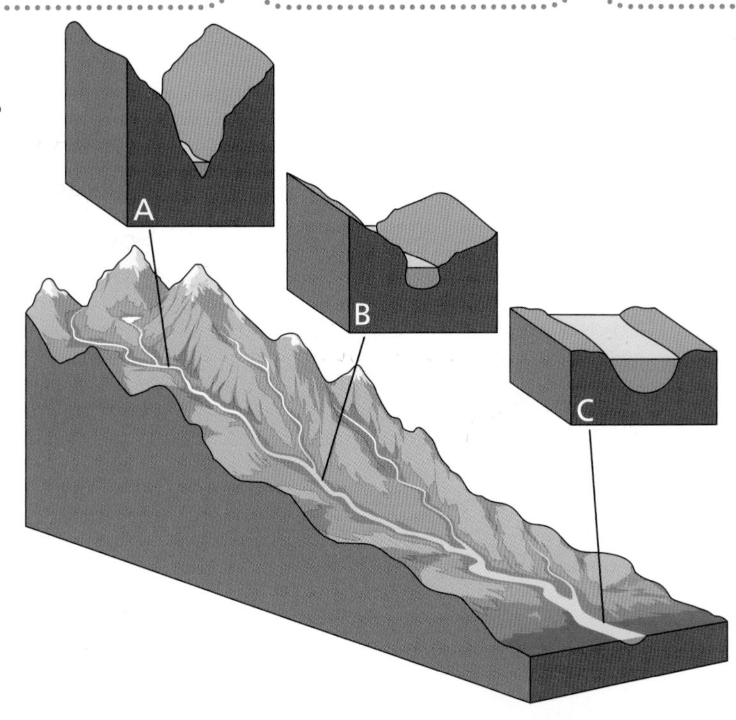

A: Youthful stage
B: Mature stage
C: Old stage

Rivers: Shaping our landscape

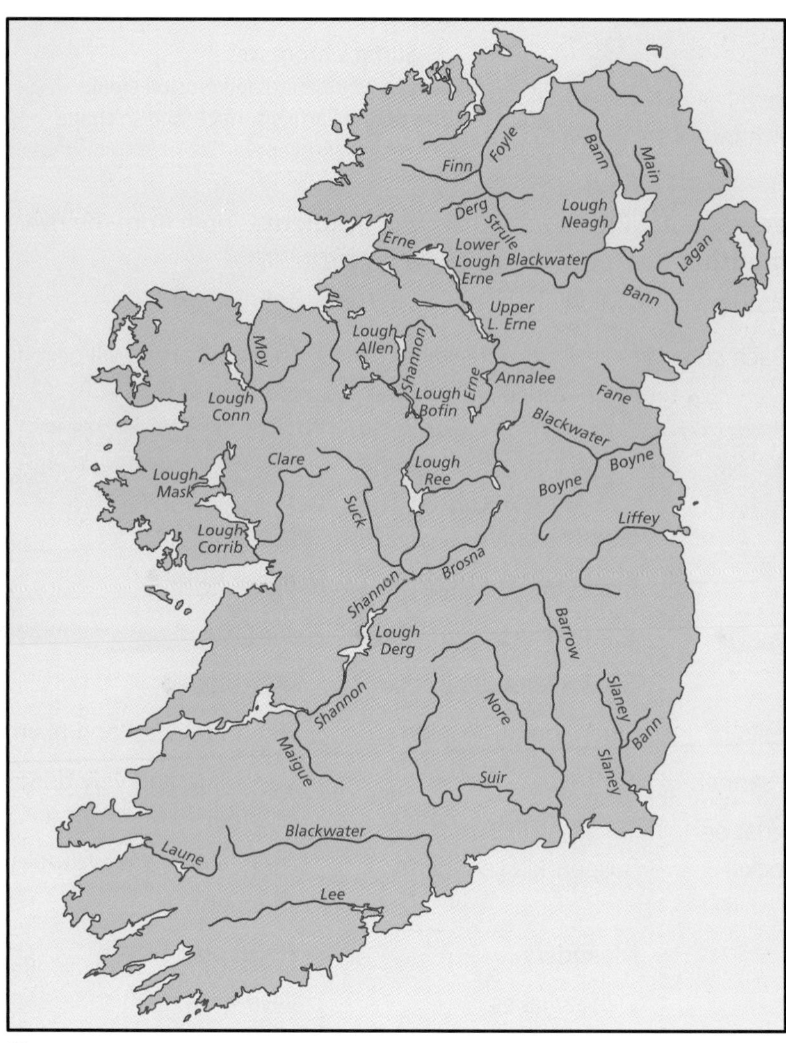

Figure 9.3 *The rivers of Ireland*

NUMERACY ACTIVITY

Go online to find the answer to these questions. Give your answers in kilometres. (Note: 1 mile = 1.6 kilometres)

(a) What is the length of the longest river in Ireland?

(b) What is the length of the river that flows through Cork City?

(c) What is the length of the river that flows through Dublin City?

(d) What is the length of the river that flows through Waterford City?

(e) What is the total length of all three rivers commonly known as the Three Sisters in Ireland?

(f) Which is longer in length
(i) the River Shannon OR
(ii) the total length of the rivers that run through the following cities – Waterford, Galway, Cork, Dublin and Kilkenny?

Rivers are of great importance to people as a **source of water**, and we also **interact** with them in other ways. We will look at the ways in which we interact with rivers later in the chapter.

ACTIVITY

Can you list four other ways people interact with rivers?

(i) Name two landforms in the mature stage of the river. Oxbow lake, meander

(ii) Name two landforms in the old stage of a river. V shaped valley, waterfall

(iii) What is the start or beginning of a river called? Source

(iv) What is a confluence point? The point where 2 rivers meet

(v) What are the main differences between the old stage and the youthful stage of a river?
Fast moving, slow moving. Heavy flow of water, slow flow

(vi) Which two characteristics of the youthful stage of a river allow erosion to occur?
Fast moving water, large amount of water

- I can explain the landforms that are commonly found along the route of a river.
- I can name and identify the three stages of a river.

The work of rivers

Learning Intentions

In this section, you will learn:

- how the processes of river erosion, transportation and deposition shape the landscape.

Erosion	Abrasion	Saltation
Transportation	Attrition	Suspension
Deposition	Solution	
Hydraulic action	Traction	

As a river travels along its course, it **shapes the landscape** in the following ways:

Erosion
The river wears the landscape away.

Transportation
The river carries the material that it has eroded.

Deposition
The river drops the material that it was carrying.

Processes of river erosion

A river **erodes** its bed and bank through the following **processes**:

Hydraulic action	The **physical force** of the moving water wears away and breaks off the rock and soil from the banks and bed of the river.
Abrasion	Small stones carried by the river **wear away** the banks and bed of the river.
Attrition	The small stones in the river are worn down and **broken up** as they hit off each other.
Solution	Rocks, such as limestone, and soil are **dissolved** by acids in the water.

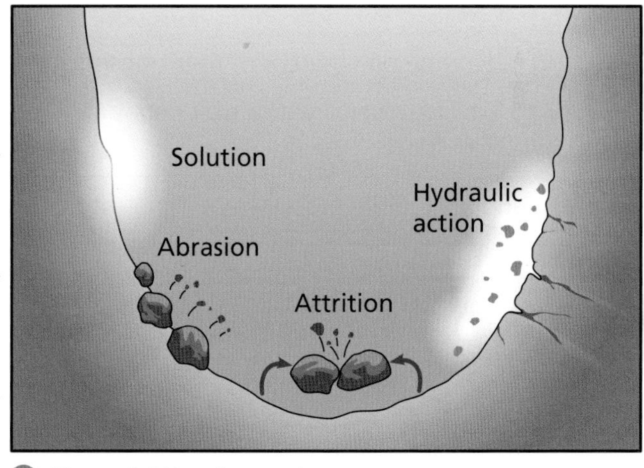

Figure 9.4 *How rivers erode*

Processes of river transportation

A-Z Load: the material that is eroded by the river and carried along in its flow.

The **transportation** downstream of eroded material occurs in a variety of ways. The method depends on the size of the material and also on the size and speed of the river. The material transported by the river is called its **load**.

The load can vary in size from small particles of **sediment** to large pieces of **stone**. The river carries its load in different ways because of the difference in **size** and **weight** of its load.

Methods of river transportation include:

Rolling	The larger stones are **rolled** along the bed of the river. This process is known as **traction**.
Bouncing	The smaller pebbles are **bounced** along the bed of the river. This process is known as **saltation**.
Suspension	Light materials such as sand and silt **float** along in the water.
Solution	Other materials **dissolve** in the water and are carried along by the river.

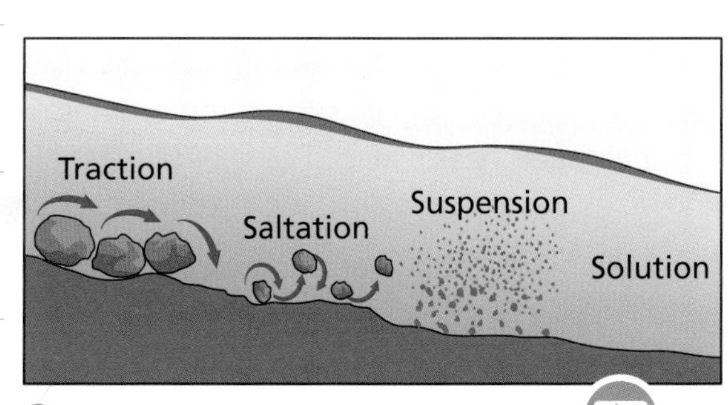

Figure 9.5 *How rivers transport their load*

Processes of river deposition

River **deposition** can shape the land by leaving **sediment** in new places. The sediment makes new land or adds to existing land.

Causes of deposition include:

- **Reduction in the river's speed**: This can happen when a river enters a lake or sea, or during a period of dry weather.
- **Increase in load size**: This can happen when a tributary joins a river, or after a period of heavy rainfall. The river then does not have the energy to carry its increased load so it drops it.
- **Reduction in the river's volume**: This can happen during a period of dry weather.
- **When the gradient levels off:** This occurs when the river reaches flatter land.

DID YOU KNOW? The Roe River in Great Falls, Montana, USA, is only 61 m long and many people consider it to be the world's shortest river.

(i) List the three ways a river shapes the landscape.

(ii) List two processes of river erosion.

(iii) List two processes of river transportation.

(iv) Explain one process of river erosion.

(v) Describe one process of river transportation.

(vi) Explain in detail why a river deposits its load.

 I understand the processes of river erosion, transportation and deposition.   

River landforms

Learning Intentions

In this section, you will learn:

- how landforms are created in the youthful stage of a river by the process of erosion
- how landforms are created in the mature stage of a river by the processes of erosion and deposition
- how landforms are created in the old stage of a river by the process of deposition.

Vertical erosion
V-shaped valley
Interlocking spurs
Waterfall
Undercutting
Overhang
Lateral erosion
Meanders
Oxbow lake
Flood plain
Alluvium
Levee
Delta
Distributary

The youthful stage (upper course)

As the river flows from its **source** through the **youthful (upper) stage**, it erodes **downwards** into the channel that is has created. This is because the **gradient** is **steep** and the river is **flowing fast**. This is known as **vertical erosion**. It causes the river channel to become **deeper**.

Vertical erosion in this highland part of the river helps to create **V-shaped valleys**, **interlocking spurs** and **waterfalls**.

V-shaped valleys

A V-shaped valley is a **steep-sided valley** in the shape of a 'V'. It is shaped by vertical erosion.

Formation:

- The force of moving water in the river cuts downwards into the river bed, making it deeper. This process is called **hydraulic action**. It creates a **deep, narrow valley**.
- **Mechanical weathering** and **mass movement** also weather the sides of the valley, breaking down rock and soil.
- The material that falls into the river is carried downstream as part of the river's **load**.

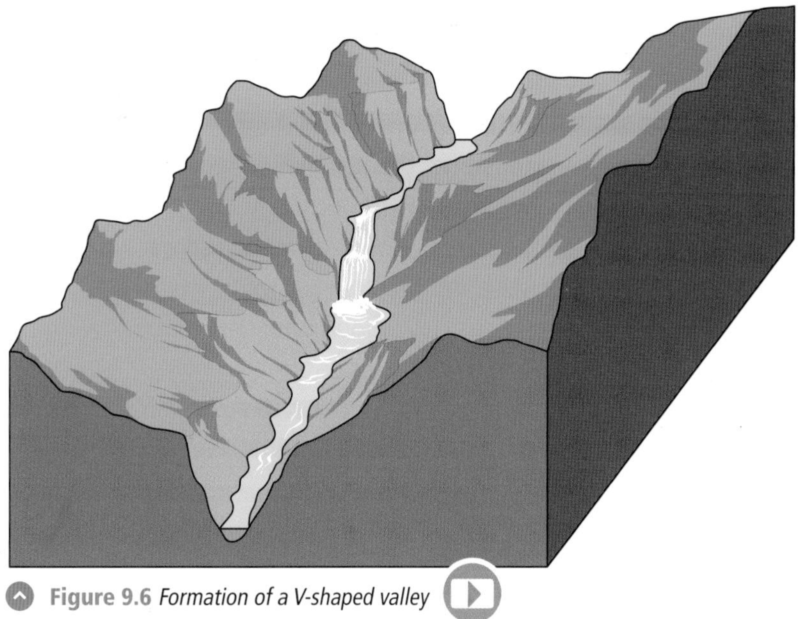

Figure 9.6 *Formation of a V-shaped valley*

Examples of V-shaped valleys: the upper course of the rivers Liffey, Lee and Moy.

Interlocking spurs

Interlocking spurs are areas of **high ground** that jut out at **both sides** of the V-shaped valley.

Formation:

- The river flows very fast in the upper course. It makes its way downhill, winding and bending around areas of **hard rock that it cannot erode**.
- The river erodes **vertically** as it winds and bends.
- This process creates areas of **high ground** on either side of the river which fit together like a zip.
- Over time, as the river continues to erode, they become more pronounced, and we call them **interlocking spurs**.

Examples of interlocking spurs: upper course of the rivers Barrow and Slaney.

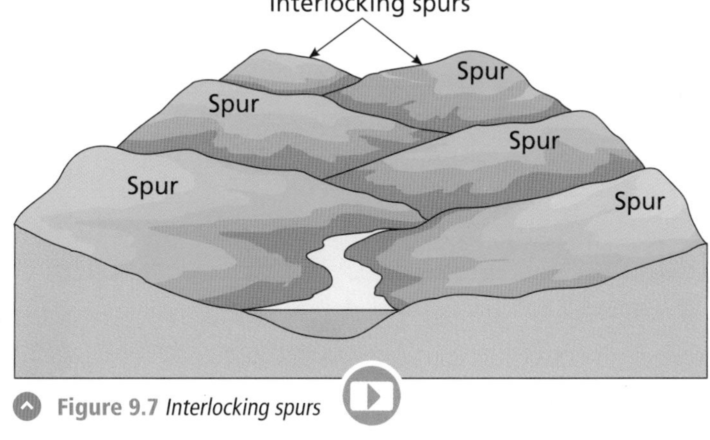

Figure 9.7 *Interlocking spurs*

Figure 9.8 *An example of a V-shaped valley, with interlocking spurs in the background*

Waterfalls

A waterfall is a **vertical drop** in the course of the river in its youthful stage.

Formation:

- When the river flows over an area where a band of **hard rock**, such as granite, lies across a band of **soft rock**, such as sandstone, the soft rock is **eroded** more quickly than the more resistant hard rock, gradually creating a **vertical drop**.
- The river falls over the vertical drop as a **waterfall**.
- This fall increases in size, and the material the river carries (its **load**) creates a deep pool, known as a **plunge pool,** at the base. This plunge pool gets bigger over time through the processes of **hydraulic action** and **abrasion**.
- The water falling into the plunge pool **splashes** against the back wall of the waterfall. The process of **solution** erodes the back wall, **undercutting** the waterfall and creating an **overhang**.
- Pressure and the force of **gravity** eventually cause this overhang to **collapse**.
- This process repeats itself over time, making the waterfall **retreat** upstream.

Examples of waterfalls: Torc Waterfall near Killarney, Co. Kerry, and Ashleigh Falls near Leenane, Co. Mayo.

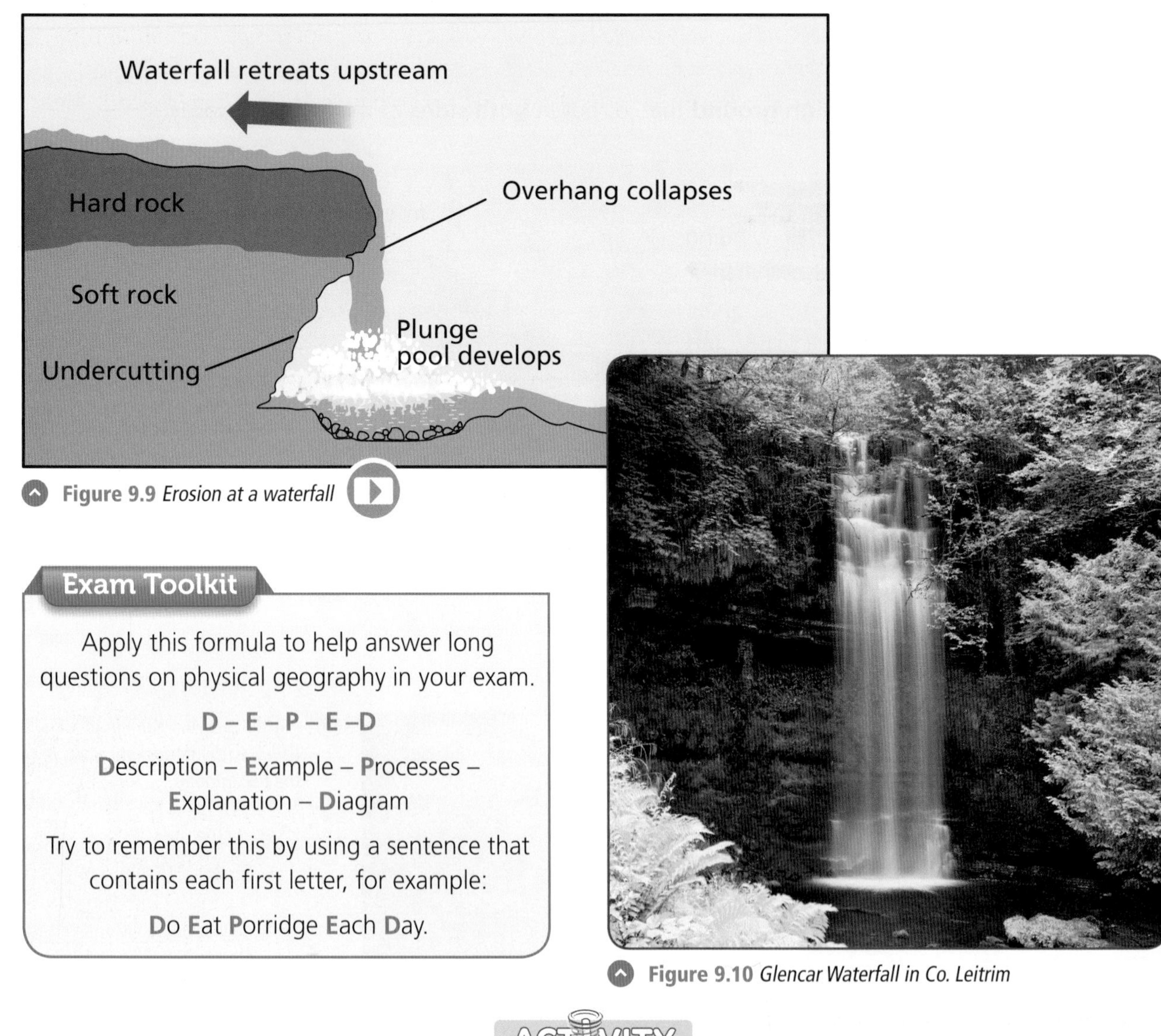

Figure 9.9 *Erosion at a waterfall*

Figure 9.10 *Glencar Waterfall in Co. Leitrim*

Exam Toolkit

Apply this formula to help answer long questions on physical geography in your exam.

D – E – P – E –D

Description – **E**xample – **P**rocesses – **E**xplanation – **D**iagram

Try to remember this by using a sentence that contains each first letter, for example:

Do **E**at **P**orridge **E**ach **D**ay.

ACTIVITY

Can you apply the D-E-P-E-D formula to explain one landform of river erosion to your classmates? Use the outline on page 40 of your Activity Book to help you.

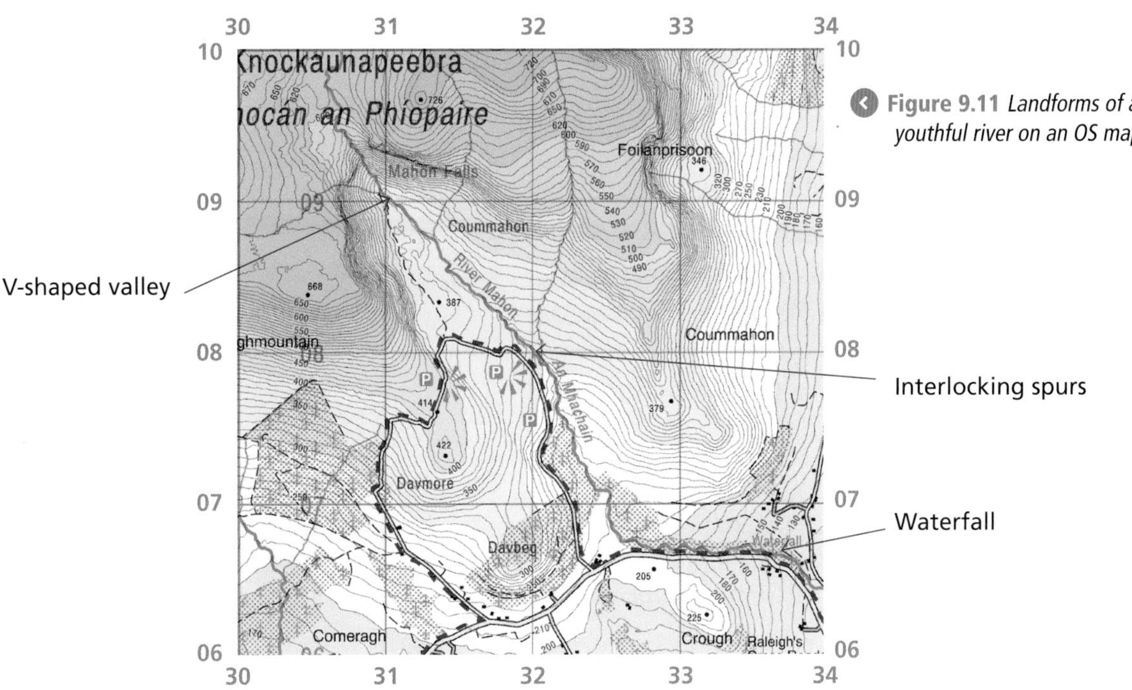

Figure 9.11 *Landforms of a youthful river on an OS map*

The mature stage (middle course)

During the **mature (middle) stage**, the river is now carrying a **greater volume** (amount) of water and as a result has **more power**. This is because **tributaries** or other rivers have joined it. Even though the gradient at this stage is not as steep as the youthful stage, the river is still **eroding**. It now erodes both **vertically** and **laterally** (sideways). Also, at this stage, the river is carrying more material in its **load**.

Meanders

Meanders are **curves** or **bends** in the river in its mature stage. Meanders are formed by **both deposition and erosion**.

Formation:

- As the river reaches its mature stage it flows more **slowly** and **lateral erosion** occurs where there is a bend in the river.
- The **hydraulic action** of the river **erodes** the bank on the **outside** of the bend, as this is where the river is flowing the fastest. The bank is also **undercut**, further eroding the outside of the bend.
- Meanwhile, the eroded material is **deposited** on the **inside** of the bend where the river is flowing more slowly (as the river has to slow down on the inside of the bend).
- With time, the bend becomes more extreme and forms the shape of a **loop**.

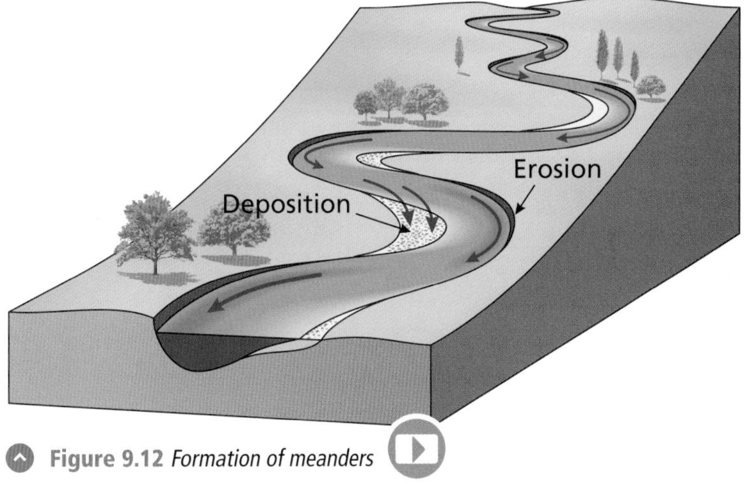

Figure 9.12 *Formation of meanders*

Examples of meanders: Meanders are found on most rivers and can be seen in the middle courses of the rivers **Shannon** and **Moy**.

Figure 9.13 *Meanders on the River Moy in Co. Mayo*

Oxbow lakes

An oxbow lake is a **horseshoe-shaped lake** that is formed when a meander is **cut off** from the river.

Formation:

- When the **neck** of a meander becomes very tight, the river can **erode** its way through the neck to take the straightest course.
- This usually happens during a **flood** when the river has a higher **discharge** and more energy.
- The loop is cut off from the main river when **sediment** is deposited at the entrances to the loop.
- The cut-off loop is called an **oxbow lake**. Over time, this lake will dry up and form an **oxbow scar**.

Examples of oxbow lakes: in the middle courses of the rivers Liffey and the Moy.

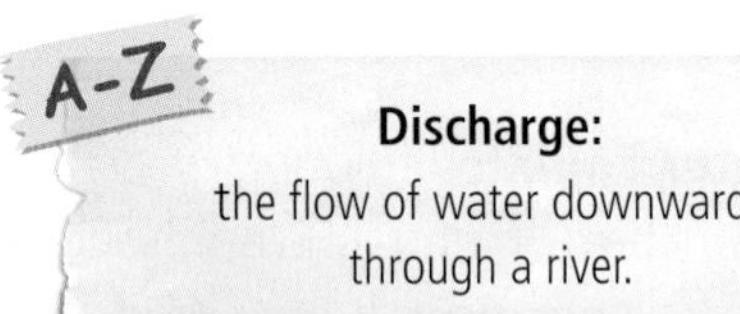

Discharge:
the flow of water downwards through a river.

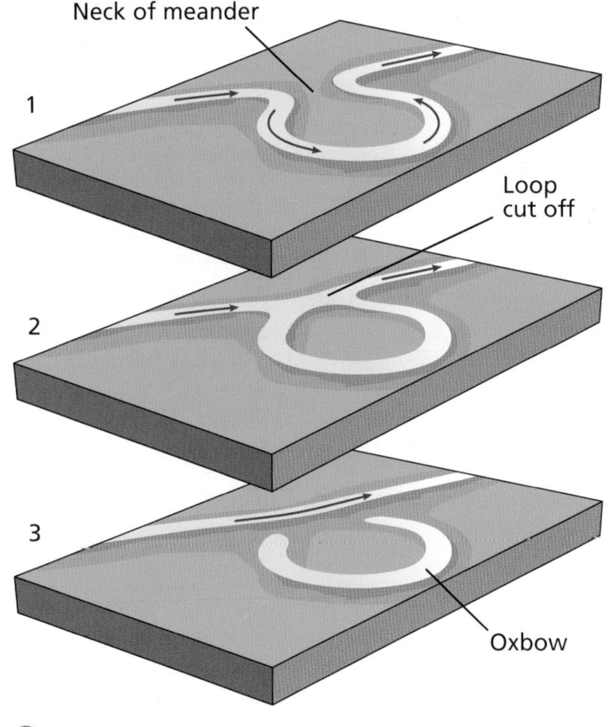

Figure 9.14 *Formation of an oxbow lake*

Figure 9.15 *Oxbow lake in central Alaska*

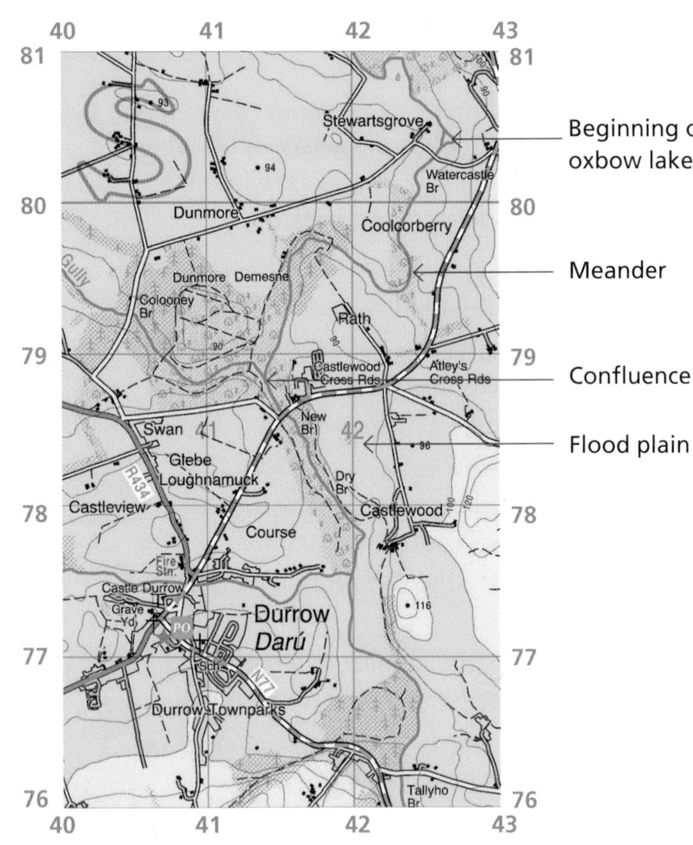

Figure 9.16 *Landforms of the mature and old stages of a river on an OS map*

The old stage (lower course)

At this stage the river is nearing the end of its course. It **flows slowly** along flat land and carries a **load** that has been eroded during the previous stages and through surface run-off. As the river is now nearing the sea, it has less energy and **deposition** has become the main process.

ACTIVITY

Why do you think there are trees planted along the course of the river in Figure 9.16? Discuss in pairs.

Flood plains

A flood plain is a **wide, flat** area of land on either side of the river in its old stage. The river is now nearing the sea, and **deposition** has become the main process.

Formation:

- The river carries a large load of sediment known as **alluvium**. During a flood, the river spreads out on both sides, and **deposits** the load it is carrying. The heaviest material is dropped off first.
- Over time, a **thick layer** of alluvium builds up on the flat land by the river. This is the **flood plain**.
- The alluvium makes the soil very **fertile** and generally good for farming.
- The highest point reached by the river when in flood is called the **bluff line**.

Examples of flood plains: the lower courses of the rivers Moy and Liffey.

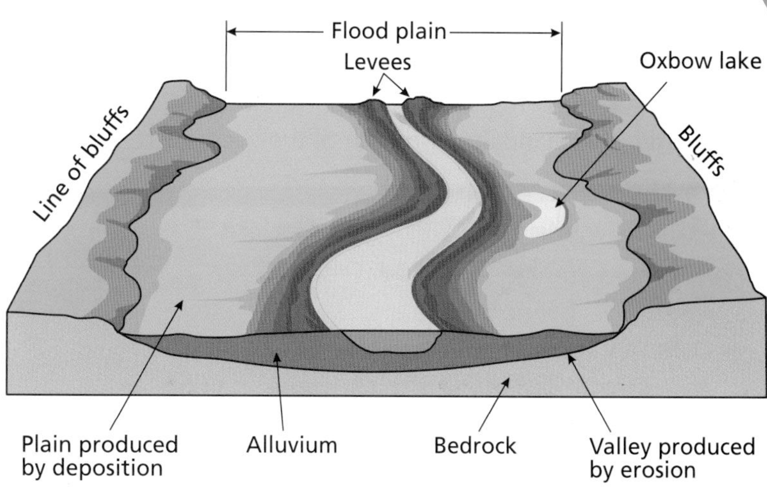

Figure 9.17 *Landforms of a flood plain*

Figure 9.18 *A flood plain during flooding*

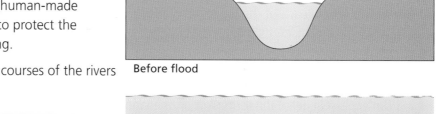

Levees

A levee is a build-up of **alluvium** on the **banks** of a river. Levees are caused by **floods**.

Formation:

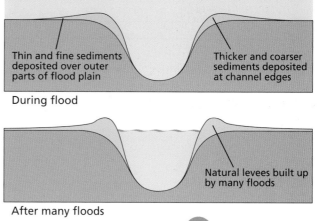

- In times of **low flow**, material is deposited on the **river bed**, raising the height of the river bed.
- In times of **flood**, the water leaves the **channel** and spreads out over the flood plain. As it does so, it loses energy and **deposits** its load.
- The coarser, **heavier** material is deposited on the river **banks**, and the **finer** material is carried further onto the flood plain.
- After many floods, the river builds a **bank** on either side. **Artificial levees** (human-made river banks) can also be used to protect the surrounding land from flooding.

Examples of levees: the lower courses of the rivers Moy and Liffey.

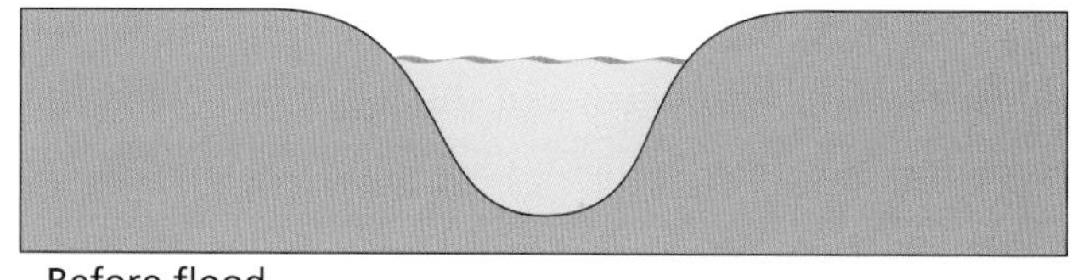

Figure 9.19 *A levee*

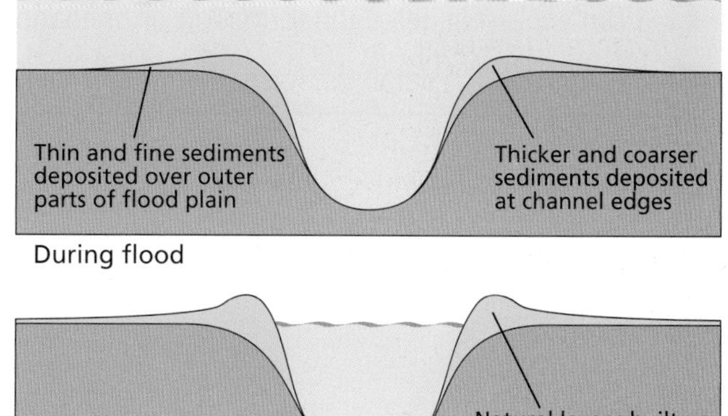

Figure 9.20 *Formation of levees*

Deltas

Deltas are **landforms of deposition** found in the old stage of a river. A delta is a **triangular** or **fan-shaped** area of land at the mouth of the river where it enters a lake or the sea.

Formation:

- The river slows down when it enters a lake or the sea and **loses energy**, causing it to **deposit** its load.
- Deltas form where river **mouths** become choked with **sediment**, causing the main river channel to **split** into many smaller channels or **distributaries** on their way to the sea.

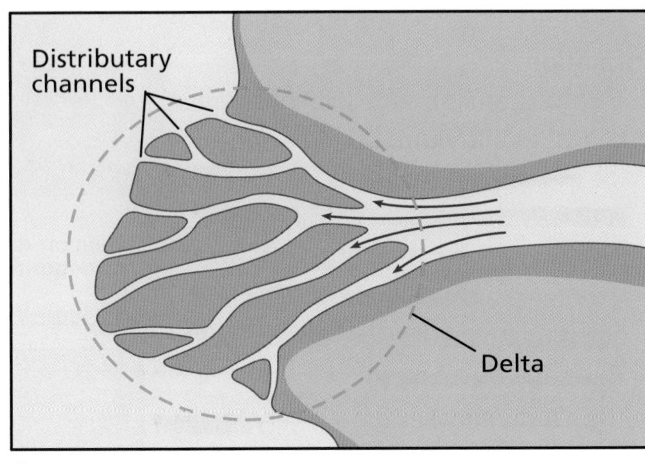

Figure 9.21 *The structure of a delta*

Deltas form only under certain **conditions**:

- The river must be transporting a **large amount of sediment**.
- The sea must have a **small tidal range** and **weak currents**.
- The sea must be **shallow** at the river mouth.

Examples of deltas: the Mississippi delta in the USA, the Ganges and Brahmaputra delta in India and Bangladesh, and the Nile delta in Africa.

Can you apply the D-E-P-E-D formula to explain one landform of river deposition to your classmates? Use the outline on page 41 of your Activity Book to help you.

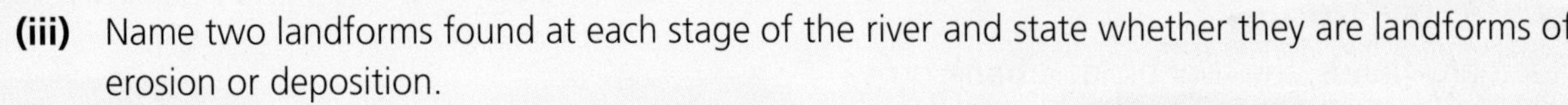

(i) Name the three stages of a river.

(ii) Why does deposition become the main process in the old stage of a river?

(iii) Name two landforms found at each stage of the river and state whether they are landforms of erosion or deposition.

(iv) Explain how each of the processes of erosion can be involved in the formation of waterfalls.

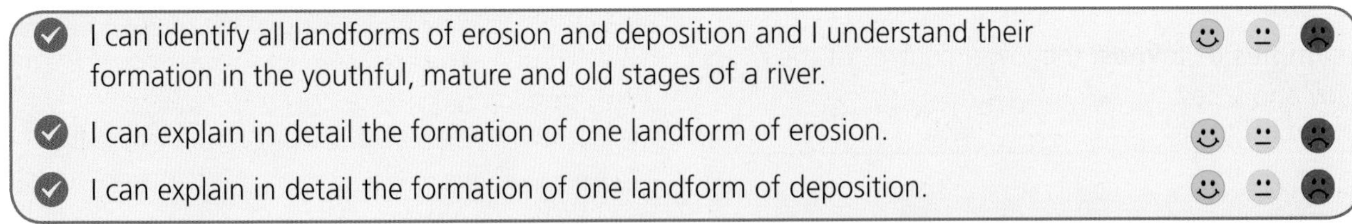

- I can identify all landforms of erosion and deposition and I understand their formation in the youthful, mature and old stages of a river.
- I can explain in detail the formation of one landform of erosion.
- I can explain in detail the formation of one landform of deposition.

People and rivers

Learning Intentions

In this section, you will learn:

- that people use rivers on a daily basis and in a variety of ways
- that these human interactions with rivers can be both beneficial and harmful.

Settlement
Pollution
Hydroelectric power (HEP)
Surface run-off

Some of the ways people interact with rivers include:

- Transport
- Tourism
- Fishing
- Settlement
- Pollution
- Hydroelectric power (HEP)
- Domestic water supply
- Flooding

Transport

Since the earliest settlers came to Ireland, rivers have been used to transport people and goods. **Waterford** is an example of a city with a **port** function which we will examine in more detail in Chapter 12. The **River Rhine** is an important transport route in Europe.

Figure 9.22 *A barge transporting goods on the River Rhine*

Figure 9.23 *An angler fishing for salmon*

Tourism

Tourists use rivers for cruising and fishing. Towns such as **Carrick-on-Shannon** and **Athlone** along the River Shannon are well-known tourist destinations in Ireland. We will learn more about rivers and tourism on page 150.

Fishing

Irish rivers are popular with anglers and many, such as the **River Moy** in Co. Mayo, are famous for **salmon fishing**. Many tourists visit Ireland for this purpose. In order to ensure that freshwater fishing is **sustainable**, anglers must have a fishing licence and follow rules set out by **Inland Fisheries Ireland (IFI)**. They set down what tackle you can use and when you are allowed to fish for certain species. We looked at responsible fishing in Ireland in Chapter 4.

Settlement

As we will learn in Chapter 12, many cities and towns have developed along **river banks** as these locations provide water, food, transport and defence.

Figure 9.24 *Limerick City developed on the banks of the Shannon*

Figure 9.25 *Waste from industry can sometimes poison rivers*

Pollution

Pollution can come from a variety of human activities

- **Farming**: When farmers spread **slurry** on their land, it can seep into rivers, polluting them and killing fish.
- **Domestic**: Waste material from **septic tanks** can seep into rivers, polluting them in a similar way.
- **Industrial waste**: If factories dump **waste** into rivers it can also cause pollution. Not only fish, but birds and animals that live close to the river may be poisoned.

Hydroelectric power (HEP)

HEP stations are often built using **dams**. The power of the water is used to generate cheap, clean, renewable energy. We looked at HEP in Chapter 5.

Domestic water supply

More than **80 per cent** of the water we use when we turn on our taps comes from our **rivers and lakes**. The rest comes from groundwater and springs. **Irish Water** is responsible for the supply of water in Ireland. You can find out more about the work that they do at www.water.ie.

Flooding

Human activity can be responsible for flooding. Cutting down trees can lead to more **surface run-off** of rainwater because there are no trees to absorb the water. It also leads to soil erosion because the trees are no longer holding the soil in place. This can mean that soil is deposited on river beds, causing the river to rise and burst its banks. Flooding is classed as a **natural disaster** and can have devastating effects on the surrounding region and its people.

CASE STUDY

Rivers and flooding: the Shannon, 2015–16

During the **winter of 2015–16**, Ireland was affected by a series of **storms** that battered the country over the course of November, December and January. **Storm Desmond** brought the largest amount of rainfall. Many parts of the country received double, and in some cases triple, the average amount of winter rainfall.

The **River Shannon and its drainage basin** was the area worst affected by the flooding. It had a major impact on urban and rural communities such as Limerick, Castleconnell, Clonlara, Carrick-on-Shannon and Athlone.

Figure 9.26 *Flooding on the Shannon at Shannonbridge, December 2015*

Why did flooding occur along the Shannon?

- Unusually high levels of **rainfall**
- **Lack of planning** and flood defences
- The **building** of residential and commercial units on flood plains
- **Poor management** of the Shannon waterway.

DID YOU KNOW? With the growing problem of climate change, and increased levels of rainfall, flooding is likely to get worse all over the world. We cannot prevent the rain from falling so we must be prepared for it by planning for it.

Immediate impact

- Thousands of **homes flooded**
- Large areas of agricultural **farmland covered** in water
- Many homes asked to boil their drinking water owing to concerns about **water quality**
- **Roads** and other infrastructure severely damaged
- **Businesses** forced to shut during the busy Christmas period
- **Livestock** lost.

Government responses

- The **army** was deployed to help with prevention of further flooding by using **sandbags** in areas and also **pumping** water on a 24-hour basis.
- Families were temporarily housed in **emergency accommodation** such as hotels.
- €16 million was given to the **local councils** in assisting with the **clean-up** and **prevention** of flooding in the immediate aftermath.
- €85 million was given to **repair damage** to roads and infrastructure.

Long-term solutions to the problem

- Better **flood defences** were put in place to prevent future flooding.
- The River Shannon was **dredged** to remove the build-up of sediment and deepen the river channel.
- The **Shannon Flood Risk Group** was established to coordinate flood control and maintain the Shannon basin.
- A national flooding **forecast** and **warning service** was set up.

Figure 9.27 *Steel fences were erected in Limerick to keep out flooding*

Imagine you have been hired by the government to research flood prevention methods around the world. Use the internet to find out what you can. You might look at flood prevention in the Netherlands and Bangladesh. Record what you learn. Get together in groups of four and write a short report outlining the best methods to prevent flooding in Ireland.

PORTFOLIO ACTIVITY 9.1

Research a flood that has occurred either locally, nationally or internationally and fill out the template on page 36 of your Portfolio.

Rivers and tourism: the Shannon

Tourism is one way in which people interact in a positive way with rivers. The **River Shannon** is Ireland's longest river and has become a **major tourist attraction** in a short period of time. It is used by **watersports** enthusiasts, **anglers** and those in leisure boats. This is mainly because the River Shannon is free from any large commercial shipping traffic. A **cruise** along the Shannon is now possible with one of the many **boat rental companies**. Tourists can travel the length of the Shannon from Carrick-on-Shannon in Leitrim all the way down to Limerick city, and enjoy the various **tourist sites** that the Shannon has to offer.

Figure 9.28 *A marina with cruising boats on the Shannon*

PORTFOLIO ACTIVITY 9.2

Imagine you are planning a family cruise along the River Shannon. Go to page 37 of your Portfolio to create an itinerary for your family.

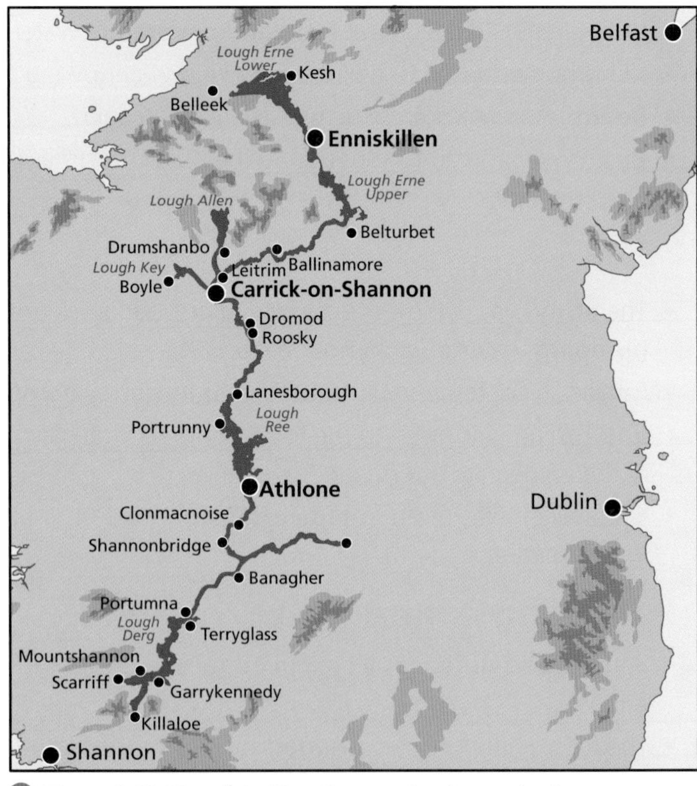

Figure 9.29 *Map of the River Shannon showing tourist sites*

 **(i)** List two ways in which people use rivers on a daily basis.

 **(ii)** Describe two ways in which people pollute rivers. What are the effects of this pollution?

 **(iii)** Why, historically, have people settled beside rivers?

(iv) What suggestions would you make to prevent future flooding of the River Shannon?

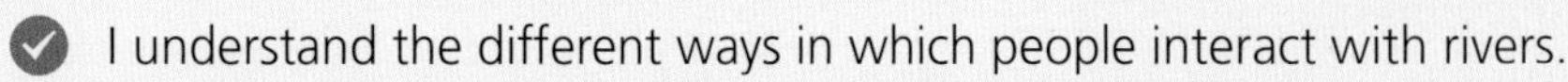

- I understand the different ways in which people interact with rivers.
- I have studied one negative and one positive way in which people interact with rivers.

Drainage features (rivers) on Ordnance Survey maps

Learning Intentions

In this section, you will learn:

- river features and drainage features can be identified on an Ordnance Survey map.

Drainage
Dendritic
Trellis
Radial
Deranged

The word **drainage** refers to how water flows in an area. On an Ordnance Survey map you can pick out rivers, streams and other drainage features that are present in the landscape. If an area is **well drained** it will attract **settlement**. A **badly drained** area might have a chaotic system of rivers and streams, bogs or marshland, and therefore **little settlement**.

Patterns of drainage

We can identify different **patterns of drainage** using Ordnance Survey maps. The most distinctive patterns of drainage are **dendritic**, **trellis**, **radial** and **deranged**.

Dendritic

Dendritic drainage systems are the most common form of drainage system. In a dendritic system, many tributary streams combine before joining the main river.

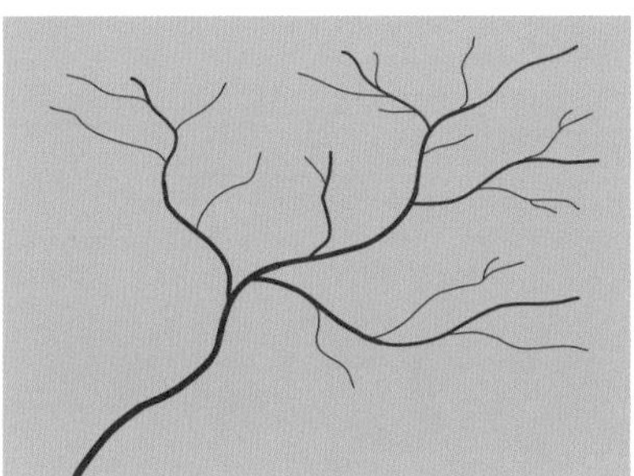

Trellis

As a river flows along, smaller tributaries feed into it from the steep slopes on the sides of mountains. These tributaries enter the main river at an angle close to 90° (right angle), creating a drainage system that looks like a trellis.

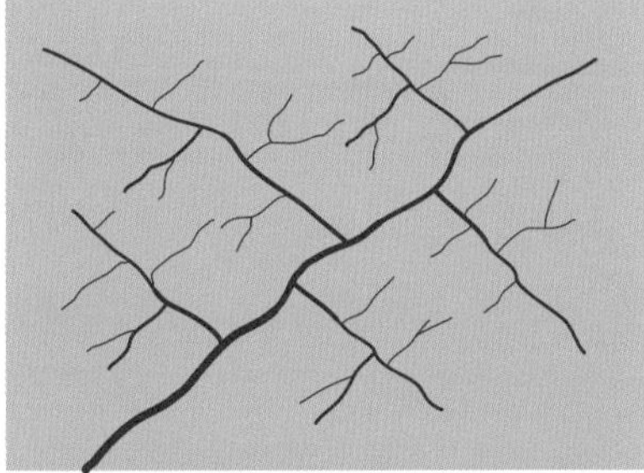

Radial

In a radial drainage system, the streams radiate outwards from a central high point. This resembles the spokes on a bicycle wheel.

High point

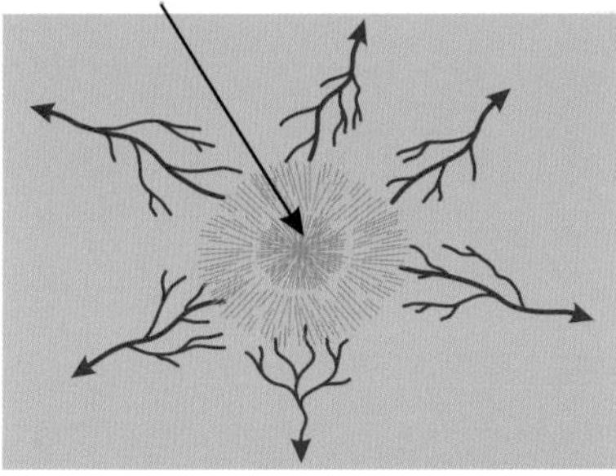

Deranged

In a deranged drainage system, there is no clear pattern to the rivers.

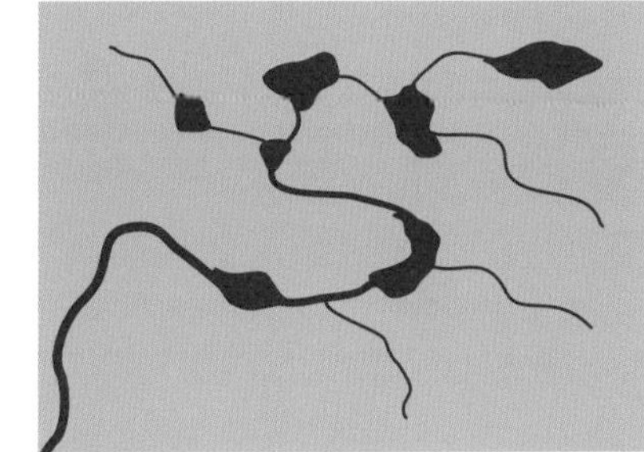

DID YOU KNOW? The term dendritic comes from the Greek word *dendron*, which means tree. As you can see, the tributaries of the river look like the branches of a tree.

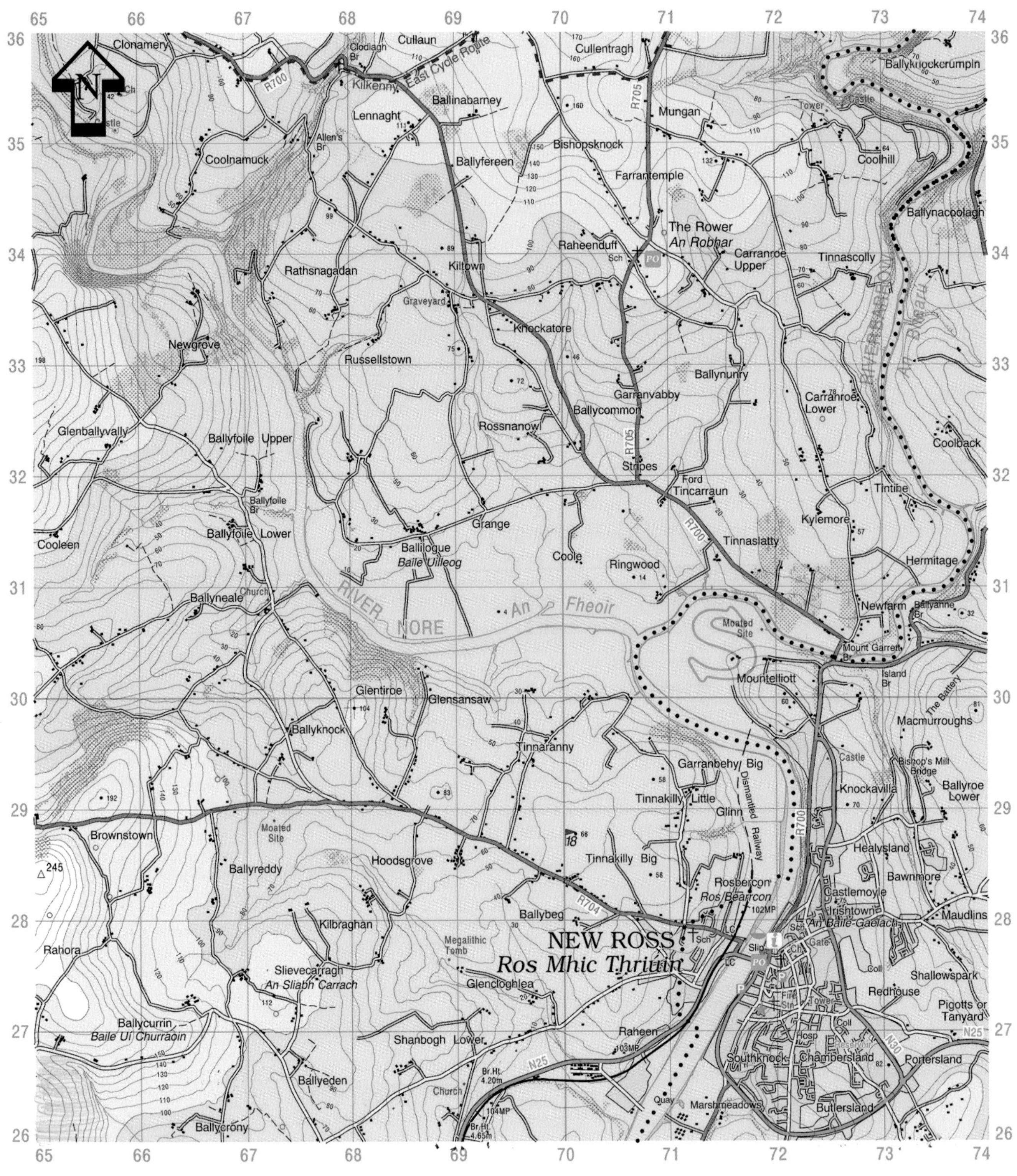

Figure 9.30 *New Ross, Co. Wexford*

Rivers and maps

Examine the Ordnance Survey map of New Ross on the opposite page and answer these questions.

1. Identify the following features on the map extract using four-figure grid references:
   - **(a)** Flood plain
   - **(b)** Dendritic drainage
   - **(c)** V-shaped valley
2. Identify the following features on the map extract using six-figure grid references:
   - **(a)** Meander
   - **(b)** Confluence point
   - **(c)** Tributary
3. On the map extract, find the length of the River Nore in kilometres.
4. On the map extract, find the area of the land south of the River Nore to the nearest km^2.
5. Draw a sketch map of the Ordnance Survey map extract and include the following:
   - **(a)** River Nore
   - **(b)** Meander
   - **(c)** Confluence point
   - **(d)** Flood plain
   - **(e)** Tributary
   - **(f)** Urban area of New Ross

✔ I can recognise river features and drainage features on an Ordnance Survey map. ☺ 😐 ☹

REVISION

The river goes through three stages – the youthful stage, the ___midior___ stage and the old stage.

Rivers shape the landscape by erosion and ___deposition___. A river erodes the landscape through four processes: hydraulic action, abrasion, ___mechanical weathiring___ and ___transportation___. It then transports its ___sediment___ by __________, __________, suspension and solution.

Different landforms form along the __________ of the river. In the youthful stage, V-shaped valleys, __________ __________ and __________ are found. In the mature stage, landforms such as __________ and __________ __________ are formed, while in the old stage, flood plains, __________ and __________ are present.

People can have both __________ and negative impacts on the river system. We can use rivers to our advantage, for example to make electricity by building __________ and __________ power stations.

Questions & Answers

Sample Question

Name **one** landform of river erosion and, with the aid of a diagram, explain how it was formed.

Sample Answer

Description – A waterfall is a landform of river erosion. It occurs when a river flows over a vertical drop.

Examples – Examples of waterfalls in Ireland are Torc Waterfall near Killarney, Co. Kerry and Powerscourt Waterfall in Co. Wicklow.

Processes – When a river flows over an area comprising a layer of hard rock above a layer of soft rock, the soft rock gets eroded quicker by the processes of hydraulic action, abrasion and solution.

Explanation – This creates a fall in the river. A plunge pool forms at the base of the waterfall due to the force of the falling water. Undercutting then takes place and creates an overhang. This overhang eventually collapses and the waterfall retreats.

Plunge pool undercuts hard rock which collapses

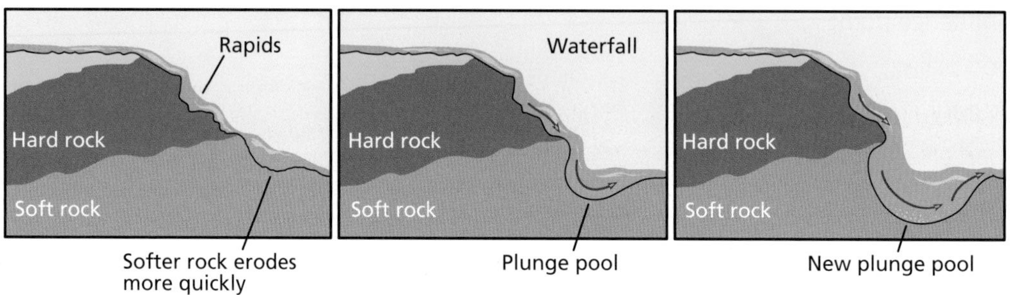

Short Questions

1. At **X** in the diagram, the river is rolling and dragging stones along the river bed (traction). This is an example of:

River erosion ☐

River transport ☐

River deposition ☐ [tick (✓) the correct box]

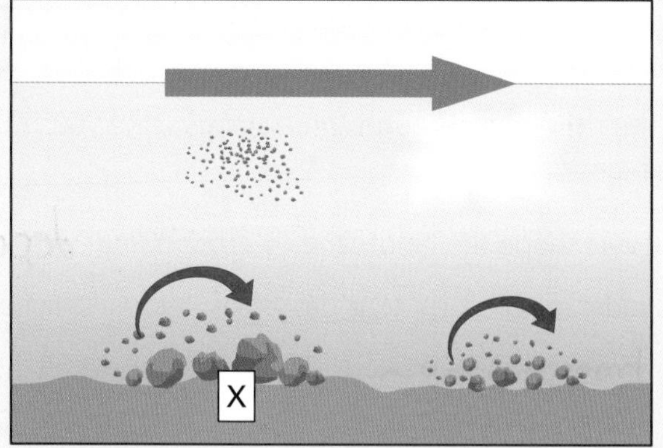

2. The diagram shows four river features that are labelled A–D.

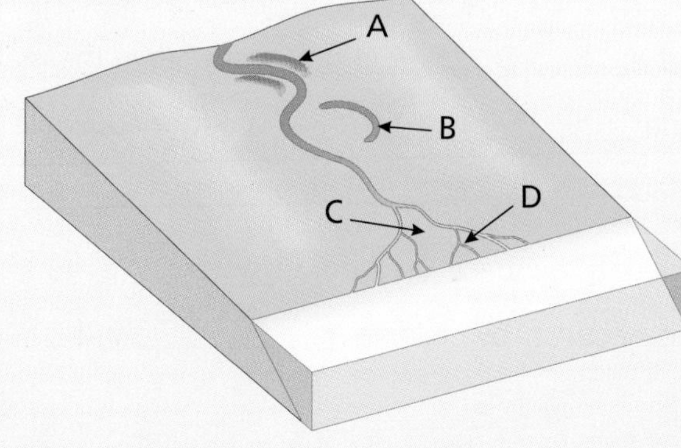

Feature	Letter
Delta	C
Oxbow lake	
Distributary	
Levee	

In the boxes provided, match each letter on the diagram with the correct feature listed in the table.

3. The diagram shows the course of a river.

Give the correct location for each of the river landforms shown on the diagram by writing the correct letter beside each landform named in the table below. One pair has been completed for you.

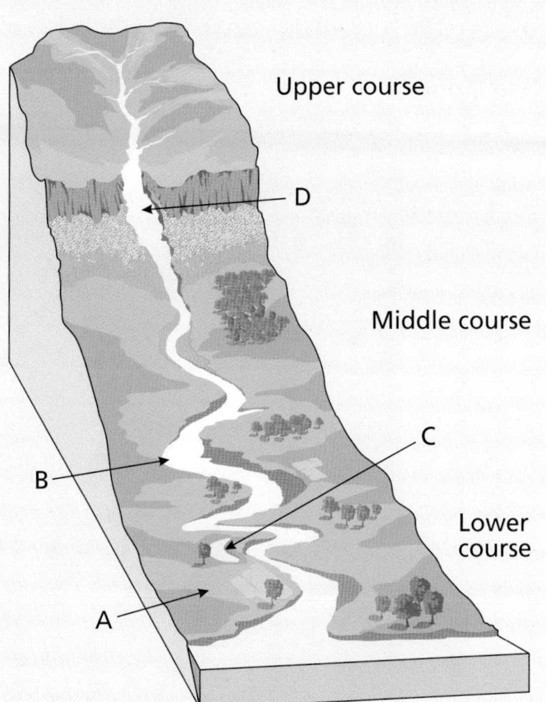

Feature	Letter
Meander	B
Oxbow lake	
Waterfall	
Floodplain	

4. The diagrams A, B and C show a river in its upper, middle and lower courses.

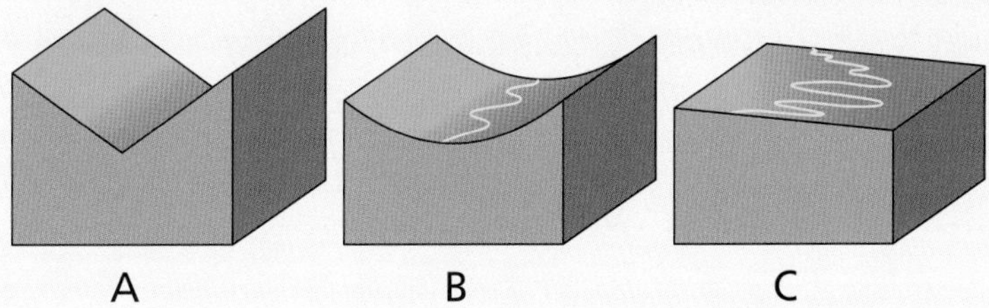

Circle the correct answer in **each** of the statements below:

(i) Lateral erosion is most common in **Diagram A / Diagram B / Diagram C**.

(ii) Deposition is most common in **Diagram A / Diagram B / Diagram C**.

(iii) Vertical erosion is most common in **Diagram A / Diagram B / Diagram C**.

5. The diagram shows river meanders. The statements below refer to the diagram.

One of the statements is correct. Tick (✓) the box opposite the correct statement.

The river is:

(i) Eroding at **B** and depositing at **A** ☐

(ii) Eroding at **B** and depositing at **C** ☐

(iii) Eroding at **A** and depositing at **C** ☐

(iv) Eroding at **C** and depositing at **D** ☐

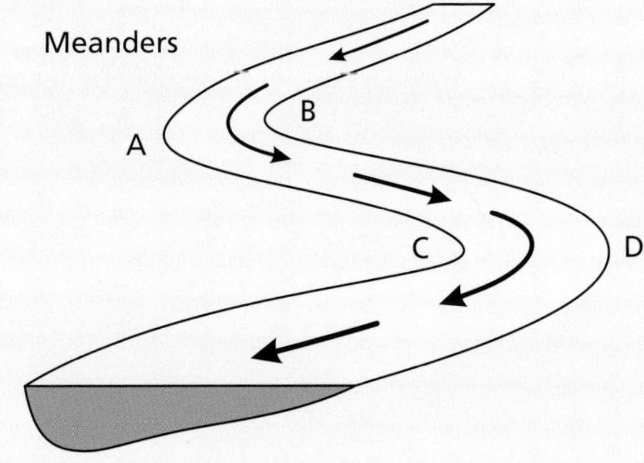

6. The photograph below shows a river bursting its banks and flooding the land nearby. Circle the correct answer in **each** of the statements below:

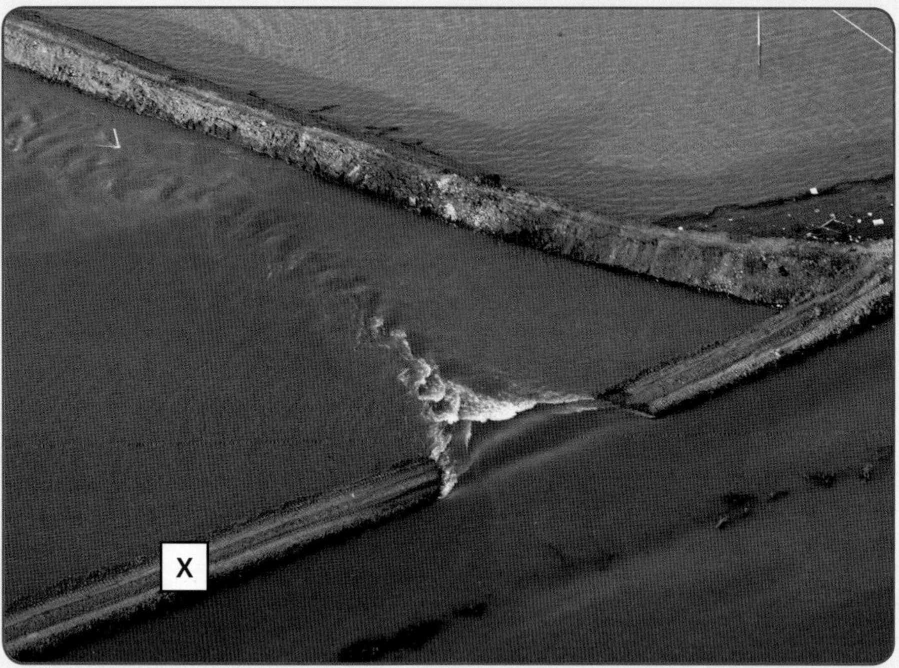

(i) The landform at **X**, where the river breaks through, is known as a **levee / delta**.

(ii) Landforms such as this are found in the **youthful / old** stage of a river.

(iii) Deposits left after such flooding are called **moraine / alluvium**.

Long Questions

1. **(a)** Name **one** landform of river erosion and, with the aid of a diagram, explain how it was formed.

   (b) Name **one** landform of river deposition and, with the aid of a diagram, explain how it was formed.

   (c) **(i)** Name and briefly explain **one** way that people use rivers.

   (ii) Name and briefly explain **one** way that people pollute rivers.

2. Rivers in times of flooding can have negative impacts on the surrounding area. Describe some of these impacts with reference to an example you have studied.

3. Describe **three** measures that could be taken to avoid flooding.

Visual Summary

Confluence
Source
Drainage basin
Tributary
Watershed
Estuary
Mouth
Common features
Youthful
Mature
Old
Stages
Rivers
Processes of erosion
Hydraulic action
Abrasion
Attrition
Solution
Processes of transportation
Solution
Suspension
Rolling
Bouncing
Processes of deposition
Reduction in speed and volume
Increase in load
Gradient levels off
Landforms of erosion
V-shaped valleys
Interlocking spurs
Waterfall
Plunge pool
Undercutting
Landforms of erosion and deposition
Meander
Oxbow lake
Landforms of deposition
Flood plains
Levees
Deltas
People and rivers
Transport
Tourism
Fishing
Settlement
Pollution
HEP
Domestic water supply
Flooding

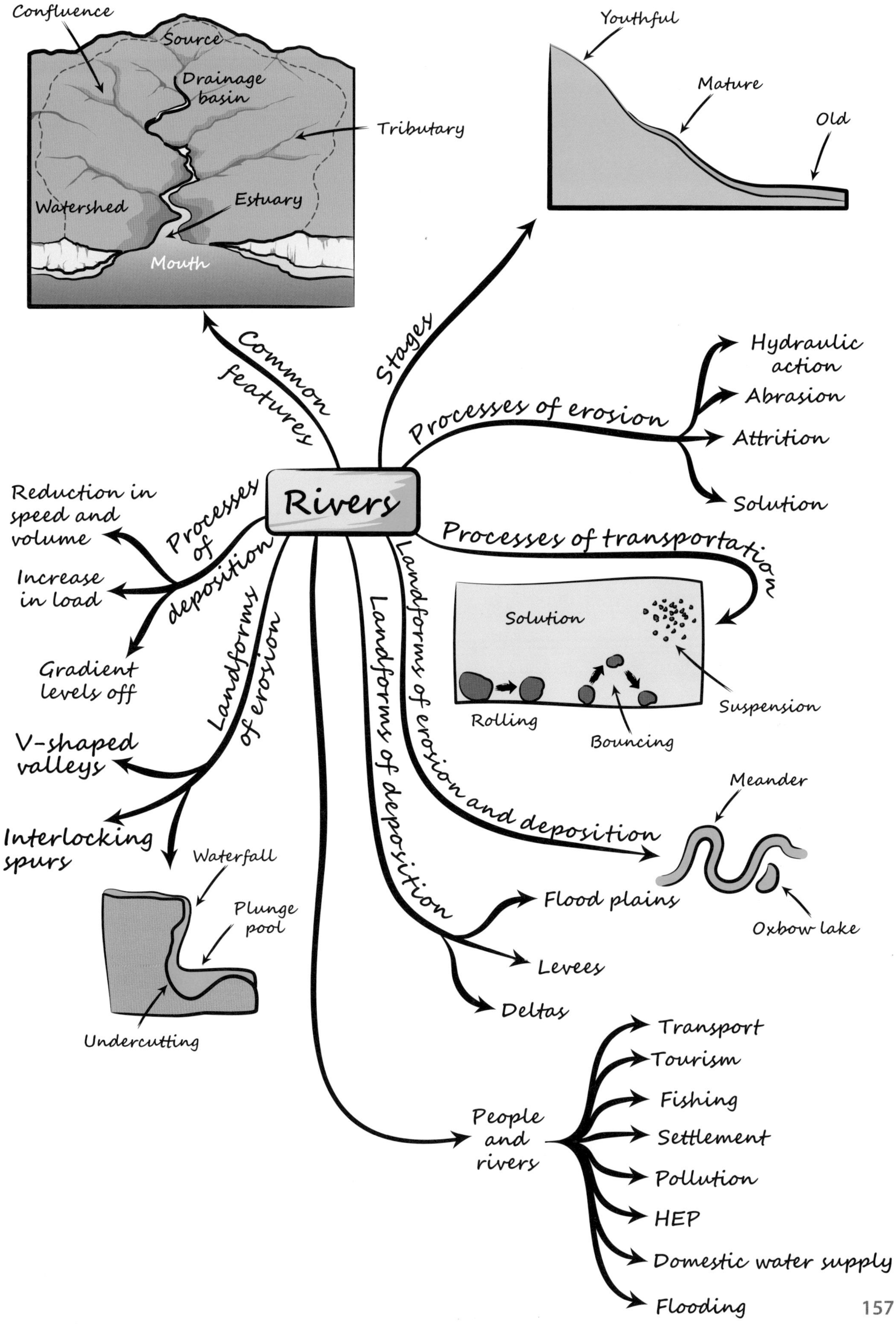

10 The Sea: How it shapes our coastline

In this chapter, you will learn:

- how waves erode, transport and deposit material along the coastline
- why erosion occurs in some places and deposition in others
- how landforms of coastal erosion and deposition are formed
- how people interact with the sea
- how human interaction affects coastlines
- how to recognise coastal landforms on Ordnance Survey maps.

ICE-BREAKER ACTIVITY

Look at the shape of the west and east coastlines on the map of Ireland on page 411. In what ways are they different? Can you suggest reasons why?

Waves

Learning Intentions

- how waves are formed
- the different types of waves that can be formed
- how waves erode the coastline.

Fetch
Swash
Backwash
Constructive waves
Destructive waves
Compression

The sea is constantly shaping the coastline. Waves **erode**, **transport** and **deposit** material along the coast.

Waves are formed by **wind** moving across the surface of the sea. The distance of open sea over which the wind blows is called the **fetch**. Waves with a greater fetch are stronger.

When waves reach **shallow** water, the front of the wave comes in contact with the seabed, causing it to **break** as it moves towards the shore.

When a wave breaks, the water that rushes up the beach is known as the **swash.** The water that returns back down the beach is known as the **backwash**.

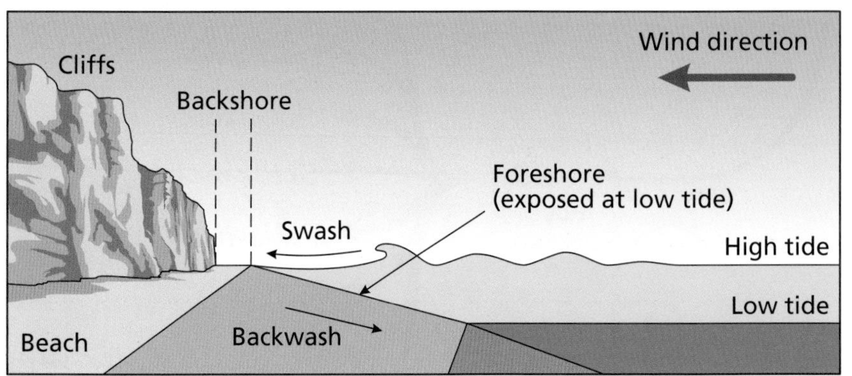

Figure 10.1 *Swash and backwash*

There are two types of waves:

1. **Constructive waves:** waves in which the swash is greater than the backwash. Constructive waves **deposit** material.

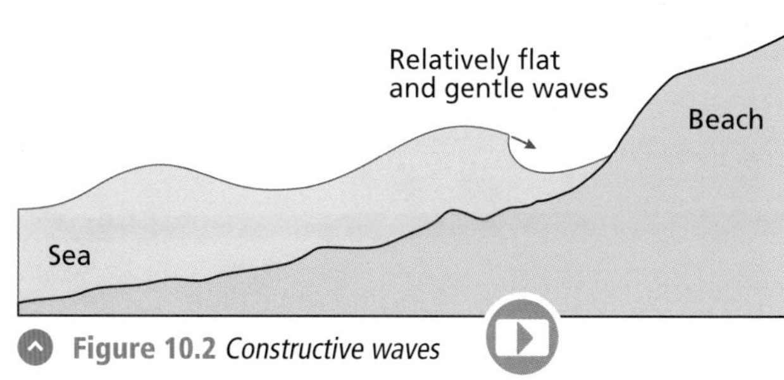

Figure 10.2 *Constructive waves*

2. **Destructive waves:** waves in which the backwash is greater than the swash. Destructive waves **erode** material and carry it away.

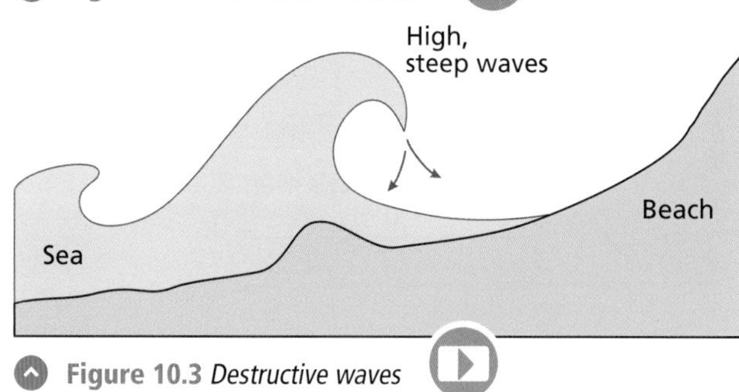

Figure 10.3 *Destructive waves*

Processes of coastal erosion

There are a number of **processes** involved in the **erosion** of the coastline:

Hydraulic action

The **physical force** of the waves breaks material off the coastline. During a **storm**, waves are stronger and their ability to erode increases.

Abrasion

Loose material (rocks and sand) is thrown against the coastline by waves. This action breaks more material off the coastline.

Compression

When waves crash against a cliff, **air** gets **trapped** in the cracks and joints on the cliff face and becomes **compressed**. When the waves retreat, the pressure is suddenly **released**. This process of compression and release happens repeatedly until the rock eventually **shatters**.

Solution

Some rocks, such as limestone and chalk, are **dissolved** by water.

Attrition

The **stones** that are carried in the water are constantly **hitting** against each other. Over time, they become worn down, smooth and rounded. This can eventually lead to the formation of **sand**.

Compression
Hydraulic action
Solution
Abrasion
Attrition

Figure 10.4 *Processes of coastal erosion*

(i) Define fetch.

(ii) Explain what happens when a wave breaks and comes ashore.

(iii) What is the difference between a constructive wave and a destructive wave?

(iv) Name and explain two processes of coastal erosion.

I understand how waves are formed and the processes that help erode the coastline.   

Landforms of coastal erosion

Learning Intentions

In this section, you will learn:

- how landforms along the coastline are formed by coastal erosion
- how to identify landforms formed by coastal erosion
- how to recognise landforms of coastal erosion on an OS map.

Bay
Headland
Sea cliff
Notch
High-water mark
Low-water mark
Undercutting
Overhang
Wave-cut platform
Wave-built terrace
Sea cave
Sea arch
Sea stack
Sea stump
Blowhole

The **landforms** associated with **coastal erosion** are described and shown below.

Bays and headlands

A **bay** is a **curved area** where the waves have eroded the coastline. A **headland** is an area of hard rock **jutting** into the sea.

Formation:

- The coastline is made up of **hard rock** and **soft rock**. As waves crash against the coastline, **soft** rock such as limestone is **eroded faster** than hard rock such as basalt.
- The processes of **hydraulic action**, **abrasion**, **compression** and, sometimes, **solution** erode the softer rock to form a **bay**.
- The **harder rock** stands out on either side of the bay to form **headlands**.
- Sometimes **beaches** form in bays.

Example of a bay: Dublin Bay.

Example of a headland: Bray Head.

Hard rock
Soft rock
Wave direction
Headland
Bay
Wave direction

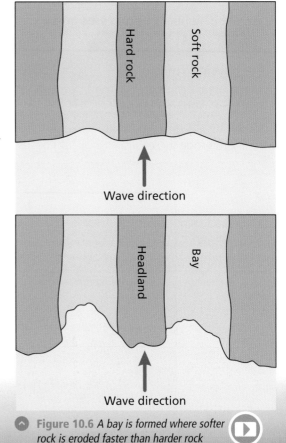

Figure 10.6 *A bay is formed where softer rock is eroded faster than harder rock*

Figure 10.5 *Bays and headlands on the north Antrim coast*

Sea cliffs

A **sea cliff** is a vertical or steep slope on the coastline. They can be seen on OS maps where **contour lines** along the coast are **very close together**.

A-Z

High-water mark and low-water mark: the levels reached by the sea at high and low tides.

Formation:

- Waves erode a **notch** at a line of weakness on the coastline between the **high-water mark** and the **low-water mark**. Over time, this notch grows larger due to the **hydraulic action** of the waves.
- **Undercutting** (the cutting of the waves into the rock base) then occurs.
- The rock above the **notch** is called the **overhang**. It is left without support and eventually **collapses**.
- As the sea **erodes** further and the rock it erodes gets higher, a **cliff** is formed.
- The processes of **compression** and **abrasion** constantly erode the cliff so that it **retreats** into the coastline.
- The rock that is left at the former base of the cliff is called a **wave-cut platform**. Material eroded from the new cliff face is then deposited on top of this platform to form a **wave-built terrace**.

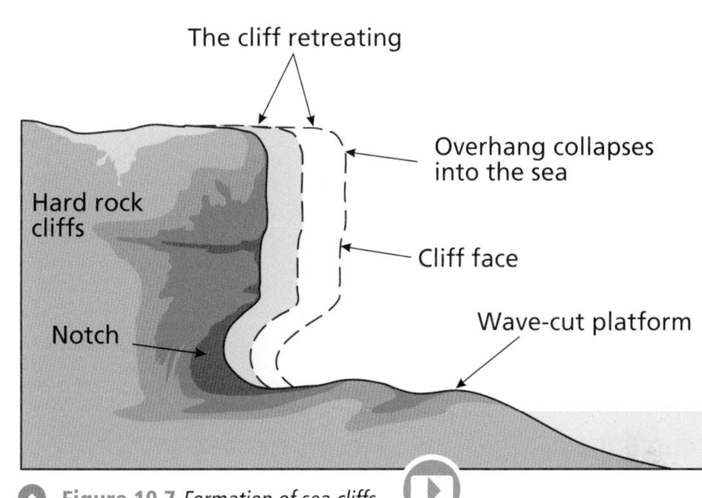

Figure 10.7 *Formation of sea cliffs*

Example of cliffs: Cliffs of Moher in Co. Clare.

NUMERACY ACTIVITY

(a) Research the highest point of (i) the Cliffs of Moher in Co. Clare and (ii) the Cliffs of Dover in England.

(b) What is the difference in height between the Cliffs of Moher and the Cliffs of Dover?

Figure 10.8 *The Cliffs of Moher*

DID YOU KNOW? The cliffs of Croaghaun on Achill Island in Co. Mayo are the highest in Ireland. They are 688 metres high.

Sea caves

A **sea cave** is a tunnel at the base of a cliff.

Formation:
The **hydraulic action** of the waves erodes a **weak spot** on the cliff face. This creates an opening in the cliff. **Compression** and **abrasion** make this opening wider and deeper until a **cave** is formed.

Example of sea caves: The caves at Ballybunion in Co. Kerry.

Sea arches

A sea arch is an **arch-shaped tunnel** that stretches through a **headland**.

Formation:
A sea arch is formed through the processes of **hydraulic action**, **compression** and **abrasion**. It forms when **two caves** develop back to back and eventually **meet**, or when **erosion** causes one cave to reach the other side of the headland.

Examples of sea arches: The Bridges of Ross at Loop Head in Co. Clare and the Bull Rock at Dursey Island in Co. Cork.

Sea stacks and stumps

A sea stack is a **pillar of rock** cut off from the cliff or headland and left standing on its own.

Formation:
A sea stack is formed when a **sea arch collapses**. Over time, the sea stack is eroded and it collapses. A **sea stump** is formed. These sea stumps can be seen at low tide.

Examples of sea stacks: Dún Briste off Downpatrick Head in Co. Mayo and Cnoc na Mara in Co. Donegal.

Blowholes

A blowhole is a **passage** that links the surface of the **cliff top** with the **roof** of a sea cave. They can be seen on OS maps as small blue circles near the coast.

Formation:
When waves crash into a sea cave, air is trapped and **compressed** inside, causing the rock in the roof of the sea cave to **shatter**. The rock eventually **collapses**, forming a **blowhole**. During stormy weather conditions, **sea spray** can be seen coming out of the blowhole.

Examples of blowholes: The Two Pistols and McSwyne's Gun on the Co. Donegal coast.

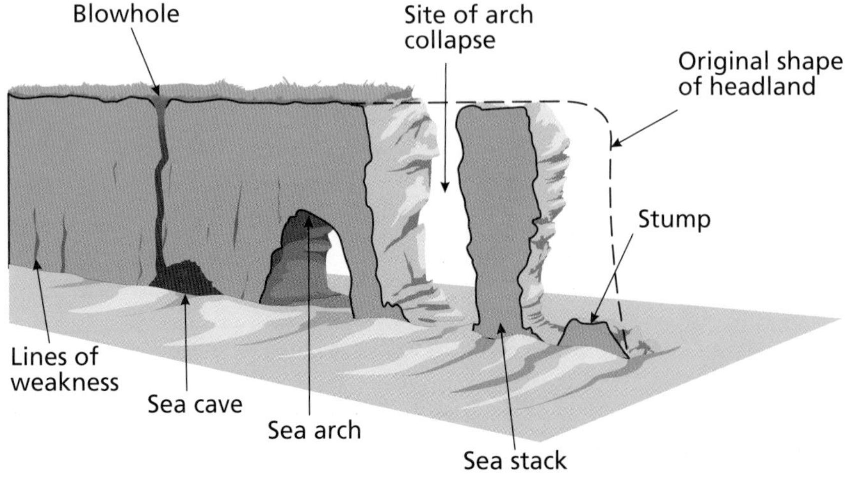

Figure 10.9 *Landforms of erosion found at a headland*

Figure 10.10 *Headland in Normandy, France, with sea cave, sea arch and sea stack*

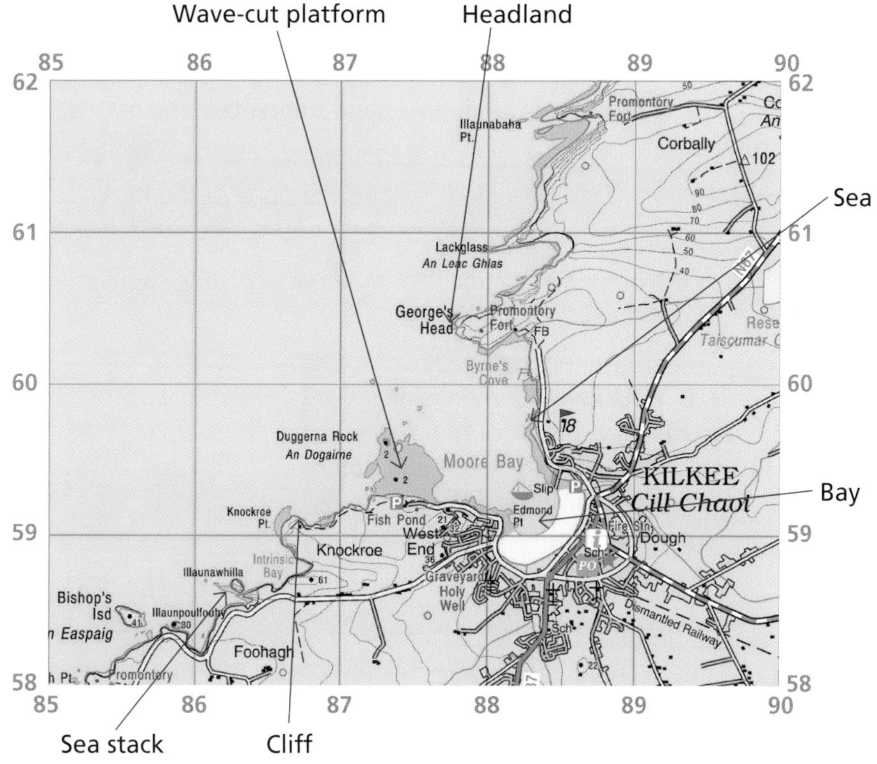

Figure 10.11 *Landforms of coastal erosion on an OS map*

Exam Toolkit

Apply this formula to help you answer long questions on physical geography in your exam.

D – E – P – E –D

Description – **E**xample – **P**rocesses – **E**xplanation – **D**iagram

Try to remember this by using a sentence that contains each first letter, for example:

Do **E**at **P**orridge **E**ach **D**ay.

Can you apply the D-E-P-E-D formula to explain one landform of coastal erosion to your classmates? Use the outline on page 44 of your Activity Book to help you.

(i) Name three landforms of coastal erosion.

(ii) How can cliffs be recognised on OS maps?

(iii) With the aid of a labelled diagram, explain how a cave can develop into a sea stack.

- I can identify features of coastal erosion. 
- I can explain the formation of two features of coastal erosion. 

Coastal transportation and deposition

Learning Intentions

In this section, you will learn:

- how material is transported along the coastline by longshore drift
- how landforms along the coastline are formed by coastal deposition
- how to identify landforms of coastal deposition
- how to recognise landforms of coastal deposition on an OS map.

Longshore drift
Prevailing wind
Storm beach
Sand dune
Sand spit
Lagoon
Sandbar
Tombolo

Longshore drift

The material **transported** by waves, such as sand, shingle, mud and eroded material, is called the **load**. The movement of the load along the coastline is called **longshore drift**.

Longshore drift involves **two** steps:

1. Waves approach and move up the shore **at an angle** (matching the direction of the **prevailing wind**). When a wave breaks, the **swash** moves the load up the shore at an angle and **deposits** some material there, and so the material is moved **along** the shore.
2. The **backwash** carries material back down the shore. This movement follows the slope of the beach, and is usually in a **straight line**.

The process is **repeated** over and over, resulting in the gradual movement of material along the shore in a **zigzag** fashion.

DID YOU KNOW? Winds are named after the direction from which they come. The most common winds that blow over an area are the **'prevailing winds'**. In Ireland the prevailing winds are south-westerly.

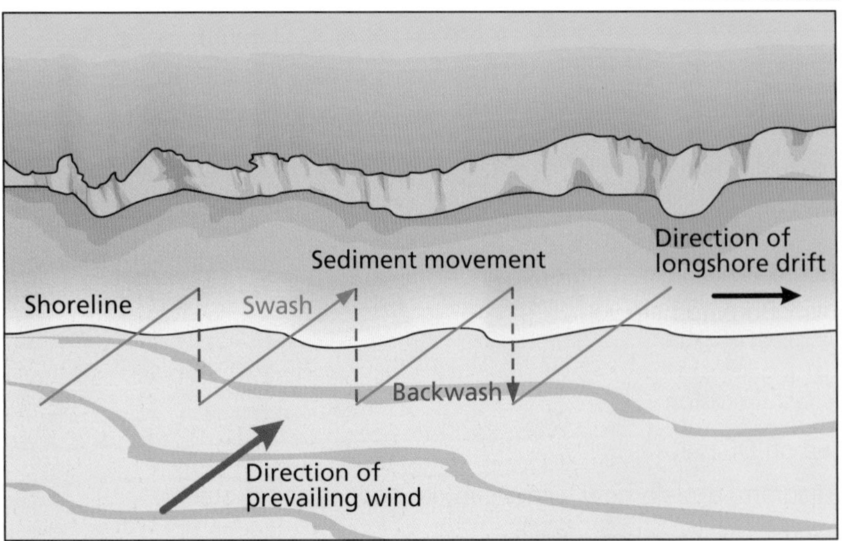

Figure 10.12 *How longshore drift works*

ACTIVITY

Can you think of ways to test if longshore drift is taking place on a shore?

Landforms of coastal deposition

Waves have **less energy** in sheltered areas like **bays**, where the slope of the shoreline is gentle. Waves **deposit** their load when they no longer have enough energy to carry it. The features associated with coastal deposition are described and shown below.

Beaches

A beach is a build-up of **sand** and **shingle** (small pebbles) that have been deposited by **constructive waves** between the **high-water** and **low-water marks**. They are yellow on OS maps.

Formation:

- When waves **break**, they lose energy and are unable to carry their load. The **swash** carries material up the shore and **deposits** it.
- The waves are unable to carry all the material back because the **backwash** is **weaker** than the swash.
- The **heaviest** material is dropped **first**, and the **finer** material is carried closer to the shoreline. Over time, this material **builds up** to form a **beach**.
- During **storms**, waves are stronger and are able to carry heavier material such as **boulders** and **rocks**. This heavy material is then deposited above the high-water line. This creates a **storm beach**.

Examples of beaches: Rosslare in Co. Wexford, Greystones in Co. Wicklow and Tramore in Co. Waterford.

Example of a storm beach: Kilkee, Co. Clare.

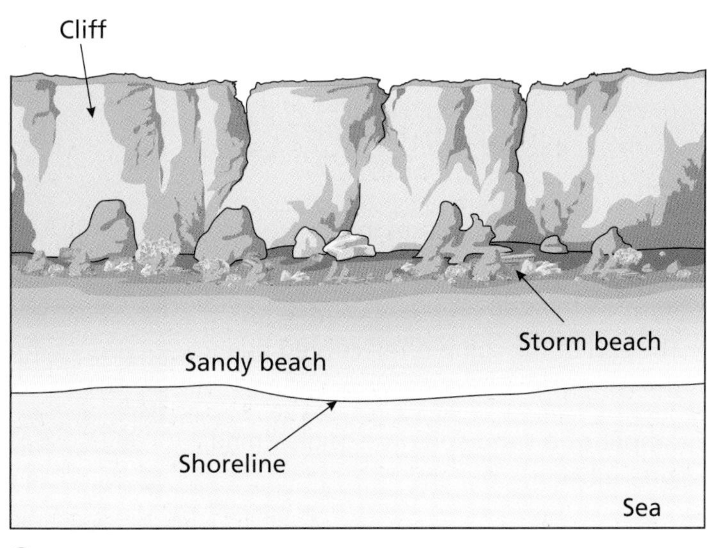

Figure 10.13 *Features of a beach viewed from the sea*

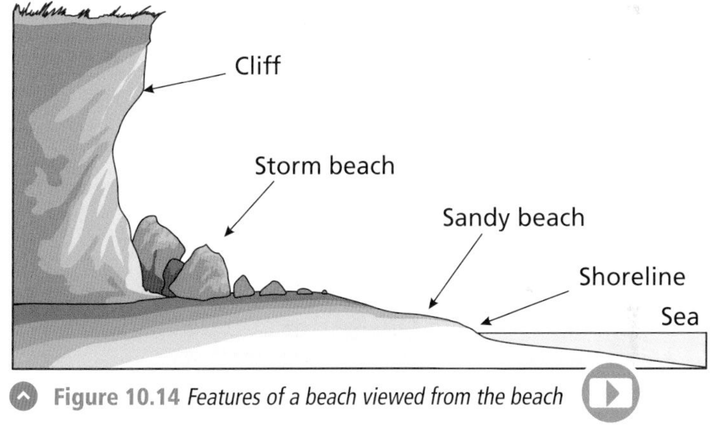

Figure 10.14 *Features of a beach viewed from the beach*

Sand dunes

Sand dunes are a **build-up of sand** at the back of the beach above the high-tide level.

Formation:

- When sand on a beach is **dried** out and blown inland by onshore winds, it gets **trapped** by a wall of **vegetation** and builds up to form sand hills or sand dunes.
- Sometimes **marram grass** is planted on the sand dunes to prevent the sand from blowing further inland. Marram grass has deep roots that help to **anchor** the sand in place.

Example of sand dunes: Castlegregory in Co. Kerry.

Figure 10.15 *A sand dune with marram grass, Stocker Strand, Portsalon, Co. Donegal*

Sand spits

A sand spit is a **long ridge** of sand or shingle that stretches across a bay and is **connected** to one side of the bay.

Formation:

- **Longshore drift** loses its energy and **deposits** the material it is carrying when it is interrupted by a sheltered **bay**.
- The material builds up over time and gradually **extends** across the bay. A **sand spit** is formed.
- As the sand spit increases in size, vegetation grows on it and a **beach** can form on the side facing out to sea.
- The end of the spit is often **curved** due to the current.

Example of a sand spit: Rossbeigh Strand near Glenbeigh, Co. Kerry.

Figure 10.16 *A sand spit at Rossbeigh Strand, Co. Kerry*

Lagoons

A lagoon is an area of water that has been **cut off** from the sea by a **sandbar**.

Formation:
A sandbar forms when a **sand spit** continues to grow across a bay until it **connects** with the other side. The bay is then cut off from the sea, and a lake, called a **lagoon**, is formed.

Example of a lagoon: Lady's Island Lake in Co. Wexford.

Tombolo
Lagoon
Sandbar
Sand spit
Longshore drift

Figure 10.17 *Landforms of coastal deposition*

Tombolos

A tombolo is a **ridge of sand** that **connects** the mainland to an **island**.

Formation:
A tombolo is formed when longshore drift creates a **sand spit** in the sheltered waters between the **mainland** and an **island**.

Example of a tombolo: Howth in Co. Dublin was once an island but is now connected to the mainland by a tombolo. Nearby Sutton is built on this tombolo.

Figure 10.18 *A tombolo connecting an island to the mainland in Scotland*

Can you apply the D-E-P-E-D formula to explain one feature of coastal deposition to your classmates? Use the outline on page 46 of your Activity Book to help you.

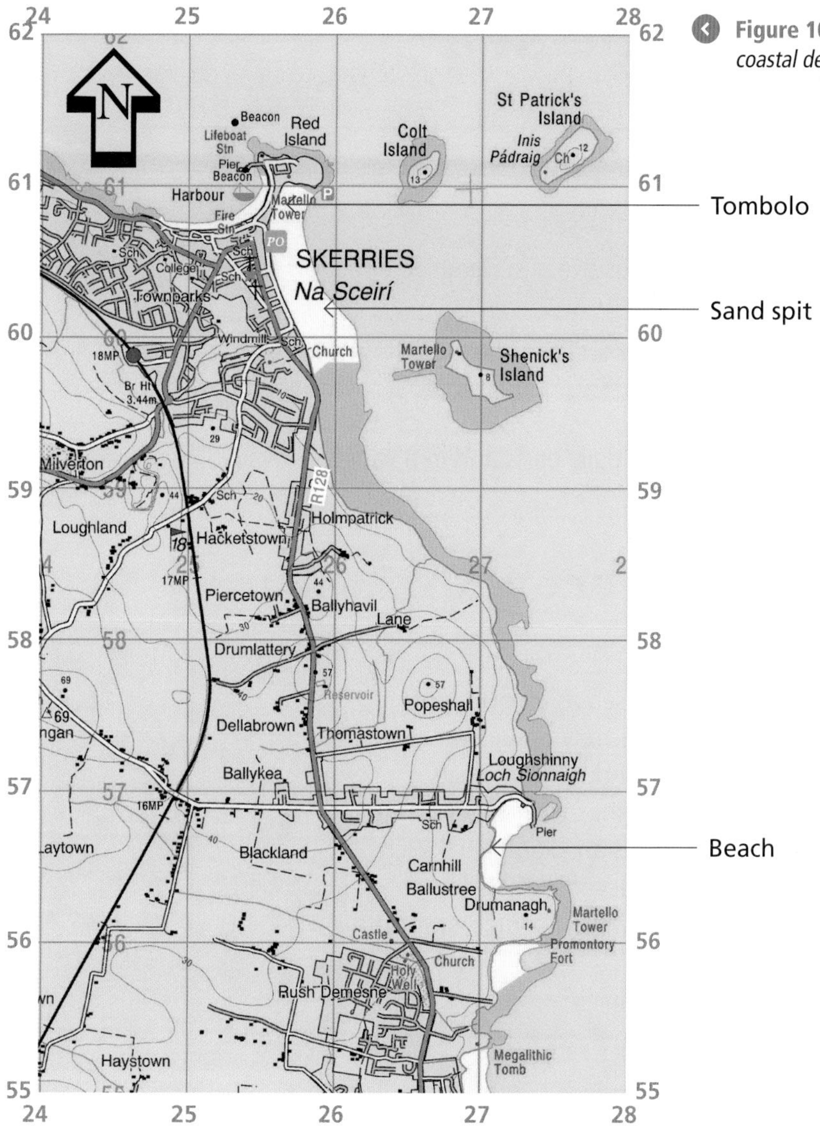

Tombolo

Sand spit

Beach

Figure 10.19 *Landforms of coastal deposition on an OS map*

ACTIVITY

Take a look at a coastal area near you on Google Maps.

Can you identify some of the features you have just learned about?

 **(i)** Name three landforms of coastal deposition.

 **(ii)** With the aid of a labelled diagram, explain the process of longshore drift.

 **(iii)** With the aid of a labelled diagram, explain how a sand spit develops into a sand bar, creating a lagoon.

- I can explain longshore drift.
- I can identify the features of coastal deposition.
- I can explain the formation of two features of coastal deposition.

People and the sea

Learning Intentions

In this section, you will learn:

- how people interact with the sea
- how people can have a positive and negative effect on the coastal processes
- about the ways people protect the coastline from coastal erosion.

Sea walls
Rock armour
Groynes
Gabions

People **interact** with the sea on a daily basis and in a variety of ways. These interactions with the sea can be both **positive** and **negative**.

How people interact with the sea

Food supply

People have always looked to the sea as a **source of food**. Many people in coastal areas rely on incomes earned from **fishing**. The fishing industry provides **jobs** on fishing trawlers and in onshore fish-processing plants. **Killybegs** in Co. Donegal is an example of such a **coastal community**. In recent decades, **fish farms** on the Irish coast have provided another source of food and income.

Figure 10.20 *Fishing boats in Killybegs, Co. Donegal*

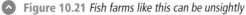

Figure 10.21 *Fish farms like this can be unsightly*

However, **overfishing** has depleted fish stocks in recent years, and many consider fish farms to be an **eyesore**.

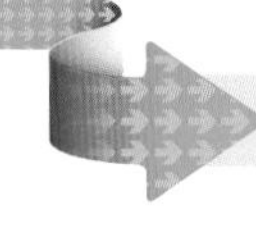

Go to Chapter 4, page 60, for more information on overfishing.

Transport

Ferries from Rosslare, Cork and Dublin transport passengers to and from the UK and France, which contributes to our **tourist industry**. Huge **cargo ships** are used to transport heavy **raw materials**, such as oil, iron, steel and other minerals by sea.

However, **pollution** can be a negative side-effect. **Oil spillages** are a constant threat and can be damaging to coastal environments.

Figure 10.22 *A cargo ship transporting containers*

Recreation

The sea and beaches provide a wide range of **recreational activities** such as surfing, kayaking and sunbathing. Coastal towns benefit when tourists are attracted to these areas. **Tourism** brings increased income and employment to areas, as well as improvements in roads and services. The **west coast** of Ireland is a prime example of an area that has benefitted from tourism.

Figure 10.23 *Surfing in Lahinch*

Figure 10.24 *Plastic containers washed up by the sea are an all-too-common sight on beaches all over the world*

This interaction can also have a negative impact. People can cause **erosion** of sand dunes by walking over them, and often leave **litter** behind after a day at the seaside. Pollution can also occur when **sewage** from tourist resorts gets into the sea.

PORTFOLIO ACTIVITY 10.1

Go to page 40 of your Portfolio and complete the research activity on the Doonbeg Golf Club.

VIDEO LESSON

Watch this video on plastic bags and pollution:

https://educateplus.ie/go/plastic-bags-marine

Now answer the following questions:

(a) What percentage of items found on beaches are made from plastic?

(b) How many items on average are found per square metre on New Zealand beaches?

(c) How many species of animals are affected by this type of pollution?

(d) Name a type of bird that is constantly affected by plastic pollution.

(e) How do plastic bags have an impact on turtles?

(f) List three plastic items that are found on beaches.

(g) How many million tonnes of plastic are we now producing worldwide?

(h) What has the town of Modbury in south Devon, England, done to help stop the problem of plastic pollution?

DID YOU KNOW? The sea level is rising around the world at a rate of 3.2 mm per year. We will learn more about this in Chapter 14.

Coastal protection

Over the years people have developed different ways to **protect** the coastline from erosion. Here are some of the methods used:

Sea walls

Sea walls break the power of incoming waves, and their **curved tops** push waves back out to sea. During storms, these concrete walls can be damaged and may need repair. Examples of sea walls can be seen at **Salthill** in Galway and **Strandhill** in Co. Sligo.

Figure 10.25 *Sea defences – a sea wall*

Rock armour

These are **large boulders** at the base of a cliff or in front of sand dunes. When a **wave breaks**, it hits the rock armour and **loses energy**. This reduces the erosion of the coastline. Rock armour is used to protect the coastline at **Tramore** in Co. Waterford.

Figure 10.26 *Sea defences – rock armour*

Groynes

Groynes are concrete or wooden structures built at **right angles** to the coastline. They extend down the shore and into the sea. They are designed to **trap sediment** carried by **longshore drift**. This ensures that **sand builds up** on the beach rather than being removed from it. Groynes can have a **negative** impact, however. If sand is trapped in one place, it means that further down the coastline there is nothing to deposit, and the waves have more power to erode.

Figure 10.27 *Sea defences – groynes at Rosslare Strand*

Gabions

Gabions are **wire cages** filled with small stones. They are placed in front of beaches or sand dunes to break the power of the waves and slow down erosion. Gabions are used to protect the beach at **Lahinch** in Co. Clare.

Figure 10.28 *Sea defences – gabions*

DID YOU KNOW? The word gabion comes from the Italian *gabbione* meaning 'big cage'.

CASE STUDY

Rosslare Strand and Rosslare Harbour, Co. Wexford

The coastal area of Rosslare consists of Rosslare Harbour and Rosslare Strand. The sea plays a huge role in the **economic activities** of the area and the results of these activities are evident.

- **Rosslare Harbour** is a famous **port**. Passenger ferries and cargo ships use it as a **transport hub** to the UK and France.
- **Rosslare Strand** is situated to the north of the port and its 8 km of sandy beaches have **Blue Flag** status. It has been an important **tourist resort** for many years.

A **sea wall** was built at Rosslare Harbour to provide **shelter** for the port and to ensure that **sediment** would not block the channel. However, this resulted in the build-up of material south of Rosslare Harbour, and a **reduction** in sand deposition on the beaches and sand dunes of Rosslare Strand. The beach began to disappear.

To tackle this issue, **gabions**, **rock armour** and **groynes** were put in place. In addition, sand was **dredged** or dragged up from the seabed about 6 km offshore and used to nourish the beach and build it up again.

This is an example of how human interaction in one area can affect another area.

Figure 10.29 *Rosslare Harbour is an important ferry port*

Figure 10.30 *Rosslare Strand*

ACTIVITY

Check out http://beachawards.ie/ to find out how a beach qualifies to get a Blue Flag.

PORTFOLIO ACTIVITY 10.2

Go to page 41 of your Portfolio and research a flood that has occurred along the coastline.

(i) List two ways people use the sea to their advantage.

(ii) List two negative impacts of people interacting with the sea.

(iii) Name and explain two methods used to protect the coastline from the power of the sea.

(iv) What negative impact can the building of groynes have?

(v) Suggest two ways in which people can interact with the coastline in a more sustainable way.

- I can give examples of how people interact with the sea.
- I can explain, using examples, how people try to protect the coastline from erosion.

Coastal landforms on Ordnance Survey maps

Tramore

Examine the Ordnance Survey map of Tramore on the opposite page and answer these questions.

1. Identify the following features on the map extract using four-figure grid references:

- **(a)** Sand spit
- **(b)** Beach
- **(c)** Wave-cut platform
- **(d)** Bay

2. Identify the following features on the map extract using six-figure grid references:

- **(a)** Cliff
- **(b)** Headland
- **(c)** Sea stack

3. Measure the area of this map that is located in subzone X.

4. What is the size of the area of water behind Tramore Strand in km^2?

5. Draw a sketch map of the Ordnance Survey map extract and include:

- **(a)** A beach
- **(b)** Tramore Strand
- **(c)** A cliff
- **(d)** A sea stack
- **(e)** A headland
- **(f)** Urban area of Tramore

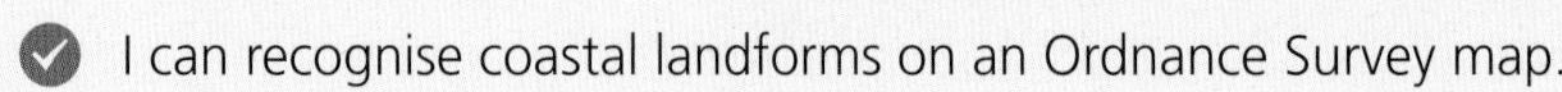

I can recognise coastal landforms on an Ordnance Survey map.

Figure 10.31 *Tramore, Co. Waterford*

REVISION

Waves can erode, ____________________ and ____________________ material along the coastline. The area of water over which the wind blows a wave is called the ____________________. When the wave comes up the beach it is called ______________, and when it goes back down the beach it is called ____________________.

The sea erodes in different ways: ____________________ action, abrasion, compressed air, ____________________ and solution. Coastal features formed from erosion include sea caves, sea ____________________, sea ____________________, headlands and ____________.

Material is often transported along the shore by a process known as ____________________ drift. The waves meet and travel up the shore at an ______________. Material is then carried straight back down the shore by the ____________________. The material therefore moves along the coastline in a ____________________ fashion.

A beach is formed when material is deposited by ____________________ waves. The ____________________ is too weak to carry away the material. Other features formed by deposition include sand ____________, sand ____________ and ____________________.

People make use of the sea as a source of ____________________ and income, to transport goods and ____________________ and for ____________________ activities. They can also have a negative impact on the coastline through, for example, ____________________.

Forms of coastal protection include sea walls, rock armour, _______________ and _______________.

Questions & Answers

Sample Question

Name **one** landform of coastal erosion and with the aid of a diagram, explain how it was formed.

Sample Answer

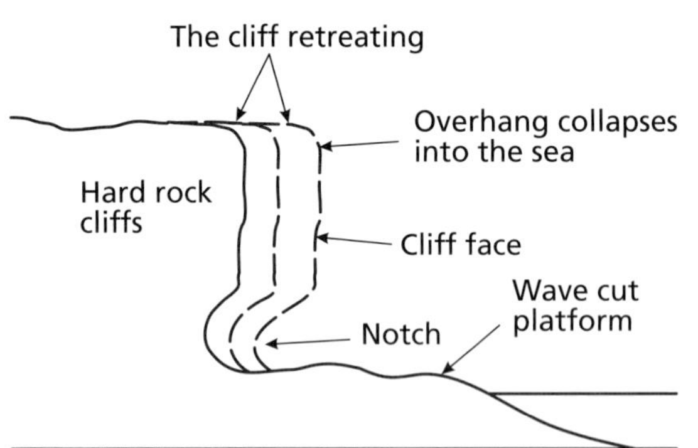

Description – A sea cliff is a vertical or steep slope on the coastline and is a landform of coastal erosion.

Example – An example of a sea cliff in Ireland is the Cliffs of Moher in Co. Clare.

Processes – Erosion: hydraulic action, abrasion, compressed air and solution.

Explanation – Waves erode a notch at a line of weakness on the coastline between the high-water mark and the low-water mark. Over time, this notch grows larger due to the hydraulic action of the waves and undercutting occurs. This process leaves the rock above the notch without support and, eventually, it collapses, forming a cliff. Because the cliff is constantly being eroded towards the land, it is said to be retreating. The rock that is left at the base of where the cliff used to be is called a wave-cut platform. The materials eroded from the cliff face are deposited on top of this platform to form a wave-built terrace.

1. Examine the photograph.

Circle the correct answer in each of the following statements:

(i) The features at **Y** are formed by the process of coastal **erosion / deposition**.

(ii) The waves that form these features are **constructive / destructive**.

(iii) Features like these are found on the west coast of Ireland. **True / False.**

2. Examine the diagram, which shows features of sea erosion. Identify each feature with the correct letter. One has been done for you.

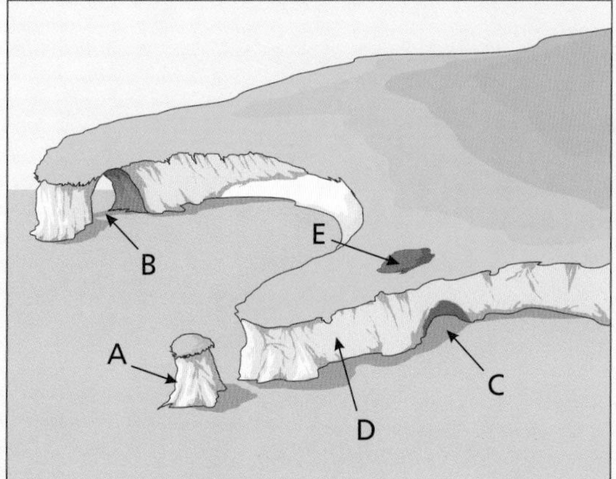

Blowhole	
Sea arch	
Sea cave	
Sea stack	
Sea cliff	D

3. The diagram below shows how material is transported along the shore.

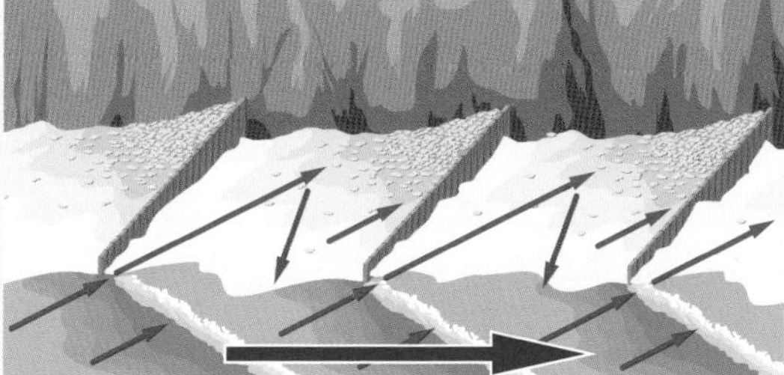

Movement of material along the shore

This process is called:

Erosion ☐

Longshore drift ☐

Suspension ☐ [tick (✓) the correct box]

4. The coastal feature in this photograph is called:

A delta ☐
A sand spit ☐
A wave-cut platform ☐
A cave ☐
[tick (✓) the correct box]

5. The feature marked X in this photograph shows a feature of coastal deposition.

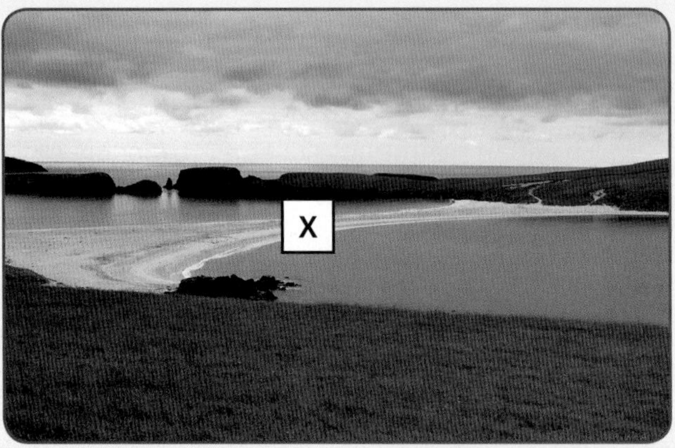

It is called a:

Sea stack ☐
Delta ☐
Tombolo ☐
[tick (✓) the correct box]

Long Questions

1. Name **one** feature of coastal erosion and with the aid of a diagram, explain how it was formed.
2. Name **one** feature of coastal deposition and with the aid of a diagram, explain how it was formed.
3. **(a)** Name and briefly explain **one** way that people use coastal areas.
   (b) Name and briefly explain **one** way that people pollute coastal areas.
4. **(a)** Name an area of Irish coastline in danger of erosion.
   (b) Describe **three** methods of coastal protection that could be used in such an area.

Visual Summary

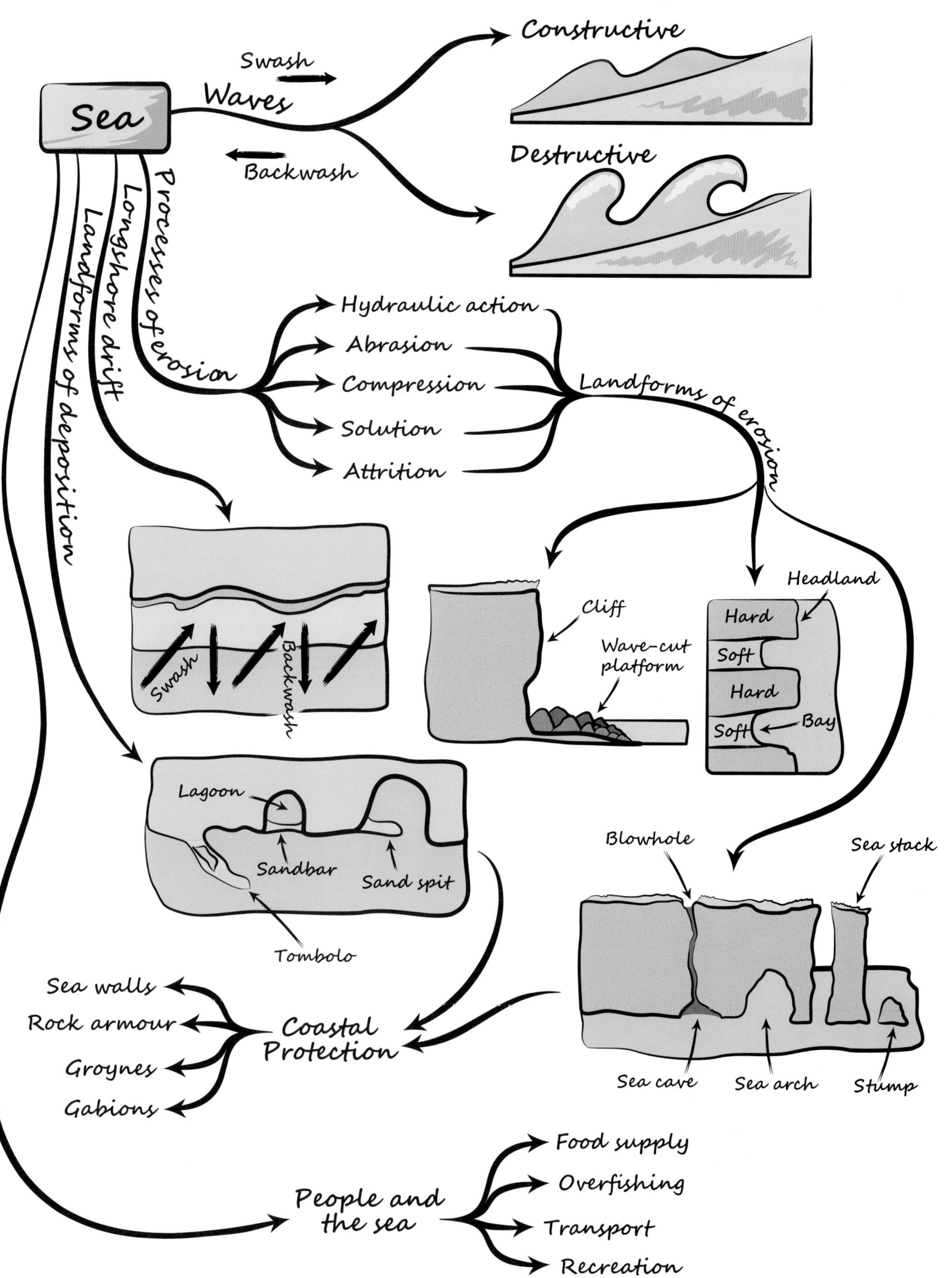
Sea
Swash
Waves
Backwash
Constructive
Destructive
Processes of erosion
Longshore drift
Landforms of deposition
Hydraulic action
Abrasion
Compression
Solution
Attrition
Landforms of erosion
Swash
Backwash
Cliff
Wave-cut platform
Headland
Hard
Soft
Hard
Soft
Bay
Lagoon
Sandbar
Sand spit
Tombolo
Blowhole
Sea stack
Sea cave
Sea arch
Stump
Sea walls
Rock armour
Groynes
Gabions
Coastal Protection
People and the sea
Food supply
Overfishing
Transport
Recreation

11 Glaciation:
The work of ice

In this chapter, you will learn:

- what causes an ice age to occur
- the processes of glacial erosion, transportation and deposition
- the landforms created by these processes
- the positive and negative effects of glaciation
- how a landscape created by glaciation can attract tourists
- how to recognise glacial landforms on Ordnance Survey maps.

Discuss the following questions in groups:

(a) What do you know about the last ice age?

(b) How do you think it came about?

(c) Why do you think it ended?

(d) Are there parts of the world still covered in ice?

Glaciation

Learning Intentions

In this section, you will learn:

- how glaciers form
- what causes an ice age
- the processes by which glaciers erode.

Glaciation	Plucking
Ice age	Friction
Ice sheet	Abrasion
Glacier	Striation

Figure 11.1 *Franz Joseph Glacier on South Island, New Zealand*

An **ice age** is a period during which large parts of several continents are covered by **ice sheets**. The last ice age to affect Ireland ended roughly **12,000 years ago**.

During that ice age, the temperatures in the northern hemisphere were so low that snow and ice did not get a chance to melt. Year after year, layers of snow and ice built up until it was compressed or **compacted** together to form huge **masses** of ice called **glaciers**.

Glaciers formed in **upland areas**. The effect of **gravity** eventually moved them **downslope**. Some glaciers melted while others joined together to form **ice sheets**. These ice sheets covered huge areas of land.

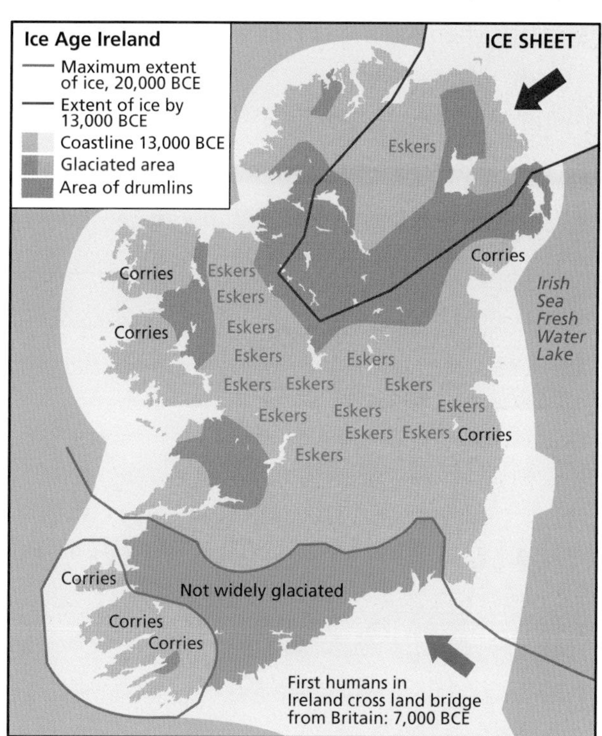

Figure 11.2 *Most of Ireland was covered by ice in the last ice age*

What causes an ice age?

We have already learned that the Earth is constantly changing because of **plate tectonics**. These changes, along with other factors, can bring about changes in **global temperatures**. We do not know for sure why ice ages occur, but some **factors** that might be important in causing an ice age include:

- **Earth's orbit and axis:** The Earth's **orbit** around the sun changes regularly from oval, or **elliptical**, to **circular**. The Earth is tilted on its **axis**, and the **angle** of its tilt is always changing. These changes happen over **tens of thousands of years** and it is thought that they have an important influence on the Earth's climate.
- **Earth's atmosphere:** When there is less **carbon dioxide** (CO_2) in the atmosphere to trap the sun's heat, **global temperatures** can drop.
- **Ocean currents:** Ocean currents **distribute heat**. When they change course, **ice sheets** can build up.

Processes of glacial erosion

Ice erodes the landscape through the processes of **plucking** and **abrasion**.

Plucking

As a glacier moves, there is **friction** between the glacier and the ground beneath it. This friction causes the bottom of the glacier to **melt**. The **meltwater** makes its way into cracks in the rocks underneath the glacier. The meltwater then **refreezes** around the rocks.

When the glacier moves, it **plucks** the frozen meltwater and the rocks from the ground. The rocks are then **carried away** with the glacier.

Abrasion

As the glacier moves, the rocks attached to it **scratch** and **scrape** the surface rock underneath and on the sides of the valley. The scratch marks left behind on rocks are called **striations**. These marks tell us the direction in which the glacier moved.

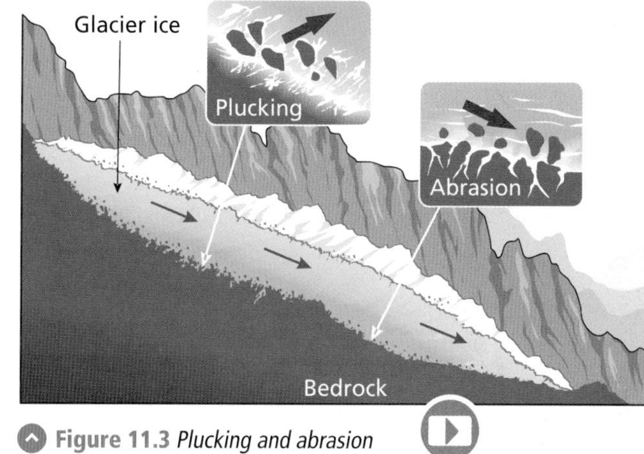

Figure 11.3 *Plucking and abrasion*

(i) When did the last ice age end?

(ii) What is a glacier?

(iii) Name two processes of glacial erosion.

(iv) How can we tell what direction glaciers travelled?

(v) Explain two factors that might cause ice ages to occur.

- I understand some of the reasons why ice ages may occur.
- I can explain the two processes of glacial erosion.

Landforms of glacial erosion

Learning Intentions

In this section, you will learn:

- how landforms of glacial erosion are created
- how to identify landforms of glacial erosion.

Cirque
Arête
Pyramidal peak
U-shaped valley
Truncated spur
Ribbon lake
Paternoster lakes
Hanging valley
Fjord

Landforms created by glacial erosion are mostly found in **upland areas**. There are many examples of these in the Irish landscape.

Cirques

A cirque is a **basin-shaped hollow** in a mountain. It looks like an armchair. It has **three steep sides** and often contains a lake. A cirque was the birthplace of a glacier.

DID YOU KNOW? Cirques are also known as corries, cooms and coums.

Formation:

- A cirque is formed when snow **accumulates** (builds up) in a hollow high up on a mountain. The snow is **compressed** to form ice.
- The ice **plucks** rocks from the sides of the mountain as it begins to move. These rocks make the hollow **deeper** through the process of **abrasion**.
- The ice eventually **overflows** from the hollow and **gravity** causes the ice to move downhill.
- The ice that is left behind melts and forms a lake in the hollow. This lake is called a **tarn**.

Figure 11.4 *A cirque with a tarn at Coumshingaun in Co. Waterford*

Examples of cirques: There are many examples of cirques in Ireland. Many can be identified by the word *coom* or *coum* in their name, for example **Coumshingaun** in the Comeragh Mountains in Co. Waterford. Another famous cirque which contains a lake is the **Devil's Punchbowl** near Killarney in Co. Kerry.

Arêtes

An arête is a narrow, **steep-sided ridge** between two cirques.

Formation:

- An arête occurs when **two cirques** form next to each other on a mountain.
- The ground between the two cirques erodes backwards. This leaves a **narrow ridge** called an arête between the two cirques.

Examples of arêtes: Coumshingaun in the Comeragh Mountains in Co. Waterford and around the Devil's Punchbowl in Co. Kerry.

Figure 11.5 *Arête with cirque and tarn below it*

Pyramidal peaks

A pyramidal peak is a **steep-sided peak** between three or more cirques.

Formation:

When **three** or more cirques form around a mountain top, a steep-sided peak remains between them.

Examples of pyramidal peaks: Comeragh Mountains in Co. Waterford and the Matterhorn in Switzerland.

Figure 11.6 *The Matterhorn in Switzerland is an example of a pyramidal peak*

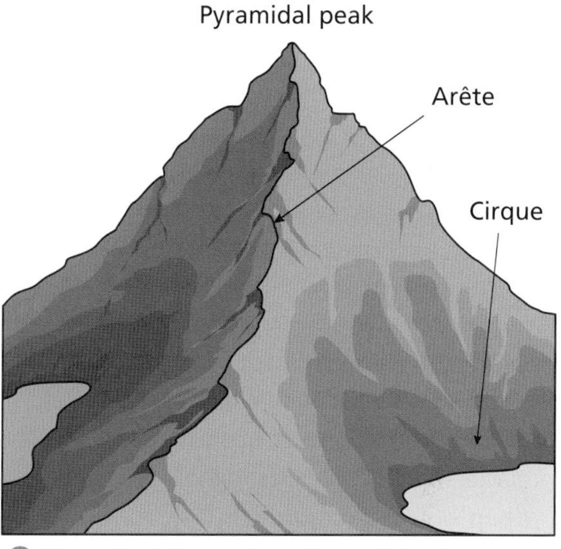

Figure 11.7 *Cirque, arête and pyramidal peak*

U-shaped valleys

A glaciated or U-shaped valley has a **wide, flat floor** and **steep sides**.

Formation:

- When a glacier moves out of a cirque and down the mountain, it follows the easiest **route** possible.
- This route is often a **V-shaped valley** that has previously been carved out by a river.
- The glacier uses **plucking** and **abrasion** to widen and deepen the valley. This changes it from a V-shaped valley to a **U-shaped valley**.
- As the glacier moves through the valley, it also cuts off the tips off the **interlocking spurs** created by the river, leaving behind **truncated spurs**.

Examples of U-shaped valleys: Glendalough in Co. Wicklow and the Gap of Dunloe in Co. Kerry.

Figure 11.8 *A U-shaped valley with truncated spurs*

Ribbon lakes

A ribbon lake is a **long, narrow lake** on the floor of a **U-shaped valley**.

Formation:

- As a **glacier** passes through the valley, it erodes patches of **softer rock** from the valley floor. This leaves behind **hollows**.
- After the ice age, the hollows fill with water to form lakes called **ribbon lakes**.
- When a number of ribbon lakes are joined together by a river they are called **paternoster lakes**. They are called this because they resemble rosary beads.

Example of a ribbon lake: Glendalough in Co. Wicklow.

Example of paternoster lakes: The Gap of Dunloe in Co. Kerry.

Figure 11.9 *Ribbon lake at Glendalough, Co. Wicklow*

(i) Can you explain why ribbon lakes got their name?

(ii) Look up photographs of paternoster lakes and rosary beads online. Do you think they look similar? Work in pairs.

Hanging valleys

A hanging valley is a smaller **glaciated valley** that **hangs** above the main glaciated valley.

Formation:

- Hanging valleys contained **smaller glaciers**. Smaller glaciers are not able to **erode** as deeply as larger glaciers. This means that hanging valleys are **not as deep** as the main valleys.
- When the glacier melts, the floor of the hanging valley is left **high above** the main valley.
- A stream drops from the high hanging valley to the low main valley as a **waterfall**.

Example of a hanging valley: The **Poulanass Waterfall** in Glendalough, Co. Wicklow drops from a hanging valley.

Figure 11.10 *A hanging valley*

Fjords

A fjord is a **drowned U-shaped valley** that is very deep and has steep sides.

Formation:

When an ice age ended, the glaciers melted and the **sea level rose**. Glaciated valleys located near the coast were drowned and became **fjords**.

Example of a fjord: Killary Harbour on the border between Co. Mayo and Co. Galway is Ireland's only fjord.

Figure 11.11 *Killary Harbour, Co. Mayo*

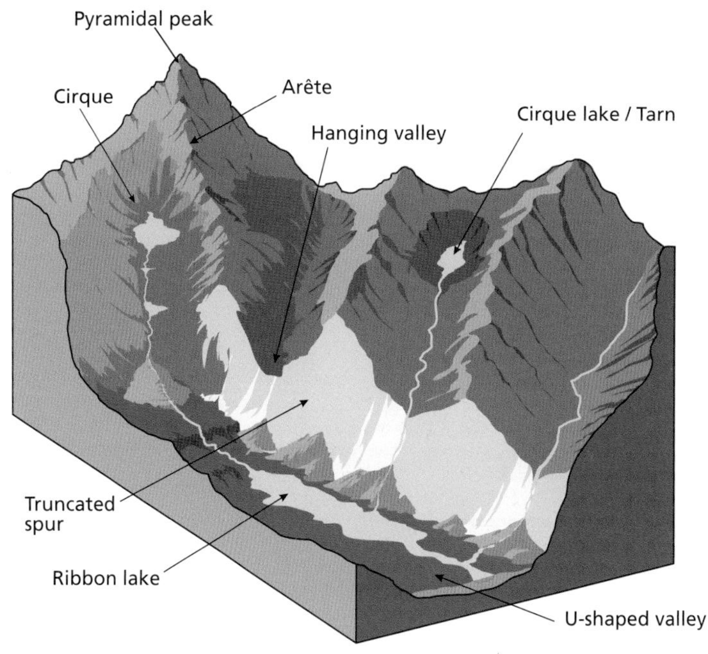

Figure 11.12 *Landforms of glacial erosion*

DID YOU KNOW? Fjord is a Norwegian word. There are many fjords along Norway's coast.

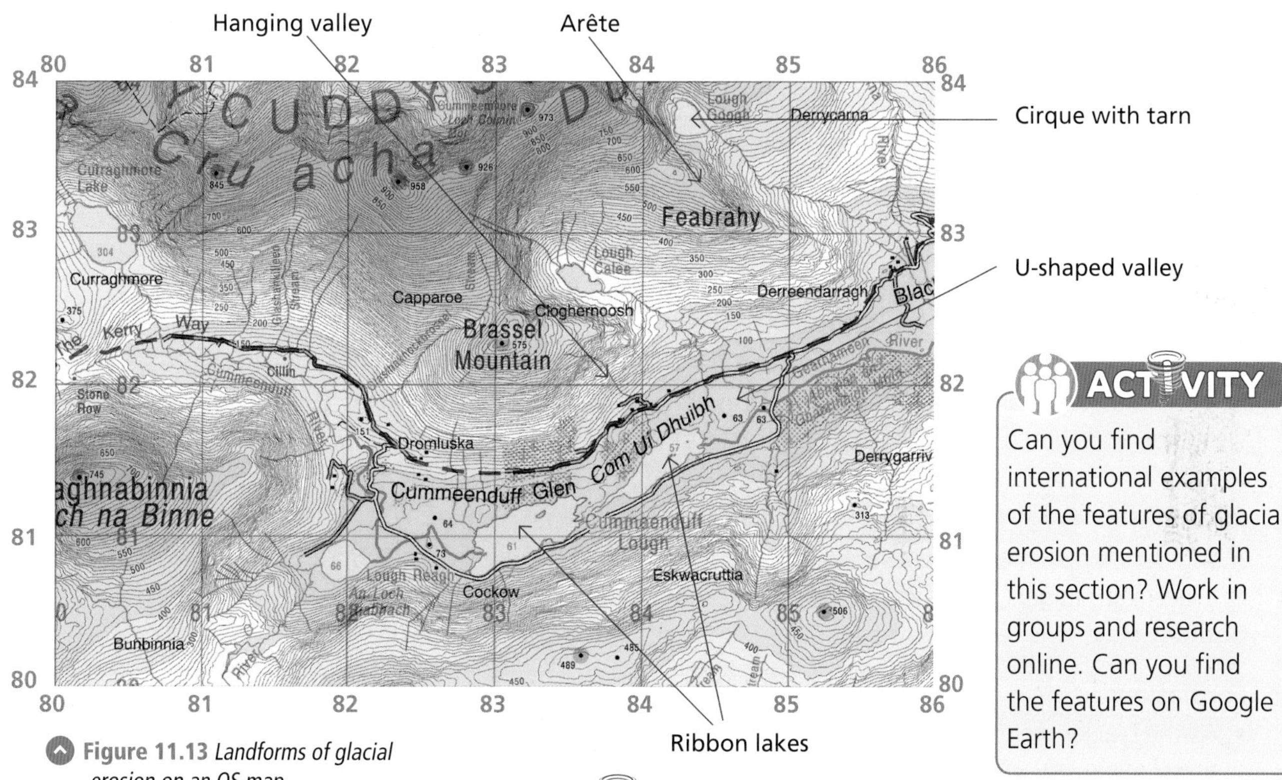

Figure 11.13 *Landforms of glacial erosion on an OS map*

ACTIVITY

Can you find international examples of the features of glacial erosion mentioned in this section? Work in groups and research online. Can you find the features on Google Earth?

ACTIVITY

Can you apply the D-E-P-E-D formula to explain one landform of glacial erosion to your classmates? Use the outline on page 51 of your Activity Book to help you.

(i) Name two landforms of glacial erosion.

(ii) Where in Ireland can you see a fjord?

(iii) What is an arête?

(iv) What landform might you expect to find at a hanging valley?

(v) Can you give any reasons why a U-shaped valley might have good places to build settlements and roads?

- I can identify landforms of glacial erosion
- I can explain the formation of two landforms of glacial erosion.

Glacial transportation and deposition

Learning Intentions

In this section, you will learn:

- how glaciers transport their load
- how landforms are created by glacial deposition
- how to identify landforms of glacial deposition.

Crevasse	Medial
Boulder clay	Terminal
Drumlin	Meltwater
Erratic	Fluvio-glacial
Moraine	Esker
Lateral	Outwash plain

How glaciers transport their load

Glaciers **carry** large amounts of material from upland areas, where they are formed, to lowland areas. They carry this **load** in the following ways:

- Material is pushed **in front** of the glacier, like a sweeping brush.
- Material is carried **on top** of the glacier.
- Material is rolled along at the **sides** of the glacier and **underneath** the ice.
- Material falls through cracks or **crevasses** in the glacier, and so is carried **within** it.

Glaciers gather and lose material along the way. The material that is **transported** by the glacier, and later **deposited** by it, is called a **moraine**. We will learn more about moraines on page 186.

Landforms of glacial deposition

When a glacier reaches **lowland** areas, the warmer temperature causes the ice to **melt**. The glacier is unable to carry its load and starts to **deposit** it. The landforms associated with **glacial deposition** are described and shown below.

Figure 11.14 *Boulder clay*

Boulder clay plains

A boulder clay plain is a **lowland area** that is covered in a layer of boulders, clay, sand and stones called **boulder clay**.

Formation:

- As the glacier melts, it **deposits** its load of eroded material consisting of **boulders**, **clay**, **sand** and **stones**.
- Boulder clay is very **fertile** and excellent for agriculture.

Example of boulder clay plains: The **Golden Vale** in Munster, known for its farms, has boulder clay soils.

Figure 11.15 *Agriculture in the Golden Vale*

Drumlins

Drumlins are **oval-shaped hills** made of **boulder clay**.

Formation:

- A drumlin forms when a glacier deposits **mounds** of boulder clay.
- The glacier then continues its journey and **smooths** the boulder clay as it moves over it.
- The **steep** slope or **stoss end** of the drumlin shows us what direction the glacier was coming from. The **gentle** slope or **lee slope** shows us what direction the glacier was travelling in.
- Drumlins usually occur in **clusters**, forming what is called a '**basket of eggs**' landscape.

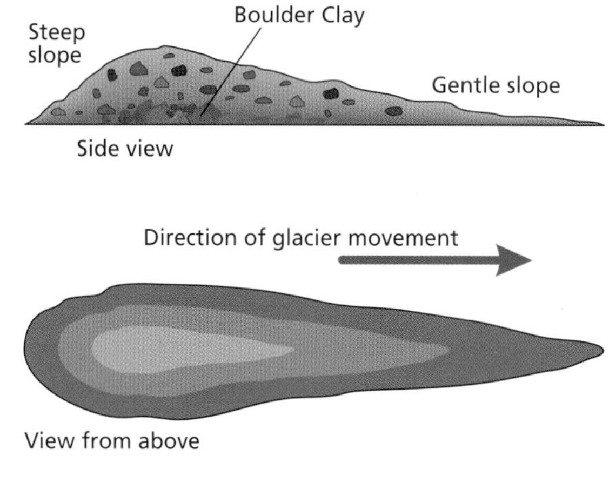

Figure 11.16 *How a drumlin is formed*

Examples of drumlins: Clew Bay in Co. Mayo and Strangford Lough in Co. Down.

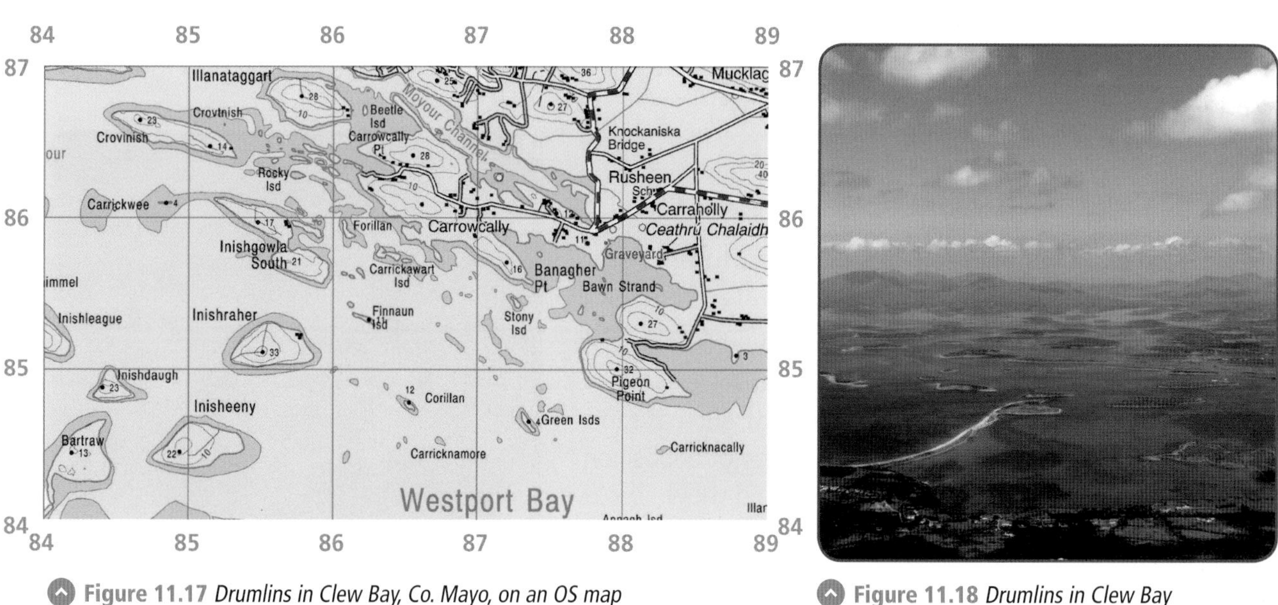

Figure 11.17 *Drumlins in Clew Bay, Co. Mayo, on an OS map*

Figure 11.18 *Drumlins in Clew Bay*

Erratics

Erratics are **large boulders** that were **transported** from their original location by a glacier and then **deposited** in an area where the **rock type** is different.

For example, there are boulders of **granite** in the **Burren**, Co. Clare, where the local rock type is **limestone**. The nearest source of granite is north Galway, which tells us that the ice sheet that passed over the Burren came from the north.

Figure 11.19 *An erratic in the Burren, Co. Clare*

Moraines

A moraine is the name given to the material transported and later **deposited** on the **valley floor** by a glacier.

Formation:

- As a glacier travels through a valley, it **drops off** some of the material that it has eroded from the upper slopes at either **side** of the glacier. This deposit is known as a **lateral moraine**. It is a **ridge** of material at the **sides** of the valley.
- When two glaciers **meet**, the lateral moraines of each glacier also meet, creating a **medial moraine**.
- Material is also moved along and deposited **underneath** a glacier. This is called the **ground moraine**.
- Finally, when a glacier **stops** moving, a ridge, made up of the material that it was pushing **in front** of it, is deposited. This material is called a **terminal moraine**. It tells us where the glacier ended.
- Other ridges of deposited material are found behind the terminal moraine and are called **end moraines**.

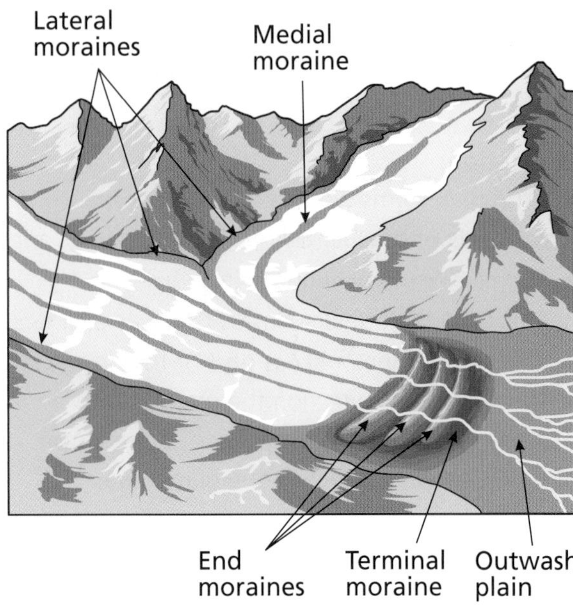

Figure 11.20 *Types of moraine*

Landforms of meltwater (fluvio-glacial) deposition

Towards the end of an ice age, global **temperatures** begin to **rise** and glaciers start melting. The **meltwater** from the glaciers carries material as it flows across the landscape.

The **heavier material**, such as stones and gravel, is deposited first, and then the **lighter material**, such as sand, is deposited. Features associated with this type of deposition are called **fluvio-glacial** and are described and shown below. 'Fluvio' comes from *fluvius*, the Latin word for river.

Figure 11.21 *An esker snakes its way through a prairie in North Dakota, USA*

Eskers

An esker is a **long, narrow ridge** of sand and gravel that winds its way along a **lowland** landscape.

Formation:

- When a glacier begins to melt, streams of **meltwater** carrying a **load** of eroded material flow through a **tunnel** that is carved out **under the glacier**.
- When the load becomes too great, some material is **deposited** on the bed of the meltwater stream.
- The stream **loses its energy** when it exits the tunnel and it deposits the remainder of its load. This forms a **ridge of sand and gravel** on the surrounding plain.
- This ridge is known as an **esker**. Roads have been built on eskers in many areas as they provide good foundations.

Example of an esker: Esker Riada in Co. Galway.

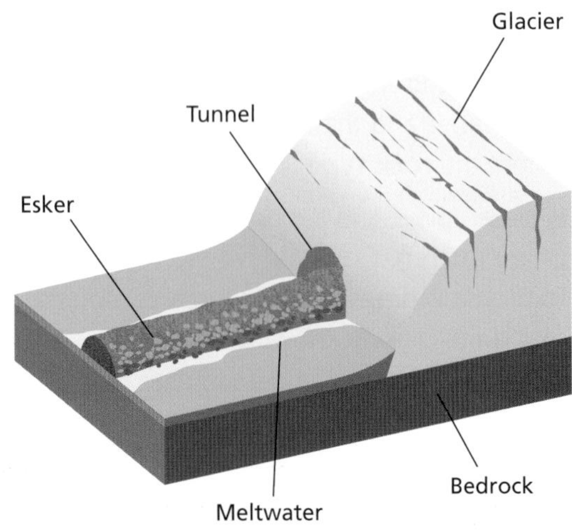

Figure 11.22 *Formation of an esker*

Outwash plains

An outwash plain is a **low**, **flat area** of land made of **sand** and **gravel**. It is found in front of a **terminal moraine** (see Figure 11.20).

Formation:

- As the glacier melts, **meltwater** carrying a load of sand and gravel flows from the front of the glacier and **spreads out** over the lowland area.
- As the meltwater loses energy, it begins to **deposit** the heavier material first, followed by the lighter material.

Example of an outwash plain: The Curragh in Co. Kildare.

Figure 11.23 *The Curragh, Co. Kildare*

Can you apply the D-E-P-E-D formula to explain one feature of glacial deposition and one feature of fluvio-glacial deposition to your classmates? Use the outline on page 53 of your Activity Book to help you.

(i) List the four ways a glacier transports its load.
(ii) What is boulder clay?
(iii) The Curragh in Co. Kildare is an example of which glacial feature?
(iv) Where in Ireland might you find a drumlin landscape?
(v) Can you explain two pieces of geographical information we can learn from erratics?

- I can explain how glaciers transport their load.
- I can identify landforms of glacial deposition and fluvio-glacial deposition.

- I can explain the formation of two landforms of glacial deposition and two landforms of fluvio-glacial deposition.

People and glaciation

Learning Intentions

In this section, you will learn:

- how people interact with and manage glacial landforms.

Agriculture
Tourism
Hydroelectricity
Glacial deposits

The **influences of glaciation** are widespread on the Irish landscape. These influences can have both a positive and a negative effect on human activity.

Benefits of glaciation

Agriculture

The **boulder clay** deposited during an ice age makes very **fertile soil** that is suitable for agriculture. The **Golden Vale** area in Munster is famous for its dairy produce.

Figure 11.24 *Agriculture in the Golden Vale*

Tourism

Beautiful **landscapes** created by glaciation are important **tourist attractions**. Lakes in glacial areas are often used for **recreational** purposes including **boating** and **fishing**. Areas such as **Glendalough** in Co. Wicklow and the **Gap of Dunloe** in Co. Kerry attract thousands of visitors each year and are an example of the relationship between the physical world and tourism.

Figure 11.25 *Pony trekking at the Gap of Dunloe, Co. Kerry*

Go to Chapter 17 to learn more about the relationship between the physical world and tourism.

PORTFOLIO ACTIVITY 11.1

Go to page 44 of your Portfolio to complete the activity on glaciation and tourism.

Hydroelectricity

Glacial lakes provide a natural reservoir for the generation of **hydroelectric power** (HEP). The HEP station at **Turlough Hill** in Co. Wicklow uses water from Lough Nahanagan, which is a tarn, to generate electricity.

Figure 11.26 *Lough Nahanagan, Co. Wicklow*

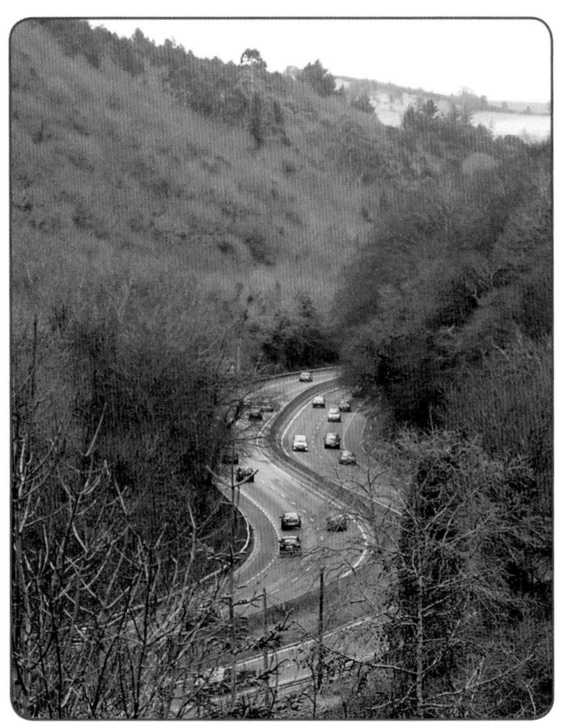

Roads

Glaciated **U-shaped valleys** provide natural **routeways** through upland areas. The **Gap of Dunloe** in Co. Kerry and the **Glen of the Downs** in Co. Wicklow are examples. Roads are sometimes built on **eskers** also. This is an example of the relationship between the physical world and transport which we will learn about in Chapter 17.

Figure 11.27 *The N11 dual carriageway goes through the Glen of the Downs*

Industry

Sand and **gravel** are taken from eskers and used in the **construction industry**. Glacial lakes provide a **water supply** for industry and urban areas.

Figure 11.28 *Gravel mining at an esker*

Negative influences of glaciation

Poor agricultural land in upland areas

Glaciers **remove** much of the **soil** cover in upland areas, often leaving them **unsuitable** for productive **agriculture**. Sheep farming and forestry may be the only options for farmers in these regions.

Figure 11.29 *Farming options are limited in upland areas*

Poor drainage

Glacial deposits such as drumlins can lead to **poor drainage**, causing **bogs** to develop in some areas.

Figure 11.30 *The melting Antarctic ice sheet will lead to a rise in sea levels*

Flooding

Although the ice sheets that once covered Ireland are long gone, today's glaciers and ice caps in the **Arctic** and **Antarctica** are **melting** at an alarming rate. This causes **sea levels** to **rise**. If they continue to rise, lowland coastal areas of Ireland will be at **risk of flooding**.

ACTIVITY

Go online to find out how quickly the polar ice caps are melting each year. What is the impact of this?

ACTIVITY

Check out 'The Action of Ice' clip at https://educateplus.ie/go/action-ice to find out more about how glaciers form and how they are affected by global warming.

 **(i)** Name one positive and one negative impact of glaciation.

 **(ii)** Name two ways that glaciation attracts tourists.

 **(iii)** How does glaciation influence farming?

 I can explain the positive and negative influences of glaciation on human activity.   

Figure 11.31 *MacGillycuddy's Reeks, Co. Kerry*

Glaciation on Ordnance Survey maps

Examine the Ordnance Survey map of MacGillycuddy's Reeks opposite and answer the following questions:

1. Identify the following landforms on the map extract using four-figure grid references:
   - **(a)** U-shaped valley
   - **(b)** Arête
   - **(c)** Ribbon lake
2. Identify the following landforms on the map extract using six-figure grid references:
   - **(a)** Cirque/corrie
   - **(b)** Tarn
   - **(c)** Hanging valley
3. On the map extract, find the area of land over 200 metres in height in km^2.
4. Draw a sketch map of the map extract showing the following landforms:
   - **(a)** U-shaped valley
   - **(b)** Arête
   - **(c)** Corrie
   - **(d)** Ribbon lake
   - **(e)** Tarn
5. What aspects of the physical glaciated landscape would attract tourists to this area?
6. What evidence is there on this OS map that tourists visit the area?

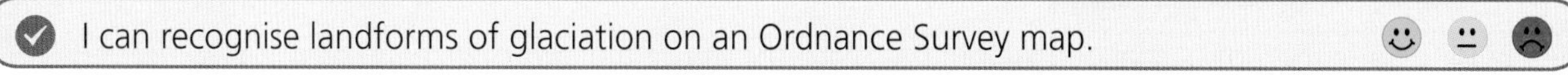

I can recognise landforms of glaciation on an Ordnance Survey map.

REVISION

The two main processes of glacial erosion are ____________________ and ____________________.
An armchair-shaped hollow in the side of a mountain is called a ____________________.
It is the result of glacial erosion. A narrow, steep-sided ridge separating two cirques is called an ____________________. When three or more cirques form on the side of a mountain, a ____________________ ______________ is formed. A _____-________________ valley is formed when a glacier erodes the sides and bottom of a V-shaped valley. A long, narrow lake on the floor of a U-shaped valley is known as a ____________________ lake. A tributary glacial valley, which has been eroded less than the main valley, is known as a ____________________ ____________________.

Material transported and deposited by a glacier is called ____________________. Melting glaciers deposit ____________________ clay and other material that can form rounded hills called ____________________. Features such as eskers and ____________________ plains are formed by meltwater deposits.

Positive influences of glaciation include ____________________ soil, ____________________ and industrial resources. ____________________ influences include poor land in ____________________ areas, poor drainage and the risk of ____________________.

Questions & Answers

Sample Question

Name **one** feature of glacial deposition and, with the aid of a diagram, explain how it was formed.

Sample Answer

Description: Eskers are a feature of glacial deposition. An esker is a long, narrow ridge of sand or gravel that winds its way along a lowland area.

Example: An example of this is the Esker Riada in Co. Galway.

Processes and Explanation: As the glacier began to melt, streams of meltwater carrying a load of eroded material flowed underneath it. When this meltwater increased in volume, a tunnel was carved out under the glacier. Eventually, some material was deposited on the bed of the meltwater stream. When the stream came out of the tunnel, it lost energy and began depositing the remainder of the load. This esker formed a ridge of sand and gravel on the surrounding plain. Roads have been built on eskers in many areas as they provide good foundations.

Diagram:

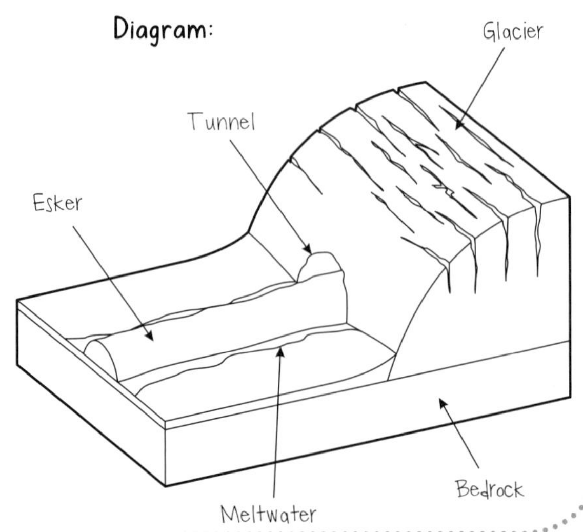

Short Questions

1. The feature shown in the diagram is formed by glacial erosion.

   It is called:

   An esker ☐
   A ribbon lake ☐
   A corrie or cirque ☐
   A drumlin ☐ [tick (✓) the correct box]

Freeze-thaw weathering

Plucking and abrasion

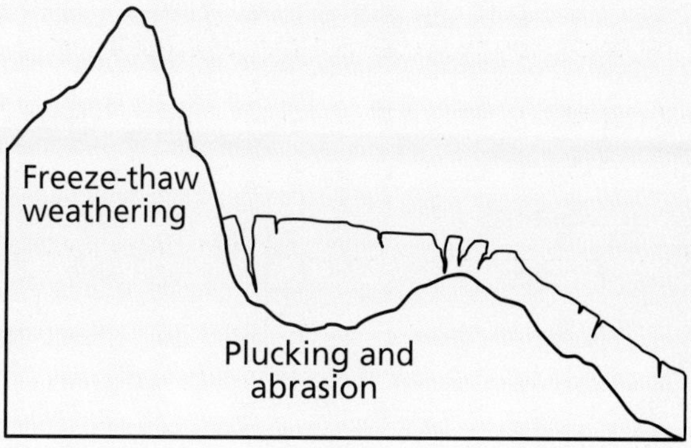

2. Examine the diagram, which shows features of glacial erosion. In the grid provided, match each of the numbers 1 to 4 in Column X with the letter of its pair on the diagram. One pair has been completed for you.

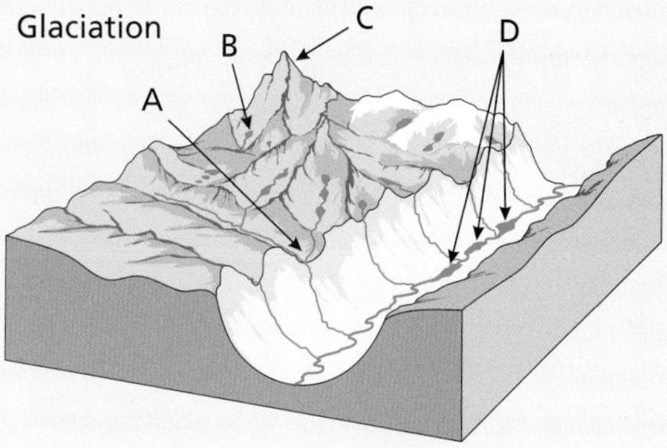

Glaciation

A B C D

Column X		Y
1	Cirque/Corrie	
2	Ribbon lakes	
3	Pyramidal peak	C
4	Hanging valley	

3. Examine the photograph.

   Circle the correct answer in each of the following statements:

   (i) The lake pictured here is a feature of glacial **erosion / deposition**.

   (ii) The lake pictured here is called **an arête / a tarn**.

   (iii) This lake is found in **upland / lowland** areas in a glacial region.

4. Which of the following are all features of glacial erosion?

   (i) Fjord, moraine, pyramidal peak ☐
   (ii) Arête, cirque, U-shaped valley ☐
   (iii) Boulder clay, cirque, hanging valley ☐
   (iv) Arête, cirque, drumlin ☐ [tick (✓) the correct box]

5. In the photograph, the deposited material indicated by the red arrows is:

   Moraine ☐
   A cirque (corrie) ☐
   A fjord ☐
   A drumlin ☐ [tick (✓) the correct box]

6. Ice sheets sometimes carried large rocks, like the one shown in this photograph, and deposited them in places where the rock type was different. These rocks are called:

Moraines ☐

Erratics ☐

Boulder clay ☐ [tick (✓) the correct box]

7. Which of the following are all features of glacial deposition?

(i) Eskers, moraines, drumlins ☐

(ii) Corries, drumlins, erratic ☐

(iii) U-shaped valleys, moraines, cirque (corrie) ☐

8. When an ice age ended, the meltwater caused the sea levels to rise, which flooded U-shaped valleys.

The feature shown in this photograph is called a:

Fjord ☐

Ria ☐

Corrie ☐ [tick (✓) the correct box]

Long Questions

1. Name **one** feature of glacial erosion and with the aid of a diagram, explain how it was formed.
2. With the aid of a labelled diagram, explain the difference between lateral, medial, terminal and end moraines.
3. Explain the processes of plucking and abrasion.
4. Briefly explain how a glacier is formed.
5. **(i)** Name and briefly explain **one** way that people benefit from the results of glaciation.

   (ii) Name and briefly explain **one** disadvantage of the results of glaciation.

Visual Summary

- **Glaciation**
  - Erosion
    - Processes
      - Plucking
      - Abrasion
    - Features

  - People and glaciation
    - Benefits
      - Farming
      - Tourism
      - HEP
    - Negative influences
      - Poor agricultural land
      - Poor drainage
  - Deposition
    - Glacial
      - Boulder clay
      - Drumlin

      - Erratics

      - Moraines → Lateral → Medial → Terminal → End
    - Meltwater
      - Eskers
      - Outwash plains

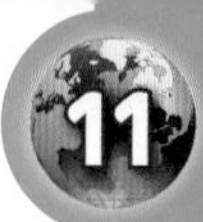

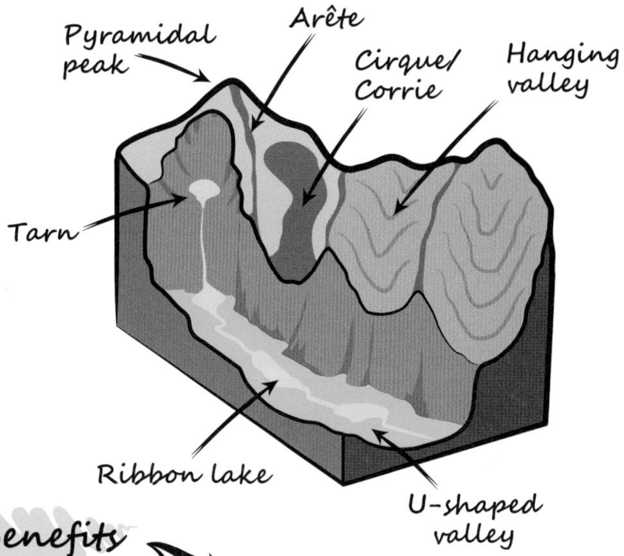

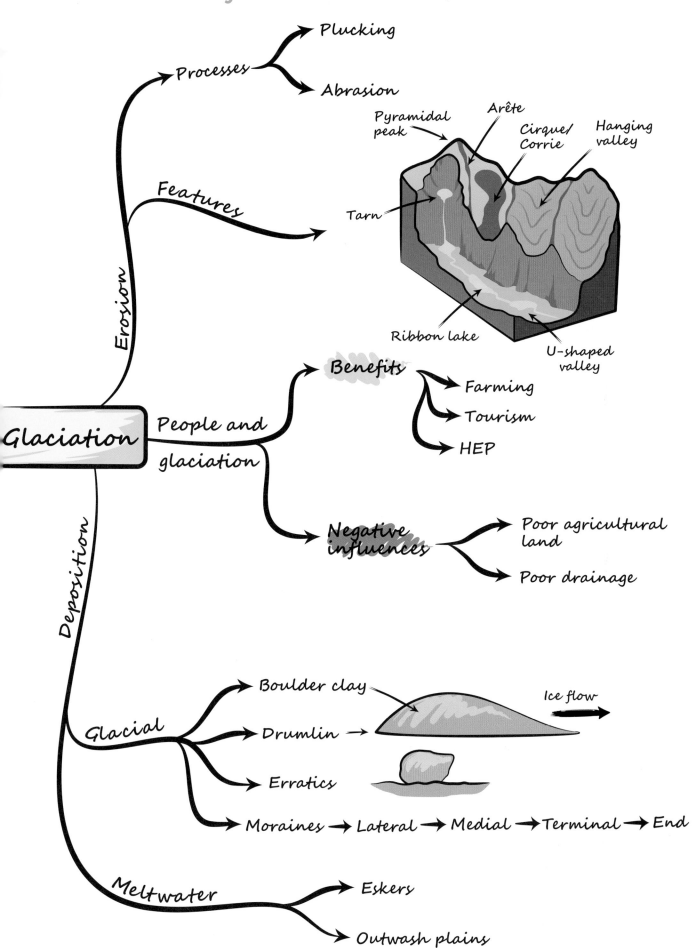

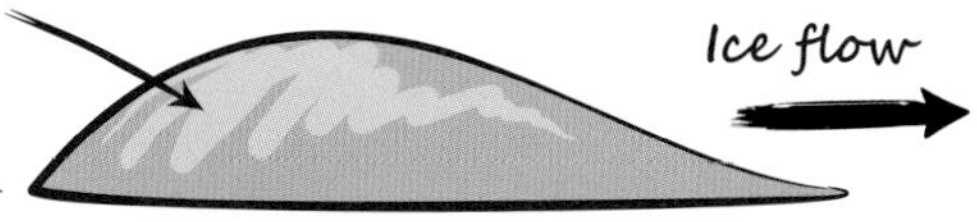

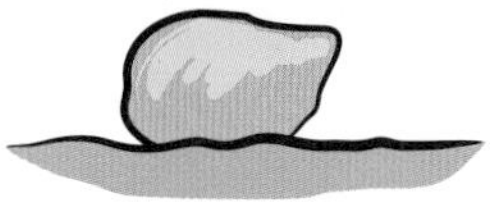

12 Settlement and Urbanisation: Where we live and why

In this chapter, you will learn:

- what settlement is
- the history of rural and urban settlement in Ireland
- the factors that affect the location of rural and urban settlement in Ireland today
- how to identify settlement on Ordnance Survey maps
- what urbanisation is
- the causes of urbanisation
- the effects of urbanisation.

ICE-BREAKER ACTIVITY

Take a look at the two images at the bottom of this page and at the bottom of the next. One is an illustration of a Celtic settlement in Ireland. The other is a photograph of Galway City today. Work in pairs and compare the two images under the following headings:

- the location of the settlement
- what activities take place in the settlement
- the size of the settlement
- what jobs the people who live there might have.

Figure 12.1 *Artist's impression of a Celtic settlement*

Introduction to settlement

Learning Intentions

In this section, you will learn:

- what settlement is
- how site affects settlement
- how situation affects settlement
- how to identify site and situation on an Ordnance Survey map.

Settlement
Population density
Population distribution
Site
Situation
Altitude
Aspect
Drainage
Bridging point
Slope
Shelter
Nodal point

Settlement refers to where people live. The places where settlements are built and the **services** (or **functions**) that settlements provide change over time.

When the first settlers arrived in Ireland about nine thousand years ago settlement was influenced by **basic needs** (e.g. food, water supply and shelter) and **communications** (e.g. transport). Today, settlement is influenced by peoples need for **services** (e.g. schools and shops) and **employment**.

Population density: how many people live in an area; it is often measured by the number of people living in 1 km^2.

If you look at Ireland's **population distribution** you will see that most people now live in towns and cities. There is a low **population density** in rural areas and a high population density in urban areas. The growth of towns and cities (settlements) is called **urbanisation**.

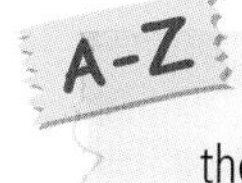

Population distribution: the spread of where people live.

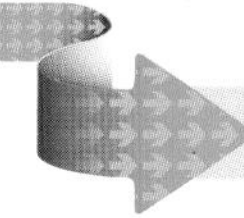

We will learn more about urbanisation on pages 210–221 of this chapter.

When examining the location of any settlement, we look at the **factors** that influence the **site** and the **situation** of the settlement.

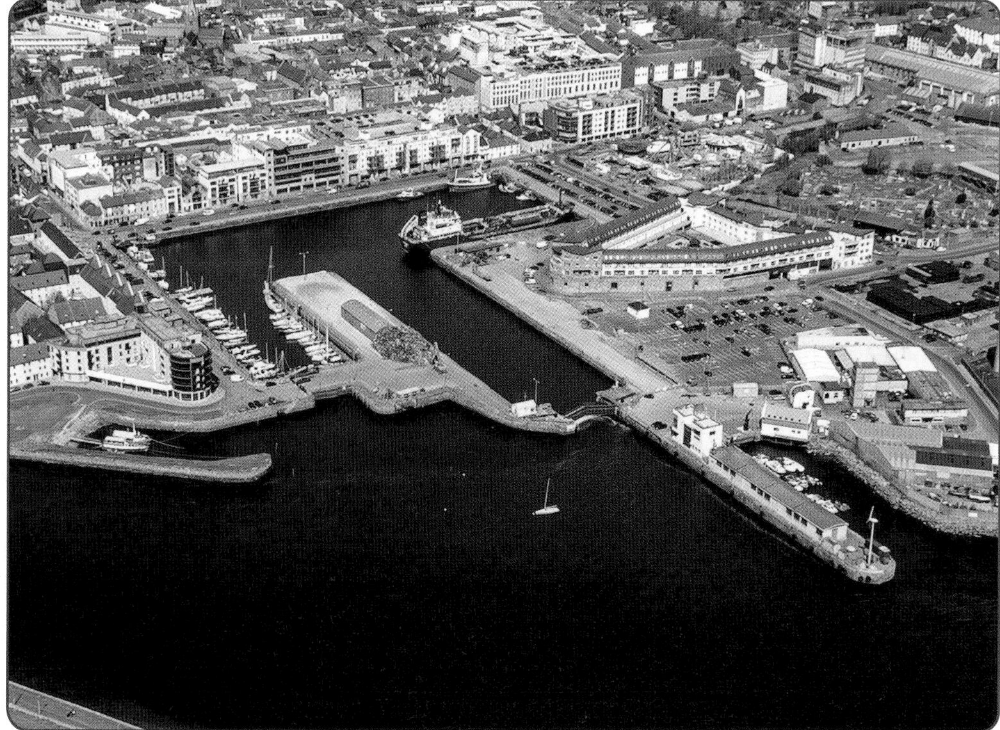

Figure 12.2 *Aerial photograph of Galway City*

Site of settlement

The **site** refers to the actual **ground the settlement is built on**. The choice of site for a settlement can be influenced by a number of **physical factors**.

Altitude

Altitude refers to the **height** of a place above sea level.

Little settlement occurs in upland areas. Conditions are too cold, wet and windy. Soils also tend to be thin and poor in upland areas due to mass movement. It is also difficult to get building materials to upland areas.

Most settlements are on **low-lying land** under 200 m. However, some ancient settlements were in upland areas for defensive purposes.

Example: **Killarney** is in a low-lying area surrounded by mountains.

Aspect

Aspect refers to the **direction in which** a place is facing.

In the **northern hemisphere** the best slopes to locate on face **south**. South-facing slopes receive the most **sunshine**, and are therefore warmer and better for agriculture.

Example: **Killybegs** is on a south-facing slope.

Drainage

Drainage refers to **natural removal of water** from an area.

Settlement occurs near **rivers**. In the past, rivers were important for **water**, **transport** and **food**. Fertile soil is also found alongside many rivers, which is good for **farming**.

Many towns also developed at **bridging points**. A bridging point is a place where it is easiest to cross a river, usually at a narrow point.

Example: **Athlone** is at a bridging point on the River Shannon

Slope

Slope refers to when land is **slanted** rather than flat. When land is very sloped it is said to be **steep**.

Settlement usually occurs on **low-lying, flat land**. Little settlement occurs on slopes. It is difficult to build any type of infrastructure on slopes.

Low-lying flat land in **river valleys** usually has very **fertile soil**, which attracts settlement. The land on slopes is not as suitable for agriculture because soils are thinner and it is more difficult to operate machinery.

Example: **Kilkenny** is located on flat land on the banks of the River Nore.

Shelter

Shelter is **protection from weather** by trees, mountains or other natural features.

Settlement on the coast is usually in **sheltered** areas such as **harbours**. **Valleys** at the foot of hills provide excellent shelter and so settlements are often found in those areas.

Example: **Dingle** is sheltered by the surrounding mountains.

Look at the site of Killybegs Town in Co. Donegal on the Ordnance Survey map opposite.

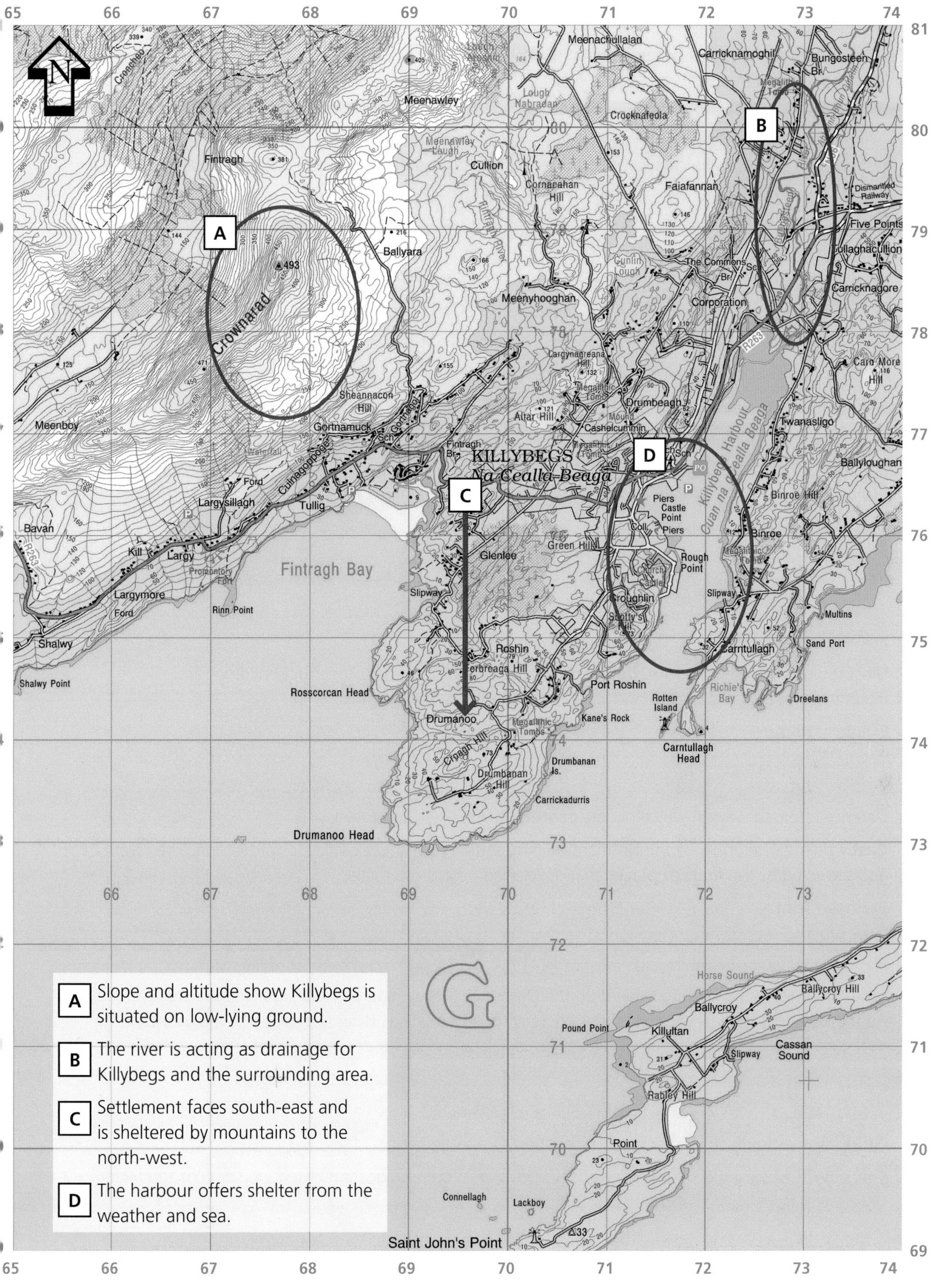

Figure 12.3 *Killybegs, Co. Donegal*

Situation of settlement

Situation refers to the **area surrounding** the settlement. The situation of a settlement can be influenced by a number of **factors**:

Nodal point

A nodal point is a location where different routes meet. It is also known as a **route focus**. These routes can be road networks, rail lines, rivers or canals.

People settled at nodal points and towns grew as a result.

Example: **Carlow**

Bridging point on a river

A bridging point is a place where it is easiest to cross a large river.

People settled at bridging points and many towns and cities have built up around them.

Example: **Carrick-on-Suir**

Coastal

Sheltered harbours, trade and fishing attracted people to coastal locations.

People settled in these coastal areas and towns developed.

Example: **Bray**

Relief

Relief describes the **height**, the **aspect** and the **slope** of an area.

Most towns developed on **low, flat, fertile land** as it was easier to construct buildings and infrastructure. Low, flat, fertile land was also better for agriculture.

Example: **Kildare**

Defence

Defence refers to ways in which people **protect** themselves from attack.

Castles were often built by the Normans. People settled near these castles for protection. They were also attracted by the **market places** that developed near these castles.

Example: **Trim**

ACTIVITY

Some of the factors above are evident on the Ordnance Survey map opposite. Use the legend on page 7 and the skills you have developed to identify why the town of Castlebar developed at this location.

(i) What is a settlement?

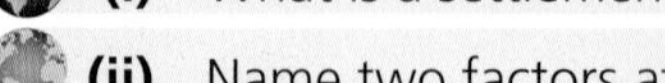

(ii) Name two factors affecting the site of a settlement.

(iii) Name two factors affecting the situation of a settlement.

(iv) Why has your local town or city developed in its current location? Mention some of the factors you have learned about in this section.

- I understand how site and situation have affected settlement.
- I can identify site and situation factors on an Ordnance Survey map.

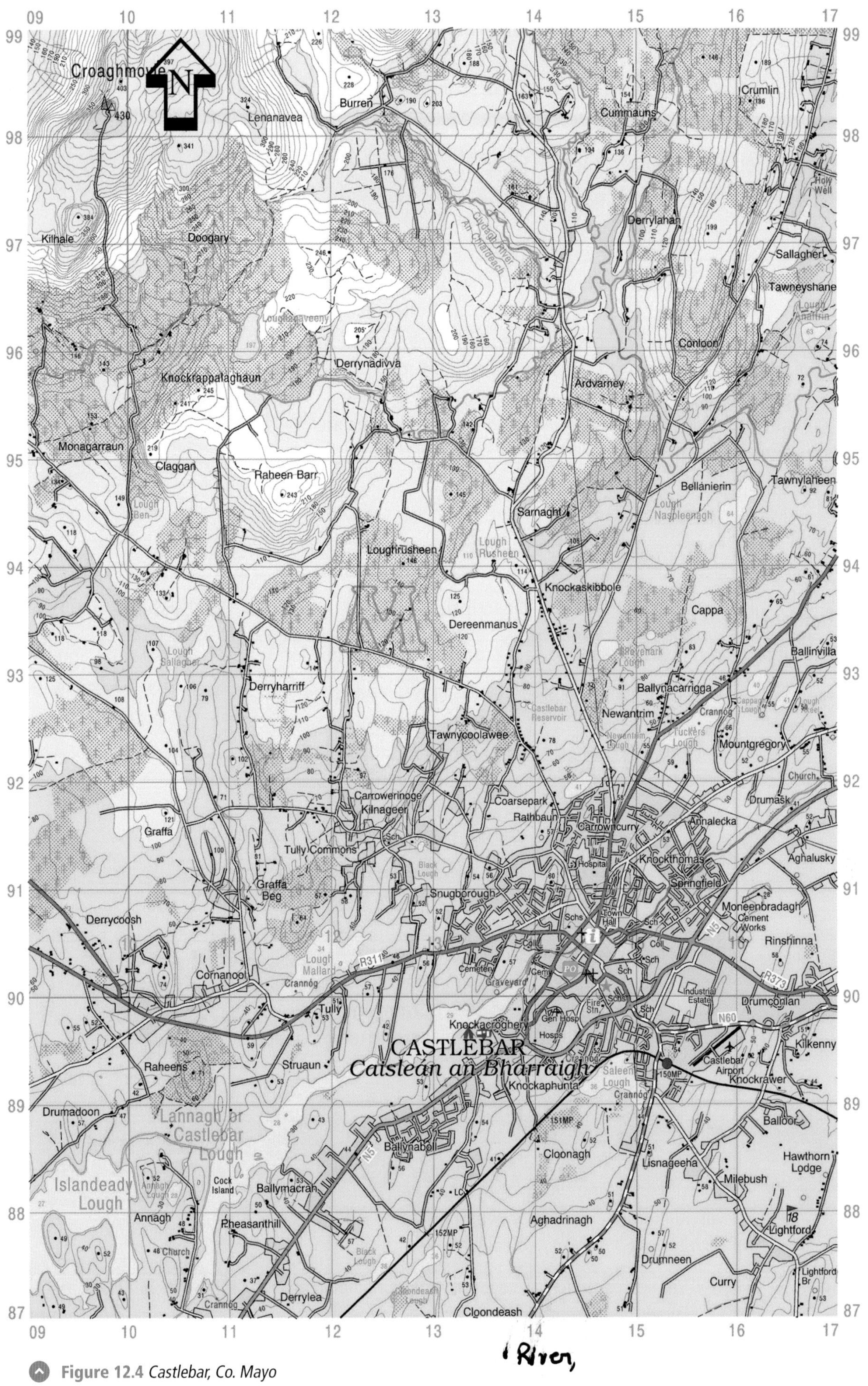

Figure 12.4 *Castlebar, Co. Mayo*

History of settlement in Ireland

Learning Intentions

In this section, you will learn:

- about the history of settlement in Ireland
- how to identify different historical settlements on an Ordnance Survey map.

Antiquity
Celtic
Viking
Norman
Plantation

If we study any Ordinance Survey map of Ireland, we will see evidence of **historical settlement**. This table describes the different types of settlement in Ireland and how to identify these settlements on Ordnance Survey maps. All historical settlements are shown on OS maps as **antiquities** with their location and name marked in red.

Antiquity:
an object, building or work of art from the ancient or historic past.

Type of settlement	Description	Evidence on OS maps
Pre-Christian	The first settlers who came to Ireland chose sites for: • **Water** – near **rivers** because they needed a water source. • **Food** – near their food sources and on **fertile land**, such as flood plains rich in alluvium. • **Defence** – locations they could **defend** when under attack: near rivers, coasts and cliffs. • **Communications** – coastal locations where settlers first arrived and at bridging points on rivers. The first settlers mainly travelled by **river**.	• Megalithic Tombs • Portal Dolmens • Cairn • Midden
Celtic	The Celts arrived in Ireland around 500 BCE. They built small **farming** settlements. Sometimes they built artificial islands on the beds of lakes called **Crannógs**. They also built defensive settlements called **forts**, often in upland and coastal areas.	• Crannóg • Forts – ring, hill and promontory • Fulacht fia • Standing Stone • Souterrain
Early Christian	**Monasteries** were built by monks after Saint Patrick brought Christianity to Ireland in the fifth century. These monasteries were often built in remote places like Glendalough in Co. Wicklow. They were important places of refuge, education and religion.	• Holy Well • Monastery • Round Tower • High Cross • Church
Viking	The Vikings came to Ireland from Scandinavia around 800 CE. They made the dangerous journey in longboats. They settled along the **coastline** of Ireland, especially at river estuaries. Examples of Viking Settlements are **Wexford** and **Waterford**.	Place names that include 'ford' (from the Norwegian word *fjord*), such as Waterford and Wexford.

Norman	The Normans invaded Ireland in the twelfth century (1169). They built great **castles** along the **banks of rivers**. They chose to settle on the banks of rivers so they could defend themselves. The Normans first arrived in the south and east of Ireland and they mainly settled there. Kilkenny City is famous for its magnificent Norman castle.	• Castle • Motte and Bailey • Moated Site • Town Walls
Plantation	In the sixteenth and seventeenth centuries, British people came to Ireland and set up towns. Parts of Ireland were planted or settled by people loyal to the king or queen of England. These towns were known as **plantation towns**. Examples of plantation towns include Portarlington and Portlaoise in Co. Laois, and Youghal and Mallow in Co. Cork.	• Fortified House • Demesne • Bawns

ACTIVITY

Can you locate and identify past historic periods of settlement on the map below?

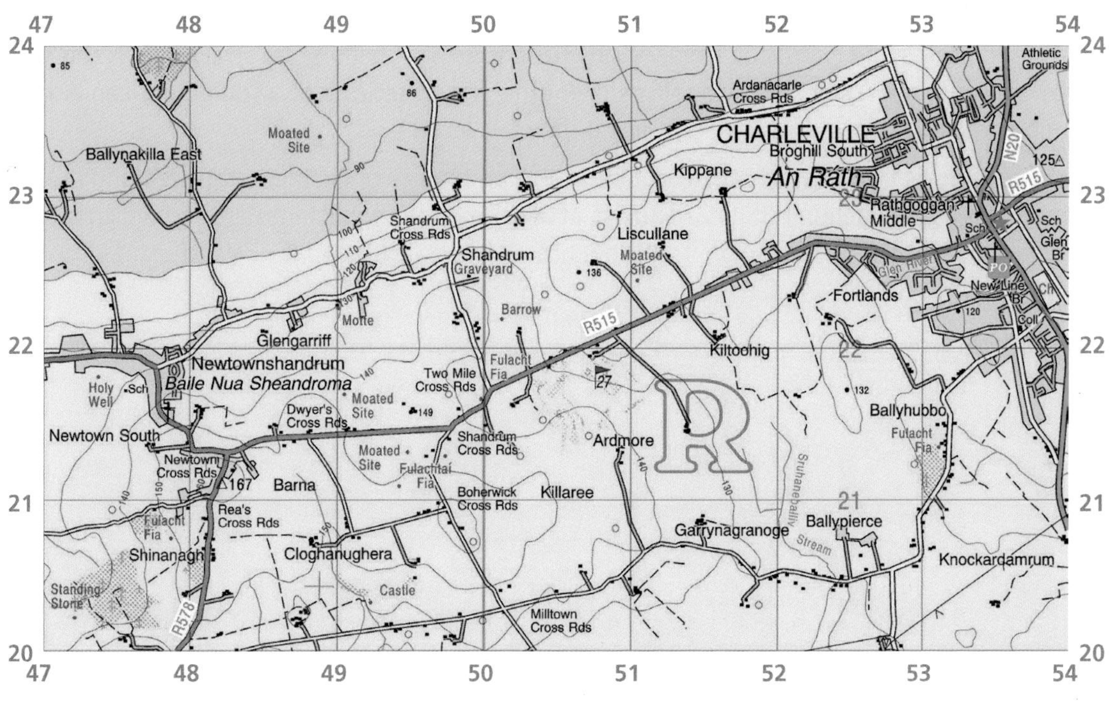

Figure 12.5 *Charleville, Co. Cork*

ACTIVITY

Can you suggest a reason why the Vikings and the Normans settled in Ireland? From what you have learned in History, can you name some antiquities or evidence from past settlements that can be found in your local area?

(i) Why did ancient settlers locate near rivers?

(ii) List two periods of historic settlement in Ireland and name an antiquity from those times.

(iii) Study the map of Castlebar on page 201 (Figure 12.4). List three pieces of evidence that show that it has a long history of settlement.

- I understand the different time periods of historic settlement in Ireland.
- I can identify those settlements on an Ordnance Survey map.

Urban settlement in Ireland today

Learning Intentions

In this section, you will learn:

- about the functions of urban settlements
- that the function of an urban settlement can change over time
- how to identify functions of urban settlements on OS maps and aerial photographs.

Function
Market
Defence
Resource
Ecclesiastical
Residential
Multi-functional

Most Irish people today live in **urban** areas. If we look around our towns and cities, we can find evidence of what attracted people to live there in the past and evidence of what attracts people to live there today.

The functions of urban settlements

Urban settlements (towns and cities) can have various **functions**. A function of a settlement is the **service it provides**. As a settlement grows and **develops** over time, the **functions** of a settlement can also **change** depending on the needs of the people living there.

The **historical functions** that towns had are not as important today. For example, the **castle** in Kilkenny no longer has a defensive function but it is a **tourist attraction**. The monasteries around which a town was once built may still exist, but the town itself now has many other functions.

Figure 12.6 *Kilkenny Castle*

Below are a list of functions and how they can be identified on Ordnance Survey maps and aerial photographs.

Function	Explanation	Evidence on OS maps and aerial photographs	Example
Market	Some towns developed as markets for farmers and traders to sell their goods. Today there are shops and other services such as banks and post offices.	• Road network leading to the town • Town square • Street names such as Market Street	Mullingar, Co. Westmeath
Defence	Some settlements began on an easily defended site such as a river. It was a place of protection which usually had a castle.	• Castle • Moated site • Town wall	Fethard, Co. Tipperary
Resource	Some towns developed around an area with a natural resource, such as coal.	• Mines	Navan, Co. Meath (zinc mine)
Ecclesiastical/ Religious	Some towns developed in places that once had an **ecclesiastical function**, like monasteries. Churches and other religious buildings still provide a **religious function**.	• Monastery • Round tower • Abbey • Church	Monasterevin, Co. Kildare
Port	Towns can also grow up around a place where ships dock. Large ports are often surrounded by settlement.	• Port • Boating activities	Limerick City
Industrial	Some towns have a long association with a particular industry. Today industrial estates provide employment for people.	• Factory • Industrial estate	Sandyford, Dublin Douglas, Cork
Residential	Towns that are close to cities and workplaces attract people to live there. These became known as **dormitory** or **commuter towns**.	• Housing estates	Ashbourne, Co. Meath
Transport	Some towns developed at **bridging points** because people had to come there to cross the river. All towns today provide transport services for people.	All forms of transport: • Road • Rail • Airports • Ports	Athlone, Co. Westmeath
Tourism and recreation	Towns can develop around a beach or other leisure facility. These are usually holiday resorts. Towns also provide **leisure facilities** for locals and facilities that attract people to visit, such as sports stadiums.	• Caravan park • Tourist information office • Hostels • Camp site • Golf course • Sports ground	Tramore, Co. Waterford

Can you identify two more Irish towns that fit into each of the categories above?

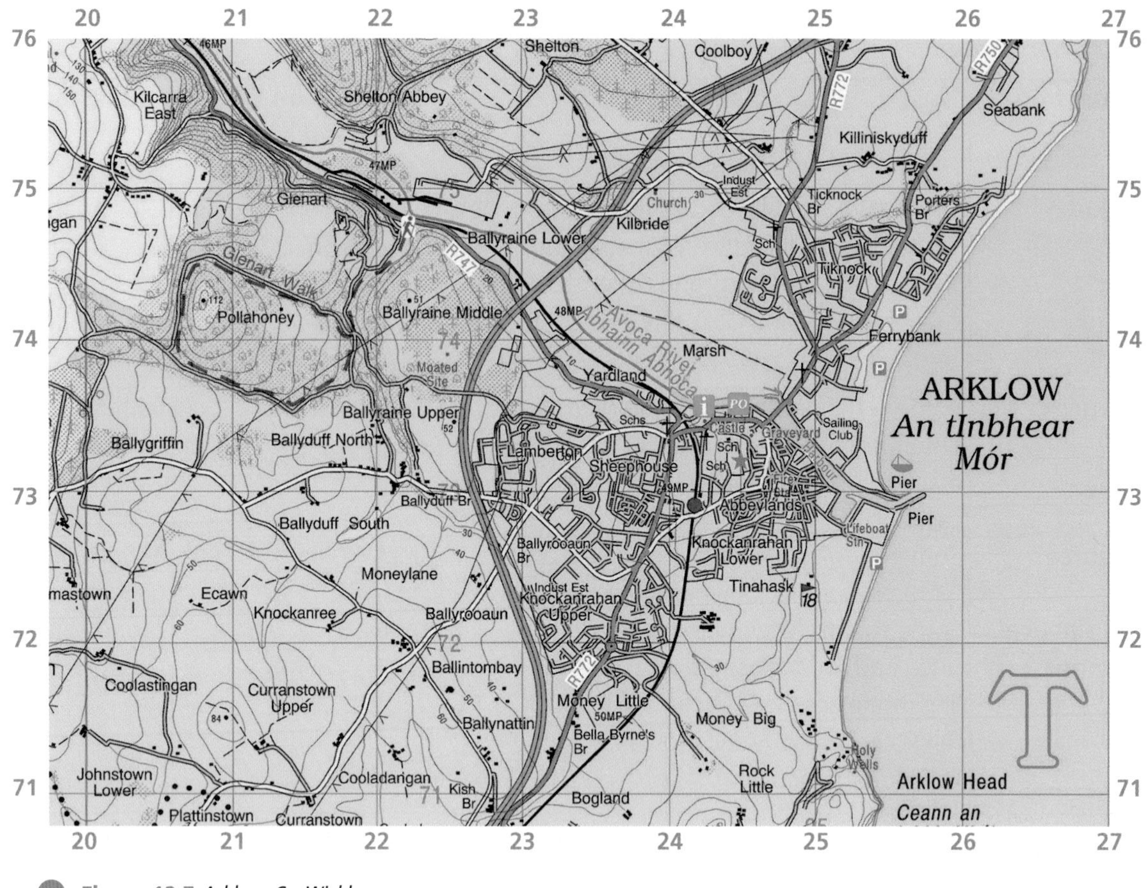

Figure 12.7 *Arklow, Co. Wicklow*

Study the map in Figure 12.7 and identify the functions of Arklow **(i)** now and **(ii)** in the past.

Look at the aerial photograph of Arklow below. Can you identify three reasons why Arklow developed at this site?

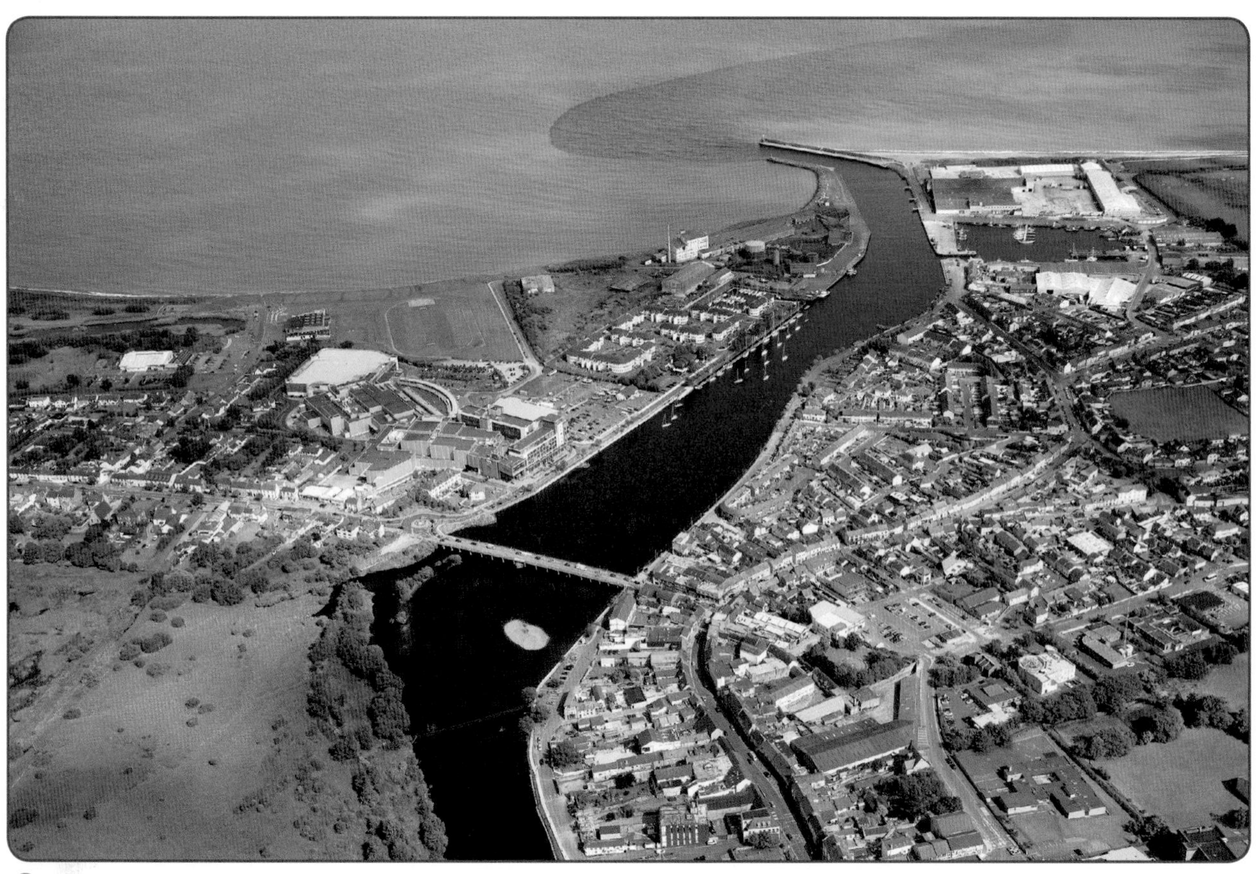

Figure 12.8 *Aerial photograph of Arklow*

Multi-functional settlement

A **multi-functional settlement** is a settlement that provides many functions for its population. Today, **all urban settlements** are multi-functional. All towns provide **services** for the people who live there and in the surrounding area, such as schools, hospitals, Garda stations and fire stations, and sometimes colleges and universities. These services also provide employment.

We will examine the many functions that Waterford City provides in the Case Study below. We will also look at how the functions of Waterford City have **changed over time**.

CASE STUDY

Multi-functional settlement: Waterford City

Waterford City is an example of a settlement that has changed its function over time. Today, the city provides many functions for its population. It is what we call a **multi-functional settlement**.

Defensive

Waterford began as a **defensive** settlement. The **Vikings** settled near Woodstown (now on the outskirts of Waterford). There is still evidence of Viking settlement in Woodstown today. The **Normans** settled in Waterford after the Vikings. They are responsible for the **walls** of the city that still stand today. The Normans built these walls to protect the city.

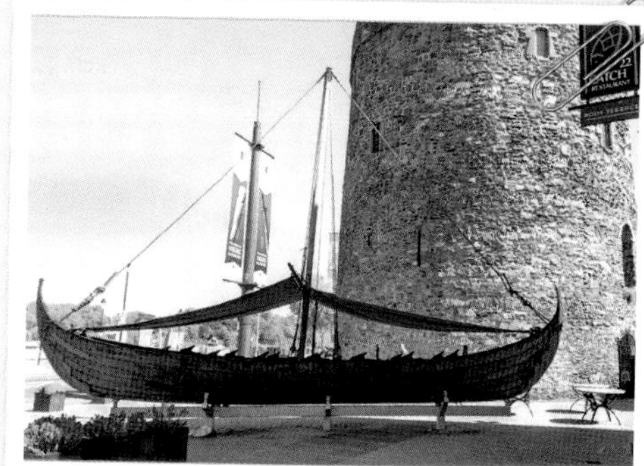

Figure 12.9 *This replica of a Viking ship is a reminder of Waterford's past*

Employment

Waterford has always been a very important place of employment. **Waterford Crystal** was a major employer in the city for decades. In recent years, large **MNCs** like GlaxoSmithKline Pharmaceuticals have located here. This has provided employment in many different industries.

Port

Waterford is one of Ireland's most important **ports**. It is the closest Irish port to mainland Europe and caters for both commercial and leisure ships. The port is excellently **serviced** by both rail and road to the rest of the country.

Waterford has many other functions today. For example, it has an important **residential function** with many suburbs around the city centre. Waterford IT, a third-level institution, also provides an important **educational function**.

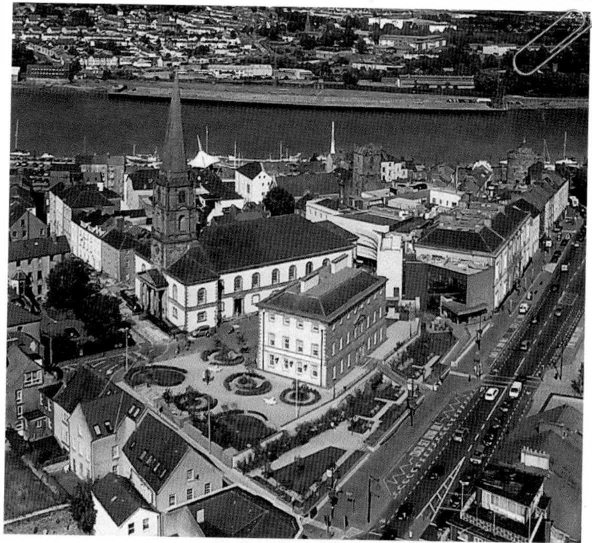

Figure 12.10 *An aerial view of Waterford*

With a classmate, research a town or city in your locality and see how its function has changed over time. Think of the following functions:

- Defence
- Market
- Religious

Does the town or city have a new function (educational, industrial, residential)?

Report back to your class on your findings.

 **(i)** What does the term 'function' mean when talking about settlements?

 **(ii)** List two functions of a settlement. What do those functions provide?

 **(iii)** 'Waterford could be described as a multi-functional settlement.' Discuss this statement, giving three pieces of evidence to justify your points.

- I understand what a function of a settlement is. 
- I understand that settlements can have multiple functions and that the functions of settlements can change over time. 
- I can identify functions of settlements on an Ordnance Survey map and an aerial photograph. 

Rural settlement in Ireland today

Learning Intentions

In this section, you will learn:

- about rural patterns of settlement in Ireland today and how to identify them on Ordnance Survey maps.

Linear
Nucleated
Clustered
Dispersed

In the past, settlements in rural areas were linked to **agriculture**. Today, less than 10 per cent of the population is involved in agriculture, yet 37.3 per cent of our population still lives in rural areas. Looking at the **patterns of rural settlement** helps us to understand this type of settlement better.

Top Tip

Houses are identified by black squares on Ordnance Survey maps.

Rural patterns of settlement

Linear

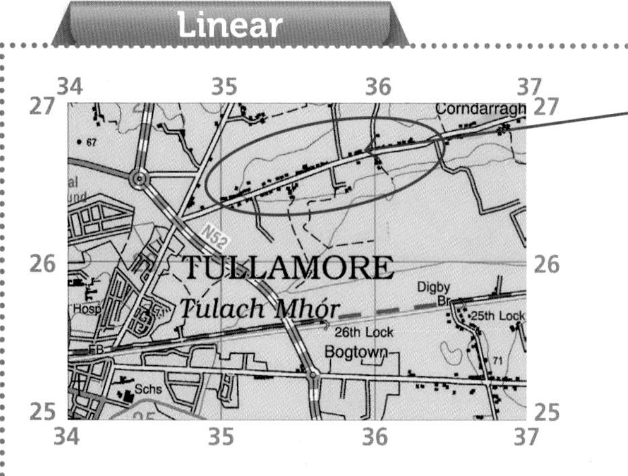

Figure 12.11 *Linear settlement*

This is when settlement is in a **line along a road**. It is also called **ribbon** settlement.

This type of settlement occurs because it allows easy access to the nearest urban area and to **services** such as water, electricity and sewerage.

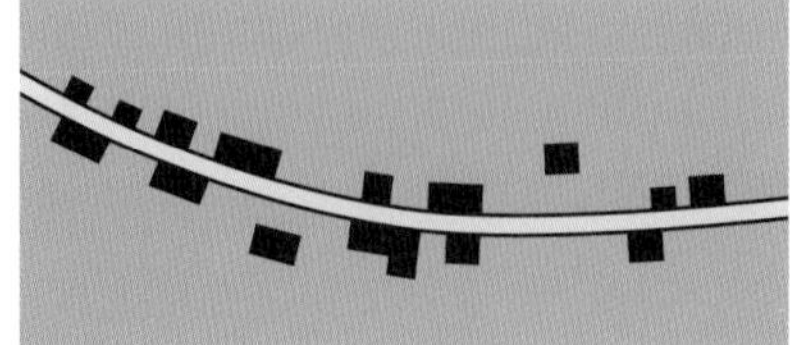

ACTIVITY

Why do some people like living in linear settlements?

Nucleated

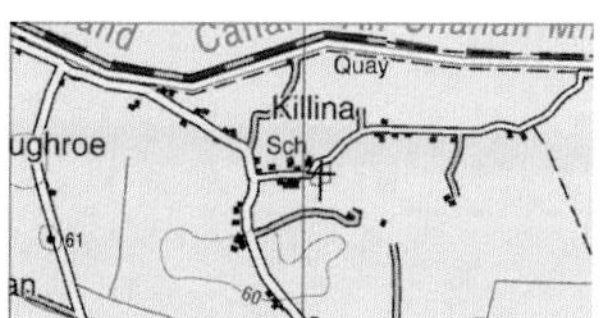

Figure 12.12 *Nucleated settlement*

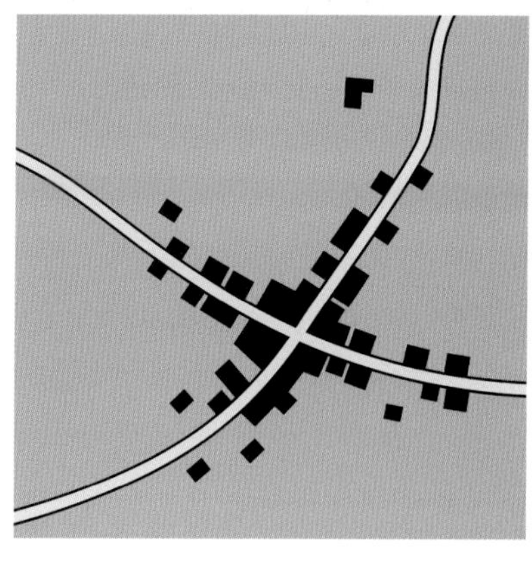

This is when settlements are **grouped** together. It is also called **clustered** settlement.

This type of settlement occurs for a number of reasons. In rural areas, some villages have developed around **crossroads**. In other cases, they have developed from *clachans* (clusters of houses), where land owned by a farmer was divided into several sites for the children.

ACTIVITY

Why do some people like living in nucleated settlements?

Dispersed

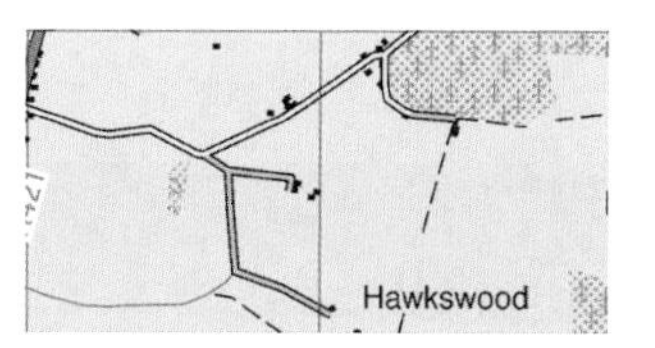

Figure 12.13 *Dispersed settlement*

This is when settlements are **spread out** and randomly **scattered**.

There is no pattern to the settlements and they are mainly **farmhouses**. The area surrounding the settlement is generally farmland. The settlement may also be in an **upland** area that is not densely populated.

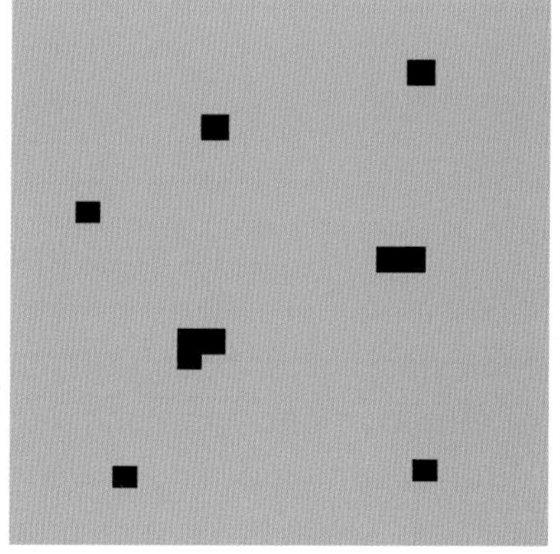

ACTIVITY

Why do some people like living in dispersed settlements?

PORTFOLIO ACTIVITY 12.1

Go to page 48 of your Portfolio to look at ways of encouraging sustainable rural development.

(i) What percentage of the population live in rural areas in Ireland?

(ii) Name one pattern of rural settlement and explain why it occurs.

(iii) Can you locate linear, nucleated, or dispersed patterns of settlement near your local area? If so name the pattern and the location. Why has this pattern of settlement taken place here?

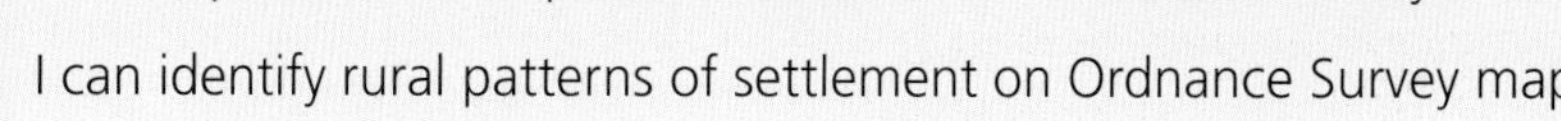

- I can explain the rural patterns of settlement in Ireland today.
- I can identify rural patterns of settlement on Ordnance Survey maps.

Introduction to urbanisation

Learning Intentions

In this section, you will learn:

- what urbanisation is
- what causes urban change
- the effects of urban change.

Urbanisation	Urban sprawl
Planning	Dormitory town
Congestion	Satellite town
Commuter	Urban decay
Rush hour	Shanty town

Urbanisation is the increase in the number of people living in towns and cities. This causes a growth in the **size** and **number** of towns and cities.

Until about two hundred years ago, most people lived in **rural** areas and worked the land. Only a small number of people lived in cities and towns. Today, almost 55 per cent of the world's population lives in **urban areas**.

Write down five reasons why more people are now living in urban areas than in the past. Compare your list with the person beside you. Share your list with the class.

Causes of urbanisation

- During the **Industrial Revolution** in the late eighteenth and early nineteenth centuries, **factories** in cities became important places of **employment**. More and more people left the countryside and moved to cities in search of work. It was during this period that the **terraced houses** found in many of our cities were built for the labourers working in nearby factories.
- More recently, factories have started to locate on the **outskirts** of towns and cities, often in **industrial estates**. This has caused the development of residential housing in the **suburbs**.

Figure 12.14 *Terraced houses in Dublin*

- Urban areas become centres for many **services**. This attracts people to live there and also provides **employment** in the service sector. **Government** departments and **civil service** offices are located here also.
- There is a wide variety of available **housing**. It can be more **affordable** to buy a house in a housing estate in a town or city than purchase a site and build a house in a rural area.
- Urban areas attract people because of the variety of **recreation** and **leisure** activities available there.

Effects of urbanisation

Cities can be great places to live. There is a lot to do. However, there are many **problems** associated with the growth of urban areas. These problems are largely down to **lack of planning**. **Facilities** and **services** for the ever-growing populations of towns and cities need to be planned for, both in Ireland and around the world. Good planning does not always happen.

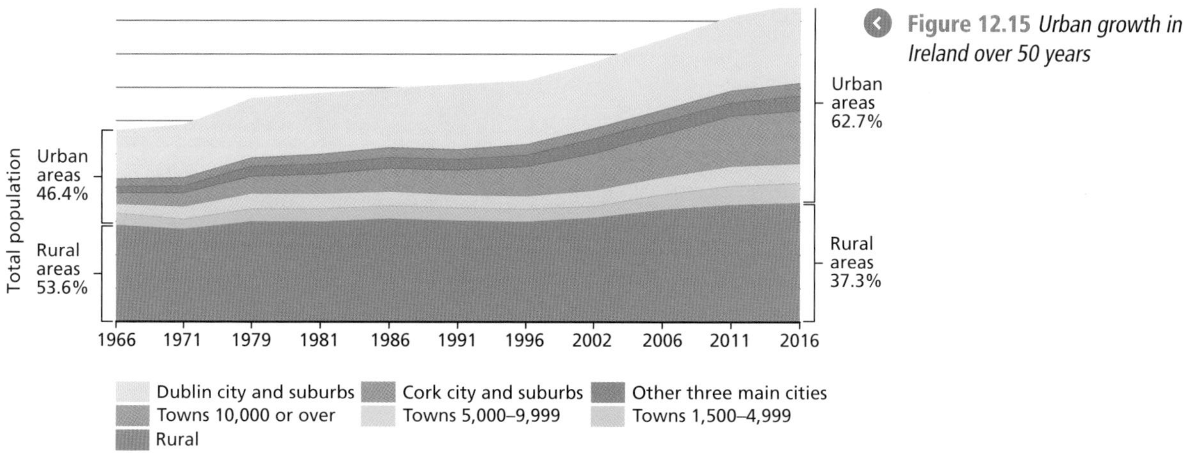

Figure 12.15 *Urban growth in Ireland over 50 years*

Traffic congestion

The **movement of people** within an urban area on a daily basis can lead to **traffic congestion**. **Commuters** are people who travel to and from work by car, bus or train. There is a **pattern** to their movement, and generally it is repeated at the same time every day. We refer to this period of time as the **rush hour**. Rush hour generally occurs from 8 a.m. to 9 a.m. and 5 p.m. to 6 p.m., Monday to Friday. Our **underdeveloped public transport** services and transport **infrastructure** causes traffic congestion.

Figure 12.16 *Gridlock on the M50 near Dublin*

How do you travel to school and how long does it take? Compare your answer with the others in your group.

Urban sprawl

Urban sprawl is the rapid **spread** of housing from the cities outwards into the countryside. As a result of this, valuable farmland and green open spaces are taken over by roads and houses. Smaller villages and towns become **absorbed** by the city, putting **pressure** on services such as water supply and sewage.

Towns around a major city can also see an increase in their population as people settle there and commute to the city for work. These **commuter towns** are known as **satellite** or **dormitory towns**. They grow at a rapid rate.

A-Z

Satellite town:
a town that is close to a major urban centre but is not part of it.

Figure 12.17 *A modern housing estate in a satellite town*

Urban decay

Many places in the city centre are **derelict** sites. This means they have been abandoned and have fallen into disrepair. While some have been redeveloped, there are still many run-down buildings in cities. These buildings may be occupied illegally by squatters and drug addicts, and can become areas of urban decline. A lot of money has been spent on improving these areas in recent years.

Figure 12.18 *A run-down street in north Dublin*

ACTIVITY

Take pictures of urban decay in your area. Show your pictures to the class.

Crime

Crime is a big issue in many inner-city areas. A lot of crime is **drug-related**. High rates of **unemployment** among young people, and a lack of services and facilities for people of all ages, make the problem worse.

Pollution

Air pollution or **smog** is also a major problem in cities around the world. It is caused by the burning of fossil fuels and fumes from traffic congestion and industrial factories. It is so bad in some cities that many residents suffer from breathing problems.

Go to Chapter 5, page 84, to learn more about smog.

Strain on resources

Growing urban population puts a severe strain on resources and services such as **sewage** and the **water supply**. The average household in Dublin uses 400 litres of water a day. This is why there are plans to bring water from the River Shannon in the west of Ireland to Dublin.

Housing

The **shortage** of housing can also be a major problem in cities around the world. In developing countries, **shanty towns** have grown to accommodate people who want to live in the city but have no chance of finding a proper house or apartment. This has led to areas of cities that have high rates of **poverty** and **crime**. In Ireland, the rapid growth of **Dublin** had led to a housing shortage in the city and has resulted in a **housing crisis**, homelessness and families living in temporary accommodation such as hotels.

Figure 12.19 *A shanty town in Cambodia*

ACTIVITY

Research the latest figures for homelessness in Ireland. Suggest three possible solutions to the homeless problem in Ireland.

Shanty town: a settlement (sometimes illegal) of poor people living in houses made from scrap materials.

 **(i)** What is urbanisation?

 **(ii)** Explain two causes of urbanisation.

 **(iii)** Explain why traffic congestion is a problem associated with urbanisation.

 I can explain what urbanisation is and the problems associated with urbanisation.  

Solutions to urbanisation problems

Learning Intentions

In this section, you will learn:

- about how people try to counteract the problems of urbanisation.

QBCs
DART
Luas
Cycle lanes
Renewal
Redevelopment

Solutions to traffic congestion

It has been proven in cities all over the world that building more roads does not solve the problem of traffic congestion. The best way to solve the problem is by encouraging people to use **public transport**.

Buses and QBCs

Buses can carry up to 80 people. If more people used buses it would take many cars off the roads each day. Buses can get to the city centre much quicker than cars because they can use **Quality Bus Corridors (QBCs)**, which are special bus lanes. There has been a big increase in the number of QBCs in Dublin and other urban areas in recent years.

Figure 12.20 *Bus lanes speed up public transport*

Light rail system

The **DART (Dublin Area Rapid Transit)** is an example of a **light rail system**. The DART line runs along the coast of Dublin Bay, from Howth or Malahide to the north of Dublin, to Greystones in Co. Wicklow. Many people travel to and from work each day on the DART. The DART Expansion Programme aims to develop the service further in the coming years.

Figure 12.21 *The DART*

Tram system

The **Luas** is a **tram** system. This type of public transport is very popular in many European cities. It is a fast and efficient method of transport. There are three Luas lines in Dublin: the Red, Green and Blue line. The Blue line is a new cross-city line that opened in 2017. It connects the Green and Red lines. The Luas service is very important as it **links** residential areas in the **suburbs** of Dublin with the **city centre**.

Look up https://luas.ie to find out what areas are serviced by the Luas and if there are plans for further development.

Figure 12.22 *The Luas*

Cycle lanes

The **Bike to Work** and the **dublinbikes** rental schemes have encouraged people to use **bicycles** as a way of commuting to and from work every day. Creating **cycle lanes** makes it safer and easier for people to cycle in the city centre.

Figure 12.23 *Bicycles for rent in Dublin*

Road improvements

Road improvements can greatly reduce traffic congestion:

- **Ring roads** mean that cars don't have to go into town centres.
- **Roundabouts** allow traffic to move more freely.
- **Pedestrian crossings** make it safer for people to walk to work and school.
- **Traffic lights** make junctions safer.
- **Yellow boxes** prevent access points from being blocked.
- **Double yellow lines** stop on-street parking that might block traffic flow.

Look at the photograph below and say what measure has been put in place to help traffic flow.

Figure 12.24 *Aerial photograph of Westport, Co. Mayo*

With the help of your teacher and classmates, draw up a list of ideas to reduce traffic congestion in your area.

Solutions to urban sprawl

Urban sprawl is a serious problem in Dublin and is of huge **threat** to the surrounding region, especially the agricultural land. One way in which the government tried to control the urbanisation of Dublin was by the development of **new towns**. One such town was **Adamstown**.

CASE STUDY

New town: Adamstown

The government decided to build a new town in Adamstown, a site 16 km from Dublin city centre, in 2003. Permission was given to build 10,000 homes for roughly 25,000 people and the **facilities** and **infrastructure** necessary for all of the people living in this new town. In fact, 1,400 houses, two primary schools and a secondary school were built.

Unfortunately, the **economic recession** hit and construction came to a stop in early 2009. This meant that the main centre, with a supermarket, library, cinema, healthcare centre, leisure centre and swimming pool, was not built.

Figure 12.25 *Adamstown train station opened in 2007*

Building started again in Adamstown in 2014. The number of planned homes has been reduced from 10,000 to 8,000. It is hoped that building will continue and Adamstown will develop into the town that was originally planned with services and facilities for the community.

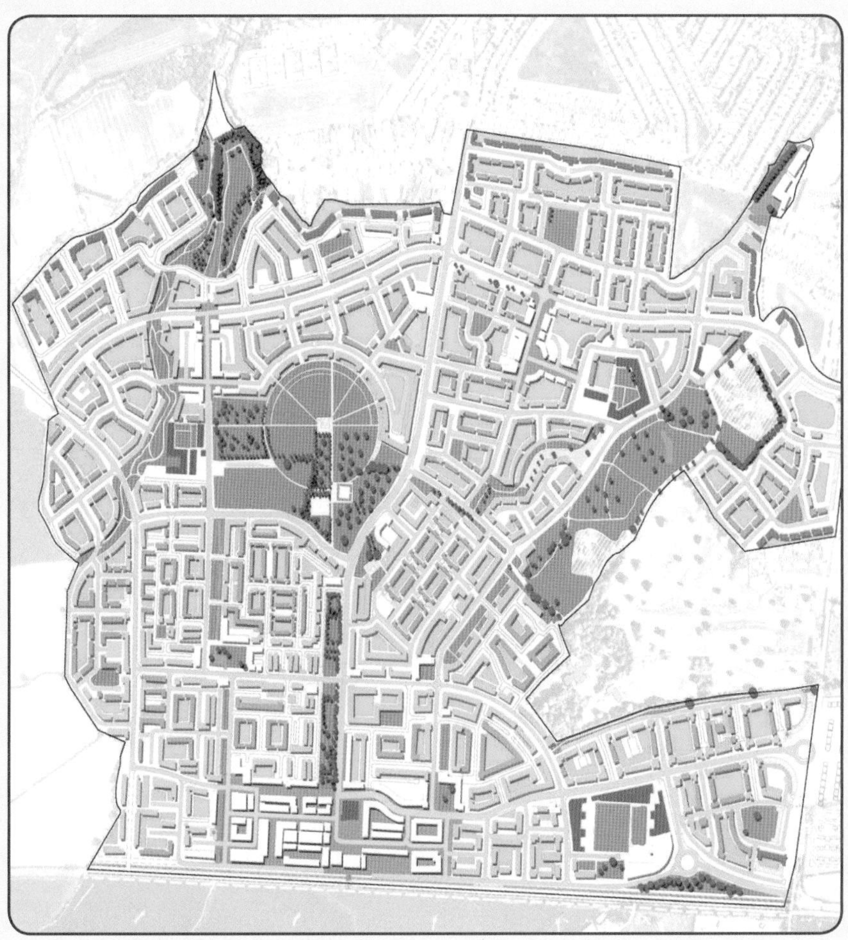

Figure 12.26 *Plans for the Adamstown development*

Solutions to urban decay

There are two solutions to urban decay – **urban renewal** and **urban redevelopment**.

Urban renewal

Urban renewal is the **improvement** of old inner-city areas. Facilities are upgraded or developed to keep the city **community** in place. Urban renewal prevents urban decay. An Irish example of urban renewal is **Ballymun** in Dublin.

Urban redevelopment

Urban redevelopment takes place when old houses, flats, shops, offices, restaurants or car parks are **knocked down**. New commercial offices and shop spaces are then built to replace them. The **residents** who had previously lived in these areas are **relocated** to the suburbs. An Irish example of urban redevelopment is the Dublin Docklands area.

Figure 12.27 *The Bord Gáis Energy Theatre is part of the redevelopment of the old Dublin docks area*

PORTFOLIO ACTIVITY 12.2

Go to page 49 of your Portfolio to research urban renewal or redevelopment in a town or city near you.

Crime

Urban renewal and redevelopment can help solve the issue of crime in cities because there are fewer derelict buildings attracting **anti-social behaviour**. Many urban areas have increased the **Garda** presence, especially at night time and during the weekend. Most urban suburbs have **neighbourhood watch groups** who report anti-social behaviour and any unusual activity in an area.

Garda Síochána

Neighbourhood Watch

Pollution

Many cities are now trying to solve the problems of pollution and smog. For example, in Beijing in China, where face masks are given to all the people when the smog is particularly bad, there is now a focus on **renewable energy**, especially solar power, to replace the coal-fired power stations and factories that cause so much of the pollution.

Housing

Solving the **housing crisis** is one of the biggest challenges for Irish politicians today. There are a number of steps that could be taken to help solve this problem:

- Build more **social housing**, owned by the state, which can be given to people who cannot afford housing.
- Ensure that **developers** are building on the land they have purchased, rather than holding on to it until prices increase.
- Restrict the use of Airbnb to make more property available to **rent**.
- **Convert** buildings that are not being used into apartments.
- Provide more **services** for the homeless.

 **(i)** Suggest two solutions to traffic congestion.

 **(ii)** Explain the difference between urban redevelopment and urban renewal.

 **(iii)** Imagine you are planning the development of a new town. What do you think are the five most important things to keep in mind?

 I can give examples of solutions to the problems associated with urbanisation.   

Focus on urban areas

Learning Intentions

In this section, you will learn:

- the different functional zones in cities
- how land use is related to land value
- the types of housing in urban areas
- what a primate city is.

Functional zone
Central Business District (CBD)
Suburbs
Land value
Building density
Apartment
Terraced housing
Semi-detached
Detached
Primate city

Functional zones in cities

If we look at the building pattern of most cities in the world, we can see that a city is divided into a number of different **zones**. Each of these zones has a different **function** or use.

The following five zones can be seen in most cities:

1. A **Central Business District (CBD)**
2. Some **smaller shopping areas**
3. A number of **shopping centres**
4. **Industrial** areas
5. **Open space** for recreation and leisure

The Central Business District

The centre of every city has a **CBD**. This is where the big banks, office blocks and department stores are located. These buildings are usually **multi-storey** buildings.

Where is the CBD in the city nearest to you?

Figure 12.28 *Dublin's CBD is located in the old docklands area*

Shopping areas

Around the **outskirts** of a city there are usually small village centres where people can do their day-to-day shopping. These small areas give people access to all the **services** they need without having to go into the city centre.

Where are there shopping areas like this in your local town/city?

Figure 12.29 *A shopping street in Dún Laoghaire, Co. Dublin*

Shopping centres

There are large shopping centres in the **suburbs** of Irish cities. The ease of access and parking facilities make them popular with customers.

Where are the shopping centres in your local town/city?

Figure 12.30 *Dundrum shopping centre in Dublin*

Industrial areas

Figure 12.31 *Industrial estate in Co. Limerick*

Where are the industrial estates in your local town/city?

Since the **Industrial Revolution**, cities have been at the centre of industry. Many goods are **manufactured** in the factories of cities. **Port** cities often have industries such as **oil refining** (Rotterdam) or **chemical factories** (Cork). This is because the raw materials and finished products for these industries are often transported by sea.

There are many **industrial estates** in the suburbs around cities. **Footloose** industries are attracted to these areas. This is because there is room to expand and land is cheaper on the outskirts of a city.

Space for recreation and leisure

Figure 12.32 *Phoenix Park is the largest enclosed public park in any capital city in Europe*

All cities need space for children to play and for people to relax and enjoy the outdoors. Most cities in Ireland have **parks** and recreational areas **within the CBD** such as the **Mardyke Arena** in Cork and the **People's Park** in Limerick. There are also many parks in the **suburban areas** surrounding Irish cities.

Where are the recreational areas in your local town/city?

Land use and land values

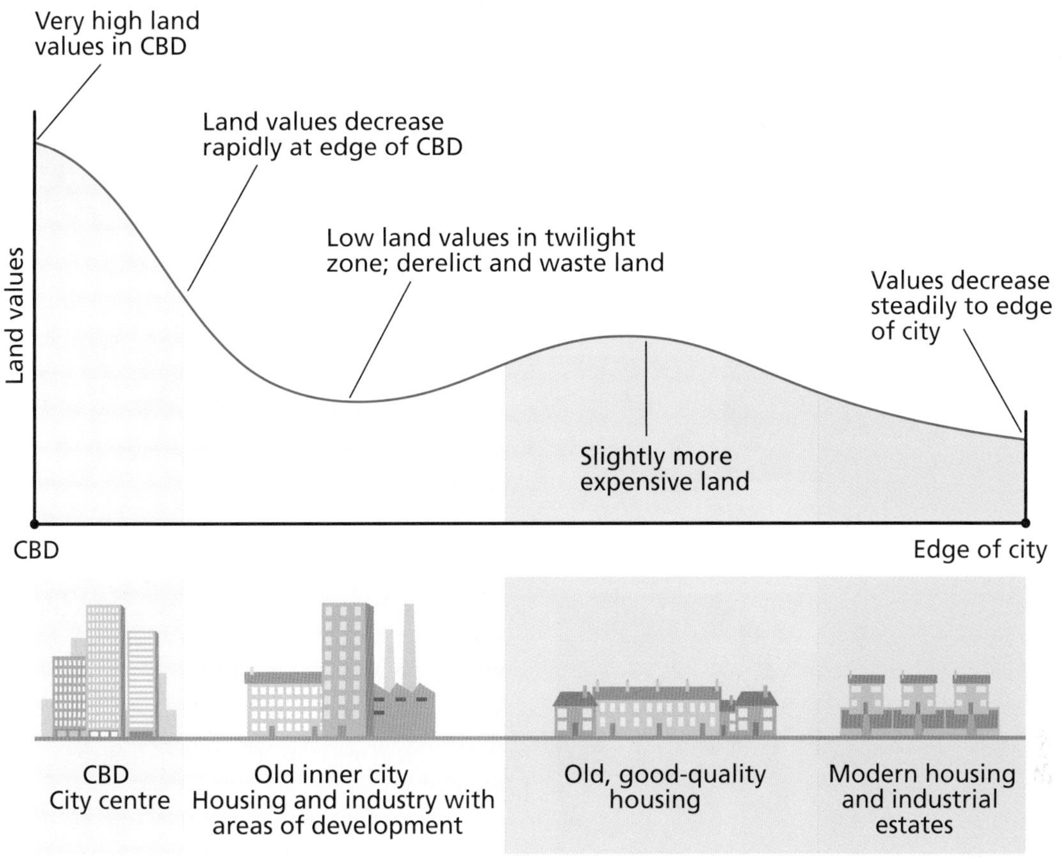

Figure 12.33 *Land values in cities*

The common pattern seen in urban areas is that **land value** and **building density** increase the nearer you get to the **CBD**. This is because it is the area of a city where there is the most **demand** for land. A shortage of available land and a strong demand means that **prices are higher** here than in other parts of the city. Due to the higher cost of land in the CBD, taller buildings are usually constructed as people try to **maximise** the land use.

ACTIVITY

Look at the aerial photograph and locate and name as many land uses as possible.

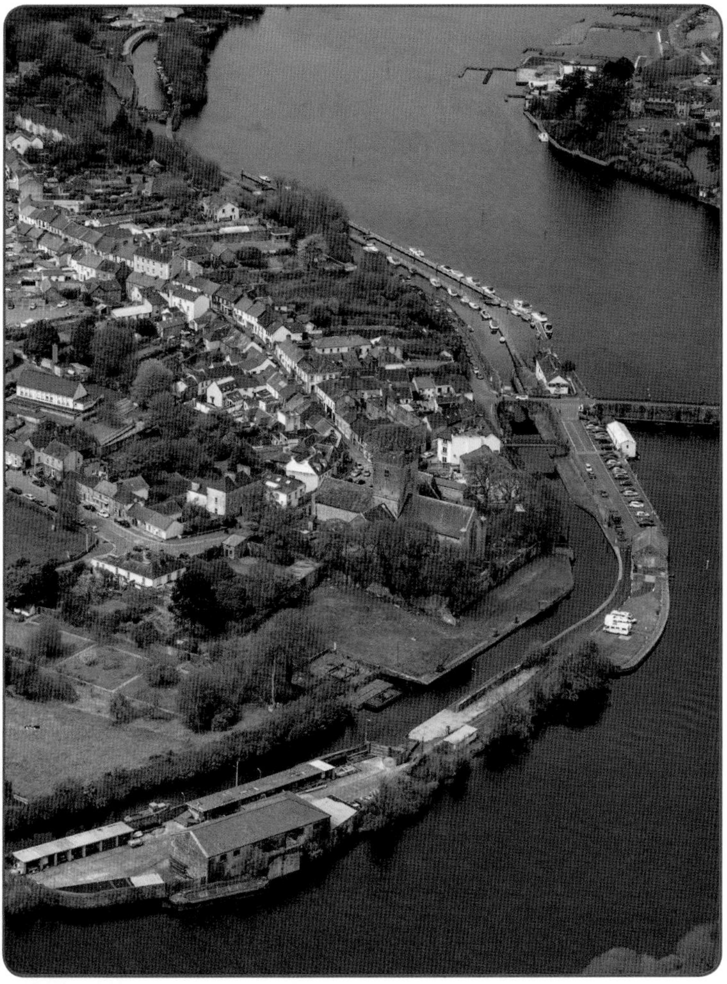

Figure 12.34 *An oblique aerial view of Killaloe, Co. Clare*

Residential housing in urban areas

Apartments and flats

Apartments are generally found close to the city centre. They are built to maximise space and are often home to young professionals working in the city. The buildings are often multi-storey in order to fit as many people into the area as possible. This is called **high-density housing**.

Figure 12.35 *An apartment block*

Terraced housing

Terraced housing can be found close to the city centre and in housing estates. These houses usually have no front garden and the front door opens on to the street. In the inner city, this type of house was used in the oldest residential housing.

Figure 12.36 *Terraced houses*

Semi-detached houses

Semi-detached housing is usually found on the outskirts of a town or in housing estates. They are built as pairs of houses with a shared wall. Semi-detached houses typically have land, such as a garden or a driveway, around them.

Figure 12.37 *Semi-detached houses*

Detached houses

Detached houses can be found in housing estates and on the outskirts of a town. They are free-standing buildings on their own site. Because there are fewer people living in a larger space, this is called **low-density housing**.

Figure 12.38 *A detached house*

DID YOU KNOW? Public housing is built by a local council, whereas private housing is built by individuals or developers.

The primacy of Dublin

A **primate city** is a city that is at least twice as big as the second biggest city in the same country. **Dublin** is a primate city because it is about five times as big as Cork. **Paris** is also an example of a primate city as it is twice as big as Marseilles, the second biggest city in France.

Figure 12.39 *Leinster House, the home of the Oireachtas*

Why did Dublin become a primate city?

1. It is where the **government** of Ireland sits.
2. It is Ireland's **main port**.
3. It is Ireland's main **transport focus** (air, sea, rail, roads).
4. It is Ireland's most important **educational**, **cultural** and **commercial centre**.

Dublin's primacy has heavily affected the **distribution** of settlements in Ireland. Many settlements have **circled** Dublin and surrounded it. The major **routeways** leading out of Dublin tend to have **linear settlement** along them. As a result of Dublin's rapid growth, the city has endured many **urban problems** such as crime, urban decay, traffic congestion and urban sprawl. It has, however, tried to solve these problems.

(i) List the five different zones in an urban area.

(ii) Explain why buildings are taller in the CBD than in the suburbs.

(iii) Explain the term primate city.

- I know what the different functional zones in cities are.
- I can explain how land value is linked to land use.
- I can recognise different types of housing in urban areas.
- I understand what a primate city is.

REVISION

Early-Irish settlers located in certain places for reasons such as water, food, ____________________ and ____________________. Factors that influence the site of settlement include ____________________, aspect, ____________________, ____________________ and shelter. ____________________ refers to the area surrounding the settlement.

The ____________________ of a settlement is the services it provides. These ____________________ over time.

There are ____________________ of settlement in rural areas. These include ____________________, nucleated and ____________________.

The ____________________ of people living in urban areas is called ____________________. Traffic ____________________ is one of the problems with this. The growth of urban areas into the countryside is called urban ____________________. Adamstown is an example of a ____________________ ____________________.

There are functional ____________________ within cities. The ____________________ Business ____________________ is in the centre and has the ____________________ buildings. Land ____________________ is highest here.

Dublin is a ____________________ city.

Questions & Answers

Sample Questions

'The function of a town may change over time.'

1. Name a town that you have studied whose function has changed.
2. Describe and explain the change in the function that has taken place.

Sample Answers

1. Navan, Co. Meath
2. Navan was originally a monastic settlement and then when the Normans invaded, it became a walled defensive town. After that period, due to its location and the many passing traders, it became a market town for the surrounding region. In 1977, with the opening of Tara Mines, the function of Navan changed to mining, which provided much employment in the area. In addition to this, the town of Navan is a satellite town to Dublin City.

1. Examine the sketch maps labelled **A**, **B** and **C**.

A 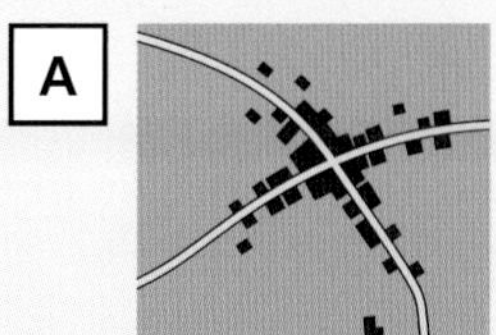

B 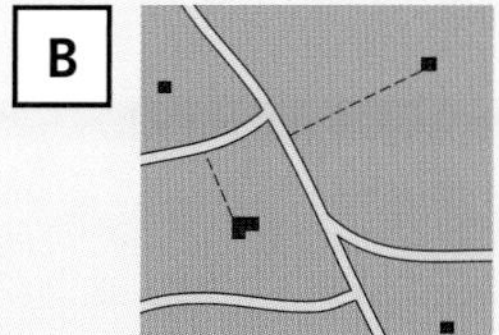

C 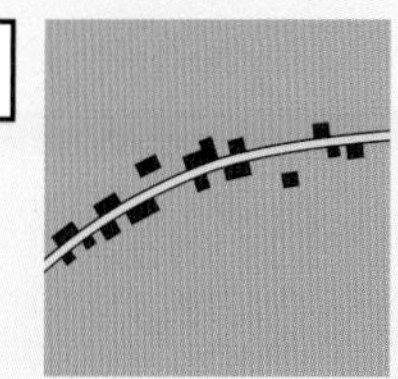

(i) The type of settlement pattern shown in **Sketch Map A** is ______________________

(ii) The type of settlement pattern shown in **Sketch Map B** is ______________________

(iii) The type of settlement pattern shown in **Sketch Map C** is ______________________

2. The type of settlement pattern shown in this picture is:

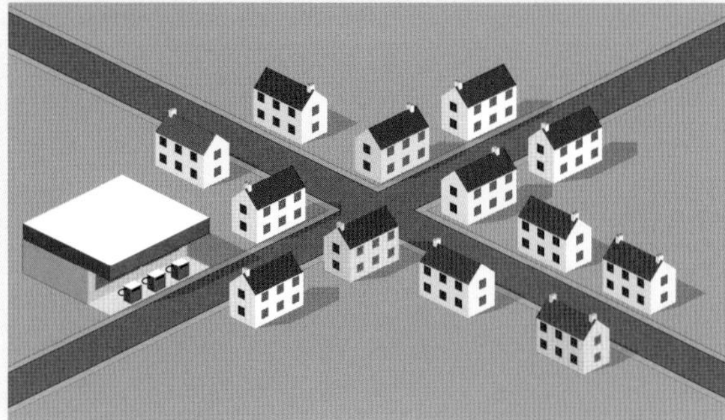

Scattered ☐

Nucleated ☐

Historic ☐ [tick (✓) the correct box]

3. Read the statements below. Which two statements are true?

(a) Dolmens, ring forts and castles are all signs of former settlement.

(b) A village which clusters around a road junction has a linear settlement pattern.

(c) The west of Ireland is more densely populated than the east of Ireland.

(d) Land values usually increase towards the centre of a city.

4. In the boxes provided, match each of the letters in **Column X** with the number of its pair in **Column Y**. One match has been completed for you.

Column X		Column Y		X	Y
A	Primate city	1	A commuter town from where people travel to work.	A	
B	Dormitory town	2	A squatter development in cities in the developing world.	B	
C	Shanty town	3	Old buildings replaced by modern structures.	C	
D	Urban renewal	4	A city that has twice the population of the next largest city.	D	3

Long Questions

1. Name and briefly explain **three** factors that influenced the location of pre-Christian settlements in Ireland.

2. Using examples of towns you have studied, describe how settlements have been influenced by historical factors.

3. 'The functions of many towns have changed over time.'
   In the case of **one** named Irish town or city that you have studied, describe how its functions have changed. In your answer refer to **three** different functions.

4. What is urbanisation? Describe **two** problems associated with urbanisation.

5. Name and describe **two** main causes of urbanisation.

6. In relation to a city you have looked at, discuss ways in which they have tried to solve the problems that come about as a result of urbanisation.

7. 'Cities can have zones within them.'
   Discuss this statement and how these zones are identified.

8. 'The nearer you go to the centre of an urban area the taller the buildings become.'
   Why is this the case? Give reasons for your answer.

9. 'Dublin is a primate city.'
   Explain this statement. How has the primacy of Dublin influenced settlement there?

Visual Summary

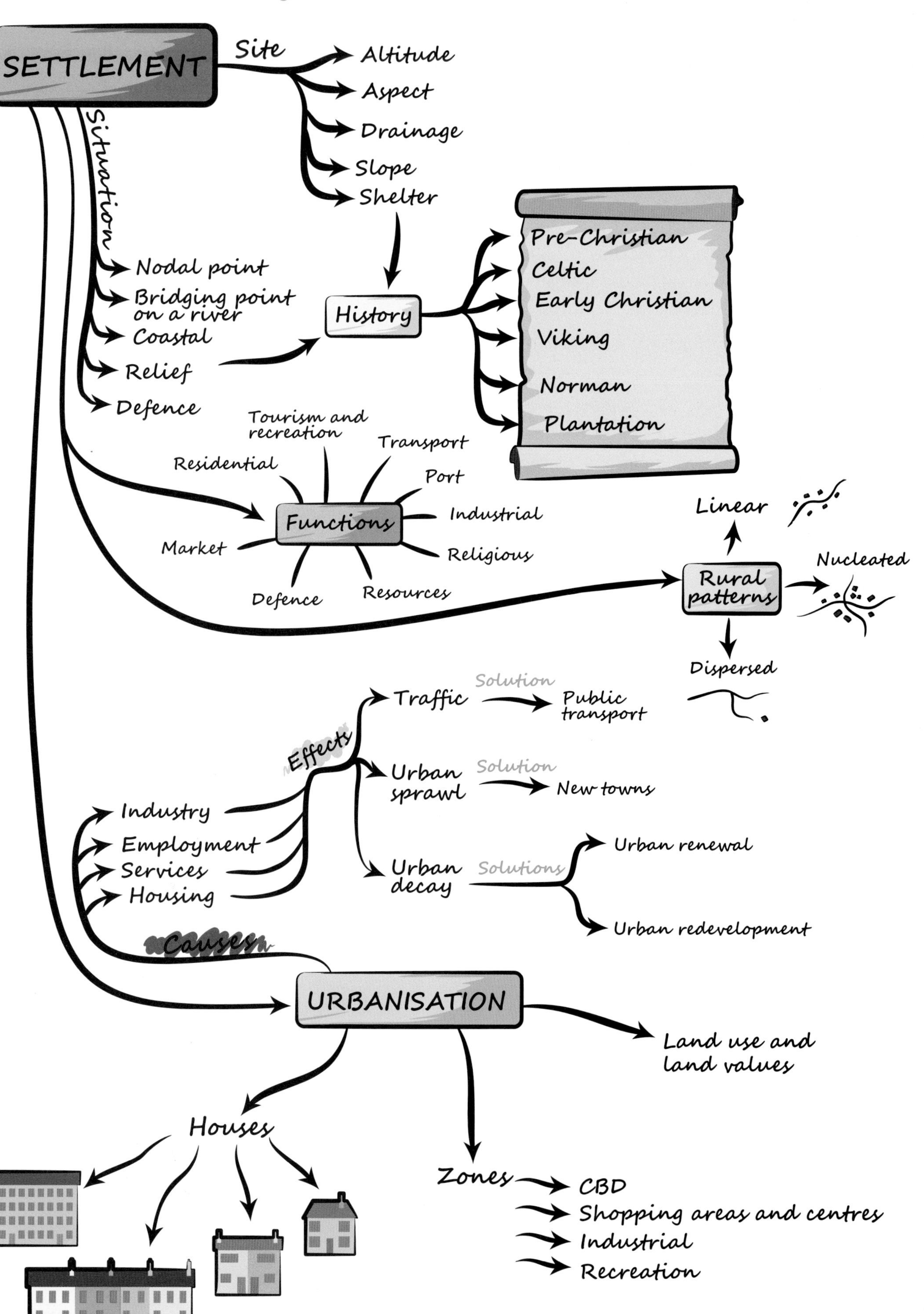
SETTLEMENT
Site
Altitude
Aspect
Drainage
Slope
Shelter
Situation
Nodal point
Bridging point on a river
Coastal
Relief
Defence
History
Pre-Christian
Celtic
Early Christian
Viking
Norman
Plantation
Tourism and recreation
Transport
Residential
Port
Functions
Industrial
Market
Religious
Defence
Resources
Linear
Nucleated
Rural patterns
Dispersed
Traffic
Solution
Public transport
Effects
Urban sprawl
Solution
New towns
Industry
Employment
Services
Housing
Urban decay
Solutions
Urban renewal
Urban redevelopment
Causes
URBANISATION
Land use and land values
Houses
Zones
CBD
Shopping areas and centres
Industrial
Recreation

13 Weather:
How it impacts on our lives

In this chapter, you will learn:

- what the atmosphere is and how the sun heats the Earth
- what causes variations in weather
- how we gather information about weather
- how to interpret data on weather maps
- how weather events form and how they impact on us.

ICE-BREAKER ACTIVITY

Watch the weather forecast for Ireland. Make a list of the elements of weather (e.g. temperature) that are mentioned. In groups, discuss how each of these aspects is measured.

The atmosphere

Learning Intentions

In this section, you will learn:

- what the atmosphere is made up of.

Atmosphere, Stratosphere, Troposphere, Ozone layer, Altitude

The **atmosphere** is a thin layer of **gases** that surrounds the Earth. Seventy-eight per cent of the atmosphere is **nitrogen**, 21 per cent is **oxygen** and less than one per cent is made up of other gases (including **argon** and **carbon dioxide**).

The atmosphere **insulates** the Earth from extreme temperatures. It traps heat and it also protects the Earth from dangerous rays from the sun.

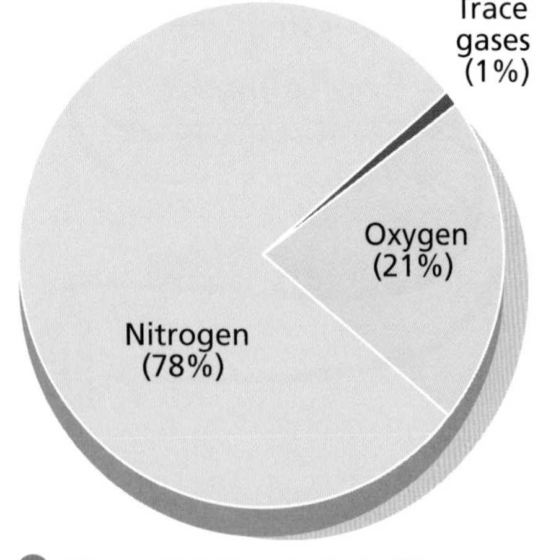

Figure 13.1 *Gases in the Earth's atmosphere*

Layers within the atmosphere

The Earth's atmosphere is about **480 km thick**, but most of it is within 16 km of the Earth's surface. There is no exact place where the atmosphere ends. It just gets thinner and thinner, until it **merges** with outer space.

There are several **layers** within the atmosphere.

The **troposphere** is the lowest layer in the Earth's atmosphere.

- It reaches from ground or water level up to about **17 km**.
- **Weather** and clouds occur in the troposphere.
- The **temperature** generally decreases as the **altitude** increases.

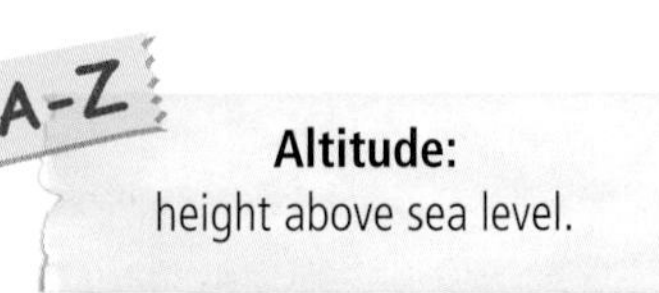

Altitude: height above sea level.

The **stratosphere** is the next layer.

- It extends from **17 km to 50 km** from the Earth's surface.
- The **ozone layer** is located in the stratosphere.
- Some of the **highest clouds** can be found in the lower stratosphere.

Go to Chapter 14, page 264, to learn more about the ozone layer.

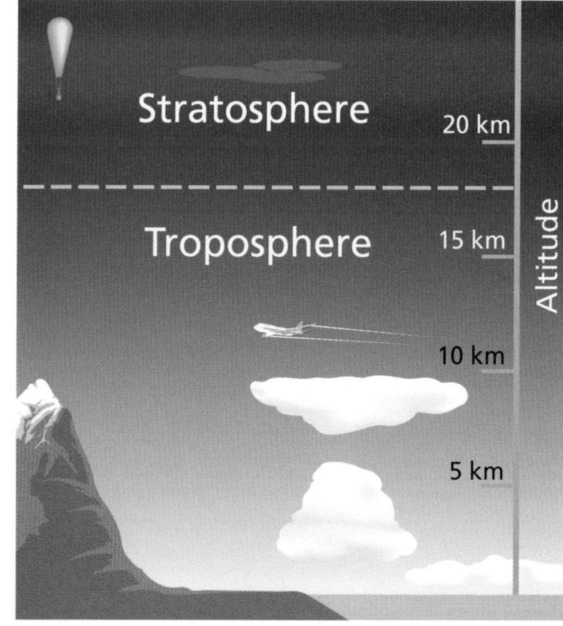

Figure 13.2 *The layers of the Earth's atmosphere*

 **(i)** Name two gases that make up the Earth's atmosphere.

 **(ii)** Name two layers in the Earth's atmosphere.

 **(iii)** Explain two differences between the stratosphere and the troposphere.

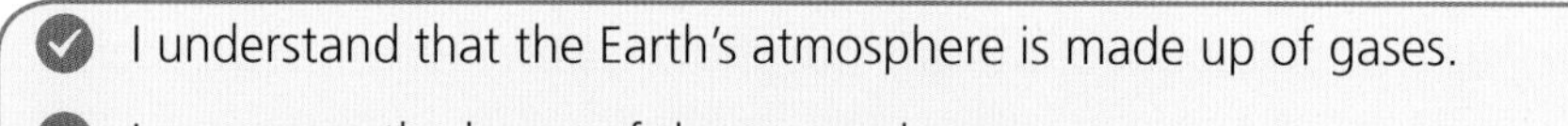

- I understand that the Earth's atmosphere is made up of gases.
- I can name the layers of the atmosphere.

The sun

Learning Intentions

In this section, you will learn:

- how the sun's energy is the main source of heat for the Earth
- how solar radiation is distributed around the globe.

Solar energy, Solar radiation, Distribution, Hemisphere, Equator, Latitude, Axis

Solar energy

Energy from the sun is called **solar energy**. Solar energy is the Earth's main source of **heat**.

The energy that travels through space from the sun is called **solar radiation**. It is transmitted in the form of light and heat. Almost all of the **energy** that the Earth uses comes from the sun.

The amount of heat kept in the **atmosphere** depends on the amount of **greenhouse gases** in the atmosphere. We will learn more about the **greenhouse effect** in the next chapter.

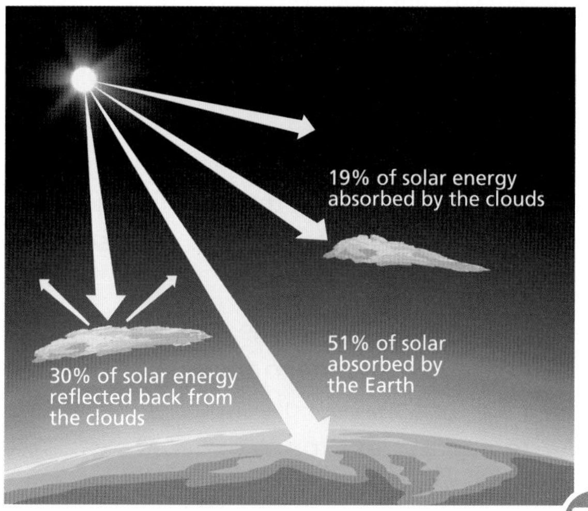

Figure 13.3 *How solar radiation heats the atmosphere*

The uneven heating of the Earth

Solar energy is **distributed unevenly** both over the surface of the Earth and within the atmosphere. Its strength depends on **latitude** and the tilt of the Earth on its **axis**.

A-Z

Distributed: positioned.

Distribution: a word used in Geography to describe where something is.

Latitude

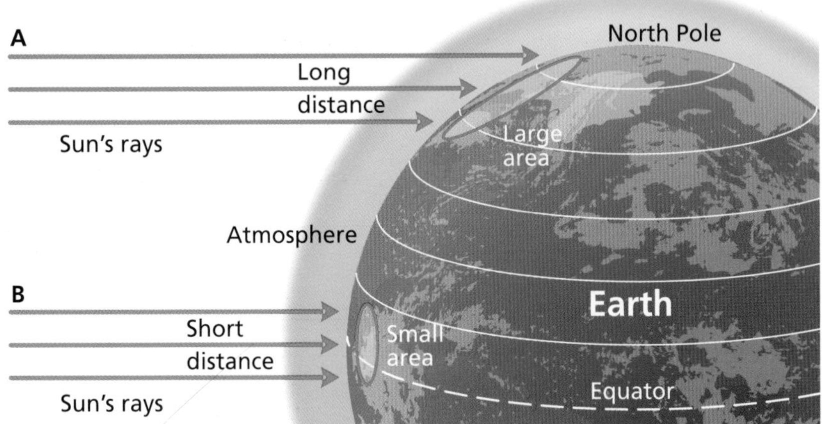

Figure 13.4 *How latitude influences the distribution of solar radiation*

ACTIVITY

Can you explain why it is colder at A than at B?

The Earth is divided into the **northern hemisphere** and the **southern hemisphere**. The imaginary line dividing these two areas is called the **equator**. The equator is used as the start point for measurement and is at 0°. The lines around the Earth that measure distance from the equator are called **lines of latitude** and they extend to the poles. The South Pole is at 90° south of the equator and the North Pole is at 90° north of the equator.

Because of the Earth's **spherical** (round) shape, the equator is closest to the **sun**. This means that areas closer to the **equator** are warmer than areas closer to the **poles**.

- The sun's rays have a **shorter distance** to travel to the equator so the heat is **more intense** here than at higher latitudes.
- The sun's rays shine **directly** on the equator and so are concentrated on a smaller area. The rays at higher latitudes are **slanted** and therefore cover a larger area and are **less intense**.

The Earth's axis

The Earth **spins** on its **axis** every 24 hours and **orbits** the sun every 365¼ days. During this time, different parts of the Earth's surface are **tilted** towards the sun. This influences the **seasons** and the **length** of the day and night.

A: During our **summer**, the northern hemisphere is **tilted towards** the sun. Days are long and we receive more **solar radiation**.

B: During our **autumn**, the northern hemisphere **begins to tilt away** from the sun. Days get shorter and **temperatures drop** as we receive less solar radiation.

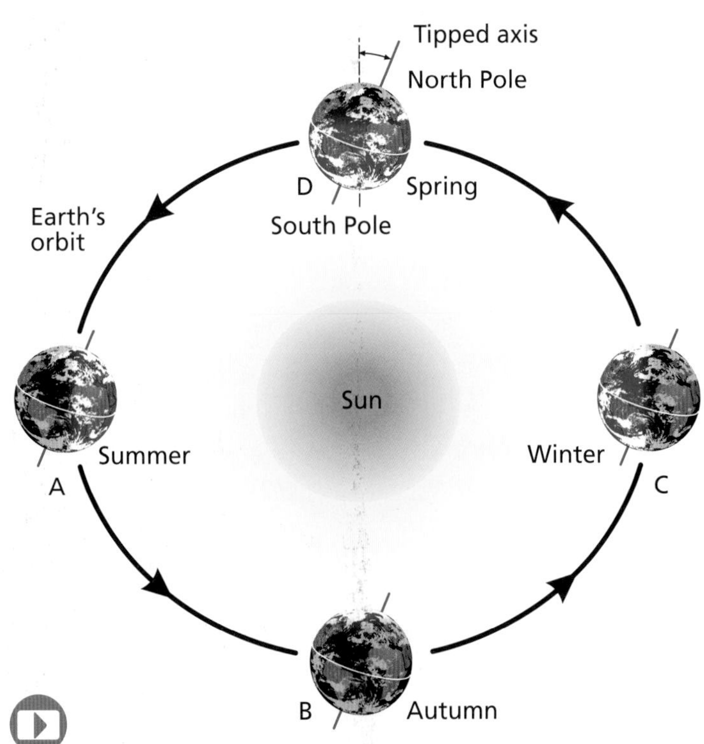

Figure 13.5 *The Earth's axis on its orbit round the sun*

C: During our **winter**, the northern hemisphere is **tilted away** from the sun. Days are short and temperatures are **low** because there is little solar radiation.

D: During our **spring**, the northern hemisphere **begins to tilt** towards the sun again and days grow longer. Temperatures **increase** with more solar radiation.

(i) What is the energy from the sun called?

(ii) Explain the term solar radiation.

(iii) Can you explain the difference in temperature and daylight hours between summer and winter in Ireland?

- I can explain the distribution of solar energy over the Earth's surface and within the atmosphere.
- I can explain the Earth's orbit around the sun.

Wind

Learning Intentions

In this section, you will learn:

- how the unequal heating of the Earth's surface leads to the movements of winds.

High pressure	Converge
Low pressure	Prevailing westerlies
Trade winds	Horse latitudes
Coriolis effect	Polar easterlies
Doldrums	

How winds are formed

The **unequal heating** of the atmosphere and the Earth's surface leads to movements of air. **Wind** is the movement of air over the surface of the Earth. Winds blow from areas of **high pressure** to areas of **low pressure**.

As we have already learned, the **equator** receives the sun's direct rays. When air is **heated**, it **expands**. This makes it **lighter** and so it **rises**. This creates areas of **low pressure** at the equator.

At about **30° north and south** of the equator, the warm air begins to **cool**. When air is cooled it becomes **heavy** and **sinks** towards the surface of the Earth. This creates areas of **high pressure**.

Between 30° latitude and the equator, **most** of the cooling, sinking air moves **back to the equator**. The **rest** of the air flows towards the **poles**.

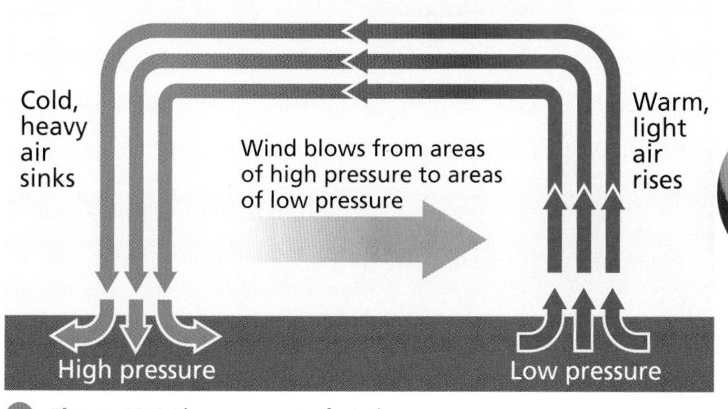

Figure 13.6 *The movement of wind*

DID YOU KNOW? Winds are named after the direction from which they come. A southerly wind blows **towards** the north.

Global winds

Trade winds

Trade winds are air movements **towards the equator**. They are warm, steady breezes that blow almost continuously. The rotation of the Earth on its axis causes what is known as the **Coriolis effect**, which makes the trade winds appear to curve towards the west, regardless of whether they are travelling to the equator from the south or north.

ACTIVITY

Go to https://educateplus.ie/go/coriolis-effect to find out more about the Coriolis effect.

The doldrums

The **doldrums** is an area of **calm** weather. The trade winds coming from the south and the north meet near the equator. As they are heated, these **converging** trade winds blow **upwards** so there is little movement of air near the surface, and so little wind.

Converge: come together.

The prevailing westerlies

Between 30° and 60° latitude, the winds that move towards the poles appear to curve to the east. Because winds are named after **the direction from which they come**, these winds are called **westerlies**. Prevailing westerlies in the northern hemisphere are responsible for many of the weather movements across Europe, and especially in Ireland.

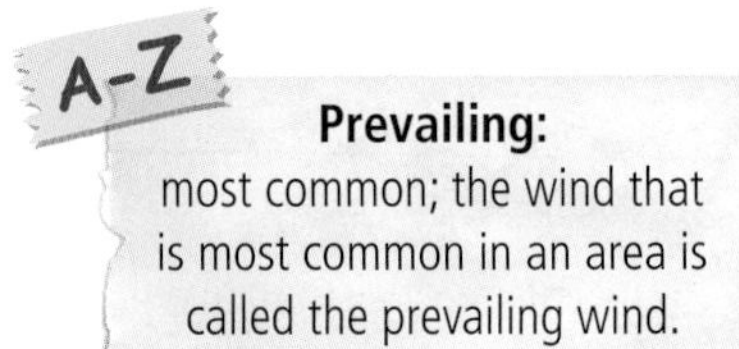

Prevailing: most common; the wind that is most common in an area is called the prevailing wind.

The horse latitudes

The **horse latitudes** are found at 30° north and south of the equator. They form a belt that blows between the trade winds and the prevailing westerlies. Horse latitude winds tend to be **weak** and encourage **clear, bright weather**.

The polar easterlies

At about 60° latitude in both hemispheres, the prevailing westerlies meet the **polar easterlies**. The polar easterlies form when the atmosphere over the poles **cools**. This cool air then sinks and spreads over the surface. As the air flows away from the poles, it is turned to the west by the **Coriolis effect**. Again, because these winds begin in the east, they are called **easterlies**.

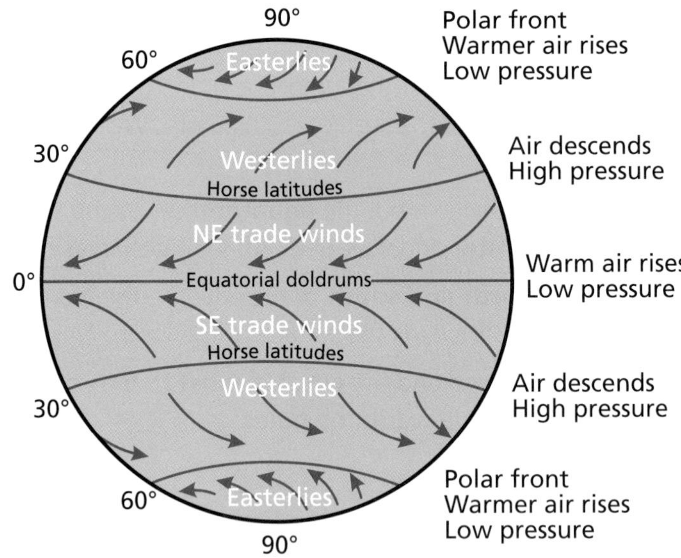

Figure 13.7 *Global wind patterns*

(i) What is wind?

(ii) Name two different types of wind.

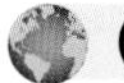

(iii) Do winds blow from areas of high pressure to low pressure or from low pressure to high pressure?

(iv) Which winds are cooler in Ireland? Polar easterlies or prevailing westerlies. Explain your answer.

- I understand how the unequal heating of the Earth's surface leads to the movement of wind. 
- I understand the main global winds. 

Ocean currents

Learning Intentions

In this section, you will learn:

- how unequal heating of the Earth's surface leads to the movements of ocean currents.

Current
Gulf Stream
North Atlantic Drift
Labrador Current

Ocean waters are always moving. The movement of water is referred to as a **current**. A current is like a river flowing though the ocean. Ocean currents occur due to:

- Differences in temperature
- The Earth rotating on its axis
- Wind

Currents can be **warm** or **cold** depending on where they flow from.

DID YOU KNOW? The Gulf Stream is 100 km wide, about 1 km deep and moves at a speed of 3.5 kph.

Warm currents

Currents flowing **from the equator** are warm. The **Gulf Stream** originates in the Gulf of Mexico and turns north-eastwards into the Atlantic Ocean, where it splits to form the warm **North Atlantic Drift** (NAD) and the cold **Canary Current**. The **NAD** flows past the west coast of Ireland where it helps to keep ports ice-free.

Cold currents

Cold currents flow from areas in high latitudes **towards the equator**. The **Labrador Current**, which flows south along the coast of north-east America, reduces the temperature of the ocean and many ports freeze over as a result.

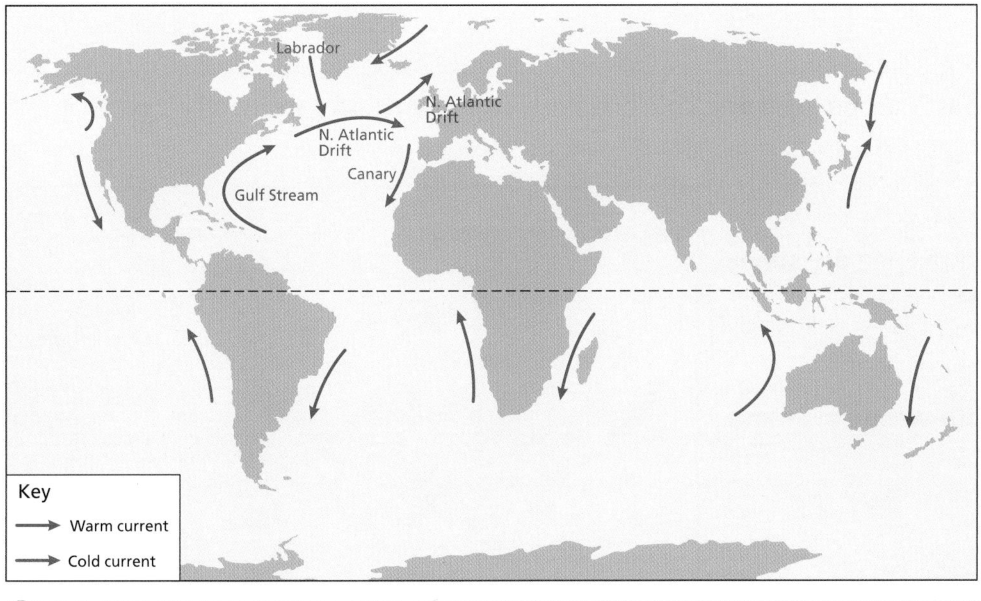

Figure 13.8 *Major ocean currents*

(i) Name one warm current.

(ii) Name one cold current.

(iii) What is a current?

(iv) What current keeps Ireland's coast ice-free? How?

I understand the heating of the Earth's surface and how it results in ocean currents.

Air masses and fronts

Learning Intentions

In this section, you will learn:

- what air masses are and how they form fronts
- about the various types of air masses
- about the different types of fronts that are formed.

WORDS
Air mass
Polar
Maritime
Tropical
Isobar
Millibar
Front
Warm
Cold
Occluded
Anticyclone
Depression

Air masses

Air masses are **large moving pockets of air** that are distinct from the surrounding atmosphere. **Warm** air masses carry more moisture or water vapour than **cold** air masses. All air masses have the following characteristics:

- They are **large**, often stretching more than 1,500 km across the landscape and extending several kilometres into the atmosphere.
- The **temperature**, **pressure** and **moisture** are similar at any point within the air mass.
- They travel across the atmosphere as a **single unit**.

Ireland experiences a range of air masses with different sources and paths. This gives us our **variable** weather. The following air masses affect Ireland:

Polar maritime

These air masses from the **north-west Atlantic** bring **cold**, **wet** air and showery conditions.

Arctic

Air masses from the **North Pole** bring **cold** weather conditions.

A-Z **Polar:** to do with the north or south poles.

Polar continental

Air masses from **north-east Europe** bring **dry**, **cold** and frosty nights and heavy **snowfall** in winter.

Tropical continental

Air masses from the **Sahara** bring **dry sunny** weather.

Tropical maritime

Air masses from the **south-west** bring **rain** all year round.

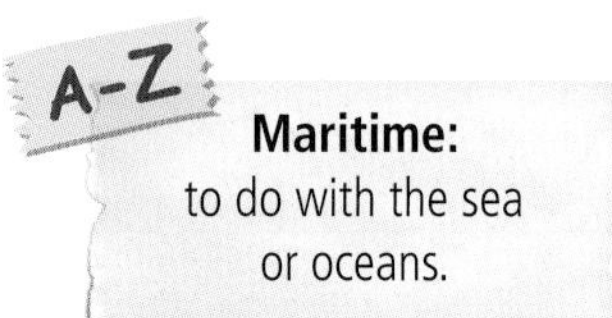

A-Z
Maritime:
to do with the sea
or oceans.

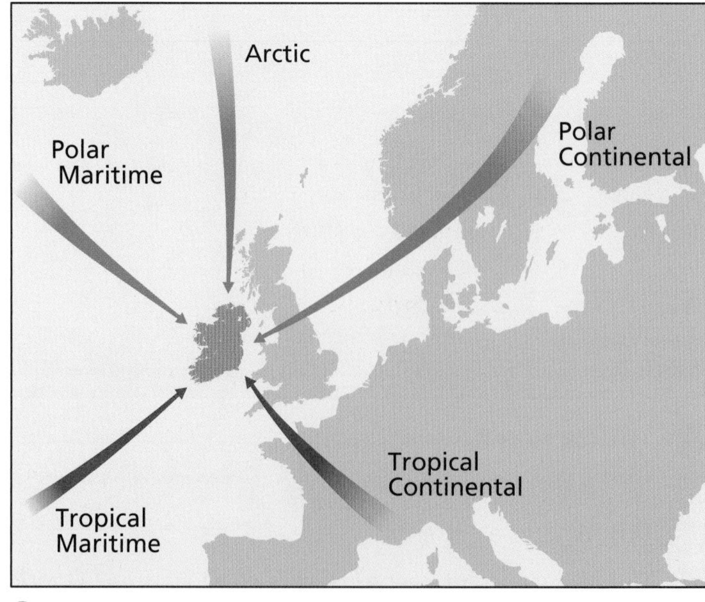

Figure 13.9 *Sources of air masses over Ireland*

Isobars and fronts

Isobars

Isobars are lines on a weather map which join together places of **equal atmospheric pressure**. In Figure 13.10 the isobar north of Ireland marked **962** represents an area of **low pressure**, while the isobar marked **1022** west of Italy represents an area of **high pressure**.

While examining isobars on this weather map of Ireland, note the following points:

- **Isobars** show areas of equal atmospheric pressure.
- Atmospheric pressure is measured in **millibars**.
- Isobars are usually drawn at intervals of **four or eight** millibars.
- The closer together the isobars are, the stronger the **wind** will be.

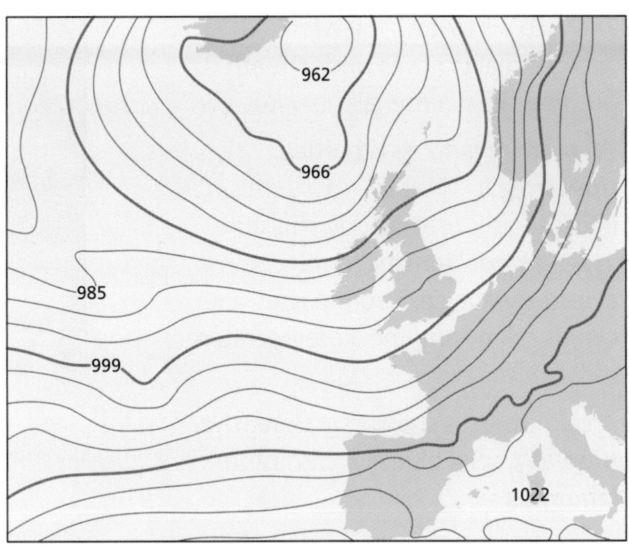

Figure 13.10 *Isobars around Ireland*

Fronts

Fronts occur where **two** different air masses **meet**.

The three different types of front are shown in Figure 13.11. These are a **warm front**, a **cold front** and an **occluded front**.

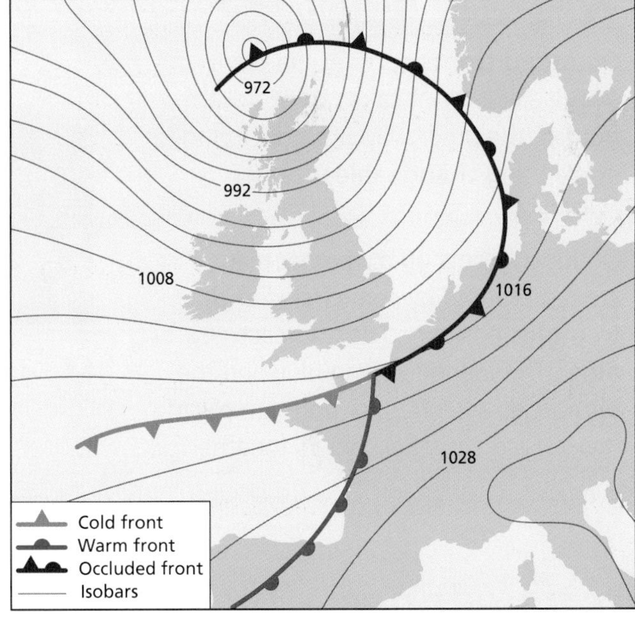

Figure 13.11 *Weather map showing isobars and fronts*

Warm fronts

Warm fronts are formed when **warm air rises over a mass of cold air**. As the warm air lifts into areas of lower pressure, it **expands, cools** and **condenses** the water vapour as wide, flat sheets of cloud. These clouds bring gentle rain.

A warm front is shown on a **weather map** as a solid red line with **red semicircles**.

Figure 13.12 *The formation of a warm front*

Cold fronts

A **cold front** occurs where a **cold air mass replaces a warmer air mass**. The cold air follows the warm air and gradually moves **underneath** it, pushing the warmer air upwards.

When the warm air is pushed **upwards**, it will **rain** heavily. This is because as it rises quickly, moisture in the air **condenses**, forming rain clouds. As the cold front passes, the clouds roll by and the air temperature is cooler.

A cold fronts is shown on a **weather map** as a solid blue line with **blue triangles**.

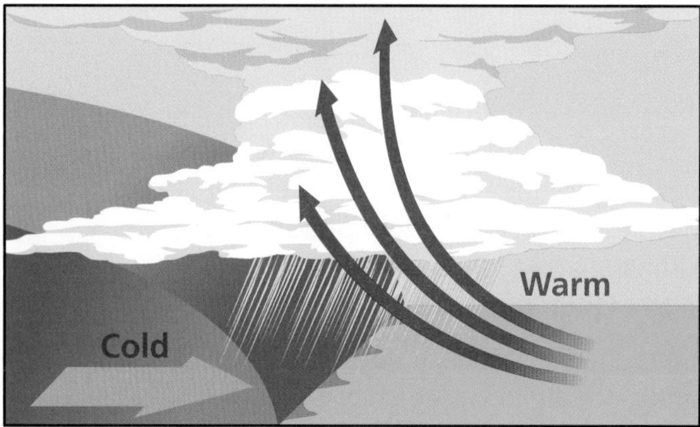

Figure 13.13 *The formation of a cold front*

Occluded front

Occluded fronts occur at the point where a cold front **takes over** a warm front or the other way around. Occluded fronts bring **changeable** weather conditions.

Occluded fronts on a weather map are represented by **semicircles and triangles** positioned next to each other. The triangles are in blue and the semicircles are in red, or both are **purple** (mixing red and blue colours together).

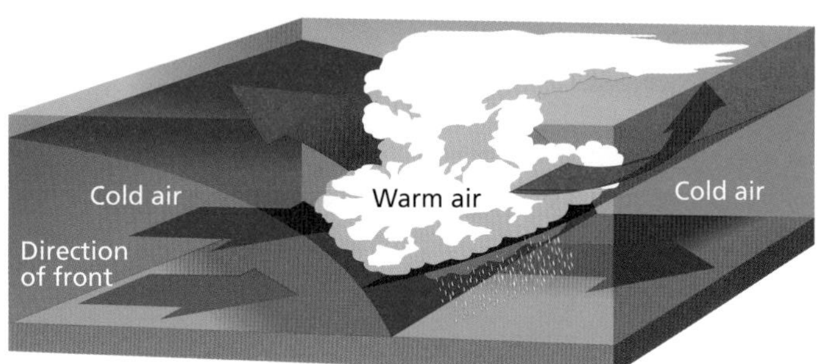

Figure 13.14 *The formation of an occluded front*

Anticyclones – high-pressure systems

This weather map is showing a high-pressure system or **anticyclone** because the highest number is in the middle circle over Ireland.

High pressure often means **dry, sunny** weather. As air **descends**, it gets warmer and increases its ability to hold moisture, so clouds do not form.

The **isobars** are well spaced, which means that winds are very **light**. Winds in a high-pressure system blow in a **clockwise direction**.

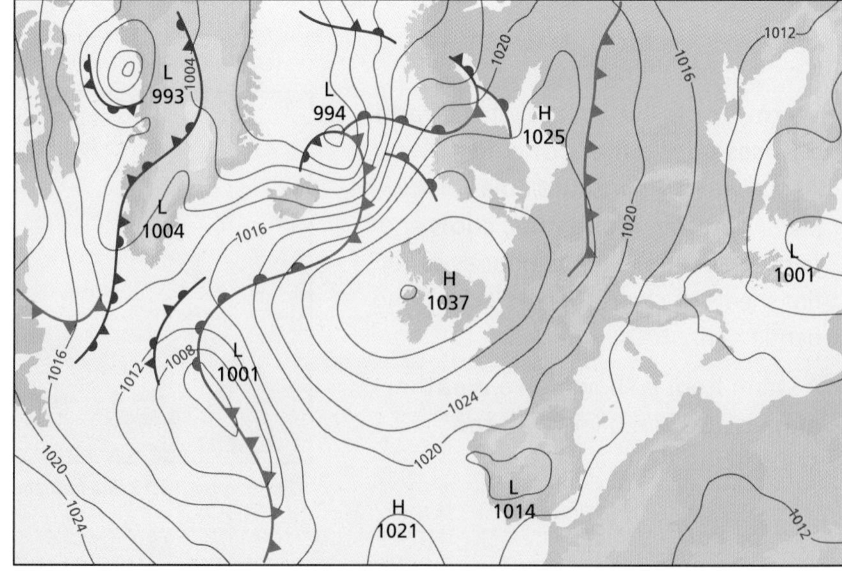

Figure 13.15 *Weather map showing high pressure over Ireland*

Depressions – low-pressure systems

We know that this weather map (Figure 13.16) is showing a low-pressure system or **depression** because the lowest number is in the middle circle over Ireland.

Ascending air typically results in low atmospheric pressure, a lot of cloud and **precipitation**, and **strong winds**. As air ascends, it cools and loses its ability to hold moisture, which results in the formation of **clouds** and rain.

The **isobars** are close together which means that winds are **strong**. Winds in low-pressure systems blow in an **anti-clockwise direction**.

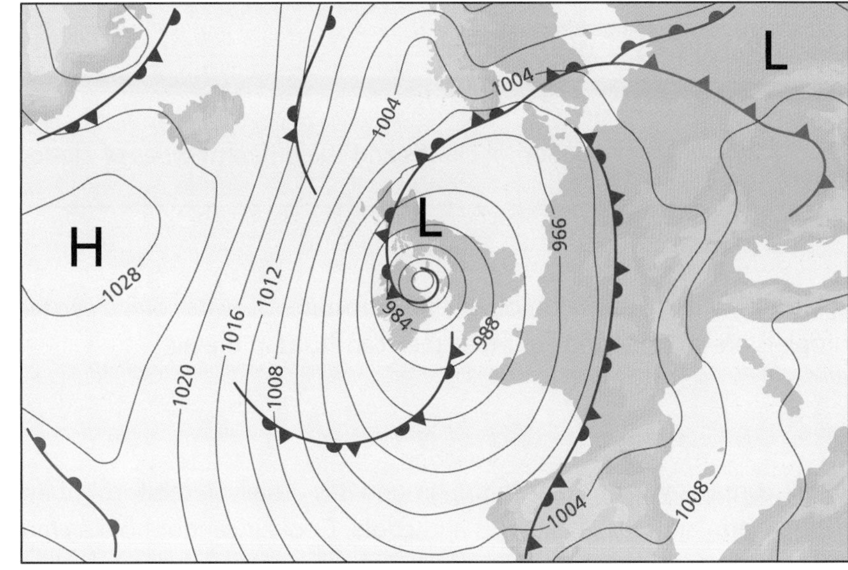

Figure 13.16 *Weather map showing low pressure over Ireland*

Anticyclone

- **Descending** air and temperatures **rise**
- **High** atmospheric pressure
- Winds blow in a **clockwise** direction
- Isobars are **well spaced** indicating **light** winds
- **Clear** skies and cold nights in winter
- **Dry** weather

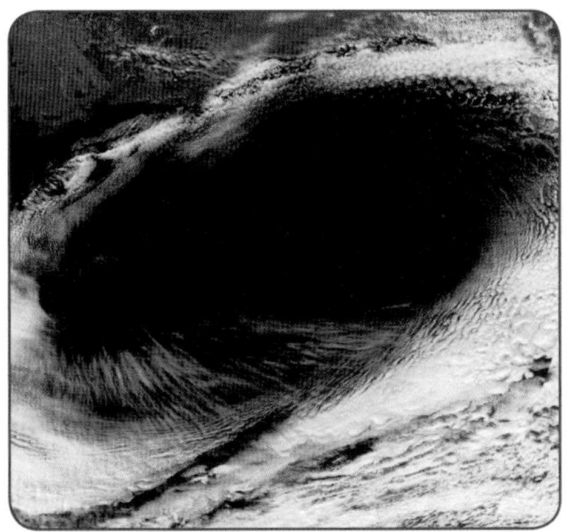

Figure 13.17 *Satellite image of an anticyclone*

Depression

- **Ascending** air and temperatures **fall**
- **Low** atmospheric pressure
- Winds blow in an **anti-clockwise** direction
- Isobars are **close together** indicating **strong** winds
- **Cloudy** skies
- **Wet** weather

Figure 13.18 *Satellite image of a depression*

(i) List two characteristics of an air mass.

(ii) Name two air masses that Ireland experiences.

(iii) Explain what a front is. Name the three types of front.

(iv) Describe the main differences between an anticyclone and a depression.

- I understand air masses and how they form fronts.
- I can explain the different fronts that are formed and I can identify them on weather maps.

Clouds

Learning Intentions

In this section, you will learn:

- about the formation of clouds and the different types of cloud.

Stratus
Cumulus
Cirrus

A **cloud** is a large collection of very tiny **droplets** of water or ice crystals held in the atmosphere. The droplets are so small and light that they can **float** in the air.

How clouds are formed

All air contains **water**. Near to the ground it is usually in the form of an invisible gas called **water vapour**. When warm air **rises**, it expands and **cools**. Cool air cannot hold as much water vapour as warm air, so some of the vapour **condenses** into tiny droplets. When billions of these droplets come together they become a visible **cloud**.

Types of cloud

There are **three** main types of cloud and each one indicates different weather conditions:

Stratus clouds

Stratus clouds occur below 2,000 m.

They look like **flat sheets** of cloud, and indicate an overcast or rainy day. These clouds are usually a uniform grey colour, and cover most of the sky.

Figure 13.19 *Stratus clouds*

Cumulus clouds

Cumulus clouds occur below 5,000 m.

They look like big fluffy balls of **cotton wool**. They usually mean that the weather will be nice. Sometimes they can look very woolly and bring heavy showers, especially in warm weather. These clouds are usually flat on the bottom, but have very **lumpy** tops. Cumulus clouds usually form alone and there is a lot of blue sky between individual clouds.

Figure 13.20 *Cumulus clouds*

Cirrus clouds

Cirrus clouds usually form above 8,000 m.

They are **wispy** clouds. Because there is very little water vapour at this height, big thick clouds cannot form. Cirrus clouds are created when water vapour forms **ice crystals**, which are very thin because of the height at which they form.

Figure 13.21 *Cirrus clouds*

 **(i)** Name two types of clouds that form.

 **(ii)** Which clouds bring the most precipitation?

 **(iii)** Draw a suitable graph to show the difference in the average height of each cloud type.

 I understand how clouds form and I can identify the various types of clouds.   

Precipitation

Learning Intentions

In this section, you will learn:

- how rainfall occurs
- about the three basic types of rainfall.

Precipitation	Frontal
Convectional	Relief
Cyclonic	Rain shadow

Precipitation is any form of water – liquid or solid – that falls from the sky. It includes rain, sleet, snow, hail and drizzle.

How rain is formed

Rain is the most common type of precipitation. Rain occurs because air has been forced to **rise**. As air rises it **cools** and loses its ability to hold water. Eventually it reaches a point where it is 100 per cent **saturated**, which means it cannot hold any more water. This is called the **dew point** and it is above this point that condensation occurs.

Condensation is the process by which the **water vapour** held in the air is turned back into water **droplets** that fall as rain.

Types of rain

There are three basic types of rain: **convectional** rain, **cyclonic** (or frontal) rain and **relief** rain.

Convectional rain

Convectional rain is common in areas where the ground is **heated** by the sun. Convectional rain can sometimes occur in **Ireland** during the **summer**. It occurs **all year** round in hot regions near the equator such as the **tropics**.

- The **warm air rises** because it is less dense.
- As the warm air rises it becomes cooler and **condenses** to form clouds.
- These clouds produce **rain**. They also occasionally produce **thunder and lightning**.

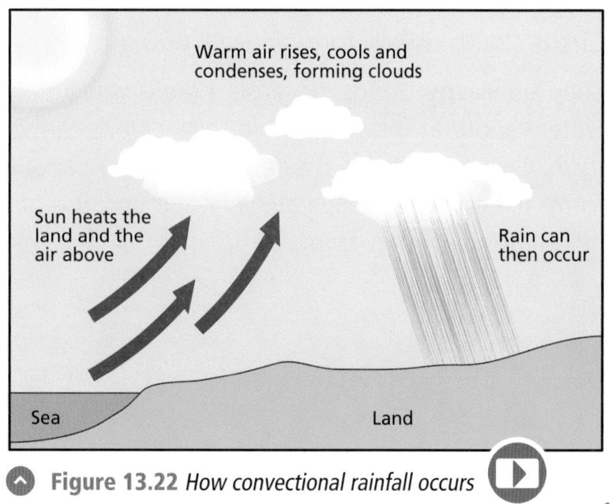

Figure 13.22 *How convectional rainfall occurs*

Cyclonic (or frontal) rain

Cyclonic rain is also called **frontal** rain because it occurs when two air masses meet, causing a front.

- The lighter, less dense, **warm air** is forced to **rise over** the denser **cold** air.
- This causes the warm air to **cool** and begin to **condense**.
- As it rises, further condensation occurs and **rain** is formed.
- Frontal rain brings a variety of clouds, which cause **moderate to heavy** rainfall.

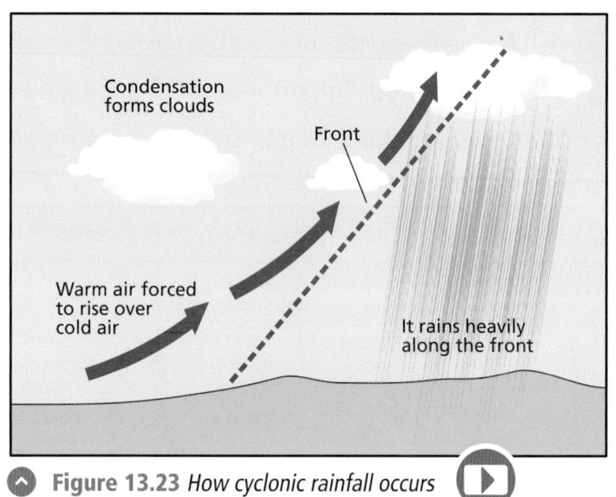

Figure 13.23 *How cyclonic rainfall occurs*

Relief rain

Relief rain is very **common** in Ireland.

- Prevailing **winds** pick up moisture from the **sea** as they travel across it, making the air **moist**.
- When this moist air reaches the **coast** it is forced to **rise** up over the coastal **mountains** and **hills**.
- This forces the air to **cool** and **condense**, forming **clouds**.
- As air continues to be forced over the mountain it drops its moisture as **relief rain**.
- Once over the mountain, the air will usually drop down the other side, **warming** as it does so.
- This means it can hold more moisture and so there is little rain on the far side of the mountain. This area is called the **rain shadow**.

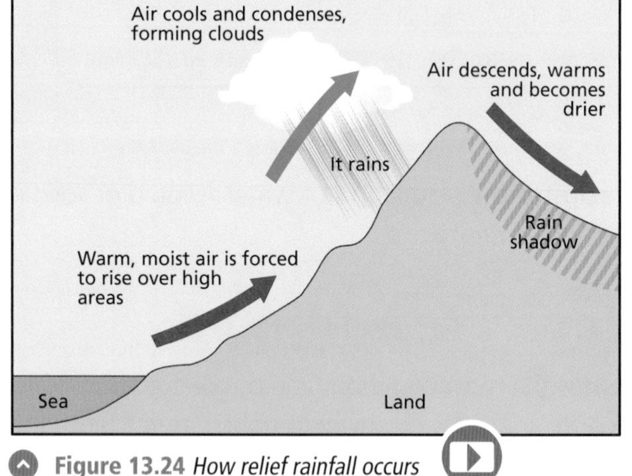

Figure 13.24 *How relief rainfall occurs*

 **(i)** Name two types of rainfall that can occur.

 **(ii)** Explain the formation of one type of rainfall.

 **(iii)** What is the socio-economic advantage of living in a rain shadow area?

- I understand how rain forms.
- I can explain convectional rain, cyclonic rain and relief rain.

Weather

Learning Intentions

In this section, you will learn:
- about weather elements and the importance of understanding weather
- about the different ways to measure and record the elements of the weather
- about the formation of a significant weather event and how people reacted to it.

Meteorologist
Weather station
Synoptic chart
Thermometer
Fahrenheit
Celsius
Isotherm
Barograph
Hectopascal
Hygrometer
Relative humidity
Stevenson screen
Anemometer
Beaufort scale
Rain gauge
Isohyet
Campbell-Stokes sunshine recorder
Isohel

Weather refers to the **state of the atmosphere** at a given time and place. **Climate** describes the common, **average weather** conditions at a particular place over a long period of time. For example, today's *weather* may be warm and sunny, but Ireland's *climate* is mild, moist and changeable.

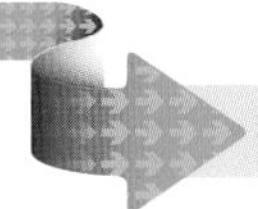
Go to Chapter 14 to learn more about the climates of the world.

Weather elements

Certain weather elements are measured constantly. These are:
- Temperature
- Humidity
- Atmospheric pressure
- Wind force
- Wind direction
- Precipitation
- Sunshine

A person who studies these elements is called a **meteorologist**.

Understanding weather

Weather forecasts

Understanding the **patterns** in weather conditions allow meteorologists to put together **weather forecasts**.

A weather forecast is a **prediction** of what the weather will be like at a particular time and place. Meteorologists study information and prepare the weather forecast. This information is gathered from sources such as **satellites**, **ships** and **weather stations**. The forecast is then put onto weather maps and charts and made available to the public.

Why is the weather forecast important?

From the clothes we wear to the journeys we take and the jobs we do, the weather has a big influence in our lives. It is important therefore that we have an idea of what type of weather to expect. The weather forecast is especially important to:
- anyone **working at sea** to make sure they are safe
- **farmers** so they can plan when to harvest crops and sow seeds
- **airlines** so they can cancel flights if the weather is forecast to be bad.

When particularly bad weather is forecast, **Met Éireann** issues weather warnings.

Weather stations

A weather station is a place with equipment and **instruments** for observing and recording the weather. Information from the weather stations in Ireland is sent to **Met Éireann**, the Irish National Meteorological Service.

Look up https://educateplus.ie/go/weather-stations. Find the weather station that is closest to your school.

Weather maps

The information gathered from weather stations is put onto weather maps called **synoptic charts**. Synoptic charts use **lines** and **symbols** to show what is happening with the weather at a given time. The lines on the charts show areas that have **equal** atmospheric pressure, temperature, sunshine or rainfall, depending on what is being measured.

Measuring weather

We will now examine the **instruments** that are used to measure the elements of weather. It is important that you know:

1. **What** it measures
2. The **name** of the instrument
3. What the **unit** of measurement is
4. **How it is shown** on the synoptic chart

Temperature

1. Temperature measures how **hot or cold** the air is.
2. The instrument used to measure air temperature is a **thermometer**.
   A thermometer consists of a glass rod with a very thin tube in it. The tube contains a liquid that is supplied from a reservoir, or '**bulb**', at the base of the thermometer. The liquid may be mercury or red-coloured alcohol. As the temperature of the liquid in the bulb increases, the liquid expands and rises up the tube.
3. The **unit** of measurement is degrees **Fahrenheit** or degrees **Celsius**.
4. **Isotherms** are lines on a weather map that join places of equal temperature.

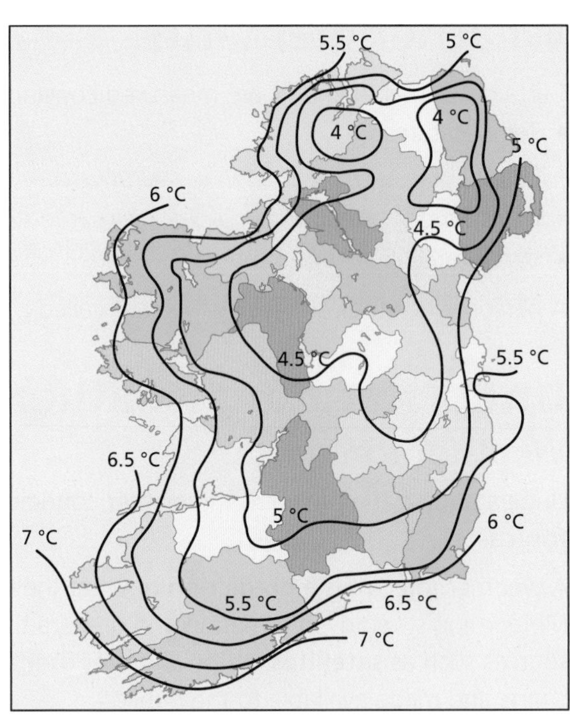

Figure 13.25 *Isotherms*

Maximum and minimum thermometers

A **maximum thermometer** measures the **highest** temperature. The mercury in the thermometer rises as the temperature increases and pushes a **pin** in the tube upwards. As the temperature drops again, the pin stays at the highest point.

A **minimum thermometer** contains alcohol and shows the **lowest** temperature. As the temperature drops, the pin in the tube drops and stays at the lowest point.

Calculating mean temperature and temperature range

The **temperature range** is the difference between the **highest** temperature and the **lowest** temperature. It can be calculated for **daily**, **monthly** or **annual** periods. The lowest temperature is subtracted from the highest temperature for whichever period is being calculated.

Highest temperature – Lowest temperature = Temperature range

The **average** or **mean** daily temperature is calculated by adding the lowest and the highest temperature for the day and dividing by two. The mean temperature is also calculated on a monthly and an annual basis.

The mean **monthly** temperature is calculated by adding the mean daily temperatures and dividing by the number of days in the month.

The mean **annual** temperature is calculated by adding the mean monthly temperatures and dividing by 12.

Figure 13.26 *A maximum and minimum thermometer*

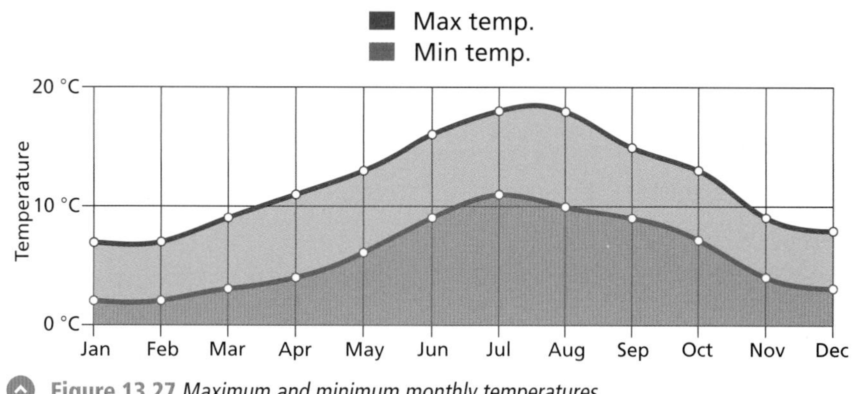

Figure 13.27 *Maximum and minimum monthly temperatures*

NUMERACY ACTIVITY

Examine Figure 13.27. Can you calculate the mean annual temperature? Calculate the mean summer and winter temperatures also.

Atmospheric pressure

1. **Atmospheric pressure** is the **weight** of the atmosphere pressing down on the Earth.
2. The instrument used to measure atmospheric pressure is called a **barograph**.

   A barograph consists of a small container with a moveable top. As the atmospheric pressure rises, the top is pushed inwards. As the pressure decreases, the top pushes back up again. A system of levers connects the top to a pen, which traces atmospheric pressures onto a **barogram**, located on a revolving drum.
3. The **unit** of measurement of atmospheric pressure is **millibars** (mb) or **hectopascals**.
4. The lines on a weather map that show areas of equal atmospheric pressure are called **isobars**.

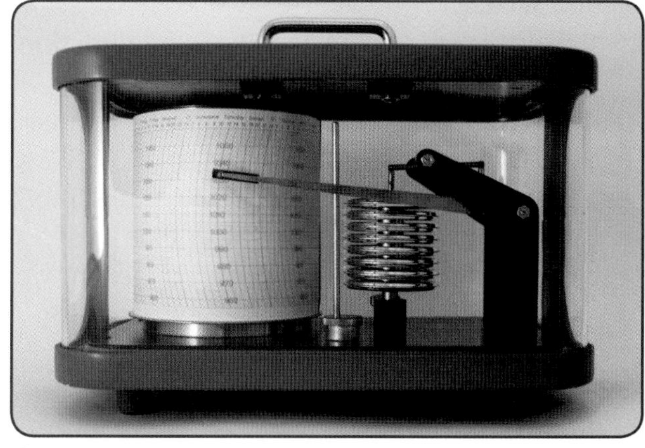

Figure 13.28 *A barograph*

Humidity

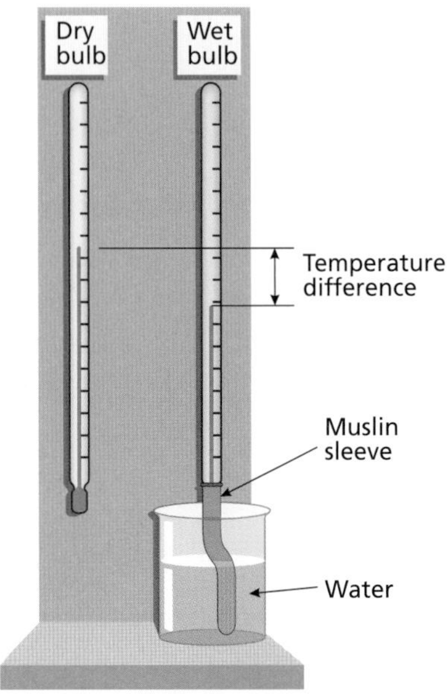

Figure 13.29 *A hygrometer with wet and dry bulbs*

1. **Humidity** is the amount of **water vapour** or moisture in the air. Warm air is able to hold more moisture than cold air. When air is unable to hold any more moisture, it is **saturated**.
2. The instrument used to measure relative humidity is a **hygrometer**. A hygrometer is a combination of a **wet** and a **dry** bulb:
   - The **dry bulb** thermometer measures the temperature of the **air**.
   - The **wet bulb** is covered by a muslin sleeve dipped in water, which keeps it **moist**. If the air is not saturated, **evaporation** will take place. This **cools** the bulb and the temperature will drop.

   The **difference** between the temperatures of the two thermometers is used to find the **amount of moisture** in the air. This is called the **relative humidity**. The greater the difference in the reading, the **drier** the air and the **lower** the relative humidity.
3. The relative humidity is measured as a **percentage** of the **maximum moisture** that could be in the air at a certain temperature. If the air has **half** the amount of **moisture** it could hold, then the **relative humidity** is **50 per cent**. When it is raining or snowing and the maximum amount of moisture has evaporated into the air, then the relative humidity is 100 per cent. The relative humidity decreases during the day as the temperature rises.
4. Humidity is shown on a weather map as a **percentage**.

Stevenson screen

The **instruments** used to measure temperature, atmospheric pressure and humidity are placed in a **Stevenson screen**. This is a box that is painted white to reflect the heat of the sun. It has slatted sides to allow air to pass through the screen. This ensures accurate readings as the instruments are not in direct sunlight.

Figure 13.30 *A Stevenson screen*

Wind direction

1. The **direction** from which the wind is coming can be measured.
2. The instrument used to measure **wind direction** is a **wind vane**.
   A wind vane is composed of an **arrow** that freely **rotates** on top of a fixed vertical rod. The letters N, S, E and W are attached to the rod to indicate north, south, east and west. The tail of the arrow is larger than the tip and this is blown **forward** by the wind, leaving the arrow pointing in the direction from which the wind is **coming**.
3. Wind direction is given by the **point of the compass from which it is blowing**.
4. Wind direction is shown using **arrows** on a map.

Figure 13.31 *A wind vane*

ACTIVITY

Can you tell what direction the wind is blowing in Figure 13.31?

Wind speed

1. The **strength** or **speed** of the wind can also be measured.
2. The instrument used to measure **wind speed** is an **anemometer**.

   An anemometer consists of three cups attached to horizontal arms. The arms are attached to a vertical rod. As the wind blows, the cups **rotate**, making the **rod spin**. The stronger the wind blows, the faster the rod spins. The anemometer counts the number of rotations, or turns, and this is used to calculate **wind speed**.
3. Wind speed is measured in **kilometres per hour** (kph). It is usually **averaged** over a short period of time because the wind speeds are not consistent, meaning they do not always blow with the same intensity.

   Wind strength can also be measured using the **Beaufort scale**. It is based on an observation of how much damage the wind causes rather than measurement. Wind strength categories range from 1 for calm to 12 for a hurricane-force wind.

Figure 13.32 *An anemometer*

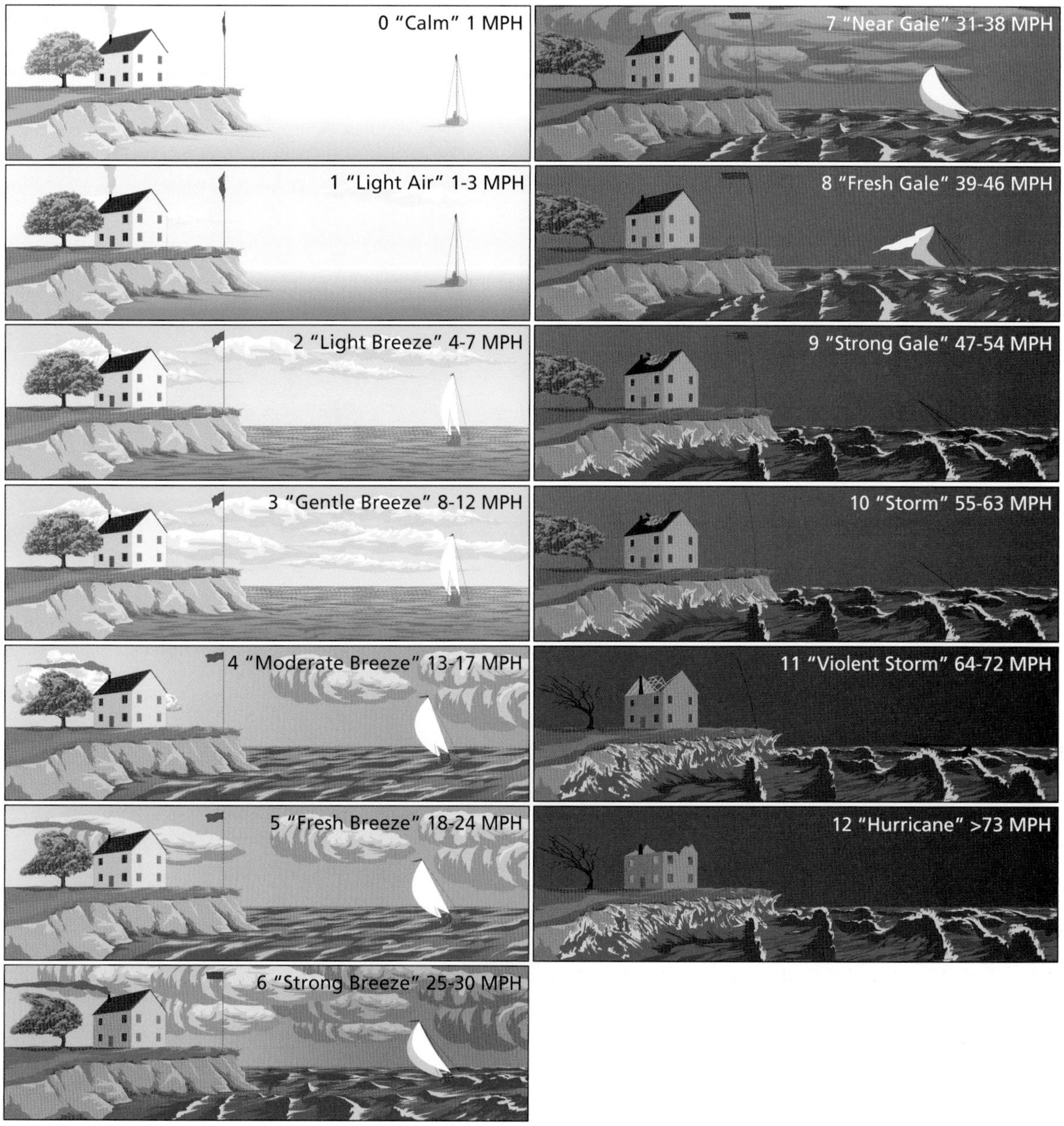

4. When the **isobars** are closer **together** on a weather map, the **wind** will be **stronger**. When they are further **apart**, the wind will be **lighter**.

0 "Calm" 1 MPH
1 "Light Air" 1-3 MPH
2 "Light Breeze" 4-7 MPH
3 "Gentle Breeze" 8-12 MPH
4 "Moderate Breeze" 13-17 MPH
5 "Fresh Breeze" 18-24 MPH
6 "Strong Breeze" 25-30 MPH
7 "Near Gale" 31-38 MPH
8 "Fresh Gale" 39-46 MPH
9 "Strong Gale" 47-54 MPH
10 "Storm" 55-63 MPH
11 "Violent Storm" 64-72 MPH
12 "Hurricane" >73 MPH

Figure 13.33 *The Beaufort scale*

Precipitation

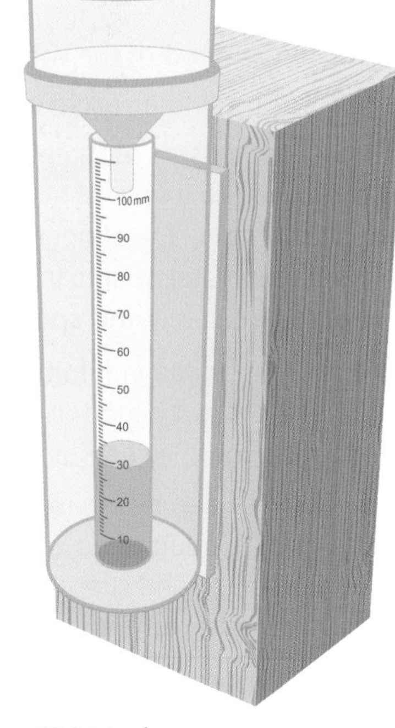

Figure 13.34 *A rain gauge*

1. **Precipitation** is any form of liquid or solid **water** particles that fall from the atmosphere and reach the surface of the Earth. It includes **rain**, **snow**, **sleet**, **hail** and **drizzle**.
2. A **rain gauge** is used to **measure** the amount of rainfall.

   A **measuring cylinder** with a **funnel** on top is placed in an **open area**, not sheltered by buildings and trees, in order to ensure an accurate reading.

   The rain falls through a funnel into the cylinder, which is marked in millimetres. When the cylinder is removed, the amount of rain that has fallen can be recorded
3. The **unit** of measurement of rainfall is **millimetres** (mm).
4. The lines on a weather map showing areas of equal rainfall are called **isohyets**.

Sunshine

Figure 13.35 *A Campbell-Stokes sunshine recorder*

1. Sunshine is when the sun's rays reach the surface of the Earth.
2. Sunshine is measured using a **Campbell-Stokes sunshine recorder**.

   A **glass sphere** focuses the sun's rays onto a spot on a sensitive **strip of paper** slotted into the semi-circular frame surrounding the ball. The sun's rays **burn** a mark on the paper. As the sun moves across the sky during the day, the burn marks move along the paper. At the end of the day, the paper can be examined to see how much the sun shone during the day.
3. Sunshine is measured in **hours per day**.
4. The lines on a weather map showing areas of equal sunshine are called **isohels**.

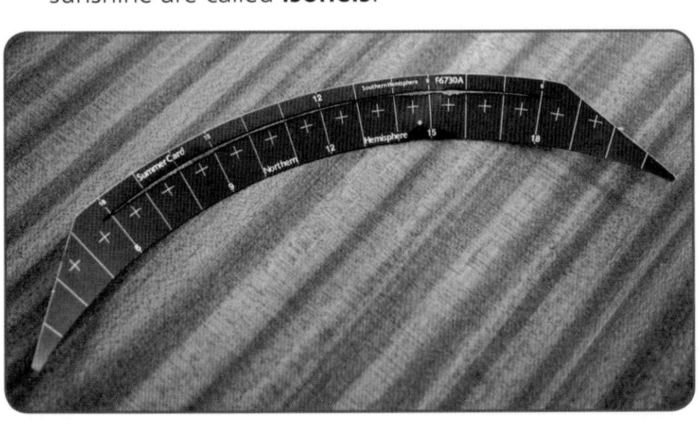
Figure 13.36 *Readout from a Campbell-Stokes recorder*

PORTFOLIO ACTIVITY 13.1

Go to page 52 of your Portfolio to find out how to make your own weather station.

CASE STUDY

Extreme weather: Hurricane Irma

A **hurricane** is a huge **rotating storm** with very strong winds and lots of rain. Hurricanes form over warm ocean water **near the equator**. When **warm** moist air **rises** upwards, it is replaced by new air. This new air then also heats up and rises and the **cycle** continues, forming clouds that rotate with the spin of the earth. Most of the time, they happen out at **sea**. When they travel towards land, the **impact** can be devastating.

Figure 13.37 *A satellite view of Hurricane Irma approaching Florida*

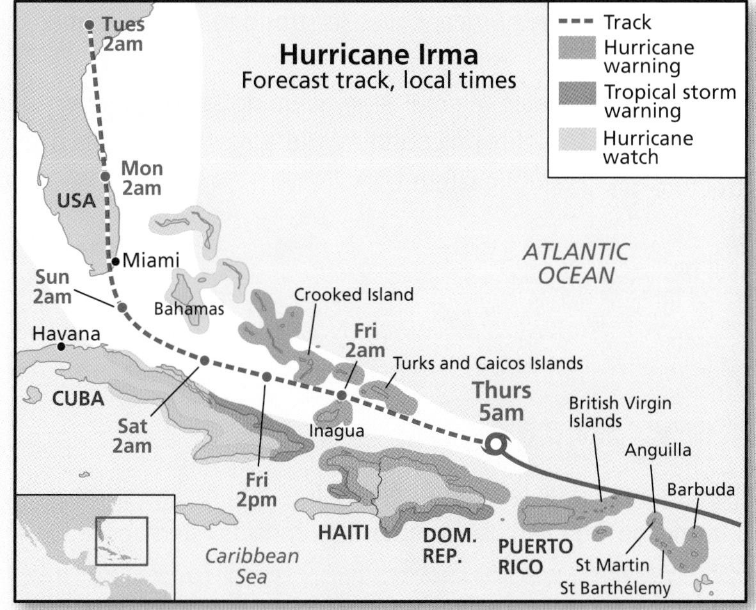

Figure 13.38 *The path of Hurricane Irma*

Hurricane Irma occurred in **September 2017**. It was one of the most powerful hurricanes ever recorded. It was classed as a **Category 5 hurricane**, the highest level of hurricane. **Wind speeds** were over **295 kph** when the Hurricane hit the Caribbean island of **Barbuda** on 6 September and these wind speeds lasted for up to 37 hours.

Figure 13.39 *Damage from Hurricane Irma on the island of St Martin*

The hurricane moved up into the state of **Florida** in the United States. When the hurricane reached Florida it had been downgraded to a Category 4 and wind speeds reduced to 210 kph.

DID YOU KNOW? September 2017 was the most active month for Atlantic hurricanes on record.

ACTIVITY

Check out these weblinks to view the progress of Hurricane Irma:

https://educateplus.ie/go/hurricane-irma-video

https://educateplus.ie/go/hurricane-irma

Impacts of Hurricane Irma

Barbuda

- 90% of buildings in the island of Barbuda were destroyed or partially destroyed.
- 60% of the population was left homeless.

St Martin

- 60% of the island's homes were destroyed.
- 1.5 million people were left without power.
- It had a huge impact on tourism in an area that receives over a million tourists each year.

Florida

- 6 million people were ordered to evacuate.
- Over 8,000 flights were cancelled.
- There were gas shortages in the region due to the evacuation.
- 40 cm of rain led to widespread flooding.
- There was damage to homes and infrastructure across the state.
- It is estimated that the cost of damage will be over $100 billion.

Overall

- 134 died because of the hurricane.
- The hurricane was so strong that it registered on seismographs in the area.
- States of emergency were declared in many Caribbean countries and across many parts of south-eastern USA.

ACTIVITY

Imagine that you and your group are members of a national response team before a hurricane strikes. Outline your responses to the threat of this hurricane. You can use some of the impacts listed above to help with your answer.

PORTFOLIO ACTIVITY 13.2

Do you remember when former hurricane, Storm Ophelia, made landfall in Ireland in October 2017? Go to page 54 of your Portfolio and write a newspaper report on Storm Ophelia.

 **(i)** List three elements of the weather that we can record.

(ii) Name the person that puts together the weather forecast.

 **(iii)** Name three instruments that are used to record elements of weather and the units of measurements they use.

(iv) What is temperature range?

 **(v)** Weather is important to people for many reasons. Can you name a person who depends on accurate weather forecasts on a daily/weekly basis for their employment and explain why?

- ✔ I can list the instruments used to measure different aspects of weather and the units they are measured in. 
- ✔ I can explain the formation and impact of a serious weather disaster. 

REVISION

The ____________________ is a thin layer of _____________ surrounding the Earth.

_______________ energy comes from the sun. The sun's energy is distributed ____________________ over the ____________________ of the Earth and the atmosphere. It varies according to ____________________ and the ________________ of the Earth on its axis. The unequal heating of the atmosphere leads to movements of _________ and ____________________ ____________________. Winds move from areas of ____________________ pressure to areas of _________ pressure. _________ ____________________ are large pockets of air. The point where they meet is called a ____________________. Cool air rising creates areas of high pressure called ____________________. Warm air descending creates low pressure systems called ____________________. The three main cloud types are ____________________, ____________________ and ____________________. The three types of rainfall are ____________________, ____________________ and ____________________.

____________________ refers to the state of the atmosphere at a given time and place. The ____________________ is the common, average weather conditions at a particular place over a long period of time. A ____________________ forecasts the weather. A ____________________ is used to measure temperature. Atmospheric pressure is measured using a ____________________. A hygrometer measures ____________________.

A _____________ _____________ shows wind direction and an ____________________ measures wind speed. A _____________ ____________________ is used to measure precipitation. A ____________________-_____________ recorder measures sunshine.

Sample Questions

1. Name the type of rainfall shown in the diagram on the right.
2. Describe how this type of rainfall occurs.

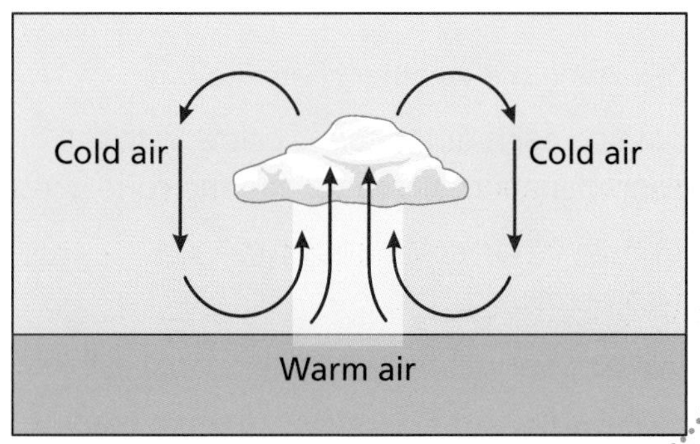

Sample Answers

1. Convectional rainfall
2. Convectional rain is common in areas where the ground is heated by the sun. Because it is less dense, warm air rises. As the warm air rises it becomes cooler and condenses to form clouds. These clouds produce rain and possibly thunder and lightning. This rain can occur in Ireland during the summer. It can be found all year round in hot regions near the equator such as the tropics.

Short Questions

1. Study the diagram showing the unequal heating of the Earth's surface by the Sun.

   Which of the following statements is **true**?

   Heat from the Sun is greatest in the northern hemisphere at **X**. ☐

   Heat from the Sun is greatest at the equator at **Y**. ☐

   [tick (✓) the correct box]

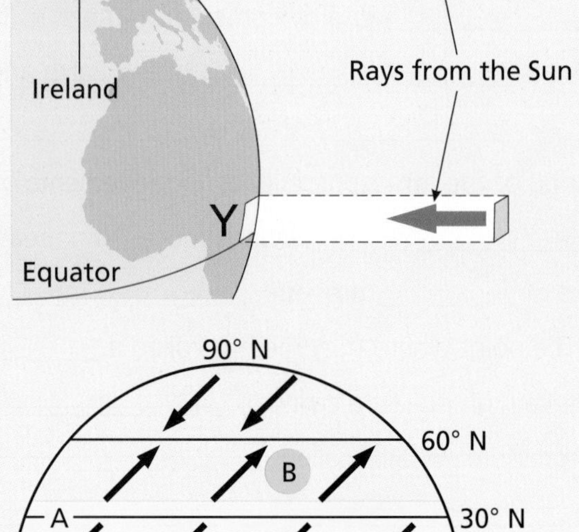

2. Examine the diagram, which shows global pressure belts and air movements.

   Circle the correct answer in **each** of the following statements:

   (i) A belt of **high pressure / low pressure** exists at the place labelled A.

   (ii) The winds at B are **south-westerlies / north-easterlies**.

   (iii) The winds at C are referred to as **cold winds / warm winds**.

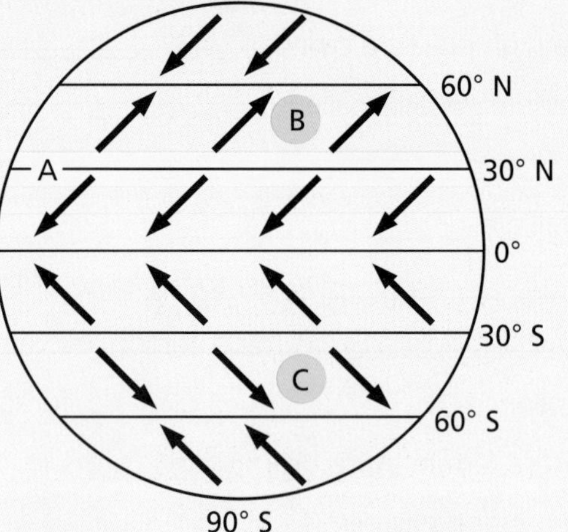

3. Examine the map.

   Circle the correct answer in **each** of the statements below.

   (i) The current at **X** is a **warm / cold** current.

   (ii) The current at **Y** is a **warm / cold** current.

   (iii) The current at **X** is called the **Labrador Current / North Atlantic Drift**.

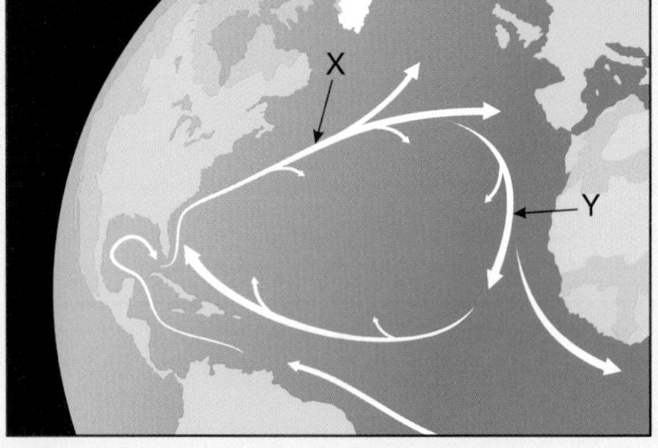

4. Examine the weather charts below.

   Match **each** of the terms below with the appropriate chart, by writing the correct letter in the spaces provided.

   Isotherms ☐

   Isobars ☐

   Isohyets ☐

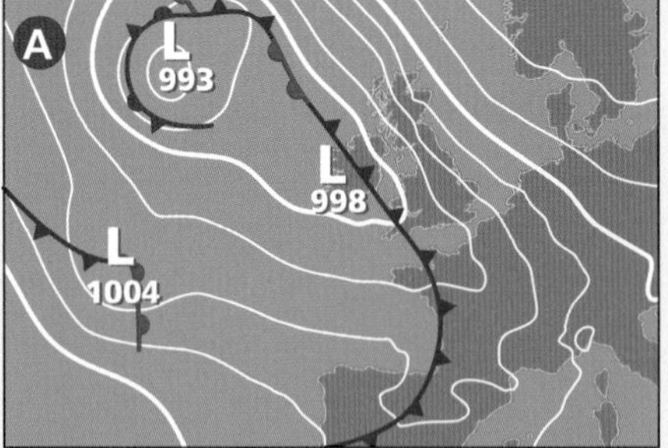

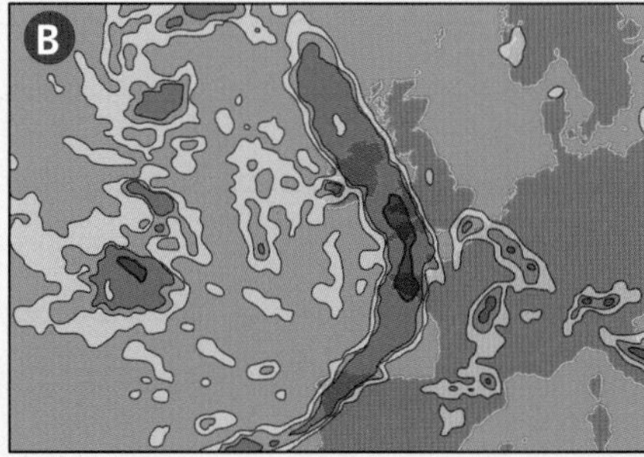

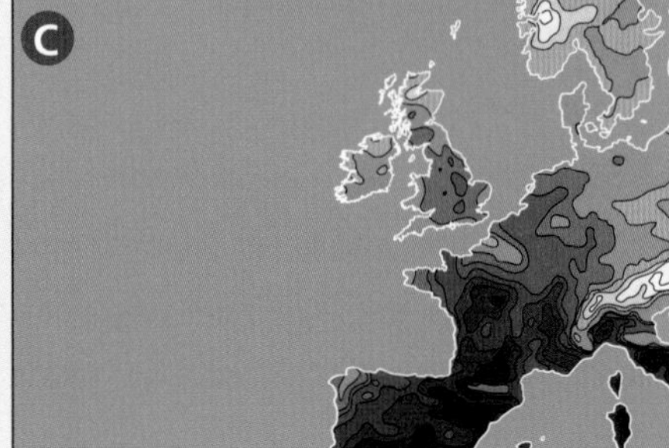

5. Examine the weather map.

In the boxes provided, match each of the letters in **Column X** with the number of its pair in **Column Y**. One match has been made for you.

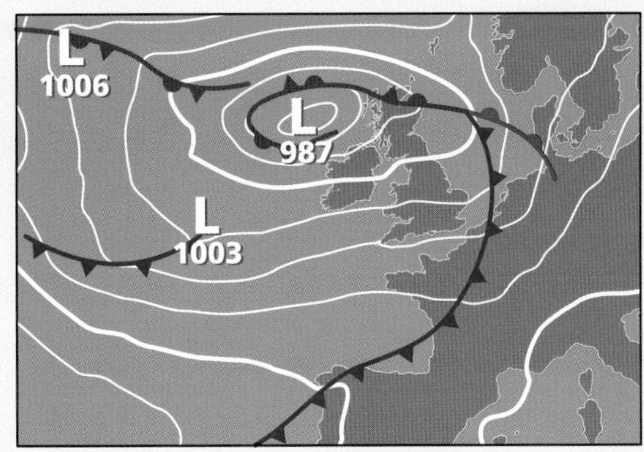

Column X		Column Y		X	Y
A		1	Depression	A	2
B		2	Isobars	B	
C		3	Cold front	C	
D	L 987	4	Warm front	D	

6. In the spaces provided, name **each** of the weather instruments that are labelled A to C in the diagrams.

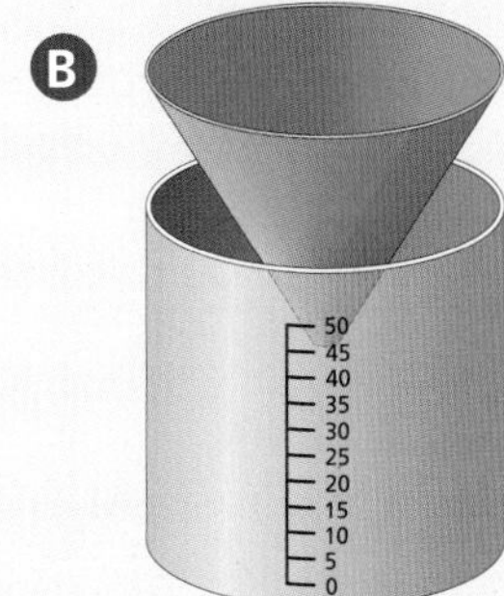

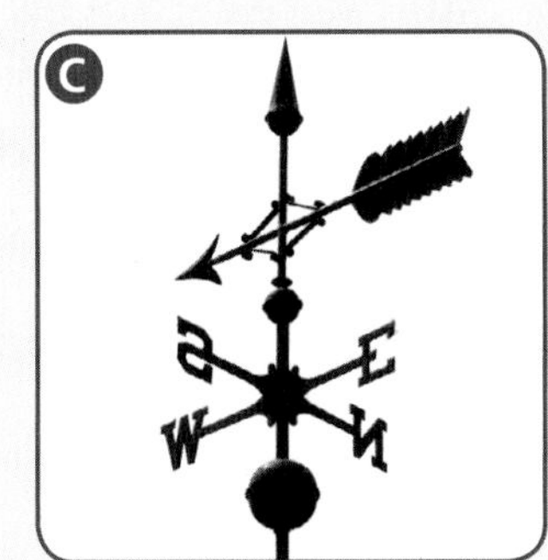

________________ ________________ ________________

7. Examine the annual temperature and precipitation graphs of Valentia, Co Kerry.

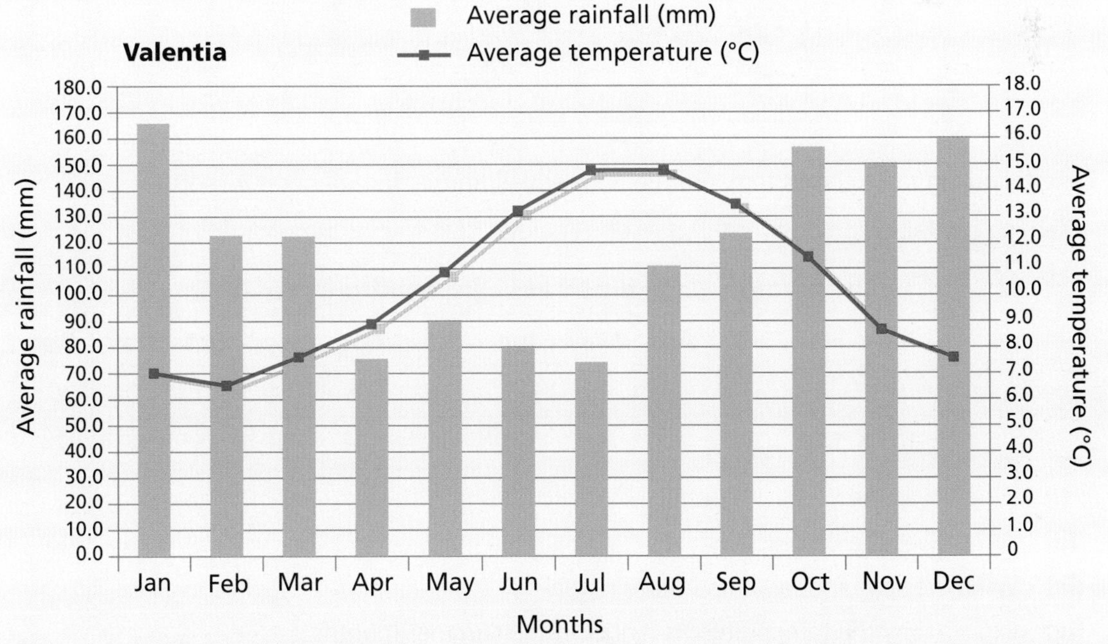

(i) According to the weather chart, which month is the coldest at Valentia? ____________

(ii) Calculate the annual temperature range at Valentia. ____________

(iii) State the precipitation in millimetres for the month of November. ____________

Long Questions

1. Study this diagram carefully. It shows how the Sun heats the Earth.
   (i) Name the line of latitude marked **A**.
   (ii) Describe why the heating effect of the Sun is different at **X** and **Y**.

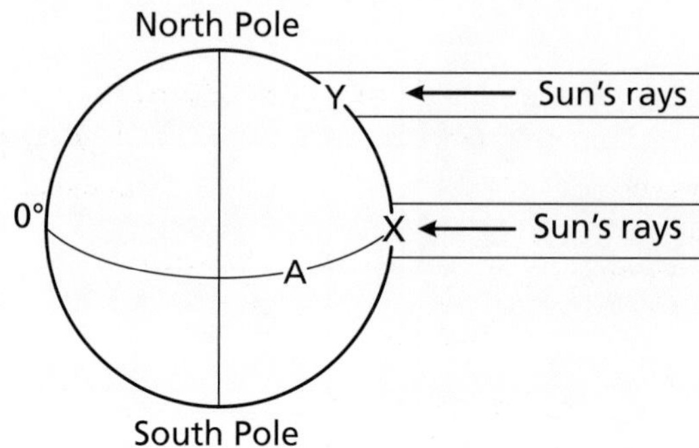

2. The weather chart shows a large cyclone or depression over Ireland.
   (i) Name **each** of the features labelled **A**, **B** and **C** on the chart.
   (ii) Describe the weather conditions which you would expect to find in the area labelled **X** on the chart. Refer briefly in your answer to atmospheric pressure, cloud and precipitation.

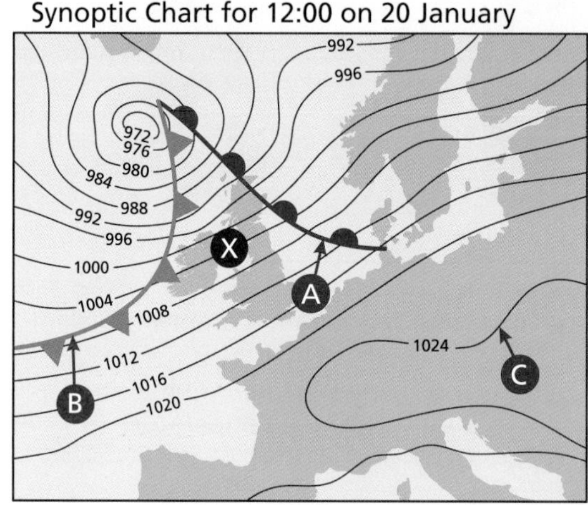

3. The following table shows temperature and rainfall figures for Shannon Airport.
   Examine the table and answer the questions below.

Temperature and rainfall at Shannon Airport for 2016													
	Jan	**Feb**	**Mar**	**Apr**	**May**	**Jun**	**Jul**	**Aug**	**Sep**	**Oct**	**Nov**	**Dec**	
Temperature	6	5	7	8	12	15	16	16	14	11	6	6	°C
Rainfall	107	144	64	42	45	68	66	107	88	35	69	74	mm

   (i) Which was the wettest month?
   (ii) Which was the coldest month?
   (iii) What was the annual temperature range?
   (iv) Explain why the temperature is higher in the summer months.

4. Draw a labelled diagram and explain how **either** relief rainfall **or** convectional rainfall occurs.

Visual Summary

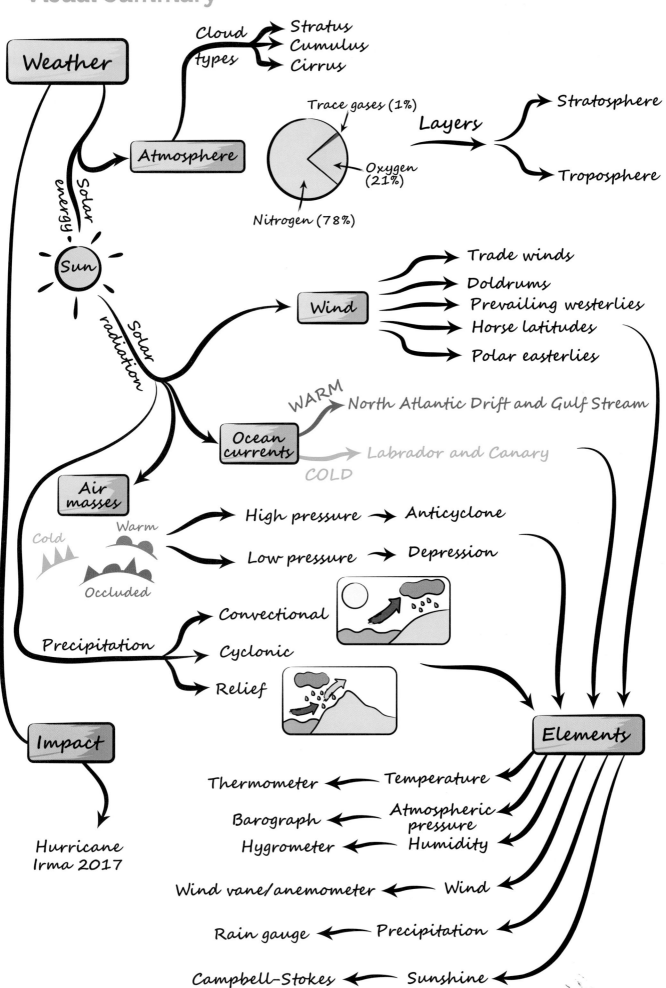

Weather
Cloud types → Stratus, Cumulus, Cirrus
Atmosphere
Trace gases (1%)
Oxygen (21%)
Nitrogen (78%)
Layers → Stratosphere, Troposphere
Solar energy
Sun
Solar radiation
Wind → Trade winds, Doldrums, Prevailing westerlies, Horse latitudes, Polar easterlies
Ocean currents
WARM → North Atlantic Drift and Gulf Stream
COLD → Labrador and Canary
Air masses
Cold
Warm
Occluded
High pressure → Anticyclone
Low pressure → Depression
Precipitation → Convectional, Cyclonic, Relief
Impact → Hurricane Irma 2017
Elements
Temperature → Thermometer
Atmospheric pressure → Barograph
Humidity → Hygrometer
Wind → Wind vane/anemometer
Precipitation → Rain gauge
Sunshine → Campbell-Stokes

Climates:
Classifying climate types and Ireland's climate

In this chapter, you will learn:

- what factors influence climate
- how to classify global climates
- what factors influence our climate in Ireland
- the causes and implications of climate change.

ICE-BREAKER ACTIVITY

Look at the pictures of Spain and northern Canada. Can you think of any reasons why it is warmer in Spain than it is in northern Canada? Work in pairs and then share your answers with the class.

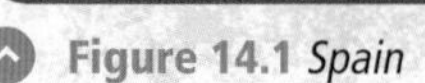

Figure 14.1 *Spain*

Figure 14.2 *Northern Canada*

Climate

Learning Intentions

In this section, you will learn:

- the factors that influence climate globally and locally.

Latitude
Prevailing winds
Air masses
Aspect
Altitude

We have already learned that **weather** refers to the state of the atmosphere at a given time and place. The **climate** is the common, **average weather conditions** across a **large area** of the Earth's surface over a **long period** of time. It is calculated using the average weather records over 30 to 35 years.

Factors that influence global climates

The characteristics of any global climate type are influenced by a number of **factors**. These include:

Latitude

Distance from the sea

Prevailing winds and air masses

Latitude

Slanted rays of sunlight

Direct rays of sunlight

Figure 14.3 *The sun's rays*

Latitude is the distance of a place **north or south** of the equator. It is measured as an **angle**, in degrees.

Areas closer to the equator are **warmer** because the sun's energy is greatest at the **equator**. The sun is closest to the Earth here, so its rays shine directly upon it and are **concentrated** on a smaller area.

The further you travel from the equator, the **cooler** it gets because the sun's rays are at an **angle** to the Earth's surface, so its heat is **spread** over a wider area. Sunlight also has to travel **further** through the **atmosphere**, so more light and heat are absorbed or scattered.

Distance from the sea

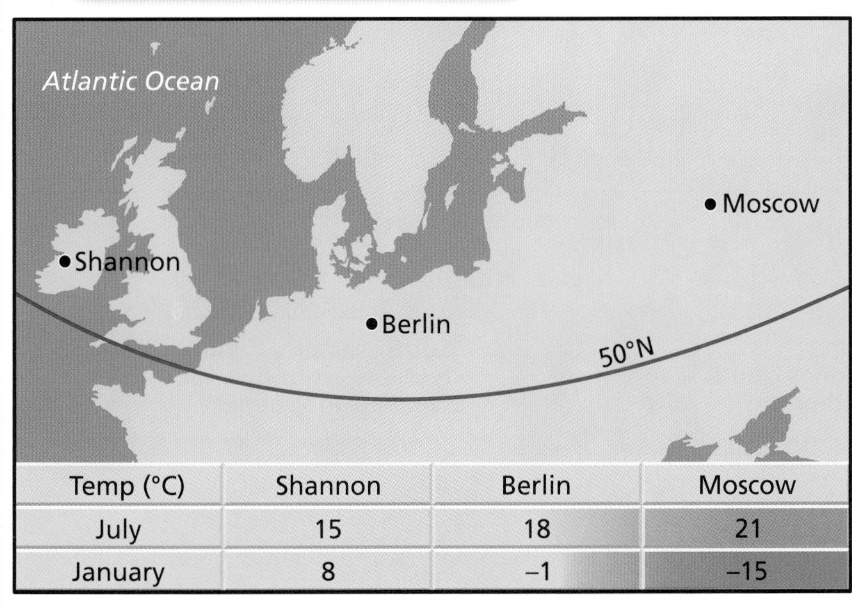

Temp (°C)	Shannon	Berlin	Moscow
July	15	18	21
January	8	–1	–15

Figure 14.4 *Average winter temperatures in Europe*

The sea takes **longer** to heat up and cool than land.

During the summer, seawater is **cooler** than land. During the **winter**, seawater is **warmer** than land because it loses heat more slowly. This means that areas **close to the sea** have **cooler summers** and **milder winters** than areas that are far away from the sea.

Prevailing winds and air masses

Winds **move** warm and cold **air masses**. Winds from the south move warm air, and winds from the north move cold air. As the air masses move over the land they influence **temperature** and **precipitation**.

The most common winds are called **prevailing winds**. Ireland's prevailing winds are **south-westerly**. The winds below influence Ireland's climate:

- **South-westerly winds** travel over the Atlantic. They are **mild in winter** because the temperature of the sea is warmer than the land. The winds are **cooler in summer** because the temperature of the sea is cooler than the land. South-westerly winds **absorb moisture** as they pass over the ocean and often bring **precipitation**.
- **Northerly** and **polar winds** are **cold** because they come from **higher latitudes**. During the winter northerly winds can bring snow.
- **Southerly winds** are **warm** because they come from **lower latitudes**. The air cools as it travels away from the equator so it loses its ability to hold moisture. Therefore, southerly winds may bring some **rainfall**.
- **Easterly winds** travel over continental Europe, so are sometimes called **continental** winds. In **summer**, when temperatures are higher, they are **warm**. In **winter**, when the temperatures are lower, they are **cold**. Easterly winds are usually **dry** winds because they travel over land.

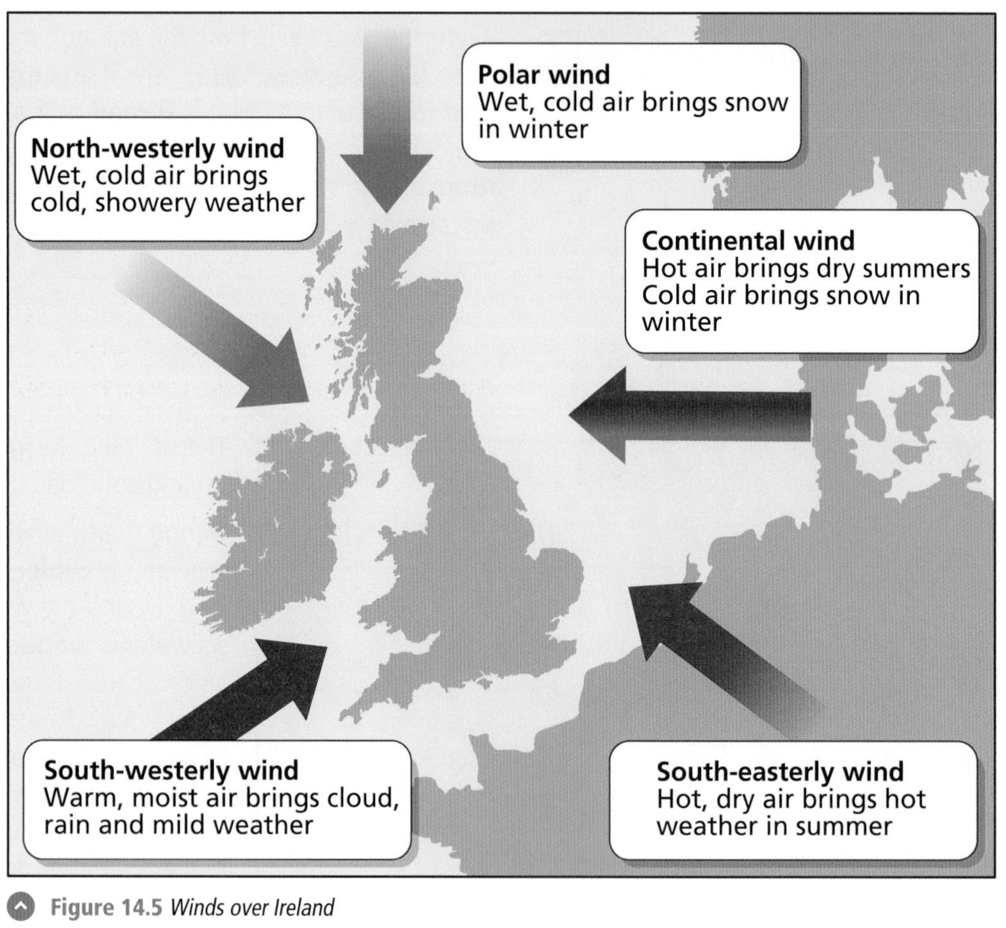

Figure 14.5 *Winds over Ireland*

Factors that influence local climates

It is possible to find **variations** of climate within a region. For example, the west of Ireland experiences more rainfall than the east, even though the climate of the whole of Ireland is cool temperate oceanic. The factors that influence climate **locally** are:

Aspect

Altitude

Aspect

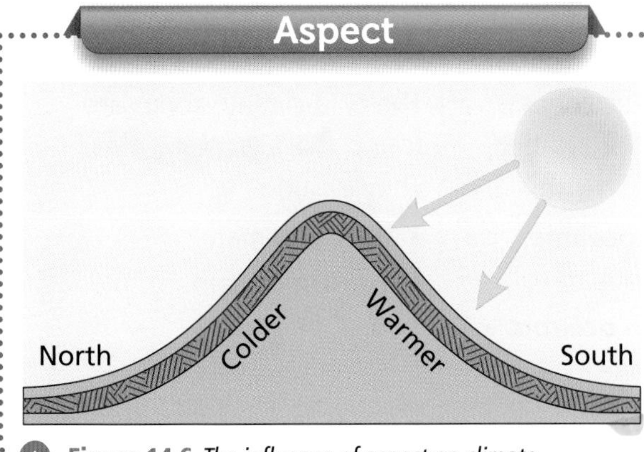

Figure 14.6 *The influence of aspect on climate*

Aspect is the **direction a slope faces** in relation to the sun.

South-facing slopes in the northern hemisphere are pointed towards the sun and are **warmer** than **north-facing slopes**, which may be in the shade.

South-facing slopes are also influenced by warm southerly **winds**. North-facing slopes may be in the path of cold northerly winds.

Altitude

Figure 14.7 *As altitude increases, temperature decreases*

Altitude is the **height** of an area **above sea level**.

The **higher** a place is above sea level, the **colder** it is. This is because the **air is thinner** at high altitudes and holds less heat. The temperature drops by about **1 °C for every 100 m** increase in altitude.

Upland areas are also more **exposed** to **wind** than lowland areas, which are sheltered by the uplands. Upland areas also experience **more rain** because as the air rises, it cools and is unable to hold moisture.

(i) Name three factors that influence climate globally.

(ii) Name two factors that influence climate locally.

(iii) Explain the terms altitude and aspect.

(iv) Explain the difference between weather and climate.

(v) Explain why Chamonix in the French Alps experiences a different climate to La Rochelle on the west coast of France, even though they are at similar latitudes.

- I can explain what climate is.
- I can explain the three factors that influence global climates.
- I can explain the two factors that influence climate locally.

Global climates

Learning Intentions

In this section, you will learn:

- how to classify global climates.

Climatic zone
Equatorial
Savannah
Temperate
Oceanic
Boreal
Tundra
Natural region

Global climates can be put into three broad **climatic zones** or categories. These are:

1. Hot climates

The hot climatic zones are found **close to the equator**. They include:

- **Equatorial** climate
- **Savannah** climate
- Hot **desert** climate

2. Temperate climates

The temperate climatic zones are found in the **mid-latitudes**. They include:

- **Cool temperate oceanic** climate (Ireland's climate)
- **Warm temperate oceanic** climate (Mediterranean climate)

3. Cold climates

The cold climate zones are found **close to the poles**. They include:

- **Boreal** climate
- **Tundra** climate

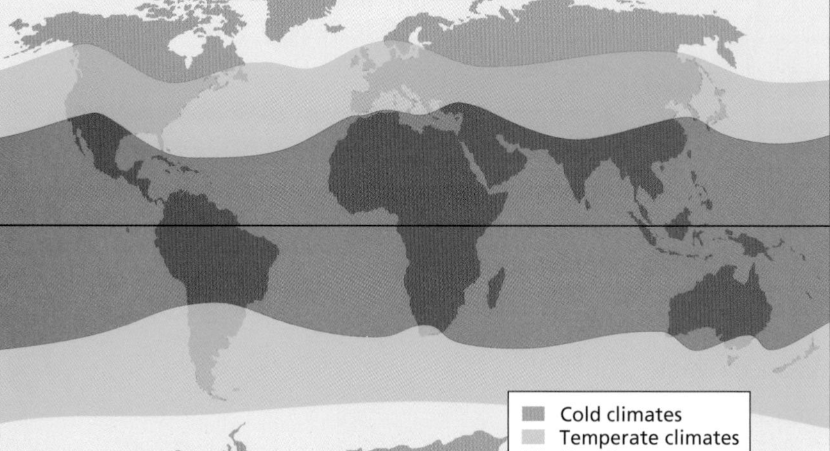

Figure 14.8 *The three broad climatic zones*

Each of the climatic zones contains a number of **natural regions**. This is an area where the climate, natural vegetation, wildlife and human activities are similar. The most important of these characteristics is **climate** because it influences the formation of the **soil** in the area, the type of **vegetation** that grows there, the **animals** that live there and what people do there. Plants and animals often have **characteristics** that are adapted to living in the conditions of their natural region.

Hot climates

The hot climates of the world are found between the **equator and 30° north and south** of the equator. They are the **equatorial**, **savannah** and **hot desert** climates.

	Equatorial climate	Savannah climate	Hot desert climate
Location	Near the equator	Between 5° and 15° north and south of equator	Between 15° and 30° north and south of equator
Characteristics			
Seasons	One season	Two seasons (dry and wet)	One season
Average temperature	27 °C annually	Dry: 30 °C Wet: 20 °C	30–50 °C
Annual precipitation	2,500 mm	750–1,000 mm	250 mm

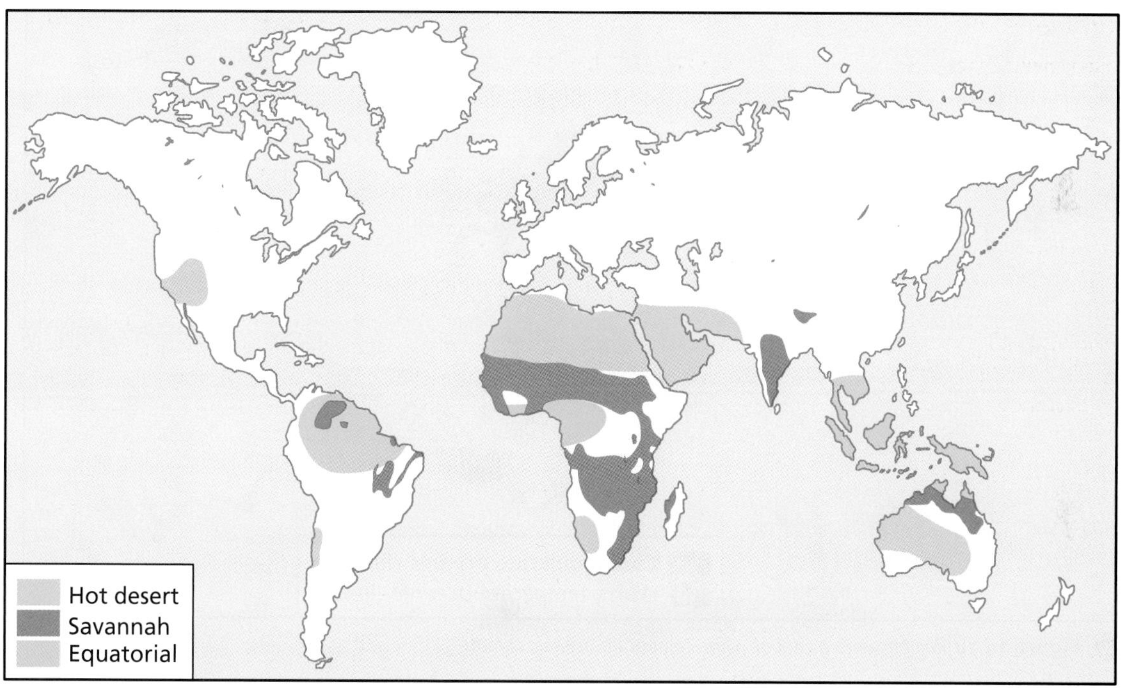

Figure 14.9 *Regions with an equatorial, savannah or hot desert climate*

ACTIVITY

Research the following online:

(a) What animals live in (i) equatorial climates, (ii) savannah climates and (iii) hot desert climates?

(b) What vegetation grows in (i) equatorial climates, (ii) savannah climates and (iii) hot desert climates?

(c) How do the animals and vegetation you've researched survive in these conditions?

Temperate climates

The temperate climates of the world are found at the **mid-latitudes**. These include the **cool temperate oceanic climate** and the **warm temperate oceanic climate**.

	Cool temperate oceanic climate	Warm temperate oceanic climate
Location	Between 40° and 60° north and south of the equator	Along the western sides of the continents and located between 30° and 40° north and south of the equator
	Characteristics	
Seasons	Four	Two
Average temperature	Summer: 14–20 °C Winter: 5–6 °C	Summer: 20–30 °C Winter: 6–8 °C
Annual precipitation	700–2,000 mm	400–700 mm

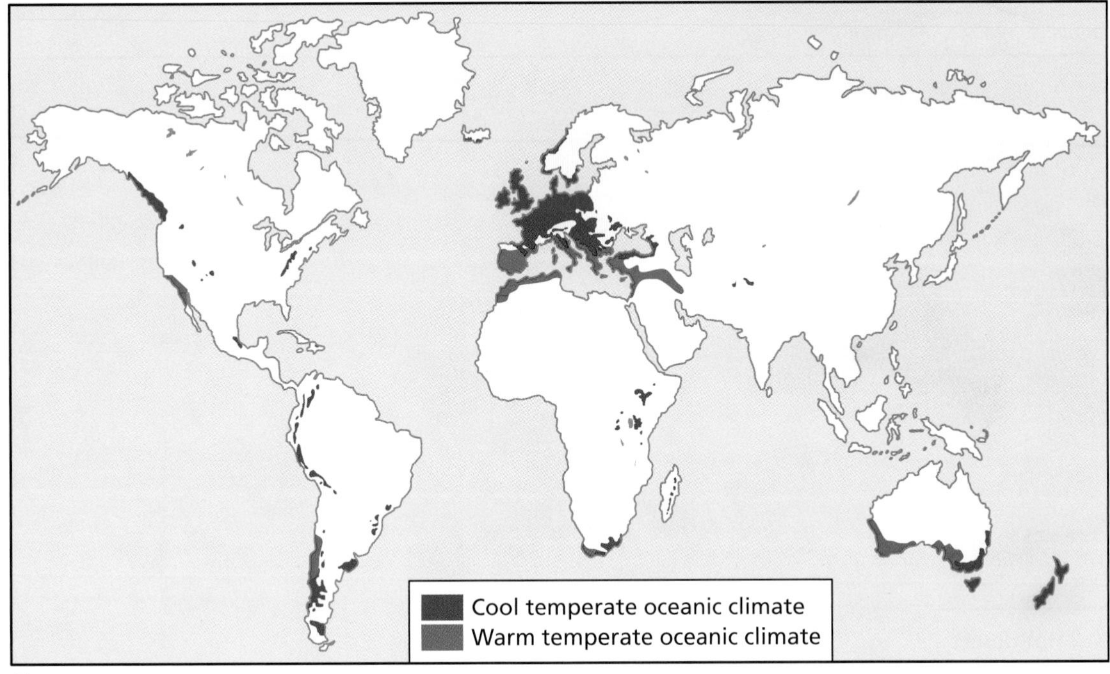

Figure 14.10 *Regions with a cool or warm temperate oceanic climate*

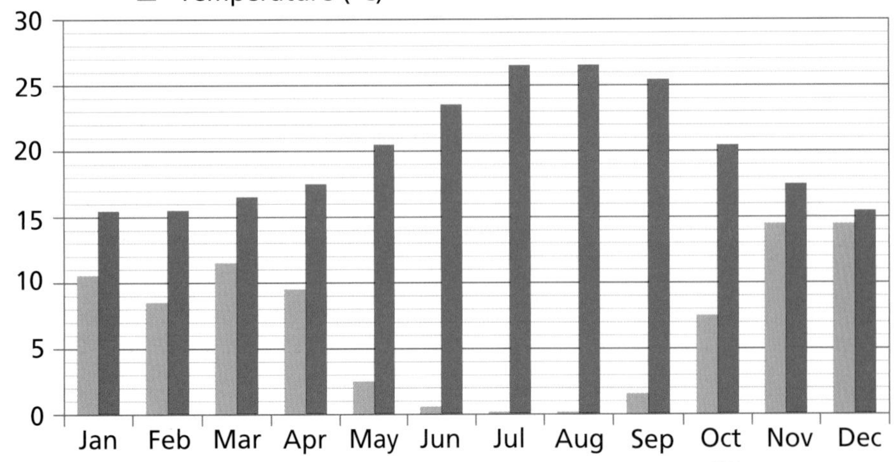

Figure 14.11 *Monthly average rainfall and temperature in Gibraltar in the Mediterranean, which has a warm temperate oceanic climate*

NUMERACY ACTIVITY

Examine Figure 14.11. What is the annual temperature range? Which are the driest months?

Cold climates

Cold climates are found **close to the poles**. These include the **boreal** climate and the **tundra** climate.

	Boreal climate	Tundra climate
Location	Northern hemisphere between 55° north of the equator and the Arctic Circle	Around the poles
Characteristics		
Seasons	Two	Two
Average temperatures	Summer: 15–20 °C Winter: –15 °C	Summer: 3–12 °C Winter: –35 °C
Annual precipitation	200–2,000 mm mostly snow	250 mm mostly snow

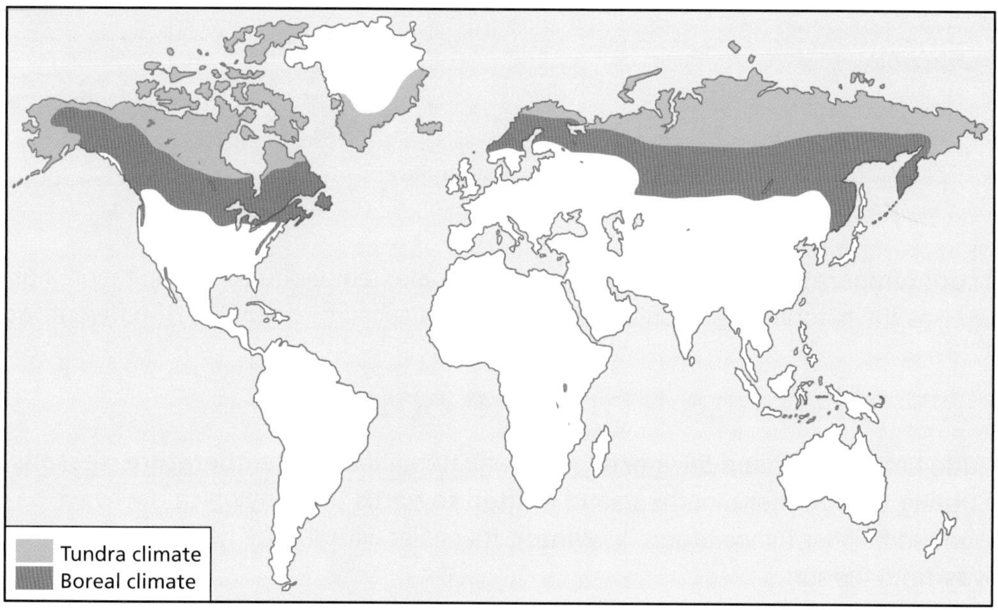

Figure 14.12 *Regions with a boreal or tundra climate*

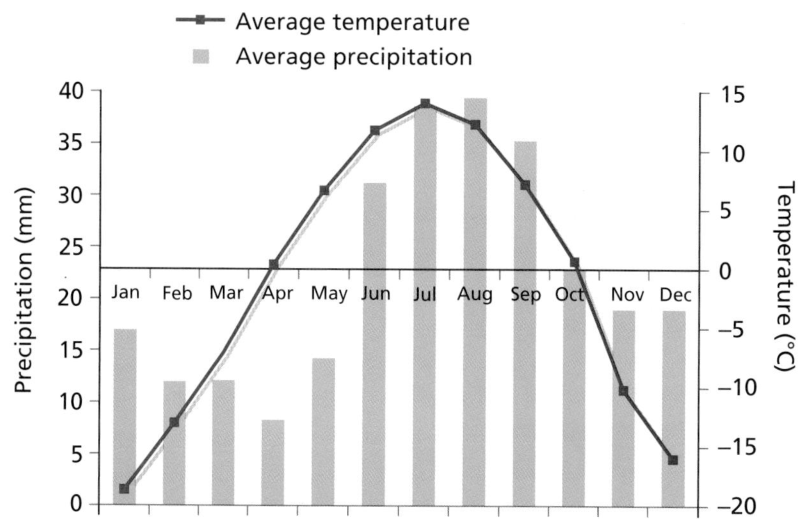

Figure 14.13 *Monthly average precipitation and temperature in the Yukon, Canada, which has a boreal climate*

NUMERACY ACTIVITY

Examine Figure 14.13. What is the annual daily mean temperature range? Which is the warmest month? Which month has the highest amount of precipitation?

PORTFOLIO ACTIVITY 14.1

Go to page 58 of your Portfolio to complete the template about a climate of your choice.

(i) Name one hot climate.
(ii) Name one temperate climate.
(iii) Name one cold climate.
(iv) What two characteristics can be used to describe any global climate?
(v) Compare the characteristics of a hot desert climate with those of the tundra climate.

- I can give examples of hot climates, temperate climates and cold climates.
- I can outline the main characteristics of each global climate type.

Factors influencing Ireland's climate

Learning Intentions

In this section, you will learn:

- the factors that influence Ireland's climate.

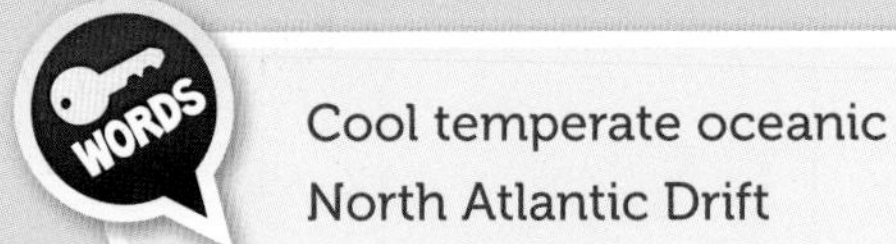

Ireland has a **cool temperate oceanic** climate. Ireland's climate (temperatures, precipitation, hours of daylight), as well as the natural vegetation and wildlife, is influenced by a number of different **factors**.

Latitude – distance from the equator

Ireland's **latitude** between **51° and 56° north** of the equator influences **temperature**, **seasons** and hours of **daylight**. During the **summer** months Ireland is **tilted towards** the sun, which is why we have longer hours of daylight and higher temperatures. In **winter**, it's cooler with shorter hours of daylight because we are **tilted away** from the sun.

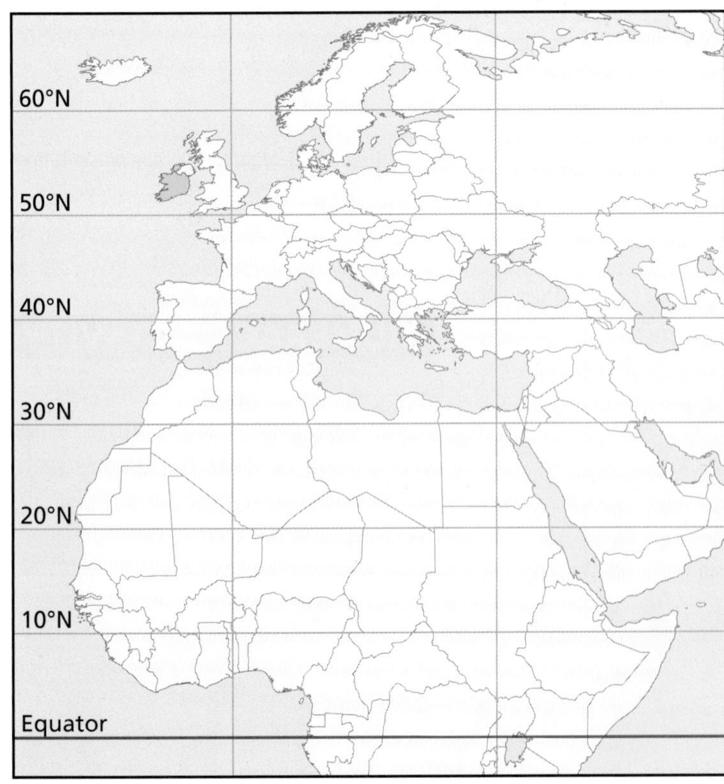

Figure 14.14 *Ireland's latitude*

Distance from the sea

Oceans and seas **heat** up and **cool** down more **slowly** than land. Areas **close to the sea** are **cooler** in the **summer** and **warmer** in the **winter** than inland areas. The average January temperature in **Cork** is 6 °C. In **Berlin**, which is at the same latitude, the average January temperature is 0 °C.

Atlantic ocean currents

Ocean **currents** are river-like **movements of water** through the ocean. They are caused by the **unequal heating** of the Earth. There are only **two types** of ocean currents – **warm** currents flowing from the equator and **cold** currents flowing from the poles.

The **North Atlantic Drift** is a warm current from the Gulf of Mexico. It keeps our **temperatures** warmer and influences **rainfall**. The eastern part of the country gets between 750 and 1,000 mm of rainfall each year, whereas the western part, which is closer to the warm current, gets between 1,000 and 1,250 mm. Mountainous areas can experience up to 2,000 mm of rainfall.

Prevailing winds

Ireland's prevailing winds are **south-westerly**. They bring **warm, moist air** from the **Atlantic** Ocean and contribute to the high amount of **rainfall** we experience in Ireland, especially in the mountainous areas of the west coast.

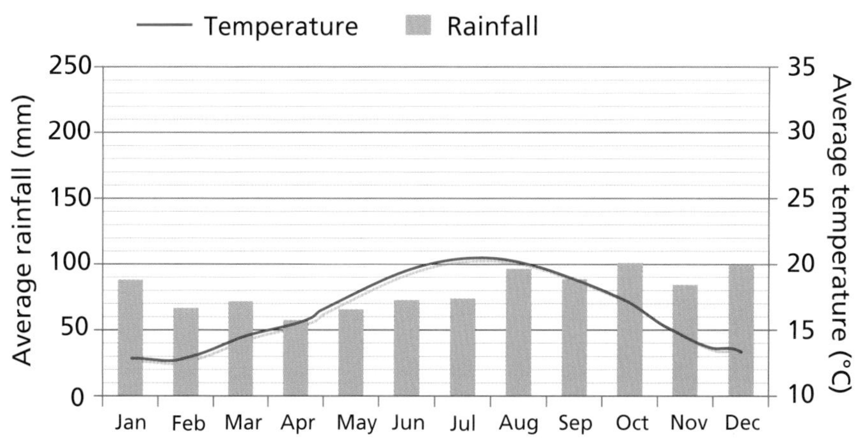

Figure 14.15 *Monthly average rainfall and temperature in Monaghan, Ireland, which has a cool temperate oceanic climate*

NUMERACY ACTIVITY

Examine Figure 14.15. What is the annual temperature range? Which month has the highest temperatures? Which month has the lowest rainfall?

 **(i)** Name the current that flows along the west coast of Ireland.

(ii) What is Ireland's prevailing wind?

(iii) Explain one reason why the west coast of Ireland gets more rainfall than the east coast.

(iv) How do currents affect the climates of places they pass by?

(v) Analyse the factors that influence why Ireland has a cool temperate oceanic climate.

I can explain the factors that influence Ireland's climate.   

Climate change

Learning Intentions

In this section, you will learn:

- about climate change
- how the greenhouse effect is causing global warming
- about the implications of climate change.

Greenhouse effect	Methane
Global warming	Nitrous oxide
Greenhouse gases	CFCs
Carbon emissions	Ozone layer
Carbon footprint	Drought
Deforestation	Desertification

Climate is constantly changing. We know that the world has gone through periods when the temperature was much warmer and much cooler than it is today. Evidence to support this can be found by studying **rocks** and **fossils** and analysing **pollen** found in ice that dates back thousands of years.

Our **glaciated** landscape tells us that Ireland was covered in ice during the last **ice age**, which ended around 10,000 years ago.

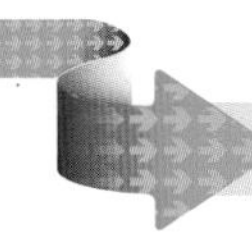

Go to Chapter 11 to learn more about glaciation in Ireland.

There are a number of natural causes for climate change, such as:

- Changing ocean current patterns
- Earth's changing orbit and tilt
- Volcanic activity blocking the sun.

However, the **hottest years** on record have all occurred **since 2000**, which tells us that the climate change that is occurring at the moment is **faster** than ever before. This is due to human activity and what is called the **greenhouse effect**.

Figure 14.16 *The effects of global warming: a dried-up reservoir in Thailand*

Work in pairs. Discuss what life might be like in Ireland in a hundred years' time if the temperature keeps increasing. How will it impact on our economic activities?

The greenhouse effect and global warming

We have already learned that the **atmosphere** is made up of various **gases**. We have also learned that the atmosphere is heated by the **sun**. Some of this heat is **absorbed** and the rest is **reflected** back into space.

Scientists believe that gases such as **carbon dioxide** and **methane** act like a blanket or **greenhouse** around the planet and **trap** some of the heat from the sun in the atmosphere. These **greenhouse gases** also absorb some of the solar radiation that is reflected back from the Earth's surface. This traps the heat and keeps it in the atmosphere.

These gases have always been present in the world's atmosphere. However, as we produce **increasing amounts** of greenhouse gases, more heat is being trapped in the atmosphere and **temperatures** are **rising**.

The Greenhouse Effect

CO_2 and other gases in the atmosphere trap heat, keeping the Earth warm.

Some sunlight that hits the Earth is reflected. Some becomes heat.

Atmosphere

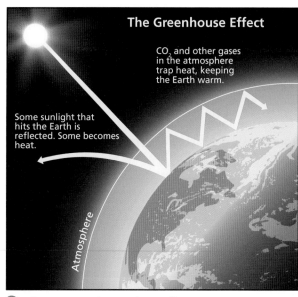

Figure 14.17 *The greenhouse effect*

Causes of global warming

The increase in the temperature of the Earth due to the greenhouse effect is called **global warming**. **Human activity** is largely responsible for the increase in greenhouse gases in the atmosphere.

- When we **burn fossil fuels** in our homes, in industry, in power stations and through various modes of transport such as cars and planes, gases such as **carbon dioxide (CO_2)** enter the atmosphere. These gases are sometimes called **carbon emissions** and the amount we produce as individuals is sometimes called our **carbon footprint**.
- **Trees** and other vegetation **absorb CO_2** and release oxygen (O_2) into the atmosphere. They act as a **carbon sink**, which is something natural or human-made that stores carbon. **Deforestation** is the removal of forests without replanting them and it is occurring at an alarming rate. The amount of **CO_2** in the atmosphere **increases** because there are **fewer trees** left to absorb it.
- The greenhouse gas **methane** is produced by **bacteria** that feast on decomposing organic matter when there is no oxygen present. This occurs in **landfills**, in **paddy fields** where rice is grown, in animal **manure** and as animals digest their food.

Figure 14.18 *Exhaust fumes from traffic*

DID YOU KNOW? The average Irish citizen releases 12.8 tonnes of CO_2 into the atmosphere each year.

Figure 14.19 *Deforestation in Borneo, Malaysia*

- As the global population increases, so too does the amount of cattle, rice production and waste. This, in turn, increases the amount of methane in the atmosphere.
- **Nitrous oxide** is produced when artificial fertilisers in the form of **nitrates** are used. This increases the greenhouse gases in the atmosphere.
- **Chlorofluorocarbons** or **CFCs** are the most dangerous of the greenhouse gases. These were used in **aerosol** cans, **foam** packaging and **refrigerators**. These gases have been phased out because of the damage they were causing to the ozone layer.

The **ozone layer** is a part of the lower atmosphere, which helps to filter out harmful **ultraviolet (UV) rays** from the sun. It is very important to wear sunscreen with UV ray protection to help avoid skin cancer.

ACTIVITY

Go to www.carbonfootprint.com to work out your carbon footprint.

Implications of climate change

- **Rising sea levels** will threaten low-lying land and the people who live and farm there.
- **Increasing temperatures** bring higher evaporation rates, which lead to **drought** and **famine** in some places such as the **Sahel** region of Africa as crops fail. Lack of vegetation cover causes soil erosion and **desertification** where land is turned into desert.
- **Weather** patterns will become **more extreme** with more regions suffering drought and flooding.
- The **skiing season** will be reduced or may even disappear altogether, which will affect the economies of mountainous areas.

Figure 14.20 *The effects of climate change: melting ice sheets*

- There will be **less meltwater** available for the production of **HEP** in places such as Norway and Italy.
- **Habitats** will be under threat and so will the **animals** that live in them as they struggle to adapt to new climatic conditions.
- There could be an increase in the number and length of **wildfires** due to rising temperatures.

Check out https://educateplus.ie/go/sea-levels. In groups, choose a country that will be affected by rising sea levels. Discuss how this might impact on the country you have chosen.

Figure 14.21 *The effects of climate change: forest fires*

Global warming and Ireland

The **Environmental Protection Agency** runs a climate change research programme which monitors climate change and the impact it has on Ireland. To date, the most obvious **signs** of global warming in Ireland are:

- Mean **temperature increase**
- **Fewer** days of **frost**
- Increase in **rain** in the north and west
- Longer **growing season**.

If global warming continues, there will be serious **environmental consequences**, including:

- Rising **sea levels**
- More intense and more frequent **storms**
- **Water shortages** in the summer.

How do you think global warming will impact on agriculture in Ireland? Discuss with your group.

Acting on climate change

Climate change **affects everyone** in every country on every continent in the world. Therefore, everyone needs to work together to **fight global warming**.

The **United Nations (UN)** held a conference in Paris on climate change in December 2015, where countries committed to take action against climate change. Each country that signed the **Paris Agreement** agreed to reduce their greenhouse gas **emissions**. However, in June 2017 the **USA withdrew** from the Paris Agreement because President Trump felt that it would damage the economy.

The UN has a set of global **priorities** that the whole world must focus on between 2015 and 2030. These are called the **Sustainable Development Goals** and they cover all sorts of global issues. Goal 13 is to take urgent action to **combat climate change** and its impacts.

All countries are encouraged to prepare for the problems climate change might bring. There are a number of steps that can be taken to prepare for the effects of climate change. Take a look at the poster on the right and make a list of the precautions we should be taking now.

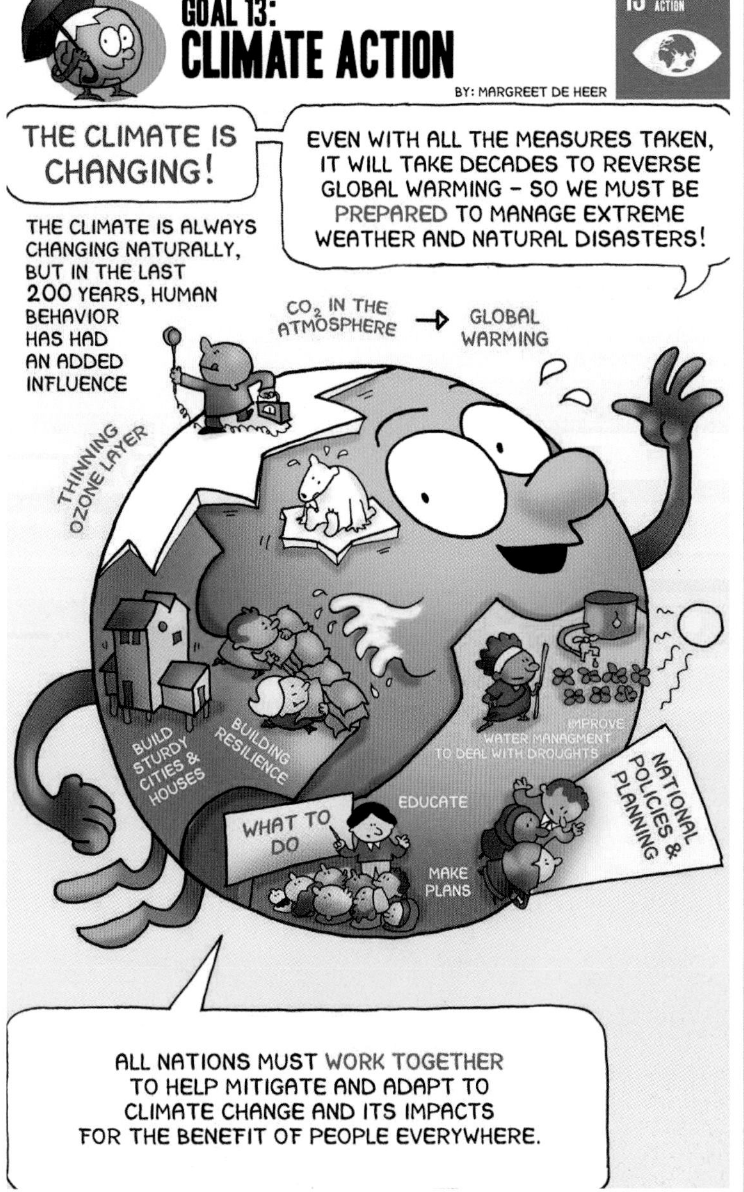

Figure 14.22 *Poster for Goal 13 of the UN's Sustainable Deleopment Goals*

In Ireland, we have committed to an 80 per cent reduction in greenhouse gases by 2050. Discuss ways that we can ensure we reach this target.

PORTFOLIO ACTIVITY 14.2

Go to page 59 of your Portfolio to complete the class charter on climate change.

(i) What is global warming?

(ii) How does burning fossil fuels cause global warming?

(iii) List three implications of climate change.

(iv) With the aid of a labelled diagram, explain the greenhouse effect.

- I understand the causes and implications of climate change.
- I can explain what is being done to tackle climate change.

REVISION

The ____________ is the common, average weather conditions across a large area of the Earth's surface over a long period of time. The ____________ of any climate is influenced by a number of factors. These include ____________, distance from the ____________ and ____________ winds and air masses. Locally, climate is influenced by ____________ and ____________. Global climates can be put into broad climatic ____________. ____________, hot desert and ____________ are examples of hot climates. Temperate climates can be found in the ____________-latitudes. ____________ and ____________ are examples of cold climates. Ireland has a cool ____________ oceanic climate. The North ____________ Drift influences Ireland's climate. There are natural and ____________ causes of climate change. The recent increase in world temperatures is called ____________ ____________. There are many ____________ of climate change, including ____________ and drought.

Sample Questions

1. **(i)** Name **one** hot climate.
   (ii) Name **one** temperate climate.
   (iii) Name **one** cold climate.
2. Factors affecting climate include:
   - Latitude
   - Distance from the sea
   - Prevailing winds and air masses
   - Altitude
   - Aspect

   Select any **three** of these factors and explain how each one affects climate.
3. Discuss **one** cause and **one** implication of climate change.

Sample Answers

1. (i) Hot desert climate
   (ii) Cool temperate oceanic climate
   (iii) Tundra climate
2. **Aspect**: Aspect is the direction a slope faces in relation to the sun. South-facing slopes in the northern hemisphere face the sun and are warmer than north-facing slopes that tend to be in the shade.

   Altitude: Altitude is height above sea level. The higher a place is above sea level, the colder it is. This is because the air is thinner in high altitudes and holds less heat. The temperature drops by about 1 °C for every 100 m increase in altitude.

   Latitude: Latitude is the angular distance of a place north or south of the equator. Areas closer to the equator are warmer than areas further from it. The equator is where the sun's energy is greatest. Because the sun is closest to the Earth here, its rays shine directly upon it and are concentrated on a smaller area. The further you travel from the equator, the cooler it gets because the sun's rays have a longer distance to travel and become slanted. As the heat is spread over a wider area, it is cooler and less intense.
3. Burning fossil fuels causes climate change. Gases such as carbon dioxide enter the atmosphere. These gases trap the heat from the sun like a blanket. As we increase the amount of greenhouse gases in the atmosphere we increase the amount of heat trapped by them and so the temperature rises.

   One consequence of climate change is rising sea levels. This will happen because ice caps and glaciers are melting as the global temperature rises. This will threaten low-lying areas and the people who live and farm there because they will be below the new sea level.

Short Questions

1. Look carefully at the climate map of Africa.

The climate type at **X** (shaded orange) is:

Cool temperate oceanic ☐

Hot desert ☐

Tundra ☐

Boreal ☐ [tick (✓) the correct box]

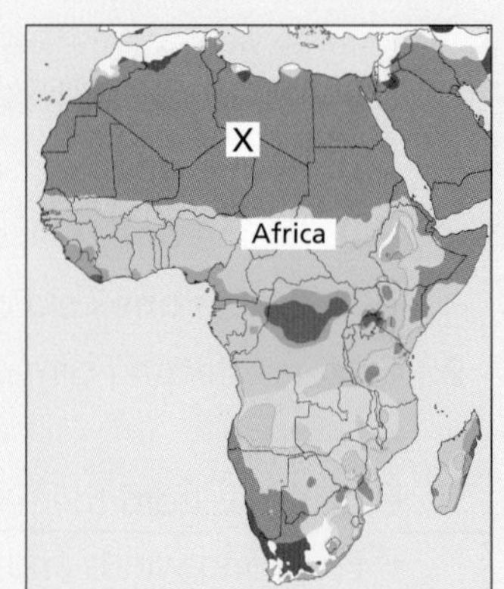

2. Ireland has a cool temperate oceanic climate. Name four factors that influence Ireland's climate

(i) ______________________________

(ii) ______________________________

(iii) ______________________________

(iv) ______________________________

3. Examine the graph below showing the monthly average rainfall and temperature in a region with an equatorial climate: the rainforest of Manaus, Brazil.

(i) Which month has the highest rainfall?

(ii) Which month has the lowest rainfall?

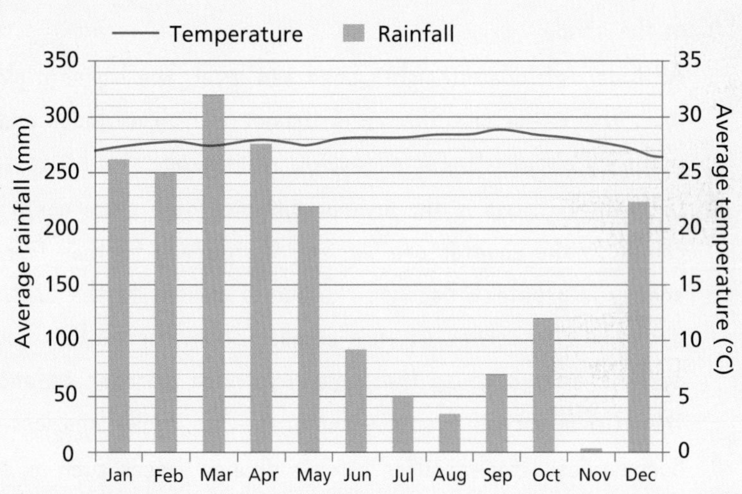

4. Examine the graph below showing the monthly average rainfall and temperature in a region with a savannah climate: the grasslands of Mali, Africa.

(i) What is the annual temperature range of the savannah?

(ii) Which month has the highest rainfall?

(iii) Which month has the lowest temperature?

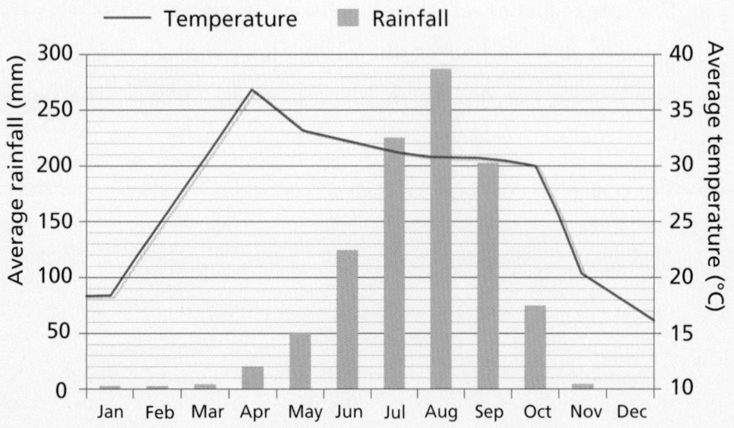

5. Examine the graph below showing the monthly average rainfall and temperature in a region with a hot desert climate: the Sahara Desert.

   (i) Which is the hottest month in the Sahara?

   (ii) What is the highest average monthly temperature reached?

   (iii) Which are the driest months?

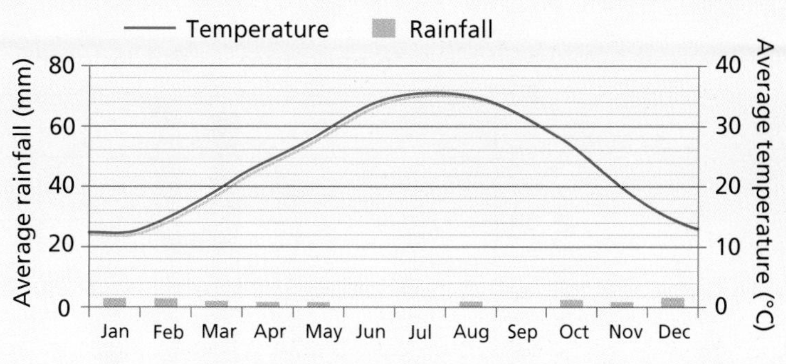

6. Examine the graph below showing the monthly average rainfall and temperature in a region with a tundra climate: Baker Lake, Canada.

   (i) What is the annual temperature range?

   (ii) Which is the warmest month?

   (iii) In which month does most of the snow fall?

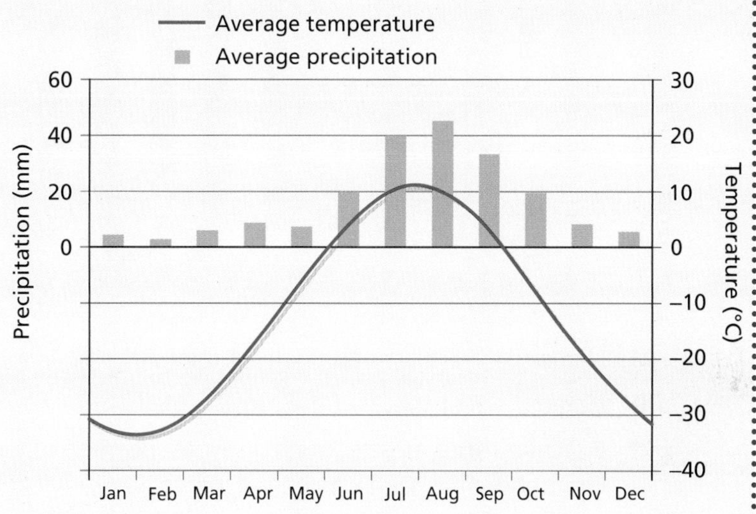

Long Questions

1. Explain why places near the equator are hotter than places near the poles. (If it helps, you can draw a diagram as part of your answer.)

2. Examine the map which shows part of Europe.

   (i) State which of the **two** places, **A** or **B**, has warmer summers and colder winters and explain why.

   (ii) Explain how the prevailing wind labelled **X** would affect the climate of the lands over which it blows.

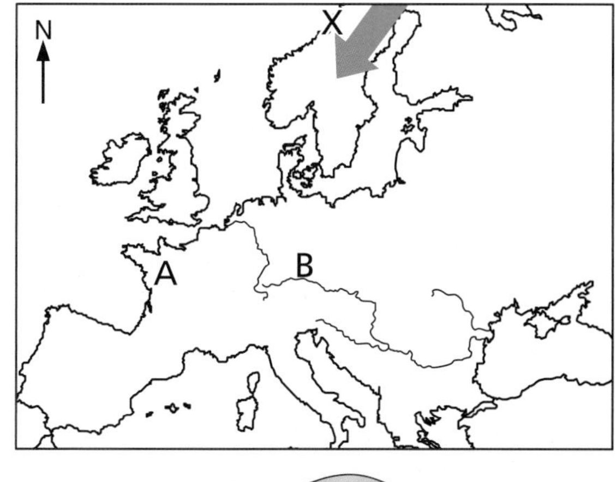

3. The diagram shows a mountainous area in Europe.

   Explain **two** reasons why you would expect the place labelled **X** on the diagram to be colder than the place labelled **Y**.

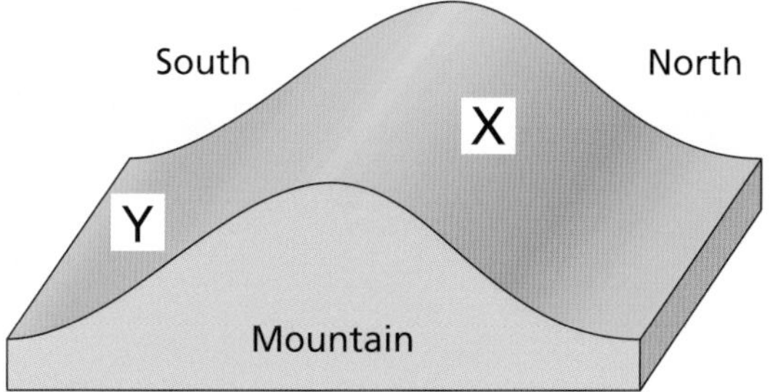

4. Some African countries suffer because climate change may result in a shortage of precipitation. The graph shows how rainfall levels changed over time in Somalia between 2001 and 2012.

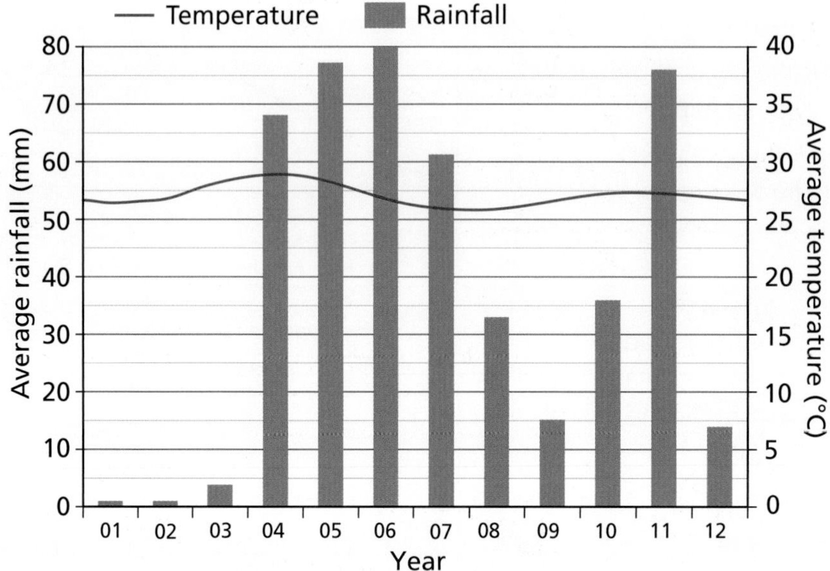

(i) Name the year that had the least rainfall.

(ii) Name the year that had the most rainfall.

(iii) Describe **three** effects which a severe shortage of rain might have on the development of a country such as Somalia.

5. Examine the map which shows the location of three of the world's climatic regions.

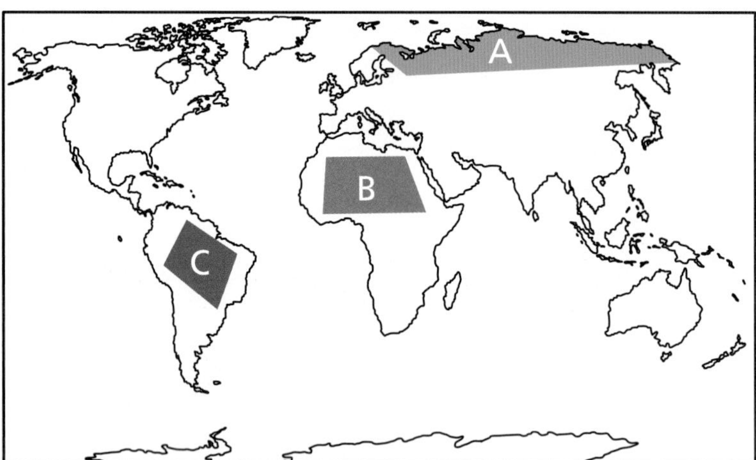

(i) Name the type of climate at each of the locations **A**, **B**, and **C**.

(ii) Explain the characteristics of Ireland's climate.

Visual Summary

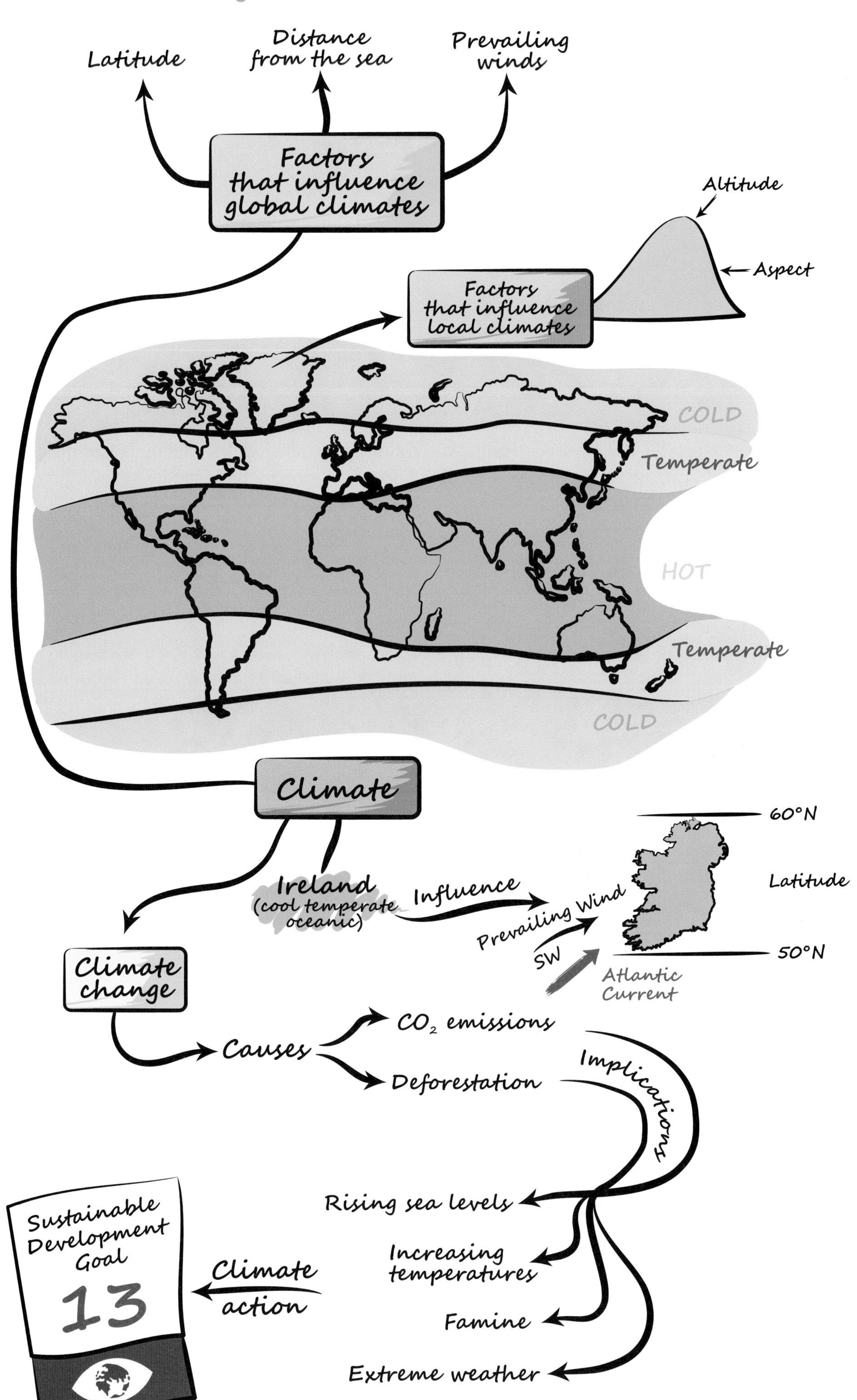

Latitude
Distance from the sea
Prevailing winds
Factors that influence global climates
Altitude
Aspect
Factors that influence local climates
COLD
Temperate
HOT
Temperate
COLD
Climate
60°N
Latitude
Ireland (cool temperate oceanic)
Influence
Prevailing Wind
SW
50°N
Atlantic Current
Climate change
CO_2 emissions
Causes
Deforestation
Implications
Rising sea levels
Increasing temperatures
Famine
Extreme weather
Sustainable Development Goal 13
Climate action

Geographical Skills for Third Years:

Ordnance Survey, aerial photograph and satellite imagery skills

In this chapter, you will learn:

- the aerial photograph and Ordnance Survey map skills you will need for Third Year
- the satellite image skills you will need for Third Year.

ICE-BREAKER ACTIVITY

Work in groups of four. Do you know what a satellite image is? Discuss with your group and write down an answer.

Go to https://educateplus.ie/go/satellite-timelapse and zoom in on your area. You will see how satellite images can show how an area changes over time. Write down three of the biggest differences from the first satellite image to the last satellite image.

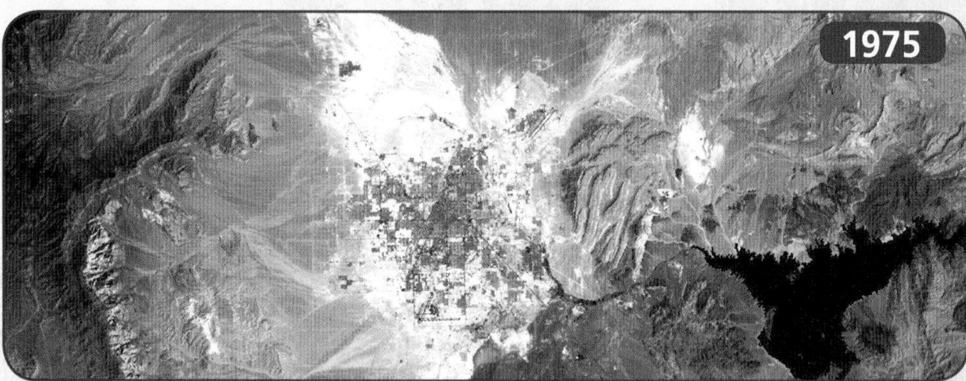

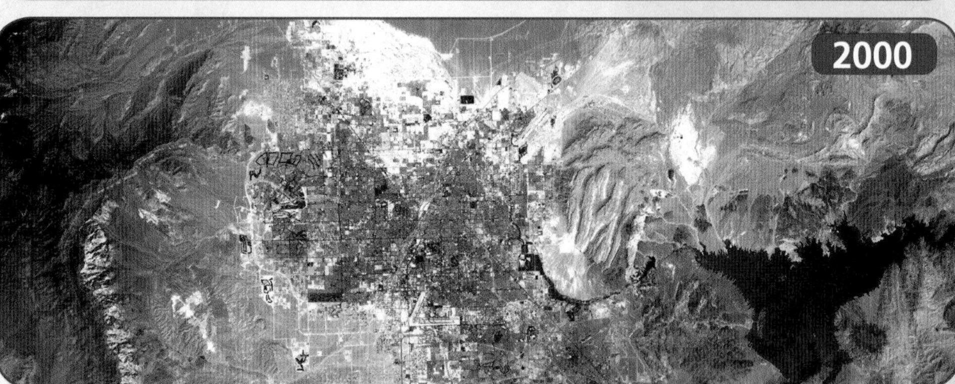

Figure 15.1 *Three satellite views of Las Vegas, Nevada, USA, showing the rapid growth of the city between 1975 and 2014*

This chapter will teach you some of the skills that you will need in your third year of Geography. Your class can dip in and out of this chapter throughout the year. Don't forget to go back and revise the skills you learned in Chapter 1 and Chapter 7. The skills you will need in Third Year are broken into three groups:

1. **Comparing aerial photographs and Ordnance Survey map skills**
2. **Aerial photograph skills**
3. **Satellite imagery skills.**

Comparing Ordnance Survey maps and aerial photographs

Learning Intentions

In this section, you will learn:

- how to compare Ordnance Survey maps and aerial photographs
- how to identify what direction the camera was pointing when an aerial photograph was taken.

Landmark

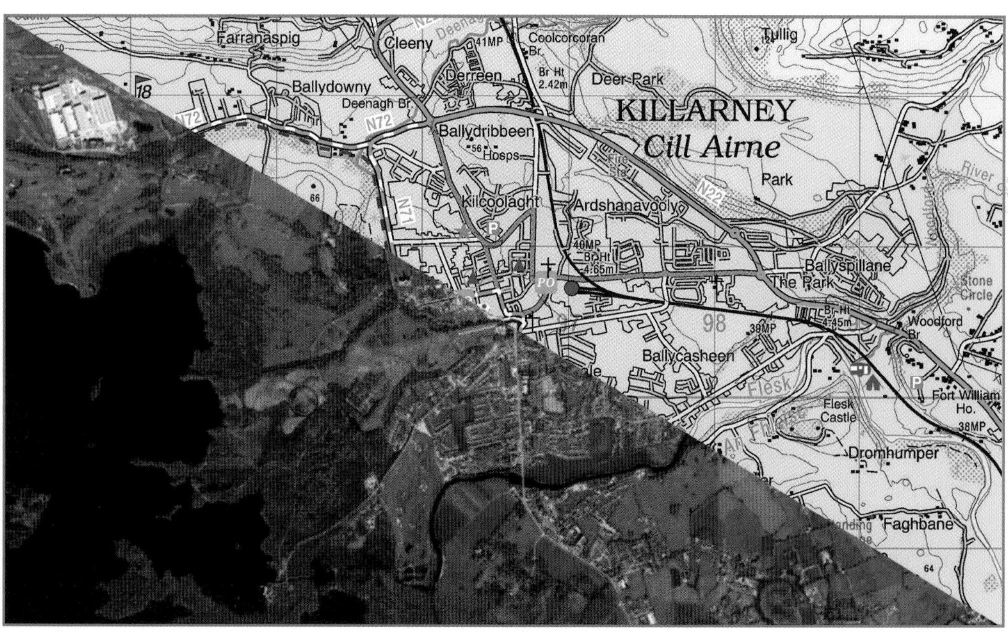

Figure 15.2 *Killarney in a vertical aerial photograph and on an OS map*

You wrote down the advantages and disadvantages of Ordnance Survey maps and aerial photographs during the Ice-Breaker activity in Chapter 7. Can you remember your group's answers?

Take a look at the table on the next page for more information on the differences between Ordnance Survey maps and aerial photographs.

	Ordnance Survey maps	Aerial photographs
Distance	Distance is exact.	Distance can only be estimated.
Location	Location can be pinpointed with grid referencing.	Location can only be given generally. It is usually given in the context of something else, e.g. the school is **south** of the church.
Legend	The use of symbols helps to identify land use.	There is no legend given so it can be hard to identify features. However, they can often be recognised quite easily.
Names	Names of places and features are given.	No place or feature names are given.
Area	Can show a large area of land.	Can show only a small area of land.
Size	Building size cannot be seen.	Building size can be seen. However, use can sometimes be unclear.
Buildings	It is not possible to be sure of the state of a building or antiquity.	An aerial photograph taken close enough can show whether or not a building or antiquity is in good repair.

Imagine you are going to Inis Oírr in the Aran Islands on holiday. Do you think it would be better to bring an OS map or an aerial photograph of the area? Explain your answer.

Direction of camera

It is possible to work out what direction the camera was pointing when an aerial photograph was taken by comparing the aerial photograph with an Ordnance Survey map. To do this:

1. Pick out features or significant **landmarks** that are evident on both: for example, a bridge, cathedral or port.
2. Pick two landmarks on the photograph and draw a straight line between them.
3. On the Ordnance Survey map identify the same two landmarks and draw a similar straight line between them.
4. Line up the photograph with the map so that the features match up.
5. By comparing the two lines you should be able to work out the direction of the aerial photograph.
6. The Ordnance Survey map shows us the direction of north, so by comparing the two, we can work out what direction the camera was pointing.

Top Tip

When answering questions on aerial photographs or Ordnance Survey maps you need to back up your statement with **evidence** from the photograph or map. Be very careful if the map or photograph you are given is an area with which you are familiar. Any personal knowledge you have will not be acceptable in your answer.

Remember **S–E–E:** make a **Statement**, give **Evidence**, and **Explain**.

- I understand the key differences and similarities between OS maps and aerial photographs.
- I can identify the direction a camera was facing for an aerial photograph using an OS map.

Aerial photograph sketch maps

Learning Intentions

- how to draw a sketch map from an aerial photograph.

Drawing a sketch map of an aerial photograph is similar to drawing a sketch of an Ordnance Survey map. Follow these **steps** when drawing a sketch map:

1. Always use a **pencil**. Colouring pencils are useful when adding features.
2. Draw the **frame**, making sure it is the same shape as the photograph you are sketching. The photograph will be either portrait or landscape.
3. Measure the width of the photograph in centimetres and divide it by two. Then measure the height of the photograph and again divide it by two. These will be the dimensions of your frame.
4. Give your sketch map a **title**. This will be the name of the place you are drawing.
5. **Divide** both the photograph (see Figure 15.3) and sketch into eight sections. Use a marker for the photograph and a light pencil for your own sketch.
6. Draw in any **physical features** on the photograph like a river, lake, coastline or upland area.
7. Then draw the outline of the **features** you are asked to show and name them.
8. Place a **key** to the sketch outside the frame, labelling the features you have put in your sketch.
9. Keep your sketch **simple**. Only put in the features you are asked to put in. (Most of these will be land uses or functions that you learned about Chapter 7: Geography Skills 2.)
10. Be as **neat** as possible.

Example: On the next page is an aerial photograph of Cobh, and a sketch map based on it. The sketch shows:

- The coastline
- A recreational area
- A church
- A residential area
- A marina.

Figure 15.3 *An oblique aerial view of Cobh, Co. Cork*

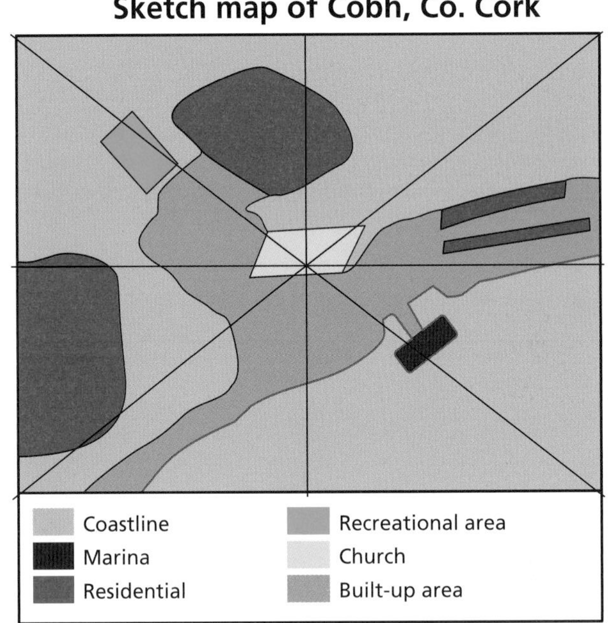

Figure 15.4 *Sketch map based on Figure 15.3*

Remember: **S**tatement–**E**vidence–**E**xplain = **S–E–E**

Example: Describe one land use that you can see on the aerial photograph of Cobh.

One of the land uses I can see on this aerial photograph is agriculture. There are green fields in the right background of the photograph. This could be pasture for cows and dairy farming. I can also see that crops have been cut in the fields in the centre background and left background. Farming is clearly an important economic activity in this area.

Figure 15.5 *An oblique aerial view of Carlow*

ACTIVITY

Look at the photograph of Carlow town above. Draw a sketch map of Carlow town showing the following:

- A river
- A bridge over the river
- A church
- A car park
- An area of terraced housing

ACTIVITY

What time of the year do you think the photograph of Carlow was taken? Give a reason for your answer.

Look at the OS map and aerial photograph of Dublin, and then answer the questions on page 280.

Figure 15.6 *OS map of central Dublin*

Figure 15.7 *Aerial photograph of central Dublin*

1. Draw a sketch map of the aerial photograph of Dublin and include the following:
   (a) River
   (b) Multi-storey car park
   (c) Green area
   (d) Main route way and bridge
   (e) Commercial area.
2. Comment on any differences in the information you can obtain from the OS map of Dublin compared with the aerial photograph, in relation to:
   (a) land use in the city
   (b) traffic management and public transport.
3. The photograph of Dublin shows the city centre and O'Connell Bridge. Using the OS map, can you work out what direction the camera was facing when the photograph was taken?

 I can draw a sketch map of an aerial photograph. 

Satellite imagery

Learning Intentions

In this section, you will learn:

- how to interpret and understand satellite imagery.

Satellite image
Satellite

Satellite images are images of the Earth taken by satellites.

Satellites are often hundreds of kilometres above the ground. They are like eyes in the sky. Satellite images can provide us with extra **information** on many of the topics we cover in our Geography course. For example, they can be used to study weather, deforestation, urban sprawl, volcanic eruptions, land use, types of agricultural land and many more topics.

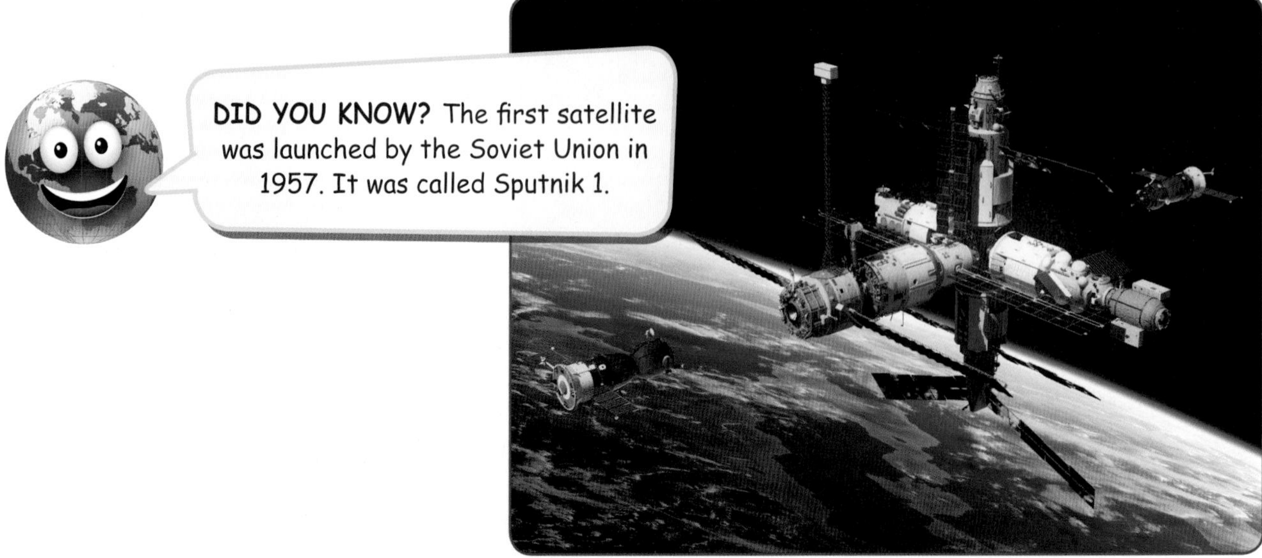

DID YOU KNOW? The first satellite was launched by the Soviet Union in 1957. It was called Sputnik 1.

Figure 15.8 *A satellite*

Here are some examples of satellite images.

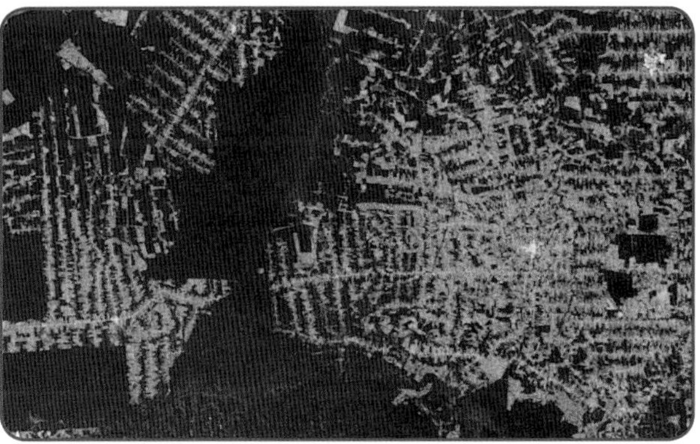

Figure 15.9 *Deforestation*

Figure 15.10 *Volcano*

Figure 15.11 *Hurricane Ophelia*

Figure 15.12 *Delta*

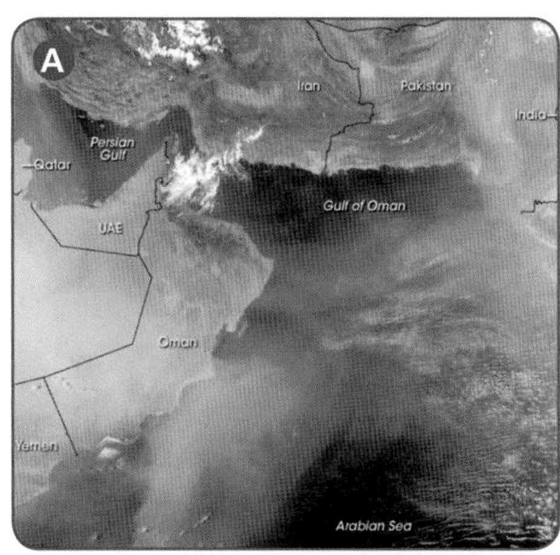

B

C

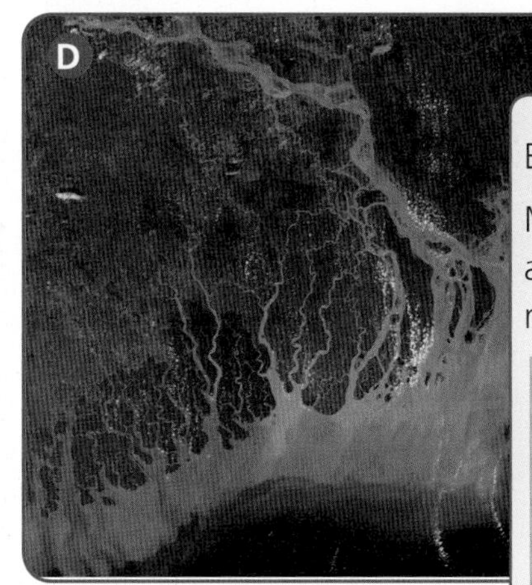

ACTIVITY

Examine the satellite images above.

Match each of the letters **A**, **B**, **C** and **D** with the description that best matches it in the table below.

Description	Letter
Delta	
Open-cast mining	
Dust storm	
Forest fire	

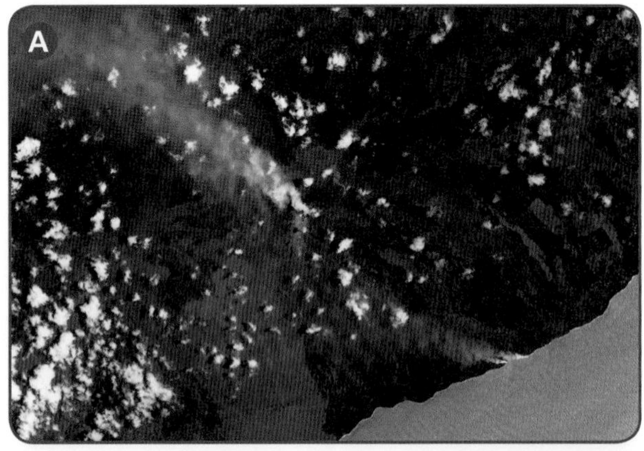

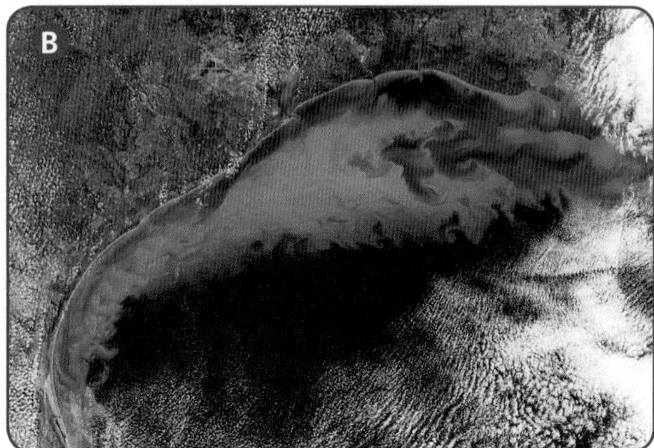

ACTIVITY

Examine the satellite images above.

Match each of the letters **A**, **B**, **C** and **D** with the description that best matches it in the table below.

Description	Letter
The Aswan Dam	
A hurricane	
A recent lava flow	
Coastal sediment	

On 31 August 2017 there were 1,738 active satellites orbiting the Earth, of which 803 were from the USA. Thousands more have lived out their useful life and become space debris.

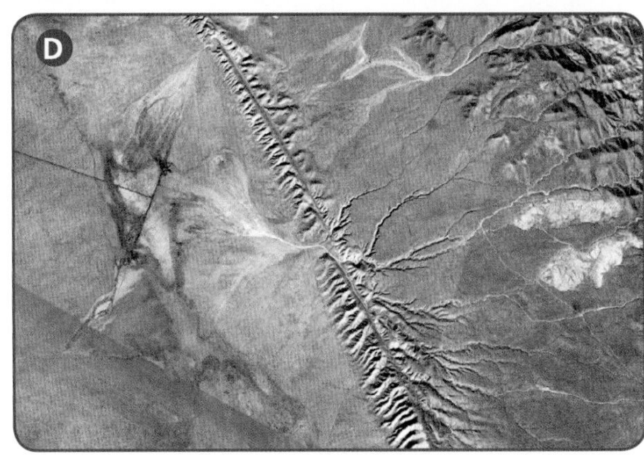

ACTIVITY

Examine the satellite images above.

Match each of the letters **A**, **B**, **C** and **D** with the description that best matches it in the table below.

Description	Letter
Oil slick in the Gulf of Mexico	
Flooding in Pakistan, 5 August, 2010	
Erupting volcano in Alaska	
San Andreas Fault in California	

I know how to interpret satellite imagery.   

Soil:
A vital natural resource

In this chapter, you will learn:

- what soil is and how it is formed
- about the different types of Irish soils (including the soil in your local area)
- about the relationship between soil and vegetation
- how soil influences economic activities
- how people interact with a natural resource like soil
- about the sustainable exploitation of soil.

ICE-BREAKER ACTIVITY

(a) Work in groups of four. Fill a third of a glass jar with a sample of soil from your area. Look at your soil sample and discuss the following questions with your group:
- What colour is the soil sample?
- What is the soil sample made up of?
- What does the soil feel like?

Record the group's findings in your copybook.

(b) Look at the soil texture chart (Figure 16.3). Do you know which soil type your sample belongs to? Record your answer in your copybook.

Soil

Learning Intentions

In this section, you will learn:
- that soil is made up of five main ingredients
- that soil texture refers to the percentage of sand,
- silt and clay particles in the soil
- about soil profiles
- that rainfall can cause leaching of minerals in soils.

Mineral	Bedrock
Humus	Horizon
Nutrients	Plant litter
Texture	Leaching
Soil profile	Hardpan

Soil is a **thin layer** of material on the Earth's surface. **Plants** have their roots in the soil and cannot grow without it. People and animals use plants as a food source, so soil is a very important **natural resource**.

Soil composition

Soil is made up of **five** main ingredients:

1. Mineral matter

2. Air

3. Water

4. Humus

5. Living organisms

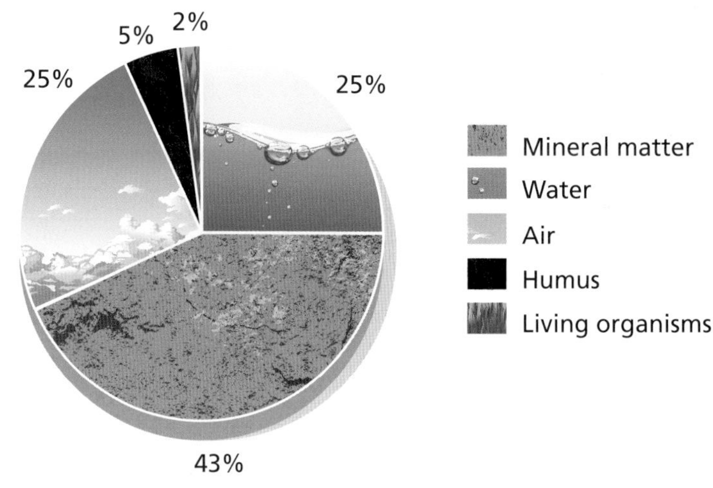

Figure 16.1 *Ingredients of soil*

1. Mineral matter

Mineral matter is the **main ingredient** in soil. It is made up of **rock particles** that have been **weathered** and **eroded**. It includes stones, sand, silt and clay. It provides the **minerals** that help plants to grow.

2. Air

Air fills the **spaces** between the particles of rock in the soil. Air contains **oxygen** and **nitrogen**. **Plants** need oxygen and nitrogen to grow. **Living organisms** need them to survive in the soil.

3. Water

Water helps to **bind** the soil together. Minerals **dissolved** in water are **absorbed** through the roots of plants and help them grow.

4. Humus

Humus is a dark, **jelly-like substance** that forms when plants and animals **decay** and rot. Humus **binds** the soil together and provides **nutrients** that make the soil **fertile**.

5. Living organisms

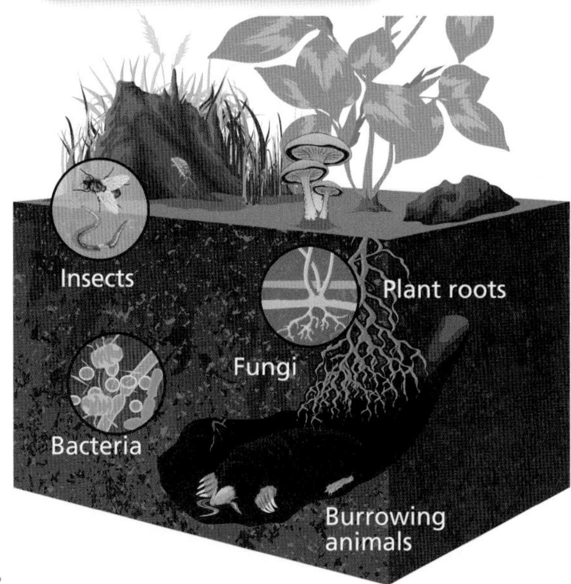

Soil is home to many types of living things, such as **earthworms** and various **bacteria**, **fungi**, **insects** and **burrowing animals**. These living organisms break down plant and animal remains (**organic matter**) to form **humus**. They also mix up the soil to make it easier for water and air to pass through.

Figure 16.2 *Living organisms in the soil*

Soil texture

Soil texture is what the soil **feels** like. The **particles** in the soil belong to three groups – **sand**, **silt** and **clay**. The texture of the soil is determined by the **percentages** of sand, silt and clay in the soil. Different minerals produce soils of different texture. If, for example, the mineral matter comes from weathered or eroded sandstone then the soil will have a sandy texture. The particles in **sand** are the **largest**, those in **clay** are the **smallest**.

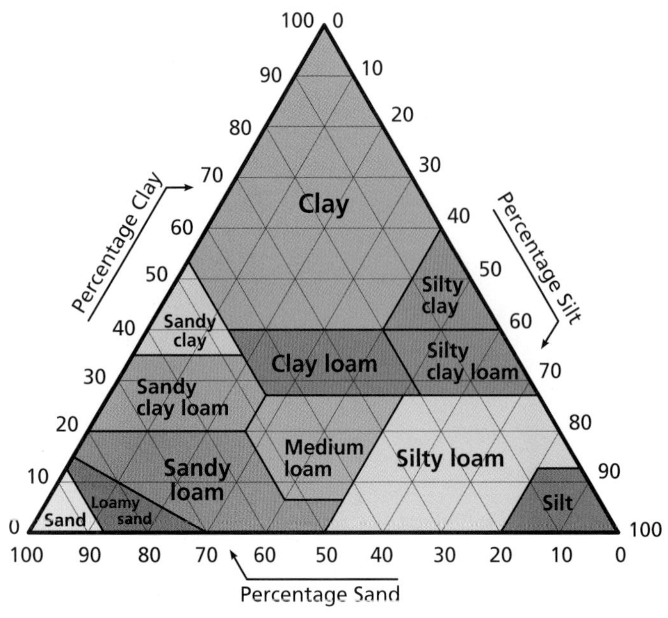

NUMERACY ACTIVITY

Take a look at Figure 16.3.

(i) What percentage sand, silt and clay is a medium loam soil?

(ii) Which soil is 30% clay, 10% sand and 60% silt?

Figure 16.3 *Soil texture chart*

Soil profiles

A soil profile is a **cross-section** of the different **layers** of soil – from the surface down to the **bedrock**.

Each layer is called a **horizon**. You can tell the horizons apart by looking at a number of things, including **content**, **texture** and **colour**.

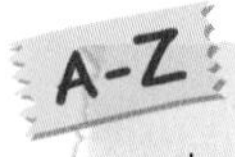

Bedrock: the bottom layer of solid rock which is usually covered with broken-down rock and soil.

O horizon

This layer contains **organic matter**. Leaves and rotting vegetation are called **plant litter** and this provides the **humus** for the soil.

A horizon

This is the **upper layer** of the soil and is called the **topsoil**. This is where most of the **organisms** in the soil live. It is usually **darker** than the other layers because it has the highest **humus** content. It is the most **fertile** part of the soil.

B horizon

This layer is called the **subsoil**. It is **lighter** in colour than the A horizon because there is **less humus** here. This layer has **more stones** because it is located closer to the bedrock and because it is protected from weathering and erosion by the A horizon.

C horizon

This is the **bedrock** or **parent material**. The lower layer consists of solid rock but the upper section may be broken down into **rock particles**. In some instances the parent material can actually be a different rock deposited on top of the bedrock by **glacial deposition**.

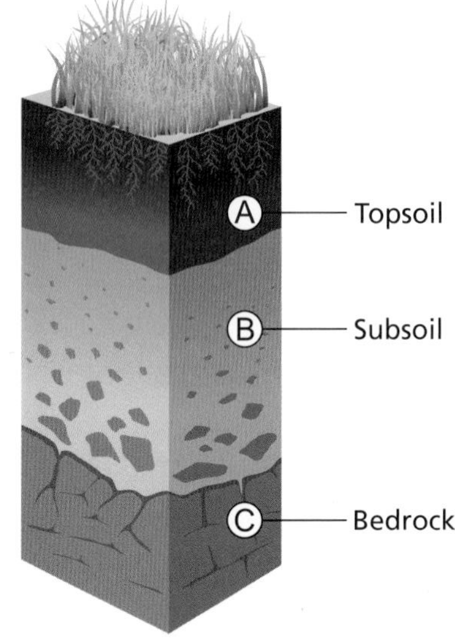

Figure 16.4 *Soil profile*

Go to Chapter 11, pages 184–187, to learn more about glacial deposition.

Leaching

When rain falls, water passes through the soil, **washing** minerals, humus and nutrients from the A horizon down into the **B horizon**. This process is called **leaching**.

Most **plant roots** are located in the **A horizon**, and leaching can sometimes interfere with their growth if nutrients are washed beyond their reach.

Sometimes, in extremely wet conditions, minerals build up at the bottom of the A horizon. They can become cemented together to create **hardpan**. This is an **impermeable layer** that water is unable to flow through, and so the soil above the hardpan becomes **waterlogged**.

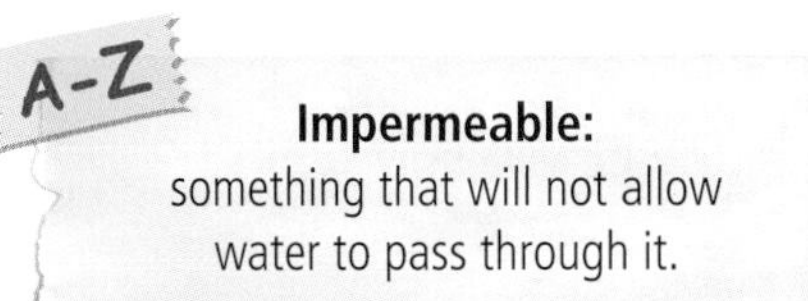

Impermeable: something that will not allow water to pass through it.

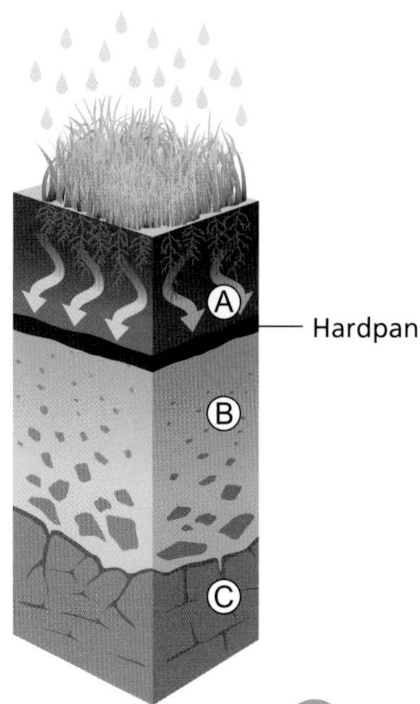

Figure 16.5 *Hardpan*

Figure 16.6 *Soil profile showing where nutrients have been leached out of the grey layer*

(i) Name the five ingredients of soil.
(ii) What percentage of a typical soil sample is water?
(iii) What is humus?
(iv) Explain the term leaching.
(v) Explain how a hardpan is formed.
(vi) Draw and label a soil profile in your copybook.

- I can explain what the five ingredients of soil are.
- I understand what soil texture is.
- I can draw and label a soil profile.
- I can explain leaching.

Soil: A vital natural resource

Soil formation

Learning Intentions

In this section, you will learn:

- about the factors that influence soil formation.

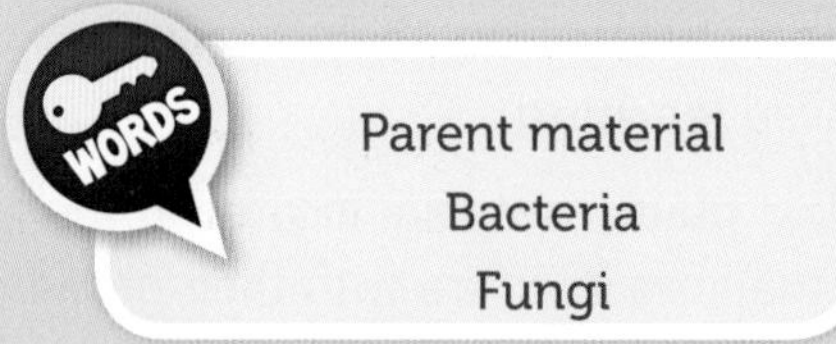
WORDS
Parent material
Bacteria
Fungi

Soil formation is influenced by a number of different **factors** which work together over a long period of time. These factors include:

- **Climate**
- **Parent material**
- **Living organisms**
- **Landscape/relief**
- **Vegetation**
- **Time**

The **interaction** of these factors leads to the formation of different **soil types**.

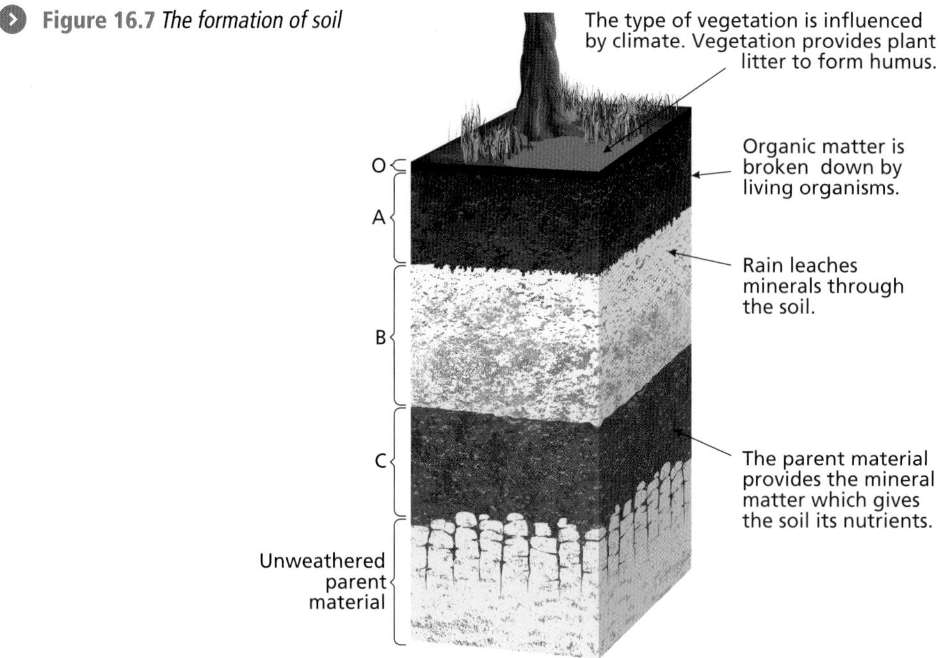
The type of vegetation is influenced by climate. Vegetation provides plant litter to form humus.
O
A
Organic matter is broken down by living organisms.
Rain leaches minerals through the soil.
B
C
The parent material provides the mineral matter which gives the soil its nutrients.
Unweathered parent material

Figure 16.7 *The formation of soil*

Climate

The rate at which parent rock is broken down to form mineral matter by **weathering** depends on the amount of **rainfall** and the **temperature**. Too much rainfall can lead to **leaching**. **Freeze-thaw** action occurs in areas with cold climates, and **chemical weathering** helps to break down the parent rock in areas with hot climates.

Climate also has an impact on the type of **vegetation** that grows there. The type of vegetation controls the breakdown of living organisms and the formation of **humus**.

Parent material

Parent material refers to the **type of rock** that is broken down by weathering to form soil. The **minerals** from the broken-down rock provide **nutrients** for the soil. Soils that form on limestone are **fertile**.

ACTIVITY

With your class:

(i) Explain why soils that form on the bedrock of limestone are very fertile.

(ii) Research the reasons why the acidity of the soil is important.

Living organisms

Living micro-organisms in the soil, such as **bacteria** and **fungi**, break down plant litter in the O horizon. This creates **humus** and makes the soil more **fertile**.

Animals, such as **earthworms** and burrowing animals, break up the soil and allow for the movements of water, humus and air through the soil. When these organisms die, they add **nutrients** to the soil.

Landscape/relief

Soils in **upland** areas are generally **thin** because of **mass movement**. They are also **poorly drained** because of heavy rainfall in upland areas.

Soils in **lowland** areas are **deeper**, well drained and generally more **fertile**. They are rich in **humus** because there is more plant litter and living organisms.

Vegetation

Vegetation in the area creates plant litter, which breaks down into **humus**. Humus makes soil **fertile**.

Areas with **deciduous** trees have more plant litter than areas with coniferous trees. That means that areas with deciduous trees have **more fertile** soils.

Time

It can take up to **four hundred years** for **one centimetre** of soil to form because the process is so slow. As soil is a **non-renewable** resource, we must make sure that we do not overexploit it.

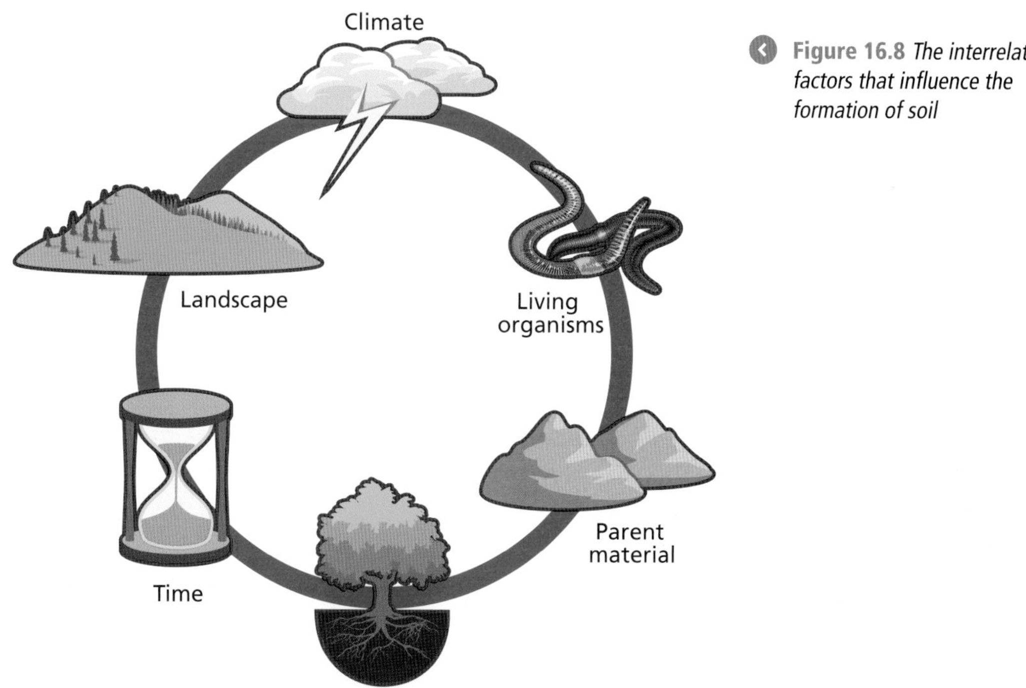

Figure 16.8 *The interrelated factors that influence the formation of soil*

 **(i)** List the factors that influence soil formation.

 **(ii)** Explain what is meant by the term 'parent material'.

 **(iii)** Explain how climate influences soil formation.

(iv) Explain why soil is a non-renewable resource.

 I understand the factors that lead to soil formation.  

Irish soil types

Learning Intentions

In this section, you will learn:

- about the different soil types in Ireland
- about the soil in your local area.

Brown earth
Loam
Deciduous
Podzol
Coniferous
Gley
Peat

There are **four** main soil types in Ireland and they can be seen on the map.

- Brown earth soils
- Podzol soils
- Gley soils
- Peaty soils

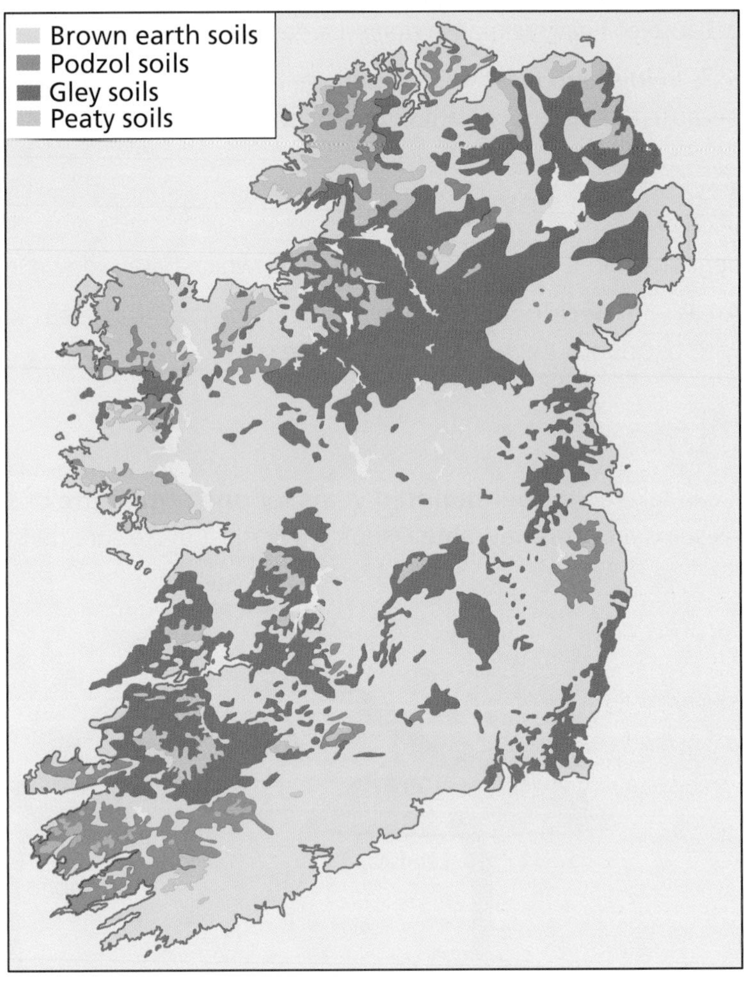

Figure 16.9 *Soil types of Ireland*

ACTIVITY

Look at Figure 16.9. Which soil type is in your area?

Brown earth soils

Brown earth soils are the **most common** soil types in Ireland. They are mostly found in **lowland** areas in the Irish midlands. Brown earth soils developed on the **boulder clay** that was deposited at the end of the last Ice Age. They contain fairly even amounts of sand, silt and clay and have a **loam** soil texture.

Loam:
an even mixture of sand, silt and clay. Loam soils have a soft, even texture and they break up easily. They are ideal for growing a variety of crops.

Figure 16.10 *Brown earth soil*

Deciduous forests developed on this soil, and the plant litter from the leaves that fell from the trees every year provided material for the formation of **humus**. This is why brown earth soil has a **dark colour**. Very **little leaching** occurs in these areas, so the soil remains **fertile**.

Over time, the forests were cleared for **agricultural** land. The land is now used for intensive **arable** and **pastoral** farming. Farmers add **nutrients** to the soil in the form of **manure** and **fertilisers** because the level of plant litter is no longer as high as it was when these soils were formed.

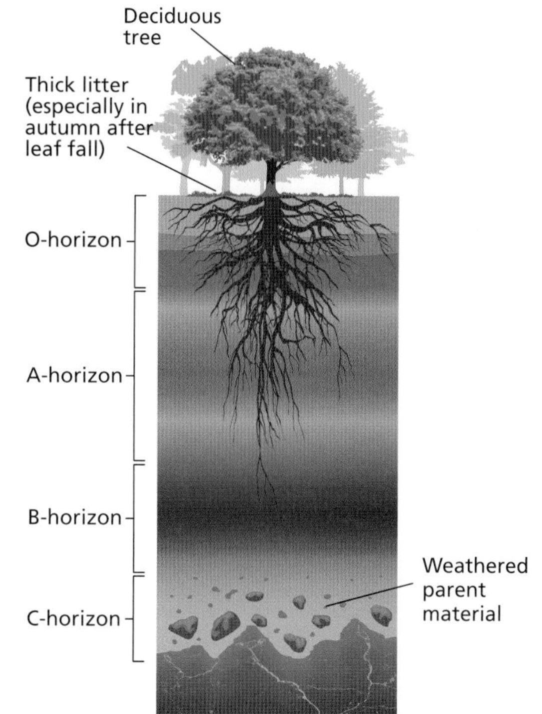

Figure 16.11 *Soil profile of a brown earth soil*

Podzol soils

Podzol soils are found on the floors of **coniferous forests** in cold and wet areas. Coniferous forest floors have little plant litter, and therefore small amounts of humus. The **cold** and **damp** conditions mean that there is also little earthworm activity.

Heavy rainfall causes a lot of **leaching**, and nutrients are washed through the A horizon, often creating a **hardpan**. This gives the A horizon a grey colour.

Podzols are quite **infertile** and **acidic**. They tend to be **heavy** soils and their texture has more **clay** particles than sand and silt. They are found in **poorly drained** upland areas of Co. Galway and Co. Cork.

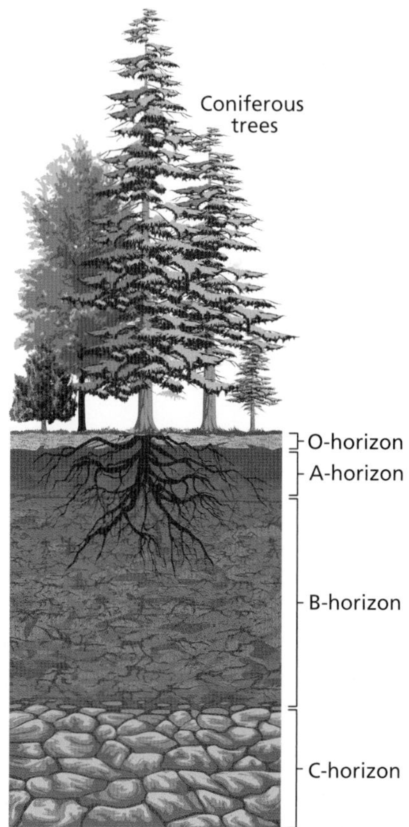

Figure 16.12 *Soil profile of podzol soil*

Gley soils

Gley soils are **grey** in colour. They develop where the bedrock, or the clay above it, is **impermeable**. They are **sticky** and **waterlogged**. This makes it difficult to grow crops on the land and so it is used only for **pastoral** farming.

Figure 16.13 *Gley soil*

Peaty soils

Peaty soils are **dark** in colour. They develop in **cold, upland** areas with **high rainfall**, and **lowland** areas with **poor drainage**. These soils are **waterlogged** and full of organic matter that has not broken down. They are a valuable source of **fuel** and are found in blanket and raised **bogs**.

Figure 16.14 *Peaty soil*

NUMERACY ACTIVITY

Work in groups of four and do the following:

(a) Fill a third of a glass jar with soil from your area. Break up any big clumps.

(b) Add water slowly and fill the jar until three quarters of the jar is full.

(c) Put the lid on and make sure it is secured tightly.

(d) Shake the jar and allow it to sit for a few days. What does it look like?

(e) Measure the depth of the soil in the jar. Then measure each layer. Work out the percentage of each layer.

(f) Check the diagram (Figure 16.3) on page 286 to see what soil type it is.

Did you correctly guess what soil type was in your area when you did the first activity in this chapter?

PORTFOLIO ACTIVITY 16.1

Go to page 64 of your Portfolio to complete the Soil Investigation activity.

ACTIVITY

Draw a table in your copybook, and use it to show the main differences between brown earths and podzol soils. Use the following headings: colour; texture; particle size; material present; location; what the soil is used for. Make sure you remember these differences!

(i) What is the most common soil type in Ireland?

(ii) Explain two differences between brown earth soils and podzol soils.

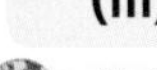

(iii) Where in Ireland could you expect to find peaty soils?

(iv) Which soil type is most suitable for farming? Why?

I understand the various types of soil found in Ireland.

Natural vegetation and soil

Learning Intentions

In this section, you will learn:

- how soil influences vegetation and how vegetation influences soil.

Natural vegetation
Soil conditions
Acidity
Lime

Natural vegetation refers to any plants or trees that grow on their own, naturally, without any form of human interference. The natural vegetation of any **region** of the Earth's surface is related to the **climate** in that region.

The type of vegetation is influenced by **soil conditions**, and soil conditions are in turn influenced by the **vegetation** growing on them

Figure 16.15 *Fields in Tipperary*

The influence of soil on vegetation

Soil influences the type of vegetation that grows in it in a number of ways:

Depth

- **Deep** fertile soils have the ability to support a wide variety of vegetation because they have a **high nutrient content**.
- **Shallow** infertile soils are more **limited** in the type of vegetation that they are able to support. Coniferous forests are often planted in such areas.

Acidity

- Some plants, such as **rhododendrons**, grow in areas with **acidic** soil.
- However, many plants do not grow in areas with acidic soil. Farmers spread **lime** on the soil to **reduce its acidity** and make it more fertile.

Drainage

- **Clay** soils can become **waterlogged** easily and farmers find it difficult to cultivate them.
- **Sandy** soils are **well drained** and have the ability to support a wide range of vegetation.

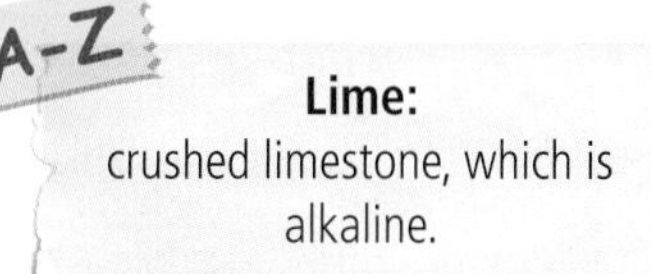

Lime:
crushed limestone, which is alkaline.

The influence of vegetation on soil

Vegetation also influences soil in a number of ways:

Plant litter

- Vegetation provides the **plant litter** to make **humus**. Brown earth soils formed under **deciduous** forests are rich in humus and **fertile**. Podzol soils formed under **coniferous** forests are **infertile**.

Soil erosion

- Vegetation **binds** the soil and **protects** it from soil erosion and mass movement. When this cover is **lost**, the soil is vulnerable and **erosion** occurs.

Leaching

- Vegetation acts as an **umbrella** and reduces the impact of heavy rain on the soil. This **reduces** the effects of leaching. Where **leaching** does occur, in areas such as the tropical rainforests, some trees have very shallow roots to access the minerals in the A horizon before they are leached down through the soil.

Figure 16.16 *Soil erosion due to lack of vegetation cover*

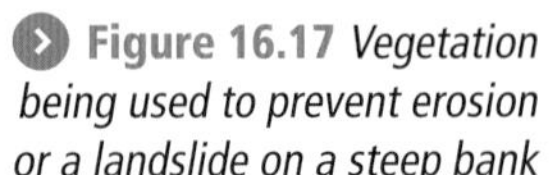

Figure 16.17 *Vegetation being used to prevent erosion or a landslide on a steep bank*

 **(i)** Explain the term 'natural vegetation'.

 **(ii)** How do farmers deal with soil that is too acidic?

 **(iii)** Explain how vegetation cover reduces the rate of leaching and soil erosion.

 I understand how soil and vegetation influence each other.   

Human interference with soil

Learning Intentions

In this section, you will learn:
- how human activities can lead to soil erosion
- about the sustainable exploitation of soil as a natural resource.

Deforestation	Semi-arid
Reforestation	Nomadic
Over-cropping	Raised bog
Monoculture	Blanket bogs
Cash crop	Biomass
Overgrazing	Biodiversity
Desertification	Cut-away bog

Soil is a very important **natural resource** and many economic activities could not take place without it. As with any natural resource, **over-exploitation** can be a problem. The biggest threat to the economic activities associated with soil is **soil erosion**. The main causes of soil erosion are **deforestation** and **intensive farming** methods.

Deforestation

Deforestation is when forest land is changed to **non-forest land**. Trees are removed for **economic purposes** (so the wood can be sold). The land that has been cleared is then used for other purposes, often for **agriculture**. This has two major effects:

1. The removal of vegetation also removes **plant litter**, which is the source of humus. This means that the soil loses some of its **fertility**.
2. The removal of the vegetation cover leaves the soil **exposed** to wind and rain, which causes soil **erosion**. The lack of vegetation cover can lead to **flooding** in lowland areas and **mass movement** in upland areas during periods of heavy rainfall

The simple solution to this problem is **forest management**. Controlled removal of trees and replacing trees **(reforestation)** will greatly reduce the impact of deforestation.

Figure 16.18 *Deforestation and soil erosion*

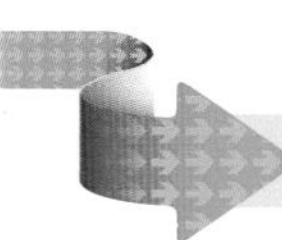

Go to Chapter 4, pages 64–66, to learn more about forestry in Ireland.

Intensive farming

Over-cropping

Over-cropping occurs when crops are **continuously** grown on the land. This means that **nutrients** are constantly being **removed** from the soil. The soil eventually loses its fertility and becomes **exhausted**. Soil should be given a chance to recover and **regain** its nutrients before more crops are planted.

Monoculture is practised in many areas, especially poorer countries. Monoculture is the growing of one single crop type, usually a **cash crop** such as coffee or cotton. It means that the same nutrients are taken from the soil over and over again. This results in the soil becoming **infertile**.

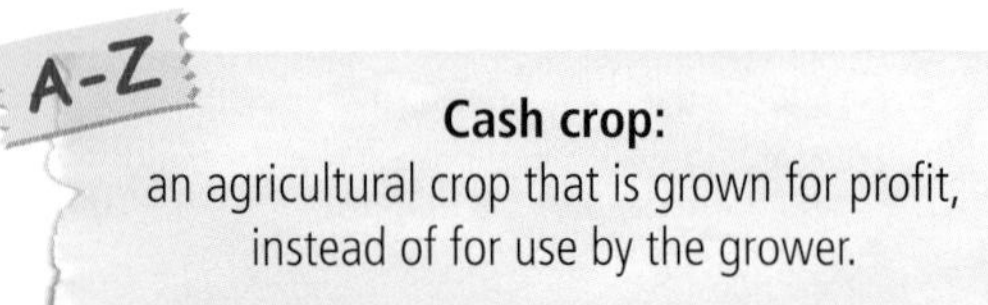

Cash crop:
an agricultural crop that is grown for profit, instead of for use by the grower.

Careful **management** and **crop rotation** will overcome these problems.

Overgrazing

Overgrazing occurs when vegetation is exposed to **intensive grazing** for long periods of time, or when **too many** cattle or sheep graze an area of land. Roots are destroyed and the soil is left bare and **exposed** to wind and rain. This causes **soil erosion**.

Changing farming practices is the most important solution to desertification, and farmers sometimes need educating about the best practices.

Figure 16.19 *The effects of overgrazing*

Solutions to desertification

There are a number of actions that can slow down and stop desertification:

- **Trees** can be planted to replace those that were cut down. This is called **reforestation**. It shelters the soil and reduces soil erosion.
- Changing **farming practices** can reduce the pressure on the soil and allow it to recover.
- Reducing the **number of animals** also reduces pressure on the soil.
- Digging **deeper wells** can provide much-needed water to support vegetation.
- **Irrigation schemes** can be put in place to increase the productivity of the land.

Go to https://educateplus.ie/go/desertification to watch a video on desertification. Discuss the video in groups of four. What was it about the video that affected you most?

CASE STUDY

Desertification: the Sahel

Desertification occurs where **land is turned into desert**. It occurs in the **semi-arid** areas that border the world's major deserts. The **Sahel** region in Africa borders the Sahara Desert.

Semi-arid areas:
dry places that receive very little rainfall (under 50 cm each year).

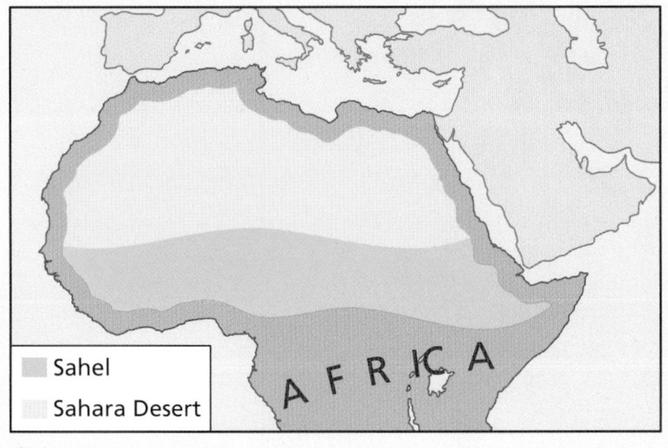

Figure 16.20 *The Sahel region*

Figure 16.21 *The Sahel in Burkina Faso*

Causes of desertification

Desertification is caused by a combination of **climate change** and **human activity**.

Climate change

Global warming has had a negative impact on the Sahel region of Africa.

- There is less rain in the Sahel and rainfall there is **unreliable**. Sometimes it does not come at all.
- There are also higher **evaporation rates** due to the high temperatures.
- These factors have led to a number of **droughts** and **famines** in the region.
- Vegetation has died and now the soil is even **less fertile**.
- In addition, rivers and waterholes have dried up, leaving **no source of water**.

Human activity

Agriculture in the Sahel was traditionally **nomadic**. However, the rapid **increase in population** in recent times means that the demand for food has grown. This has led to more **intensive farming** and increased pressure on the land.

A-Z

Nomadic:
moving in groups from place to place in order to find grazing for their animals.

- Farmers have increased their herd numbers, leading to **overgrazing**. This destroys the roots of what vegetation there is and the soil becomes **infertile**.
- Farmers have started growing **cash crops**, such as coffee, for export, instead of traditional crops that are more suitable for the region.
- When trees and shrubs are cut down for **fuel**, the soil is left exposed and **soil erosion** occurs.

Results of desertification

Desertification is causing serious problems in the Sahel region of Africa.

- Grassland has been changed into desert, forcing people to **migrate** and put pressure on the land to which they relocate.
- The soil is **no longer fertile** and is unable to support agriculture. This results in **crop failure** and the death of millions of animals due to the lack of food and water.
- **Famine** has forced millions of people to live in **refugee** camps, where they struggle to survive.

CASE STUDY

Bord na Móna: sustainable exploitation of Ireland's peat bogs

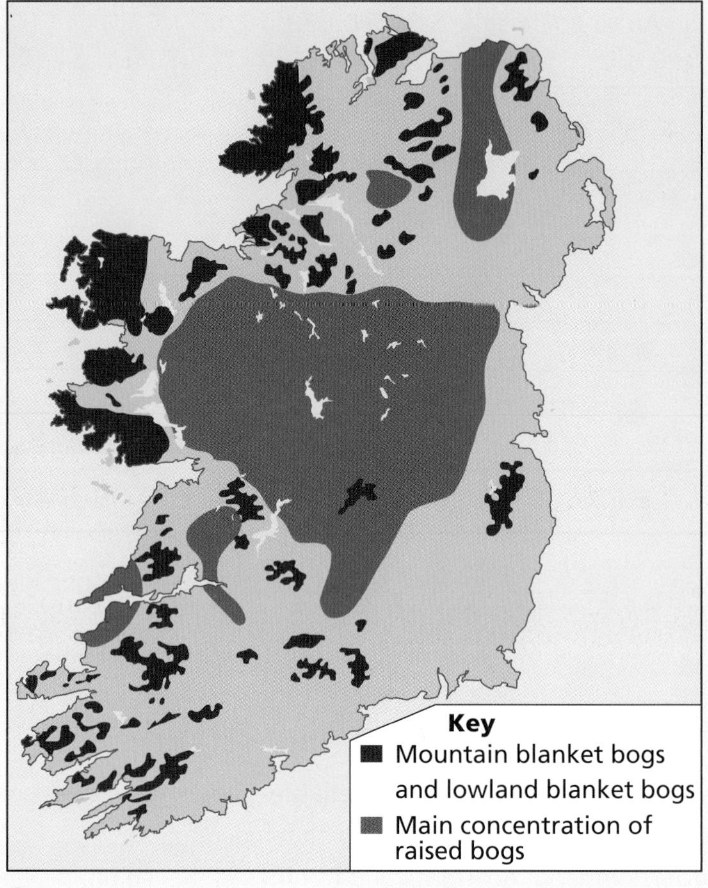

Figure 16.22 *The two types of bog in Ireland*

Peat is a **non-renewable natural resource** that has been exploited in Ireland for hundreds of years. It has been a valuable source of **heating** and **energy**. We have **two types** of peat bogs in Ireland.

Raised bogs

- Found mostly in the midlands of Ireland
- About 8 metres deep
- Owned and harvested by families and industries

Blanket bogs

- Found mainly in western counties
- About 3–4 metres deep
- Mostly owned and harvested by families

Traditionally, the turf was cut using a ***sleán***, and many summer days would be spent harvesting the **turf**. The turf would then be dried out and brought home for the winter.

In 1946, **Bord na Móna** was established by the government to exploit and harvest peat on an industrial scale. Since then, 50,000 hectares of bogland under its control have been harvested, and burned at three **power stations** to generate **electricity**. That is an area about twice the size of the Burren.

Figure 16.23 *Sleán*

However, as peat is a **non-renewable resource** this rate of exploitation is **unsustainable**. Because of this, Bord na Móna will cease to extract peat for energy production in **2030**. Instead, it will focus on renewable energy sources such as **wind**, **solar** and **biomass** energy. It will also work with ecologists to restore the bogs and increase the **biodiversity** of these habitats.

Biomass:
a fuel made from organic materials (e.g. sawdust and agricultural waste). It is a renewable and sustainable source of energy. It can be used to generate electricity.

Biodiversity:
a term used to describe the variety of life found in a particular habitat. A lot of variety is usually a sign of a healthy habitat.

VIDEO LESSON

Watch this video about Bord na Móna and then answer the questions below:

https://educateplus.ie/go/bord-na-mona

(a) What does Bord na Móna hope to achieve by 2030?

(b) How many wind farms do they intend to build?

(c) How much land will be assigned a land use other than harvesting peat?

(d) Name three types of renewable energy mentioned in the clip.

Why bogs are ideal locations for the production of renewable energy

When the peat has been removed from bogs they are called **cut-away bogs**. Cut-away bogs are **ideal locations** for wind farms, solar panels and growing crops for biomass energy production.

- The land is **flat** and therefore easily **accessible**.
- The exposed landscape means there is **no shelter** from the wind.
- There are few **residential** areas nearby, so there would be little objection to the construction of a wind farm or solar energy panels.
- The existing **power stations** previously run off peat could be **adapted** to use renewable energy.
- The existing **light railways** could be used to access the wind farms and solar panels.

Figure 16.24 *Wind farm on a bog in Caithness, Scotland*

 **(i)** Name the two types of peat bog in Ireland.

 **(ii)** Explain the term 'deforestation'.

 **(iii)** How can intense farming practices cause soil erosion?

(iv) Suggest two ways to avoid soil erosion.

- I can explain the impact humans have on soil.
- I understand the need for sustainable exploitation of soil.

REVISION

Soil is a thin layer of ________________ on the Earth's surface in which plants have their ________________. It is a very important ________________ ________________.

Soil is made up of five main ingredients: ________________ ________________, ____________, ________________, ________________ and ________________ ________________. Soil ________________ depends on the amount of sand, ____________ and clay in the soil.

A ____________ ________________ is a cross-section of the different ________________ of soil, from the surface down to the ________________. Each layer is called a ________________. When rain falls, ________________ from the A horizon are washed down into the __________ ________________. This process is called ________________.

The most common soils in Ireland are the ________________ ________________ soils. These soils form under ________________ forest and are ________________ soils.

Podzol soils form under ________________ forests and leaching often creates a ________________ between the A horizon and the B horizon.

Plants and trees that grow naturally are called ________________ ________________. ____________ influences vegetation and ________________ influences soil. Soils are affected by people through ________________ and ________________ farming methods that lead to ____________-________________ and ________________.

Questions & Answers

Sample Questions

1. Examine the diagram of a soil profile. Name the layers labelled X, Y and Z.
2. Describe the composition of any **one** soil you have studied.

Sample Answers

1. X = A Horizon; Y = B Horizon; Z = C Horizon
2. The soil I have studied is brown earth soil.

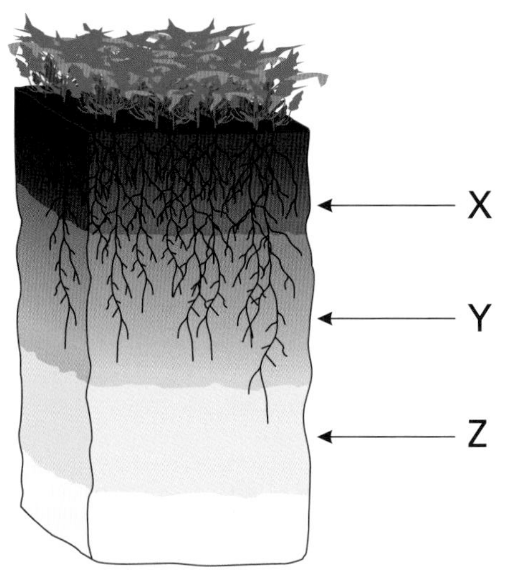

Brown earth soils have a high humus content. This is because they formed in areas where there was deciduous forest. When the leaves fall off the trees, they provide plant litter for the soil. This rotting vegetation is broken down by the organisms in the soil to make a dark, jelly-like substance called humus. Humus binds the soil and provides nutrients that make the soil fertile.

Brown earth soils are home to many types of living things, such as earthworms and various bacteria, fungi and insects. These living organisms break down the organic matter to form humus, and mix up the soil to make it easier for water and air to pass through. They make the soil more fertile.

1. Choose **three** terms from the box to fill the gaps in the extract below.

leaching	humus	podzols
micro-organisms	mineral particles	hardpans

The breakdown of plant litter into __________________ helps to fertilise soil. Processes such as __________________ may damage soil fertility by causing nutrients to seep below the reach of plant roots. __________________ are a type of soil commonly found in damp highland areas in Ireland.

2. The divided bar chart shows the composition of soil.
Label the pie chart, using the information on the divided bar.

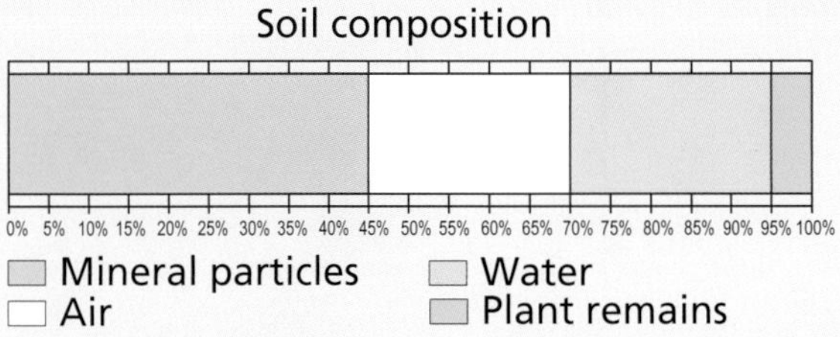

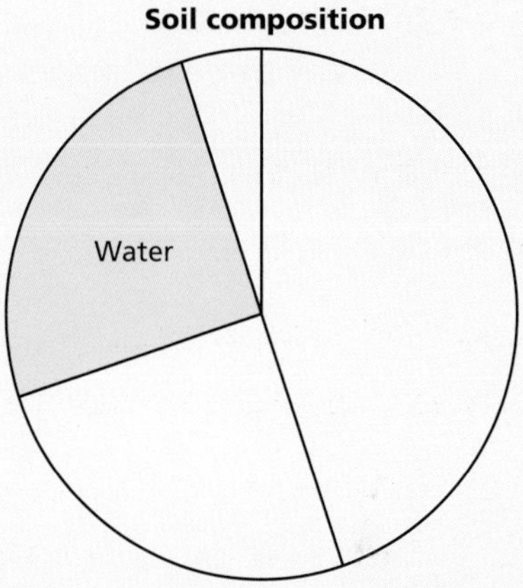

3. Plant litter provides soil with:

Rock particles ☐
Moisture ☐
Humus ☐
Podzols ☐ [tick (✓) the correct box]

4. Leaching is:

Removing vegetation by the spread of deserts ☐
Bringing water to irrigate dry land ☐
When plant nutrients and minerals are washed deep into the ground and plant roots cannot reach them ☐
Creating electric power from running water ☐ [tick (✓) the correct box]

5. This diagram shows a typical soil profile.
The feature shown at **X** is:

Bedrock ☐
Humus ☐
Hardpan ☐ [tick the correct box]

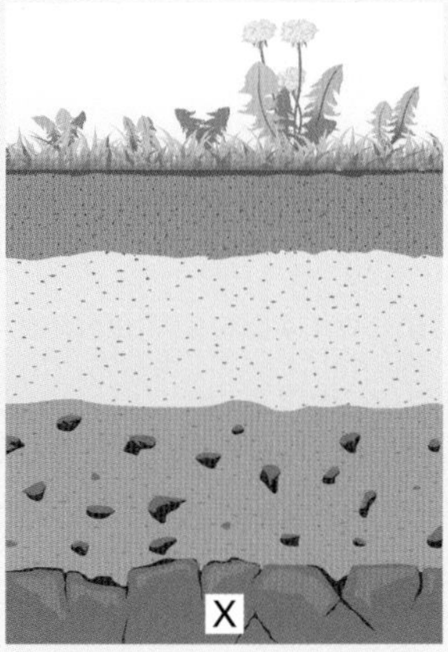

Long Questions

1. Describe the importance of any **three** of the following in the composition of soil:
   - Mineral matter
   - Water
   - Air
   - Humus
2. Explain the term leaching. How does leaching have a negative impact on vegetation growth?
3. Briefly explain how **three** different factors influence the formation of soil.
4. Examine the map, which shows some of Ireland's principal soil types.
   - **(i)** Identify the most common soil type in the south-east of Ireland.
   - **(ii)** Choose **two** Irish soil types and describe any **three** differences between them.

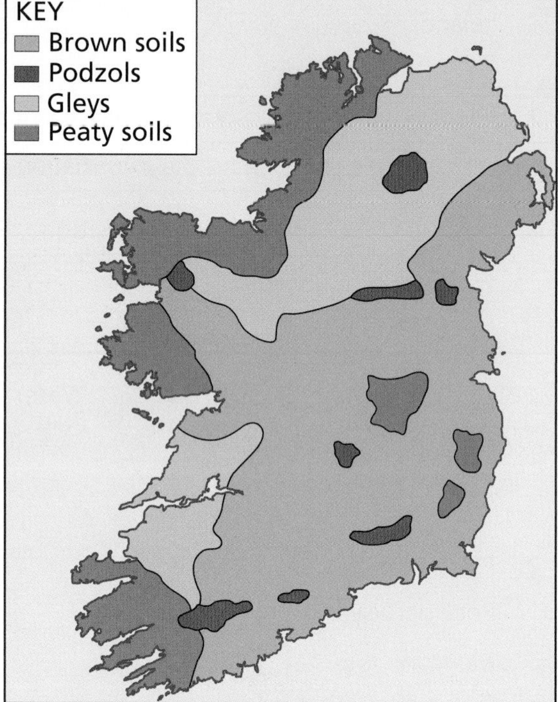

5. 'Soil influences the type of vegetation that grows in an area and the vegetation influences the soil.' Discuss this statement with reference to soil types you have studied.
6. Describe **three** ways that humans cause soil erosion.
7. **(i)** Explain **two** ways soil is important to humans.
   (ii) 'Soil erosion and desertification can occur as a direct result of human activity.' Suggest **three** things that could be done to reduce the impact of human activity on soil erosion and desertification.
8. **(i)** Why is the exploitation of peat by Bord na Móna no longer sustainable? Give **two** reasons for your answer.
   (ii) Explain **three** reasons why the peat bogs owned by Bord na Móna make suitable locations for the production of renewable energy.

Visual Summary

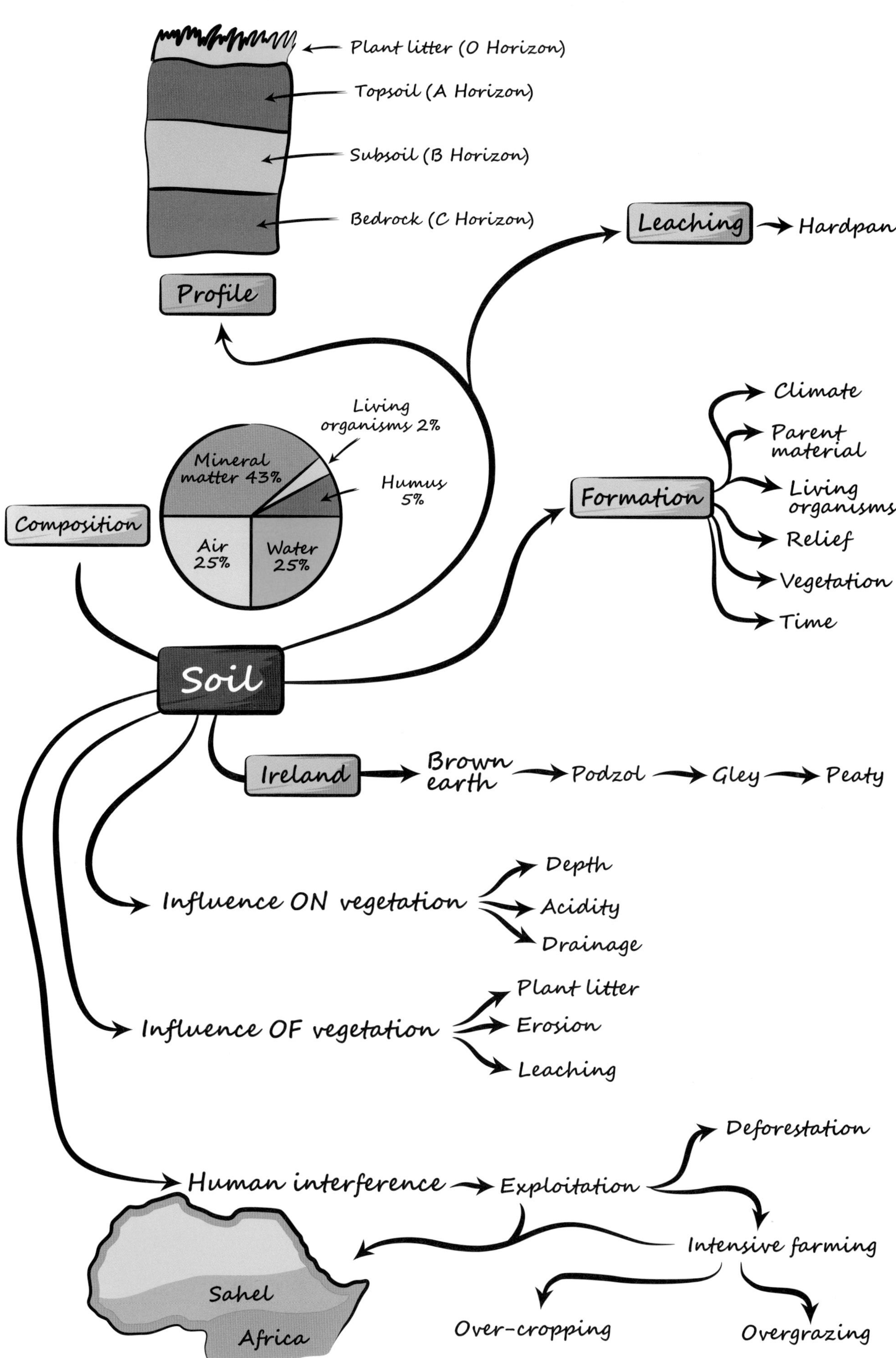
Plant litter (O Horizon)
Topsoil (A Horizon)
Subsoil (B Horizon)
Bedrock (C Horizon)
Profile
Leaching
Hardpan
Living organisms 2%
Mineral matter 43%
Humus 5%
Air 25%
Water 25%
Composition
Formation
Climate
Parent material
Living organisms
Relief
Vegetation
Time
Soil
Ireland
Brown earth
Podzol
Gley
Peaty
Influence ON vegetation
Depth
Acidity
Drainage
Influence OF vegetation
Plant litter
Erosion
Leaching
Human interference
Exploitation
Deforestation
Intensive farming
Over-cropping
Overgrazing
Sahel
Africa

17 Tertiary Economic Activities:

Transport and tourism

In this chapter, you will learn:

- about tertiary economic activities
- that tourism and transport are examples of service industries in the tertiary sector
- how tourism and transport are linked with each other and the physical world.

ICE-BREAKER ACTIVITY

Think of an area you are familiar with that is popular with tourists.

(a) List the reasons why tourists are attracted to this area.

(b) What are the benefits of tourism to this area?

(c) Is tourism causing any problems in this area?

(d) List the different ways tourists could get to this area.

Tertiary economic activities

Learning Intentions

In this section, you will learn:

- what tertiary economic activities are.

KEY WORDS

Services
Facilities
Interrelationship

Tertiary economic activities involve providing **services** and **facilities** to people.

Examples of tertiary economic activities include **education**, **law** and **health**.

Services:
systems or activities that supply a public need (e.g. transport, electricity, education).

Facilities:
something that the public can use such as a picnic area or a sports ground.

Figure 17.1 *Tourists at the Cliffs of Moher, Co. Clare*

Tourism and transport are also tertiary economic activities. We are going to look at the **interrelationships** between tourism, transport and the physical world in this chapter.

Interrelationship:
how things are linked with and influence each other.

ACTIVITY

Most of the population in developed countries works in the tertiary economic sector. In the developing world it can be less than 10 per cent. Suggest why this might be the case.

 **(i)** Define tertiary economic activities.

 **(ii)** Define services.

(iii) Define facilities.

 **(iv)** Give three examples of tertiary economic activities.

Tourism

Learning Intentions

In this section, you will learn:

- about the importance of tourism to Ireland and Europe.

Attractions
Fáilte Ireland
Discover Ireland
Amenities

Tourism is a very important **tertiary** economic activity because it contributes valuable **income** to the economy. Tourist **services** and **facilities** are often located in regions which offer various **attractions**. Such regions include:

- Areas of **natural beauty**
- **Beaches** and **coastlines**
- Regions offering **recreational** and **sporting** facilities
- **Cities**

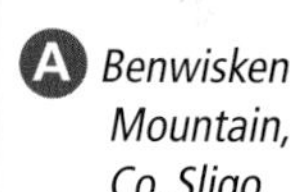

Figure 17.2

A Benwisken Mountain, Co. Sligo

B Sellerna Beach, Cleggan, Co. Galway

C Leopardstown Racecourse

D Cork City

ACTIVITY

Can you match each picture to the type of tourist region mentioned above?

There has been a growth in tourism over the years. Can you make a list of reasons why? Work in groups of four. You can record your thoughts under the following headings: euro, transport, law, internet, package holiday, mindfulness. Present your findings to the class.

Tourism in Ireland

According to the Department for Transport, Tourism and Sport, over **8.8 million** tourists visited Ireland in 2016. They spent more than **€8 billion**. That makes tourism one of Ireland's most important economic activities.

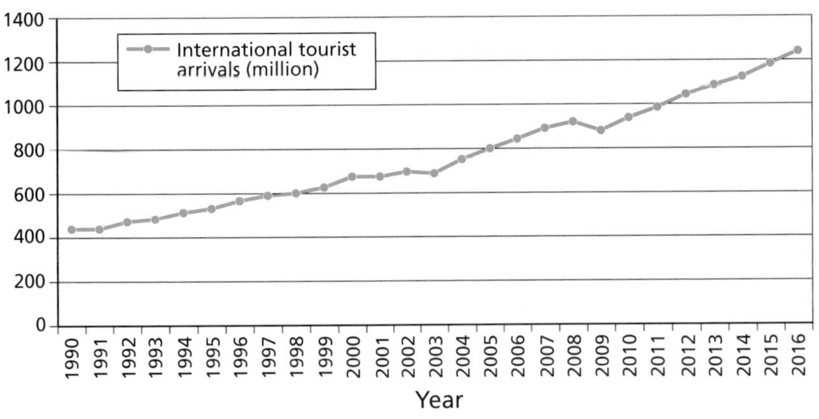

Figure 17.3 *Growth in tourism measured by international arrivals*

ACTIVITY

Look at Figure 17.3. Investigate what happened in 2008–09 that might have caused a drop in tourism globally.

Ireland has a number of agencies dedicated to developing tourism in the country. These include **Fáilte Ireland** and **Discover Ireland**.

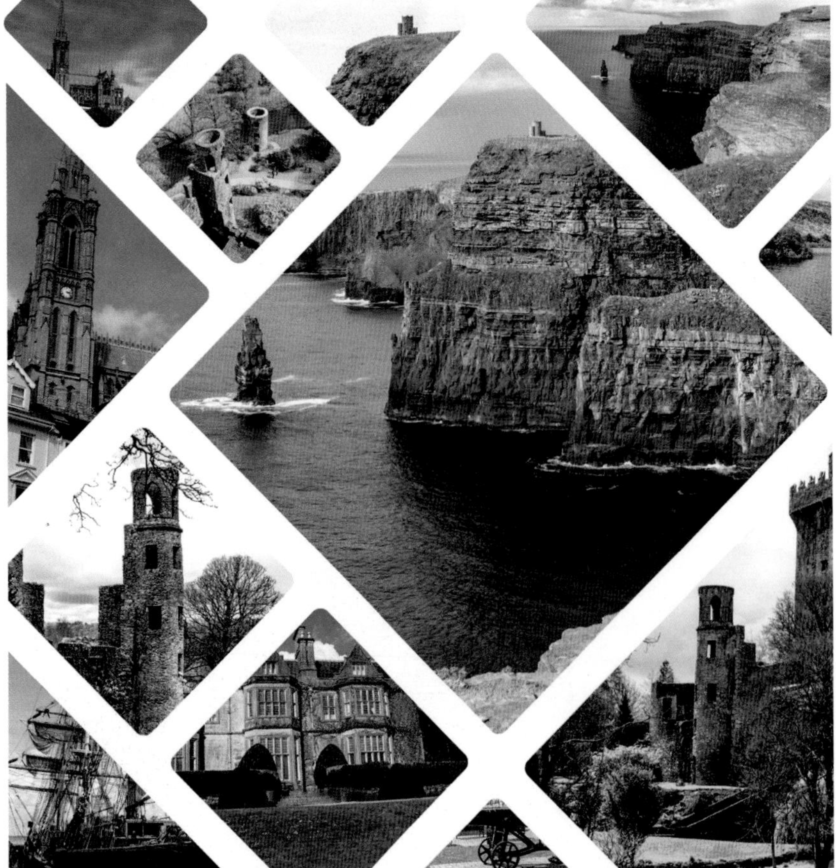

Figure 17.4 *Some of Ireland's main tourist attractions*

ACTIVITY

Imagine a friend from another country is coming to visit you. Check out the websites www.failteireland.ie and www.discoverireland.ie and make a list of the top five things you think they should do while they are here. Compare your list with others in your class to see if you have any of the same ideas.

Ireland has a wide range of tourist facilities or **amenities**. They provide the **services** needed by tourists, such as hotels, restaurants, visitor centres, transport facilities, sports facilities and more. Towns that are popular with tourists have **tourist information offices** providing information about all the amenities and attractions of the area.

NUMERACY ACTIVITY

Look at the Tourism Facts and Figures under the Research page on www.failteireland.ie. Write down how many tourists visited your area and how much money (revenue) they brought to your area.

Tourism in Europe

Climate is an important factor in making some regions attractive for tourism.

- **Switzerland** attracts tourists during the winter for **winter sports** such as skiing and snowboarding. During the summer months, the slopes provide excellent **hiking** and **hillwalking** routes.
- **Spain** attracts tourists for a variety of reasons, mostly because it is a suitable destination for those looking for **sun holidays**.

 **(i)** Name two government agencies responsible for tourism in Ireland.

 **(ii)** How many tourists visited Ireland in 2016? What was it worth to the economy?

 **(iii)** Why are tourists attracted to Ireland? List two reasons.

(iv) How can climate influence people's choice of holiday?

 **(v)** Discuss why it is important for the Irish government to invest in tourism.

I understand the importance of tourism to Ireland and Europe.   

The physical world and tourism in Ireland

Learning Intentions

In this section, you will learn:

- that tourism, transport and the physical world are interrelated
- about the influence of Ireland's physical landscape on tourism
- about the impact of tourism on the physical world
- about the importance of sustainable tourism
- about the influence of tourism on transport.

Sustainable tourism
Ecotourism
Accessibility

Ireland is world-renowned for being the land of the 'Céad Míle Fáilte'. While **Dublin** is our top tourist destination, with over 5.6 million visitors in 2016, Ireland's variety of **physical landscapes** and beautiful scenery is what attracts overseas **tourists** to Ireland.

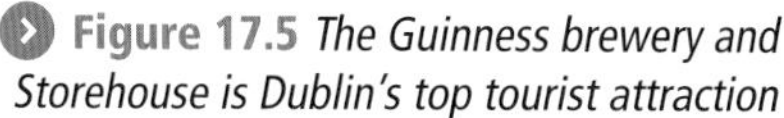
Figure 17.5 *The Guinness brewery and Storehouse is Dublin's top tourist attraction*

We are now going to learn about how the physical landscape **influences** tourism and the activities available to tourists in different areas around Ireland. We will then examine how tourism can, in turn, impact on the physical environment. Finally, we will look at the importance of **sustainable tourism** and the impact of tourism on transport.

Influence of Ireland's physical landscape on tourism

Areas of natural beauty

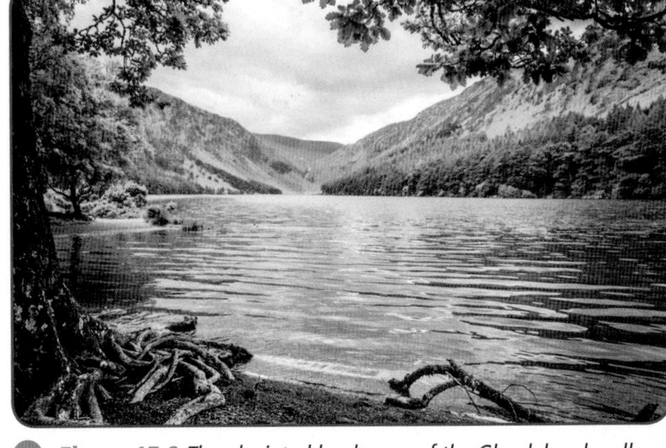

Figure 17.6 *The glaciated landscape of the Glendalough valley, Co. Wicklow*

- The **Burren** in Co. Clare is a karst region that you studied in Chapter 4. This is a beautiful landscape of exposed **limestone** rock and underground caves. It attracts tourists every year from both Ireland and abroad.
- Ireland's **mountains**, such as the Wicklow Mountains, attract hillwalkers and other tourists. Many mountainous regions have spectacular valleys that were carved out by moving ice after the last ice age, such as **Glendalough** in Co. Wicklow.
- Ireland's **rivers and lakes** are popular among tourists. Boat trips on the River Shannon and water sports are among the many attractions on offer.

Beaches and coastline

Ireland's coastline is a huge attraction for tourists. Coastal **erosion** and **deposition** have created a rugged shoreline of spectacular cliffs and sandy beaches.

Go to Chapter 10 for further information about coastal erosion and deposition.

Figure 17.7 *The cliffs at Benbane Head, Co. Antrim*

- The west coast of Ireland has been shaped by the Atlantic Ocean. High **sea cliffs** offer terrific views of the ocean at various places around the west coast. The cliffs in Achill, Co. Mayo (668 m) and the Slieve League cliffs in Donegal (598 m) are among the highest cliffs in Europe.
- The coastlines of Kerry and west Cork are very popular with tourists. The famous **Ring of Kerry** attracts many visitors each year.
- Co. Clare is home to the **Cliffs of Moher**, one of the most popular tourist attractions in Ireland, and the beach at Lahinch is popular with surfers.
- The **Wild Atlantic Way** is a tourism trail along Ireland's Atlantic coast first launched in 2014.
- The east coast of Ireland has some of Ireland's best beaches. South-east Ireland is known as '**the sunny south-east**' because it gets more hours of sunshine than the rest of the country. Fáilte Ireland promotes tourism in the region through an initiative called **Ireland's Ancient East**.

ACTIVITY

Check out https://educateplus.ie/go/blue-flag-beaches to find out more about the beaches in Ireland that have been awarded Blue Flag status for their cleanliness, water quality, safety and level of environmental protection.

Recreational and sporting facilities

Activity-based holidays are growing in popularity every year and Ireland offers a wide range of activities for tourists.

- Ireland has some of the best **golf courses** in the world, including the K Club in County Kildare and Ballybunion in Co. Kerry. The success of Irish golfers internationally has helped to promote this type of tourism. Many of these golf courses are built on sand dunes and wonderful parkland areas.
- Adventure holidays are also increasing in popularity, and outdoor **adventure centres** such as Delphi Mountain Resort in Co. Galway offer activities such as surfing, abseiling and canoeing.
- Ireland has many trails for **hillwalking** and **cycling**. The Great Western Greenway is a 42 km stretch of pathway between Westport and Achill Island in Co. Mayo, suitable for walking and cycling, with many facilities along the way.
- With a huge network of rivers and lakes, Ireland attracts **anglers** from all over the world. The River Suir at Caher in Co. Tipperary is one of the best places in Europe to fish for wild brown trout, and the Blackwater River that flows through Munster is one of Ireland's best rivers for salmon fishing. The waterways throughout Ireland also lend themselves to boating and other water-based activities.

Figure 17.8 *Tralee Golf Club, Co. Kerry*

Figure 17.9 *Cyclists above Lough Na Fooey, Co. Galway*

Cities

Dublin, Cork, Galway, Waterford and Kilkenny are all popular for **city breaks**, both for Irish people and tourists travelling from abroad.

ACTIVITY

Write a blog about how to spend 24 hours in any of the cities mentioned above. What attractions, tours, restaurants and hotels would you recommend?

Impact of tourism on the physical environment.

Although tourism is a huge economic positive for Ireland, there are many **downsides** to it. The areas of natural beauty, beaches and coastlines must be **protected** and looked after, to make sure tourism is **sustainable** and to make sure the environment is not damaged. **Impacts** of tourism on the physical environment include the following:

Pollution

Tourism brings an increased flow of traffic and vehicles such as rental cars, buses and camper vans. The exhaust **emissions** damage the air quality and lead to **air pollution**. This has a big impact on the natural environment of areas of natural beauty and coastlines.

A large number of tourists means more **waste** to be disposed of. **Litter**, especially plastic, is a constant problem in tourist areas such as beaches, as we saw in Chapter 10 (see page 169).

Destruction of scenery

Areas that were once famous for their spectacular beaches and wonderful scenery have suffered because of the **infrastructure** that must be built for tourists. Apartments, holiday homes, hotels and roads are frequently built in these areas. They can spoil the landscape and destroy what once was an area of beauty. This can be seen around Ireland in many coastal towns, as well as abroad, for example on the coast of **Spain**.

Figure 17.10 *High-rise hotels and apartment blocks in Benidorm on the Costa Blanca, Spain*

Flora and fauna

Tourism can have a big impact on **wildlife**. Large numbers of people visiting an area can affect the animals and plants there. This is especially true of activity holidays such as hiking, boating and cycling. For example, visitors to the Burren in Co. Clare can damage the rare plants and the physical environment they depend on.

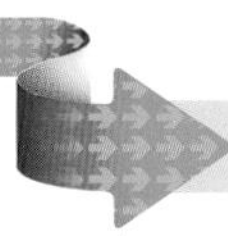

Go to Chapter 6, page 95, to read more about tourism in the Burren.

Imagine a new tourist centre is planned for your area. Divide into two groups. One group should list the positive impacts of bringing new tourists to the area. The other group should list the negative impacts.

Present your thoughts to the class. Take a class vote on whether or not the tourist centre should be built.

Sustainable tourism

Ecotourism: sustainable and responsible travel that aims to avoid having a negative effect on the environment.

In response to the damage caused to the physical world by tourism, we have seen a huge growth in **ecotourism**.

There are many things tourists can do to ensure that their trip is not harming the physical world.

- Support tourist services that use **green energy** such as solar panels and wind energy.
- Avoid using cars. Use **public transport**, cycle or walk where possible.
- **Avoid using plastic**. Reuse water bottles and containers. Always take your rubbish with you.
- Don't pick flowers and stick to official paths where possible.
- Use **local guides** and tour operators.
- Support local and organic produce.

Check out www.irelandecotourism.ie to find out more about ecotourism in your county.

ACTIVITY

Watch this video about ecotourism in Inishbofin: https://educateplus.ie/go/inishbofin. Make a list of the steps taken to promote ecotourism on the island.

Figure 17.11 *Camping cabins like these in Cushendall, Co. Antrim, are often used by tourists who want to minimise their impact on the environment*

Impact of tourism on transport

When tourists are choosing a destination for their holidays one of the main factors they must consider is **accessibility**. In other words, how easy is it to reach the destination? The impact of tourism on transport can be seen in the following ways:

- **Regional airports** are developed with chartered flights specifically for tourists, for example Faranfore and Knock in Ireland, Alicante in Spain and Faro in Portugal. This service can be used by locals as well as making it easier for tourists to access parts of Ireland outside Dublin.
- A modernised **road network** is built to deal with increased traffic due to tourism. Roads linking tourist resorts and ring roads around towns to deal with congestion are often built. The N21 road to Kerry has seen many improvements, including the bypass of Castleisland in 2010.
- Services on **rail systems** are improved, with more frequent departures during the peak season. Iarnród Éireann often puts extra coaches on their trains in the summer to cater for the increased numbers.

PORTFOLIO ACTIVITY 17.1

Go to page 68 of your Portfolio to research two tourist destinations, one in Ireland and one abroad.

 **(i)** Name two areas of natural beauty in Ireland that tourists visit.

 **(ii)** Explain two ways in which the physical landscape attracts tourists to Ireland.

(iii) Explain two ways that tourism impacts on the physical landscape.

(iv) List and explain ways to promote tourism without impacting on the physical landscape.

- I understand that tourism, transport and the physical world are all interrelated.
- I understand how the physical landscape influences tourism in Ireland and the impact tourism has on the physical landscape as a result.
- I understand the importance of sustainable tourism.
- I understand how tourism influences transport.

Transport

Learning Intentions

In this section, you will learn:

- that transport, tourism and the physical world are interrelated
- about Ireland's transport network
- about the influence of the physical landscape on transport
- about the influence of transport on the physical world
- about the influence of transport on tourism.

Communication links
Transport network
Transport infrastructure
Route
Boundaries
Transport Infrastructure Ireland

The movement of people and goods between settlements leads to the development of **communication links**. These links include **roads**, **railways**, **rivers**, **canals** and **airports**. Together they form a **transport network**.

We are now going to learn about Ireland's **transport network**. We are then going to learn about how the physical landscape **influences** transport and how transport influences the physical landscape. Finally, we will look at how transport influences tourism.

Ireland's transport network

In recent years, Ireland's transport network has been greatly improved due to **government investment**. In 2015, the government announced a €10 billion investment in **transport infrastructure** as part of the **2016–22 capital plan**. Some recent projects include:

- M7 Dublin–Limerick
- M8 Dublin–Cork
- M4/M6 Dublin–Galway
- M1 Dublin–Belfast
- M9 Dublin–Waterford
- M17/18 Tuam–Gort–Limerick
- The upgrading of the M50 motorway around Dublin City
- The construction of **ring roads**, by-passing the majority of large towns in Ireland.

In 2018, the government announced **Project 2040** – a long-term investment project, which includes a plan to develop all transport infrastructure in Ireland.

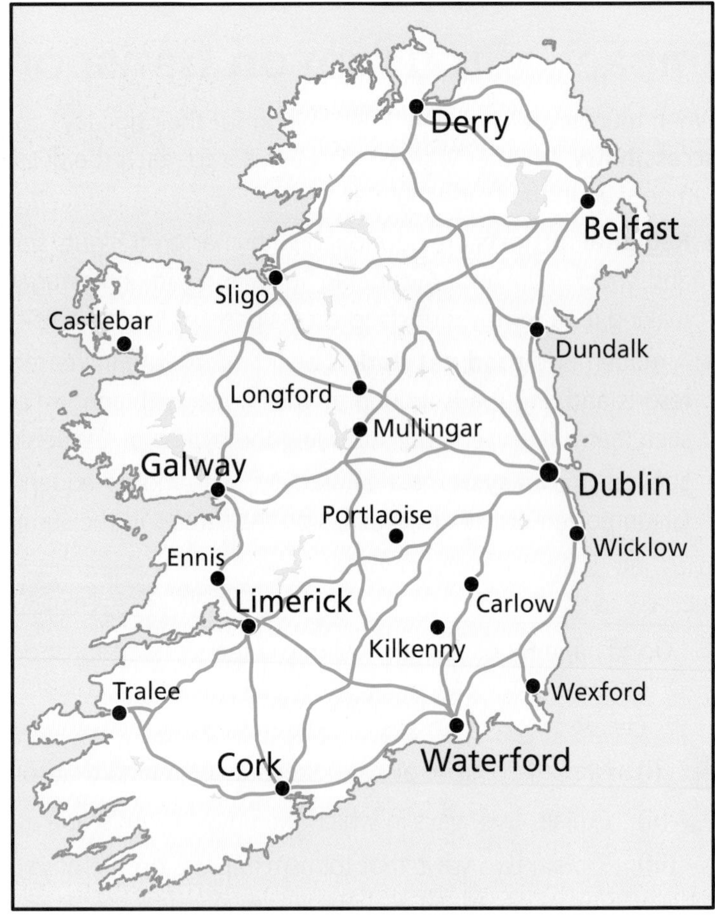

Figure 17.12 *Ireland's network of major roads*

Influence of the physical world on transport

The **physical landscape** influences the type of transport that can be developed in an area. The first **roads** in Ireland were built in ancient times, by the **Celts**. Although they were nothing like the smooth-surfaced roads we are used to today, they created the basis of many of the roads that make up the Irish transport network. The **routes** of these roads have changed very little over the centuries. The easiest and most cost-efficient route is the preferred option.

Boundaries

Today, when **Transport Infrastructure Ireland** decides on the route of a new road or motorway, **compulsory purchase orders** are issued to landowners affected. This means that they **have to sell** the land through which the road will pass to the NRA. Understandably, this causes **conflict** because it has a huge impact on the livelihood of local landowners, especially **farmers**.

Many of Ireland's roads **wind** through the countryside, for no apparent reason. This is because when they were originally constructed it was between the **boundaries** of farms to avoid dividing up farmland where possible.

Figure 17.13 *Tunnels under major roads can be built where farmland has been divided*

Coast

Figure 17.14 *The Greenway in Co. Mayo follows the route of the old Westport–Achill railway*

If you look at a map of Ireland you will notice that there are **settlements** all along the Irish coastline. Many of these settlements were **fishing** and **trade** towns and villages in the past. Indeed, some of them still are. These settlements needed communication links, which is why we see **coast roads** all around the Irish coastline. Erosion of the coastline has damaged some of these roads and new roads have been built to replace them.

In the late nineteenth century, many Irish coastal towns were connected to larger regional towns by **rail**.

- One example is the **Ballybunion to Listowel** line in north Kerry. This railway line was used to transport people, cattle and sand and connected with the Limerick–Tralee railway line in Listowel.
- Another example is the **West Clare Railway**, which operated from 1887 to 1961. This railway line connected the coastal towns of Kilkee and Kilrush with Ennis, with stops in Lahinch, Milltown Malbay and Ennistymon.

As road transport increased in popularity, these railways closed as they were no longer **cost-efficient**.

Mountains

Figure 17.15 *The Conor Pass, Co. Kerry*

Building roads in mountainous regions is challenging and **costly** because getting the material needed up the mountain is very difficult. When planning the route the main factor to be considered is finding the easiest route with the most gentle **gradient**. Roads in upland areas **zig-zag** up the slope. They avoid going directly uphill because, in the past, animals would not have been able for it, and today car engines would not be able for it.

Gaps and valleys carved out by **glaciers** are sometimes used as routes. The **Conor Pass** in Co. Kerry is Ireland's highest mountain pass.

Sometimes, the easiest route is **through** the mountain. An example is the **Great St Bernard Tunnel** through the Alps which runs from Martigny in Switzerland to Aosta in Italy. This reduces the journey time and avoids the mountain pass, which is often closed in winter because of heavy snowfall.

Eskers

An esker is a feature of **glacial deposition** (see page 186). Sand, gravel and boulders were deposited by water flowing under ice sheets and these low-lying ridges were exposed when the glacier melted at the end of the last ice age. Eskers are suitable for roads because they provide natural **foundations** and because the land around them is often boggy and unsuitable for road construction.

Esker Riada, which stretches from Galway to Dublin, is an example.

Rivers

Many transport routes follow the path of a **river valley** as the route has already been carved out naturally. Where part of the course of the river flows through a flood plain, you will notice that the route moves up beyond the **bluff line** (the highest point reached by a river when in flood) to avoid flooding.

When transport routes need to cross rivers, the narrowest point on the river is chosen as the **bridging point**. Settlements often develop at these locations. Most towns in Ireland are also bridging points.

Figure 17.16 *A road and a railway following the path of a river valley*

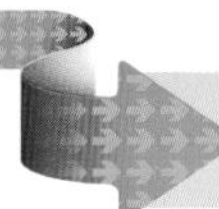

Go to Chapters 9–11 to remind yourself of what you have learned about rivers, the sea and glaciation.

Influence of transport on the physical world

Transport can have **negative impacts** on the physical world.

ACTIVITY

Can you think of any negative impacts of road or railway line construction? Remember what you learned on page 97 of Chapter 6: Weathering and Mass Movement.

Transport also brings traffic, which burns **fossil fuels**. These emit greenhouse gases, which contribute to **global warming** and **climate change**.

Go to Chapter 14 to learn more about global warming and climate change.

Influence of transport on tourism

Accessibility

If tourism is important to an area then transport links need to be developed so that tourists can **access** the area. The **accessibility** of areas plays a huge role in the development of tourism. More tourists visit **Dublin** and the surrounding area than any other part of Ireland. This is because there are **flights** from a lot more places coming into Dublin than to smaller airports like Knock, Shannon and Cork.

NUMERACY ACTIVITY

Investigate how many passengers pass through Dublin Airport, Shannon Airport, Knock Airport and Cork Airport every year. Draw a suitable graph to display your findings.

Means of transport

The **type of transport** available in an area also influences tourism.

Some tourists prefer to travel by **car** and use **ferries** for international travel. The south-east has benefited from this type of tourism, as has the mainland of Europe. The **Channel Tunnel** makes it easy to move between France and the UK.

Figure 17.17 *Rosslare Europort*

Cities with a well-developed **transport infrastructure** attract tourists because it's so easy to get around. **London** and **Paris** are huge tourist destinations where visitors can use special travel cards to use the bus, train and underground.

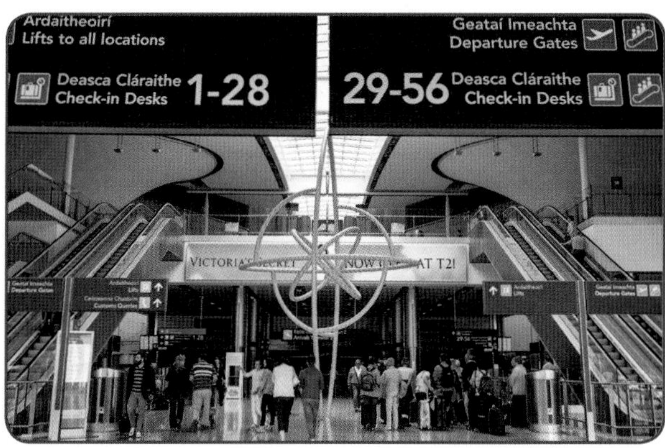

Figure 17.18 *Dublin Airport*

ACTIVITY

Pick an EU airport of your choice and investigate its importance to its surrounding region. What benefits does it bring to the area?

(i) List two types of communication links between villages/towns/cities.

(ii) List three projects carried out by the government to improve transport in Ireland.

(iii) Explain two ways the physical landscape influences transport.

(iv) Explain two ways that transport influences the physical world.

(v) Describe the ways in which transport influences tourism.

- I understand that tourism, transport and the physical world are all interrelated.
- I understand how Ireland's transport network has developed.
- I understand the influence of the physical landscape on transport and the influence transport has on the physical world.
- I understand how transport influences tourism.

Tourism and transport on Ordnance Survey maps

Learning Intentions

In this section, you will learn:

- that tertiary economic activities can be identified on Ordnance Survey maps
- about the interrelationship between the physical world, transport and tourism on Ordnance Survey maps.

Tertiary economic activities like tourism and transport services are evident on Ordnance Survey maps.

For example, tourist services like **tourist information offices**, **picnic areas** and **viewpoints** can be seen clearly on Ordnance Survey maps. The attraction of areas of natural beauty, like **lakes** and **mountains**, are also visible on Ordnance Survey maps.

Transport routes can also be seen on Ordnance Survey maps. Roads can be identified by their names and categories:

- **M** roads are motorways.
- **N** roads are national primary or secondary roads.
- **R** roads are regional roads.

Other evidence of transport facilities, such as **railway stations**, **airports** and **harbours** can be identified using grid references.

The **influence** of the physical landscape on tourism and transport services can also be easily seen. For example, roads following **coastlines** and **river valleys**.

Figure 17.19 *Carrick-on-Shannon, Co. Leitrim*

1. Identify **four** means of transport tourists could use to visit the town of Carrick-on-Shannon. Give evidence to justify your answer.
2. Using map evidence, explain **three** different types of recreational activities available to tourists in this area.
3. What evidence is there on this map of aspects of the physical world which might be of interest to tourists?
4. Using map evidence, explain **two** ways that the physical landscape has influenced transport on this map.

Remember

Statement, Evidence and Explain (SEE). See Chapter 15, page 274.

- I can recognise tertiary economic activities on Ordnance Survey maps.
- I can identify the links between the physical world, transport and tourism on Ordnance Survey maps.

REVISION

Tertiary economic activities involve the provision of ____________ and ____________. One of the most important tertiary activities is ____________.

Many people are employed in the tourist industry in Ireland, and the money that tourists spend here is vital to our ____________. Tourists are attracted to Ireland for a number of reasons including its ____________ and ____________ ____________. Ireland has a number of agencies that look after tourism in Ireland. These include ____________ Ireland. Towns that are popular tourist areas usually have a tourist ____________ ____________.

Tourism can have many impacts on the physical environment, including ____________ ____________ from traffic, the ____________ of scenery and damage to ____________ and fauna. ____________ is tourism of the most sustainable and responsible sort. It is travel that aims to avoid having a negative effect on the environment.

When tourists are choosing a destination for their holidays one of the main factors they must consider is ____________. Ireland's transport ____________ has greatly improved over recent years thanks to the government's 2016–22 ____________ ____________.

Questions & Answers

Sample Questions

1. Name **two** types of tourist region.
2. Explain **two** impacts of tourism on the physical world.
3. Explain **one** way that tourism impacts on transport and **one** way that transport impacts on tourism.

Sample Answers

1. Two types of tourist region are areas of natural beauty such as the lakes of Killarney and beaches and coastal areas, such as Tramore in Co. Waterford.
2. Two impacts of tourism on the physical world include destruction of scenery and damage to flora and fauna.

   Tourists need accommodation and this leads to the building of hotels, holiday homes and apartments. These can be an eyesore and are often poor quality buildings which destroy the natural beauty that made the area a tourist attraction in the first place.

   Tourism also impacts greatly on the flora and fauna in tourist areas. Animals are forced from their natural habitat. The unique flowers that grow in the Burren are trampled on and picked by hikers.
3. Tourism impacts on transport in a positive way. It can lead to the development of better transport in an isolated area so that tourists can access that region. Roads can be greatly improved while regional airports can be developed to help tourists, therefore improving transport.

   Transport also has an impact on tourism. Access is the key to tourism, and people will travel to areas if they can get there without any problems. If the access is good, tourism will prosper.

Short Questions

1. The graph shows the numbers of tourists who visited a coastal resort in Spain in the course of a year.

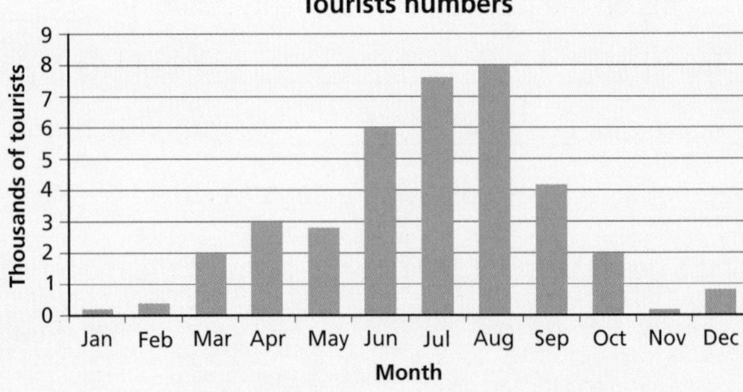

   (i) Which is the 'peak' or busiest tourist month at this coastal resort?

   (ii) Give two reasons why you think June, July and August were the busiest months.

2. Look at this chart, showing where foreign visitors to Ireland each year come from.

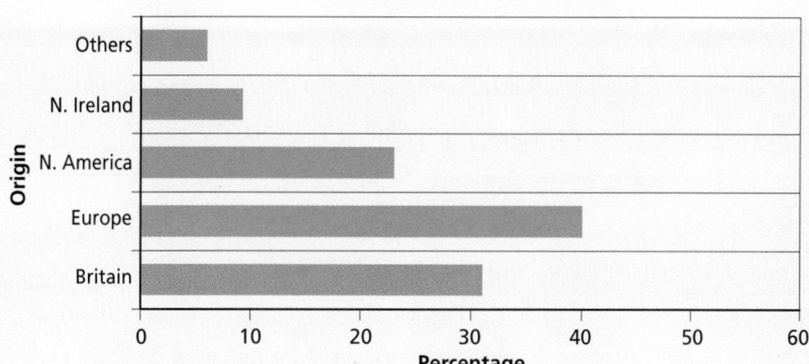

What percentage of visitors comes from Europe?

12% ☐

40% ☐

21% ☐ [tick (✓) the correct box]

3. Which of the following jobs is a tertiary (service) activity?

Farmer ☐

Miner ☐

Office secretary ☐

Steelworker ☐ [tick (✓) the correct box]

4. Examine the table showing overseas visits to Ireland and answer the questions.

Holidaymakers (000s)	2011	2012	2013	2014	2015	2016
Britain	961	941	979	1,057	1,254	1,423
Mainland Europe	1,041	1,120	1,227	1,314	1,612	1,699
North America	591	634	718	803	926	1,041
Rest of World	167	184	220	219	243	242
Total	**2,760**	**2,879**	**3,144**	**3,393**	**4,036**	**4,406**

(i) Which year had the most overseas visitors to Ireland?

(ii) Suggest a possible reason for the decrease in the number of tourists from Britain in 2012.

(iii) Draw a graph to show the increase in total tourist numbers between 2011 and 2016.

5. Which of the following are **all** examples of people involved in tertiary activities?

Hairdresser; teacher; farmer; truck driver; doctor ☐

Priest; pop singer; chimney sweep; taxi driver; teacher ☐

Taxi driver; professional footballer; shipyard worker; miner; travel agent ☐

Forestry worker; shopkeeper; mechanic; solicitor; bakery worker ☐

[tick (✓) the correct box]

6. Which of the following is not a road in Ireland

M7 ☐

D 243 ☐

R 243 ☐

N 20 ☐ [tick (✓) the correct box]

Long Questions

1. **(i)** Name a popular tourist destination in Ireland.

   (ii) Explain **two** reasons why tourists are attracted to this destination for their holidays.

2. **(i)** With the help of the photographs given from the Discover Ireland website, describe **two** tourist attractions/activities available in Ireland.

   (ii) Describe **one** way in which tourism has helped your local area.

3. Many countries and regions are important for tourism.

   (i) Name **one** such country **or** region.

   (ii) Explain **three** reasons why tourism is important in the area you have named.

4. **(i)** Name **four** reasons why tourists come to Ireland.

   (ii) Large-scale tourism may have **unwelcome impacts** on some tourist areas. Describe **two** such impacts.

5. 'Transport influences tourism and tourism influences transport.'

   Discuss this statement using three examples.

6. Discuss how each of the following influences transport routes in Ireland: mountains, rivers and the coastline.

7. One piece of sustainable travel advice is 'Take only pictures, leave only footprints'. Do you agree with this advice? Give **three** points to explain your answer.

Visual Summary

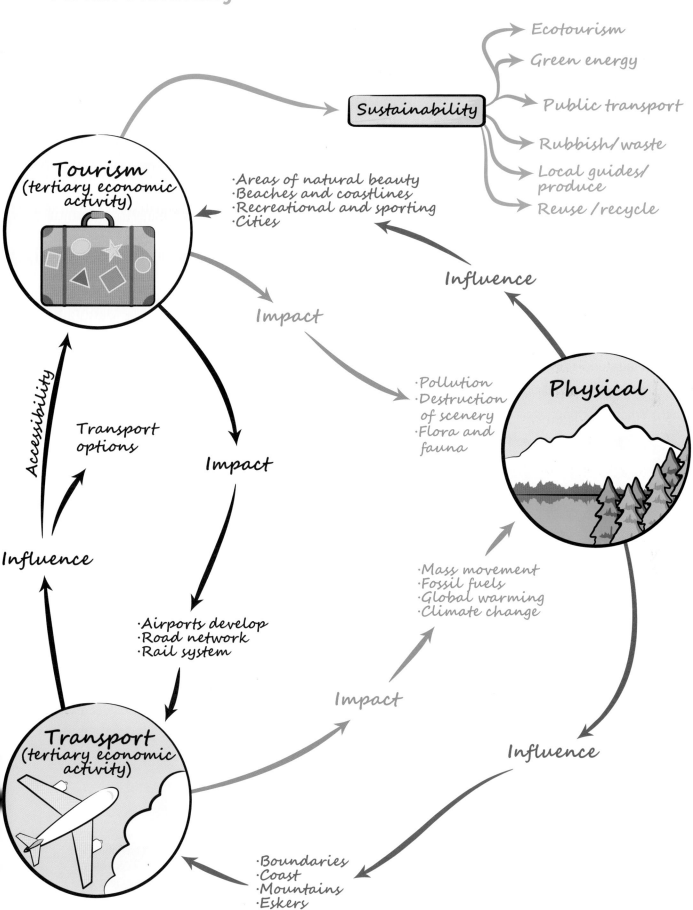

Sustainability
Ecotourism
Green energy
Public transport
Rubbish/waste
Local guides/ produce
Reuse / recycle

Tourism (tertiary economic activity)

- Areas of natural beauty
- Beaches and coastlines
- Recreational and sporting
- Cities

Influence

Impact

- Pollution
- Destruction of scenery
- Flora and fauna

Physical

Accessibility

Transport options

Impact

Influence

- Airports develop
- Road network
- Rail system

- Mass movement
- Fossil fuels
- Global warming
- Climate change

Impact

Transport (tertiary economic activity)

Influence

- Boundaries
- Coast
- Mountains
- Eskers
- Rivers

18 Population: How population changes over time

In this chapter, you will learn:

- how the world's population has increased throughout time at an uneven and fluctuating rate
- the factors that influence the rate of population change
- how the demographic transition model can help us to understand population change
- how a population pyramid shows the gender and age structure of a country
- about population change in Ireland
- about population change in a developing country.

ICE-BREAKER ACTIVITY

With the student next to you, answer the following questions:

(a) What is the population of Ireland?

(b) What is the population of your county?

(c) What is the population of Dublin City?

(d) What is the population of the United Kingdom?

(e) What it the population of Sierra Leone? Can you identify Sierra Leone on a world map?

World population growth

Learning Intentions

In this section, you will learn:

- about the world's population growth throughout history
- how to calculate population change.

Fluctuate	Migration
Birth rate	Natural increase
Death rate	Natural decrease

There are more than 7.6 billion people living in the world today.

There weren't always 7.6 billion people living in the world. If you examine Figure 18.1 on the next page you will see that the world's population grew at an **uneven** rate, right up until the 1700s. When population figures increase and decrease at an uneven rate like this, it is called **fluctuation**.

Fluctuate: increase and decrease at an uneven rate.

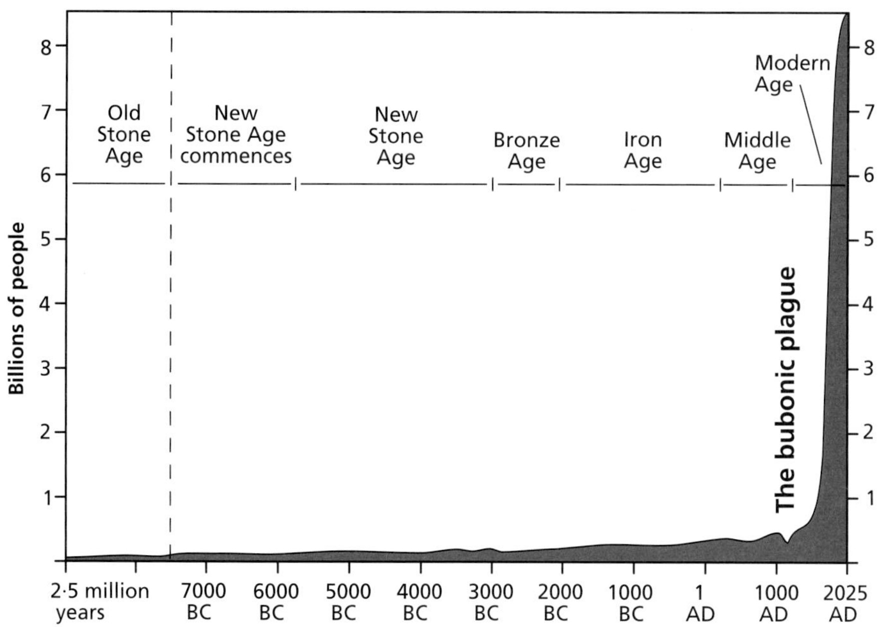

Figure 18.1 *World population growth through history*

ACTIVITY

Can you think of reasons why the world's population fluctuated? Think about what might have been happening in history during these times. Can you see the impact of the bubonic plague (the 'Black Death') during the Middle Ages on the world's population?

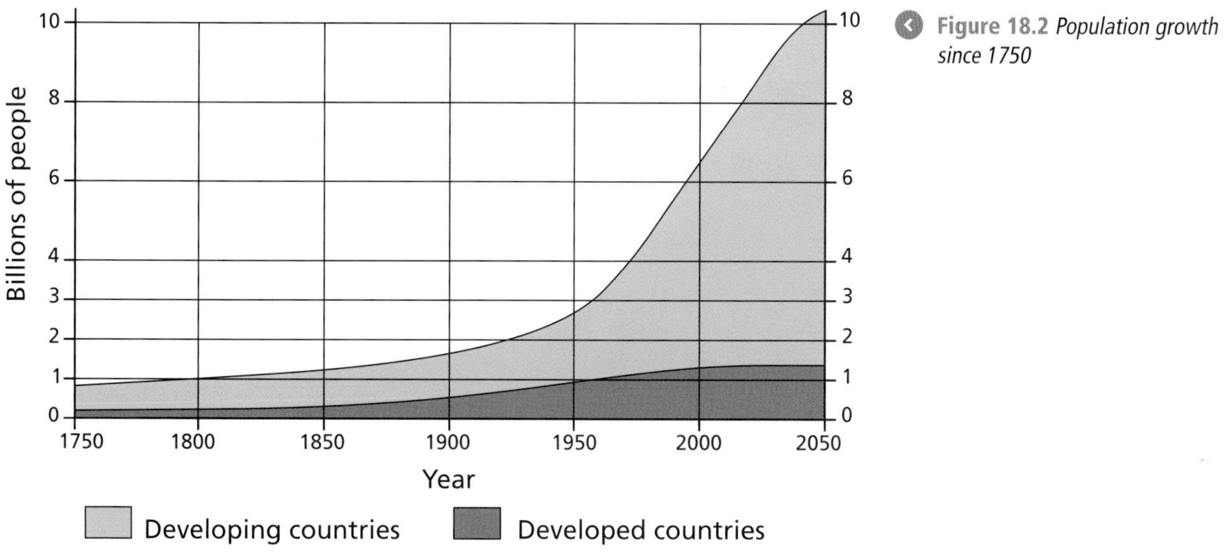

Figure 18.2 *Population growth since 1750*

As you can see from Figure 18.2, the world's population remained under a billion up until **1750**. It then began to **increase rapidly**. This is because the number of people born was higher than the number of people who died. At around this time, the **agricultural and industrial revolutions** occurred. This meant that there was more food available and people lived longer.

You will also see that the most **rapid population growth** has occurred **since 1950**. Most of this population growth is in poorer countries in the **developing world**. Population growth in Europe is much slower, and in some countries the population is even in **decline**.

ACTIVITY

Check out https://educateplus.ie/go/world-population to find out what the population was when you were born.

Calculating population change

The global rate of population growth is now 1 billion every 15 years. The three main causes of population change are:

Births	These are measured using the **birth rate**.
Deaths	These are measured using the **death rate**.
Migration	These are measured using the **movement** of people in and out of an area.

A-Z

Birth rate:
This is the number of babies born per 1,000 people in the total population in one year.

A-Z

Death rate:
This is the number of deaths per 1,000 people in the total population in one year.

- If more people are born than die in a year, the population grows. This is called a **natural increase**.
- If more people die than are born in a year, the population drops. This is called a **natural decrease**.

Because the increase or decrease is measured **per 1,000**, we put the figure over a thousand to get the percentage increase or decrease.

For example: The birth rate in Ireland in 2016 was 13.5 per 1,000 of the population. The death rate was 6.4 per 1,000. The natural increase can be calculated as follows:

$$\text{Birth Rate} - \text{Death Rate} = \text{Natural Increase}$$
$$13.5 - 6.4 = 7.1 \text{ per } 1{,}000$$

$$\frac{\text{Population increase} \times 100}{1{,}000} = \text{Natural increase percentage}$$
$$\frac{7.1 \times 100}{1{,}000} = 0.7\%$$

Any other changes in population are due to people either moving into that place or leaving it. This is called **migration**.

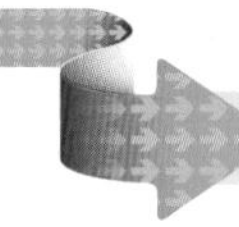

Go to Chapter 19 to learn more about migration.

NUMERACY ACTIVITY

(a) Below is a table showing birth rates and death rates in 2016. Can you fill in the blanks?

Country	Birth Rate	Death Rate	Natural Increase	Natural Decrease
Ireland	13.5	6.4	7.1	
Sierra Leone	36.7	10.6		
Germany	8.5	11.6		
China	12.4		4.7	

(b) In **2006** the birth rate in Ireland was 16.7. The death rate was 6.7.

(i) Calculate the change in Ireland's birth rate and death rate over the last ten years.

(ii) Did the population of Ireland naturally increase or decrease between 2006 and 2016?

 **(i)** What is the global rate of population change?

 **(ii)** Define the term birth rate.

(iii) Define the term death rate.

(iv) Do you think Ireland's population is growing fast or slow? Give reasons for your answer.

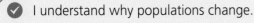

- I understand why populations change.
- I can calculate whether a population is increasing or decreasing.

Factors that influence the rate of population change

Learning Intentions

In this section, you will learn:

- about the factors that influence the rate of population change in a country.

Agricultural Revolution
Potato blight
Baby boom
Civil war
Healthcare
Sanitation
Life expectancy
Family planning
Infant mortality rate

NUMERACY ACTIVITY

Find out if the birth rate is increasing or decreasing in your class.

(a) Ask the students in the class how many siblings are in their family.

(b) Ask students how many brothers and sisters their parents or guardians have.

(c) Compare the figures and see if there is a drop in family size.

List any reasons why this might be happening.

A number of factors influence the rate of population change. These include:

- Food supply
- Health
- War
- Education
- Technological development
- The place of women in society

Food supply

A growing population needs an increasing food supply. The **Agricultural Revolution** brought about population growth because it made more food available. **Machinery** and **new farming practices** allow farmers to produce more food. **Fertilisers** and **pesticides** allow farmers to grow more crops which means that there is **more food** available and less chance of famine. This lowers the death rate and the population grows.

Before the **potato blight** in Ireland, the population was growing because of the constant food supply. However, being so dependent on one food source caused a **famine**, as most of the population had nothing to eat. People died of starvation and emigrated during the **Great Famine** in the 1840s. This caused the population to drop.

In countries such as **Sierra Leone** in West Africa, the population is vulnerable to diseases because many people don't get the necessary nutrition from their food sources. In Sierra Leone, nearly half the population is without a regular food supply.

Figure 18.3 *Spraying fertiliser on a bean crop in Australia*

War

War obviously **increases the death rate** in an area. It also **decreases the birth rate** because young people are away in times of war. It also puts a **strain** on health services, water supplies, sanitation and farming. This can also lead to higher death rates.

The population of Germany decreased during the First and Second World Wars. There was a **baby boom**, however, when soldiers returned from the wars.

Many parts of **Africa** are war-torn at present, affecting population levels in those countries. **Civil war** in Sierra Leone between 1991 and 2001 meant that there was little or no investment in development. Many people died because of the conflict, causing the population to decline.

Figure 18.4 *Civil war in Rwanda, 1994*

ACTIVITY

Choose a country that is currently at war. Examine the impact of the war on the population of the country you have chosen. Find out what you can about the death toll, migration and famine in the area.

Technological development

Figure 18.5 *Lettuces being grown using robotic technology*

Technology has led to an increase in food supply. **Tractors** and machinery have made farming more productive. **Irrigation schemes** provide much-needed water to grow crops in areas that suffer from drought. Technology has also improved people's health. **Medical equipment** and new **drugs** mean that people live longer. All of this reduces death rates and causes the population to grow.

In **Ireland**, we rely on technology in the primary, secondary and tertiary sectors. Our developed **IT sector** makes us an attractive base for MNCs. This improves employment prospects and **attracts migrants**, causing the population to increase.

Over half the population of **Sierra Leone** lives below the poverty line. This means that the population there doesn't have the money to invest in technology. It is difficult to develop agriculture, industry and services without technology. This means that people continue to have large families to help with the workload and look after them when they get older. This causes the population to grow.

Health

A good **healthcare system** lowers the death rate. **Vaccines** and **antibiotics** are widely available in developed countries, and people now survive illnesses and diseases that previously caused widespread deaths. **Access** to doctors and hospitals also decreases the death rate.

The availability of **clean drinking water** reduces the spread of disease, as does proper **sanitation.** Many of the fatal diseases that are widespread in the developing world rarely occur in richer countries like Ireland because our **living conditions** are so much better.

Sanitation:
facilities to dispose of human waste in a safe way, such as sewerage systems and toilets.

Every child born in **Ireland** has access to free vaccines, which is why **life expectancy** here is **81.5** years.

In **Sierra Leone** only 60 per cent of the population has access to clean water, leading to deaths from diseases such as diarrhoea, typhoid and cholera. This is why **life expectancy** in Sierra Leone is just **51** years.

Life expectancy:
the average number of years a person is expected to live.

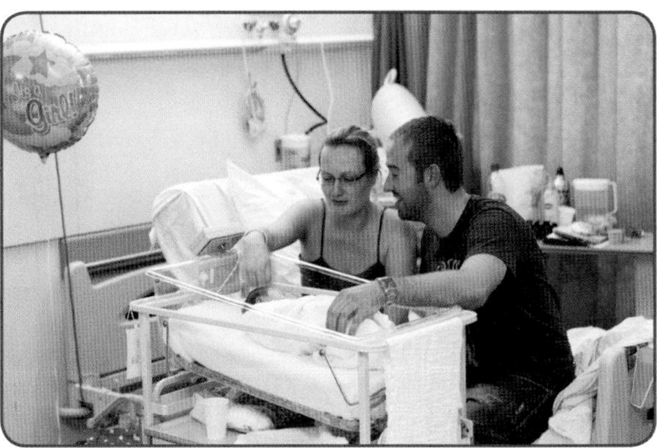

Figure 18.6 *Maternity hospitals in the developing and developed worlds. Left: Malawi; Right: Ireland*

Work in groups of four. Look at the photographs above of maternity hospitals in Malawi and Ireland. Discuss the differences.

Education

Education leads to lower birth and death rates. If people are educated they are more likely to have smaller families. They understand **family planning** methods better and raise healthier children. Educated people often know more about a healthy diet, personal hygiene and sanitation and how all of these things can help their children to live long, healthy lives. This is why education is a priority in the **Sustainable Development Goals**.

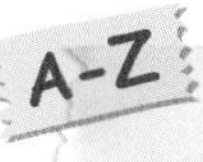

Family planning:
the awareness of birth control, and the planning and spacing of the number of children that a family might want.

In **Ireland** all children have access to education where they learn about healthy living and family planning. People choose to have **smaller families** so that they can balance family life with a career.

In **Sierra Leone**, even though the government recognises the importance of education, just 65 per cent of children finish primary school. This is a huge concern because access to education helps to reduce poverty and can help in the fight against **HIV/AIDS** and other diseases.

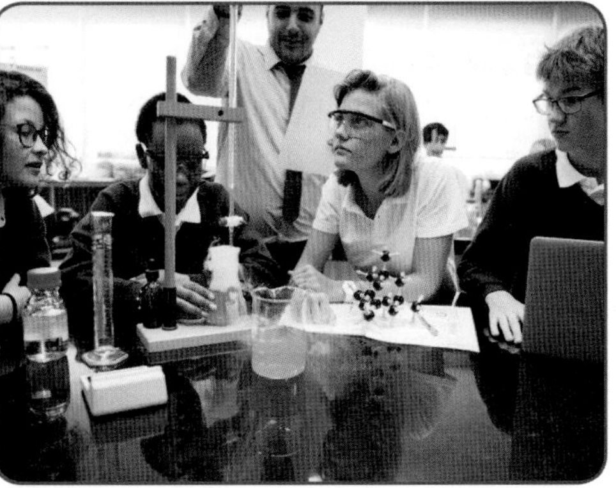

Figure 18.7 *Classrooms. Top: Kenya; Bottom: Ireland*

The role of women in society

Figure 18.8 *Mother and children in Mali, West Africa*

The **role or status of women** in society has a huge influence on population growth. As a country **develops** and women become more educated, they also gain **equality** and often choose to have smaller families. The **birth rate** then drops.

Here in **Ireland**, many women have a **career** outside the home and plan their families so they can work. Our population is rising slowly as women choose to have **fewer children**.

In less developed countries, like **Sierra Leone**, the main role of the woman is that of a **mother**. Women tend to get married at a young age, and men expect them to have **large families**. Because many of these women are **uneducated**, they do not know about family planning. In Sierra Leone 33 per cent of girls don't go to school.

One of the reasons for the **high birth rate** is that parents want to ensure they have children to earn money, and to look after them when they are old. High **infant mortality** rates mean that women have more children in order that some survive.

Infant mortality rate:
the number of children under the age of one who die for every 1,000 children born in that year.

Aoife lives in Ireland and Fatu lives in Sierra Leone. Write a short conversation between them to show how their lives differ. Discuss things like morning time, getting to school, and after-school activities. Work in pairs. Perform the conversation in front of the class.

 **(i)** List two factors that impact the rate of population change.

 **(ii)** How does technology increase food supply? How does an increase in food supply influence population growth?

(iii) Define the term infant mortality.

 **(iv)** Choose one of the factors that influences population change. Explain how that factor should be addressed in the developing world in order to slow population growth.

 I understand the factors that lead to population growth in developed and developing countries.   

The demographic transition model

Learning Intentions

In this section, you will learn:

- the different stages in the demographic transition model
- about different views on the future of population growth.

Demographer
Demographic transition model
Fluctuating
Expanding
Senile
Pessimistic
Optimistic

People who study changes in population are called **demographers**. They have come up with a model to help us understand how a population changes over time called the **demographic transition model**.

This shows the changes in the birth rates and death rates of a country over time.

The five stages of the demographic transition model are as follows:

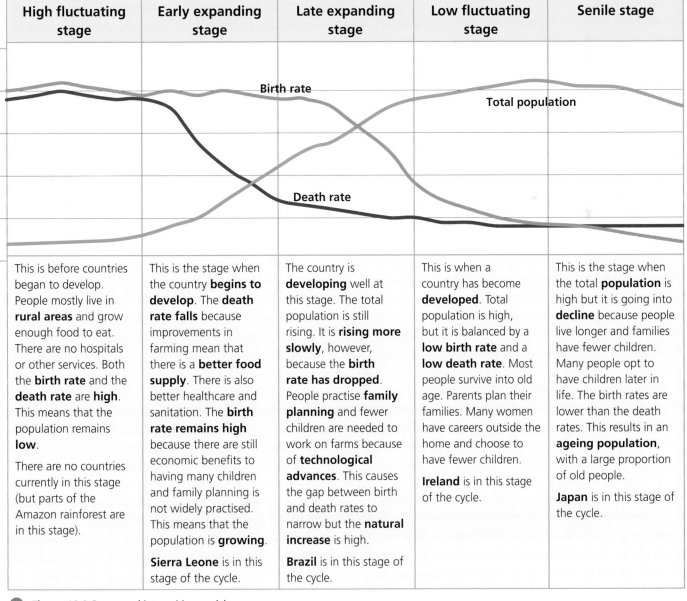

STAGE 1 High fluctuating stage	STAGE 2 Early expanding stage	STAGE 3 Late expanding stage	STAGE 4 Low fluctuating stage	STAGE 5 Senile stage
	Birth rate Death rate		Total population	
This is before countries began to develop. People mostly live in **rural areas** and grow enough food to eat. There are no hospitals or other services. Both the **birth rate** and the **death rate** are **high**. This means that the population remains **low**. There are no countries currently in this stage (but parts of the Amazon rainforest are in this stage).	This is the stage when the country **begins to develop**. The **death rate falls** because improvements in farming mean that there is a **better food supply**. There is also better healthcare and sanitation. The **birth rate remains high** because there are still economic benefits to having many children and family planning is not widely practised. This means that the population is **growing**. **Sierra Leone** is in this stage of the cycle.	The country is **developing** well at this stage. The total population is still rising. It is **rising more slowly**, however, because the **birth rate has dropped**. People practise **family planning** and fewer children are needed to work on farms because of **technological advances**. This causes the gap between birth and death rates to narrow but the **natural increase** is high. **Brazil** is in this stage of the cycle.	This is when a country has become **developed**. Total population is high, but it is balanced by a **low birth rate** and a **low death rate**. Most people survive into old age. Parents plan their families. Many women have careers outside the home and choose to have fewer children. **Ireland** is in this stage of the cycle.	This is the stage when the total **population** is high but it is going into **decline** because people live longer and families have fewer children. Many people opt to have children later in life. The birth rates are lower than the death rates. This results in an **ageing population**, with a large proportion of old people. **Japan** is in this stage of the cycle.

Figure 18.9 *Demographic transition model*

Population growth in the future

Opinion is divided as to the **future rates** of population increase. Some people believe that the numbers will continue to increase rapidly while others believe that the rate of increase will slow down.

Pessimistic view

The **pessimistic view** is that the population will continue to rise at an **explosive rate** and reach over 11 billion people by 2050. We call this the pessimistic view because such numbers would put enormous **pressure** on land and food supplies.

Optimistic view

The **optimistic view** is that birth rates will drop as education and healthcare become more widely available in areas with the highest population growth. Optimists believe that people will have **smaller families** and while the population will continue to grow, it will only reach 11 billion by the end of the century.

 **(i)** What is the name given to people who study population?

 **(ii)** What is happening the population (birth rate and death rate) in stage 2? Why?

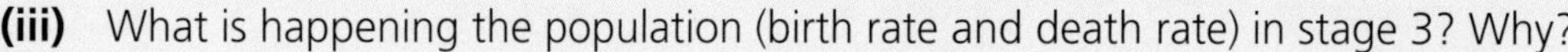
(iii) What is happening the population (birth rate and death rate) in stage 3? Why?

 **(iv)** Can you think of any disadvantages for a country that enters the senile stage?

(v) What impact do you think the growth in population has on the world and its resources?

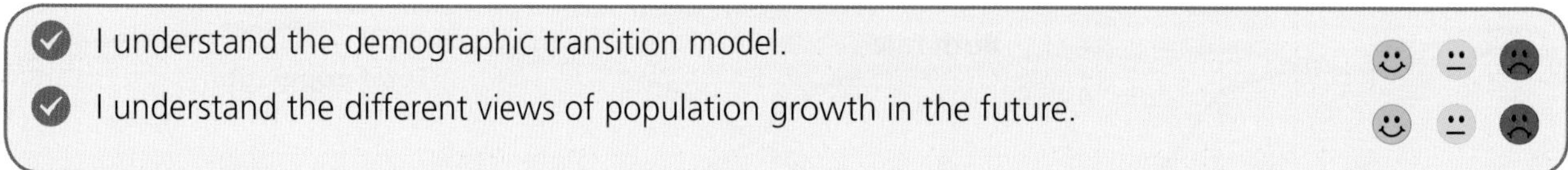

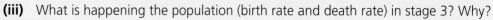

- I understand the demographic transition model.
- I understand the different views of population growth in the future.

Population pyramids

Learning Intentions

In this section, you will learn:

- that population pyramids can be used to analyse the age and gender profile of a country's population
- how population pyramids can be used to plan for the future.

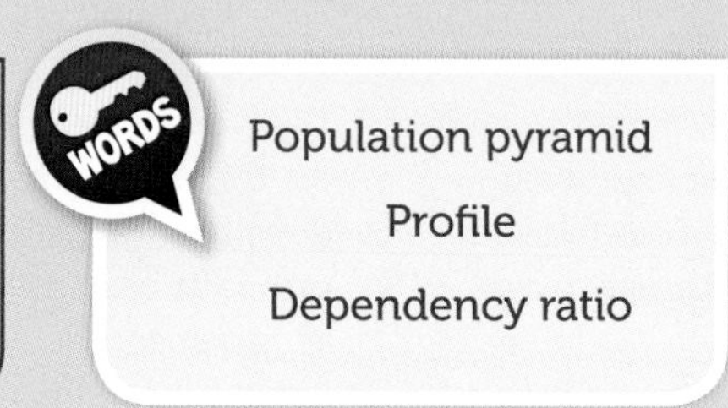

When looking at the population of any country, the two major **characteristics** that stand out are the **gender** and **age profiles** of that population. This can easily be seen by examining **population pyramids**.

Population pyramids show the **number or percentage** of the population, both male and female, in each **age group**. Each bar on the pyramid represents the number of people in a **five-year age band**. One side of the pyramid shows males, the other shows females.

By examining the population pyramid of Ireland, a developed country, and Sierra Leone, a less developed country, we can see what **information** they provide.

The population pyramid on the next page shows us the **gender and age profiles** of the Irish population in 2017. The information is provided in **percentages**.

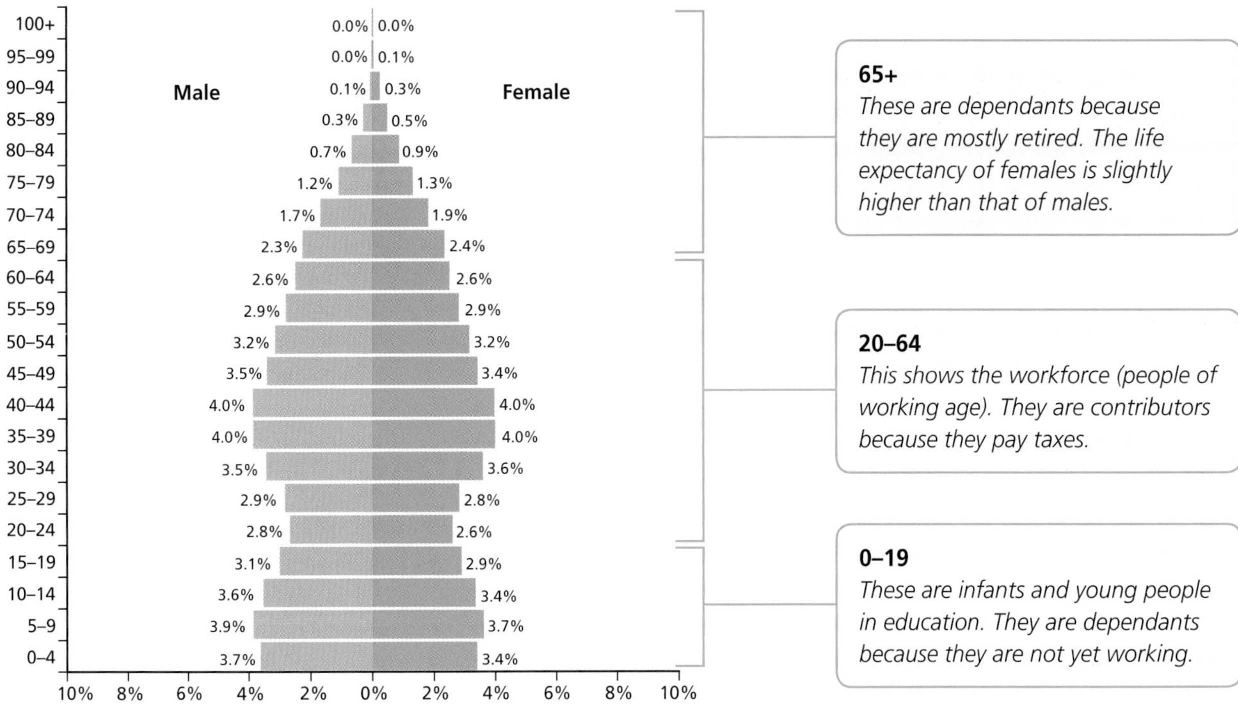

Figure 18.10 *Population pyramid of Ireland*

ACTIVITY

Examine the population pyramid and answer the following questions:

(a) What is the total percentage of males and females in the 0–4 age group and in the 5–9 age group? Is the birth rate rising or falling? Explain your answer.

(b) Why do you think life expectancy is higher for women than men in Ireland?

(c) What is the total population over 65 years of age? What services will people in this category require?

(d) Can you explain why the 20–24 category is narrower than those beside it?

Now let's look at the population pyramid for a **developing** country, **Sierra Leone**. You will notice that the population pyramid of a less economically developed country looks more like a **pyramid**.

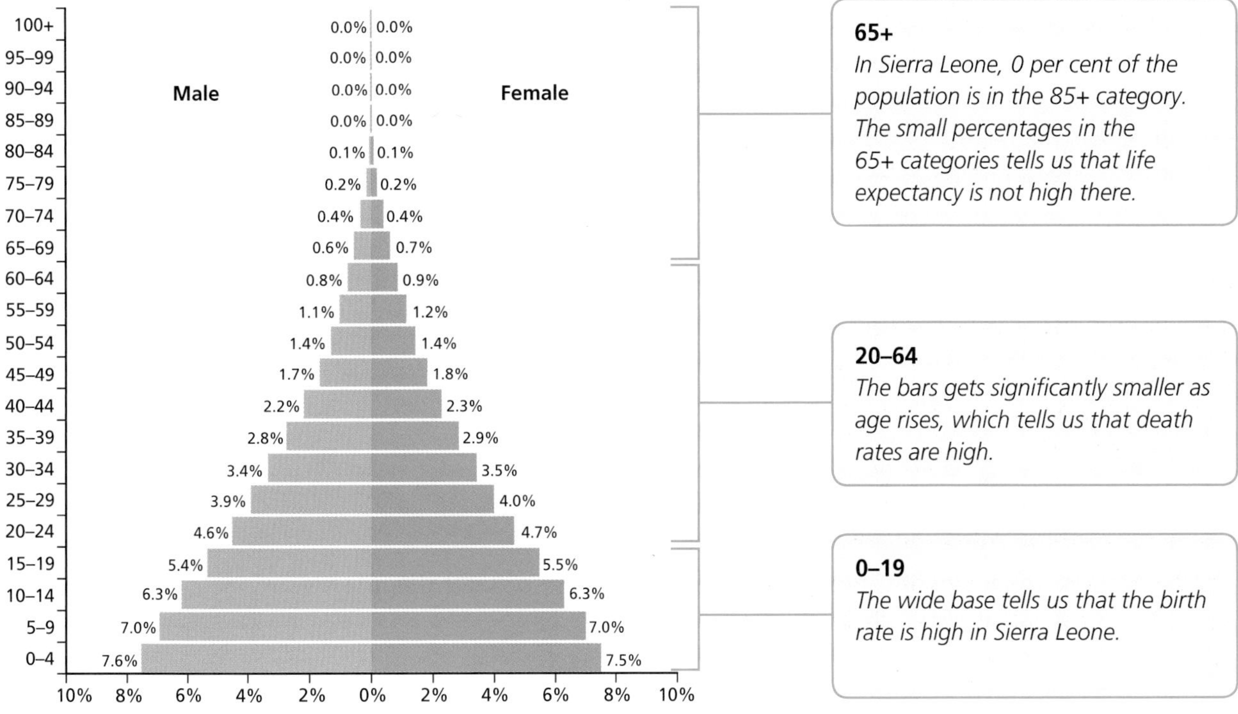

Figure 18.11 *Population pyramid of Sierra Leone*

ACTIVITY

Examine the population pyramid of Sierra Leone and answer the following questions:

(a) What is the total percentage of the population over 60 years of age? Why do you think life expectancy is this low in Sierra Leone?

(b) Calculate the total percentage of the population of Sierra Leone under 20 years of age. Compare this with the population over 60 years of age.

(c) Can you list some problems that might be associated with Sierra Leone having a population pyramid like this?

Why do we study population pyramids?

Population pyramids are a very **useful tool** for governments and other agencies when **planning** for the future needs of the population. They can help determine what **services** will be required. For example:

- If **birth rates are high**, the government may need to plan for the extra pressure put on **education** services.
- If the number of people contributing to the **workforce is low**, there might be a need to bring in **migrants** to fill the needs of the economy.
- If the population is **ageing**, the government needs to ensure there will be enough **healthcare** facilities to take care of their needs in the future. We can see this by looking at how many people are going to be retiring in the near future.
- Population pyramids give us an idea of the **dependency ratio** so the government can plan how much money they will need to look after the elderly and the young.

A-Z

Dependency ratio:
the number of people not working in the older and younger age groups compared to the number of people in the middle groups who are working.

Look at the population pyramids for Ireland and Sierra Leone. If you were a member of the government in each of these countries, what would you do to plan for the next ten years? Present your suggestions to the class.

 **(i)** What two characteristics can we see on population pyramids?

 **(ii)** What are the two dependent groups on a population pyramid?

(iii) Explain the term dependency ratio.

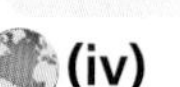 **(iv)** Explain the difference between the population pyramid of Ireland and Sierra Leone under the following headings:

- Birth rate
- Death rate.

I know how to read population pyramids.  

I understand how population pyramids can be used to plan for the future. 

Population change

Learning Intentions

In this section, you will learn:

- how and why Ireland's population has changed over the years
- about population change in Sierra Leone, a developing country.

Census
Great Famine
Colony
Fertilty rate

Ireland

Ireland's population according to the **census** of 2016 was **4,761,865 million**. This is an increase of 3.8 per cent since the census of 2011. There has been a **natural increase** of 196,613 people in Ireland since 2011. Ireland is a developed country. The population is **growing slowly**.

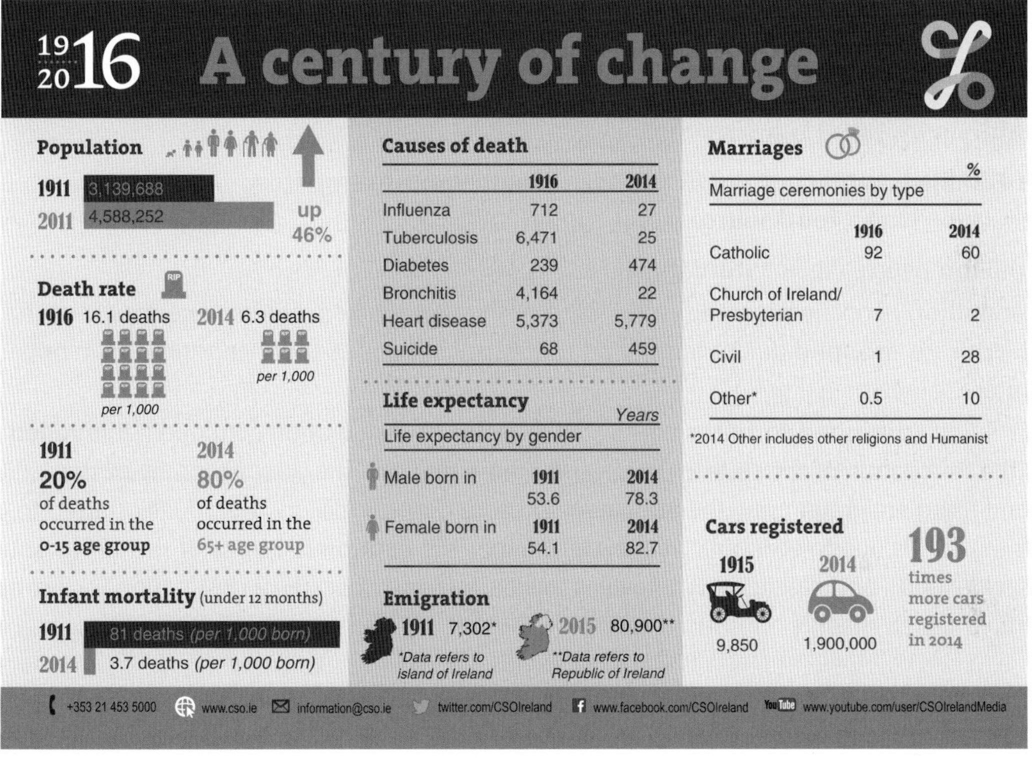

1916
2016
A century of change
%
Population
1911 3,139,688
2011 4,588,252
up 46%
Death rate
RIP
1916 16.1 deaths per 1,000
2014 6.3 deaths per 1,000
1911
20% of deaths occurred in the 0-15 age group
2014
80% of deaths occurred in the 65+ age group
Infant mortality (under 12 months)
1911 81 deaths (per 1,000 born)
2014 3.7 deaths (per 1,000 born)
Causes of death
1916 2014
Influenza 712 27
Tuberculosis 6,471 25
Diabetes 239 474
Bronchitis 4,164 22
Heart disease 5,373 5,779
Suicide 68 459
Life expectancy
Years
Life expectancy by gender
Male born in 1911 53.6 2014 78.3
Female born in 1911 54.1 2014 82.7
Emigration
1911 7,302*
*Data refers to island of Ireland
2015 80,900**
**Data refers to Republic of Ireland
Marriages
%
Marriage ceremonies by type
1916 2014
Catholic 92 60
Church of Ireland/ Presbyterian 7 2
Civil 1 28
Other* 0.5 10
*2014 Other includes other religions and Humanist
Cars registered
1915 9,850
2014 1,900,000
193 times more cars registered in 2014
+353 21 453 5000
www.cso.ie
information@cso.ie
twitter.com/CSOIreland
www.facebook.com/CSOIreland
www.youtube.com/user/CSOIrelandMedia

Figure 18.12 *Chart from Ireland's Central Office of Statistics*

ACTIVITY

Look at the chart above, which gives information about how the population of Ireland has changed in the last hundred years or so. Then answer these questions:

(a) What was the percentage increase in population from 1911 to 2011?

(b) What was the death rate percentage in the 0–15 age group in 1911? Why do you think it was so high?

(c) Why has life expectancy greatly increased in Ireland for males and females?

(d) Why do you think tuberculosis was a huge killer in 1916 and is not today?

Population before the Great Famine

Before the **Great Famine**, Ireland's population was **rising rapidly**. People had a constant food supply, farmers sub-divided their land among all their sons so there were lots of small farms and people married young and had large families.

In **1841** the population of Ireland was over 8 million, with **6.5 million** in the area that is now the Republic.

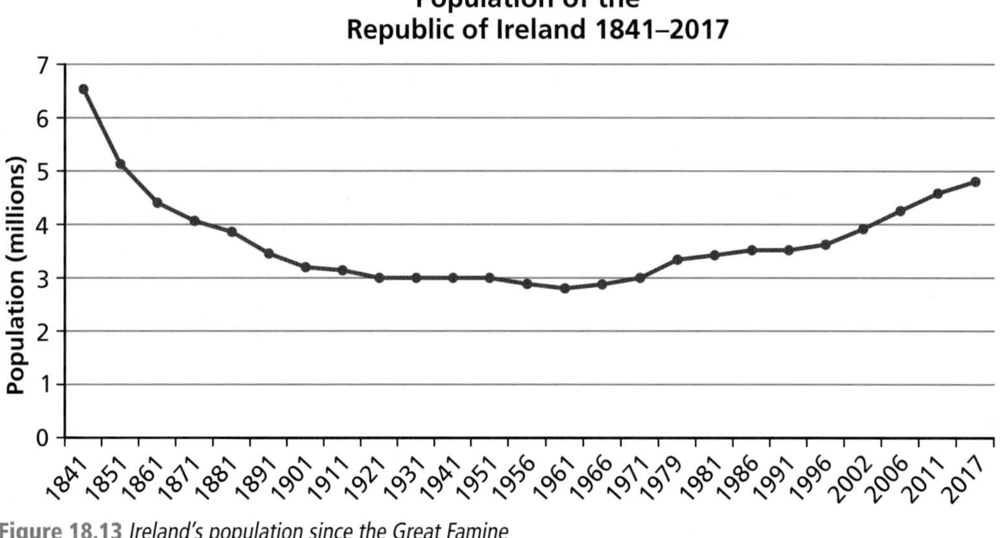

Figure 18.13 *Ireland's population since the Great Famine*

Population after the Famine

The **Great Famine** occurred from 1845 to 1852 when the **potato** crop failed because of blight. This cut off the population's main **food source**.

- Over a **million** people died of **starvation**.
- A further **million** people **emigrated** to the UK and the USA. The emigrants were mostly young couples so the **birth rate dropped** during this period too. Many farmers abandoned their land in hope of a better future somewhere else.
- The population **continued to fall** as birth rates dropped and emigration continued. It **levelled off** around the foundation of the state in 1922 at around **3 million**. The poor economy of the 1950s and 1960s and rising emigration saw the population drop to under 3 million. It gradually started to grow again in the 1970s due to economic and social change. The **economic boom** of the 1990s and early 2000s saw Ireland's population grow to over 4 million as Ireland became a destination for **economic migrants** in search of work.

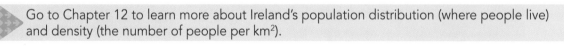

Go to Chapter 12 to learn more about Ireland's population distribution (where people live) and density (the number of people per km²).

Sierra Leone

Sierra Leone was a **colony** of Great Britain from 1808 to 1961, forming part of the province of West Africa. Since **independence**, its population has grown from 2.3 million in 1961 to 7.3 million in 2017. The population change can be seen in the graph on the right:

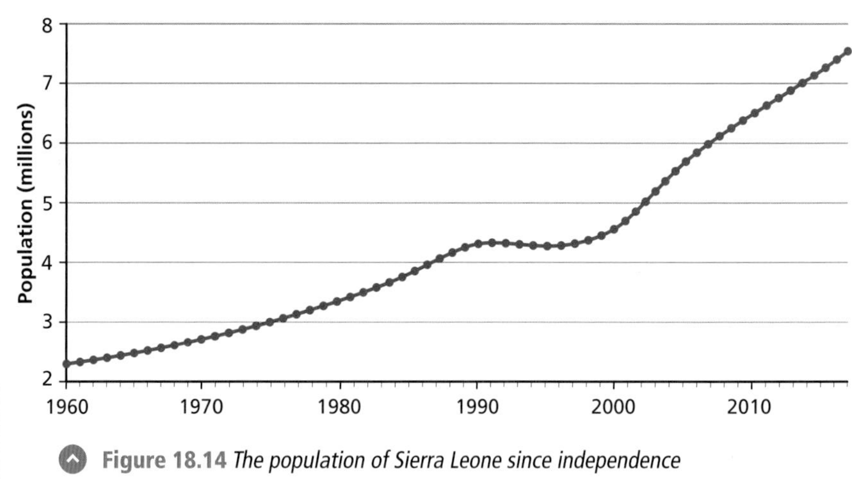

Figure 18.14 *The population of Sierra Leone since independence*

ACTIVITY

There was a civil war in Sierra Leone. Can you work out which decade it occurred in from studying this graph?

There are many **reasons** for Sierra Leone's continuing population growth:

- There is a **high fertility rate** of almost five children per woman because people want large families.
- There is a **low** level of **contraceptive use**.
- Women start having children in their **late teens**.
- There are high levels of **illiteracy**.
- Sierra Leone has been a source of and destination for **refugees**.
- Sierra Leone's **civil war** internally displaced as many as two million people.
- The **conflicts** that occurred in the country since independence have meant that governments have not been **prioritising** education and basic health services.

It is estimated that Sierra Leone's population will rise to almost **10 million** by 2030.

Fertility rate:
the average number of babies born per woman.

Figure 18.15 *Young mother and her baby in a refugee camp in Sierra Leone*

Figure 18.16 *Domestic life in Freetown, Sierra Leone*

(i) What was the population of Ireland before the Great Famine?

(ii) What was the population of Ireland in 2017?

(iii) Give two reasons for the population growth of Sierra Leone.

(iv) How did life expectancy change in Ireland between 1911 and 2014? Suggest three reasons for this change.

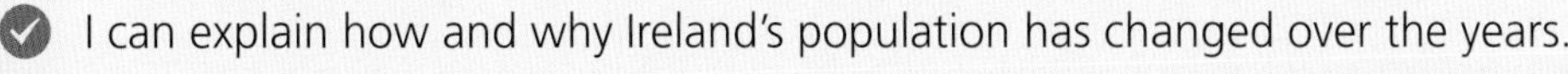
I can explain how and why Ireland's population has changed over the years.  

I can explain how and why the population of a developing world country has changed.  

How could your local area respond to the possible problems created by rapid population growth? Go to page 72 of your Portfolio to create an action plan.

REVISION

The population of the world is over ____________________ ____________________. This has ____________________ over time. If the ____________________ ____________________ is higher than the death rate, then the population ____________________. If the death rate is higher than the ____________________ ____________________ then the population ____________________.

The factors that influence population change are ____________________, ____________________ ____________________, ____________________, ____________________ ____________________, ____________________, and the role of ____________________ in society. People who study population change are called ____________________. They have developed a model called the ____________________ ____________________ model to help us understand how a population changes. Ireland is currently in the ____________________ ____________________ stage.

The graph used to show the gender and age profile of a population is a ____________________ ____________________. The ____________________ ratio is the number of older people and youths compared to the number of people working. ____________________ mortality rate is the number of children who die under the age of one for every 1,000 children born in that year. ____________________ ____________________ is an indicator of how long a person can expect to live.

Questions & Answers

Sample Questions

1. Name **one** country with a population structure similar to Pyramid A.
2. Name **one** country with a population structure similar to Pyramid B.
3. Explain **one** reason why Pyramid B has a wider base than Pyramid A.
4. Name **two** uses of population pyramids

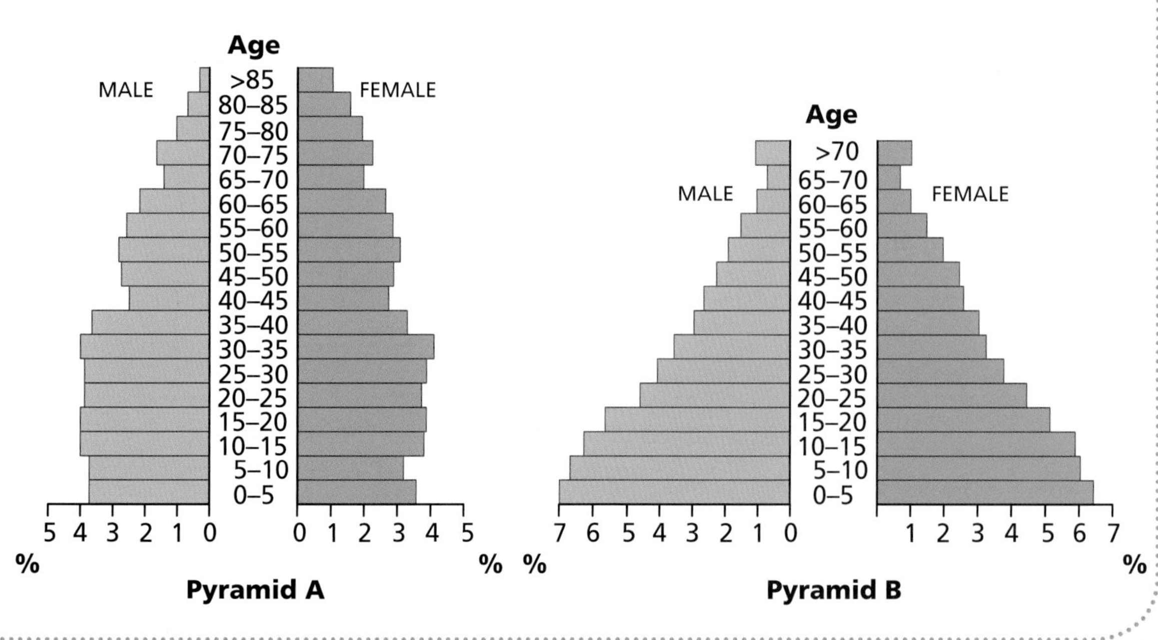

Sample Answers

1. A developed country such as Ireland has a population structure similar to Pyramid A.
2. A developing country such as Sierra Leone has a population structure similar to Pyramid B.
3. Pyramid B has a wider base than Pyramid A because it has a higher birth rate.
   This is because people in Country A are more educated than people in Country B and are aware of family planning so they have fewer children.
   It is also because women have a stronger role in society in Country A than in Country B and choose to have a career before they have children. This makes the birth rate lower in Country A than in Country B.
4. Population pyramids can be used to plan for the educational needs of the population.
   Population pyramids can also be used to see what percentage of the population is contributing to the workforce and what percentage of the population is dependent.

Short Questions

1. The diagram shows changes over time in a country's birth rate and death rate. The statements below relate to the diagram.

Indicate whether each statement is true or false by circling the true or false alternatives.

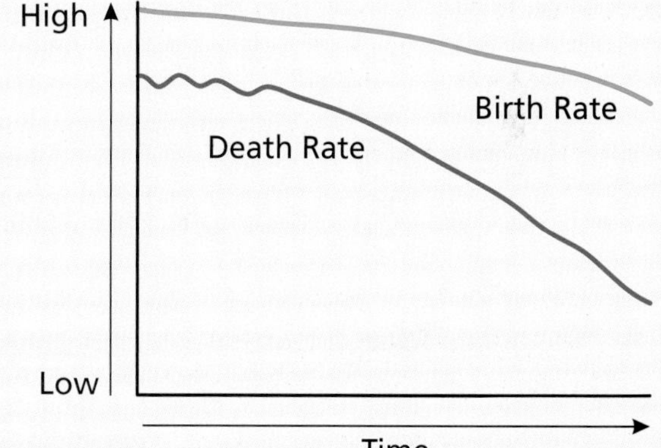

(i) The death rate fluctuated (went up and down) at first and then fell quite rapidly. **True / False**

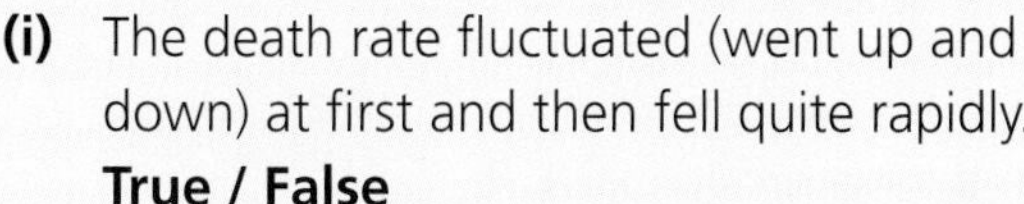

(ii) The birth rate fell more rapidly than the death rate. **True / False**

(iii) This country has a natural increase in population. **True / False**

2. Examine the Demographic Transition Model below.

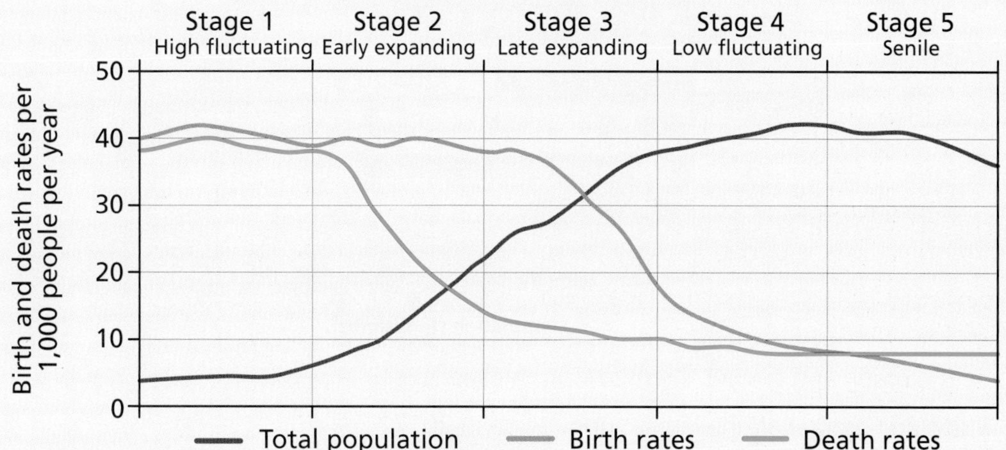

In Stage 1, total population growth is slow because:

Death rates are low and birth rates are high. ☐

Both birth and death rates are high. ☐

Death rates are high and birth rates are low. ☐ [tick (✓) the correct box]

3. The diagram shows the population pyramid of Ireland for 2017.

Use the population pyramid to indicate which of the statements are true.

A All children under the age of four make up 4% of the population.

B The age group with the greatest number of people is the 5–9 age group.

C Females tend to live longer than males.

D There are roughly equal percentages of men and women in the 25–29 age group.

E Teenagers (age 10–19) make up 13% of the total population. The correct statements are:

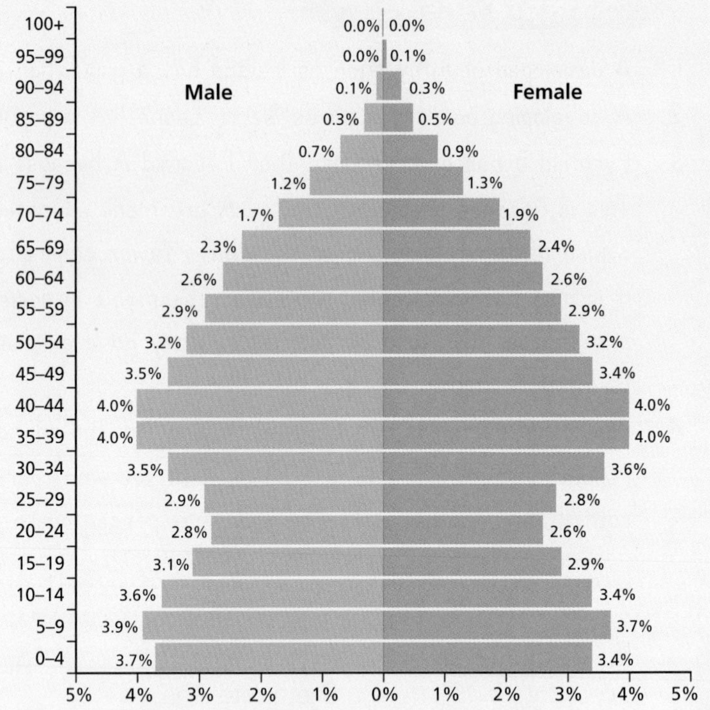

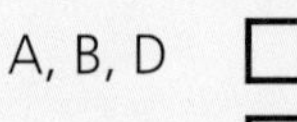

A, B, D ☐

A, C, E ☐

B, C, D ☐

C, D, E ☐ [tick (✓) the correct box]

4. The graph below shows the total Irish population by age group in 2017.

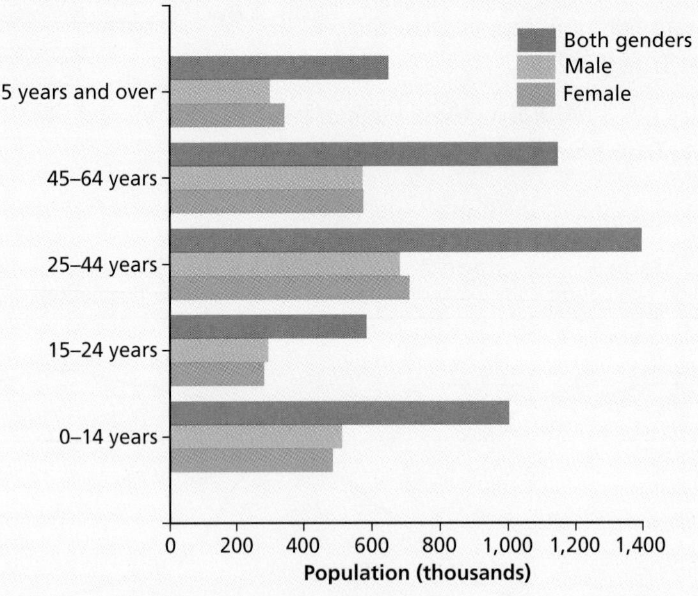

Examine the graph and answer the following questions:

(i) Which age group had the largest population in 2017?

(ii) Which **two** age groups make up the dependent groups?

1. ____________________

2. ____________________

(iii) Do men or women have a higher life expectancy? Account for your answer.

5. Match each of the letters in **Column X** with the number of its pair in **Column Y**. One match has been made for you.

	Column X		Column Y	X	Y
A	Natural decrease	1	The average number of people per square kilometre	A	3
B	Population density	2	The number of live births per 1000 of the population in one year	B	
C	Population explosion	3	When the death rate is higher than the birth rate	C	
D	Birth rate	4	Very rapid population growth	D	

Long Questions

1. (i) Name **one** reason why world population began to rise from 1800 onwards.
   (ii) What will the world population be in 2050?
   (iii) Explain **two** problems associated with the predicted growth of the world population.

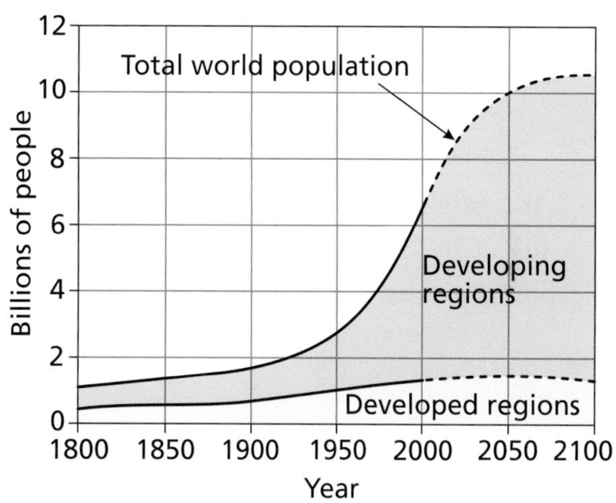

2. Explain the following terms: birth rate; death rate; natural increase; natural decrease.

3.

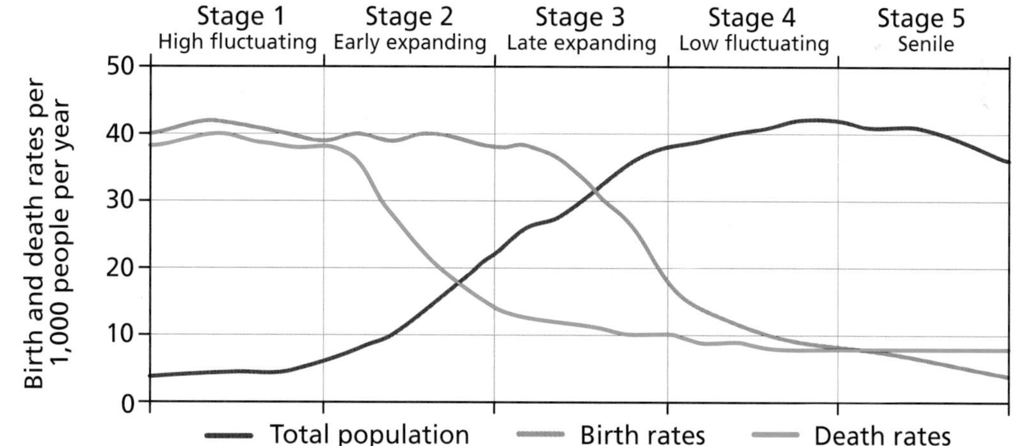

(i) What name is given to this diagram?
(ii) At which stage of the diagram is the death rate at its highest?
(iii) At which stage of the diagram is the total population growing most rapidly?
(iv) At which stage is there a natural decrease in the population?
(v) Briefly explain each of the following:
– Why the death rate fluctuates (goes up and down) at Stage 1.
– Why the death rate declines rapidly at Stage 2.
– Why the birth rate declines at Stage 3.

4. Name and describe **three** factors that influence the rate of population change. Use examples of countries you have studied to support your answer.

5. What are the optimistic view and the pessimistic view of population change in the future? Which view do you think is the most likely? Give **two** reasons to justify your answer.

6. Examine these two diagrams which show the population structure of two countries.

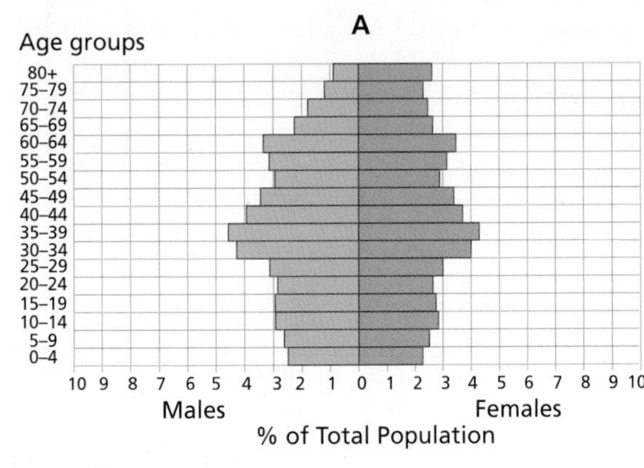

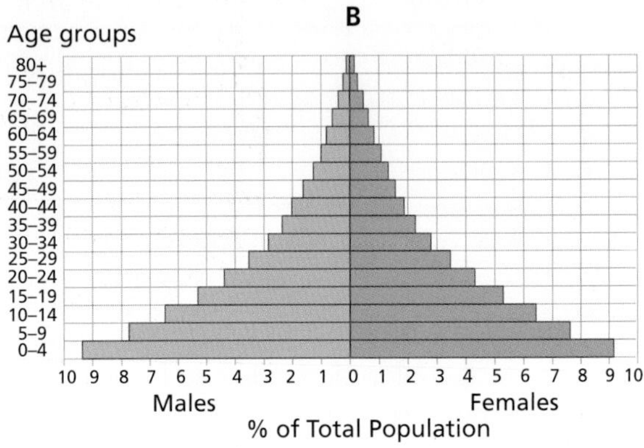

(i) What are these diagrams called?

(ii) Which one shows the population structure of a developing country.

(iii) Describe **two** major contrasts (differences) between the population structures of these two countries. You should refer to birth rates, death rates and life expectancy in the two countries.

7. Examine the population pyramid for Ireland in 2050.

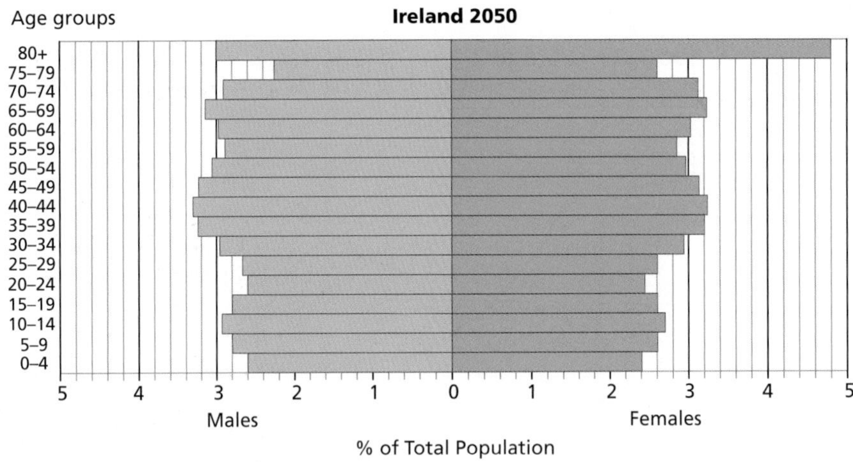

(i) What percentage of the population will be in the 80+ age group in 2050?

(ii) Explain why life expectancy will be longer in 2050.

(iii) Name **two** ways in which governments use population pyramids. Use examples from countries you have studied to support your answer.

Visual Summary

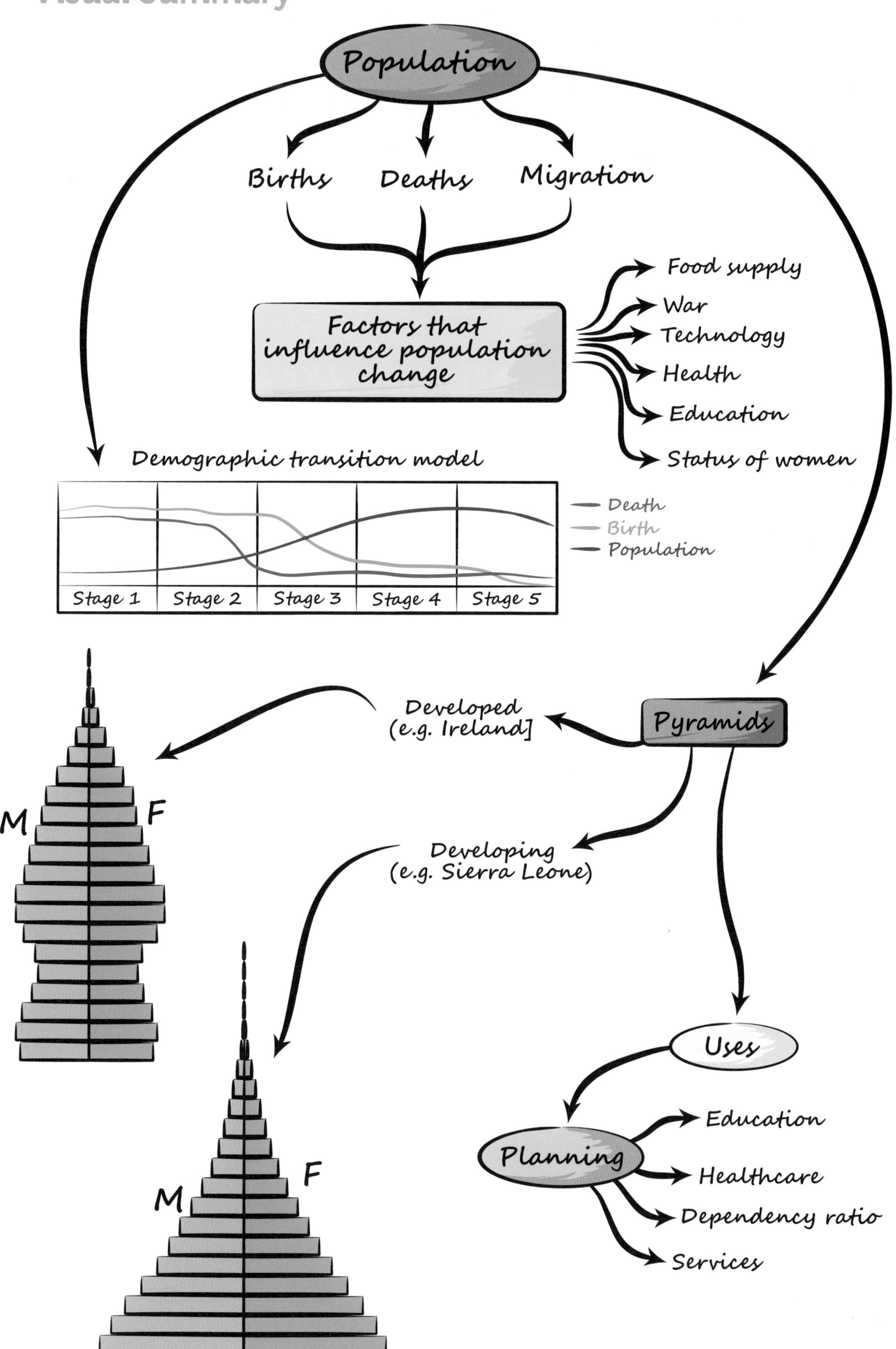
Population
Births
Deaths
Migration
Factors that influence population change
Food supply
War
Technology
Health
Education
Status of women
Demographic transition model
Death
Birth
Population
Stage 1
Stage 2
Stage 3
Stage 4
Stage 5
Pyramids
Developed (e.g. Ireland]
M
F
Developing (e.g. Sierra Leone)
M
F
Uses
Planning
Education
Healthcare
Dependency ratio
Services

19 Migration: People on the move

In this chapter, you will learn:

- what migration is
- about the causes and consequences of migration.

ICE-BREAKER ACTIVITY

(i) List five reasons why people might want to move from a place.
(ii) List five reasons why people might be attracted to move to a place.
(iii) Compare your list to the person next to you and circle the ones in common.
(iv) Work as a class to create a complete list.

Migration

Learning Intentions

In this section, you will learn:

- what migration is
- about the causes (push and pull factors) of migration
- about barriers that can stop migration
- about the consequences of migration.

Migration	International
Migrant	Push factor
Emigrant	Pull factor
Immigrant	Voluntary
Refugee	Forced
Asylum	Visa
Internal	Brain drain

Migration is the movement of people from one place to another. A person who leaves one place for another is called a **migrant**. Migration has happened throughout history and it continues today.

Do you know anyone who has migrated? Write down a few points about why they migrated. Discuss with the person next to you.

Internal migration

Internal migration is when people migrate **within the same country** or region. For example, moving from the west of Ireland to Dublin. Most migration is internal migration.

International migration

International migration is when people migrate **from one country to another**. For example, moving from Ireland to Australia.

Migrants are both **emigrants** and **immigrants**:

- A person who leaves one country to live in another is called an **emigrant**.
- A person who comes to live in one country from another is called an **immigrant**.
- For example, an Irish person who moves from Ireland to Australia is an emigrant from Ireland and an immigrant to Australia.

Figure 19.1 *Emigration is also immigration*

Figure 19.2 *Irish emigrants: the Dubai Celts GAA team*

Causes of migration

Migration can be caused by **economic**, **social**, **political** or **environmental** factors.

- **Economic migration**: moving to find work or follow a particular career path
- **Social migration**: moving somewhere for a better quality of life or to be closer to family or friends
- **Political migration**: moving to escape political persecution or war
- **Environmental migration:** causes include natural disasters such as flooding or famine.

Figure 19.3 *Political migration: refugees from Syria arriving at a Greek island, 2015*

Someone who feels they cannot return to their country because they might be persecuted can apply for **refugee** status in another country. This is also called seeking **asylum**. A refugee cannot be forced to return to their home country under the **United Nations convention** on the status of refugees. **Political** and **environmental** migrants are often **refugees**.

When people have to flee their homes for one reason or another, they often end up in **refugee camps** until they can return home or find a host country to live in.

PORTFOLIO ACTIVITY 19.1

Go to page 76 of your Portfolio to research and write a report on a refugee camp.

The reasons for migration can be divided into **push factors** and **pull factors**:

- A **push** factor is what makes someone want to leave a place.
- A **pull** factor is what attracts people to live in a place.

Push factors

- lack of job opportunities
- lack of services
- lack of safety
- high crime
- crop failure
- drought
- flooding
- poverty
- war

Pull factors

- higher employment
- more wealth
- better services
- good climate
- safer/less crime
- political stability
- more fertile land
- lower risk from natural hazards

Migration usually happens as a result of a **combination** of these push and pull factors.

Migration can be **voluntary** or **forced**:

- **Voluntary** migration is when people **choose** to migrate. For example, someone might decide to move to another area to improve their chances of getting a good job.
- **Forced** migration is when people do not have a choice and **have to migrate**. For example, someone who moves due to war or famine.

Individual migration

Individual migration is when a person chooses to move from one place to another. This usually happens when a person feels they will have a better **quality of life** somewhere else. Examples of this type of migration include people moving from the west of Ireland to Dublin, and Irish people moving abroad to places like Australia.

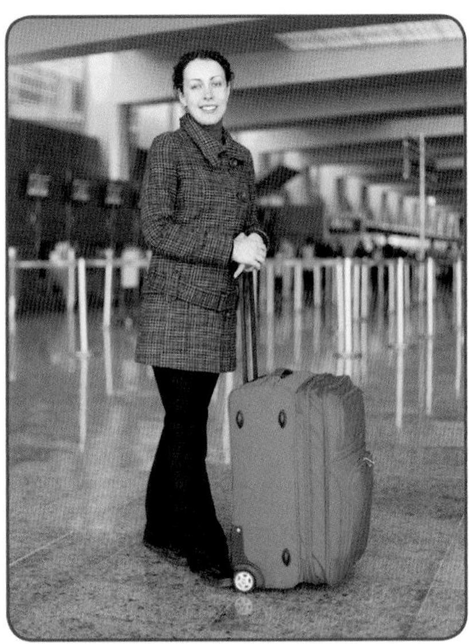

Figure 19.4 *People often emigrate in the hope of finding a job somewhere else*

Push factors

- **Unemployment**: There may be a lack of job opportunities. This is especially true in times of **economic recession**.
- **Lack of services**: Education and healthcare services might not be widely available.
- **Lack of facilities**: As the population of rural areas declines, so do the facilities available for the local people. Many young people migrate because of the limited social life in many rural areas.

Pull factors

- **Employment**: People are attracted to areas where jobs will be available to them. Many young people move to Dublin, Ireland's capital and **core region**, where there are career opportunities, especially in the **services sector**. Other young people emigrate to Australia, Canada and the USA where there are jobs in a variety of sectors, including the **construction industry**.
- **Better services**: People migrate to places where there is access to **education** and **healthcare**. Many people who migrate from the west of Ireland to Dublin to attend **third-level colleges** end up staying in the region because this is where most of the jobs are.
- **Better facilities**: People migrate if they think they will have a better **quality of life** in another area. The pull factors that encourage people to move to Dublin and abroad include a better **social life**, a better standard of living and, in the case of moving abroad, better **weather**.

ACTIVITY

Read the story of the two migrants below. Make a list of the push and pull factors that influenced their migration.

Adnan's Story

Adnan is a 14-year-old boy from Syria. Before the war he lived on a farm with parents and his brother and sister. Their house was destroyed in the fighting and his baby sister was killed. His family fled their home and crossed the border into Lebanon. They now live in a refugee camp with 140,000 other Syrians. The UN Refugee Agency (UNHCR) gave them basic supplies such as blankets, cooking utensils and soap. Adnan fears that he will never be able to return to his homeland and now dreams of starting a new life in Europe.

Sean's Story

Sean is 24 years old and from Co. Carlow. He graduated from university in Dublin with a degree in English and History and went on to become a qualified teacher. Since then he has had difficulty finding work. He got some work subbing in various schools in Dublin but he found that with the high rent he was paying he didn't have much money. He heard about a job in a school in Dubai and went for an interview. The school offered him a job and free accommodation. Sean moved to Dubai to start his new job in August.

ACTIVITY

Imagine you have emigrated. Write a letter to a friend who still lives in the place where you were born. Explain why you migrated and how you feel about your new life.

Figure 19.5 *Much of the Middle East has been a war zone in recent years. Syria and Lebanon were mentioned in Adnan's story. Can you find them on this map?*

Barriers to migration

Sometimes there are **barriers** to migration. These barriers may stop people from moving even though they want to. Barriers to migration include:

- **Poverty**: There may not be enough money available to migrate.
- **Personal reasons**: People may have ties to their families that prevent them from moving. Perhaps there will be no one to look after their parents if they choose to leave.
- **Visas**: Some countries require foreigners to get a visa before they can enter the country. People may not be able to get a visa for the country they wish to migrate to.

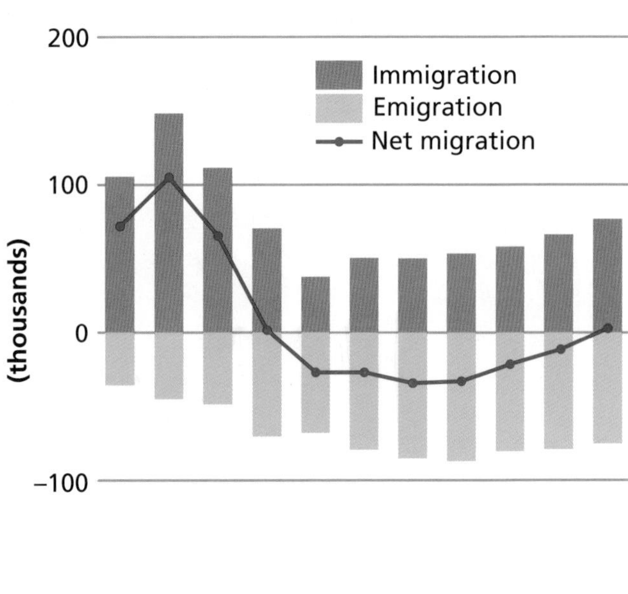

Figure 19.6 *Migration in Ireland, 2006–16*

ACTIVITY

The graph above shows the migration pattern in Ireland from 2006 to 2016. Study the graph and answer the following questions.

(a) Why do you think emigration was so low in 2006?

(b) Emigration peaked in 2012–13. Why do you think this happened?

(c) Why were there so few immigrants in 2010?

(d) What impact did migration have on the population in 2014? Did that change by 2016?

Consequences of migration

The impact of migration on the place left behind

When large numbers of people choose to migrate from an area, it has a huge **impact** on that area. This area is sometimes referred to as the **donor region**, as the area is giving people to another area.

- **Marriage rates** go into decline and **birth rates** drop. This may lead to schools closing down if there are not enough students.
- Other **facilities** may also close and sports clubs may find it difficult to keep their teams going. During the **recession** in Ireland many GAA clubs in rural Ireland found it difficult to put together a team because so many young people had emigrated.
- It becomes more difficult to attract industry because there is a '**brain drain**' of young people.
- Farms become **less productive** without young people to develop them. The average age of farmers in Ireland is 56 years and only 25 per cent of farmers are under 45 years old. This means that farmers tend to use more **traditional methods** which may not be so productive.

Figure 19.7 *Small schools in rural areas are forced to close when pupil numbers drop*

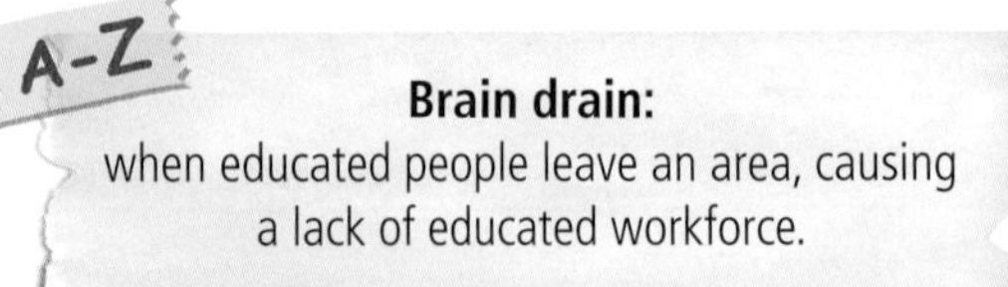

Brain drain:
when educated people leave an area, causing a lack of educated workforce.

The impact of migration on the place people move to

Immigrants make valuable contributions to places they move to.

- They bring a wide range of **skills**, and add to the workforce.
- Because they pay taxes, they increase government **revenue**. During its economic boom from 2002 to 2006, Ireland benefitted greatly from immigrant workers paying tax.
- They bring new cultural elements to a country, including food, customs and language. We have seen Ireland develop into a **multicultural society** in recent years.

Figure 19.8 *An Irish Chinese take-away: the culture of immigrant communities often enriches the host region*

However, when the population of a region increases because more people are settling there, it puts **pressure** on that region to provide for the demand on **services** and **facilities**. This area is also referred to as the **host region**. This is because the area is hosting the people who come to live there.

- **Services**: The **demand** for healthcare services and places in school increases. The government must provide adequate services to fill the needs of the growing population.
- **Housing**: An increase in population means that there is a growing **demand** for housing. **House prices** rise as demand grows. This may lead to the development of **overspill** or **dormitory towns** to provide housing for these people.
- **Facilities**: Transport links and **infrastructure** may need to be developed to cope with the growing demand. This puts a lot of economic pressure on the host area.

PORTFOLIO ACTIVITY 19.2

In Ireland almost every family has a member who has migrated to or from or within Ireland. Go to page 78 of your Portfolio to prepare an interview with a member of your family who has migrated.

(i) What is migration?
(ii) What is internal migration?
(iii) What is international migration?
(iv) What is a push factor of migration? Give an example.
(v) What is a pull factor of migration? Give an example.
(vi) Describe one impact of migration on a host region.
(vii) Describe one impact of migration on a donor region.
(viii) If you were to migrate in the morning, where would you migrate to? List the push and the pull factors.

- I understand what migration is.
- I can explain the causes of migration (push and pull factors).
- I can explain the barriers that can stop migration.
- I can explain the consequences of migration.

Organised migration

Learning Intentions

In this section, you will learn:

- what organised migration is and examples of where it occurred
- about the consequences of organised migration.

Organised migration is the **planned** movement of people by a government. The **plantations** of Laois-Offaly, Munster and Ulster are examples.

CASE STUDY

Organised migration: the Plantation of Ulster

As you may have learned in your History course, the Plantation of Ulster began in 1609 when English and Scottish Protestants settled on land that was taken from the native Irish.

Causes

- The British crown wanted to rule the whole island of Ireland and **reward** its loyal servants by giving them land.
- Britain wanted to spread the **Protestant religion** to Catholic Ireland and spread English customs.

ACTIVITY

Check out https://educateplus.ie/go/plantation-ulster to find out more about the Plantation of Ulster.

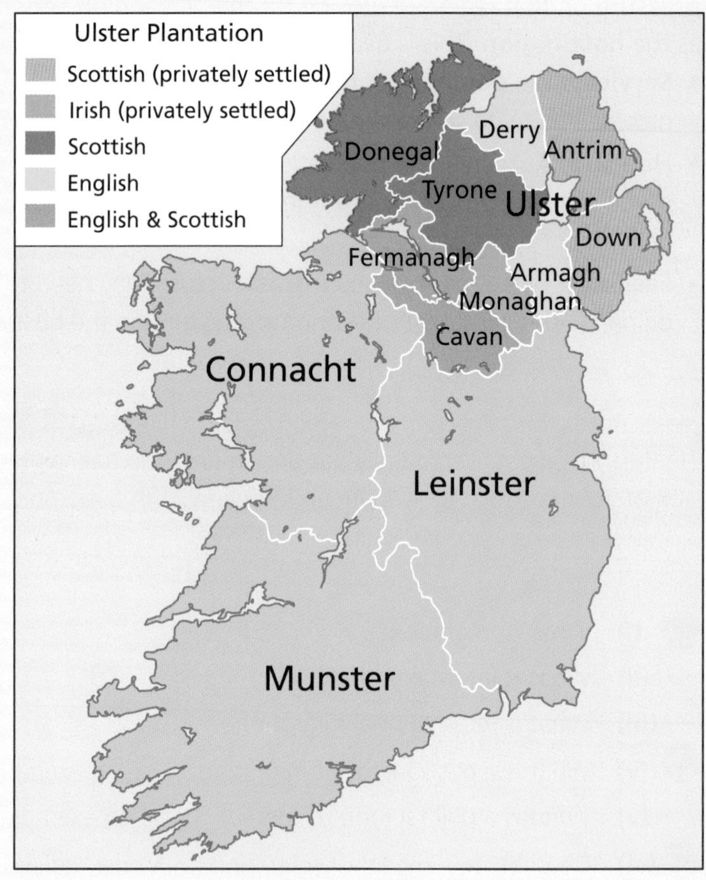

Figure 19.9 *The Plantation of Ulster*

Consequences

- **Planned towns** with market squares such as **Coleraine** and **Londonderry** (also known as **Derry**) were built.
- The settlers brought with them new ideas about farming and **improved farming practices**.
- Irish was replaced by **English as the first language** of the majority of people.
- The planters brought with them English and Scottish **culture** and **traditions**.

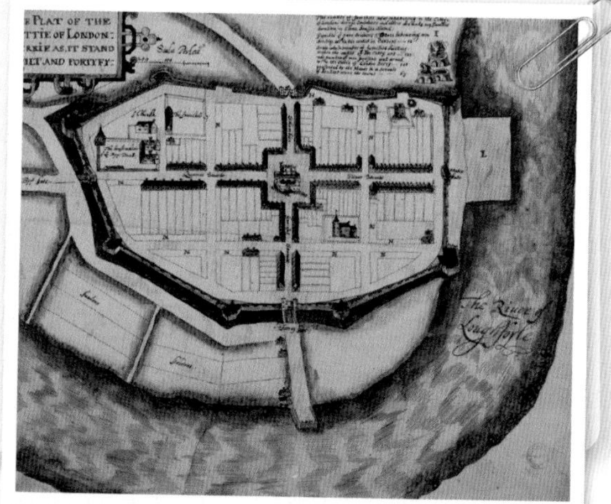

Figure 19.10 *The planned town of Derry*

- **Protestantism** and **Presbyterianism** were introduced to Ulster. They are still the majority religions in Northern Ireland today. Catholics are in the minority.
- It led to **tension** between Protestants and Catholics. There was a period of **conflict** for 30 years from 1968 until the **Good Friday Agreement** was signed in 1998. The mostly Protestant unionists wanted to remain part of the UK and the mostly Catholic nationalists and republicans wanted to be part of the Republic of Ireland. There is still tension between the two sides in Northern Ireland today.

The European **colonisation** of Central and South America and the migration of Jews to Israel after World War II are other examples of **organised migration**. You may have studied them in your History class.

(i) Name two organised migrations that occurred in the past.
(ii) Why did the Ulster Plantation take place?
(iii) What were the impacts of the Ulster Plantation?
(iv) Do we have organised migration today? Give reasons to justify your answer.

I can explain the causes and consequences of organised migration.

REVISION

________________ is the movement of people. A person who leaves one country to live in another is an ________________. A person who arrives in a country from another is an ________________. A ________________ is someone who has had to flee their home and is seeking ________________. The things that attract people to a place are ________________ factors. The things that make people leave are ________________ factors. ________________ migration is when a person makes the decision themselves to move. ________________ migration is when someone does not have a choice. Sometimes there are ________________ which stop people from migrating. Migration has an ________________ on the place left behind. When the educated young people leave an area it is called a ________________ ________________. The Plantation of Ulster is an example of ________________ migration.

Questions & Answers

Sample Questions

1. Name **one** example of an individual migration you have studied.
2. Describe **one** push factor associated with this individual migration.
3. Describe **one** effect of migration on the area from which people have migrated.

Sample Answers

1. One example of an individual migration I have studied is a young Irish person emigrating to Dubai to take up a teaching job.
2. One push factor is employment. This young person was not able to get a permanent job. Because of the lack of job security they decided to emigrate.
3. The brain drain associated with this type of migration means that it is very difficult for schools to get substitute teachers. There are also fewer young people to make up teams for sports clubs all over the country because they are emigrating out of Ireland to find better opportunities abroad.

Short Questions

1. Migration can be caused by push and pull factors.

   Circle the correct answer in each statement.

   (i) Civil war and unrest are a **push / pull** factor.

   (ii) Excellent job opportunities are a **push / pull** factor.

   (iii) A mild climate is a **push / pull** factor.

2. In the boxes provided, match each of the letters in **Column X** with the number of its pair in **Column Y**. One match has been made for you.

Column X		Column Y	
A	Emigrant	1	Religious or political persecution
B	A push factor	2	A person who migrates into an area
C	Immigrant	3	A person who migrates out of an area
D	A pull factor	4	A promise of freedom

X	Y
A	
B	
C	
D	4

3. The table below shows a push factor, a pull factor and a barrier to human migration.

Immigration law	Unemployment	Better services

Complete each of the following sentences using the correct term from the table above.

A push factor is _________________________________.

A pull factor is _________________________________.

A barrier to migration is ____________________________.

Long Questions

1. Describe **three** push and pull factors which might encourage someone to migrate from the west of Ireland to Dublin.

2. **(i)** Explain any **two** of the following terms:
   - Emigration
   - Immigration
   - Barriers to migration.

   (ii) Explain why forced migration occurs, with reference to an example you have studied.

3. **(i)** Name **one** example of organised international migration.

   (ii) Describe **two** reasons why this organised migration took place.

   (iii) Describe **one** long-term effect of this migration in the destination country.

Visual Summary

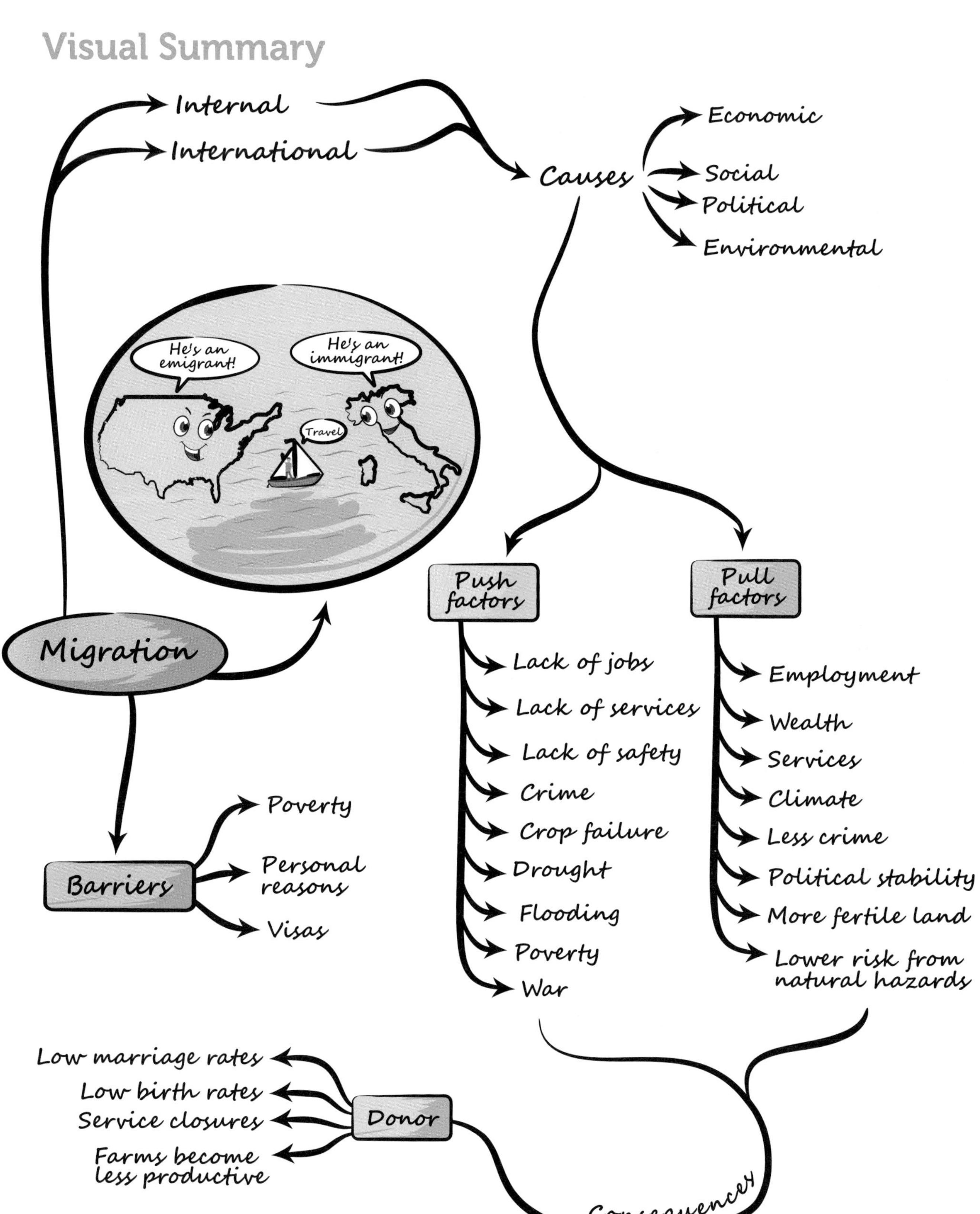

20 Economic Inequality: A world divided

In this chapter, you will learn:

- how countries are classified according to their economic development
- about the inequalities between the economies of rich developed countries and poor developing countries
- about development assistance/aid
- about the different life chances of young people in a developed country and a developing country.

ICE-BREAKER ACTIVITY

Divide into groups of four and look at the images below. The first photograph is of young people in Ireland. The second photograph is of young people in Mali. Make a list of (i) how young people's lives in Ireland and Mali are the same, and (ii) how young people's lives in Ireland and Mali are different.

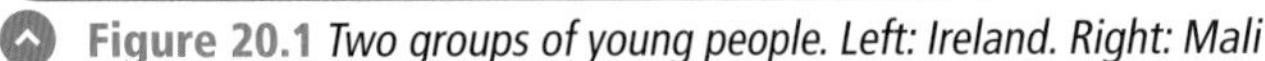

Figure 20.1 *Two groups of young people. Left: Ireland. Right: Mali*

Levels of economic development

Learning Intentions

In this section, you will learn:

- that countries can be classified into different groups according to their economic development
- how we measure levels of economic development.

In transition
World Bank
Gross National Income
Per capita
Human Development Index
Indicator
Standard of living

When we study different countries we can see that some countries are richer than others. This unequal distribution of wealth is called **economic inequality**.

Countries can be divided into **three categories** according to their economic development:

1. Developed economies

2. Economies in transition

3. Developing economies

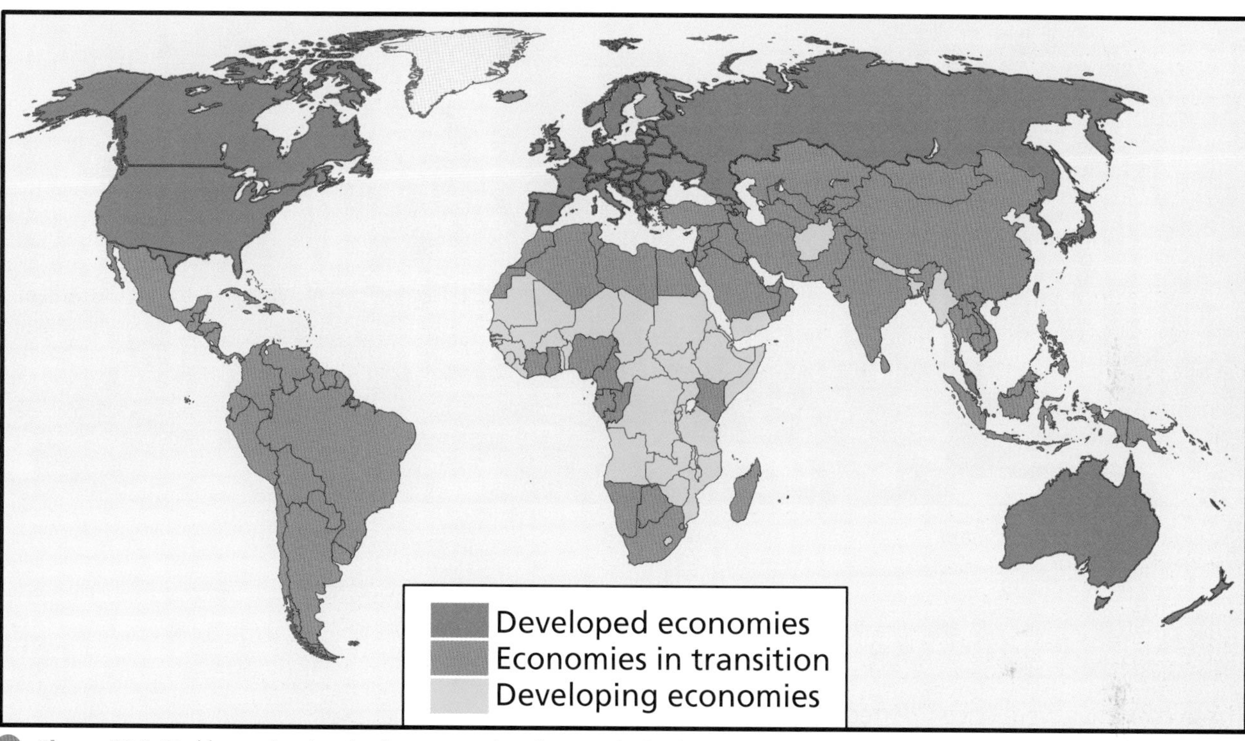

Figure 20.2 *World map showing the three categories of economic development*

1. Developed economies

The **economies** of these countries are **very strong**.

- These countries are well-developed and **wealthy**.
- They are also heavily **industrialised**.
- The majority of the **workforce** is employed in the **secondary** and **tertiary** sectors.
- Developed countries have good **healthcare**, a high standard of **education** and a high-quality **infrastructure**.

Countries with developed economies are mainly located in the **northern hemisphere**. However, Australia and New Zealand are also developed economies.

Figure 20.3 *New York City, USA*

2. Economies in transition

The economies of these countries are often known as **tiger economies**.

- **Industrialisation** is occurring rapidly in these countries because of a growth in employment in the **secondary sector**.
- The focus in these countries is mainly on **exporting** goods.
- **Wages** are increasing slowly.
- Increased wealth has led to an improved **standard of living**.

Countries with economies in transition include **Brazil**, **China** and **Mexico**.

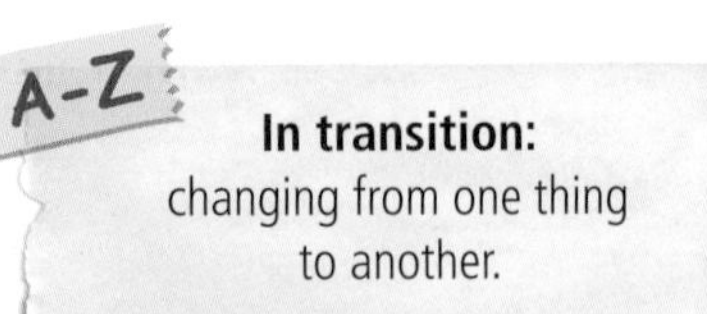

In transition: changing from one thing to another.

Figure 20.4 *São Paulo, Brazil*

3. Developing economies

These countries were once referred to as **Third World** countries.

- The economies of these countries are **reliant on primary-sector activities** such as farming.
- They have little or no involvement in secondary and tertiary sectors, and **poor infrastructure** makes it difficult to attract industry.
- Large numbers of their populations are living in **extreme poverty**.
- These countries tend to be affected by **famine**, **war** and **high birth rates**.

Countries with developing economies are mainly located in the **southern hemisphere**. Examples include Sudan and Ethiopia.

Figure 20.5 *Khartoum, Sudan*

Measuring economic development

World Bank categories

The **World Bank** is changing the way it measures economic development. It now measures levels of economic development mainly by looking at a country's **Gross National Income (GNI)** per person.

DID YOU KNOW? The World Bank is an international organisation made up of about 180 countries. It takes money from governments and other people and gives loans and grants to countries in need.

A country's **GNI** is all of the income earned by a country's residents and businesses at home and abroad. To get the **GNI per person** (also known as **per capita**), the country's GNI is divided by the total population of the country. Ireland's GNI per capita in 2016 was **$52,560**.

The World Bank has come up with four new categories based on countries' GNI per capita:

- High-income economies: $12,476 or more
- Upper middle-income economies: between $4,036 and $12,475
- Lower middle-income economies: between $1,026 and $4,035
- Low-income economies: less than $1,025.

Note: All measurements are in US dollars, as it is the currency usually used in the global economy.

NUMERACY ACTIVITY

Calculate the range of GNI per capita in (i) upper middle-income economies and (ii) lower middle-income economies.

According to the World Bank, the higher the GNI per capita figure, the more developed that country and its economy are.

Per Capita GNI 2016 in US dollars	
Norway	$82,330
US	$56,180
Australia	$54,420
Ireland	$52,560
Brazil	$8,840
Uganda	$660
Sierra Leone	$490

ACTIVITY

Identify the countries listed above on a map of the world. What do you notice about where they are located?

ACTIVITY

Divide into groups of three. Do you think income is the best way to measure a country's level of development? What else should be examined, in your opinion?

Write down your answers and then swap them with another group. Do you agree with the other group's answers?

Human Development Index

Another way of measuring economic development is the **Human Development Index (HDI)**. Countries can be compared to each other based on a number of **indicators**, including:

- literacy
- life expectancy at birth
- standard of living.

Standard of living is calculated using **Purchase Power Parity (PPP)** as well as income. PPP is all about how valuable money is in a country. For example, €10 gets you more in Brazil than in Ireland but gets you more again in a developing country like Sierra Leone.

Country	Life expectancy at birth	Literacy	Standard of living (PPP in $)	HDI	HDI rank
Australia	82.5	99.0%	42,822	0.939	3
Norway	81.7	100.0%	67,614	0.949	1
Ireland	81.1	99.0%	43,798	0.923	8
Brazil	74.7	92.6%	14,145	0.754	79
Sierra Leone	51.3	48.1%	1,529	0.420	179

NUMERACY ACTIVITY

Look at the table of HDI ratings above, then answer these questions:

(a) Calculate the difference in life expectancy at birth between Ireland and Sierra Leone. Can you suggest reasons for this difference?

(b) Calculate the difference between PPP in Ireland and Norway. Can you suggest reasons for this difference?

 **(i)** Give one example each of a developed economy, an economy in transition and a developing economy.

 **(ii)** List three indicators used in measuring economic development using the Human Development Index.

 **(iii)** Evaluate which method, GNI or HDI, is better when measuring economic development.

- I can classify countries into different groups according to their economic development. 
- I understand that there are different methods of measuring economic development. 

The North–South divide

Learning Intentions

In this section, you will learn:

- that there are huge inequalities between the economies of rich developed countries and poor developing countries
- some of the reasons for economic inequality
- some solutions to economic inequality.

Inequality	Commodity
Exploitation	Plantation
Subsidy	Cash crop
Colonialism	Protectionism
Neo-colonialism	Dependency
Debt	Fair trade
Corruption	Aid

In groups, suggest three reasons why countries in the South tend to be poor and countries in the North tend to be rich. Share your idea with the other groups in the class.

Whichever method of measuring **economic development** you use, there is a clear **gap** between the richer developed countries and the poorer developing countries. We sometimes refer to this as the **North–South divide**. This is because the wealthier countries are generally in the northern hemisphere and the poorer countries are generally in the southern hemisphere.

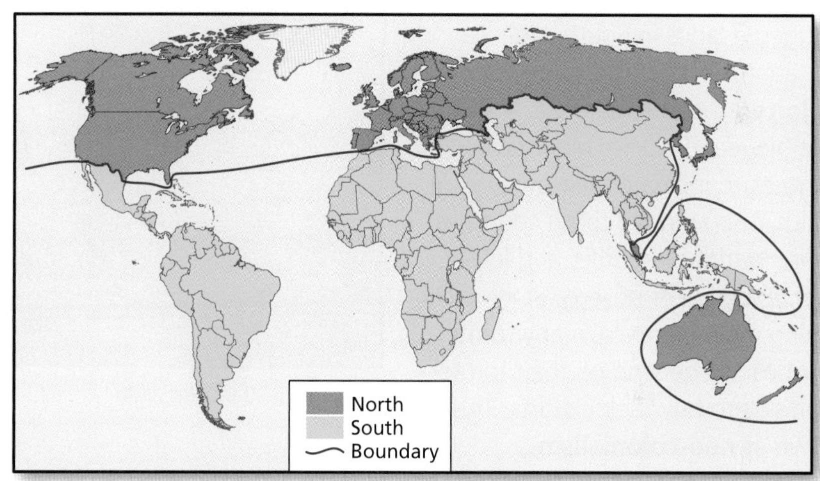

Figure 20.6 *A world divided – rich and poor*

Reasons for economic inequality

There are many reasons for the divide that exists in our world today. For many years, developed countries have **exploited** the vulnerable, developing countries. This **exploitation** continues today. Other **factors** have also helped in creating the divide between the world's rich and poor.

Trade

Many wealthy countries buy **raw materials** from developing countries at low prices. They then process these materials into **finished goods**, which have a much higher value than the raw material.

For example, coffee beans grown in Colombia are sold to companies in Ireland where they are **processed** into coffee and sold at a much higher price than what was paid for the beans.

Many **multinational corporations** (MNCs) exploit countries in this way. Because crops like coffee beans are seen as a **cash crop** in developing countries, the people there can become **dependent** on just a few exports.

ACTIVITY

Can you make a list of other commodities that are bought from developing countries?

In addition, MNCs sometimes set up business in these poorer countries to take advantage of the **low wages** they can pay workers. This makes the MNCs **more profit**.

In some developed European countries such as Ireland, farmers receive **subsidies** from the EU for their produce. Farmers from the developing world cannot compete with the subsidised prices in the developed world.

Subsidy:
money paid to farmers (or others) to keep prices low while guaranteeing their income.

Figure 20.7 *A Shell oil rig in Nigeria*

Colonialism

During the **Age of Exploration** from the fifteenth to the seventeenth century, many European countries conquered lands in South America and later in Africa. The colonists **exploited** the raw materials and mineral wealth in the colonised countries to increase their own wealth. This stripped those countries of their natural resources and left them in a state of poverty. Since gaining independence, many former **colonies** still depend on their former colonisers to buy their exports. This is known as **neo-colonialism**.

Figure 20.8 *Colonialism*

ACTIVITY

What is the message of the cartoon above? Discuss in pairs.

Debt

Many developing countries **owe** foreign banks huge sums of money because they have borrowed money to help develop the country. This is called **debt**. Money that should be used to provide basic healthcare and education is often used to **repay** loans.

Corruption

Some developing countries have **corrupt** leaders. These leaders often take money intended for important services like healthcare and education and use it to increase their own personal wealth or buy weapons instead.

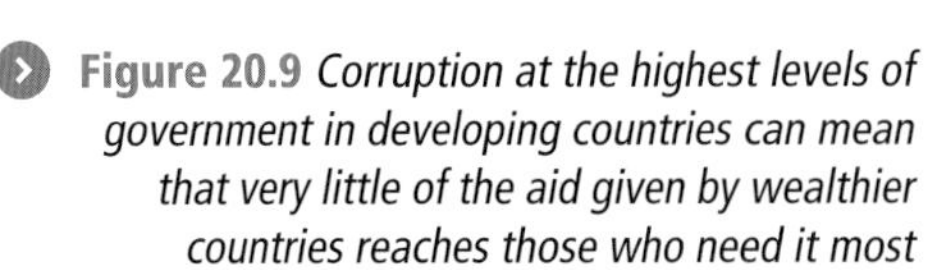

Figure 20.9 *Corruption at the highest levels of government in developing countries can mean that very little of the aid given by wealthier countries reaches those who need it most*

CASE STUDY

Exploitation: the coffee trade

Coffee is a worldwide **commodity**. This means that it is a raw material that is **bought and sold** on world markets. Coffee is produced by **processing** coffee beans. These coffee beans grow in many developing countries such as Colombia, Brazil, Uganda, Kenya and the Ivory Coast. Over **20 million** people are employed in the coffee industry.

DID YOU KNOW? Coffee is the second most traded commodity in the world. Can you guess what the most traded commodity is?

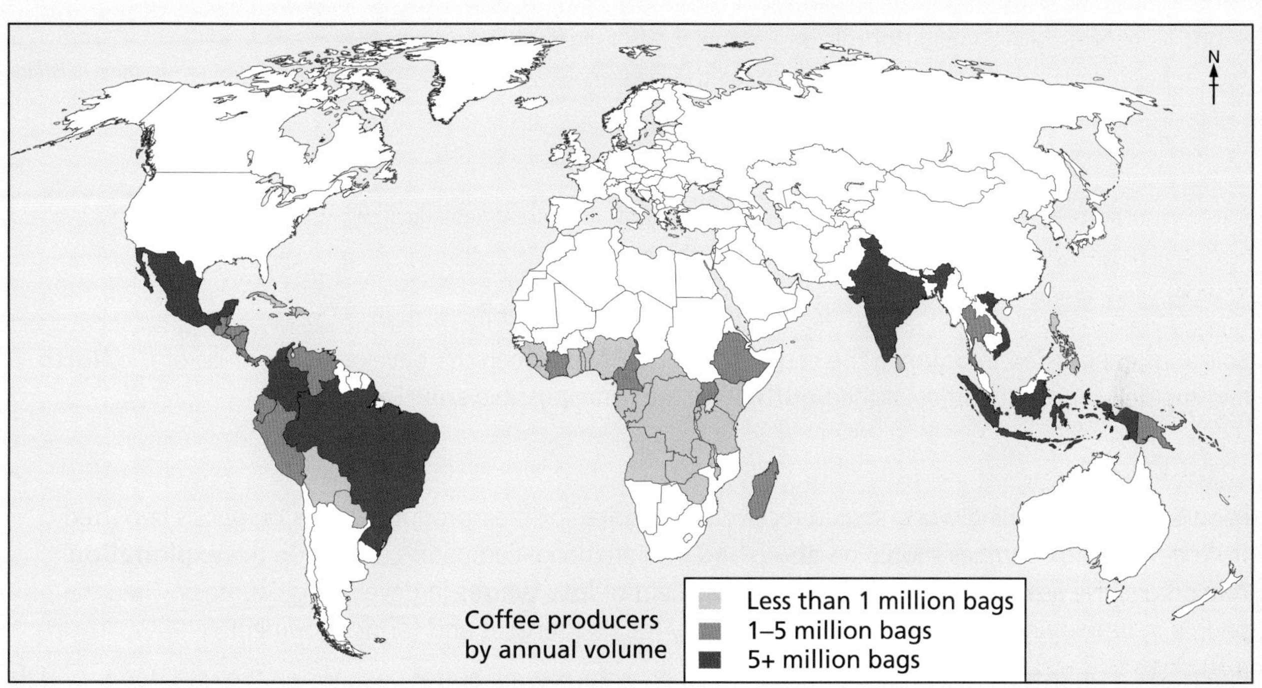

Figure 20.10 *Coffee-producing countries of the world*

How coffee is grown

Plantations: Coffee **plantations** are large areas of land where coffee beans are produced. They are often owned by foreign companies who pay very low wages to the workers.

Local farms: In some countries, local farmers also produce coffee beans as a **cash crop**.

Cash crop:
an agricultural crop that is grown for profit, instead of for use by the grower.

Exploitation of coffee-producing nations

Price

Companies pay very little to farmers for their coffee beans. They then process these beans into coffee in their own countries and sell it at a large profit. Therefore, the farmers do not get a f**air price** for their product.

Figure 20.11 *Coffee production in Uganda*

Protectionism

Developed countries look after their own needs and profits. They put high **taxes** on the importation of processed coffee. This makes it difficult for developing countries to make a profit from processing the coffee themselves. Developed countries often use other methods to make it difficult too. For example, when Brazil started to process its own coffee the USA threatened to stop giving it aid.

Dependency

Some developing countries can have an **over-dependency** on coffee production because it is such an important crop to the country's economy. As a result of this dependency, the failure of a coffee bean crop can lead to huge **poverty** in the country.

Figure 20.12 *Coffee consumption in Ireland*

Solutions to economic inequality

Solutions are needed to **balance** the economic inequality between the developed countries of the **North** and the developing countries of the **South**. Here are some possible **solutions**.

Fair trade

People in the developing world should receive a **fair price** for their produce. **Taxes** on goods imported from developing countries should be **abolished**. Multinational companies must stop the **exploitation** of workers, the use of **child labour** and the payment of **low wages** in developing countries. Then the people in developing countries would have money for vital services and for development.

Fairtrade is an **international movement** which gives **farmers** a better deal. When they sell goods on fair trade terms they get a **better price**, which allows them to improve their lives. If you buy a product with the **Fairtrade** logo, you know that the farmers who produced it got a better price for it.

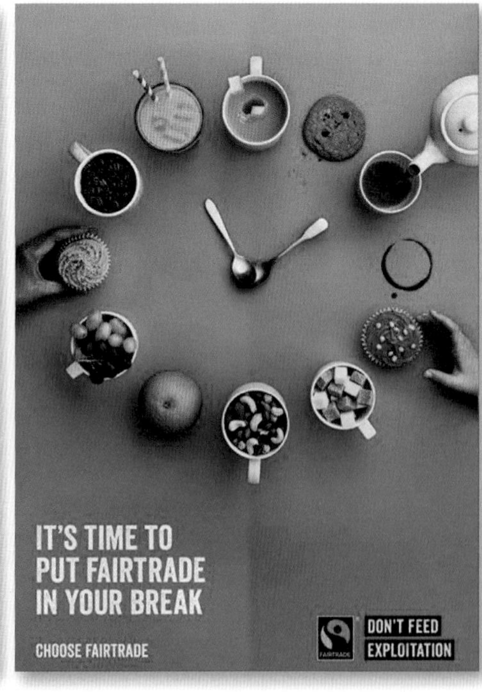

Figure 20.13 *Fairtrade posters*

ACTIVITY

Examine the posters on the left:

(a) Can you list some Fairtrade products?

(b) Explain why you should choose Fairtrade products.

Debt

The **loans** given to developing countries could be cleared. These loans come with high interest rates, and many countries cannot afford the repayments. In 2005, the developing world owed over $500 billion.

A call for an end to world debt in 2005 resulted in some countries having their debt cancelled. For the 18 countries that qualified under this new initiative, **debt cancellation** brought impressive results. For example, it was reported that Zambia used savings to increase its investment in health, education and rural development.

However, 2017 figures show that countries in the developing world still owe more than **$4 trillion** to the World Bank. **Angola** is Africa's largest exporter of oil, and yet in 2016 the government spent almost half (44 per cent) of its revenue repaying debt.

Aid

The developing world needs **assistance** from richer countries. This is called **aid**. It is essential that aid reaches its intended targets within the developing world and is not taken by greedy and corrupt politicians. If aid is focused on education, then communities can learn to help themselves. We will learn more about assistance/aid in the next section.

 **(i)** List three reasons why there is an economic divide between the developed and developing worlds.

 **(ii)** How does debt impact on economic development?

 **(iii)** How could governments in the developed world ensure that trade is fairer for developing countries?

- I understand that inequality exists between the developing and developed worlds.  
- I understand the reasons why inequality exists and can give some possible solutions.  

Development assistance/aid

Learning Intentions

In this section, you will learn:

- about the different types of development assistance/aid
- about Ireland's overseas aid programmes
- about the positive and negative aspects of assistance/aid.

Non-government organisation (NGO)
Tied aid
Bilateral aid
Multilateral aid
Irish Aid
Gender equality
Governance
Human rights

Development assistance/aid is given by wealthier, developed countries to poorer, developing countries. Aid can come in the form of money, food and medicines and can be given in a number of different ways.

In Ireland, the government as well as a number of **non-government organisations (NGOs)** give aid to poorer countries. NGOs receive government funding but also depend on the general public to make charitable donations.

Types of aid

Emergency aid / humanitarian aid

This is aid in the form of food, water, medicines and basic supplies given **following a natural disaster** such as an earthquake or famine. Emergency aid can also be given in times of war.

Figure 20.14 *UN soldiers distributing food to displaced people in Haiti after an earthquake in 2010*

Development aid

This type of aid provides help over a **long period** of time. It focuses on the development of **healthcare**, **education** and **infrastructure** in a country. It can be in the form of money or personnel, such as teachers and nurses.

Tied aid

This type of aid comes with **conditions**. It may mean the poorer, developing country will have to purchase certain products from the richer, developed country in order to receive aid. These products can include weapons and ammunition. This type of aid is not always good for a developing country.

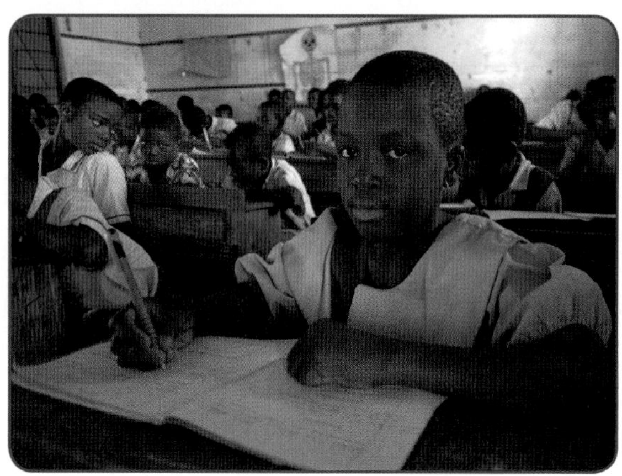

Figure 20.15 *Children in developing countries benefit from aid*

Bilateral aid

Aid from **one country directly to another country** is called bilateral aid. The aid the Irish government provides to Ethiopia is an example of this type of aid.

Multilateral aid

Aid provided by **organisations** such as the United Nations, the World Bank and the European Union is called multilateral aid. Governments of member states contribute money for development programmes run all over the world.

Positives and negatives of aid

There are many arguments for and against the giving of aid.

Positives

- In times of **natural disasters**, emergency aid is vital in saving lives.
- **Healthcare** and **education** improve drastically when development aid is given, and the money is spent in the right way.
- **Relationships** can be forged between two countries, creating better links and improvements within the poorer country.
- NGOs can help **develop the skills** of local people.

Negatives

- Countries can become very **dependent** on aid. This can result in countries not developing themselves.
- **Corruption** can lead to aid being stolen and not reaching its intended target.
- Tied aid can result in the richer, developed country benefiting, rather than the poorer, developing country.
- Aid can lead to huge amounts of money being spent on arms and weapons. This in turn can lead to **wars**.

PORTFOLIO ACTIVITY 20.1

Should Ireland spend so much money helping countries in the developing world? Go to page 82 of your Portfolio to prepare a speech about whether that expense is justified.

Ireland's overseas aid programmes

The **Irish government** spends a certain amount of its annual budget on bilateral, multilateral and emergency aid for developing countries. The Irish government's programme for overseas development assistance (ODA) is called **Irish Aid**. In 2016, the government provided €723 million in ODA. This money was spent on Irish Aid programmes and it was given to NGOs as grants. For example, the NGO **Trócaire** received €19 million from Irish Aid in 2016.

Trōcaire

CASE STUDY

Ireland's overseas aid: Irish Aid in Ethiopia

Ethiopia is one of the poorest countries in the world. Irish Aid has been working in Ethiopia since 1994. Irish Aid focuses on those most at risk and encourages local people to get involved in their communities.

- Irish aid to Ethiopia in 2016: €35.5 million
- Population of Ethiopia: 99.4 million

Figure 20.16 *Irish Aid has been working in Ethiopia since 1994*

Food and agriculture

The population of Ethiopia depends heavily on **agriculture** for survival. However, because of climate change, **droughts** are becoming more common. If drought leads to crop failure, it can mean that millions of people need humanitarian aid. Irish Aid helps farmers to use better farming methods. These include improved **technology**, **seeds** that are resistant to drought, **conserving water** and **irrigation**. In 2015, the farmers in some of the programmes produced 40 per cent more food even though there was a drought.

Irish Aid works with other organisations to provide a **work-for-food programme**. This allows people to exchange their labour for food or cash. Over six million people benefit from the programme every year.

Figure 20.17 *Farmer in Tigray, Ethiopia*

Equality issues

Irish Aid supports **gender equality** in all its partner countries. The Ethiopian Women's Lawyers Association gives free legal aid to women affected by violence with the help of Irish Aid. In 2015, Irish Aid started to support the Ethiopian Centre for Disability in setting up a workshop and cooperative for people with disabilities.

HIV/AIDS

In 2016, 7 per cent of Irish Aid's budget was spent helping to tackle the AIDS/HIV epidemic. It is estimated that over 700,000 people live with the disease in Ethiopia. It is also estimated that over a million children have been made orphans by the disease. It is good that more people in Ethiopia now know their HIV status. By 2016, 43 per cent of men and 40 per cent of women had voluntarily had an HIV test.

Governance

Of Irish Aid's budget to Ethiopia, 6 per cent is spent on **governance** issues. That includes helping people hold local officials to account and supporting NGOs that work in the area of **human rights**. This means that Irish Aid makes sure money reaches its proper target and that corruption is tackled effectively.

An Roinn Gnóthaí Eachtracha agus Trádála
Department of Foreign Affairs and Trade

Emergency aid

In 2016, Irish Aid spent €194 million on **emergency aid**, responding to emergencies in many different countries, including floods in Malawi, an earthquake in Nepal, drought in Ethiopia and the huge numbers of refugees from Syria, South Sudan and Nigeria. Assistance included tents and blankets, water and sanitation, and counselling for those affected by the crises.

Ireland's non-government organisations (NGOs)

Ireland has many **NGOs**, many of which are supported by Irish Aid, that contribute aid to poorer, developing countries. These organisations do not give money directly to the governments of developing countries. Instead, they **help** people in local communities, and **educate** them so that in the future they will be able to provide for their own needs. Examples of Irish NGOs include **Trócaire**, **Concern**, **Bóthar** and **Goal**.

ACTIVITY

Research an example of the work that an Irish NGO does in the developing world. Present your findings to your class. Create a poster for your selected NGO, highlighting your findings on it.

(i) List three types of aid.

(ii) Name two countries assisted by Irish Aid.

(iii) What is an NGO? Give two examples of NGOs.

(iv) What work do NGOs do?

(v) Suggest ways of overcoming the negative impacts of aid.

- I can explain the different types of aid. 
- I can give examples of Ireland's overseas aid programmes. 
- I can explain the positive and negative impacts of aid. 

Life chances in the developed and developing worlds

Learning Intentions

In this section, you will learn:

- how the life chances of a young person in the developing world differ from those of a young person in the developed world.

Child mortality
Infant mortality
Life expectancy

The **economic inequalities** that we have looked at in this chapter mean that almost half the world's population live on less than $2 a day. A fifth of children in the developing world live in **extreme poverty**. This includes half the children in sub-Saharan Africa and over a third of the children in south Asia.

The world's poorest people have **little or no access** to health, education and other basic **services** that we in the developed world take for granted. The realities of living in a country with a **developing economy** limit their choices and chances in all sorts of areas.

A young person in a **developed** country like Ireland will have very different chances in life compared with a young person in the **developing** world. We will now examine just how different these **life chances** are.

Figure 20.18 *Getting water. Left: Africa. Right: Europe*

Gender equality

Gender equality means that every person has **equal opportunities**, whether they are **male or female**. Although women don't always experience equality in the developed world, there are **laws** protecting women and making gender bias and **discrimination** illegal. A girl born in Ireland can expect to go to school and university, get a job, own property, vote and enjoy the same freedoms and opportunities that men have. This is not the case in many parts of the world.

In the **developing world**, although the law usually treats men and women equally, traditional attitudes mean that women are often **treated unequally in practice**. One third of girls in the developing world are married before they are 18, and girls living in poor households are twice as likely to marry before the age of 18 as those from better-off families.

DID YOU KNOW? In sub-Saharan Africa women make up 75 per cent of the farm workers, and yet they own only 1 per cent of the land.

Women in the developing world are more at risk of **domestic violence**. For example, 87 per cent of women in Afghanistan report that they have experienced it. In some countries, such as Mali and Uganda, 77 per cent of women believe that domestic violence is acceptable in some circumstances.

You have already learned about the United Nations' **Sustainable Development Goals** (see Chapter 14, page 265). Goal 5 of the Sustainable Development Goals is to achieve **gender equality**. Research what is being done to achieve this goal.

Look up https://educateplus.ie/go/gender-inequality and discuss in class other issues of gender inequality that exist in the world today.

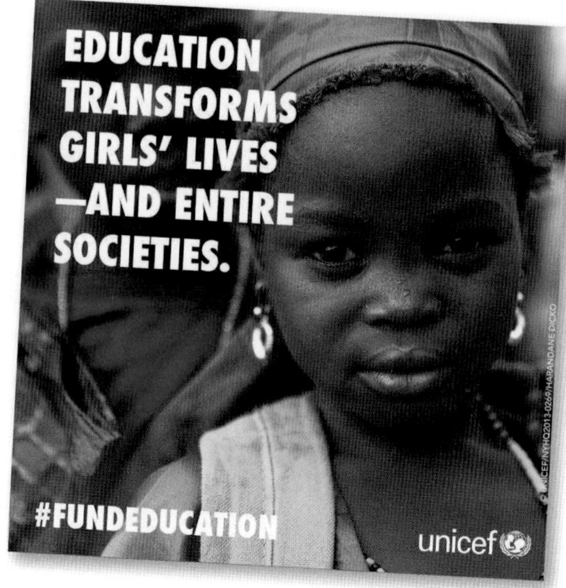

Figure 20.19 *A poster produced by UNICEF, the part of the United Nations that helps children in developing countries*

Education

There are currently 263 million children aged 6–17 out of school, most of them in the developing world. Education is a right that we sometimes take for granted in the developed world. In most developed countries, like Ireland, there is **free access** to education for all.

In Africa, 42 per cent of children will **drop out** of school before finishing their education. There are many **reasons** for this. Parents might not be able to afford to keep their children in school. Children might be needed to work to contribute to the family's **income**. The high **HIV/AIDS rates** in sub-Saharan Africa means that many children lose one or both parents and have to work.

Education of girls is a particular problem in the developing world, with many dropping out of school to get **married** or because of **teenage pregnancy**. Goal 4 of the Sustainable Development Goals is to ensure a quality education for all.

CASE STUDY

Fighting for education: Malala

Malala Yousafzai is a young woman from Pakistan, a country that has one of the highest percentages of children not in school in the world. She wrote a blog for the BBC about what her life was like when the Taliban were in power in her part of the country. The Taliban is an extreme Islamic group. They view education, especially the education of girls, as a threat to their cause. When girls were banned from going to school Malala spoke out against this in her blog.

Figure 20.20 *Malala Yousafzai met the US president, Barack Obama, in 2013*

In 2012, Malala was shot by the Taliban on her way home from school because they did not like her speaking out about her experiences as a young girl in Pakistan. Malala survived this attack and used the publicity it received to highlight the issue of girls in education. In 2014, she received the Nobel Peace Prize for her work as an activist for children's education.

Think about how important your education is to you. If you could not go to school, consider how this would impact on you, your family and your community. Work in pairs and write down a list.

Employment

We have already studied the three **sectors** of employment – primary, secondary and tertiary. In **developed countries** like Ireland, most people work in the **tertiary sector**. **Access to education** here increases our chances of getting a job when we are older.

Figure 20.21 *Children breaking bricks in Bangladesh*

We know that most of the people in the **developing world** work in the **primary sector**. Many earn very low wages.

In many countries, **children** make up a large part of the **workforce**. In 2016, **152 million** children between the ages of five and 17 were working. While that number is dropping, it is still a huge issue in many developing countries. If children are not educated, then the chances of them finding employment that will provide them with a good standard of living are slim.

Unemployment is a serious problem, and yet getting a job does not mean escaping poverty. Without **economic growth** there will never be enough good jobs available, and so there is less incentive to get an education.

Goal 8 of the Sustainable Development Goals is about promoting economic growth and creating decent work opportunities for everyone.

ACTIVITY

Why is finding a job important? Why might it be difficult for a person in the developing world to find a job? Suggest what can be done to improve their chances of getting a job.

ACTIVITY

Check out www.stopchildlabour.eu to find out about global campaigns to stop child labour and get children into school.

Healthcare

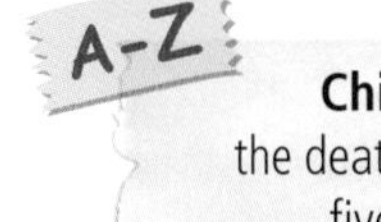

Child mortality: the death of children under five years of age.

Life expectancy in Ireland is 81 years. This is because we have access to **healthcare**, a plentiful **food supply** and are **educated** about a healthy lifestyle and balanced diet. Children in Ireland and other developed countries are **vaccinated** against diseases such as measles and tuberculosis, which caused high **child mortality** rates in the past.

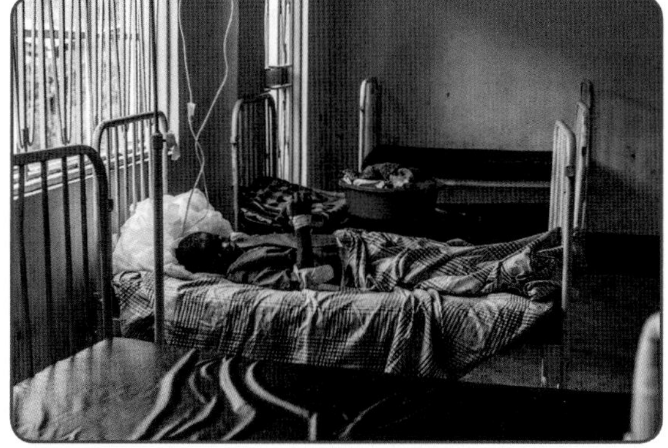

Figure 20.22 *Children's hospital ward in Uganda*

Young people in the developing world have very different experiences. Of the world's **undernourished** people, 98 per cent live in the developing world. The risk of a child dying before their fifth birthday is **eight times higher** in Africa than in Europe. The greatest health risks in Africa are from bronchitis and pneumonia, HIV/AIDS, malaria and diarrhoea. These diseases can often be prevented with good **sanitation**, clean **drinking water**, better **education** and a strong **healthcare** system.

ACTIVITY

Go to https://educateplus.ie/go/sustainable-goals and research Sustainable Development Goals 3 and 4. How is your life different to those of young people living in the developing world? Discuss with your group and make a list of five ways in which your life chances are different.

CASE STUDY

A young woman in sub-Saharan Africa: Hajah Conteh

Figure 20.23 *Hajah*

Hajah Conteh lives in Freetown, Sierra Leone. When Hajah was 13, she was going to school and her mother was paying her fees. When her mother could no longer pay her fees and find lunch for her, a man agreed to support her. The agreement was that as soon as Hajah finished school they would marry. But at 15, Hajah became pregnant. Pregnant girls were not allowed go to school, so Hajah dropped out and marriage was her only option.

More women die in childbirth in Sierra Leone than in any other country in the world, and the **infant mortality** rate is very high. In theory, the government provides free healthcare to pregnant women, but the resources aren't always available. Hajah didn't get any health checks when she was pregnant. She survived childbirth, but her baby didn't.

Hajah hopes she may have a second chance. She may be able to finish her education thanks to an initiative led by UNICEF. Her dream is to become a seamstress and make clothes for people.

Find out more about Hajah at https://educateplus.ie/go/sierra-leone

ACTIVITY

How would Hajah Conteh's life have been different if she lived in Ireland? Consider the following: gender equality, healthcare, education and employment.

PORTFOLIO ACTIVITY 20.2

Go to page 84 of your portfolio to write an information sheet about one of the United Nations' Sustainable Development Goals and how it could be achieved.

(i) How much of the world's population lives on less than $2 a day?

(ii) Which of the Sustainable Development Goals deals with gender equality?

(iii) Explain why infant mortality is high in some developing countries.

 I can explain how my life chances differ from those of a young person in the developing world. 

REVISION

Economic inequalities can be seen in three different types of countries: developed, developing and economies in ____________________. We can find out how developed countries are, by calculating the ____________________ ____________________ ____________________ (GNI) or ____________________ ____________________ ____________________ (HDI). The development of economies can be affected by trade, ____________________, debt and ____________________.

Wealthier countries can help poorer countries by giving ____________________.

____________________ aid is aid given from one government to another. When a country gives aid to an organisation like the EU or the UN it is referred to as ____________________ aid. Voluntary organisations can also help in distributing aid. These are called ____________________ ____________________ ____________________ (NGOs).

When countries receive aid to help with the effects of a natural disaster, this is called ____________________ aid. Aid that is given to help with education and health is referred to as ____________________ aid. When poorer countries have to give something in return for the aid they receive it is called ____________________ aid.

The ____________________ Development ____________________ (SDG's) are a set of targets that aim to deal with global issues such as economic inequality.

Questions & Answers

Sample Questions

1. Explain **two** reasons why the level of economic development is lower in the 'South'.
2. Name **two** ways in which this can be addressed.

Sample Answers

1. Unfair trade and debt are two reasons why economic development is slower in the South. Unfair trade has resulted in poorer countries – and the workers in those countries – being exploited and not receiving a fair price for their goods. Many countries in the South owe huge debts to countries in the North. This means countries in the South cannot afford to spend money on important services such as education and health as they are crippled by the huge debt they owe.
2. One way in which this can be addressed is by introducing fair trade. Workers must receive a fair price for their goods, which are then processed and sold at a much higher value. The clearing of world debt would also help address the divide and give poorer countries in the South a chance to develop and spend money on the services that are essential, such as education, transport and healthcare/medicines.

Short Questions

1. The map shows the percentage of population that are undernourished throughout the world.

Write down the percentages of population that are undernourished in the following countries.

(i) Ireland

(ii) Brazil

(iii) Sierra Leone

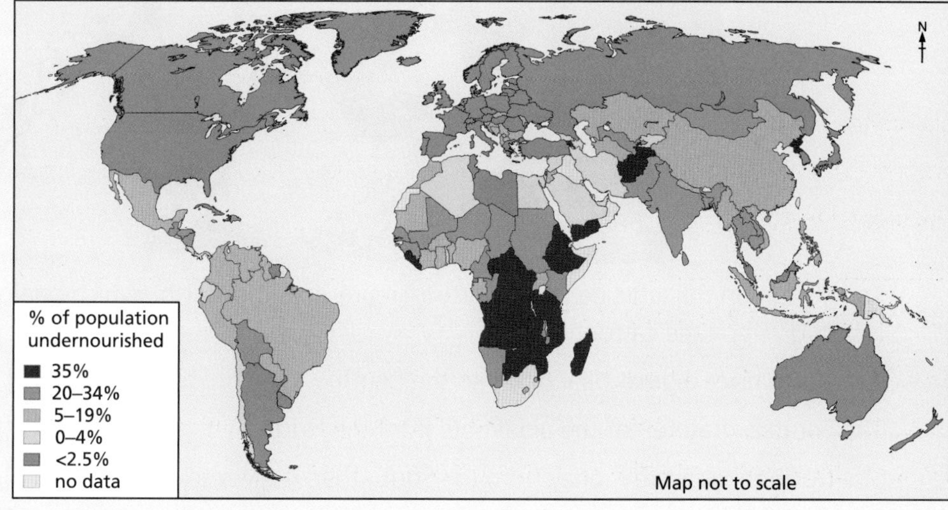

2. There is a general view that the world is divided into 'the rich North' and 'the poor South'.

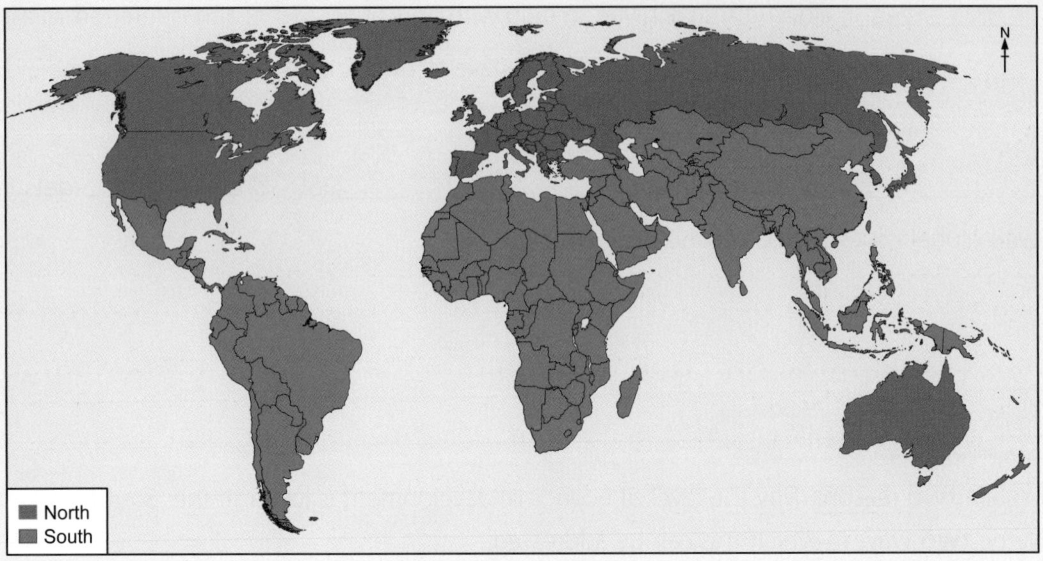

In the South:

The countries owe very little money to banks. ☐

The population is decreasing. ☐

Most people work in offices and shops. ☐

Many young children die from hunger and disease. ☐ [tick (✓) the correct box]

3. Name **three** types of aid given by richer countries to poorer countries.

(i) ____

(ii) ____

(iii) ____

4. The cartoon refers to the relations between the North (Developed) and the South (Developing World).

The person on the left side of the cartoon represents the North. Which one of the messages below is best given by the cartoon?

The North gives a great deal of aid to the South. ☐

The South is grateful for the aid it gets from the North. ☐

The North takes more money from the South than it gives to the South. ☐

The South is better off because of its relations with the North. ☐

[tick (✓) the correct box]

5. In the boxes provided, match each letter in Column **X** with the number of its pair in Column **Y**. One pair has been completed for you.

	Column X		Column Y	X	Y
A	Aid given by the Government of Ireland to the Government of Ethiopia	1	Bilateral Aid	A	1
B	Trócaire, Concern, Oxfam	2	Emergency Aid	B	
C	Aid given through organisations such as the United Nations	3	NGOs	C	
D	Medicine, shelter and food	4	Multilateral Aid	D	

6. The map shows average daily calorie intake in different countries.

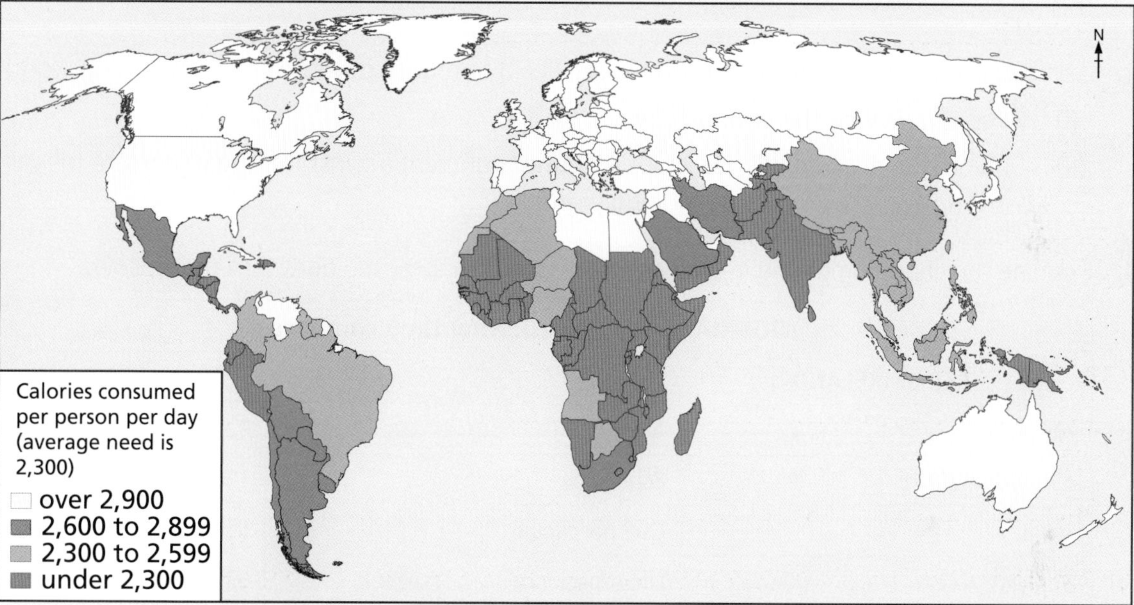

Write the daily calorie intake per person in each of the following countries:

(i) Ireland ________________

(ii) Brazil ________________

(iii) Ethiopia ________________

Long Questions

1. Explain **three** reasons for the divide that exists between the North and the South.

2. Study the diagram below which shows how the income from coffee is divided between the groups involved in its production and marketing.

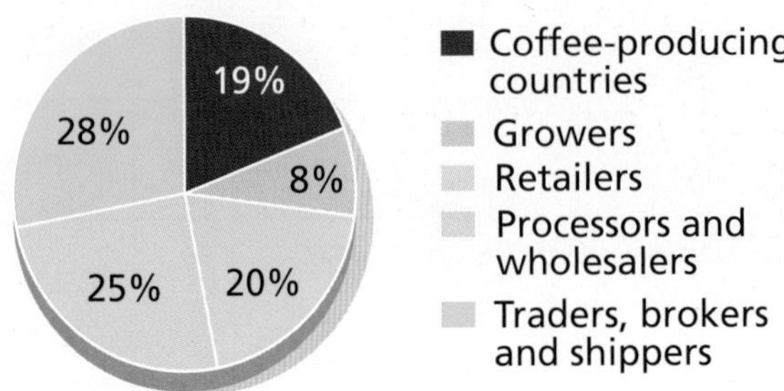

In relation to coffee or another commodity you have studied, explain **two** ways in which the division of income causes problems for the developing countries involved.

3. Some countries such as Ireland provide bilateral aid to reduce poverty in the developing world.
   (i) What is meant by the term 'bilateral aid'?
   (ii) Outline **one** argument in favour of and **one** argument against the use of aid as a means of assisting countries of the developing world.

4. Examine the chart comparing Ireland and Nigeria and answer the questions that follow:

NIGERIA and IRELAND: How they compare		
REP of IRELAND		**NIGERIA**
70,280 km^2	Area	923,768 km^2
4.7 million (2017)	Population	186 million (2017)
$65,871	GDP per capita	$5942
80.9 yrs	Life expectancy	53.05 yrs
6	Infant mortality rate (per 1,000)	112
6	Maternal mortality (per 100,000)	700
0.1% (2,200 people)	People living with HIV/AIDS	5.0% (27m people)
219	Doctors per 100,000	19
99%	Access to essential drugs	10%

   (i) Select from the chart **three** statistics showing that Nigeria is less developed than Ireland.
   (ii) Outline **two** types of aid Ireland could provide to Nigeria to help it develop.
   In your answer, name the type of aid and discuss the likely effects of each.

5. Describe **three** possible solutions to economic inequality.

6. Outline **three** ways in which a person in a developed country has better chances in life than one in a developing country.

Visual Summary

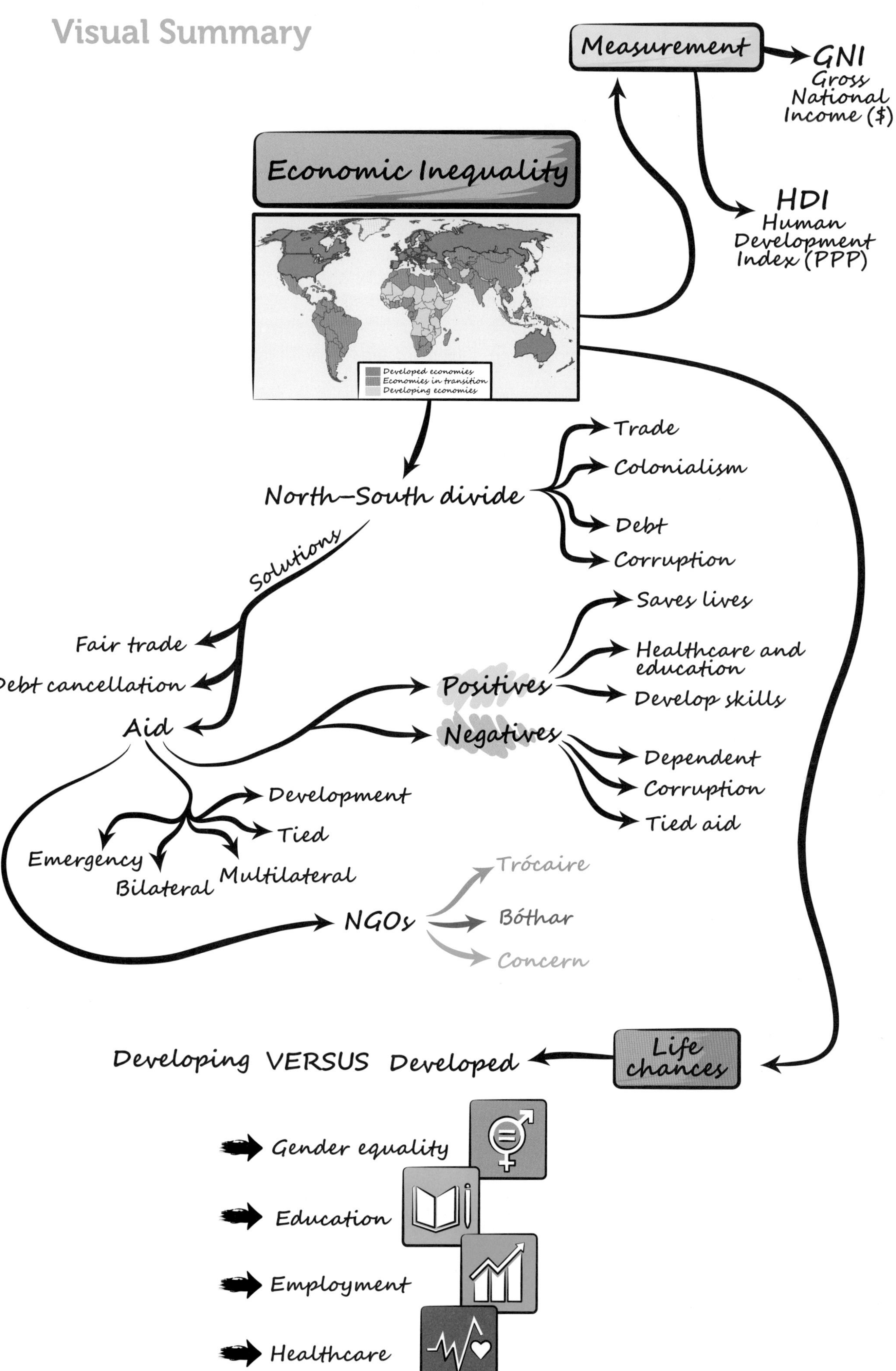
Measurement
GNI
Gross National Income ($)
HDI
Human Development Index (PPP)
Economic Inequality
Developed economies
Economies in transition
Developing economies
North–South divide
Trade
Colonialism
Debt
Corruption
Solutions
Fair trade
Debt cancellation
Aid
Positives
Saves lives
Healthcare and education
Develop skills
Negatives
Dependent
Corruption
Tied aid
Development
Tied
Emergency
Bilateral
Multilateral
NGOs
Trócaire
Bóthar
Concern
Developing VERSUS Developed
Life chances
Gender equality
Education
Employment
Healthcare

21 Globalisation: Living in an interconnected world

In this chapter, you will learn:

- what globalisation is
- that different parts of the world are connected through globalisation
- the positive and negative impacts of globalisation
- how globalisation is interlinked with population, settlement and human development.

ICE-BREAKER ACTIVITY

Draw a table with two columns in your copybook. In one column, write down five things you did yesterday. In the other column, write down all the global connections. For example:

Action	Global connection
I listened to music on my smartphone while walking into school.	My smartphone was made in China and I was listening to Taylor Swift from the USA.

Introduction to globalisation

Learning Intentions

In this section, you will learn:

- what globalisation is
- the factors that influence globalisation.

Globalisation
Interconnected
Interdependent
Conference call
Call centre
Popular culture
Trade agreement

What is globalisation?

Globalisation is the way that people and places are **interconnected** with other people and places around the world.

We are all **connected**. For example, we might have family members living in Australia, travel in a car made in Japan, use a mobile phone assembled in China and watch movies made in the USA. The list goes on and on.

Globalisation makes the world feel smaller. It also makes people and places more **dependent** on one another. When people and places are dependent on one another we say they are **interdependent**.

Figure 21.1 *A woman in front of shops in Shimla, India*

Look at the photograph on the previous page. Identify the signs of globalisation in the photograph.

Globalisation began when people first started to move around the world and **trade** with each other. There was a rapid increase in the speed of globalisation in the twentieth century, and into the present century.

Factors that influence globalisation

Transport

The improvement of transport means **goods**, **produce** and **people** can be transported around the world on a daily basis.

- Goods and fresh produce are transported daily on container ships and cargo planes.
- MNCs can fly their employees to their international offices.

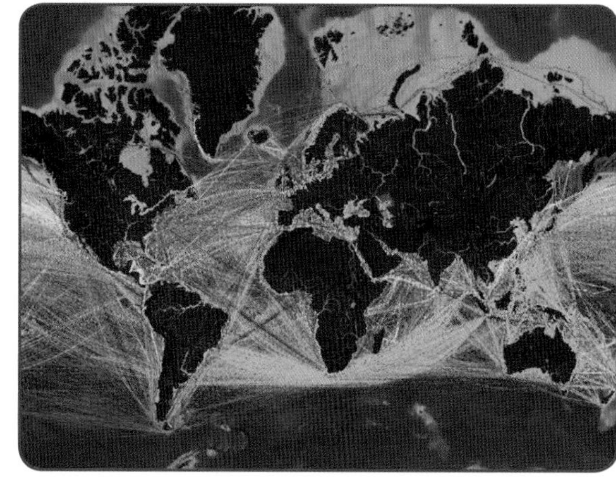

Figure 21.2 A map showing the *movement of cargo ships across the world*

Communication

High-speed **broadband**, **mobile phones**, **satellites** and **TV** means there can be **immediate communication** from any part of the world to another.

- Employees in different parts of the world can talk on **conference calls**.
- **Call centres** can be located in a different country from the company's customers. For example, when we phone insurance companies and banks, we could be speaking with someone in a call centre in India or the Philippines.

Figure 21.3 *Business meetings can happen online with people all over the world*

Politics

Since the end of the Second World War we have seen more **cooperation** between countries. The United Nations, European Union and the World Trade Organization are all examples of **international organisations** that bring countries closer together.

Many political leaders have realised that we all need to work together. This has resulted in agreements between countries, including the **Sustainable Development Goals** and the UN **Declaration of Human Rights**.

Popular culture

Popular culture involves our **everyday pastimes**. The clothes we wear, the music we listen to and the TV shows we watch are all examples. We are influenced by fashion from Paris, music from South America and TV shows from Australia. Popular culture makes the world feel smaller. It also spreads ideas so we feel closer to people and cultures all over the world.

Go to page 88 of your Portfolio to think about the music you listen to and its global connections.

Economy (trade)

Trade agreements between countries means that goods can flow quickly and freely between countries. The **EU** is an example of a **free trade area**.

We have seen how important the free movement of people and goods can be in the recent **Brexit** negotiations. As Britain planned to leave the EU, our biggest concern in Ireland was maintaining trade with all parts of the UK, and how the border between us, especially with Northern Ireland, should be controlled.

 **(i)** List five factors that influence globalisation.

 **(ii)** Explain two reasons why political cooperation is important today.

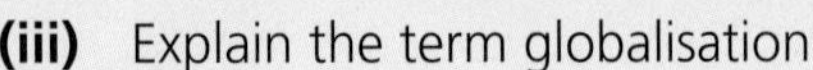

(iii) Explain the term globalisation.

 **(iv)** Describe two ways in which the internet has influenced globalisation.

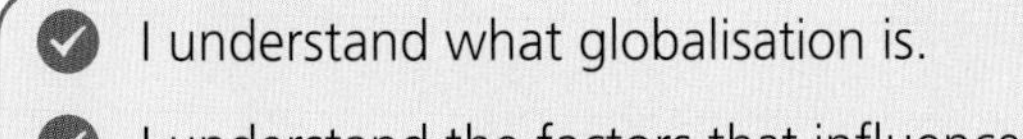

- I understand what globalisation is.
- I understand the factors that influence globalisation

Impact of globalisation

Learning Intentions

In this section, you will learn:

- that globalisation has positive and negative impacts.

WORDS
Multinational companies (MNCs)
Job security
Monoculture
Food miles
Cultural diversity

We have learned that globalisation has a huge impact on our daily lives and on the economy. It is difficult for us to imagine a world without globalisation. While there are many **positive effects** of globalisation, there are also **negative impacts**.

MNCs

Multinational companies bring **employment** and **investment** to both developed and developing countries.

- When **skilled** employees are required, MNCs will choose to locate in **developed** countries with an educated workforce. Ireland has a highly skilled workforce, as well as low corporation tax to help attract MNCs.
- Where the work is **labour-intensive**, such as in the textile industry, MNCs are more likely to pick **developing countries**, where the **cost of labour** is much lower.
- As a result, MNCs can **widen the gap** between developing and developed countries rather than closing it. This can make globalisation a **negative** force.
- There is also little **job security** with MNCs. They can move about freely from country to country, but they keep their profits in their headquarters, which are usually in developed countries.

(a) Name one MNC with a factory in Ireland.

(b) How many workers do they employ?

(c) Examine the benefits to the Irish economy.

Figure 21.4 *The world in MNC logos*

Food

Figure 21.5 *Look at the labels: the food you eat comes from all over the world*

We can now buy almost any type of food at any time of year. This is because foods can now be **transported** quickly from one country to another country. This means that we no longer have to depend on certain seasons to grow certain crops, as we can **import** them from anywhere in the world. For example, we can buy apples grown in Ireland and harvested in autumn for part of the year, but we can also buy apples from France, South Africa, South America and New Zealand during the rest of the year.

As a result, certain crops become very valuable on the global market. The negative impact of this is **monoculture**: the growing of just one crop.

- In **developing countries** especially this can eventually destroy the quality of the soil, making it difficult to grow crops.
- Growing **cash crops** in the developing world can also mean that there isn't enough space for locals to grow food for themselves, so that they have to buy food at higher prices or, in some cases, go hungry.
- In **developed countries** monoculture leads to the reliance on fertilisers, which is harmful to the environment.

We must also think about '**food miles**' – how far the food we consume has travelled. What impact does this have on the environment?

ACTIVITY

How far does your food travel? Go to www.foodmiles.com to research the answers.

Work with a partner to write a list of some of the advantages of buying locally produced food.

Environment

Globalisation has increased our reliance on and consumption of **fossil fuels**. Some of the reasons for this are that:

- people **travel** more often and longer distances
- the goods we use have to be **transported** on a daily basis
- **energy** is needed to power industries around the globe, as we saw in Chapter 5.

As we have seen in previous chapters, this has an enormous impact on the **environment** through pollution, global warming, acid rain, smog, deforestation and rising sea levels.

On the other hand, globalisation has also increased our **awareness** of climate change and has resulted in the **Sustainable Development Goals**. The goals are helping countries to work together to ensure that we all live in a more sustainable way.

Figure 21.6 *Cargo planes can deliver goods all round the world in a short time*

Economic inequality

As we saw in Chapter 20, globalisation can lead to an **unequal** world. Developing countries are often **exploited** by the developed world. Developed countries are getting wealthier while developing countries are being left behind. This **widens the divide** in the world between rich and poor.

For example, MNCs often locate in developing countries to take advantage of **cheaper labour**. Workers in India, for example, are usually paid much lower wages than workers in Ireland.

Culture

The **sharing** of ideas, experiences and cultures is a positive result of globalisation. We all have a lot to learn from each other. We have already learned that Ireland is a **multicultural** society because of migration.

Globalisation does threaten **cultural diversity**, however. As popular culture is shared more and more and we all use the goods produced by MNCs, the cultures of different countries become more and more alike.

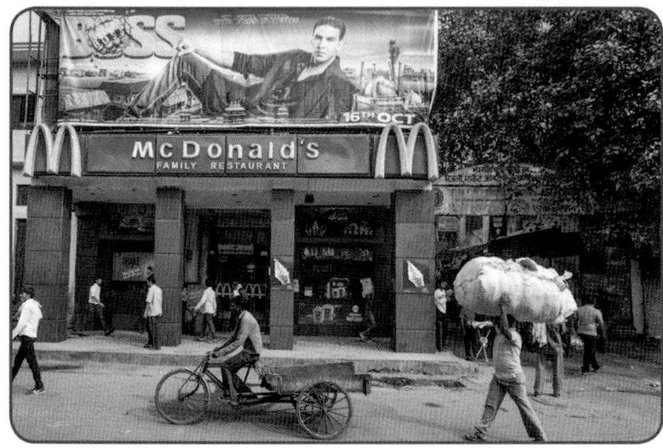

Figure 21.7 *Delhi, India*

Figure 21.8 *Galway, Ireland*

Look at the two photographs above. One shows a street in India, the other a street in Galway. In groups, discuss the differences and similarities between the two. Share your thoughts with the class.

 **(i)** List two positive impacts of globalisation.

(ii) List two negative impacts of globalisation.

(iii) Why might MNCs decide to relocate to a less economically developed country?

(iv) Explain how globalisation is increasing economic inequality.

I can explain how globalisation impacts on people all over the world.   

Globalisation and the world we live in today

Learning Intentions

In this section, you will learn:

- how globalisation is linked to population, settlement and human development
- what the future of globalisation may be.

Population
Settlement
Migration
Human development

Globalisation influences population, settlement and human development. We will now take a closer look at this.

Globalisation and population

In Chapter 18, we learned about **population**. Population is influenced by globalisation.

The movement of **people**, **knowledge** and **ideas** has spread awareness about health and family planning. It has greatly **reduced the gap** in fertility rates and death rates between developed and developing countries. Because of globalisation, we see more countries progressing to stages 3 and 4 of the **demographic transition model**.

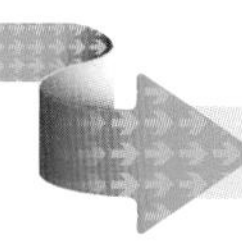

Go to Chapter 18, page 329, to learn more about the demographic transition model.

In **Ireland**, we have seen the impact of globalisation on our population.

- Our population **increases** during times of economic **prosperity** as people **migrate** to Ireland in search of work. These people bring their cultures and traditions such as food and music which influences Irish society.
- Our population **declines** during periods of economic **recession** as people migrate to other countries in search of work. The Irish have a strong influence on the places they move to. They bring with them culture and traditions such as Gaelic games, traditional music and dance.

Figure 21.9 *Shops like this, which cater to the needs of an immigrant community, have become common in Irish cities*

Globalisation and settlement

In Chapter 12, we learned about **settlement and urbanisation**. Patterns of settlement all over the world today are **influenced** by globalisation, but those influences are very different in the developing and developed worlds.

Figure 21.10 *A St Patrick's Day parade in Japan*

The developed world

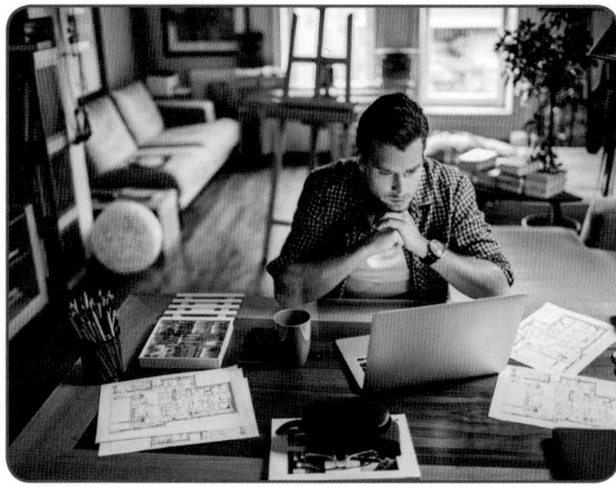

Figure 21.11 *Working from the comfort of your living room*

In the **developed world**, as we have learned, people choose to live in urban areas because of **work**, **services** and a better **social life**. The presence of regional headquarters of **MNCs** or of big global **brands** in the shops increases the attraction of big cities, and **accelerates urbanisation**.

However, it is important to note that globalisation has also given people more **choice** about where they can live. A lot of business is now conducted over the **internet** and an increasing number of people are able to **work from home** or smaller branch offices. Globalisation means that they don't always have to live where their company's office is. There is also an increasing number of **entrepreneurs**, who work independently, and they can work from almost anywhere if they have a good broadband connection available to them. Nevertheless, they often choose to live in urban areas because there are people there who they can work with and learn from in order to develop their businesses.

The developing world

Figure 21.12 *A slum area in Nairobi, Kenya*

The effect of globalisation on settlement patterns in the **developing world** is more negative. **Urbanisation** is happening at a **faster rate** in the developing world. Many people move to urban areas in the developing world out of a sense of desperation. The **push factors** behind rural-to-urban migration are many. Rather than stay in what they perceive to be backward rural areas, where they might not have enough food to eat, no chance of an education or a job, people move to cities in the **hope** that they might find something better. Therefore, the **slums** in cities such as Nairobi in Kenya and Mumbai in India are constantly growing.

Globalisation and human development

Globalisation has made all global citizens **interdependent**. The actions of people in one place can impact on people in another place. For example, choosing to buy **fair trade** products means that we are helping to make sure that the farmers that grow the produce are getting a fair deal. Therefore, as global citizens we have a **responsibility** to each other.

Globalisation develops at an uneven rate because of the **gap** between developed and developing countries. As we saw in Chapter 20, this gap exists because of:

- Unfair trade
- Colonisation
- Debt
- Corruption

The global community needs to try and close this gap between developed and developing countries so globalisation can have a positive impact on everyone's lives.

We have seen how countries have **joined together** to fight climate change and global warming and to reduce our carbon footprint in Chapter 14 on climate. These same countries now need to take action to make sure there is a level playing field for all countries.

The future of globalisation

While the **positive and negative impacts** of globalisation can be debated, there is no doubt that globalisation is here to stay. One of the greatest challenges for governments today is dealing with the pressures associated with the **high population densities** in some of the world's cities. These issues include:

- Overcrowding
- Lack of housing
- Shortage of clean water
- Pollution
- Lack of open space.

It is important that we recognise the negative impacts of globalisation so that we can protect our **cultural diversity** and **environmental biodiversity** and work towards global **economic equality**.

Figure 21.13 World leaders at the 2017 G20 summit of the world's wealthiest nations, intended to create economic stability across the globe. How many do you recognise?

PORTFOLIO ACTIVITY 21.2

Globalisation is a very controversial topic. Go to page 89 of your Portfolio to draw up your own list of its advantages and disadvantages.

ACTIVITY

Your teacher will hand out two sticky notes to each student. Write down two ways that globalisation has linked you to another part of the world. Place your sticky note on a map of the world and explain your connection to the rest of the class. Remember to link your connection to globalisation.

(i) List three things we must consider when looking at the future of globalisation.

(ii) Explain how globalisation has reduced the gap between developed and developing countries in terms of fertility rates and death rates.

(iii) Discuss three ways globalisation has influenced us in Ireland.

- I can evaluate how globalisation is interlinked with population, settlement and human development.
- I can discuss the possible future of globalisation. 

REVISION

The ____________ between different parts of the world is called ____________.

There are many ____________ that have influenced globalisation, including

____________, ____________, ____________, ____________

and ____________ ____________.

Globalisation has a huge ____________ on our lives. We should consider

____________ ____________ when we purchase food because of how it is

transported. Globalisation can increase economic ____________ because developing countries can be ____________. We are all influenced by ____________ culture such as music and ____________.

Globalisation has influenced population by helping countries progress to ____________ 3 and 4 of the ____________ transition model. It also influences rural-to-____________ migration.

Questions & Answers

Sample Questions

1. Explain the term 'globalisation'.
2. Examine **three** factors that have influenced globalisation.

Sample Answers

1. Globalisation is the way that different parts of the world are connected, making the world feel smaller.
2. (a) Globalisation is influenced by communications. Because of the internet and other modern communications, it is now easy to keep in contact and work with people living all over the world.

   (b) Globalisation is influenced by transport. Fresh produce can be transported by air so that it doesn't go off and MNCs can fly their employees to any of their offices all over the world.

   (c) Globalisation is influenced by politics. Governments are realising that we are all dependent on each other. It is important that we cooperate with each other and organisations such as the UN and WTO bring countries closer together.

Short Questions

1. Which of the following is **not** a global organisation?
   (a) UN – United Nations
   (b) WTO – World Trade Organisation
   (c) GAA – Gaelic Athletic Association
   (d) IFA – Irish Farmers' Association
2. Which of the following is **not** influenced by globalisation?
   (a) Music
   (b) Movies
   (c) Trade
   (d) Glaciation
3. Circle the correct answer.
   (a) Globalisation is about **independence / interdependence**.
   (b) A positive impact of globalisation is increasing **awareness of issues / consumption of fossil fuels**.
   (c) A negative impact of globalisation is **job creation in developing countries / job losses in developed countries**

Long Questions

1. Explain **three** ways that globalisation has influenced multinational companies.
2. Why has there been an increase in globalisation in the past 50 years?
3. 'There are positives and negatives to globalisation.' Discuss this statement with reference to **three** topics you have studied.
4. Explain briefly how globalisation has affected settlement in the developed and developing worlds.

Visual Summary

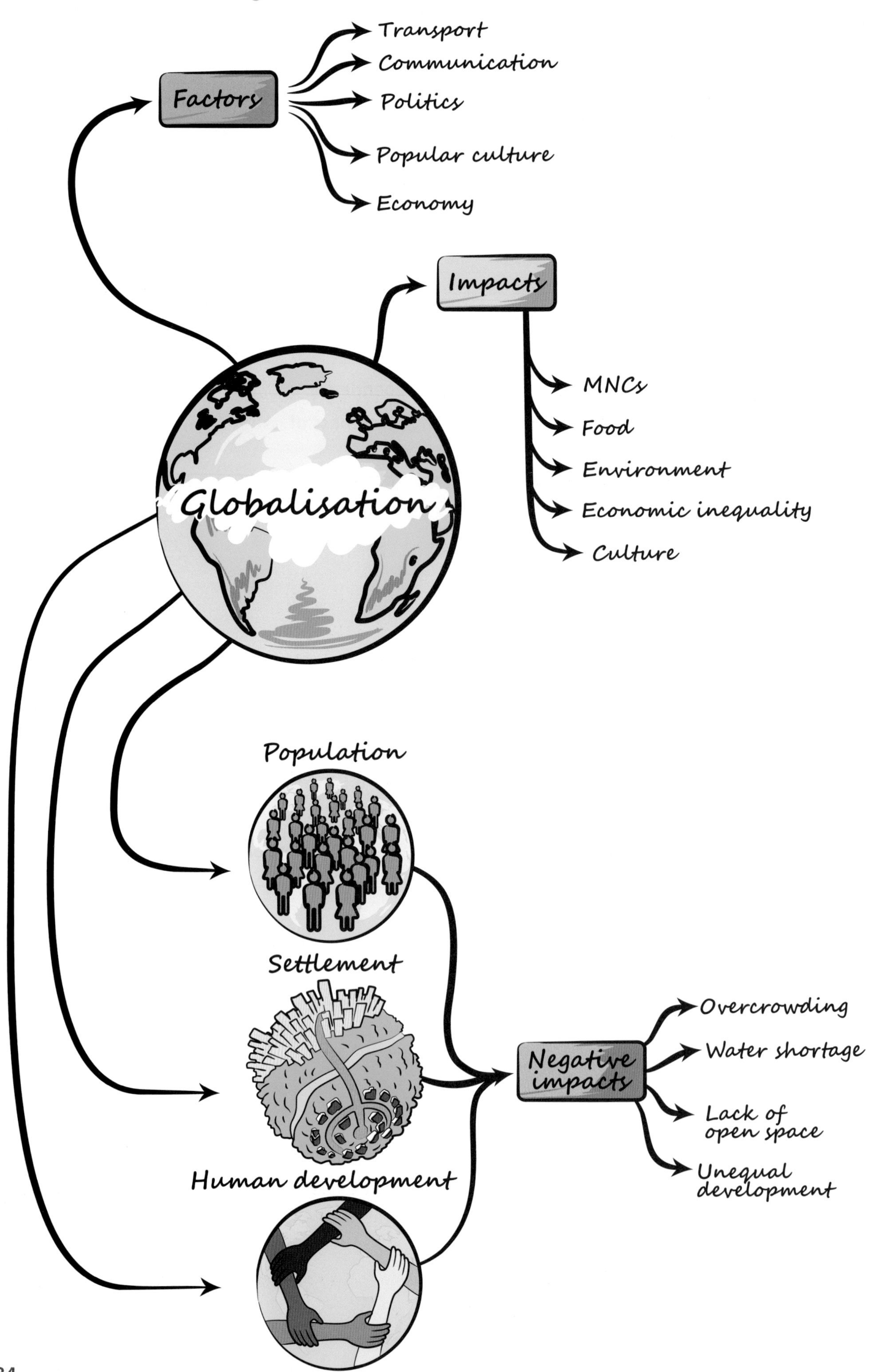

Factors
Transport
Communication
Politics
Popular culture
Economy
Impacts
MNCs
Food
Environment
Economic inequality
Culture
Globalisation
Population
Settlement
Human development
Negative impacts
Overcrowding
Water shortage
Lack of open space
Unequal development

Key Words

Chapter 1

		Page
Area	The size of a surface, the amount of space inside a boundary; to find the area, multiply the length by the width	18
Bar chart	A diagram where the values are shown by the height or length of lines or rectangles of equal width	14
Cardinal points	One of the four main points of the compass: north, south, east or west	9
Cartographer	A person who makes maps	3
Compass	An instrument used to calculate direction	9
Contour	Lines on a map showing areas of equal height	8
Data	A collection of facts	14
Easting	Vertical line on an OS map, giving coordinates; the numbers get higher as you go further east	4
Grid reference	Method of indicating an exact location on an OS map	5
Legend	Panel explaining what the symbols on a map represent; also called a key	6
National grid	A system of coordinates or set of squares used by the OSI and printed on OS maps	4
Northing	Horizontal line on an OS map, also giving coordinates	4
Percentage	Parts per hundred (e.g. 25 per cent means 25 per 100)	18
Pie chart	A graph in a circular shape; the data is shown in slices or sectors	15
Ratio	How much of one thing there is compared to another thing	4
Scale	A term used to describe the relationship between the size of an area of land and the size of a map of the same area	4
Spot height	A number and a black spot on a map to show the height of a hill or a mountain	8
Subzone	A subdivision of a zone; a box on the national grid	4
Summit	The highest point of a hill or mountain	8
Trend graph	Graph that uses one or more lines to show a trend or pattern for data over a period of time using two axes (X and Y)	16
Triangulation pillar	Triangle shape on a map showing where a concrete pillar is located on a mountain peak or hilltop	8

Chapter 2

		Page
Active volcano	A volcano that erupts regularly (e.g. Mount Etna in Sicily)	25
Aftershock	Small tremors that follow an earthquake	28
Alpine	Period of folding about 30 to 35 millions years ago when the Alps and Himalayas were formed	32
Anticline	Downward fold	32
Armorican	Period of folding when the Eurasian Plate and African Plate collided about 250 million years ago	32

		Page
Caledonian	Period of folding when the Eurasian Plate and the American Plate collided about 400 million years ago	32
Cone	The shape of a volcanic mountain after layers and layers of lava have poured out	24
Constructive boundary	Where two plates are separating and creating new crust	22
Continental drift	The process whereby the Earth's plates move and carry the continents with them	22
Convection currents	Circular movement of magma in the mantle, which rises, moves to the side then drops again	21
Core	Centre of the Earth	21
Crater	The opening at the top of the vent of a volcano	24
Crust	Outer layer of the Earth	21
Destructive boundary	Where two plates are colliding and destroying crust	22
Dormant volcano	A volcano that has not erupted for a long time but might again (e.g. Mount Vesuvius in Italy)	25
Epicentre	The point on the Earth's surface directly above the focus of an earthquake	28
Extinct volcano	A volcano that will not erupt ever again (e.g. Croghan Hill in Co. Offaly)	25
Fault line	A long, deep crack in the Earth's crust, often between tectonic plates (also called simply a fault)	22
Focus	The location in the Earth's crust where an earthquake occurs	28
Geothermal energy	Heat energy produced by and stored in the Earth	25
Geyser	Hot spring that gushes from the Earth in a volcanic zone	25
Lahar	River of mud when ash from a volcano mixes with melting snow	25
Lava	Magma when it has reached the surface	24
Magma	Molten rock that flows in convection currents within the Earth's mantle	21
Magma chamber	A chamber below the vent of a volcano, containing a reservoir of magma	24
Mantle	The layer of Earth located under the crust	21
Mid-ocean ridge	The constructive boundary where two plates are pulling away from each other	24
Pangaea	The huge land mass where the continents were once joined	22
Passive boundary	Where two plates are sliding past each other	22
Plate	The pieces of the Earth's crust that sit on top of the mantle	21
Plate boundary	The line where two plates meet	21
Plate tectonics	The study of plates and their movements	22
Richter scale	A measure of the intensity of earthquakes	29
Sea-floor spreading	The seabed widening because plates are separating to form new crust under the sea	22
Seismograph	An instrument that records the intensity of earthquakes	29
Seismologist	A person who studies earthquake activity	29
Socio-economic	To do with both social factors (i.e. people) and economic factors (i.e. money) and how they relate to each other	25
Subduction	When plates collide and the heavier plate is pushed under the lighter plate	22
Sustainability	Using the Earth's resources in a responsible way so that they are still available for future generations	26
Syncline	Upward fold	32
Tremor	A shaking or vibrating movement	28
Tsunami	A large, destructive sea wave caused by an earthquake on the ocean floor	29
Vent	A narrow tube in a volcano, through which magma flows	24

Chapter 3

		Page
Basalt	Igneous rock formed from lava cooling above the surface of the Earth	40
Building materials	Rocks/minerals extracted from the Earth's surface for building purposes	45
Cement	To bind or stick together	42
Compress	To press tightly together and make smaller	42
Crystal	A solid form of mineral	40
Deposit	To lay down or drop; the load laid down by water, waves or ice	42
Energy	Source of power	44
Exploit	Use something in order to benefit from it	44
Extrusive	Rock formed above the surface of the Earth	40
Galvanise	To coat iron or steel with a protective layer of zinc	47
Granite	Igneous rock formed from slowly cooling magma below the surface	40
Heat	The energy an object has because of the movement of its molecules	43
Hexagonal	Something with six sides	40
Igneous	Rock formed from the cooling of molten magma or lava	39
Intrusive	Rock formed below the surface of the Earth	41
Limestone	Sedimentary rock formed from particles of shells and the remains of skeletons of sea creatures	42
Marble	Metamorphic rock formed when limestone is put under great heat and pressure	43
Metamorphic	Rock that has been changed by extremes of heat and pressure	43
Mineral	A naturally occurring element, usually found in the ground	38
Mining	The process of obtaining coal or other minerals from below the Earth's surface	45
Natural resource	Something in the natural world that people can use to their advantage, such as land, rivers and seas	44
Ore	Rock from which valuable metals or minerals can be extracted	47
Permeable	Something that allows water to seep or pass through	42
Pressure	Continuous physical force exerted on or against something	43
Quarrying	The extraction of rock from the surface of the Earth using large machinery or explosives	45
Quartzite	Metamorphic rock formed when sandstone is put under great heat or pressure	44
Sandstone	Sedimentary rock formed from sand that has been worn away from the Earth's surface	42
Sediment	Matter that settles to the bottom of a liquid	42
Sedimentary	Rock formed when material is deposited and compacted	39
Soluble	Something that dissolves in water	42
Strata	Layers of rock	42

Chapter 4

		Page
Agriculture	The practice of farming, including the growing of crops and the rearing of animals	61
Aqueduct	Human-made channels used to pipe water from one area to another	58
Arable farming	The growing of crops	62
Canal	Waterway built by people for shipping, travel or irrigation	58
Coillte	Semi-state body which owns and manages half of the forests in Ireland	66
Condensation	The tiny droplets formed when water vapour in the air rises and cools	55
Coniferous	Trees that keep their leaves/needles all year round (e.g. spruce, pine)	65
Conservation zone	A protected area	61

		Page
Continental shelf	Seabed surrounding a continent, up to 200 metres deep	59
Dairy farming	The keeping of cows for milk, butter, cheese, etc.	62
Deciduous	Trees that lose their leaves in winter (e.g. beech, birch, oak)	64
Deforestation	The clearing of all trees from an area by burning or cutting	66
Evaporation	When the sun heats up water in rivers, lakes, oceans, trees and plants and turns it into water vapour	55
Filtering	A process whereby water is cleaned	56
Finite	Having an end, can run out (e.g. fossil fuels)	52
Fluoride	A chemical added to water to help stop tooth decay	56
Horticulture	The growing of vegetables, flowers, fruits, salad, etc.	62
Infinite	Resources that can be used over and over again (e.g. wind, solar energy)	52
Inputs	The things needed to begin a process in a system	62
Irrigation	The artificial watering of land	57
Livestock	Cattle, sheep, pigs, horses	62
Natural resources	Things in the natural world that people can use to their advantage, such as land, rivers and seas	52
Non-renewable	Something that cannot be replaced once used (e.g. oil, gas and coal)	52
Outputs	The products or results of a system	62
Over-exploitation	Using a resource too much	59
Overfishing	To fish so much that the fish stocks are reduced	60
Pastoral farming	The grazing of sheep or cattle	62
Photosynthesis	The process whereby plankton convert the sun's energy into food energy	59
Plankton	Tiny organisms that drift on ocean currents and are eaten by fish	59
Potable water	Water that is safe for people and animals to drink	54
Precipitation	Moisture from the atmosphere that reaches the Earth as rain, snow, sleet, hail or dew	55
Primary	Economic activity using the Earth's resources (e.g. rocks, soils, water)	52
Processes	Tasks or jobs done within a system	62
Reforestation	The planting of trees on areas of land that were once covered by forest but were affected by deforestation	66
Renewable	Energy sources that can be used again and again (e.g. wind, solar, water, geothermal)	52
Run-off	Water that has fallen on the Earth and runs off the soil into oceans, lakes or rivers	55
Secondary	Economic activity that involves processing raw materials into products	52
Semi-state body	An organisation partly owned and run by the government	66
Teagasc	Semi-state body that offers advice and assistance to the agricultural sector	66
Tertiary	Economic activity that involves providing a service to people	52
Tillage	The production of crops	62

Chapter 5

		Page
Acid rain	Formed when sulfur dioxide and nitrogen oxide are released into the atmosphere, through the burning of fossil fuels	83
Biofuel	Fuel produced from biomass which can be used to power engines	79
Biomass	Organic material (e.g. sawdust and agricultural waste) that can be used to generate electricity	79

		Page
Coal	Non-renewable energy source used for heating, powering electricity stations, etc.	76
Dependent	Relying on something	72
Energy resources	The resources that the physical world provides us with that we can make energy from	71
Fossil fuel	Fuel formed from decomposing plants and animals (e.g. coal, oil)	72
Gas	Non-renewable energy source used for heating homes, cooking, etc.	74
Geothermal power	Energy created by using the heat from the Earth's crust	78
Global warming	The increase in the temperature of the Earth due to the greenhouse effect	83
Greenhouse gases	Gases such as carbon dioxide and methane that act like a blanket around the planet and trap heat from the sun in the atmosphere	83
Hydroelectric power	Electricity created by using the force of falling water	77
Hydropower	Hydroelectricity; energy produced using the force of falling water	80
Megawatt	A unit of electrical power equal to one million watts	80
Nitrogen oxide	An atmospheric pollutant	83
Non-renewable	Something that cannot be replaced once used (e.g. oil, gas and coal)	72
Oil	Non-renewable energy source used for running cars, heating homes, flying aircraft, etc.	72
OPEC	Organisation of the Petroleum Exporting Countries	73
Peat	A fuel made of decayed plants and other organic matter found in bogs; important source of heating and energy	76
pH value	A scale of measurement of how acidic or alkaline a substance is; the lower the pH value, the more acidic the substance is	83
Renewable	Something that can be used again and again (e.g. wind, water, geothermal power)	77
Reservoir	An artificial lake that is used to store a large supply of water for use in people's homes, businesses, etc.	81
Smog	Pollution that occurs when smoke from burning fossil fuels is combined with sunlight and heat	84
Solar cell	An object that captures the heat and light from the sun and converts it into electricity	78
Solar panel	A collection of solar cells which can be put onto a roof	78
Sulfur dioxide	A colourless, pungent, toxic gas formed by burning sulfur in air	83
Turbine	A machine where liquid (water) or gas (wind) flows through and turns a wheel with blades in order to produce power	77
Wind farm	Several modern wind turbines grouped together in one area	78

Chapter 6

		Page
Avalanche	The rapid movement of snow and ice down a slope	100
Bedding plane	The horizontal spaces between the layers or strata in limestone rock	93
Bog burst	Sudden movement of saturated bogland down a slope	98
Calcite	A white or colourless mineral consisting of calcium carbonate	94
Calcium carbonate	A colourless or white crystalline compound, $CaCO_3$, occurring naturally (e.g. chalk, limestone, marble)	91

		Page
Carbonation	Type of chemical weathering in which limestone is broken down by the carbonic acid in rainwater	91
Carbonic acid	A mixture of rainwater (H_2O) and carbon dioxide (CO_2)	91
Cavern	An underground cave whose opening is also underground	93
Chemical weathering	When rocks are dissolved because of a chemical reaction, e.g. carbonation	91
Clint	Blocks of limestone left in between the grikes	92
Denudation	The wearing down of the Earth's surface by erosion or weathering	89
Erosion	The breakdown and removal of material by water, wind or ice	90
Fluctuating	Increasing and decreasing at an uneven rate	90
Freeze-thaw action	Type of mechanical weathering where rock is broken down due to water in cracks repeatedly freezing and thawing	90
Gradient	Steepness of a slope	97
Grike	Grooves or gaps between the limestone blocks	92
Hydraulic action	The physical force of moving water	93
Joint	The long vertical crack in limestone rock	92
Karst	A limestone area with surface and underground features made by chemical weathering	92
Lahar	River of mud when ash from a volcano mixes with melting snow	98
Limestone pavement	The surface of a karst landscape	92
Mechanical weathering	The physical breaking up of rocks into smaller pieces by putting pressure on the rock (e.g. freeze-thaw action)	90
Mudflow	Fast-moving river of rock, soil and water down a slope	98
Regolith	Rock fragments that have broken away from solid rock through weathering and erosion	97
Saturated	When something has taken in all the water it possibly can	98
Scree	Small pieces of rock created due to mechanical weathering	98
Soil creep	Slow movement of soil down a slope due to gravity	98
Stalactite	Icicle-shaped structure which hangs from the roof of a cave under an area of limestone, made from deposits of calcite	94
Stalagmite	Icicle-shaped structure which grows upwards from the floor of a cave, made from deposits of calcite	94
Swallow hole	Holes through which rivers in limestone areas disappear underground	93
Terracette	A step formed after soil moves downslope due to soil creep	98
Weathering	The breakdown and decay of rocks by mechanical and chemical processes	90

Chapter 7

		Page
Angle	The viewpoint from which something is seen	114
Background	The area or scenery behind something; the top of a photograph	115
Compound	A slope that is steep in places and not steep in other places	109
Concave	All or part of a slope that gets increasingly shallow as you go downhill	109
Convex	All or part of a slope that gets increasingly steep as you go downhill	109
Cross-section	A view into the inside of something made by cutting through it	110
Foreground	The part of a view that is nearest to the observer; the base of a photograph	115
Function	The service something provides (e.g. a school serves an educational function; a church serves a religious function)	117

		Page
Horizon	The line at which the Earth's surface and the sky appear to meet	115
Infrastructure	The systems and facilities that support a factory, settlement, community or nation (e.g. transport, communication, sewage, water, electricity)	111
Irregular area	An area on an OS map that is not a rectangle	108
Land use	Any use of land (e.g. a school)	111
Oblique	Indirect or from a diagonal or slanting direction; in photography, the camera is at an angle	114
Regular area	An area on an OS map in the shape of a rectangle	108
Settlement	A place where people have settled (e.g. hamlet, village, town, city)	111
Site	The actual ground on which something is built	111
Slope	A surface of which one end or side is at a higher level than another	109
Vertical	Up and down; in photography, the camera is pointing straight down	114

Chapter 8

		Page
Carcinogenic	Something that has the potential to cause cancer	132
Finished product	Product that is ready for market	122
Footloose industry	An industry that is not tied to a specific location	129
Foreign direct investment (FDI)	When multinational companies locate their bases in other countries, including Ireland	130
Globalisation	The way that people and places are interconnected with other people and places around the world	130
Heavy industry	Industry where heavy or bulky raw materials are used (e.g. smelting, oil refining)	126
Incinerator	A facility used to burn waste	132
Industrial estate	Site at the edge of an urban area that is set aside to be used by industries, with high level of services and within easy reach of the transport network	129
Industrial inertia	When an industry stays at its original location even though the reasons for locating there no longer apply	129
Inputs	The things needed to begin a process in a system	122
Labour force	People who are able to work	124
Light industry	Manufacturing activity that uses moderate amounts of raw materials to produce goods (e.g. fashion, electronics)	126
Manufacturing	Changing raw materials into a product that a customer wants	123
Markets	A place where goods are bought and sold; also, a group of people who buy goods	124
Multinational company (MNC)	A company with a base in more than one country	130
Outputs	The products or results of a system	122
Policy	A plan or course of action	125
Processes	Tasks or jobs done within a system	122
Raw materials	The basic materials from which a product is made	124
Semi-finished product	Product that has undergone some processing but requires further processing	122
Services	Systems or activities that supply a public need (e.g. transport, electricity, education)	125
System	A way of doing something or describing how something is done	122
Transport	The movement of people, materials or goods from one place to another	124
Waste management	Processes involved in dealing with waste	132

Chapter 9

		Page
Abrasion	Erosion caused when loose material in the load carried by water wears away the land	139
Alluvium	Material transported and deposited by a river when it floods	145
Attrition	Erosion caused when small stones in the load carried by water bump against one another	139
Confluence	The point at which two rivers or streams join together	136
Course	The route a river takes to the sea	136
Delta	Landform of deposition found in the old stage of the river, triangular in shape at the mouth of the river where it enters the sea or lake	146
Dendritic drainage	Shaped like a tree, where smaller tributary streams combine before joining the main river	151
Deposition	The laying down or dropping of the material that the river, sea or glacier has transported	139
Deranged drainage	Where there is no clear pattern to the river system	151
Distributary	Smaller channel which carries water to the sea through the delta	146
Drainage	How water flows in an area; the natural removal of water from an area	151
Drainage basin	The area of land drained by a river	136
Erosion	The breakdown and removal of material by water, wind or ice	139
Estuary	The part of a river mouth that is tidal	136
Flood plain	A wide, flat area of land on either side of the river in its old stage that is covered in water when the river floods	145
Hydraulic action	The physical force of moving water	139
Hydroelectric power (HEP)	Renewable energy created by using the force of falling water	148
Interlocking spurs	Areas of high ground that jut out at both sides of a V-shaped valley	141
Lateral erosion	The eroding sideways into the channel of a river	143
Levee	A build-up of alluvium on the banks of a river, caused by floods	145
Meanders	Curves or bends in the river in its mature stage	143
Mouth	The point where a river comes to the end, usually when entering the sea	136
Overhang	Something that sticks out or hangs over another thing	142
Oxbow lake	A horseshoe-shaped lake that is formed when a meander is cut off from the river	144
Pollution	Any contamination of air, soil, water and environment which makes it harmful to humans	148
Radial drainage	Where streams radiate outwards from a central high point, resembling the spokes of a wheel	151
Saltation	The bouncing movement of stones in a flow of water	139
Settlement	A place where people have settled (e.g. hamlet, village, town, city)	148
Solution	A mixture of water and the materials dissolved in it	139
Source	The beginning or start of a river	136
Surface run-off	The flow of water that occurs when excess rainwater flows over the surface of the Earth into a river or stream	148
Suspension	Light materials such as sand and silt that float along in the water	139
Traction	The rolling movement of stones in a flow of water	139
Transportation	The movement of material that the river has eroded	139
Trellis drainage	Where tributaries enter the main river at an angle close to 90 degrees	151
Tributary	A stream or smaller river that flows into a larger stream or river	136

		Page
Undercutting	Cutting or wearing away the part below or under something	142
V-shaped valley	A steep-sided valley in the shape of a 'V', shaped by vertical erosion	137
Vertical erosion	The eroding downwards into the channel of a river	140
Waterfall	A vertical drop in the course of the river in its youthful stage	142
Watershed	The area of high ground which separates two drainage basins	136

Chapter 10

		Page
Backwash	Water moving back down the beach to return to the sea	158
Bay	A curved stretch of coastline that has been eroded by waves	160
Blowhole	A passage that links the surface of the cliff top with the roof of a sea cave	162
Compression	When air gets trapped in cracks and joints on a cliff face and becomes compressed; when the waves retreat, the pressure is released	159
Constructive waves	Where the swash is greater than the backwash, leading to the deposition of material	159
Destructive waves	Where the backwash is greater than the swash, leading to the erosion of material	159
Fetch	The open area of sea across which a wave travels; the larger the fetch, the larger the wave	158
Gabions	Wire cages filled with rocks and small stones to break the power of the waves approaching the beach or sand dunes	170
Groynes	Concrete or wooden structures built at right angles to the coast to trap sediment carried by longshore drift, in order to prevent the removal of sand from the beach	170
Headland	A land area of hard rock jutting into the sea	160
High-water mark	A line marking the highest level reached by water at high tide	161
Lagoon	A shallow sea inlet cut off from the sea	166
Longshore drift	The zigzag movement of material carried by waves along a coastline	164
Low-water mark	A line marking the lowest level reached by water at low tide	161
Notch	An indentation at a point of weakness on an edge or surface	161
Overhang	Something that sticks out or hangs over another thing	161
Prevailing wind	The most common wind that blows over an area	164
Rock armour	Large boulders placed at the base of a cliff or in front of sand dunes	170
Sand dune	A build-up of sand at the back of the beach above the high-tide level	165
Sand spit	A long ridge of deposited sand or shingle joined to the coastline at one end	166
Sandbar	Deposited sand and shingle that extends across and closes off a bay	166
Sea arch	A tunnel that goes into and through a headland	162
Sea cave	A tunnel into a sea cliff	162
Sea cliff	A vertical or steep slope on the coastline	161
Sea stack	A pillar of rock formed when the roof of a sea arch collapses	162
Sea stump	An eroded sea stack, often only visible at low tide	162
Sea walls	High concrete walls that break the power of incoming waves	170
Storm beach	The heavier materials such as boulders and rocks that are carried above the high-water line by waves during storms	165
Swash	The powerful movement of a breaking wave up a beach	158
Tombolo	A ridge of sand or shingle joining an island to the mainland	166
Undercutting	Cutting or wearing away the part below or under something	161
Wave-built terrace	A terrace built up from eroded sediments on top of a wave-cut platform	161
Wave-cut platform	A narrow, flat area at the base of a retreating sea cliff, created by the action of waves	161

Chapter 11

		Page
Abrasion	Erosion caused when loose material in the load carried by ice or water wears away the land	179
Agriculture	The practice of farming, including the growing of crops and the rearing of animals	187
Arête	A steep mountain ridge separating two cirques	181
Boulder clay	A mixture of clay and rocks deposited by a glacier	184
Cirque	A hollow in a mountain with three steep sides, formed by glacial erosion; also called a corrie, coom or coum	180
Crevasse	A deep crack in a surface	184
Drumlin	A low, oval mound or small hill, typically one of a group, consisting of compacted boulder clay shaped by past glacial action	185
Erratic	A rock or boulder that differs from the surrounding rock and is believed to have been brought from a distance by glacial action	185
Esker	A long ridge of glacial material deposited when a glacier melted	186
Fjord	A glacial valley that was flooded by the sea	182
Fluvio-glacial	To do with the water flowing from a melting glacier	186
Friction	The resistance that one surface or object encounters when moving over another	179
Glacial deposits	Mixture of unsorted sediment deposited after the melting of a glacier	189
Glaciation	The processes and landforms caused by the movement of glaciers	178
Glacier	A slow-moving mass or river of ice	179
Hanging valley	A smaller glaciated valley that hangs above the main glaciated valley, often containing a waterfall	182
Hydroelectricity	Electricity created by using the force of falling water	188
Ice age	A period during which large parts of several continents are covered by ice sheets	179
Ice sheet	Large expanse of ice	179
Lateral	To the side	186
Medial	Towards the middle	186
Meltwater	The water flowing out from under the glacier as it melts	186
Moraine	Deposited material found in the lowlands of glacial valleys	186
Outwash plain	A broad, flat area of land created when glacial meltwater deposited its load of sand and gravel	187
Paternoster lakes	Two or more ribbon lakes linked by a river in a U-shaped glacial valley resembling rosary beads	182
Plucking	Glacial erosion where rock fragments are pulled out of a valley floor by moving ice	179
Pyramidal peak	A steep mountaintop created by three or more cirques meeting around a peak	181
Ribbon lake	Long, narrow lake on the floor of a U-shaped valley	182
Striation	Scratch marks left behind on rocks after the glacier has moved over them, showing the direction it moved in	179
Terminal	At the end of something	186
Tourism	When people travel to a place for leisure	188
Truncated spur	Interlocking spur which has been eroded by a passing glacier	181
U-shaped valley	A valley with a wide, flat floor and steep sides carved out by moving ice	181

Chapter 12

		Page
Altitude	The height of a place above sea level	198
Antiquity	An object, building or work of art from the ancient or historic past	202
Apartment	A room or set of rooms for people to live in within a larger building	220
Aspect	Direction a place faces in relation to the sun	198
Bridging point	A place where it was easy to cross a river (e.g. shallow water, narrow stretch)	198
Building density	The number and size of buildings on a given area of land	219
Celtic	To do with the people who arrived in Ireland around 500 BCE	202
Central Business District (CBD)	The commercial and often geographic heart of a city	217
Clustered settlement	Settlement where buildings are grouped together	209
Commuter	A person who makes a regular journey to and from a place of work or study	211
Congestion	When large numbers of vehicles are moving on roads at the same time, causing traffic jams	211
Cycle lanes	Lanes on the road reserved for cyclists	214
DART	Dublin Area Rapid Transit; a train which runs along the coastline of Dublin Bay from Howth to Greystones	213
Defence	Protection against attack	200
Detached house	A house that is not joined to any other house	220
Dispersed settlement	Settlement where houses and buildings are spread over a wide area	209
Dormitory town	A town that people leave during the day to work elsewhere	211
Drainage	How water flows in an area; the natural removal of water from an area	198
Ecclesiastical	To do with the church or its clergy	205
Function	The service something provides (e.g. a school serves an educational function; a church serves a religious function)	204
Functional zone	Area of a city where a particular type of activity takes place (e.g. industry, retail)	217
Land value	The value or worth of a piece of land	219
Linear settlement	Settlement where houses are built in a line along a road	208
Luas	The tram system in Dublin	213
Market	A place where goods are bought and sold; also, a group of people who buy goods	205
Multi-functional	Having several purposes	207
Nodal point	A central location where different routes meet	200
Norman	To do with the people who invaded Ireland in the twelfth century who originally came from Normandy in France	203
Nucleated settlement	Settlement where houses and buildings are grouped around a central point	209
Planning	Preparation for the future	211
Plantation	An organised colonisation when settlers are sent by their ruler to live somewhere else	203
Population density	How many people live in an area; it is often measured by the number of people living in 1 km^2	197
Population distribution	The spread of where people live	197
Primate city	A city that is at least twice as big as the second biggest city in the same country	221
QBCs	Quality Bus Corridors; special lanes on a road reserved for buses	213

		Page
Redevelopment	When old houses, flats, shops, offices, restaurants or car parks are knocked down and new spaces are built in their place	216
Renewal	Upgrading and improvement of the old inner-city areas	216
Residential	To do with where people live	205
Resource	Something in the natural world that people can use to their advantage	205
Rush hour	The movement of commuters to and from work by car at a specific time each day	211
Satellite town	A town that is close to a major urban centre but is not part of it	211
Semi-detached house	A house that is joined to another house on one side only	220
Settlement	A place where people have settled (e.g. hamlet, village, town, city)	197
Shanty town	A settlement (sometimes illegal) of poor people living in houses made from scrap materials	212
Shelter	Protection from the weather by trees, mountains or other natural features	198
Site	The actual ground on which something is built	198
Situation	The area surrounding a settlement	200
Slope	A surface of which one end or side is at a higher level than another	198
Suburbs	The outskirts of a town or city, mainly used for housing	218
Terraced housing	Houses built together in a row which share walls on each side	220
Urban decay	When areas of a city have been abandoned and have fallen into disrepair	212
Urban sprawl	The spread of a town or city into the surrounding countryside	215
Urbanisation	The increase in the number of people living in towns and cities	210
Viking	To do with the people who came to Ireland in longboats from Scandinavia around 800 CE	202

Chapter 13

		Page
Air mass	Large moving pocket of air	232
Altitude	The height of a place above sea level	226
Anemometer	Instrument used to measure wind speed	243
Anticyclone	A high-pressure system	234
Atmosphere	A thin layer of gases that surrounds the Earth	226
Axis	An imaginary line around which a body rotates	228
Barograph	Instrument used to measure atmospheric pressure	241
Beaufort scale	A scale used to measure wind strength	243
Campbell-Stokes sunshine recorder	Instrument used to measure the number of hours of sunshine per day	244
Celsius	The unit of measurement of air temperature commonly used in Europe	240
Cirrus clouds	Thin and wispy clouds that occur above 8,000 metres	237
Cold front	Front formed when a cold air mass replaces a warmer air mass	234
Convectional rain	Rain that is formed when warm air rises and condenses, common in areas where the ground is heated by the sun	238
Converge	Come together	230
Coriolis effect	The rotation of the Earth on its axis which makes the trade winds appear to curve towards the west, regardless of whether they are travelling to the equator from the south or north	230
Cumulus clouds	Clouds that look like big fluffy balls of cotton wool and indicate good weather, occurring below 5,000 metres	236
Current	The movement of water like a river through the ocean	231
Cyclonic rain	Rain that occurs when two air masses meet and form a front	238

		Page
Depression	A low-pressure system	235
Distribution	A word used in Geography to describe where something is	228
Doldrums	An area of calm weather where the trade winds from the north and south meet near the equator	230
Equator	An imaginary circle around the Earth that is equidistant from the North Pole and the South Pole	228
Fahrenheit	The unit of measurement of air temperature commonly used in the USA	240
Front	The place where two air masses meet	233
Frontal rain	Rain that occurs when two air masses meet and form a front	238
Gulf Stream	A current originating in the Gulf of Mexico and moving north-eastwards into the Atlantic Ocean	231
Hectopascal	A unit of measurement of atmospheric pressure	241
Hemisphere	The half of the sphere of the Earth above or below the equator	228
High pressure	A condition of the atmosphere in which the pressure is above average (e.g. an anticyclone)	229
Horse latitudes	Found at 30° north and south of the equator, where winds are weak	230
Hygrometer	Instrument used to measure relative humidity	242
Isobar	Line on a weather map which joins together places of equal atmospheric pressure	233
Isohel	Line on a weather map showing areas of equal sunshine	244
Isohyet	Line on a weather map showing areas of equal rainfall	244
Isotherm	Line on a weather map that joins places of equal temperature	240
Labrador Current	A cold current which flows south along the coast of north-east America	231
Latitude	Position north or south of the equator, measured in degrees	228
Low pressure	A condition of the atmosphere in which the pressure is below average (e.g. a depression)	229
Maritime	To do with the sea or oceans	232
Meteorologist	A person who studies the weather	239
Millibar	A unit of measurement of atmospheric pressure	233
North Atlantic Drift	A warm ocean current from the Gulf of Mexico that runs along the west coast of Ireland	231
Occluded front	Front formed where a cold front takes over a warm front or the other way around, bringing changeable weather conditions	234
Ozone layer	Part of the lower atmosphere, which helps to filter out harmful ultraviolet rays from the sun	227
Polar	To do with the north or south poles	232
Polar easterlies	Found at 60° north and south of the equator, they are cold winds from the poles	230
Precipitation	Moisture from the atmosphere that reaches the Earth as rain, snow, sleet, hail or dew	237
Prevailing westerlies	Winds from the west, the most usual winds that blow over Ireland	230
Rain gauge	Instrument used to measure the amount of rainfall	244
Rain shadow	The area on the opposite side of the mountain to where relief rain falls	238
Relative humidity	A percentage of the maximum moisture that could be in the air at a certain temperature	242
Relief rain	Rain that falls as moist air rises over mountains	238
Solar energy	Energy from the sun	227
Solar radiation	Energy transmitted from the sun as light and heat	227

		Page
Stevenson screen	A box used to hold instruments measuring temperature, atmospheric pressure and humidity	242
Stratosphere	The upper layer of the atmosphere, extending from 17 km to 50 km above the Earth's surface	227
Stratus clouds	Clouds that look like flat sheets and indicate an overcast or rainy day, occurring below 2,000 metres	236
Synoptic chart	A weather map that contains information gathered from weather stations, using lines and symbols to show what is happening with the weather at a given time	240
Thermometer	An instrument used to measure air temperature	240
Trade winds	Warm, steady breezes that blow towards the equator	230
Tropical	To do with the tropics around the equator	232
Troposphere	The lowest region of the atmosphere, extending from the Earth's surface to a height of about 17 km	226
Warm front	Front formed when warm air rises over a mass of cold air	233
Weather station	A place with equipment and instruments for observing and recording the weather	240

Chapter 14

		Page
Air masses	Large moving pockets of air	254
Altitude	The height of a place above sea level	255
Aspect	Direction a place faces in relation to the sun	255
Boreal climate	A cold climate found in the northern hemisphere between 55° north and the Arctic Circle	259
Carbon emissions	Gases emitted from the burning of fossil fuels	263
Carbon footprint	The amount of carbon emissions we produce as individuals	263
CFCs	Chlorofluorocarbons, one of the most dangerous greenhouse gases, were once used in aerosol cans, foam packaging and refrigerators	264
Climatic zone	A geographical zone with a similar climate throughout	256
Cool temperate oceanic climate	Climate found between 40° and 60° north and south of the equator; the climate of Ireland	256
Deforestation	The removal of forests without replanting them	263
Desertification	Lack of vegetation cover causes soil erosion and land is turned into desert	264
Drought	A prolonged period of abnormally low rainfall, leading to a shortage of water	264
Equatorial climate	Climate of areas near the equator	257
Global warming	The increase in the temperature of the Earth due to the greenhouse effect	263
Greenhouse effect	When carbon dioxide and other gases in the atmosphere trap heat, keeping the Earth warm	263
Greenhouse gases	Gases, including carbon dioxide and methane, that contribute to the greenhouse effect	263
Latitude	The distance of a place north or south of the equator, measured in degrees	253
Methane	A greenhouse gas produced by decomposing organic matter	263
Natural region	An area where the climate, natural vegetation, wildlife and human activities are similar	256
Nitrous oxide	A greenhouse gas produced when artificial fertilisers in the form of nitrates are used	264
North Atlantic Drift	A warm ocean current from the Gulf of Mexico that runs along the west coast of Ireland	261
Oceanic climate	A climate affected by the oceans	258

		Page
Ozone layer	Part of the lower atmosphere, which helps to filter out harmful ultraviolet rays from the sun	264
Prevailing winds	The most common winds that blow over an area	254
Savannah climate	Climate of areas between 5° and 15° north and south of the equator	257
Temperate climate	Climate of the areas located in the mid-latitudes, between 40° and 60° north and south of the equator	258
Tundra climate	A cold climate in areas located around the north and south poles	259

Chapter 15

		Page
Landmark	A feature (e.g. building, bridge, cathedral) that is easy to see and can help a person find the way to a place near it	274
Satellite	An artificial body placed in orbit round the Earth or another planet in order to collect information or for communication	280
Satellite image	Image of the Earth taken by a satellite	280

Chapter 16

		Page
Acidity	How acidic or alkaline a substance is	293
Bacteria	A very large group of micro-organisms	289
Bedrock	The bottom layer of solid rock which is usually covered with broken-down rock and soil	286
Biodiversity	Term used to describe the variety of plants and animals in a particular habitat	299
Biomass	A fuel made from organic materials (e.g. sawdust and agricultural waste) that can be used to generate electricity.	299
Blanket bog	Shallow bog found in the west and mountainous areas of Ireland	298
Brown earth soils	Soils that developed on boulder clay; the most common soil type in Ireland	290
Cash crop	An agricultural crop that is grown for profit, instead of for use by the grower	296
Coniferous	Trees that keep their leaves/needles all year round (e.g. spruce, pine)	291
Cut-away bogs	Bogs from which the peat has been removed	299
Deciduous	Trees that lose their leaves in winter (e.g. beech, birch, oak)	291
Deforestation	The removal of forests without replanting them	295
Desertification	Lack of vegetation cover causes soil erosion and land is turned into desert	297
Fungi	Organisms such as mould or mushrooms that are important in breaking down organic matter	289
Gley soils	Soils that develop where the bedrock, or the clay above it, is impermeable; they are sticky and waterlogged.	292
Hardpan	The build-up of minerals at the bottom of the A horizon that become cemented together to form a hard impermeable layer	287
Horizon	A specific layer of soil or subsoil in a soil profile	286
Humus	Fertile part of the soil formed when plants and animals decay	285
Leaching	The process whereby rain water passes through the soil, washing minerals, humus and nutrients from the A horizon down into the B horizon	287
Lime	Crushed limestone, which is alkaline	293
Loam	An even mixture of sand, silt and clay, ideal for growing a variety of crops.	290
Mineral	A naturally occurring element, usually found in the ground	285
Monoculture	The growing of one single crop type	296
Natural vegetation	Plant life that grows in an area without any human interference	293

		Page
Nomadic	Moving in groups from place to place in order to find grazing for their animals	297
Nutrients	Substances that provide nourishment essential for life and growth	285
Over-cropping	When crops are continuously grown on land and nutrients are constantly being removed from the soil	296
Overgrazing	The practice of grazing too many animals on the land for too long, resulting in damage to the vegetation and erosion	296
Parent material	The underlying geological material (e.g. bedrock) on which soil horizons form	288
Peat	Brown material made of decomposed vegetable matter	298
Plant litter	Leaves and rotting vegetation	286
Podzol soils	Infertile soils found on the floors of coniferous forests in cold and wet areas	291
Raised bog	Deep bog found in the centre of Ireland	298
Reforestation	The planting of trees on areas of land that were once covered by forest but were affected by deforestation	296
Semi-arid	Region that receives very little rainfall and struggles to support vegetation, often found on the fringes of deserts	297
Soil conditions	Factors that determine the suitability for planting or growing a crop (e.g. depth, acidity, drainage)	293
Soil profile	A vertical cross-section of soil from the ground surface to the parent rock	286
Texture	The feel, appearance or consistency of a substance	285

Chapter 17

		Page
Accessibility	How easy it is to reach a destination	311
Amenities	Facilities that provide the services needed by tourists (e.g. hotels, restaurants and visitor centres)	307
Attractions	Places of cultural, historical or natural interest where tourists visit for leisure and enjoyment	305
Boundaries	Lines which mark the limits of an area; dividing lines	312
Communication links	How people move from place to place (e.g. roads, railway)	311
Discover Ireland	Organisation operated by Fáilte Ireland that features listings for Irish accommodation, activities, events and tourist attractions	306
Ecotourism	Sustainable and responsible travel that aims to avoid having a negative effect on the environment	310
Facilities	Something that the public can use such as a picnic area or a sports ground	304
Fáilte Ireland	The National Tourism Development Authority, whose role is to support the tourism industry in Ireland	306
Interrelationship	How things are linked with and influence each other	304
Route	A way or course taken in getting from a starting point to a destination	312
Services	Systems or activities that supply a public need (e.g. transport, electricity, education)	304
Sustainable tourism	Tourism capable of being continued with minimal long-term effects on people and the environment	310
Transport infrastructure	The framework of transport in a country, including roads, railways, ports and airports	312
Transport Infrastructure Ireland	A state agency in Ireland responsible for national road and public transport infrastructure, established in 2015	312
Transport network	A set of connected communication links	311

Chapter 18

		Page
Agricultural Revolution	A period of technological improvement in agriculture that occurred during the eighteenth and early nineteenth centuries	325
Baby boom	Rapid increase in birth rates	326
Birth rate	The number of babies born per 1,000 people in the total population in one year	324
Census	An official count of the population of a country	333
Civil war	War between different sides within one country	326
Colony	A country or area under the full or partial political control of another country and occupied by settlers from that country	334
Death rate	The number of deaths per 1,000 people in the total population in one year	324
Demographer	A person who studies population change and structure	329
Demographic transition model	Theory linking population changes to developments in the economy, education and healthcare	329
Dependency ratio	The number of people not working in the older and younger age groups compared to the number of people in the middle groups who are working	332
Expanding stage	When the population is increasing	329
Family planning	The awareness of birth control, and the planning and spacing of the number of children that a family might want	327
Fertility rate	The average number of babies born per woman	335
Fluctuate	Increase and decrease at an uneven rate	322
Fluctuating stage	When the population is increasing and decreasing at an uneven rate	329
Great Famine	Famine in Ireland in the 1840s that reduced the country's population through starvation and emigration	334
Healthcare	The organised provision of medical care to individuals or a community	326
Infant mortality rate	The number of children under the age of one who die for every 1,000 children born in that year	328
Life expectancy	The average number of years a person is expected to live	327
Migration	When people move from one place to another to live	324
Natural decrease	When more people die than are born in a year	324
Natural increase	When more people are born than die in a year	324
Optimistic view	The idea that birth rates will drop, people will have fewer children, the population will grow more slowly and reach 11 billion by the end of this century	330
Pessimistic view	The idea that the population will continue to rise at an explosive rate and reach over 11 billion people by 2050	330
Population pyramid	A graph or diagram that shows the distribution of age and gender in a country's population	330
Potato blight	Disease in potatoes that led to the Great Famine	325
Profile	The number of people of different ages or genders in a population	330
Sanitation	Facilities to dispose of human waste in a safe way, such as sewerage systems and toilets	326
Senile stage	When the population is high but decreasing; birth rates are lower than death rates	329

Chapter 19

		Page
Asylum	The protection granted by a state to someone who has left their home country as a political refugee	343
Brain drain	When educated people leave an area, causing a lack of educated workforce	346
Colonisation	The settlement by a powerful country of a weaker country or territory	349
Emigrant	A person who leaves one country to live in another	343
Forced migration	When people do not have a choice and have to migrate (e.g. due to war or famine)	344
Immigrant	A person who comes to live in one country from another	343
Internal migration	When people migrate within the same country	342
International migration	When people migrate from one country to another	342
Migrant	A person who leaves one place for another	342
Migration	When people move from one place to another to live	342
Plantation	An organised colonisation when settlers were sent by their ruler to live somewhere else	348
Pull factor	A factor that attracts people to live in a place (e.g. higher employment, better services, good climate)	344
Push factor	A factor that makes people want to leave a place (e.g. lack of job opportunities, war, poverty)	344
Refugee	A person who has been forced to leave their country in order to escape war, persecution or natural disaster	343
Visa	An endorsement on a passport indicating that the holder is allowed to enter, leave or stay for a specified period of time in a country	346
Voluntary migration	When people choose to migrate (e.g. for a better job)	344

Chapter 20

		Page
Aid	Assistance given by rich countries to projects in the developing world	361
Bilateral aid	Aid from one country directly to another	362
Cash crop	An agricultural crop that is grown for profit, instead of for use by the grower	359
Child mortality	The death of children under five years of age	367
Colonialism	When a powerful country takes control of a weaker country and settles some of its people there	358
Commodity	A raw material that is bought and sold on world markets	359
Corruption	Dishonest behaviour by people in power for personal gain	358
Debt	Something, typically money, that is owed to another person or organisation	358
Dependency	A reliance on something	360
Exploitation	Making full use of something and getting benefit from it	359
Fair trade	An international movement which aims to give farmers in developing countries a better price for their products, allowing them to improve their lives	360
Gender equality	When every person has equal opportunities, whether they are male or female	364
Governance	The action or manner of governing a state or organisation	364
Gross National Income (GNI)	All of the income earned by a country's residents and businesses at home and abroad	355
Human Development Index	A way to compare countries with each other based on indicators such as literacy, life expectancy at birth and standard of living	356
Human rights	Rights which should belong to every person (e.g. free speech, education)	364
In transition	Changing from one thing to another	354

		Page
Indicator	A thing that shows the state or level of something	356
Inequality	Unequal access to opportunities	357
Infant mortality	The death of children under the age of one	368
Irish Aid	The Irish government's programme for overseas development assistance	363
Life expectancy	The average number of years a person is expected to live	367
Multilateral aid	Aid provided through organisations such as the UN	362
Neo-colonialism	The way in which former rulers still influence the countries they once colonised	358
Non-government organisation (NGO)	Organisation that receives some money from government but is not run by government (e.g. voluntary agencies that provide assistance to projects in the developing world)	361
Per capita	Per person	355
Plantation	Large farm where a particular crop is grown (e.g. coffee)	359
Protectionism	The practice of shielding a country's domestic industries from foreign competition by taxing imports	360
Standard of living	How wealthy a group of people is and what they can afford to buy	356
Subsidy	Money paid to farmers (or others) to keep prices low while guaranteeing their income	358
Tied aid	Aid which comes with conditions attached	362
World Bank	An international financial organisation that gives loans and grants to countries in need	355

Chapter 21

		Page
Call centre	An office in which large numbers of telephone calls are handled, especially the customer service functions of a large organisation	375
Conference call	A telephone call in which someone talks to several people at the same time, often in different countries	375
Cultural diversity	The existence of a variety of cultural or ethnic groups within a society	378
Food miles	How far the food we eat has travelled from its place of origin	377
Globalisation	The way that people and places are interconnected with other people and places around the world	374
Human development	The process of increasing people's freedoms and opportunities and improving their wellbeing	380
Interconnected	Linked in different ways	374
Interdependent	Two or more people or places being dependent on each other	374
Job security	When one's job is secure and one is unlikely to have it taken away	376
Migration	When people move from one place to another to live	378
Monoculture	The growing of one single crop type	377
Multinational companies (MNC)	Companies with a base in more than one country	376
Popular culture	Our everyday pastimes, including the clothes we wear, the music we listen to and the TV programmes we watch	375
Population	All the inhabitants of a particular place	379
Settlement	A place where people have settled (e.g. hamlet, village, town, city)	379
Trade agreement	An agreement between countries about the movement of goods and services	376

Index

A

abrasion
- glacial 179, 180, 181
- river 139, 142
- sea 159, 160, 161, 162

Achill Island 161
acid rain 25, 82–4
Adamstown, Dublin 215
aerial photographs 114–20
- Arklow, County Wicklow 206
- Ballina, County Mayo 118
- Carlow town 277
- Charleville, County Cork 118
- Cobh, County Cork 276
- Cork City 117
- Dublin City 279
- functions, identification of 117–18
- Galway City 197
- Killala, County Mayo 116
- Killaloe, County Clare 118, 219
- land uses, identification of 117–18
- locations, naming of 115
- Mitchelstown, County Cork 119
- oblique photographs 115
- OS maps and 273–4
- rural functions 118
- seasons, identification of 116
- sketch maps 275–80
- transport on 119
- types of 114–15
- urban functions 117
- vertical photographs 114

Africa 358, 361, 365, 366, 367, 368
- *see also* Ethiopia; Sahel; Sierra Leone

Age of Exploration 358
agriculture 61–4, 187, 325
- in Ethiopia 363
- in Iceland 26
- monoculture 296, 377
- in mountainous areas 33, 189
- sustainable 53–4, 295–6
- *see also* farming

air masses 232, 233, 234, 254
air pollution 84–5, 212, 216, 309
Alpine mountains 32
altitude 198, 226, 255
Angola 361
Apple 128
Ardnacrusha 80
arêtes 181, 183
Arklow, County Wicklow 206
Armorican mountains 32
Atlantic ocean currents 231, 261
atmosphere 226–7
atmospheric pressure 241
Aughinish Island 127
avalanches 29, 33, 98, 100

B

Ballina, County Tipperary 118
Barbuda 245, 246
barograph 241
basalt 38, 40, 160
bays 160
beaches 165
biodiversity 299
biomass energy 79, 299
blowholes 162
bog bursts 82, 98
bogs 76, 81, 82, 189, 292, 298–9
Boliden Tara mine 47
Bord na Móna 298–9
boulder clay plains 184
brain drain 346
Bray, County Wicklow 108
Burren, County Clare 42, 91–3, 95–6, 185, 308, 310

C

Caledonian mountains 32
Campbell-Stokes sunshine recorder 244
carbon dioxide (CO_2) 66, 91, 179, 226, 263
carbon sink 263
carbonation 91–5
Carlow town 277
Carrauntoohil 19, 33
Carrick-on-Shannon 316
cartographers 3
Castlebar, County Mayo 201
caverns and caves 93–4
Celtic settlements 196, 202
census (2016) 333
Central Business District (CBD) 217, 219
Central Valley Project, California 58
Charleville, County Cork 118, 203
charts
- bar charts 14–15
- pie charts 14, 15–16

chemical weathering 90, 91, 95
child mortality 367
China 76, 78, 84, 85, 99, 216, 354
- Three Gorges dam 77, 81

chlorofluorocarbons (CFCs) 264
cirques 180, 181, 183
Cliffs of Moher, County Clare 161, 308
climate change 66, 83, 149, 262–4, 265, 297
climates 252–5
- altitude and aspect 255
- Atlantic ocean currents 261
- boreal 259
- cold climates 256, 259
- cool temperate oceanic 258, 260
- distance from the sea 253, 261
- equatorial 257
- global 66, 83, 253–4, 256–9
- hot 256, 257
- hot desert 257
- Irish 260–1
- latitude 253, 254, 260

local 255
savannah 257
temperate 256, 258
Tundra 259
warm temperate oceanic 258
winds/air masses 254
Clonmel, County Tipperary 112
clouds 236–7
coal 45, 76
coasts
deposition, landforms of 165–7
erosion, landforms of 160–3
erosion, processes of 159
protection of 170
transportation 164
Cobh, County Cork 276
coffee trade 359–60, 372
Coillte 66
colonialism 358
Common Agricultural Policy (CAP) 63
communications 375
Conteh, Hajah 368
Coriolis effect 230
Cork City 117
Corporation tax 125, 128, 130
Corrib gas field 74, 75–6
corruption 358
Crag Cave, Castleisland 93
crime 216
Croagh Patrick 90
cultural diversity 378, 381
culture 378

D

D-E-P-E-D formula 142, 163
deforestation 66, 263, 281, 295
deltas 146, 281
demographers 329
demographic transition model 329, 379
desertification 264, 296–7
developing world 365
aid 361, 362, 363–4
corruption and 358
debt and 358, 361
education of girls 366
exploitation 359–60
globalisation and 380
women and 328, 365–6
Dingle Harbour, OS map 6
doldrums 230
drumlins 185, 189
Dublin City 221, 278, 279, 307

E

Early Christian settlements 202
Earth 21–2, 228–9
core 21, 22
crust 21, 22
magma 24
mantle 21, 22
orbit 228
structure 21–2
earthquakes 20, 22, 28–31
economic activities 51–2, 122–34
primary 51, 52
secondary 51, 52, 122–34
tertiary 51, 52, 304–16
economic development
levels of 352–4
measurement of 355–6
North–South divide 357–8
World Bank categories 355
economic inequality 357–61, 365, 378
ecotourism 310
education 327, 366, 367
emergency aid 364
emigrants 343
employment 367
energy 45–6, 71
biomass 79, 299
coal 46, 76
consumption in USA 87
electricity, Ireland 87
fossil fuels 72
gas 45, 74–6
geothermal 25, 26, 78
Home Energy Usage (SEAI) 86
hydroelectric power 77, 80–1
non-renewable 71, 72–6, 299
oil 45, 72–4
peat 76, 298–9
production, effects of 82–5
renewable 71, 77–82, 216
solar 78
wind 78, 81–2
environment
energy production, effects of 82–5
globalisation and 377–8
impact of farming 63
Environmental Protection Agency (EPA) 265
erosion 89, 90
coastal 159–63
river 137, 139, 143
soil 294, 295
erratics 185
Esker Riada 186, 313
eskers 186, 188, 189, 313
Ethiopia 363–4
exploitation 359–60

F

factories
government policy 125
labour force 124, 127, 128
location of 124–5, 127, 128
markets 124, 127
raw materials 124, 127
services 125
transport facilities 124, 127, 128
Fairtrade 360
farming 61–4, 296
arable (tillage) 62, 63
cash crops 296, 297, 359
dairy 62, 63
environment, impact on 63
horticulture 62
inputs 62
livestock 62, 63
mixed 62, 63
outputs 62
overgrazing 97, 100, 296, 297
pastoral 62, 63
processes 62
types of 62–3
see also agriculture
fishing 59–61, 168
overfishing 60, 168
rivers and 147
sustainable 61
fissures 24
fjords 182–3
flood plains 137, 145
flooding 148, 149, 189
Florida 245, 246
fluvio-glacial deposition 186–7
fold mountains 20, 32–4
food miles 377
food/food supply 61, 168, 325, 326
calorie consumption 371
globalisation and 377
Forest Service 66
forestry 33, 64–5, 66

fossil fuels 16, 17, 44–5, 72, 82–5
freeze-thaw action 90, 288

G

Galway Wind Park 81
gas 45, 74–6
gender equality 365, 366
geography 1–3
geothermal energy 25, 26, 78
geysers 25, 26
Giant's Causeway 28, 40
glaciation 178–90
  deposition 184–7
  effects of 187–9
  erosion 179–83
glaciers
  plucking 179, 181
  transportation 184
Global Goals for Sustainable Development 57
global warming 263–4, 265, 297
globalisation 374–81
  factors affecting 375–6
  future of 381
  human development and 380
  impact of 376–8
  population and 379
  settlement and 379–80
Good Friday Agreement 349
Google 130
granite 40–1
graphs 14, 15, 16–17
Great Famine 333–4
greenhouse gases 66, 83, 263
Gross National Income (GNI) 355

H

headlands 160
health/healthcare 326–7, 367
HIV/AIDS 327, 364, 366, 372
horse latitudes 230
housing 212, 216, 220, 347
human development, globalisation and 380
Human Development Index (HDI) 356
humidity 242
Hurricane Irma 245–6
hydraulic action 93, 139
  rivers and 141, 142, 143
  waves and 159, 160, 161, 162
hydroelectric power (HEP) 77, 80–1, 148, 188

I

ice age 179, 182
Iceland 22, 24, 26–7
igneous rocks 39, 40–1, 357
immigrants 343
incinerators 132
industrial inertia 129
industry 180, 189
  factory location 123,–5, 127, 128
  footloose industry 129
  heavy industry 126, 127
  industrial estates 129
  industrial inertia 129
  in Ireland 123
  light industry 126, 128
  multinational corporations 130–1
  types of 126–9
  see also factories
infant mortality rates 328, 333, 368
Inniscarra Dam 80
interlocking spurs 137, 141, 181
interrelationship 304
Irish Aid 363–4
Irish Conservation Box 61
Irish Water 55
irrigation 57–8, 296, 326, 363
isobars 233

J

Japan 30, 31, 329

K

karst landscapes 92–6
Killala, County Mayo 116
Killaloe, County Clare 118, 219
Killarney, County Kerry 273
Killybegs, County Donegal 168, 198, 199

L

lagoons 166
lahars 25, 98, 99
lakes
  glacial lakes 188, 189
  oxbow lakes 137, 144
  ribbon lakes 182
Lambay Island 28
land use 219
land values 219
landslides 99
Las Vegas, Nevada 272
latitude 228, 253, 260
levees 137, 145
life expectancy 327, 331, 333, 356, 367
lime 293
Limerick city water supply 56
limestone 42, 45
limestone pavement 92
longshore drift 164

M

McMonagle Stone 46
maps 3
  see also Ordnance Survey maps
marble 43, 45
maritime 232
mass movement 97–100
  controlling 100
  factors affecting 97
  types of 98–100
meanders 137, 143
measurement 18–19, 120–1
  area 18
  distance 120
  height 19
  mean 121
  percentages 18
  range 121
  ratio 120
mechanical weathering 90
meltwater landforms 186–7
metamorphic rocks 39, 43
Mid-Atlantic Ridge 22, 24, 26
migration 342–9
  barriers to 346
  causes of 343–5
  consequences of 346–7
  organised 348–9
mining 45, 46, 47
Mitchelstown, County Cork 119
MNCs *see* multinational corporations
Moment Magnitude Scale 29
Moneypoint, County Clare 76
monoculture 296, 377
moraines 184, 186
Mount Rushmore 41
Mount St Helens, USA 24, 25, 27, 99
mountaineous areas 33
mudflows 98

multinational corporations (MNCs) 130–1, 207, 326, 357–8, 376–7, 380

N

Naas, County Kildare 131
natural disasters 27
natural resources 52
- fish 59–61
- forestry 64–5
- non-renewable 52
- renewable 52
- water 54–7

neo-colonialism 358
Nevado del Ruiz, Colombia 99
Nigeria 372
nomadic 297
non-government organisations (NGOs) 361, 364
Nore River 152
Norman settlements 203, 207
North Atlantic Drift 261

O

ocean currents 179, 231, 261
oil 45, 72–4
Ordnance Survey Ireland (OSI) 4, 7
Ordnance Survey maps 3–13, 106–13
- aerial photographs and 273–4
- area calculation 108
- Arklow, County Wicklow 206
- Bray, County Wicklow 108
- Burren, County Clare 96
- cardinal points 9
- Carrick-on-Shannon, County Leitrim 316
- Castlebar, County Mayo 201
- Charleville, County Cork 203
- Clonmel, County Tipperary 112
- coastal landforms 163, 167, 172
- colours 8
- compass 9
- contours 8
- cross-section 110
- Dingle Harbour, County Kerry 6, 10
- directions 9
- distance measurement 107
- Dublin City 278
- eastings 4
- four-figure grid reference 5
- glaciation 183, 190–1
- grid reference 5–6
- height 8
- hydroelectric power stations 79
- industries on 131
- Killybegs, County Donegal 199
- land uses 111
- legend 6, 7
- MacGillycuddy's Reeks, County Kerry 190
- measuring distance 107
- Naas, County Kildare 131
- national grid 4
- New Ross, County Wexford 152
- north 9
- northings 4
- power stations 76
- ratio 4
- river landforms 143, 144
- rivers 151–3
- scale 3, 4, 108
- six-figure grid reference 5
- sketch maps 10–13
- slopes 109
- spot heights 8
- subzone 15
- summit heights 8
- symbols 6
- tourism 315–16
- triangulation pillar 8
- Wicklow Mountains 34
- wind farms 79

outwash plains 187
overgrazing 97, 100, 296
oxbow lakes 137, 144

P

Pacific Ring of Fire 23
Pangaea 22
Paris Agreement 265
peat 76, 298–9
pH value 83
photosynthesis 59
pillars 94
Plantation of Ulster 348–9
Plantations 203
plate boundaries 20, 21, 22
plate tectonics 22
- continental drift 22
- convection currents 21
- earthquakes 22
- fault lines 22
- mid-ocean ridges 22, 23, 24
- subduction 22

plates 20
- continental 20, 21
- oceanic 20, 21

plunge pools 142
politics 375
pollution 84–5, 148, 168, 212, 216, 309
popular culture 375
population
- birth and death rates 324
- demographic transition model 329, 379
- family planning 327
- fertility rate 335
- globalisation and 379
- infant mortality rate 328
- in Ireland 333–4
- life expectancy 327
- in Sierra Leone 334–5

population pyramids 330–2
Pre-Christian settlements 202
precipitation 55, 237–8, 244
Presbyterianism 349
primate city 221
protectionism 360
Protestantism 349
Purchase Power Parity (PPP) 356
pyramidal peaks 181

Q

quarrying 45, 46
quartzite 44, 46

R

rain/rainfall 237–8, 258, 261
reforestation 66, 295, 296
refugees 343, 345, 364
regolith 97, 98, 99
Rhine River 147
Richter Scale 29
river landforms 137, 140–6
- mature stage (middle course) 137, 143–4
- old stage (lower course) 137, 144–6
- youthful stage (upper course) 137, 140–3

river processes
- deposition 137, 139, 140, 143, 145, 146
- erosion 137, 139, 143
- transportation 139

rivers 136–56
- angling/fishing 147
- discharge 144
- drainage patterns 151
- features of 136
- flooding 149–50
- of Ireland 138
- load 139, 141, 142, 143, 144
- Nore River 152
- OS maps 151–3
- people and 147–8
- pollution of 148
- stages of 137, 140–6
- tourism 147, 150
- transport 147
- the work of 139–40

roads 188
rocks 38
- building materials 45
- extrusive 40
- igneous 39, 40–1
- intrusive 40, 41
- metamorphic 39, 43
- mining 46–7
- quarrying 46
- sedimentary 39, 42–3
- uses 44–6

Rosslare, County Wexford 171
rural settlements 208–9
RUSAL Aughinish Alumina 127

S

Sahel 264, 296–7
St Martin Island 245–246
San Andreas fault 22, 28, 29, 283
sand dunes 165
sand spits 166
sandstone 42–3, 46
sanitation 326, 367
satellite images 272, 280–3
satellite towns 211
saturated 98, 237
sea
- arches 162
- caves 162
- cliffs 161
- high-water mark 161
- levels 170, 182, 189, 264
- low-water mark 161
- people and 168–9
- stacks 162
- stumps 162
- walls 170

sedimentary rocks 39, 42–3
seismographs 29
seismologists 29
semi-state body 66
settlements 196–209
- dispersed 209
- globalisation and 379–80
- in Ireland 202–9
- linear 208
- multi-functional 207
- nucleated 209
- rural 208–9
- sites of 198
- situation of 200
- urban 204–6

Shannon River 56, 149–50
shopping areas/centres 217–18
Sierra Leone 325, 326, 327, 328, 331, 334–5
sketch maps 10–13, 275, 276
smog 84–5, 212
socio-economic factors 25
soil 284–99
- composition 285
- formation 288–9
- human activity and 295–6
- leaching 287, 294
- profiles 286
- texture 285–6
- vegetation and 289, 293–4

soil creep 98
soil erosion 284, 294, 295
soil types
- brown earth 290–1
- gley soils 66, 292
- Irish 290–2
- loam 290
- peaty 292
- podzol 291

solar energy 78, 227–8
stalactites 94
stalagmites 94
Stevenson screen 242
subsidy 358
sulfur dioxide 25, 83, 84
sun 227–9
sunshine 244
Sustainable Development Goals 57, 265, 327, 366, 367, 375, 378
Sustainable Energy Authority of Ireland (SEAI) 82
swallow holes 93
Syria 343, 345

T

Taliban 366
Teagasc 66
technological development 326
terracettes 98
tombolos 166
tourism 188, 305–11
- ecotourism 310
- environment and 309–10
- in Europe 307
- in Iceland 26
- in Ireland 95, 306–11
- mountaineous areas 33
- OS maps and 315–16
- physical landscape and 308–9
- rivers and 147, 150
- the sea and 169
- sustainable 310
- transport and 311, 314–15

trade 357
- coffee trade 359–60
- EU free trade area 376
- fair trade 360, 380
- globalisation and 376

Tramore, County Waterford 173
transport 213–14, 311–16, 375
- buses and QBCs 213
- cars 84
- cycle lanes 214
- globalisation and 375
- Irish network 312
- light rail system 213
- physical world and 312–14
- railways 313
- rivers 147
- road improvements 214
- sea 168
- tourism and 311, 314–15
- traffic congestion 211, 213–14
- tram system 2 13

Transport Infrastructure Ireland 312
tsunamis 29, 30
turbines 77

U

U-shaped valleys 181, 188
UN Declaration of Human Rights 375
UN Sustainable Development Goals 57, 265, 327, 366, 367, 375, 378
United Nations (UN) 265

- urban areas 217–18
- urban decay 212, 216
- urban renewal/redevelopment 216
- urban settlements 204–6
- urban sprawl 211, 215
- urbanisation 210–15, 380

V

- V-shaped valleys 137, 141, 181
- vaccines 326, 327, 367
- valleys
  - hanging 182
  - U-shaped 181, 188
  - V-shaped 137, 141, 181
- Viking settlements 202, 207
- volcanic islands 22, 24
- volcanic mountains 22, 24–5
- volcanoes 20, 23–8
  - eruptions, responses to 27
  - gases 25
  - geothermal energy 25, 26
  - geysers 25
  - lahars 25, 99
  - magma chamber 24
  - Pacific Ring of Fire 23
  - socio-economic effects 25, 26
  - types of 25

W

- war 326
- water 54–7, 148
  - drinking water 326, 367
  - in Ireland 55–7
  - irrigation schemes 57–8
  - Limerick city supply 56
  - sustainable development goals 57
- water cycle 54–5
- water quality 149
- water treatment plant 56
- waterfalls 137, 142
- Waterford City 207
- waves 158–9
  - backwash 158, 164
  - constructive 159
  - destructive 159
  - swash 158, 164
- weather
  - anticyclones 234, 235
  - atmospheric pressure 241
  - depressions 235
  - elements 239
  - forecasts 239–40
  - humidity 242
  - measurement 240
  - precipitation 237–8, 244
  - sunshine 244
  - temperature 240–1
- weather fronts 233–4
- weathering 89, 90
  - chemical 90, 91
  - denudation 89
  - mechanical 90
- Wegener, Alfred 22
- Wicklow Mountains 32, 33, 34, 66, 308
- wind energy 78, 81–2
- wind farms 78, 79, 81, 82, 299
- winds 164, 229–30, 242, 243, 254, 261
- women, in developing world 328, 365–6
- World Bank 355, 372
- world population 322–4
  - birth rate 324
  - change 324
  - death rate 324
  - education and 327
  - family planning 327
  - food supply and 325
  - growth 322–3, 330
  - health and 326–7
  - rate of change 325–8
  - technological development and 326
  - war and 326

Y

- Yousafzai, Malala 366

Ireland: Political

11° A 10° B 9° C 8° D 7° E 6° F

Communications
Railway
Motorway
Road
Main airport

Administration
Boundaries
International
Internal

Cities and towns
National capital
Administrative capital
Other town

0 25 50 75 km

Conic Equidistant projection

ATLANTIC OCEAN

Colonsay
Jura
Lochgilphead
SCOTLAND
Islay
Kintyre
Arran
Campbeltown
UNITED KINGDOM
North Channel

Portrush
Ballycastle
Coleraine
Buncrana
Ballymoney
Limavady
Derry
DERRY
Letterkenny
ULSTER
ANTRIM
Larne
Ballymena
Lifford
Strabane
NORTHERN IRELAND
DONEGAL
Magherafelt
Carrickfergus
Antrim
Bangor
Killybegs
Donegal
TYRONE
Cookstown
Newtownabbey
Omagh
Belfast
Newtownards
Ballyshannon
Bundoran
Lisburn
Dungannon
Lurgan
Portadown
Portaferry
FERMANAGH
Enniskillen
Banbridge
Downpatrick
Sligo
LEITRIM
Armagh
Monaghan
ARMAGH
DOWN
Newry
Newcastle
Clones
Ballina
SLIGO
MONAGHAN
Warrenpoint
Castleblayney
Kilkeel
Cavan
MAYO
Boyle
Carrick-on-Shannon
CAVAN
Carrickmacross
Dundalk
Castlebar
LOUTH
ROSCOMMON
Westport
LONGFORD
Longford
CONNACHT
Kells
Drogheda
MEATH
Navan
Irish Sea
Balbriggan
Skerries
Roscommon
Trim
FINGAL
Mullingar
Tuam
WESTMEATH
Swords
Malahide
Athlone
DUBLIN CITY
Dublin
GALWAY
Clara
Lexlip
SOUTH DUBLIN
Dún Laoghaire
Ballinasloe
Tullamore
KILDARE
DÚN LAOGHAIRE-RATHDOWN
Galway
Tallaght
OFFALY
Newbridge
Naas
Bray
Loughrea
Kildare
Mountmellick
LEINSTER
Birr
Portlaoise
Wicklow
LAOIS
Roscrea
Athy
WICKLOW
IRELAND
Ennis
Nenagh
Carlow
Arklow
CLARE
Templemore
Tullow
CARLOW
Thurles
Muine Bheag
Kilrush
Kilkenny
Gorey
Limerick
TIPPERARY
KILKENNY
Cashel
Enniscorthy
LIMERICK
Listowel
Tipperary
WEXFORD
Newcastle West
New Ross
MUNSTER
Clonmel
Carrick-on-Suir
Rathluirc
Wexford
Tralee
Castleisland
Mitchelstown
Waterford
Dingle
KERRY
WATERFORD
Tramore
Mallow
Fermoy
Killarney
Dungarvan
St George's Channel
Cahirciveen
CORK
Youghal
Macroom
CORK CITY
Cork
Midleton
Cobh
Bandon
Kinsale
Bantry
Clonakilty
Skibbereen

6 5 4 3 2 1

56° 55° 54° 53° 52°

11° A 10° B 9° C 8° D 7° E 6° F

Ireland: Physical

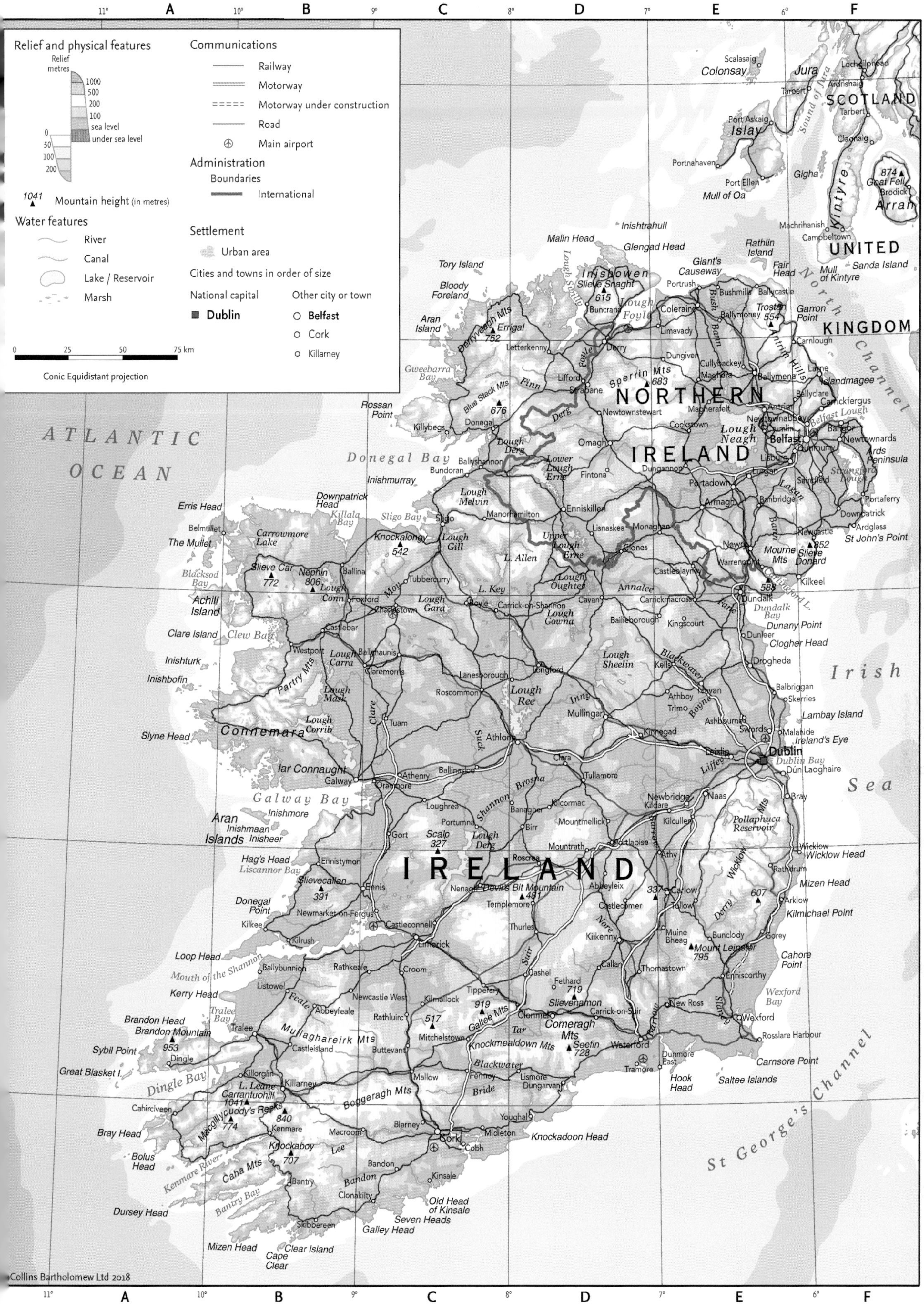

Relief and physical features

Relief metres

1000
500
200
100
sea level
under sea level
0
50
100
200

1041 Mountain height (in metres)

Water features

River
Canal
Lake / Reservoir
Marsh

Communications

Railway
Motorway
Motorway under construction
Road
Main airport

Administration

Boundaries

International

Settlement

Urban area

Cities and towns in order of size

National capital: **Dublin**

Other city or town: **Belfast**, Cork, Killarney

0 25 50 75 km

Conic Equidistant projection

Europe: Political

Europe: Physical

B.H.	BOSNIA AND HERZEGOVINA
K.	KOSOVO
L.	LIECHTENSTEIN
LUX.	LUXEMBOURG
M.	MONTENEGRO
MAC.	MACEDONIA
NETH.	NETHERLANDS
S.M.	SAN MARINO
SW.	SWITZERLAND
V.C.	VATICAN CITY

World's largest countries

		Population
1	**China**	1 417 504 000
2	**India**	1 339 180 000
3	**United States of America**	324 459 000
4	**Indonesia**	263 991 000
5	**Brazil**	209 288 000
6	**Pakistan**	197 015 000
7	**Nigeria**	190 886 000
8	**Bangladesh**	164 669 000
9	**Russia**	143 989 000
10	**Mexico**	129 163 000
11	**Japan**	127 484 000
12	**Ethiopia**	104 957 000
13	**Philippines**	104 918 000
14	**Egypt**	97 553 000
15	**Vietnam**	95 540 000

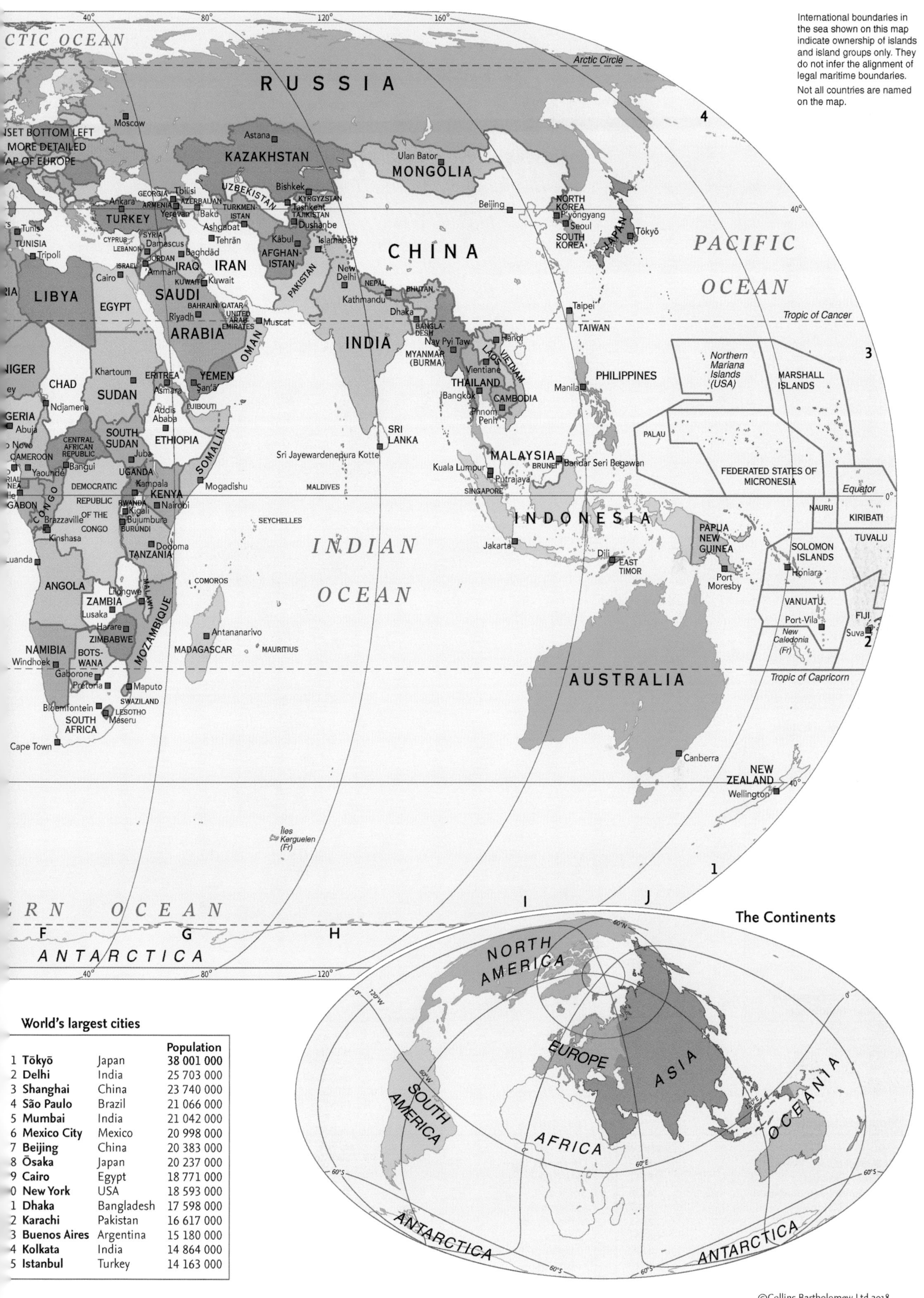

World's largest cities

			Population
1	**Tōkyō**	Japan	**38 001 000**
2	**Delhi**	India	25 703 000
3	**Shanghai**	China	23 740 000
4	**São Paulo**	Brazil	21 066 000
5	**Mumbai**	India	21 042 000
6	**Mexico City**	Mexico	20 998 000
7	**Beijing**	China	20 383 000
8	**Ōsaka**	Japan	20 237 000
9	**Cairo**	Egypt	18 771 000
0	**New York**	USA	18 593 000
1	**Dhaka**	Bangladesh	17 598 000
2	**Karachi**	Pakistan	16 617 000
3	**Buenos Aires**	Argentina	15 180 000
4	**Kolkata**	India	14 864 000
5	**Istanbul**	Turkey	14 163 000

Mountain heights

	metres
Mt Everest (China/Nepal)	8848
K2 (China/Pakistan)	8611
Kangchenjunga (India/Nepal)	8586
Dhaulagiri I (Nepal)	8167
Annapurna I (Nepal)	8091
Cerro Aconcagua (Argentina)	6961
Cerro Ojos del Salado (Arg./Chile)	6893
Chimborazo (Ecuador)	6310
Denali (Mt McKinley) (USA)	6190
Mt Logan (Canada)	5959

Island areas

	sq. km
Greenland	2 175 600
New Guinea	808 510
Borneo	745 561
Madagascar	587 040
Baffin Island	507 451
Sumatra	473 606
Honshū	227 414
Great Britain	218 476
Victoria Island	217 291
Ellesmere Island	196 236

Continents

	sq. km
Asia	45 036 4
Africa	30 343 5
North America	24 680 3
South America	17 815 4
Antarctica	12 093 0
Europe	9 908 5
Oceania	8 844 5

eans

	sq. km
:ific Ocean	166 241 000
antic Ocean	86 557 000
lian Ocean	73 427 000
:tic Ocean	9 485 000

Lake areas

	sq. km
Caspian Sea	371 000
Lake Superior	82 100
Lake Victoria	68 870
Lake Huron	59 600
Lake Michigan	57 800
Lake Tanganyika	32 600
Great Bear Lake	31 328
Lake Baikal	30 500
Lake Nyasa	29 500

River lengths

	km
Nile (Africa)	6695
Amazon (S. America)	6516
Chang Jiang (Asia)	6380
Mississippi-Missouri (N. America)	5969
Ob'-Irtysh (Asia)	5568
Yenisey-Angara-Selenga (Asia)	5550
Huang He (Asia)	5464
Congo (Africa)	4667
Río de la Plata-Paraná (S. America)	4500
Irtysh (Asia)	4440

AUTHORS' ACKNOWLEDGEMENTS:

Jason and Norma would like to thank their friends and families for all the support and patience while writing this book. They would also like to thank their colleagues and students in St Munchin's College and Laurel Hill Colaiste FCJ for their encouragement and for helping pilot some of the ideas in the book.

For permission to reproduce photographs and maps, the author and publisher acknowledge the following copyright holders:

© ALAMY LTD: Cultura Creative (RF) / Alamy Stock Photo 2TR; Art Directors & TRIP / Alamy Stock Photo 2CR, 354B; age fotostock / Alamy Stock Photo 19; Arterra Picture Library / Alamy Stock Photo 26TR; OVIA IMAGES / Alamy Stock Photo 46BR; Design Pics Inc / Alamy Stock Photo 47TR, 137CR, 184B, 187BR, 218TL; Panther Media GmbH / Alamy Stock Photo 51; Peter Titmuss / Alamy Stock Photo 55; imageBROKER / Alamy Stock Photo 58CR, 102 (cracked rock), 150; LOU Collection / Alamy Stock Photo 60BR; Doug Baxter / Alamy Stock Photo 64; Naomi Roe / Alamy Stock Photo 65CL; NOAA / Alamy Stock Photo 73TL, 245TR; RGB Ventures / SuperStock / Alamy Stock Photo 73TR; Overflightstock Ltd / Alamy Stock Photo 76TR; Hans Blossey / Alamy Stock Photo 80CR, 118B, 148TR, 197, 219; John Kehely / Alamy Stock Photo 80BR; Paul Glendell / Alamy Stock Photo 83BL; Mark Leach / Alamy Stock Photo 83BR; Holmes Garden Photos / Alamy Stock Photo 93; Chris Howes/Wild Places Photography / Alamy Stock Photo 95 (B); Kay Roxby / Alamy Stock Photo; Aurora Photos / Alamy Stock Photo 100CR; Whiskybottle / Bigstock.com 104, 194TR; David Lyons / Alamy Stock Photo 116; Stephen Power / Alamy Stock Photo 127CR; Trevor Chriss / Alamy Stock Photo 129BR; Justin Leighton / Alamy Stock Photo 130TL; Kristoffer Tripplaar / Alamy Stock Photo 130TR; FLPA / Alamy Stock Photo 144CL; A.P.S. (UK) / Alamy Stock Photo 145CR; Martyn Evans / Alamy Stock Photo 149BR; ZUMA Press Inc / Alamy Stock Photo 156, 305 (C), 335TR; DWImages Ireland / Alamy Stock Photo 165; Gary Crabbe / Enlightened Images / Alamy Stock Photo 166TR; Brad Mitchell / Alamy Stock Photo 168TR, 308BR; Bob Daemmrich / Alamy Stock Photo 169CL; Adrian Turner / Alamy Stock Photo 170TL; Pam Biddle / Alamy Stock Photo 170BR; keith morris / Alamy Stock Photo 171TR; Maurice Savage / Alamy Stock Photo 171CR; Jon Arnold Images Ltd / Alamy Stock Photo 176T; Pearl Bucknall / Alamy Stock Photo 180; Gavin Dronfield / Alamy Stock Photo 181TR; Dave Ellison / Alamy Stock Photo 181BR; Phil Crean A / Alamy Stock Photo 182TR, 315; Vincent Lowe / Alamy Stock Photo 182BR; geogphotos / Alamy Stock Photo 184CR; Tom Bean / Alamy Stock Photo 186; Peter Horree / Alamy Stock Photo 188TR Chasingthelight Images / Alamy Stock Photo 189CR; Roger Allen Photography / Alamy Stock Photo 189CL; Peter Cavanagh / Alamy Stock Photo 211BR; Radharc Images / Alamy Stock Photo 217CL, 310BR, 379CR; Irina Dmitrienko / Alamy Stock Photo 235CR; Pablo Paul / Alamy Stock Photo 242CR; Netherlands Defence Ministry / Alamy Stock Photo 245CR; DAVID J SLATER / Alamy Stock Photo 264CR; Mark Boulton / Alamy Stock Photo 292CR; Grant Heilman Photography / Alamy Stock Photo 294BR; aeropix / Alamy Stock Photo 295; JJ pixs / Alamy Stock Photo 297; Paul Felix Photography / Alamy Stock Photo 298; Steven Sheppardson / Alamy Stock Photo 299BR; Bernard Golden / Alamy Stock Photo 304; Justin Hannaford / Alamy Stock Photo 309TR; George Munday / Alamy Stock Photo 309CR; Clive Collie / Alamy Stock Photo 312; Nick Scott / Alamy Stock Photo 314BR; bildbroker.de / Alamy Stock Photo 320TR; Radius Images / Alamy Stock Photo 325; Eva-Lotta Jansson / Alamy Stock Photo 321TL; Ian Miles-Flashpoint Pictures / Alamy Stock Photo 327TR; Jake Lyell / Alamy Stock Photo 328, 359, 365CL; dbimages / Alamy Stock Photo 345TL; Danita Delimont / Alamy Stock Photo 347; Bill Cheyrou / Alamy Stock Photo 352CL; Samy / Alamy Stock Photo 352CR; Eye Ubiquitous / Alamy Stock Photo 358TR; Novastock / Alamy Stock Photo 365TR; 506 collection / Alamy Stock Photo 366BR; Zsolt Repasy / Alamy Stock Photo 367BR; DestinationImages / Alamy Stock Photo 374; Anja Schaefer / Alamy Stock Photo 375CR; Peter Probst / Alamy Stock Photo 375BR; dpa picture alliance archive / Alamy Stock Photo 378TR; Hemis / Alamy Stock Photo 378CL; PIB / Alamy Stock Photo 381 / © BARROW COAKLEY AERIAL PHOTOGRAPHY (BARROWCOAKLEY.IE): 214B / © BIGSTOCK.COM: Bragin Alexey / Bigstock.com 59 (A); jamstock / Bigstock.com 49 (B); prill / Bigstock.com 49TR; only_fabrizio / Bigstock.com 49CR; upthebanner / Bigstock 49BR, 91B, 101; ssuaphoto / Bigstock.com 53 (G); imajik / Bigstock.com 57BL; Hank Shiffman / Bigstock.com 68TL; Palych1378 / Bigstock.com 68BR; WendyAt / Bigstock.com 102 (monument); Severas / Bigstock.com 103; goodstock / Bigstock.com 124CL; ilfede / Bigstock.com 168CL; Speedfighter / Bigstock.com 170TR; Chrismp / Bigstock.com 175; kated / Bigstock.com 178; Steven Gaertner / Bigstock.com 181CL; sjabrown / Bigstock.com 182CR; ril / Bigstock.com 189TL; Eishier / Bigstock.com 193CR; Patrick Poendl / Bigstock.com 193BR; Kartouchken / Bigstock.com 194CR; Pyma / Bigstock.com 204; presian1801 / Bigstock.com 220TL; longlens / Bigstock.com 220 (terrace); mbtaichi / Bigstock.com 220BR; kikkerdirk / Bigstock.com 294CL; Fotokon / Bigstock.com 296; Birgit Urban / Bigstock.com 320TL; riganmc / Bigstock.com 320CL; Andrushko Galyna / Bigstock.com 320CR; Paha_L / Bigstock.com 344; **t:** David Snyder / Bigstock.com 362CR / © BÓTHAR: 364BR / © CARTOONSTOCK.COM / NILSSON-MAKI, KJELL: 358BR / © CENTRAL STATISTICS OFFICE: 333 / © COLLINS BARTHOLOMEW LTD 2018: 410–417 / © DUBAI CELTS GAA: 343CL / © FAIRTRADE: 360 (BL, BC) / © PAUL FITZGERALD (POLYP.ORG.UK) 'GOLD DIGGERS': 358CR / © GETTY IMAGES: Gary Braasch/CORBIS/Corbis via Getty Images 27CR; John Barr / Liaison 27BR; Jacques Langevin/Sygma/Sygma via Getty Images 99CR; Liu Zhongjun/CHINA NEWS SERVICE/VCG via Getty Images 99BR; Italy Fire Department/Anadolu Agency/Getty Images 100TR; Michelle McMahon 132; ALEXANDER JOE/AFP/ Getty Images 326TR; Olivia Acland / Barcroft Images / Barcroft Media via Getty Images 335CR; Mehedi Hasan/NurPhoto via Getty Images 367TR; KAZUHIRO NOGI/AFP/Getty Images 379BR / © GOOGLE EARTH: 273 (photograph), 281 (B, D), 282 (D) /

© JOHN HERRIOTT (IRELANDAERIALPHOTOGRAPHY.COM): 117, 118T, 119, 206B, 276, 277, 279 / © INSOMNIA IRELAND: 360TR / © IRISH AID / TESFAYE EJIGU: 363BR / © IRISH AID: 364TR / © IRISH EXAMINER: 128CR / © ISTOCKPHOTO.COM: luoman / iStockphoto.com 66; oaltindag / iStockphoto.com 377TL; Geber86 / iStockphoto.com 380TR / © LIMERICK CITY AND COUNTY COUNCIL 56 (both) / © MARINE CONSERVATION SOCIETY: 169BR / © MARTYN TURNER: 370 / © MCMONAGLE STONE: 46TR, 46CR / © NASA: 29TR, 235CL, 272 (all), 281 (TR, CL, A, C), 282 (A, B, C), 283 (all) / COURTESY OF THE HOUSES OF THE OIREACHTAS: 125CR, 221 / © O'MAHONY PIKE ARCHITECTS: 215B / © ORDNANCE SURVEY OF IRELAND / GOVERNMENT OF IRELAND: 4 (all), 6, 7, 8 (colour, summit heights, BR), 9 (north), 10T, 12, 34, 76CR (both), 79 (CL, CR), 96, 108, 109 (all maps), 110, 112, 131, 143TL, 144CR, 152, 163CL, 167, 173, 183, 185C, 190, 199, 201, 203, 206T, 208, 209 (both), 273 (map), 278, 316 / © RTÉ ARCHIVES: 31, 143BR, 299CR / © RUSAL AUGHINISH ALUMINA: 127BR / © SHANNON PROPERTIES: 218CL / © SHUTTERSTOCK INC: 115; bluedog studio / Shutterstock 1BR; Papa Annur / Shutterstock 25TR; Aleksandar Todorovic / Shutterstock 25BR; Lautz / Shutterstock 26CR; Puripat Lertpunyaroj / Shutterstock 26BR; Prometheus72 / Shutterstock 29BR; OBJM / Shutterstock 30TR; Tatiana Popova / Shutterstock 33TR; Mike Pellinni / Shutterstock 33BR; mariva2017 / Shutterstock 39CL; Jantana / Shutterstock 39C; Creative Idea / Shutterstock 39CR; woe / Shutterstock 40TR; Ocskay Bence / Shutterstock 40CR; Mrs_ya / Shutterstock 40BR; stenic56 / Shutterstock 41TR; critterbiz / Shutterstock 41CL; Aleksandr Pobedimskiy / Shutterstock 42TR, 43BR; nevio / Shutterstock 42CR; michal812 / Shutterstock 42BR; Maurizio De Mattei / Shutterstock 43TR; Sakdinon Kadchiangsaen / Shutterstock 44; anuphadit / Shutterstock 45TR; eyeidea / Shutterstock 45CR; Walter Bilotta / Shutterstock 45BR; Ksander / Shutterstock 47CR; Olaf Speier / Shutterstock 52TL; Frame China / Shutterstock 52TC; AVAVA / Shutterstock 52TR; M. Niebuhr / Shutterstock 53 (A); M Rutherford / Shutterstock 53 (B); Repina Valeriya 53 (C); nikkytok / Shutterstock (D); Split Second Stock / Shutterstock 53 (E); Marian Weyo / Shutterstock 53 (K); Photomarine / Shutterstock 60BL; Sara Winter / Shutterstock 62TL; Ratthaphong Ekariyasap / Shutterstock 62TC; Humannet / Shutterstock 62TR; Radu Cadar / Shutterstock 62 (A); Official / Shutterstock 62 (B); JP Chretien / Shutterstock 62 (C); Heath Johnson / Shutterstock 62 (D); Igor Stramyk / Shutterstock 62 (E); Bildagentur Zoonar GmbH / Shutterstock 63CR; Travel Stock / Shutterstock 68TC; Iakov Filimonov / Shutterstock 68BL; Samo Trebizan / Shutterstock 68BC; Mimadeo / Shutterstock.com 71CR; Oil and Gas Photographer / Shutterstock.com 71BR; Syda Productions / Shutterstock.com 72 (A); Africa Studio / Shutterstock.com 72 (B); Bilanol / Shutterstock.com 72 (C); StudioSmart / Shutterstock.com 72 (D); Sophie James / Shutterstock.com 74; Aerovista Luchtfotografie / Shutterstock.com 76TR; Teerayut Somprasong / Shutterstock 77; Diyana Dimitrova / Shutterstock.com 76CR; Aleksandar Tasevski / Shutterstock.com 79TR; Axel Jung / Shutterstock.com 83BC; Hung Chung Chih / Shutterstock.com 85; Jesus Keller / Shutterstock.com 86; ronnybas / Shutterstock.com 89; Maria_Janus / Shutterstock.com 92CR, 313TR; Fulcanelli / Shutterstock.com 92BL; Fat Jackey / Shutterstock.com 94B; OE993 / Shutterstock.com 95 (A); Mark Carthy / Shutterstock.com 95 (D); AlessandraRC / Shutterstock.com 100CL; Kev Llewellyn / Shutterstock.com 114; Werner Muenzker / Shutterstock.com 122BL; Dragon Images / Shutterstock.com 122BC; vdimage / Shutterstock.com 122BR; Sitthichai Suntuang / Shutterstock.com 124TR; LandFox / Shutterstock.com 124CR; michaeljung / Shutterstock.com 124BL; Millionstock / Shutterstock.com 125TR; Pavel L Photo and Video / Shutterstock.com 126C; Zeynep Demir / Shutterstock.com 126BR; mariakraynova / Shutterstock.com 128TR; Neil Mitchell / Shutterstock.com 129TR, 137C; Lloyd Carr / Shutterstock.com 130CR; SvetMedvedeva / Shutterstock.com 141; PHB.cz (Richard Semik) / Shutterstock.com 142; michelmond / Shutterstock.com 145BL; Pecold / Shutterstock.com 147CR; Conny Sjostrom / Shutterstock.com 147CL; neenawat khenyothaa / Shutterstock.com 148CL; shutterupeire / Shutterstock.com 161; StevanZZ / Shutterstock.com 163T; tcly / Shutterstock.com 168BR; Remizov / Shutterstock.com 169TR; SADLERC1 / Shutterstock.com 170BR; Martin Fowler / Shutterstock.com 185BR; Eoghan McNally / Shutterstock.com 210; OlegD / Shutterstock.com 212CR; Mick Harper / Shutterstock.com 213CR; lonndubh / Shutterstock.com 213BR; Ungor / Shutterstock.com 214TR; Ewelina Wachala / Shutterstock.com 220 (semi-detached); konstantinks / Shutterstock.com 236CR; dachnarong wangkeeree / Shutterstock.com 236BR; Martchan / Shutterstock.com 237; Darryl Sleath / Shutterstock.com 241; beeboys / Shutterstock.com 242BR; Sarah Camille / Shutterstock.com 243; vulcano / Shutterstock.com 252CL; Megapress / Alamy Stock Photo 252CR; Gil.K / Shutterstock.com 256CL; kropic1 / Shutterstock.com 256C; outdoorsman / Shutterstock.com 256CR; 24Novembers / Shutterstock.com 262; LanaElcova / Shutterstock.com 263CR; Rich Carey / Shutterstock.com 263BR; macknimal / Shutterstock.com 264B; 3Dsculptor / Shutterstock.com 280; Antonov Roman / Shutterstock.com 287; ChrisVanLennepPhoto / Shutterstock.com 290; ianmitchinson / Shutterstock.com 305 (A); Gabriela Insuratelu / Shutterstock.com 305 (B); Madrugada Verde / Shutterstock.com 305 (D); Anton_Ivanov / Shutterstock.com 307; ROUSSELLE Xavier / Shutterstock.com 308; Mile Atanasov / Shutterstock.com 310TR; Lukasz Pajor / Shutterstock.com 313CR; Cozyartz Digital Media / Shutterstock.com 314TR; Beros919 / Shutterstock.com 326CL; Joseph Sohm / Shutterstock.com 327CR; Rawpixel.com / Shutterstock.com 327BR; Nicolas Economou / Shutterstock.com 343BR; Vadim Martynenko / Shutterstock.com 345TR; mariolav / Shutterstock.com 353; Filipe Frazao / Shutterstock.com 354T; Stocked House Studio / Shutterstock.com 377CR; Martin Good / Shutterstock.com 378CR; John Wollwerth / Shutterstock.com 380CR / © TRÓCAIRE: 363TR / © THE IRISH TIMES: 75TR, 75CR, 149TL, 211CR, 213TR, 215TR, 217BL, 218BL / © UNICEF/UNI202458/KASSAYE: 368 / © UNICEF: 366 / © UN: 362TR / © UN / GLOBAL GOALS: 57CR, 69 (both), 265 / © DAVE WALSH (DAVEWALSHPHOTO.COM): 212T / © WIKICOMMONS: 68TR, 137CL, 188CR, 249CL, 292TR, 348.

The authors and publisher have made every effort to trace all copyright owners, but if any material has inadvertently been reproduced without permission, they would be happy to make the necessary arrangements at the earliest opportunity, and encourage owners of copyright material not acknowledged to make contact.